Sociology

Relationships That Make a World

Marjorie E. Donovan
Pittsburg State University, Kansas

Juan L. Gonzales Jr.
California State University, Hayward

Harry L. Humphries
Pittsburg State University, Kansas

KENDALL/HUNT PUBLISHING COMPANY
4050 Westmark Drive   Dubuque, Iowa 52002

Copyright © 1998 by Marjorie E. Donovan, Juan L. Gonzales, Jr., and Harry L. Humphries

ISBN 0-7872-3269-5

Printed in the United States of America
10 9 8 7 6 5 4 3 2 1

Dedication

In Memory of

John Edward Donovan	Alice Flora Truax Humphries
Ruth Christine Walker Donovan	Harry Robert Humphries

Contents

Chapter 5
Culture: Cultural Relations That Make a World 165

Chapter 6
Socialization: Internalization of Relationships That Make a World 209

Chapter 7
Gender and Society 265

Chapter 8
Social Structure of the Family   297

Chapter 9
Stratification and Society   321

Chapter 10
Race and Ethnicity: Relationships That Make a World   347

Chapter 11
Crime and Deviance: Nonconforming Relationships That Make a World   393

Chapter 12
Groups, Organizations, Bureaucracy, and Work: Relationships of Power and Exchange That Make a World 447

Preface

As we prepare to enter the next century and the next millennium, we cannot help but to reflect and to wonder what the future of life in human communities and societies will be like, both in the United States and in the global community. Some of us are of the opinion that things have improved over the course of the past two or three decades and over the course of the last century. Others are quick to point out the rise in rates of poverty and of hate crimes and of urban unrest over the last half of the 1990s in the United States, and the end of the Cold War and the concomitant rise of ethnic violence in many parts of Africa, Central and Eastern Europe, and in the newly emerging states of the former Soviet Union. These events are of great concern to the American public. As a result, many Americans are troubled by the future of social life as they look toward the future.

One of the primary objectives of this book is to provide an academic background for understanding the social relationships, history, and culture that constitute everyday social life. The hope is that with an exposure to ways of knowing that are embedded within a liberal arts tradition, that people will be able to arrive at a new level of understanding and cooperation. It is our belief that education can provide a key to understanding the relationships that make a world and that such an understanding will promote greater tolerance and acceptance of cultural diversity and more responsible functioning in the natural, social, political, technological, and economic environments.

The genesis of this book is the sociological tradition. Therefore, sociological theory and methodology serve as its substructure. We situate the sociological frame of reference within the broader context of a liberal arts education. Consequently the scope and orientation of this book are based on a strong interdisciplinary, multicultural approach. Our survey of social life therefore has a strong historical orientation that relies on the sociological method to examine the social issues of the day, the economic, political, and cultural forces that affect social minorities and majorities in the global community, in communities within the United States, and in our intimate primary groups.

As a result of the interdisciplinary, theoretical, empirical, and methodological approach of this book, the reader will learn both to appreciate and critically to assess the research findings of scholars from various academic backgrounds. For this reason, social life is studied from the perspective of the sociologist, historian, anthropologist, economist, demographer, psychologist, social worker, and political scientist.

The first chapter provides an overview of the ways in which the liberal arts and sociology can benefit students personally. It also introduces students to a theme developed in John Steinbeck's *Grapes of Wrath,* where migrant workers who stopped every night on their way to a new life in the West formed relationships out of their common need for solidarity and physical safety. Steinbeck's theme of cohesion, conflict, leadership, exchange, rule making and unmaking—relationships that make a world, is maintained throughout the text as a way of understanding social life.

Every chapter of the book demonstrates the links between theory and research. Students are presented with sociological concepts that they see both in their daily lives and in scholarly research. Each chapter is gender sensitive and multicultural. Consequently, the authors use the most current research as well as classical studies to illuminate the ongoing processes of sociology as they are manifest in the daily lives of both minority and majority groups in American society and elsewhere. American minority groups that are highlighted in this textbook, include white ethnics, Latinos, Asian Americans, Native Americans, and African Americans. Additionally, gender issues are integrated into each chapter. Also, one chapter is devoted to the analysis of gender and another to the analysis of racial and ethnic relations, both in the United States and in other societies.

We are sure that students will appreciate the clear writing style of the book and the systematic presentation of material within each chapter. Each chapter presents a wealth of demographic and economic data to help students understand the past and plan for the future in a highly complex and diverse world. Tables, figures, and graphs are used extensively in each chapter and box readings highlight important aspects of social life, including the contributions made by women and persons of color to the sociological enterprise.

Instructors, whether on the quarter or semester systems, will find the multicultural, gender sensitive, interdisciplinary approach of this book refreshing. The organization and presentation of materials in each chapter are based on years of teaching experience at the community college level, the college level, and the university level, both in the United States and in other countries. Instructors will like the ability to customize the use of this textbook to better fit their needs and preferences as well as those of their students. Instructors may spend more than one week on topics of their selection. Instructors will discover that they can key their lectures to the topics presented in each chapter and still emphasize the topics and theories that they feel are the most important for their students to learn and absorb.

Instructors will find the ample bibliography and the suggested readings at the end of each chapter particularly useful, as these can serve as a working bibliography for student papers and research projects. The list of key terms and important names at the end of each chapter will help students focus on the important concepts and ideas presented in each chapter. In addition, the multiple-choice and true-false questions found at the end of each chapter provide students with yet another way of learning the material. In field testing this book, we have found that when we use these very same questions as exam questions, there is still a considerable distribution of scores, and students experience a significant reduction in evaluation apprehension. A key to the true-false and multiple choice questions is available to instructors who adopt this textbook.

Students and instructors will find the learning exercises at the end of each chapter useful and refreshing. The learning exercises can be assigned as in-class or as out-of-class learning opportunities. Field testing this book reveals that students perceive that answering these exercises helps them to process the material and to retain it. Instructors perceive that having students answer these questions in a non-threatening format—e.g., as a "take-home" opportunity wherein students can re-write their answers as many times as they want within a specified time frame—enhances their critical reasoning abilities.

Students and instructors will find the Internet Resources at the end of each chapter useful. While it is true that many URLs (Uniform Resource Locators), the "addresses" of Web sites, change frequently, those that we use in this book have been somewhat stable. We selected them for that reason. These resources are fun for students to explore and they are educational. We have found it useful to reserve a college computer lab for a class period or two and to "walk" the students through some of the sites and through some of the internet exercises.

In many chapters, the last set of learning exercises is a menu of Sociology and the Iternet Exercises. These have been designed so that they are student friendly, even if the students or their instructors are cyberphobic (i.e., have a fear of computers). Many students have never "surfed the Web" or "gone online." They have heard of the Information Superhighway but have not traveled it. These exercises provide a fun, educational opportunity for students so that they can become familiar with, and more adept at utilizing, this important technological tool. Students use their growing sociological imagination to analyze information found on the Web sites. Some of us, as Instructors, have found it useful to let students themselves select which Sociology and the Internet Exercises they will execute. For these instructors, the course syllabus merely stipulates that each student is responsible for turning in a certain number—say, three—Sociology and the Internet Exercises by a specified date. Students seem to like having a choice. Other instructors, of course, prefer to be more structured in utilizing these assignments.

In addition to the clear academic orientation of the textbook, the general reader will discover a distinct gender and ethnic feeling in the presentation of facts and information. This strong gender and ethnic sensitivity derives from our personal knowledge and experiences of gendered social life and of ethnic and racial groups. It should be clear that this book is not only the result of many years of formal education, research, and teaching, it also derives from the economic data to help students understand the past and plan for the future in a highly complex and experiences of individuals who have lived in the culture.

Marjorie E. Donovan
Juan L. Gonzales, Jr.
Harry L. Humphries
July, 1998

Acknowledgments

Marjorie E. Donovan, Juan L. Gonzales, Jr., and Harry L. Humphries thank a number of individuals and institutions that contributed to the developmental ideas and to the writing of this book.

T.Y.G.

Marjorie E. Donovan

I thank my parents, John Edward Donovan and Ruth Christine Walker Donovan, without whose love, support, encouragement, and sacrifice this work would not have been possible. I thank Buddy, Sheba, and Lucia for their loyal and true companionship. I owe a special debt of gratitude to Olivia Logue. I thank my many instructors and my students.

I thank the Kansas Board of Regents for granting me a semester's sabbatical leave that afforded me the opportunity to work on a preliminary draft of parts of this manuscript. I thank Orville Brill, Dean of the College of Arts and Sciences, for his support. I thank Randy Rosenbaum, Printing Services, for his unflagging assistance and support, without which I do not know how I would have completed this arduous project. I am indebted to William Frances Shea for his friendship and encouragement and to Joseph Isaac Lipson for modeling the joys and passion of the life of the mind. I am indebted to C.H. Patton for modeling the joys of teaching sociology. I thank Jim Cooke for his encouragement and friendship. I thank Bob, Susan, Gracie, and Smudge Deckhart, whose friendship and support made this arduous task more manageable and without whose insights into natural health it may not have been possible. I thank Chris Fogliasso, Peggy and Walter Smith, and Janice Tillman. I thank Steve Shepherd, friend and home-computer mentor; Waymon Jenkins; Sherri Flood and Curt Benelli at ASSI Computers; Robert A. Walter, Dean, Learning Resources; Richard Samford, Interlibrary-Loan Librarian; Doug Stehle, Bibliographic-Instruction Librarian; Cynthia Pfannenstiel, Coordinator of Public Services; Susan Johns, Circulation Librarian; Leon H. Mayhew; Juan Gonzales; Linda Marie Fritschner; Margaret Bierly; and Susan Cooper. Special thanks to Kendall/Hunt Publishing Company. I thank Cheryl Lewis for the many hours of careful editing. Her efforts made this a better book. I owe a special debt of gratitude to John Finley Scott.

Harry L. Humphries

I owe a debt of gratitude to the Kansas Board of Regents for granting me a year's sabbatical leave from Pittsburg State University. I wrote a preliminary draft of several chapters of this text while on sabbatical leave at Kazan State University, Russian Federation from August 1994, to June 1995. Professor Orville Brill, Dean of the College of Arts and Sciences, has been supportive of this work. I thank the United States Information Agency for the Fulbright-Hays grant that allowed me to study and to teach abroad. I thank Ms. Natasha Rudakova, now a doctoral student in anthropology at Stanford University, for her insights into culture. Natasha's parents, Vladimir and Anna, opened their hearts to me, making my stay in Kazan delightful and gratifying. I thank Edward Akmetshin, now a doctoral in sociology at the University of Chicago, who was invaluable as a translator and interpreter. Edward unselfishly allowed me into the world of the Tatar people. I also acknowledge the help of Professor Alexander Salagaev, Kazan State University, at whose kitchen table we spent many hours discussing Russia's past and its ominous future. Most importantly, I thank the numerous introduction to sociology students in Russia, Finland, and America, all of whom provided numerous comments and insights helpful in formulating the context of this work.

Ms. Donna Dutcher, law student at Harvard Law School, provided feedback on various preliminary drafts. Ms. Jill Campbell Docherty edited several chapters. Thank you for the thorough and fast work. Professor Robert Backes, Physics Department, read many of the preliminary chapters. Carl Slawski, Professor of Sociology at California State University, Long Beach, provided many of the theoretical insights found in this book.

I thank Linda K Humphries, my wife, for her love and support. Linda read and reread many drafts of this manuscript. Linda shared new ineas concerning adult learning.

I owe a debt of gratitude to Albert J. Szymanski (1941-1985) who provided me insights into many of the intellectual issues that inform this book.

Juan L. Gonzales Jr.

I would like to thank my graduate research assistant, Kari Adams, for all of the time she spent in the campus library and on the web to make my contribution to this volume possible. And I would also like to thank Rosa Gonzales for her continued support of all my research and writing projects.

In addition I would like to acknowledge the contribution made by Minu Mathur to our chapter on "Crime and Deviance" and the contribution of Vibha Chandra to our chapters on "Gender" and "Stratification and Society."

Our Lives, Liberal Arts and the Uses of Relationships That Make a World

In the evening, sitting about the fires, the twenty were one. They grew to be units of the camps . . . Every night relationships that make a world, established; and every morning the world torn down like a circus.

John Steinbeck, *The Grapes of Wrath*

■   ■   ■

The first goal of this book is to assist students to function responsibly in their natural, social, political, technological, and economic environments. Its developmental ideas are the product of over forty years of teaching introduction to sociology in colleges and universities in this country as well as abroad.

During the course for which this is the required text, please reflect on the following issues. (Yes, you will have an opportunity to put your reflections in writing nearer the end of the course!) Consider what an education is, how it can affect a person's self-concept and view of the world; how education can re-focus a person's sense of well being; how an education can affect a person's ideas about work, leisure, values, and the life of the mind.

- Consider what "human nature" is as it is defined and expressed throughout this textbook and course.
- Consider what "work" and "leisure" are as they express or satisfy human nature.

- Consider what your education means in reference to the views you have of human beings and in terms of what you have learned from your families, communities, and society.

Choices

You always will be faced with choices. (Will you study for the big test scheduled for 8 a.m. Monday morning in Chemistry 101, or will you go on that ski trip with your friends? Will you take college courses in research methods, data analysis, and statistics even if they are not required for your academic major or minor? What you learn in these courses would be of use to you in the job market.)

An informed, rational choice is influenced by a full knowledge of the consequences and implications of the choices one makes. An introduction-to-sociology course can help you make informed choices in your life by affording you the opportunity to understand how social systems operate.

Liberal-Arts Education

When survey researchers ask students why they are attending college, the modal (i.e., most frequently occurring) response is: "So I can get a better job when I graduate than I otherwise would be able to get." Perhaps that also is why you are attending college, or perhaps it is at least part of the reason why you are doing so.

Research on the relationship among education, occupation, income, and employment status (e.g., employed, unemployed, underemployed) confirms that it *is* necessary to have an education and high-order cognitive skills in order to get, to keep, and to be promoted in well-paying jobs (Bishop, 1994). In the United States in 1993, males between ages 25 to 34 had earnings of roughly $33,000 per year if they were college graduates, which is more than 50 percent greater than the earnings of male high-school graduates, and more than 200 percent greater than the earnings of male high-school dropouts (Decker, Rice, and Moore, 1997). The corresponding figures for females are similar.

Data also support the observation that occupational success is facilitated by knowing how to apply generalizations, principles, theories or rules to new social situations and/or to the real world (Murnane, Willett, and Levy, 1995). An introduction-to-sociology course can help you to acquire and to hone these abilities. (Yes, these abilities can be learned, which is demonstrated by Harry Edwards' story, which you shortly will read.) In other words, a second goal of this book is to encourage you to think critically, to reason and to analyze. After all, learning to do those things is at the very heart of a liberal-arts education.

A liberal-arts education is broadly based, and it enables the individual to be **critically self-conscious**. To be **critically self-conscious** means to be able to perceive things (including yourself) as broken down into their fundamental constituent parts. This ability includes being able to perceive the social world as consisting of more than one element. Throughout this text, you will have many opportunities to analyze and to synthesize information.

Three basic assumptions inform this textbook.

- First, if we want to understand any society, we must first comprehend its history. This text is written within the context of the history of both Western Europe and the United States.

- Second, comparison is central to critical understanding. If we want critically to understand, we must have something or someone for comparison. In this text, we compare the society of the United States with other societies, past and present.

- Third, if we want to understand any society, we must first discern the processes of which it is composed. To use a metaphor, laws of nature (e.g., gravity, and entropy) govern the universe. Understanding these natural laws has enabled human beings to do many things. It is not an easy task, as we will see, to discern and to understand the social forces or processes that govern human societies. We accomplish (or at least pursue) this formidable task by using a particular method (which we will come to recognize as the scientific method) and by using a perspective, a sociological one.

Sociology as the Study of Patterns of Social Relations: Ties That Bind

We want you to develop an understanding of contemporary social issues. In this textbook you will learn various sociological paradigms by means of which you may analyze social issues both past and present. A **paradigm** is a fundamental framework for making sense out of (and for attributing meaning to) happenings, events, and objects in the social world. (Throughout this text, you will have many opportunities to demonstrate, in writing, your growing sociological awareness of various contemporary social issues). This understanding is facilitated by appreciating that there are several types of relationships and interactions that bind a group together and that further the pursuit and attainment of individual and collective goals.

John Steinbeck, a famous American novelist, understood this. In *The Grapes of Wrath* (1939: 213), John Steinbeck observes that "In

Learning Exercise 1.1

True-False Questions (Adapted from Goode, 1997: 14-15 ff)

Please answer each of the following questions by circling either "True" or "False." Unless otherwise indicated, all questions refer to the United States today.

1. Among all age categories in the U.S., *the elderly* are most likely to be victimized by violent street crime.
   (A) True   (B) False

2. Statistically speaking, the probability of being murdered is just as high in a small town as in a big city.
   (A) True   (B) False

3. Females are more likely to *attempt* suicide but males are more likely to *commit* suicide.
   (A) True   (B) False

4. Of all males who have had a homosexual experience to the point of orgasm, only *a small percent* of them develop a homosexual self-identity, shun females as sexual partners, and engage exclusively in same-sex sexual activity.
   (A) True   (B) False

5. Most murders are *intra-racial* (i.e., whites who murder tend to murder whites, African Americans who murder tend to murder African Americans, etc.).
   (A) True   (B) False

6. In the *world* today, the most prevalent mode of transmission of AIDS (acquired immune deficiency syndrome) and of the HIV virus (the human immune deficiency virus) is via *homosexual* sexual contact.
   (A) True   (B) False

7. During Prohibition (1920 - 1933), alcohol consumption in the United States actually *increased*.
   (A) True   (B) False

For correct answers, please turn page upside-down.

Correct Answers: 1. False, 2. False, 3. True, 4. True, 5. True, 6. False, 7. False

3

the evening, sitting about the fires, the twenty were one. They grew to be units of the camps . . . Every night relationships that make a world, established; and every morning the world torn down like a circus." What Steinbeck is referring to is the growth of social organization in the night-time camps that migrant laborers formed each night on their way to California or while traveling around in California during the dust-bowl years of the 1930's.

That quote, of course, is part of a much larger passage in which he describes in perceptive terms what is involved in making a world. Steinbeck describes how collections of people who hadn't known each other at all, would, just in this special context of traveling as a migrant, recognize that they in fact had a great deal in common, and would form, on the spur of the moment as it were, small societies, with everything that the term "society" implies. Thus, Steinbeck, in some detail, describes within the camps the growth of fellow feeling (**solidary order**); the growth of rules and of sanctions (**normative order**); the emergence of leadership (**imperative order**); and the growth of a division of labor (**exchange order**). He describes, in other words, *all those relationships that make a world.* A great deal of human conduct is to be understood in terms of these categories of experience; in terms of playing roles in these categories of experience; in terms of humans trying to create, to reinforce, to affirm, to solidify, to tear down, and even to replace those systems.

Sociology describes and analyzes the components of social organization, that is, the basic categories of experience that make a world. This analysis is accomplished at one or more of three levels—the small-scale or **micro** level; the large-scale or **macro** level; and the in-between or **meso** level.

The sense of the "we" is one of the kinds of relationship that makes a world. It's one of the things in the camps that Steinbeck describes that make him feel it would not be an exaggeration to say that in the evening, sitting around the campfire, the twenty were one, because this sense of identity, of solidarity, of loyalty, of "**we-ness**" developed. The concept of solidarity is illustrated throughout the text. We belong to groups like our families, to whom we are

loyal and from whom initially we receive our identity. The family is one of many relationships that make a world.

Sociology also focuses on another thing that Steinbeck says makes a world—rules, norms, and sanctions. These concepts of norms and of normative order are analyzed throughout this text. **Norms** are rules of behavior that have negative and positive sanctions attached to them. A **negative sanction** is a punishment; a **positive sanction** is a reward.

Almost from its very beginnings, sociology has focused on another thing that Steinbeck says helped to make these migrant camps worlds or societies—leadership. Leadership emerges in the nighttime camps. Leadership is a form of what the German sociologist Max Weber calls **domination,** the right to command and the duty to obey. Chapter 12 (Groups, Organizations, Bureaucracy, and Work: Relationships of Power and Exchange That Make a World) analyzes the various forms of domination that constitute imperative order. Imperative order—its sources, manifestations, and relationships with other forms of social organization—is explicitly addressed in Chapter 12, under the heading of Imperative Order in Human Groups. Chapter 12 also focuses on exchange relationships in social life.

The major transformations we are witnessing in the world today are analyzed throughout this text in terms of the relations among the processes of solidary order, normative order, imperative order, and exchange. These transformations include, but are not limited to, those occurring in the countries of the former Soviet Union; in Bosnia and Serbia; in many of the nations of Africa and of the Middle East. A basic understanding of relationships that make a world helps make intelligible transformations in social worlds both at the macro and micro levels. Thus, sociology even helps us to understand cultural diversity both within the United States and globally.

More Ways Sociology Can Benefit You Personally

A sociological perspective also benefits you personally by assisting you in accomplishing the following (Macionis, 1996):

1. **Confront your familiar understanding of yourself and of others,** so you can critically assess the validity of your views. For instance, most of us who answered the true-false quiz in Learning Exercise 1.1 probably framed our answers on the basis of what we supposed was "true" or "false." When American sociologist Erich Goode asked questions like these to students enrolled in his undergraduate social deviance course in the autumn of 1995, the average percent of correct answers was a shade under fifty percent (49.7 percent). In other words, *the probability that a student would answer a question correctly was* about 50%, or, as a statistician might say, *no better than pure chance.* A student would have answered just as well by flipping a coin to arrive at an answer. What percent of correct answers did you get?

   Professor Goode only asked questions to which there were clear, more or less undisputed answers. Research findings consistently indicate the correct answer to each of the above questions. Of course, if you choose to believe what you *think* is true, even when solid research demonstrates that it is false, you are free to do so. In that case, however, you need to be very clear to yourself and to others that you are holding a *personal* opinion, not one based on solid, representative, verified, and replicated observation. Throughout this text, including in Chapter 4 (Human Inquiry and Research Methods), you are introduced to procedures, ways of knowing, and resources that assist you in identifying problems and in locating appropriate resources by means of which you may fashion logical and reasonable responses.

2. **Detect the opportunities and constraints that characterize the modern world.** The Information Society has arrived. In the twenty-first century knowledge is power and to have power is to be a more effective "player." One variety of power is what might be called "word power." The person who writes well possesses a scarce skill that is widely valued in the market place. Part of writing well is having a rich vocabulary. Whenever you do not know the meaning of a word, look it up in a dictionary. Read the definition of the word. Construct a sentence in which you use that word. By such small yet painstaking steps a vast vocabulary is built.

   Another variety of power is the ability to distinguish relevant from irrelevant information when you are required to solve problems. This book provides you with opportunities to distinguish relevant from irrelevant information within a problem-solving context.

3. **Take control.** The appreciation of social dynamics afforded by a sociological perspective can serve as a catalyst for personal empowerment. What sociologists term personal empowerment is sometimes called an **internal locus of control** by social psychologists. When one has an internal locus of control, one views oneself as captain of one's own ship, as master of one's own life and fate. When one has an **external locus of control,** one views oneself as buffeted about by forces over which one has no control. One is a mere ball on the pool-table of life, caroming in one direction or another, depending on what the cue ball does.

   When one has an internal locus of control, one is an active participant in life rather than a passive observer. For some, this means embracing society as it is and taking advantage of both the opportunities and constraints (Ruggiero and Taylor, 1997). For others, empowerment means changing the way things are. In both cases, identifying the processes that maintain social order and those that undermine it is a first step in assessing the consequences for us personally.

4. **Participate effectively in the challenges of living in a diverse world.** Some of you might say, "I don't want to live in a diverse world." Well, welcome to a diverse world, anyway! North America represents only 5 percent of the world's population (United Nations, 1996); and, as Table 1.1 indicates, during your lifetime, the characteristics of the population of the United States itself will radically change. Table 1.1 indicates, for instance, that in 1995 persons of Hispanic origin (who may be referred to by sociologists as **Latinos**) comprised about

10 percent of the U.S. population. Latinos are expected to constitute fully one person in four (25%) by the year 2050. The corresponding figures for persons of Asian descent are four percent and nine percent, respectively (U.S. Bureau of the Census, 1996).

If you live in a large city in the United States today or are gainfully employed in the global economy, or even if you are an entrepreneur, you probably work for or with people (either as customers or as co-workers) who at first glance may appear dramatically different from you. A sociological perspective assists us both to appreciate and to flourish within the context of diversity.

5. **Depersonalize the personal.** Many of us have family members or friends who have been unemployed. Perhaps you are attending college after having experienced unemployment yourself. Becoming and being unemployed are personal, intense challenges. Yet many people have only a vague idea as to why they themselves became unemployed.

Right now 800 million people in the world are either recently unemployed or currently underemployed because of technological change (CIA World Fact Book, 1995). It is not their "fault" that they lost their jobs. This often-searing experience was *not* due to one or more personal defects, such as being lazy, drunk, abrasive, or inept. After all, we are not born with crystal balls that allow us to see into

the future. A sociological perspective, though, serves as a crystal ball of sorts: it enables us to see how numerous social forces affect our personal lives. Without a sociological perspective, we might not even *perceive* the social forces that influence us. *A sociological view helps make the invisible visible to us.* It is a relief to understand that losing your job is not your fault and is not a personal failing. A sociological perspective equips us so that we can better grasp what we need to know to become employable and to remain employed. A sociological perspective helps us to take control of our lives.

Recent survey research informs us what the top ten career prospects are predicted to be in this country by the year 2005, about seven years from now. These fast-growing and lucrative employment opportunities are presented in Table 1.2.

There are at least four ways in which sociology can benefit you, personally, in obtaining and in preparing you for one of these careers. First, all of these occupations are in the "helping" professions. They require you to understand people. Not only are such occupations gratifying and well paying, but in this country they are part of the shift in employment from the manufacturing sector to the service sector of the economy. Sociology helps you obtain these occupations by making you aware of the different needs of a diverse group of people who will seek out your services.

Second, these occupations focus on communication, a topic of considerable importance in sociology. Interpersonal and cultural com-

TABLE 1.1. Asian and Hispanic Resident Population as a Percent of the U.S. Population, 1995, and Projections for Selected Years, 2000 to 2050 _____

Date	Ethnicity	
	Asian	*Hispanic Origin*
1995	3.5	10.3
2000	4.1	11.4
2010	5.1	13.8
2015	5.6	15.1
2025	6.6	17.6
2050	8.7	24.5

Source: U.S. Bureau of the Census, *Statistical Abstract of the United States 1996* (116th edition) (Washington, D.C.: U.S. Government Printing Office, 1996), Tables 12 and 13, page 14.

munication are topics covered in this textbook. Even computer engineers have to be able to work within a group situation in solving problems. For example, they have to be able to communicate with their colleagues, many of whose ethnic backgrounds differ from their own. Sociology enhances our understanding of the processes of leadership, exchange, normative, and solidary order within such groups.

Third, all of these occupations require that you know how to conduct and/or to be literate consumers of research methods. Knowing how to conduct research is a skill that increasingly is required in many occupations. Some sociology majors even have become marketing specialists by learning research methodologies.

Fourth, occupations in corrections, law enforcement, and residential counseling are specialties directly related to the field of sociology. Understanding the fundamentals of sociology is imperative for successful community policing and detective work. These specialties are offered in many colleges and universities in this country through departments of sociology and social work. Even in many social-work programs, numerous sociology courses are either required or recommended.

As we have seen, there are many practical uses of sociology. A main reason for you to learn the principles of sociology, of course, is to be an educated person. As we have indicated, critical thinking is a primary focus of this textbook. As authors and educators we want

you to achieve maximum competence in listening and speaking skills, reading, writing, critical thinking, synthesizing data, and manipulating symbols. Throughout this textbook, those learning objectives are achieved by giving you the opportunity to strengthen your abilities in recognition and recall, interpretation and analysis, and in the application of concepts and theories to solving problems encountered in the real world. Let us now briefly address each of these domains. Please pay special attention to items with check marks (✔).

- **Recognition and Recall**
  - ✔ You should be able to reveal main themes in what you read. Remember: practice makes progress.
  - ✔ Each chapter has in **bold,** concepts that are relevant for you to understand. At the end of each chapter these concepts are again brought to your attention.
  - ✔ At the end of each chapter there are learning exercises that give you the opportunity to practice using and applying these concepts.
- **Interpretation and Analysis**
  - ✔ You should be able to connect sociological concepts with your own ideas, values, and behaviors and with the ideas, values, and behaviors of others.
  - ✔ If you experience frustration in understanding the material or if you disagree with the material presented, you should

TABLE 1.2. Future Occupational Growth in Ten Selected Occupations _____

Occupation	Projected number of job openings by 2005	Projected percent increase in jobs, 1994–2005	Estimated first-year salary, in U.S. dollars
Systems Analyst	481,000	92	43,000
Computer Engineer	191,000	90	38,500
Physical Therapist	96,000	80	31,900
Residential Counselor	158,000	76	35,600
Occupational Therapist	47,000	72	36,700
Paralegal	74,000	58	25,600
Special-Education Teacher	262,000	52	30,000
Amusement and Recreation Attendant	211,000	52	16,900
Corrections Officer, Law Enforcement	194,000	51	24,900
Speech-Language Pathologist and Audiologist	52,000	46	26,000

Source: US Bureau of Labor Statistics, 1996.

be able to identify and to discuss the source(s) of your disagreement and/or frustration. In accomplishing these ends, you should demonstrate logical argument and support the points you make.

■ **Application**
  ✔ You should be able to reflect on the reading materials in relation to what you know from your own experiences. Can you identify with some of the concepts explained in the text?
  ✔ You should be able to argue for or against the propositions or main themes in this text. For example, are we "constrained by society" or are we "free do as we please?"
  ✔ You should be prepared to be able to explain these ideas to a variety of others: to your parents, loved ones, or the telephone operator.

At the end of each chapter there are learning exercises for you to complete. In some chapters you even have the option of watching and then analyzing movies or videos to demonstrate to the instructor (and to yourself!) your comprehension of the materials. There are also in-class exercises that can be turned in for a grade. At the end of each chapter actual multiple-choice and true-false questions are presented, so that you may have yet another way of assessing your grasp of the material.

Study

If you want to be the best automobile mechanic and to make the most money as a mechanic, you study with the best mechanics and read the best literature. If you want to be the best brain surgeon, you study with the best brain surgeons and go to the best medical school. You certainly would not want to take your car to an incompetent automobile mechanic, nor would you want to submit to surgery at the hands of an incompetent brain surgeon. In short, a key to success in anything, including love, is an authentic desire to want to learn. To quote the famous sociologist, Karl Marx:

> If you want to enjoy art, you must be an artistically cultivated person; if you want to exercise influence over other people, you must

be a person with stimulating and encouraging effect on other people . . . if you love without evoking love in return . . . that is if your loving as a loving person does not produce reciprocal love. . . . then your love is impotent—a misfortune. (Marx, 1844, *Economic and Philosophic Manuscripts*, as cited in Tucker, 1978: 105)

Two important things that Karl Marx is telling us are (1) that there are no shortcuts to success and (2) that if we want to succeed at anything, we must have a *desire to learn.* Studying is a key to success for most of us. As Marx tells us and as Harry Edwards tells us later in this chapter, the key to success is our desire or passion to learn. Some students, however, do not possess the *skills* for learning even when they have the *desire.* Do not despair: skills can be learned. If you now lack the skills to learn, honestly acknowledge that fact and do something about it. In other words, be proactive. It is up to you actively to construct your education. Others cannot do it for you. Do not expect to become an educated person by rotely consuming (memorizing) information and knowledge. If that's all you do, you will transform yourself into a hack. To be educated, you need to be able to make sense out of what you learn, to apply it, to use it as a tool, *and* to cherish it *as an end it itself.* In constructing your education, we encourage you to make the most of the following three resources at your disposal:

■ *Time Management* Carpe diem! (Seize the day!) Do not procrastinate. Plan each day down to the hours and minutes in reference to what you need to accomplish. Look ahead to what needs to be done. Studying requires time, time that is unencumbered by other things. The verb "to study" originally comes from the verb "to worship." It is time you set aside for one important thing. Consider studying as a holy activity. Just say "No" to unholy activities.

■ *Words, concepts, ideas, and other things you do not understand* Obtain a college dictionary. Use it. Write down words, ideas, and other things you do not understand. Look them up. Ask questions in class. Visit your professors during office hours; they are more than happy to visit with you. Start using words you have just learned in your daily speech. Make sure you also use them in your writing assignments.

- *Professors* Your instructors are here to instruct and to help you learn. No matter what subject you are taking, professors are at your disposal. Most professors are delighted when you come by the office to visit. We like to get to know you.

Many students think of us as teachers only; but many of us, as our Ph.D.'s indicate, are also specialists in our own field. We have studied certain academic areas that are not familiar to most lay persons. We conduct scientific research and write scholarly papers. We "claim skill in or knowledge of" our field (Davies, 1976: 562); in short, we not only teach, we profess. If you have difficulty with the course materials professors can assist you in finding out what you need to know. By attending the college or university of your choice, you have direct access to your professors. Do not short-change yourself: make use of this valuable resource.

The heart of the matter is that *your education is up to you*. To use another metaphor: while society has dealt you your hand, you still have the opportunity to play the game. Harry Edwards, now a famous American sociologist, came to understand this when he was a young, poor, struggling African-American student in a largely white world that he deeply distrusted. We've quoted a long passage from his autobiography in Box 1.1.

Harry Edwards now is a famous professor of sociology at the University of California, Berkeley. He pioneered a specialty in American sociology that is known as the sociology of sport. If you watch a football game played by the San Francisco Forty Niners, for whom Harry Edwards consults, you might notice him standing along their sidelines.

BOX 1.1

Harry Edward's Story

At Fresno City College that semester I took history, psychology, English composition, speech, sociology, health, and track and field—seventeen units. Coach Ginsburg bought my books for me and took me on a tour of the campus, pointing out where each class was located. . . .

It didn't take long for me to discover that old attitudes and habits are very hard to break. Academically and athletically, I found the challenge of changing directions formidable. I found trusting and working with my new coach as challenging as the academic tasks. Nonetheless, I became very fond of Coach Ginsburg, though I never really got to know him—perhaps because I never let him get close enough to really know me. I was always amused to catch him staring at me. And then one day he told me what he was thinking. "What is Edwards's real story?

He drops in here from two thousand miles away, yet has never moved so much as an inch toward anyone." I simply shrugged my shoulders and smiled.

Academically, my greatest struggle was with myself. The last book I'd read cover to cover was my sixth-grade reader at Dunbar Elementary School. Since that time, I'd grown to hate reading. I found it boring, tedious, and pointless.

But now I was confronted with six courses requiring a total of thirteen thick books, and in every course the examinations and reports were based almost solely on the readings. The readings had to be done and it had to be done efficiently.

At first, I slipped further and further behind the assigned reading schedules. And worse, I could remember virtually nothing of what I *was* able to complete. This became so frustrat-

ing that I began to copy, word for word, everything I read. I found that I could retain more but was able to get less read.

I then began underlining the "important" information from each reading assignment. I typically ended by underlining virtually every line in a chapter, and I still failed to increase my retention.

I visited each of my professors only to find that I had tried everything they could suggest. One, the history instructor, speculated that perhaps I had overestimated my ability to handle the workload, the college transfer curriculum, or both—a notion I respectfully "shined on" (dismissed) because I had no choice. *I had to handle them.* I had to take every course on my schedule. I had no alternative but to keep trying, to keep reading and rereading, underlining and taking more notes, and then rereading again. The routine consumed more and more time, to the point that by midterm exam week I was only getting three hours of sleep a night.

Finally, I cracked. I was in the college library trying to study for my history examination. I knew what the instructor suspected about my ability to do the work, and not only was I determined to do well in history because I had to do well, but I was equally determined to prove him wrong. In fact, I knew he was wrong. But I couldn't remember much of what I had read; I couldn't retain the material. I slammed the book shut and began to sob—six feet eight inches tall by now and 240 pounds, sitting in the library crying into my hands out of pure frustration. . . .

Looking through a veil of tears that would not stop flowing, my eyes skipping over several blocks of underlined material, I read something that I had known since my earliest years at Denverside Elementary School: "Columbus discovered America . . . and he and his small band of weary men . . . encountered people they thought to be Indians."

I rubbed my eyes — once, twice, three times until they were dry—and read the statements again. I thought that there must be some mistake. It suddenly seemed patently absurd to me that a lost Italian traveling on Spanish papers, who did not know where he was going, who did not know where he was when he got there or where he had been when he returned to Spain, should be credited with "discovering" America—especially when there were people standing onshore watching him get off the boat!

I turned quickly to other sections of the book. I found that other Europeans had "discovered" other places already inhabited by other people. I learned that George Washington, the Father of our Country, the champion of freedom, justice, and human dignity, was a devout slave owner.

I discovered that Thomas Jefferson, who coined the Declaration of Independence, who penned the phrase, "All Men are created equal and endowed by their creator with certain unalienable rights . . . Life, Liberty and the Pursuit of Happiness"—this Thomas Jefferson had not only owned slaves but was accused of siring children by at least one Black slave woman—Sally Hemmings—and then turning around and enslaving his own children!

I read more. And more. More rapidly now, gulping down sentences, paragraphs, and then entire pages, searching out that hidden assumption, that key, that linchpin, following that thread of logic that held the story together. And the more I read, the more I realized that there was a story, an argument implicit within every sentence, every paragraph, and every chapter of the book. And the character of the argument, the nature of the story depended upon the perspective of the person who wrote the book and how that person wanted the reader to view the subjects covered.

The more I read, the more excited I became. I soon found that there was a message, a story, somebody's point of view implicit in every book I had been assigned in the course. *I had learned to read critically.* And unless one is reading critically, one is not reading at all. It be-

came clear that until then, I'd been saying the sentences rather than synthesizing and interrelating their meanings into ideas, and then critically analyzing—on the spot—the consistency of those ideas. I'd mistaken mastering the medium for comprehending the message. It was as if I'd been listening to a speaker and hearing only the words rather than *what was being said.* Little wonder I had difficulty retaining what I read. I may as well have been trying to memorize an unalphabetized dictionary word for word. . . .

"Two exam books? You're bluffing, Edwards. You know, these are not going to be graded by the pound," . . .

"I was surprised at the caliber of your work, Edwards. But don't let the midterm grade go to your head. My first exam is always a Mickey. You should probably know too that you have a long way to go—but you *do* think. You're crude, but you *do* think. Let me know if I can help you."

His words resounded through my head—"You *do* think . . . You *do* think . . . You *do* think . . ."—finally meshing with one of my father's favorite philosophical quotes, ". . . *therefore I am,*" and one his most often voiced aspirations for his children—"Somebody!"

. . . I felt as if I had stepped from the cold, damp, darkness of a cave into the bright, warm sunshine for the first time in my life. I could read and understand those books! I could think, and what was more, I *loved* it; I'd rediscovered a passion, a joy in learning that been lost since my elementary school days . . . (Excerpted from Harry Edwards, 1980: 102-106. Italics in original.)

Key Concepts

domination	negative sanction	solidary order
exchange order	norm	the macro level
external locus of control	normative order	the micro level
imperative order	personal empowerment	the ways that sociology can
internal locus of control	positive sanction	benefit you personally
Latinos	relationships that make a world	to be critically self-conscious

Internet Resources

gopher://INET.ed.gov:12002

Document: Gopher Menu. At this site, select **Eric.src**

ERIC is a clearinghouse for educational material. Below we list some ERIC publications related to enhancing one's study skills and to coping with the stress of the college experience. ERIC's URL is **gopher://INET.ed.gov:12002** Once you are in the ERIC web site, you will be asked to enter a keyword. At the query prompt, simply enter the title of the publication you want. You could try entering the number listed to the left of each title, below. That is supposed to work. If the number does not work, as sometimes happens, do not panic. Simply enter the title at the query prompt. This generally works for me.

Number	*Title*
ED250696	Vocabulary
ED291205	Critical Presentation Skills—Research to Practice
ED300805	Note-Taking: What Do We Know About the Benefits?
ED301143	Learning Styles
ED302558	Improving Your Test-Taking Skills
ED284526	Reducing Stress Among Students

http://www.census.gov/population/www/pop-profile/profile.html

Document: U.S. Census Bureau's Population Profile of the United States: 1995

Scroll to the end of document and use the icons there to access information.

http://www.odci.gov/cia/publications/factbook/country.html

Document: The CIA World Fact Book, Table of Contents for All Countries

This Central Intelligence Agency (CIA) site contains information on the world—the world unemployment rates, population size for the world, and so forth. It also contains information by country. Scroll down to the "W" section and click on **world.** This will bring you to the global information part of the site. Browse here: click on people, economy, military, transnational issues, etc.

http://www.prb.org/

Document: The Population Reference Bureau Home Page

The Population Reference Bureau provides data related to population and population growth around the planet.

http://www.educom.edu/web/pubs/review/reviewArticles/31231.html

Document: Jeremy J. Shapiro and Shelley K. Hughes, "Information Literacy as a Liberal Art," ***Educom Review,*** Vol. 31, No. 2, (March/April) 1996.

Job searching on the Internet:

Website	URL
1998-1999 Occupational Outlook Handbook, Finding a Job and Evaluating a Job Offer	http://stats.bls.gov/oco/oco2004.htm
Social Science Job Resources	http://osiris.colorado.edu/POLSCI/RES/job.html
Job Search by Field	http://www.uwsp.edu/stuserv/career/fields.htm
International Job Opportunities	http://www.cc.emory.edu/OIA/stwork_abroad.html
Health and Human Services	http://www.os.dhhs.gov/psc/hrs/

Learning Exercise 1.2

Writing Assignment

Write a five-page, typed, double-spaced paper. Please staple it in the upper-left hand corner. In this assignment, your are to write a response to the following issues:

1. Recognition and Recall
   - Narrate Edwards' story, especially the change that occurred in his reading ability.
   - Characterize Edwards with special attention to his background, lifestyle, and values.
2. Interpretation and Analysis
   - You should be able to infer what benefits a sociological perspective might be in understanding Edwards' experiences that night at the library.
   - You should be able to explain *why* Edwards became a good student: what became different in his performance?
   - You should be able to explain "thinking" as Edwards comes to perform it and to perceive it.
3. Application
   - Are your experiences or perceptions anything like those Edwards describes?
   - Have you ever, yourself, made a discovery like his? (We call this a personal paradigm shift.)

■ ■ ■

Learning Exercise 1.3

Internet Assignment

Use Alta Vista or Yahoo! as a search engine. Go to the following Web site: *http://www.mdv.gwdg.de/~unamed/amiland.html.* From this site you can find colleges and universities in the United States that offer bachelor and higher degrees in the United States, Canada, and other countries. You can also find community colleges in the USA, Canada, and Europe.

1. Visit your college or university's Web site Home Page. Spend some time browsing there. How does your college or university's projected image match your own experiences as a student? What are the similarities, the differences? Please tell us about it. What do you think accounts for the discrepancies that you perceive?
2. If you could go to any college/university in the world, which would it be? (If you *are* attending the college or university of your dreams, you are to select another one that also is high up on your list of the best places to attend college.) Visit its Web page. Spend some time browsing there. In what ways is this college's projected image similar to and different from the experiences you have had at the college you are attending? Please tell us about it.

■ ■ ■

Multiple-Choice Test

1. If one is critically self-conscious, one is able to perceive _____.
   A. things as broken down into their fundamental constituent parts
   B. the fundamental constituent parts of one's self
   C. the social world as consisting of more than one part or element
   D. all of the above
   E. none of the above

2. Which of the following fundamental assumptions inform this textbook?
   A. We need to comprehend a society's history if we want to understand that society.
   B. Comparison is not necessary for critical understanding.
   C. If we want to understand a society, we need to be able to discern the processes of which it is composed.
   D. All of the above.
   E. Only (A) and (C)

3. Relationships that make a world include _____ order.
   A. normative
   B. imperative
   C. exchange
   D. solidary
   E. all of the above

4. Leadership is an example of what German sociologist Max Weber would call _____.
   A. normative order
   B. solidary order
   C. exchange order
   D. imperative order

5. Sociology analyzes social organization at the large-scale or _____ level as well as at the small-scale or _____ level.
   A. micro; macro
   B. macro; micro

6. If one has a(n) _____ one views oneself as master of one's own life and fate and is an active rather than a passive observer.
   A. internal locus of control
   B. external locus of control

7. North America represents _____ percent of the world's population.
   A. one
   B. five
   C. fifteen
   D. twenty-five
   E. thirty

8. The right to command and the duty to obey refers to _____.
   A. solidary order
   B. domination
   C. ritual
   D. anomie
   E. all of the above

9. Which of the following is the perspective taken by the authors regarding your education?
   A. Fortune is fickle, so don't bother getting an education.
   B. Your education is up to you; while society has dealt you a hand, the game is still yours to play.
   C. If you do not possess the *skills* for learning, do yourself a favor and drop out of school right now, so that you do not squander your time.
   D. Make the most of the resources at your disposal, including your professors and time management.
   E. Both (B) and (D)

10. A framework for understanding the world is a _____.
    A. paradigm
    B. hypothesis
    C. blind guess
    D. double-blind study

11. This sociologist pioneered the specialty area in American sociology known as the sociology of sport.
    A. Karl Marx
    B. Erich Goode
    C. Harry Edwards
    D. Max Weber

CHAPTER 2

The Impact of Social Structure

The mind that has conceived a plan of living must never lose sight of the chaos against which that pattern was conceived. That goes for society as well as individuals.

Ralph Ellison, *Invisible Man*

■ ■ ■

My father was born October 31, 1901, in Monrovia, Kansas, just northeast of Topeka. He was born in his father's farmhouse. He had two sisters and a brother. The brother died at birth. His father was a sharecropper who shared land with an African-American family. They used domesticated animals to plant and to harvest their crops. Often, when his parents toiled in the fields, a black woman would feed both families at lunch and dinner. When my father was old enough, he helped his parents plant and harvest their crops. In return he received a meal, a place to sleep, and he had the comforts of family life. Through cooperation with the African-American family, they survived. Of course, the majority of the crop went to the white landlord from whom they rented the land.

They had no electricity. The toilet facility was an outhouse. It was common for children to die in their first year of life due to infectious diseases. When he was a child, there were no antibiotics. When people had earaches, they just suffered. My father wore a hearing aid all of his adult life due to childhood ear infections.

He played baseball, football, did his homework, and after dinner, sang songs for entertainment with his family. He left the farm for

what he assumed would be a better life in the city when he was 17 years old. When he left home, his father "broke the plate" on which his son had eaten his meals.

He and his black childhood friend jumped on a freight train they thought would take them to Kansas City. Little did they know they would end up in Denver, Colorado, since the train headed west, not east. It was in Denver where my father last saw his childhood friend; the Army my father joined to "help save democracy" would not accept black folks. After three years in the Army he received an honorable discharge. He became a Protestant minister, marrying my mother during the Great Depression.

From my father's perspective, life in American society changed significantly in the 89 years he lived and from his perspective the changes, on balance, were not positive. This viewpoint is expressed in one of his sermons given at the graveside of one of his life-long friends, John, who passed away in 1984:

Changes came over the world in the last 50 years. Two wars John and I did not understand: Korea and Vietnam. There have been changes in the home where children spend more time watching TV and playing video games rather than helping others and doing their chores. Changes in morals: many say that marriage is outmoded. Changes in education: children have no discipline and bring guns to school. Changes in the life of our cities: not safe to go out at night, cities are now dead at night. Only 15 years ago it was hub-cap stealing; now it is violent crimes and murder. (Harry R. Humphries, unpublished sermon, 1984)

From my father's perspective, social forces operating in his lifetime contradicted the *traditional values* he had learned while being reared at the turn of the century in a cohesive rural farming community in the American heartland.

How do individuals cope, organize, and reorganize their lives when social change occurs? What happens when your old ideas about the world no longer help you to understand both personal and world events? My father turned to a religious paradigm to understand these changes. A religious paradigm was his vantage point, by means of which he could understand his own behavior and evaluate the behavior of others. Religion informed his understanding of the disintegration of rural American society and its transformation into one far more urban and industrial.

Influences of Groups on Human Behavior and Perception

Sociology is the *scientific study of how and why we form groups, live together in small ones* (like our families) *and in larger ones* (like the military) *and it encompasses the functioning of whole societies and the social, economic, cultural, political, and technological relationships within, between, and among societies.* We will discuss **science** and the scientific method as a way of knowing later. Let us now note that as used by sociologists, a **group** refers to a collection of two or more individuals with the following characteristics:

- *Shared goal.* Members of the collectivity share one or more goals: earning three hours of college credit; learning how to bake a cake or use a word-processing or data-

analysis software program; making a bomb, winning a battle, and so forth.
- *Solidarity.* Members of the collectivity have a sense of "we-ness" and perceive themselves as different, for better or worse, than persons who are not members of the collectivity. The following sentiments, while apparently disparate, indicate solidarity: "Poor us who are taking Chemistry 101 from Professor Godzilla!" "Lucky us who get to take Comparative Literature from Professor Edwards! He makes the subject matter spellbinding and memorable."
- *Sustained interaction.* Members of the collectivity interact over a sustained period of time. Even in a college class that meets for only fifty minutes a day, three days a week, for sixteen weeks, sustained interaction occurs. In contrast, persons who do not know each other and who simply happen to be in the same place at the same time (such as persons in an elevator, people waiting on a busy street corner for the light to turn green so that they may cross the street) are not characterized by sustained interaction.

If two or more persons do not share all three characteristics, they are not a group. There are several collections of two or more persons that are not groups. One of these collections is a **social category,** that is, a plurality of persons who do not form a group but who have at least one similar social characteristic or status in common, e.g., sex, age, race. Examples of social categories would be females, males, working women, computer scientists, the unemployed, missionaries, teenagers, etc.

Social structure refers to stable and recurring patterns of social relations. People live in networks of social structure and in networks of groups. *It is through these networks that people cope, organize, and reorganize their lives.* Sociologists are interested in social structure—how groups are put together—because it influences our behaviors and perceptions. Let us now share with you a few examples of the influence of social structure on human social behavior.

Vietnam Veterans and Dopers

Sociologist Lee Robins, a research professor of sociology at Washington University School of Medicine in St. Louis, Missouri, wanted to know why some returning Vietnam veterans were able to stay drug free and why others did not (1974). Almost half of the American enlisted men who fought in Vietnam tried one or more addictive drugs. According to her survey of men returning to the U.S. during an autumn month of 1971, one out of three had experimented with opium, and the figures were similar for heroin. Most sociologists predicted a high rate of drug use and of re-addiction to these types of drugs after the soldiers returned home. Yet, as Robins says:

> To our great delight and to the government's great surprise, we found that most of these men had little trouble with drugs after they got back. It turned out that among men who had been addicted in Vietnam, only about seven percent were re-addicted after they got back. *This is an absolutely unheard of low rate as compared to the experience in the United States, where about two-thirds of addicts have usually relapsed within six months after treatment.* (Robins, as cited in Restak, 1988: 119. Italics added.)

Her research challenged the conventional or common-sense wisdom that "once an addict, always an addict." That common-sense prediction has not been born out. A really interesting question is why some persons who try drugs can walk away from them while others become and remain addicted. After isolating the psychological reasons why American soldiers experimented with and used drugs and why they stayed "clean," sociologists concluded that a major influence was the soldiers' *primary group* membership.

According to *Charles Horton Cooley* (1909/1962) who introduced the term, a **primary group** has common standards of behavior or values and direct, frequent contact among its members. "The members of a primary group engage in a wide variety of activities with each other and many aspects of each individual's personality are involved" in her or his "relations with other members of the group" (Theodorson and Theodorson, 1969: 178). Relations among members of a primary group are *ends* in themselves, not means to ends. Members of a primary group are interested in and know about a wide range of aspects

of each others' lives and they have a broad range of mutual rights and duties. In other words, the relationship is a *diffuse* one. The "family and the small, old-fashioned neighborhood" in large cities or in small towns are examples of a primary group (Theodorson and Theodorson, 1969: 178). These groups are considered as primary because they have both the earliest and most profound influence on a person's socialization and development. If a group is not primary, it is a **secondary group.**

While in Vietnam, the soldier's primary group was supportive of experimenting with and using drugs and even looked upon *not* using drugs as deviant. That was the definition of the situation that soldiers carried about with them while in Vietnam. In other words, using drugs, including narcotics, helped them to "feel part of the group" and to be "one of the crowd" (Robins, 1974: 31, 32). As Robins notes,

> Seventy-one percent reported that at least half of the men in their units smoked marijuana regularly. Only 3% were not aware of its regular use among their fellow soldiers. Thus, while only 21% had associated with regular marijuana users *before* service [in Vietnam], 97% knew marijuana smokers in Vietnam . . . [and] the proportion with acquaintances who used narcotics jumped from 9% before service to 95% in Vietnam. (Robins, 1974: 25. Italics added.)

Most of the soldiers were discharged from the Army within eight days of their return to the United States, and they changed more than their uniforms. They changed primary groups. They returned to their hometowns and resumed their pre-service primary-group friendships. Only 15 percent of them maintained *any* primary-group contacts they had formed in Vietnam. Their primary-group members now were neither tolerant of nor encouraging with regard to drug use, which is a major reason why comparatively few of them became re-addicted to drugs.

Our Best Friends, Family, and Loved Ones

English sociologist *Michael Argyle* (1994) wanted to find out why some English teenagers went on to college and later became occupationally successful and others did not. After reviewing the psychological reasons, Argyle discovered that among those who became occupationally successful a primary group, like the family, increased the intellectual stimuli in their childhood environment. This process, he claims, increased both the child's intelligence and emotional bonding with parents, which in turn facilitated language and motor development. Parents who provide encouragement for their toddlers and young children, who provide them with positive rewards, and who set for them definite direction for appropriately high-risk yet independent tasks produce children who internalize *achievement motivation* in the conventional social order as part of their identity and who are able problem solvers.

Argyle (1994) and Emmy Werner and Ruth Smith (1989) note that middle and high schools are places where teenagers make "best friends." On the basis of **longitudinal data** (data on the same persons across time), these authors argue that our best friends may transcend the influence of our ethnic and class backgrounds. **Peer groups,** primary groups composed of persons with roughly equal status, provide some teenagers with needed emotional support in place of family members who do not do so. A best friend's advice may constitute the impetus for a teenager to change the direction of her or his life. Due to their best friends, working-class children may view and even get to know a world they might not otherwise see and share in social experiences they otherwise might not enjoy—as in visiting a museum; going to a ballet, symphony or opera, and vacationing with their best friend's family. Their best friend's aspiration to attend college may become theirs too.

A **reference group,** as coined by *Herbert Hyman* (1942), is a group or social category whose members we use to evaluate our own behavior. Reference groups serve three functions: (1) *normative,* in that they let the individual know what behaviors, attitudes, beliefs, and values are appropriate; (2) *evaluative,* in that they provide a standard of comparison by means of which an individual may reach an appraisal of her/his abilities and behavior; and (3) *identity,* in that an individual has some sense of identity with the reference group, even if the individual does not belong to it and even

if the individual's conception of the group and its values is inaccurate. American teens, who may feel estrangement from their own parents, tend to listen to their peers and to follow their advice. Best friends thus allow teenagers to project into the future and to evaluate their life chances. For teenagers, then, a peer group is a reference group (Giordano, 1995). From peer groups, Argyle demonstrates, teenagers change the directions of their lives as they prepare to enter into the adult world of work.

Social Structure and Physiological Response: the Autokinetic Effect

On a clear starry night, have you ever looked up at the heavens only to see one or more stars jiggling about? You knew that stars do not *jiggle; yet, you saw them do just that!* Some years ago a researcher named *Muzafer Sherif* took advantage of this phenomenon, known as the **autokinetic effect,** to study the impact of the presence of others on norm formation and on perception (1937). The *auto* (self) *kinetic* (movement) phenomenon refers to the apparent movement of a fixed point of light in the dark.

If you had been a research subject in Sherif's classic experiment, you would have agreed to sit in a dark room. About fifteen feet in front of you a point of light suddenly appears. In a few seconds, you see it *move* erratically. Then it stops moving as quickly as it had started. And then it disappears.

You are asked to estimate how far it moved. You offer "Seven inches," even though you are not highly confident about your response. There are no visual perceptual standards by means of which you can orient yourself; it's *dark.* The experimenter repeats the procedure. The second time you see the light, you say: "Five inches." After several repetitions, your responses come to average around your own personal norm of, say, nine inches.

The next day, you return to the laboratory. You are joined this time by two other research subjects who had the same experience as you the day before. When the room is dark, the spot of light appears, moves, and then disappears. To your surprise, you hear "Three inches" as a response from one research subject and "One inch" from the other. Somehow you manage to utter your response of "Nine inches." With successive repetitions of this communal experience, both on this day and on the next two days, a new group norm emerges that is different than the individual norm of any of the participants. According to the testimony each member gives after the experiment is over, the participants do not consciously alter their estimations after hearing the estimates of the other members; they simply continue to give their own estimates and to hear the estimates of others.

The really interesting part of this research for sociologists comes when the people are later re-tested alone. The research subjects continue to give the *group* norm as their estimate of how far the light moved. Even a year later, the research subjects still carry with them in the "alone" situation the definition of reality that had been constructed and arrived at in the group setting. Status occupying in a group influences something as basic as our perception, even when group members are *not* immediately present (Rohrer, Baron, Hoffman, & Swander, 1954).

O. J. Simpson: What Do You Think?

O. J. Simpson was, essentially, a great runner. This was how a bow-legged kid with rickets escaped the slums where he was born, how a football super-star had become a national icon, always out-running his obstacles. "I'll tell you," he used to say, "my speed has always been my best weapon. So if I can't run away from whatever it is, I don't need to be there."

But there was never a run like last week's final play. . . . [H]e wasn't really trying to escape. He just wanted his mother. . . . He found his blocker in his faithful friend and longtime teammate Al Cowlings, and together . . . they eluded the police who had come to take O.J. into custody on charges of first-degree murder. . . . (Nancy Gibbs, 1994: 29)

Whether you think O. J. Simpson is not guilty or guilty of the criminal charge of murdering his estranged wife, Nicole Simpson, and her friend, Ronald Goldman, is largely dependent on your ethnic-group membership. Every nationally representative, scientific opinion poll, taken from the time Mr. Simpson's criminal trial began, through the rendering of the not-guilty verdict, and for months thereafter, shows that white and African-American opinions regarding the guilt or innocence of Mr. Simpson are *mirror images* of each other (Whitaker, 1995: 30, 34; Gottlieb, 1995: A12; *Jet*, July 25, 1994: 16-18). In **mirror-image perceptions** persons attribute commendable attributes to themselves and lamentable attributes to those outside of their sense of "we-ness." As David Myers observes: "Each side . . . presumes that *our* beliefs *follow* from the facts while *their* beliefs *dictate* their interpretation of the facts" (Myers, 1993: 563; Italics in original). Thus, a poll taken by CBS News immediately after the not-guilty criminal verdict showed that 60% of whites believed Mr. Simpson was *guilty*, while 90% of African Americans believed him to be *not guilty* (Gottlieb, 1995: A12). While African-American college students celebrated his acquittal of criminal charges, white students were dismayed.

This divergence of perception is understandable sociologically. As in Sherif's experiment, people in the United States carry around with them and use as their definitions of reality those that have been arrived at and forged in their group experience. In several chapters in this textbook we look at some of the ways in which, even in the 1990s, the group experiences in the United States of many male and female African Americans, and of many females across racial and ethnic boundaries, differ dramatically from those of other Americans. When group experiences diverge markedly, sociologically we would expect their definitions of the situations also to differ markedly.

When we study human behavior scientifically, we also learn that we tend to perceive ourselves in favorable terms, a tendency, which is known as the **self-serving bias**. Additionally, we also tend to perceive in favorable terms both the *groups* and *social categories* we use as positive reference groups and those to which we belong, which is known as a **group-serving bias** or the **ultimate attribution error** (Myers, 1993; Hewstone, 1990; Pettigrew, 1979, 1980). One of its manifestations is a tendency to give members of the groups and social categories to which we belong and which we use as positive reference groups the benefit of the doubt in situations where the evidence may be perceived as ambiguous. These insights also help us better to understand the racial or ethnic divergence of opinion in the O.J. Simpson case.

Various Ways of Understanding Human Behavior

Let us now continue our introduction to the sociological perspective by means of a socio-logical parable. This particular parable is a contemporary version of an old elephant story and it illustrates that *the way we know is important.*

In this version of the elephant story, four blind persons enter a room in which their task is to describe an object other than the walls and door, using their hands, ears, and noses as data-collection devices. They do not know it, but the object they are to describe is an ele-phant. The first person hugs one of the huge legs of this gigantic animal and announces that the object is a huge tree with fetid bark. The second, grabbing the elephant's swinging trunk, responds that the object obviously is . . . a fire hose! The third, gripping a tusk, answers that the object in question certainly is a smooth tubular-shaped rock projecting from the ceil-ing. Clutching the elephant's ear, the fourth person describes the object as an exceedingly large leaf.

Had one of the persons in the parable been a sociologist, she or he may well have felt the entire animal and then made the following assessment: "In order to understand the object, we must discern *all* its parts. We cannot under-stand this animal by perceiving and attending only to one "part"—the ear, the tusk, the leg, trunk, and so forth. Each part, while important, is but a segment of the whole. We need to understand the functions of each part and the relations among the parts and why those rela-tions occur. Since the whole is more than the sum of its parts, we also need to understand *the larger context in which this animal lives.* What does this animal *do,* what is its place and function in the larger picture? What are its interactions with others of its own species (**conspecifics**) and with other species? How does the animal engage in dispute resolution, find and keep a mate, reproduce, relate to the young and old of its species, defend itself

against predators? Why do those processes operate the way they do? What are the rules (norms) by which this animal lives and relates to conspecifics? How are these rules enforced? How is leadership structured in the community in which the animal lives and in the larger community? What is the exchange order like in the community in which this animal lives? How is access to scarce yet widely-valued goods and services handled in this animal's community? Why is access to scare yet widely valued goods and services handled in that particular manner? What is this animal's rela-tionship with technology: is it a tool user, or is it used *as* a tool by other conspecifics or by other species? What are its processes of mean-ing attribution and of socialization? If there is more than one sex or gender, what is the nature of the relationships between the sexes/gen-ders? Why are gender relations structured in that particular manner? What are the relations between the old and young of its own species? In short, we must come to an understanding of how this animal impacts its community and the wider community and how they influence the animal. Only then will we begin to have a satisfactory understanding of this life form."

Basically, as the sociologist in the elephant parable demonstrates, *sociology* is the scientific study of how we form groups, live together in small ones, like our families, and in larger ones, like the military. It encompasses the function-ing of whole societies and the social, economic, cultural, political and technological relation-ships within, between, and among societies.

How do sociologists accomplish such ambitious feats? How do we gain reliable and valid knowledge about the social world? Part of the answer is presented in Chapter 4 (Human Inquiry and Research Methods) which focuses on the meth-odologies (tools) used by sociologists in our endeavor to gain knowledge about the social world. Another part of the answer is found by examining the academic specialty area known as **epistemology,** the science of knowing and of knowledge—its origins, nature, and limits (Babbie, 1995: 18; Rubin and Babbie, 1993: 6).

Let us now focus on human inquiry as an activity that we engage in every day of our lives. We first look at the nature of knowledge and at the processes (ways) we use in our everyday lives to gain it. Then, we look at science as a way of knowing, at which point we discuss the scientific method. Finally, we conclude our excursion into the area of epistemology by examining some of the common errors we make in normal, everyday knowledge building and at what makes science as a way of knowing different. The thrust of this entire section is that *the way we know is important.*

On the Nature of Knowledge

Practically all people are interested in predicting their future life chances, whether for the short or long term. If I get in my car and start driving cross-country from New York City, will my car, a 1979 coup that I rarely have serviced, make the trip without breaking down? In our everyday lives, we seem content to use reasoning that is both **causal** (interested in ferreting out cause and effect) and **probabilistic.** We will return to the concepts of causality and probability in Chapter 4 (Human Inquiry and Research Methods), but let us now briefly discuss each of these points in turn.

- *Causal reasoning.* We learn to look for causes among those factors that precede the effect in time. "Why did I get an 'F' on my Physics 101 test? The class meets at 8 A.M., and I am a 'night person' and I failed to wake up in time for the class. During the past three weeks, I actually missed class more often than I attended. I didn't read the textbook until the night before the exam." We learn, in other words, to ferret out cause and effect and to perceive the relationship between them. "If I read the textbook, go to lectures regularly, study, and get plenty of sleep, I get better grades on my tests than when I fail to do these things."
- *Probabilistic reasoning.* Patterns of cause and effect are not a matter of 100% certitude, but a matter of more or less. For instance, we learn that when we study for many hours spread out over many days we usually get better grades than when we only cram for the exam the night before the test, *but not always.* When we put a lot of time and effort into a term paper, we tend to get a good grade on it, but not always.

In studying "how we know" it is important to distinguish between understanding and predicting. *It is possible to predict without understanding.* I can predict that, if the wiring in my house is in good condition, and if I pay my utility bill, and if there is a properly functioning light bulb in a lamp that also works properly, and if the city's electrical plant is functioning properly, then when I turn on the light switch, the light bulb will provide illumination. I can accurately make that prediction, yet I do not understand electricity or why it works the way it does. In our day to day lives, we frequently predict without understanding. If we only predict, we know *what* will happen. If we understand, we know *why* it happens. As sociologists Allen Rubin and Earl Babbie phrase it: "If you can understand why things are related to one another, why certain regular patterns occur, you can predict even better than if you merely memorize what those patterns are" (1993: 7). The process of human inquiry, then, has as a goal the answering of both the "what" (description) and the "why" (understanding) questions.

The Ways We Know

In our daily lives frequently we gain knowledge not by engaging in direct inquiry ourselves but by accepting at face value and as accurate the information that others give us. Some sources of "second-hand knowledge" include tradition, experts or authority, magic, religion, and philosophy. We now address each of these in turn.

1. *Tradition.* Each one of us is born into a culture that is chuck-full of explanations about how the world works and why it works that way. We might learn that we should mount and dismount a horse on the horse's left side and to do otherwise is dangerous. We learn that we should divide certain plants only in the spring, because to do so in another season might injure or even kill the plants. We learn that we should not go swimming within an hour of eating, because to do otherwise might generate body cramps, the effect of which could prove lethal. Although we might test a few of these "truths," most of us simply accept a great number of them as "true." An advantage of tradition as a form of

human inquiry is efficiency. Tradition saves us a lot of time, which is an inelastic resource. By accepting as "true" the second-hand wisdom of tradition, we are freed to expend our attentional resources on other matters.

If we are bold enough to buck tradition by seeking a newer understanding of something that practically everybody accepts as "true," we are likely to be accused of being on a "fool's errand." When sociologist Lee Robins (1974) looked into the accuracy of the traditional wisdom that told us "Once an addict, always an addict," she was accused of being on a fool's errand. Nonetheless, her research demonstrated the inaccuracy of that particular tradition and it came up with an explanation of *why* the tradition was inaccurate: the strength of primary-group ties. Similarly, when one of the authors of this textbook undertook doctoral research on the relationship between high school and growth of the white-collar occupational structure in the United States between the end of the Civil War and World War I (1870–1910), even some members of the dissertation committee thought it was a fool's errand. After all, "everybody knew" (i.e., tradition—in this case, functionalist theory—held) that the high schools expanded to fill the demand for an army of white-collar workers. Again, as it turned out, tradition was inaccurate. Empirical data repeatedly failed to support tradition. Instead, the data supported the interpretation that the crucial variables were racial and ethnic stratification. If one were a native-born white male, one could get a white-collar job *without* a high-school education; while if one were foreign-born or African American, a high-school education was necessary but not sufficient to obtain white-collar employment (Donovan, 1977).

A **variable** is a characteristic that has different degrees of magnitude or different categories. Thus, sex or gender is a variable, whose categories are male and female; education is a variable, and one may have different amounts of it.

2. *Experts or Authority.* As a way of knowing, accepting information as accurate on the authority of even highly-regarded "ex-

perts" is problematic. Experts can be incorrect. They can be incorrect even when they are speaking about an area of their own expertise, as is illustrated in the following example:

A renowned . . . molecular biologist at the University of California at Berkeley—member of the prestigious National Academy of Sciences, who was California's Scientist of the Year in 1971–Dr. Peter Duesberg stated as late as 1988 that AIDS is not caused by a virus. Furthermore, Dr. Duesberg declared that tests used to detect Human Imunodeficiency Virus (HIV) antibodies are a waste of time, and that, "If somebody told me today that I was antibody positive, I wouldn't worry one second" (Gibbs, 1991: 27. Italics in original.)

It is important that you learn to keep an open mind about cherished beliefs and theories and about research that might challenge them. It is also important that you keep an open mind about the "new" knowledge that is offered to replace the old. The new research also may be incorrect. For those among us desirous of finding "magic bullets" (instant answers), learning to tolerate ambiguity may be painfully difficult; yet, practice makes progress and part of a liberal-arts education is learning not to close inquiry prematurely.

3. *Magic.* Another way of knowing is through magic. **Magic** refers to the use of rituals that are believed to be successful in manipulating supernatural forces for a desired result. In magic, if the proper ritual is performed appropriately by the designated functionary (who is referred to as a **shaman** or priest by sociologists and as a "witch doctor" by some Hollywood moviemakers) the supernatural forces are compelled to do what is asked of them. For example, if they are feeling unwell the **Yanomamo,** an ancient hunting and gathering tribe in South America, believe that the use of hallucinogenic drugs brings them good spirits who heal them.

In fact, there is wide-spread belief in **exuvial magic** in hunting and gathering societies, the types of societies in which humans have lived for most of their existence on earth. *Exuviae* is a Latin word that literally translates as the cast-off of skins or coverings of various animals, including snakes. More generally, the term refers to any part of an animal—a cast-off scab, eyelash, strand of hair, or an entire organ (such as the heart, liver, etc.). In exuvial magic, if a shaman has even a part of a person (her or his exuviae) the shaman can control the entire person by performing certain rituals.

Lest we succumb to the error of supposing that hunting and gathering societies have a corner on magic as a way of knowing, let us recall that in the U.S. many people are superstitious and will not walk under a ladder, will not step on a crack on the sidewalk, and believe that the number 13 is bad luck. As you may have noticed, many tall buildings have no 13th floor. Furthermore, as Theodorson and Theodorson (1969: 238) remind us, the "[c]rude and intellectually unsophisticated application of religious and scientific philosophies often are considered to become or to border on magical practices."

4. *Religion.* As a way of knowing, **religion** is viewed by sociologists and by anthropologists as differing from magic. The difference lies in *the relation between the supplicant and the supernatural.* In magic, as we have seen, the supplicant (or, more precisely, the shaman) is viewed as being in control: If the shaman performs the appropriate ritual correctly, the supernatural forces are viewed as being compelled to do what is asked of them. In contrast, in religion, the deity (or deities) are viewed as being in control. The individual or priest (or shaman, rabbi, mullah, etc.) may perform the appropriate ritual correctly and god(s) may refuse to grant what is requested. The god(s) answer, in other words, but their answer may be "No."

Religion is a phenomenon found in virtually all societies. Virtually all religions provide answers to the relationship between humans and the supernatural. When humans ask: "Why am I here? What is this all about? Why am I living?" religion provides answers. All religions have this in common (Weber, 1963/1922). The answers religions provide are called a **theodicy,** an explanation of the relationship between humans and the gods (the supernatural) (Weber, 1963/1922).

5. *Philosophy.* As a way of knowing, **philosophy** has a broad focus and is concerned with the problem of value and of ethics and aesthetics. It is also concerned with the nature of knowledge, meaning, truth, reality, and the ultimate nature of humans and of humans' relation to the universe. If you're interested in the meaning of life, philosophy has a lot to say. Philosophy does use the findings of the empirical sciences. However, philosophical inquiry is concerned mainly with clarifying conceptual problems that are seen as underlying all academic disciplines, including sociology. In this way, philosophy is interested in the analysis of basic concepts, assumptions, axioms, and procedures in all academic fields of inquiry. Philosophy, as an organized way of knowing, agrees upon certain domain assumptions concerning logical reasoning. One domain assumption specifies that one needs to use a clear method to search for knowledge. Whereas religion and magic may have logic or rules for discovering knowledge (other than agreeing to basic assumptions), philosophy and philosophers consistently use analysis, criticism, and logical reasoning to discover knowledge and the nature of truth.

6. *Science and Scientific Method.* As a way of knowing **science** attempts to develop general principles about a finite range of phenomena on the basis of observations made through the senses (sight, hearing, touch, etc.). Each of these principles is stated as an hypothesis (a testable statement) that can be investigated by any competent person and either accepted or rejected on the basis of empirical data. In other words, you do *not* have to be a rocket scientist "to do science." You can do it; your next-door neighbor can do it; any competent person can do it. As a way of knowing, *the goal of science is prediction,* and **science is based on several assumptions** (Theodorson & Theodorson, 1969: 369):

■ There is a real world.
■ By using the scientific method (please see

below) the biases and values of the observer can be relatively controlled.

- A reasonable degree of objectivity is possible.
- It is possible to derive objective knowledge about the world through the senses (sight, touch, etc.).
- The truth or validity of knowledge is confirmed by the similar observations of many persons using the same methods.
- When there are differences in what is observed, the judgment of a scientific community determines which empirical observations are accepted.
- Empirical facts are a necessary but not sufficient part of science; in other words, facts alone do *not* constitute science.
- To have meaning, facts must be ordered in some way, analyzed, related to other facts, and generalized. In other words, *theory construction* is a vital part of science. Theory provides the means for ordering facts, relating them to other facts and to the findings of other researchers, and for interpreting facts. (What do they mean or signify?)
- Scientific findings and principles are constantly open to criticism, further testing, and revision within a tradition of non-dogmatic knowledge. The thrust of this list is that the interrelated generalizations that constitute the body of *scientific knowledge do not reflect personal opinion* or personal idiosyncrasy or even personal experience. They reflect the consensus of a scientific community whose members use a method known as the *scientific method.*

The **scientific method** refers to building a body of scientific knowledge through observation, generalization, and verification. While we will return to the concept of the scientific method in Chapter 4 (Human Inquiry and Research Methods), let us now briefly list and discuss six steps that together constitute a way of knowing that is referred to as the scientific method.

Steps in the Scientific Method

1. *Define the research problem.* Define the research problem. What is the purpose of this study—exploration, description, demonstration of cause and effect, replication, or what? Why should sociologists be concerned with this problem or issue? Towards what end or ends do we study it? What are the empirical or theoretical gaps in the literature? How should sociologists benefit from studying this issue in terms of theory or social policy?

2. *State the problem in terms of a particular theoretical framework and relate it to relevant findings of previous research.* State the theory or theories that are applicable to your study. How does past research relate to what you want to study? What are their findings? What are the strengths and weaknesses of the already-existing studies?

3. *State the research problem as an hypothesis or as hypotheses.* An **hypothesis** is a tentative, testable statement asserting a relationship between two or more variables; the statement is intended to be tested empirically and either verified or rejected. A scientific hypothesis is derived from a theoretical system and from the results of prior research. In this step, you devise a hypothesis or hypotheses relating to the problem or issue in which you are interested, utilizing previously accepted theoretical principles and insights.

4. *Decide upon the appropriate procedure or procedures (methodology, methodologies) for gathering the data that you will use to test your hypothesis.* This step will be discussed in greater detail in Chapter 4 (Human Inquiry and Research Methods). For now, it is enough that you know that you formulate an appropriate research design in this step, a research design appropriate to the problem you have selected. Your formulation of a research design will proceed according to the principles of the scientific method. In this step you spell out in detail how you are going to conduct your research. Others need to read the details of how you conducted your research in order to be able to make an assessment of its merits and adequacy.

5. *Collect the data.* In this step you actually collect the data. The precise nature of this step will vary depending on what kind of study you are conducting. Is it a mailed

questionnaire? An experiment? Field work (participant observation)?

6. *Analyze the data.* In this step the data are analyzed to ascertain if the hypothesis is verified or rejected. Also, in this step, you relate the conclusions of your study to the original body of theory with which you started your exploration, and indicate whether your findings support the theory or whether the theory needs to be modified in light of your findings (and the findings of others).

If you generate knowledge by using these steps, the knowledge you have created is called *scientific* and you have been engaging in an enterprise known as *science.* To repeat: **scientific knowledge** is *knowledge generated by means of the scientific method.* If you follow the procedures of the scientific method, you are "doing science." If you do not follow those procedures, you are *not engaging in science.* Remember: *How we know is important.*

In our day-to-day lives we continually try to know and to understand the world. The way we go about it, however, makes it likely that we will make mistakes. While we have not attempted to create a list that is either all-inclusive or mutually exclusive, let us now mention at least some of the common errors we make due to the haphazard methods we use and then indicate some of the ways that the scientific method protects inquiry from those pitfalls (Rubin and Babbie, 1993: 11-17).

Common Errors in Everyday Inquiry and How the Scientific Method Helps Us to Avoid Them

1. *Inaccurate observation.* If we want to understand something, we need to be able to describe it. Accurate description requires keen observation. Let's face it: in our daily lives, many of us are fairly sloppy observers. For instance, every day when I go to the building where I teach my classes, I need to climb three flights of stairs. I have made that climb for almost a decade, and yet I would not be able to tell you how many stairs are in each flight or even how many stairs there are altogether. *Can you think of an example of sloppy observation from your daily life? Tell us about it.*

2. *Overgeneralization.* In our attempts to make sense out of the world, we look for patterns. Patterning is the opposite of chaos. Patterning is some type of order. In our attempts to discover patterns, we often assume that a few similar instances indicate a pattern.

   For example, I was struck recently by a remark made by a young male college student in my introduction to sociology class. He made the statement that "Feminists are ugly (physically unattractive)." When I asked him *how he knew that,* his reply was that he had gone to a campus demonstration on the subject of women's rights recently and he had noticed that some of the coeds who were participating in the rally were physically unattractive. That, he noted, was the basis of his statement. *Can you think of an instance when, on the basis of just a few similar events, you have overgeneralized?*

   The scientist guards against the error of overgeneralization by committing in advance to a sufficiently large sample of observations. The way in which the sample is constructed also is important. The sample should be representative of the *entire* population in question. Replication of inquiry, which means repeating the study, provides yet another safeguard. Do other researchers, using similar methods on similar populations, arrive at similar conclusions?

3. *Selective perception.* As with the student in my introductory sociology class, if we have a belief that two or more events are related, we are more likely to notice and to recall confirming instances. People are not generally inclined to seek information that might disprove their beliefs. The scientific method provides two safeguards against this common error. First, the research design specifies in advance both the number and kind of observations that are to be made and that are to constitute the basis on which conclusions are made. We might select a hundred people to interview with regard to their position on whether they thought

President Clinton had acted in a sexually-inappropriate manner with Paula Jones while he was Governor of Arkansas. Even if the first five people we interviewed gave similar answers, we would interview all one hundred persons and we would record all observations. Only then would we analyze the data and base our conclusions on all the observations. Second, if scientists overlook something that contradicts their conclusion, their colleagues in the scientific community will certainly bring it to their attention. Doing so is a service that scientists perform for each other and for the body of scientific knowledge. Part of any scientific socialization is learning to define and to accept the process of correction as "simply taking care of business" and not as "a personal affront."

4. *Illogical reasoning.* In our daily lives illogical reasoning is another device that enables us to hold onto our cherished beliefs even in face of potentially disconfirming evidence. Suppose you are prejudiced against Jewish people. And then one rainy day your car breaks down on the freeway. You have no phone in the car, no spare tire, and you are stranded. The person who stops and offers you a lift to the nearest repair shop is someone whom you suppose is Jewish. One way to keep one's prejudice in this situation is to dismiss contradictory evidence with a stroke of illogic, as in "Well, that's just the exception that proves the rule." Worse yet, although the best of us may stray into illogical reasoning from time to time, many of us get defensive if someone points it out to us. Scientists avoid this pitfall by using systems of logic consciously, explicitly, and systematically.

For scientists, reasoning logically is a conscious activity. Should they falter, their colleagues will point out the errors to them.

5. *Emotional investment in a particular point of view.* In our daily lives, we may become emotionally invested in a particular way of viewing the world and become closed to other viewpoints or to contrary evidence. There is a bumper sticker that you probably have seen that says something on the order of: "God said it, I believe it, and That settles it!" the bumper sticker proclaims that the car's owner subscribes to a particular religious paradigm as a vantage point for making sense out of the world and that it is useless to try to change the owner's viewpoint.

For scientists, a firm commitment to the principles or steps of the scientific method works against too much emotional investment in a particular viewpoint. Nonetheless, scientists have been known to succumb to this particular error; and, those who are so afflicted often fail to perceive it in themselves. Their colleagues who compose the scientific community are not all so blind. They point out the error. This corrective process occurs not only in private correspondence but in public arenas. Letters to the editor in international science journals and research articles in widely-read and in widely-cited academic journals carry these exposés. Those who make decisions regarding the funding of scientific research projects read these media and take their content into account in arriving at funding decisions. So, even in face of individual or *personal* denial, the organized profession exacts conformity to the standards of the scientific method.

Human Behavior: Individual and Group-Level Perspectives

BOX 2.1

Mac's Story

Mac was well known by his friends as a kind and generous person. Only thirty-nine years old, he appeared to be in his late fifties. He and his friends would gather behind the Union 76 gas station every day to share bottles of wine, consuming every drop until they were ready once again to panhandle "spare change" from tourists in the old market area of Charleston, South Carolina.

Mac was skillful. He always made sure he looked the grubbiest, had the most offensive smelling breath and would always stand at least two feet in front of his customers. He always approached every stranger with a smile and a courteous request "Can you spare some change partner? I haven't eaten for days." Mostly older women would respond—some with fifty cents, but usually with a dollar. After collecting enough "change" to purchase more wine, they once again would pass the bottle around behind "Union 76" as they called it.

Precisely at 5 PM every Friday the Charleston Metropolitan Police would pick up Mac and his friends, arresting them for drunkenness and disorderliness, vagrancy, suspicion of begging, and being a public nuisance. You see, on the weekends, Mac and his friends would sober-up, eat some jail food, have their health problems looked at, and gets plenty of sleep. By this time everyone in old Charleston knew Mac and his friends. He and his friends only disturbed tourists' business on weekdays; business was slow then, especially during the winter months.

Being arrested so many times did not deter Mac; it had become a ritual with the police. In fact the police and merchants relied on Mac and his friends to keep an eye out for strangers at night who might break into their tourist shops full of expensive this and that's. Mac and his friends provided services both to the merchants and to the police; in return they received

food, health care, and a warm place to sleep for two or three nights a week. What more could one person ask for?

One Wednesday afternoon, the police received a call from a tourist that drunks were causing a disturbance near the "Baskin and Robins" ice-cream store. The police arrived to find Mac already dead. In fact, Mac had been dead for hours. His friends were doing their best to revive him and to call the attention of others to Mac's plight. The police reported that Mac laid in the gutter while tourists stepped over and around him. His friends found him only after he had not predictably returned with "change" to purchase more wine.

Mac was gone though. The police, merchants and his friends donated money to have him buried and they of course paid their "last respects." Mac, you know, was kind, courteous, and generous. (Harry L. Humphries, 1982. Unpublished field notes.)

Bystander Intervention Research: Random Acts of Kindness?

Were we just casually to observe Mac's situation we might conclude that Mac's end was "one he deserved." He was for all intents and purposes, as well as literally, "a bum," a person who seeks to avoid work and who seeks to live off others (Morris, 1969: 175). His life, at first glance, appears disorganized and chaotic, strange and unfamiliar.

As a way of knowing, sociology—which describes and analyzes the micro, meso, and macro levels and components of social organization—affords us a different view of Mac and his world. When put into *sociological* perspective, we perceive structure and order in Mac's world.

What type of questions, issues, and analyses would sociologists use to understand Mac, his behavior and world? Why did he lay dead for hours in a gutter while hundreds of people walked over and around him? What happened to random acts of kindness? Are Americans callous and apathetic?

A sociologist might begin to understand Mac, his world, and his "end" by indicating that acts of kindness are not *random. They are socially structured.* This was demonstrated, for instance, in the path-breaking research on by-stander intervention conducted by sociologist Bibb Latané and his colleagues (Latané and Darley, 1968; Latané and Nida, 1981). This research demonstrated that for intervention to occur in an emergency situation, three factors must be present. If even one is missing, intervention does not occur.

What are these three factors? First, the potential intervener must *perceive the event.* Sounds simple and easy, doesn't it? It's actually more complicated than might at first glance appear. Many people fail to notice many things, for many reasons, just one of which is that we have limited attentional resources (See, for instance, Myers & Myers, 1980; Keirsey & Bates, 1984; Squire, 1987; Minsky, 1986). Second, the potential intervener must *define the situation as an emergency.* The process whereby one examines and evaluates a situation before arriving at a decision regarding the meaning and nature of a situation and before deciding which actions and behaviors are appropriate is referred to by sociologists as **the definition of the situation.** The social and psychological response to help victims requires that others define the situation as an emergency. It could be many other things. For instance, some years ago, one of the authors of this textbook was walking in a somewhat "seedy" part of the state capitol of one the most populous, most urban states in this nation with a fellow sociologist, when she noticed two men assisting a third who was prostrate on the ground. "Look," she said, "There are two men assisting an injured person in need!" Her older, wiser, more street-wise companion responded: "Wise up. They're 'rolling' [robbing] a drunk!" In other words, her definition of the situation was inaccurate. If one defines a situation as other than an emergency, one fails to intervene.

Third, the potential intervener must *decide if she/he has the responsibility to intervene.* In the example above, both Marjorie and her companion who were strangers to the person who was getting mugged decided that a near-by police officer was the more appropriate person to lend assistance. So, even though they both noticed the event and eventually defined it as an emergency, neither of them intervened to help a stranger in need. Each decided that the responsibility for intervention belonged to someone else.

Latané and Nida's (1981) research also demonstrates that an individual accepts responsibility for intervention in a situation defined by the individual as an emergency only when (a) no one else is around and (b) when the victim and the potential intervener are acquaintances. If others whom they do not know are present (strangers) in the emergency situation, there is a shifting of responsibility (called "diffusion of responsibility" by those who conducted this research). If others who are friends, colleagues, and acquaintances are present in the emergency situation, they are likely to act instantly if they know the victim.

Why Mac did not receive help is therefore three-fold. His friends were not around, the others who were around did not define the situation as an emergency, and they thought others should take responsibility. In public places, large numbers of strangers impede others from helping strangers in agony.

What should also be pointed out is that while Mac was virtually homeless and, by all accounts, heartily condemned by many segments of society simply for being a "bum," he nonetheless had strong social relationships with his friends, the down-town merchants, and the municipal police. Every night and every day Mac and his friends made a world. It was Mac's world, where one's identity was based on sharing with others, caring for them, and being cared for by them. In other words, Mac was part of *solidary order*—he and his friends shared a sense of we-ness, as they did with the merchants and the municipal police. He was a member of a group governed by rules (*normative order*). These norms included the sharing of wine, panhandling, and a general distaste for anything "normal." Due to his prowess as a flawless and skillful panhandler, Mac was also the group leader (*imperative order*).

The reciprocal informal relationships Mac and his friends had with the merchants (sleeping space in exchange for keeping an eye on the store) and municipal police (informing about potential burglars in exchange for a nice place to sleep, good food, and free health care on weekends) reveal the presence of an *exchange order* between Mac's world and old Charleston society.

The Study of Suicide and Divorce

The single most stressful event in the lives of many human beings is the loss of a loved one through death, especially a family member. The sense of loss frequently is profound for individuals, families, and their communities. Particularly if the cause of death is suicide in the United States, those immediately and even indirectly affected invariably ask "Why?" Of course, at other times and in other places, such as in feudal Japan and in ancient Rome, suicide was defined as an honorable and/or redemptive ritual. In the contemporary United States and in a large portion of the modern Western world, suicide frequently is viewed as problematic. When it occurs, those affected tend to ask "Why?"

A *common–sense* answer is that the person who committed suicide was deeply distressed. Through a reconstruction of the personal tragedy, people guess at what led to this sad event. After close examination, many people eventually rationalize the other person's behavior. In the United States, some would even conclude that, as an adult of sound mind, one has a personal right freely to choose to end one's own life.

From a *psychological and/or psychiatric perspective,* the causes of suicide are often linked to clinical depression and personal crisis. From a *medical perspective,* suicide may be viewed as caused by a chemical imbalance in the brain that, in turn, causes clinical depression and/or flaws in cognition.

Sociologists, on the other hand, view suicide and its causes differently. As scientists, they make markedly different assumptions and use different methods to investigate the causes of suicide. For example if we look at suicide rates and categorize them, we observe a *pattern.* Please see Table 2.1. In 1993, the most recent

year for which statistics are available, the rate of suicide for single white Protestant middle- and upper-middle-class males (21.4) is more than *four times* as great as that of their female counterparts (5.0) and almost *twice* as large as that for lower-class African-American males (12.5). The lowest rate of suicide is for African-American females (2.1), whose rate is less than half that of white females (5.0).

TABLE 2.1. Suicide Rates per 100,000 Population in the United States, by Race and Sex, 1993

Race and Sex	Suicide Rate
Total population	11.3
White males	21.4
White females	5.0
Black males	12.5
Black females	2.1

Source: U.S. Bureau of the Census, *Statistical Abstract of the United States, 1996* (116th edition) (Washington, D.C.: Government Printing Office, 1996), pp. 93, 101.

As human beings, we all suffer tragedies in our lives, smaller ones and significantly larger ones. *What accounts for the high suicide rate among those who are financially well off and who, in terms of life satisfaction* (Please see Chapter 9, Stratification and Society), *are the happiest, or at least supposedly the most satisfied, members of society* (Argyle, 1987, 1991, 1992, 1994)? *Why should they take their own lives at a much higher rate than those nearer the bottom of the stratified order? What explains this apparent anomaly?*

French sociologist Emile Durkheim (1858-1917) developed a sociological explanation of suicide that makes the apparent anomaly understandable in terms of social cohesion and the normative order in a social setting. Let us now examine Durkheim's explanation of suicide (1897/1966).

Durkheim's explanation of suicide consists of four main points. First, Durkheim argues that society is a complex entity of social structures. Some of these social structures, including the family, religion, work, school, and friendship systems, provide individuals with social support. He terms these **supportive social systems.** These systems of support positively integrate individuals into communities and into their society. In other words, individuals become bonded with society through these social systems of support.

Second, there are different patterns of solidarity in different social settings. Forms and patterns of solidarity can vary both across societies and within them. Third, the behavior of individuals is influenced and constrained by their social environments.

Fourth, suicide rates are a function of the strength of the normative order and of the solidary ties between the individual and the conventional social order (solidary order). When these ties are strong, suicide is deflected. For instance, what occurs to individuals when personal tragedy happens in agricultural societies? In agricultural societies, Durkheim argued, the moral norms of the community are in place for providing both social and spiritual support. Hence, the individual is supported and protected by a system of kinship assistance. In this setting, a personal loss or tragedy may be experienced by, and receive support from, the whole kinship. Many small traditional farming communities in American society are still organized this way.

However, if the ties between the individual and the supportive social systems are either too strong or too weak, the individual is at increased risk of suicide. These dynamics, according to Durkheim, explain why suicide is more likely to occur among Protestants than Catholics or Jews, why single men have higher suicide rates than married men, and why suicide rates are higher in modern societies than in more traditional ones.

If the solidary ties between an individual and the collectivity are extremely strong, the individual will sacrifice her or his own life for the collectivity. Durkheim terms this action **altruistic suicide.** *Kamikaze* pilots during World War II are an example. These young men were the *divine wind*, from the Japanese words "kami," meaning "god" and "kaze," meaning "wind." They piloted aircraft loaded with explosives and crashed them into Allied warships. Altruistic suicide is motivated by a desire to serve the perceived needs of the group, and it is found in societies that tend to deemphasize the importance of the individual.

According to Durkheim, suicide rates in the latter half of the nineteenth century in various countries were highest among Protestants,

lowest among Jews, and Catholics were in-between. In contrast to Catholicism or Jewry, Protestantism emphasizes an individualistic ethos in which individuals are viewed as responsible for their own salvation. Durkheim terms this a "cult of egoism." It places a heavy (overwhelming) burden on the individual, and the group itself is not strong enough to provide the individual with adequate emotional and spiritual support outside of her/himself. In other words, the group is not sufficiently *integrated* (cohesive) to be able communally to mitigate the individual's sense of personal responsibility and guilt for perceived moral weakness and failure (sin). As a result, the individual's sense of personal responsibility and guilt become overpowering, and the individual seeks refuge in suicide. **Egoistic suicide,** then, is due to a strong value system, weak group integration, and to an overwhelming sense of personal responsibility. While Catholicism and Jewry have strong value systems, they also have a less individualistic ethos, more integrated communities, and cohesive social systems of support that prove highly valuable when their members experience personal troubles.

Durkheim's argument also extends to marital status. Married men are more integrated into society than are single men. Single men commit more suicide because they lack a feeling of belonging. *Think of social situations in which a single male would feel as if he were "a third wheel" (less than welcome) in a social setting. Have you, or anyone you know, ever experienced anything like this?*

Durkheim argued that in modern industrial societies, traditional curbs on individual behavior had declined, a condition he referred to as **anomie.** Durkheim's concept of **anomie,** sometimes translated from French into English as "normlessness," refers to norms being in flux, guidelines for acceptable behavior no longer being clear. The term anomie does not necessarily imply a collapse or absence of imperative order or of political authority. Such a situation would be called **anarchy.** In anomie, one or more norms that previously had regulated human behavior effectively either have become irrelevant and/or no longer applicable; they are in flux or weakened.

Durkheim's empirically based argument is

that, due to lack of effective restraints, many appetites become insatiable. Guidelines (norms) regarding "how much is enough," no longer are clear. One's level of frustration at not being able to satiate one's (economic, social, sexual, etc.) appetites can lead or drive one to suicide, which he termed **anomic suicide.**

Durkheim's insights thus explain high rates of suicide among persons who, in an objective sense, may be viewed by others as economically (or socially, occupationally, etc.) successful. Because standards of behavior no longer are clear (anomie), and because so many appetites are perceived as insatiable, how does one actually know that one *is* successful? How does one gauge *how successful* one has become? Is one as successful as one's neighbor or best friends? The rapid rise of an individual's expectations in defining what constitutes success, coupled with the continuing elevation of those expectations, make it difficult to come to a lasting assessment of whether one actually *is* successful and what level of success one has achieved. Doubts may surface. Is one merely a *has been* or even on the brink of being on the way *down* the ladder of success? Why doesn't "success" *feel* like one thought it would? These and related anxieties, while appearing merely existential to some, may actually lead people to take their own lives. *Do you know anyone whose suicide may be considered anomic? Everybody has a story. Tell us his or her story.*

Durkheim's analysis would explain the lower suicide rate in the United States of African-American females (in comparison to white females) as due to their higher integration into kinship, family, and community social relations. Carol Stack's study, *All My Kin* (1975) demonstrates that in urban areas African-American women form pseudo-kinship social relations as social systems of support.

Divorce in the United States

Individuals usually do not get married with the intention of going through the process of divorce two or three years later. Their intentions are to stay married. If the rate of divorce were 1 or 2 for every 100 marriages per year, then logically we could speak of divorce as a *personal* or psychological problem of individuals. We look at the domains of personal disposi-

tion or personal dynamics for the causes of a *personal problem:* perhaps the two individuals never should have married, or perhaps they had poor communication skills, and so on. But when the divorce rate during the first two years of marriage is about 50 for every 100 marriages performed, then sociologists view it as a *public issue* and as falling under the purview of sociological analysis. As sociologists, we look at the domains of macro social-structural relations for the causes of public issues. As we discuss in Chapter 8 (Family), rates of divorce may be understood sociologically as a function of macro-level social relations. In that sense, then, divorce is *not* a personal matter.

A point that will be made in a variety of contexts throughout this book is that many social phenomena—marriage, divorce, spousal abuse, suicide, to name but a few—that we may be accustomed to perceiving as personal, individual, or psychological challenges may also be viewed sociologically as being a function of social-structural relations.

Sociology and Related Behavioral Disciplines

Sociology is just one of the *behavioral sciences*, which sometimes are referred to as social sciences. Other behavioral sciences include psychology, anthropology, political science, economics, history, and social work. The various behavioral sciences tend to ask different questions, use different paradigms, and focus on different "parts" of the social and behavioral world. Sometimes they even use different methodologies. Each of these sciences, including sociology, contains specialty areas sometimes are referred to as the "divisions" or "branches" of an academic discipline. The boundaries between specialty areas *within* an academic discipline and boundaries *between* the behavioral sciences are somewhat arbitrary. These boundaries also are a matter of perception. Nonetheless, territorial disputes do occur both within and between disciplines.

We now take a look at several of the behavioral sciences and at some of the specialty areas within them. This short survey should aid us to appreciate that these disciplines are best perceived *not* as *contradictory* but as *complementary*.

One discipline is not "right" and the others "wrong." To use a metaphor, each discipline is like a "blindfolded" person endeavoring to understand the "elephant" of human behavior.

- *Psychology* concentrates on the individual. As a way of knowing, psychology focuses on the biological, psychological, and behavioral processes that occur *within* an individual. Some of the specialty areas within psychology include social psychology, learning psychology, educational psychology, developmental psychology (including child development), cognitive psychology, clinical psychology, and experimental psychology. Psychological practice varies considerably. Some psychologists are primarily concerned with mental processes such as emotions, perceptions, intelligence, memory, and learning.

Sociology and psychology converge in several areas, including the areas of socialization and deviance. What many psychologists study as "abnormal psychology," sociologists study as "deviant behavior." Although sociologists and psychologists use some of the same research methods, psychologists tend to rely more heavily on experimental research, in which they manipulate a variable (such as race, gender, presence or absence of eye-witness testimony) to see what effect it has. Sociologists tend to rely more heavily on the method of survey research, which is a useful tool for gathering information on large numbers of people. Through survey research, sociologists gather **base-rate information,** that is information that describes most people.

- *Anthropology* is the study of the culture and social structure of a community or society (Lachmann, 1991; Theodorson & Theodorson, 1969: 13). There are four main branches of anthropology. *Physical anthropology* is concerned with the biological aspects of being human. It has two main subfields: paleontology, the study of fossil evidence, by means of which human evolution is reconstructed and studied, and *neontology*, the study of the "comparative biology of the living primates" (Lachmann, 1991: 216). By viewing human beings as one of many mammals, physical anthropology forces the behavioral sciences to adopt a broad view of "human nature." *Cultural anthropology,* sometimes termed *social anthropology*, is the study of the social life of human groups. It has two main tasks. One of these is **ethnography,** the description of the life and culture of people in particular social groups. If you read E.E. Evans-Pritchard's ethnographic accounts of the Nuer (1940, 1951), a people living in the Sudan, you find out what it is like to live among the Nuer. The second specialty area of cultural anthropology is *ethnology*, which develops generalizations about the cultural practices, structural relations, and social patterns found in human societies. *Archaeology* is a third branch of anthropology, which seeks to understand the social, cultural, and physical aspects of humans. Archaeology is almost exclusively concerned with the past. Archaeology's subfields include *prehistoric* archaeology which focuses on human societies that left no written records and *classic* archaeology which is concerned with reconstructing the way of life of ancient, literate civilizations such as ancient Mesopotamia and Sumer, ancient Greece, and ancient Rome. A fourth branch of anthropology is *linguistic anthropology.* It is concerned both with the relationship among spoken language, culture, and social behavior and with the relationship among language, thought, and reality. All of the branches of anthropology have had a big impact on the development of sociology as an academic discipline.

- *Political Science* focuses on the administration and organization of government, its history, and theory. The concept "administrative region"—sometimes referred to as "administrative area" or **"administrative system"**—refers to a territorial unit such as an unincorporated area, town, city, county, or state which is defined by its political boundaries. Political scientists study how individuals form political opinions, develop political parties, and participate in politics. One form of political participation, of course, is voting. Some political scientists study voting behavior.

Many political scientists in the United states adhere to a paradigm called pluralism. **Pluralism** is a paradigm that assumes that **power,** the ability to get one's way in the face of opposition (Weber), is widely dispersed in society. Theorists who follow this perspective are known as **pluralists.**

Political science and sociology converge in the area of **political order** (sometimes also called the imperative order). The political order refers to those complexes of norms and expectations of behavior (**roles**) that serve to maintain social order, to provide the means for changing the legal or administrative systems, and to exercise the power to compel conformity to the existing structure of authority. **Authority** refers to legitimate power.

Traditionally, political science has shared with sociology an interest in the abstract qualities of the political order. While political science traditionally has focused on the formal behavior of the citizenry (as manifested in voting, office holding, and the like), sociology has focused on the ways in which power is socially organized. Sociology studies power in many settings other than at the voting booth. Sociology studies power in such structures as work organizations, families, voluntary organizations, and youth gangs.

- *Economics* is the scientific study of the economic order. The **economic order** refers to complex of roles and norms organized about the production, distribution, and consumption of goods and services. The economic order provides for the material needs (food, shelter, etc.) and demands (e.g., for electronic consumer goods) of the members of society. Economists tend to study cost efficiency; how goods and services are produced and distributed; and market forces—what markets are, how they are created, changed, and sustained. In short, economists are interested in much more than just the **economy,** the dominant form of economic activity in a society. Examples of different types of economies are hunting and gathering economy, nomadic pastoral economy, horticultural economy, settled agricultural economy, and modern industrial economy.

Sociology and economics converge in their interests in the social relations involved in economic behavior. Much of the work of the German sociologist Max Weber (1864-1920) is considered as relevant for economics as for sociology (e.g., *The Protestant Ethic and the Spirit of Capitalism,* 1904-1905; *Economy and Society,* 1922). The same may be said for much of the work of sociologist Thorstein Veblen (1857-1929). In *Theory of the Leisure Class* (1899) he developed an economic sociology of capitalism, in which he was critical of capitalism, the power of the corporation, and the elite capitalist class, which he termed "the leisure class," and which he saw as characterized by ostentatious waste, idleness, and conspicuous consumption.

Sociology emphasizes the social, cultural, and political framework within which economic activity takes place. This includes an interest in the comparative historical study of economic systems in different societies, including how and why they change. Sociological analysis focuses on the patterns of norms, roles, and values that characterize economic activity in a particular society and on the relationship between the economy and other aspects of societal organization (such as the political order, family, religion, and education, as well as gender, ethnic, age, and racial stratification).

- *History* is the study of humans' historical past, from the emergence of writing to the present. It is frequently held that history is the study of specific events largely for their own sake. Sociology, as we have seen, is interested in the development of generalized principles of human relations. *A specific event is of sociological significance only to the extent that it can be related to patterns of events that yield such principles.* History, unlike sociology, is largely a descriptive discipline. Moreover, historians focus mainly on written history, neglecting "prehistory" as the object of their research. Thus they neglect about 99.9 percent of human history.
- *Social Work* is a professional field concerned with the application of sociological, psychological, and legal principles to alleviate individual and group (e.g., family) distress. Its focus is helping clients who are

defined as in need of social services. Social-work practice deals with a variety of challenges. These challenges relate to the social organization of the community and to the client's level of integration within it. The individual client may be a person or a group, such as a family or youth group, or some other collectivity, such as a neighborhood.

Historically in the United States, social workers were "agents of social change," whereas now they have a tendency to be perceived by many audiences as "agents of social control." As a discipline, social work relies upon the theoretical literature of other disciplines to inform social work practice.

Sociology as an Academic Discipline

Let us now turn our attention to the behavioral science of sociology. As a scientific way of knowing, sociology is a product of the political, economic, cultural, and intellectual turmoil of Western Europe during the eighteenth century. We will analyze the rise of sociological theory and examine the contributions of the person who is widely regarded as the founder of modern sociology, Isador Auguste Marie François Xavier Comte (1798-1857), usually referred to as *Auguste Comte* (sounds like "Kahhmt"). Then we focus on three major thinkers who provide the theoretical foundations for modern sociology—*Emile Durkheim* (1858-1917), *Karl Marx* (1818-1883), and *Max Weber* (1864-1920). We then conclude with an examination of the development of sociology in the United States, wherein we explore several major paradigms within American sociology today. These include symbolic interactionism (which has many varieties, including labeling theory), structural functionalism (sometimes referred to as "functionalism," "consensus" or "order" theory), and social conflict theory (which also has many varieties).

The Enlightenment

The eighteenth century in Western Europe, sometimes referred to as **the Enlightenment,** witnessed the development of a philosophical movement concerned with the critical examination of previously accepted doctrines, paradigms, and institutions from a point of view known as **rationalism.** Rationalism refers to the doctrine that reason and systematic, logical thinking yield "truth" and knowledge, and that, as a way of knowing, they are superior to empirical investigation and experience. Although rationalism itself came under attack and was eventually replaced by positivism during the eighteenth century in Western Europe, it nonetheless gave rise to an important philosophical movement in honor of which an entire century is named.

Auguste Comte (1798-1857)

Prior to the eighteenth century in Western Europe, religion was a major paradigm for understanding human social behavior. This paradigm came under attack and was displaced in eighteenth century Western Europe first by rationalism and then by **positivism,** a term introduced into sociology by Auguste Comte. Positivism refers to a philosophic position that science can deal only with observable entities known directly by experience and perceived by the senses. The positivist aims to formulate general laws or theories that express relationships between phenomena. The researcher collects empirical data and uses empirical observation and experiments to demonstrate that a social phenomenon does or does not fit a particular theory. Comte maintains that sociology could and should be scientific, by which he means that it should deal only with propositions (hypotheses) that are empirically testable. The researcher "explains" social phenomena by empirically *demonstrating that they are specific instances of general laws or regularities.* The positivist tradition in modern sociology stems from Comte's formulations.

Auguste Comte was a student of *Claude Henri Saint-Simon* (1760-1825), who also was a positivist and who believed that it is possible to discover the laws of social change and of social organization. Because many, although by no means all, of Saint-Simon's ideas were influential in Comte's thinking, many persons refer to both of them—Saint-Simon and Comte—as the founders of modern sociology. Saint-Simon argued that the direction of modern society—at least modern society in his day—should be in the hands of scientists and industrialists, and *not* in the hands of clerics, lawyers, and bureaucrats whom he viewed as unproductive parasites. Saint-Simon's ideas took root in Auguste Comte's fertile mind before Comte finally broke off association with him; Comte perceived consensus to be an essential social process and Saint-Simon did not.

The term sociology first was used publicly in the fourth volume of Comte's *Cours de Philosophie Positive* (1838), which was published in English in 1896 under the title, *The Positivist Philosophy of Auguste Comte.* Comte emphasized an historical, comparative approach to sociology. He also employed an organic analogy and argued as follows:

> [S]ociety, through the division of labour . . . became more complex, differentiated, and specialized. The division of labour, along with language and religion, created social solidarity, but also created new social divisions between classes and between the private and public domains (Abercrombie, Hill, and Turner, 1994: 79).

Writing more than twenty years prior to the publication of Charles Darwin's *Origin of Species* (1859), Comte viewed society and ways of knowing as having passed through three stages, which he termed the *theological* (or fictitious) stage, the *metaphysical* (or abstract) stage, and the *scientific* (or positivist) stage. Comte also believed that all existing sciences could be rank-ordered into a hierarchy. Comte viewed the new science of sociology as the jewel in the crown: it was situated at the top of the ranking.

According to Comte, sociology should study social change, which he termed **social dynamics.** Comte also believed that society consists of many "parts," and that these parts are interrelated. Some of the parts are vital to society, including the family, the political order, the economy, and religion. These institutions provide for stability and order in society. Comte termed the sociological study of institutions that provide for stability and order in society **social statics.**

While some of Comte's ideas appear arcane and perhaps even humorous to the modern reader, his thought is important. His views regarding the interconnectedness of the ele-

ments of the social order anticipate and even set the stage for the later development of structural functionalism as a school of thought (or paradigm) in sociology. His ideas also influenced the thought of Emile Durkheim and the writings of Karl Marx.

Emile Durkheim (1858-1917)

Emile Durkheim also is a positivist who advocates the adoption in sociology of the scientific method, the formulation of laws (theories) concerning the causal relations among social phenomena, and a focus on social structure as a causal agent. Durkheim argues that the way a group is put together—its social structure—has important social and psychological effects.

Durkheim was born into a rabbinical family in Strasbourg, France, just two miles west of the German border. He was educated in both Germany and France and his studies included law, philosophy, and social science. He was greatly influenced by the French intellectual tradition of Jean Jacques Rousseau (1712-1778), C. H. Saint-Simon, and Auguste Comte. His work is marked by an opposition to the utilitarian tradition in British intellectual thought, which references social action and social phenomena to the motives and actions of individuals through the exercise of individual free will. Durkheim adopts a collectivist perspective throughout his works, maintaining that groups are more than the sum of their parts. The sociological method, according to Durkheim, is to deal with social facts.

Durkheim defines a **social fact** as a social phenomenon that is distinct from individual, biological, and psychological phenomena. A social fact, according to Durkheim, is *not* to be explained in terms of individual, biological, or psychological forces. Social facts are to be explained in terms of other social facts.

According to Durkheim, social facts refer to social phenomena that are external to the individual and which constrain the individual's behavior. Social facts have three defining characteristics: (1) they are external to the individual; (2) they are coercive, in that they constrain an individual's actions; and (3) they are objective, in the sense that they are not simply a product of subjective definitions. The subject matter of sociology, according to Durkheim, is social facts. This thinking had a great impact on Karl Marx.

Durkheim was the first professor of sociology at the University of Bordeaux. He also later lectured in sociology at the Sorbonne in Paris, France, where he remained until his death in 1917.

Durkheim's interests, like those of Marx and Weber, are historical and comparative. His scholarship combines collective empirical observation with theoretical insight. Throughout his works there is a concern with and focus on social solidarity (sometimes termed cohesiveness) and social change. He studied the implications of the presence, absence, and strength of social bonds between the individual and the collectivity. What happens if the social bonds are too strong, too weak, absent, or disintegrating? What social factors influence social cohesion? What is the role of ritual and of religion in relation to cohesion? What is the relation and potential relation between occupations and social cohesion, even at the global level? These are some of the social questions that Durkheim's work addresses.

Karl Marx (1818-1883)

Karl Marx (1818-1883) was born to Jewish parents in Germany. There was much Anti-Semitism (prejudice and discrimination against Jews) in Germany at that time. His father later converted to Protestantism and all family members were baptized as Protestants. Marx was educated in Germany. As a student at the University of Bonn and the University of Berlin, his main academic interest was philosophy. He was profoundly influenced by the ideas of the German philosopher *Georg Wilhelm Friedrich Hegel* (1770-1831).

In Marx's view, the basis or foundation of society is the economy. He referred to the economy as the **substructure.** All other "parts" of society—norms, social classes, stratification, education, religion, the political order, ideas, the family, the exchange order, gender relations, and so forth—are called the **superstructure.** *The superstructure is viewed as determined (or at least as heavily influenced) by the economy.* Thus, power, for Marx, also is viewed as derived from the substructure. Those who own

the means of production have power; those who sell their labor lack power. He also believed that in a capitalist society, political and economic decisions—at the micro, meso, and macro levels—are made within the context of unequal *exchange relationships* between those who have power and those who lack power.

According to Marx, the **economic means of production** refer to the property necessary for economic production. These might consist of spears and digging sticks in hunting and gathering society, factories in early industrial societies, and so forth. Marx appreciated that people have social relations not only with other people but also with **institution**s (complexes or bundles of norms). According to Marx, there are essentially two objective relations possible when it comes to the economic means of production: one either owns or does not own them. It is in terms of this objective relationship that Marx defines social class. If one *owns* the economic means of production, one belongs to the class he calls the **bourgeoisie.** If one works for the bourgeoisie—that is, if one sells one's labor to those who own the means of production—one belongs to the class known as the **proletariat.**

For Marx, the economic and political interests of the social classes are both different and antagonistic. For instance, in capitalist society, the proletariat wants a larger share of the fruits of their labor and the bourgeoisie does not want to give it to them. The proletariat wants greater control over the relations of production (e.g., finger guards on the sausage-making machinery), and the bourgeoisie does not want to grant it to them. Marx labeled the powerlessness of the proletariat as **alienation.** The proletariat feel disassociated from the results or fruits of their labor, and, by extension, from society. Marx believed that the proletariat, due to their lack of ownership of the means of production and their lack of control over the work process, inevitably would experience alienation.

The situation, however, was not without hope of change. Marx developed a materialistic interpretation of social change and of history known as **historical materialism.** For Marx, social change and history come about as a result of a dialectical process. The concept of **dialectic** expresses the view that change depends on the clash of contradictions. Out of the clash of contradictions emerges something new, a synthesis. The dialectical process is viewed by Marx as involving three stages or phases, which he terms **thesis** (the way things are), **antithesis** (the clash of contradictions), and **synthesis** (the emergence of something new). With the passage of time, what once was new becomes "old hat," the status quo, the way things are.

In capitalist society, according to Marx, class conflict reaches its high point. There would ensue a class struggle wherein, ultimately, a victorious proletariat would usher in a classless society. The dialectical process thus is a continuing process. The Marxian dialectical viewpoint holds that the prime cause of social change and of history is the economic order. For Marx, all history is the history of class conflict.

Marx's ideas have been a major influence on the intellectual and political history of the twentieth century. They also have had a large influence on the development of modern sociology.

Max Weber (1864-1920)

Max Weber was born in Germany. He spent much of his early life in Berlin. His early academic training was in economic and legal history, but he developed a consuming interest in sociology.

A key to Weber's many analyses of the modern world is his concept of **rationalization,** which he defines as the substitution of explicit formal, written, rules and procedures for earlier spontaneous, arbitrary, capricious approaches. In other words, rationalization refers to the development of greater standardization, coordination, and consistency in organizational structure. In the political order, rationalization may manifest itself in the decline of **patrimonial rule** (arbitrary, capricious, erratic, idiosyncratic decisions of rulers) and its replacement by a standardized stem of consistent rule (e.g., parliamentary democracy). A prime example of rationalization is bureaucracy, a form of social organization that Weber analyzes in terms that still inform contemporary research and theory.

Weber perceived that rationalization was born and first became embodied in Calvinistic Protestantism, a social movement of the 16th century in Western Europe. He wrote a path-breaking book, *The Protestant Ethic and the Spirit of Capitalism* (1904-1905/1930) in which he both elucidates and documents these insights. This book was written, at least in part, in reaction to what he perceived as Karl Marx's economic determinism. American sociologist Randall Collins presents an analysis of the rise of capitalism in Japan that is similar to Weber's thesis (1998). In contrast to Marx, Weber believes that ideas, including religious ideas, can be an important cause of social change and of economic development. Weber followed up this particular study with other analyses of the religions of China, India, and Judaism that remain classics to this day in the sociology of religion (1951, 1958, 1952).

Weber observes that communities have three scarce yet widely valued resources at their disposal which they could attach to positions as rewards. He refers to these as **class** (people who share roughly similar life chances), **status** (deference, esteem, honor), and **power** (the ability to get one's way in the face of opposition). According to Weber, the relationship among class, status, and power is both variable and an empirical question. Weber rejects what many scholars perceive as the economic determinism of Marx.

Weber also debates or disagrees with both Marx and Durkheim regarding methodology. Weber argues that a comprehensive understanding of society must take into account both the objective aspects of social organization as well as the subjective motivations of actors. He refers to subjective understanding as **verstehen,** a German word which translates into English as "empathetic understanding." Symbolic interactionists draw heavily on Weber's insights and emphasize empathetic understanding as an important way of knowing (Goode, 1997).

The Development of Sociology in the United States

The theoretical legacy of Marx, Durkheim, and Weber served as a springboard for sociological analysis in the United States. As in Western Europe, so, too, in this country sociology emerged as an academic discipline in the wake of tumultuous social, political, economic, and intellectual change. Please read Box 2.2. Early American sociologists focused on substantive areas and on social patterns similar to those studied by their European counterparts: the rise of urban poverty, migration from rural to urban areas, and immigration. However, American sociology was influenced by two factors that did not have a big impact on the development of sociology in Europe: pragmatism and individualism. **Pragmatism** is a philosophical view widely credited to William James (1842-1910) and John Dewey (1859-1952) that stresses that concepts and actions should be analyzed and evaluated in terms of their practical consequences. In this view, actions designed to accomplish a desired goal are appropriate by reason of the goal they are designed to achieve *and need no theoretical rationale.* Even if there were one or more theories in terms of which the proposed actions logically could be expected to produce the desired results, these *theories are unnecessary* according to pragmatism. A pragmatist would say, "If it works, do it."

A marked collectivist emphasis, as we have seen, has characterized European sociology: social action and social phenomena should be explained in terms of social facts. Sociology in the United States, in contrast, was influenced to a far greater extent by the ethos of **individualism.** As a concept, individualism gives priority and to one's own wants, desires and goals over those of the group and to defining self in terms of personal attributes (Myers, 1993:213). Some observers maintain that the dual emphases of individualism and pragmatism are particularly noticeable within the U.S. sociological tradition of symbolic interactionism as well as in research conducted by the methods of participant observation and ethnography. Due in large part to these dual emphases, much of American sociology has had little impact on European sociology. Many European sociologists simply dismiss much American sociology since they perceive it "as consisting of jargonized trivialities" (Ian Robertson, as quoted in Lachmann, 1991: 285).

--- BOX 2.2 ---

Snapshot Portrait of the United States, 1860 to Turn of Twentieth Century

The years between 1860 and the turn of the twentieth century mark the emergence of sociology in the U.S. What was going on then? A partial picture would include observations such as the following: Industrialization and urbanization were rampant, as was migration from small towns to the industrial cities. This country appeared as a land of golden opportunity to millions of downtrodden people who immigrated to our shores, first from Great Britain, Ireland, and Western Europe, and then, in the latter nineteenth century, in droves from Eastern Europe and from what would become in later years the Soviet Union. Immigration from the Far East was important particularly in the western States. This country grew into an industrialized world giant through the sweat of immigrant labor. The nation was recovering from the Civil War that had torn it apart. Laissez-Faire capitalism was increasingly subjected both to federal regulation and to union representation of the industrial labor force. Capitalist owners strenuously fought unionism. Immigrant labor was used to break strikes. Business, once largely the purview of small farmers and mom-and-pop businesses grew bigger. Big business continued to grow and became more international in scope. Economic busts wracked the economy. The urban poor were evicted in large numbers from their homes. Disease, riots, and political activism convulsed large industrial cities. Charles Darwin's *Origin of Species* (1859) spawned theories that explained that the poor were poor because they were inferior and that the rich were rich because they were superior. The Temperance movements emerged and gained strength nationally. Jim Crow reigned in the American south and anti-immigrationist legislation barred immigrants from many jobs in northern cities. Religious revivals swept the country. American Indians were subjugated and segregated on reservations. Suffragettes engaged in collective social action to secure the vote. The large industrial prison emerged as a form of social control. This is only a partial portrait of the larger picture against which sociology emerged and developed.

American Sociology: A Sociology of Immigrants and Multi-Culturalism

American sociology emphasizes practical results and empirical investigation. It quickly flourished in urban areas such as Chicago. American sociologists there and in other large industrial cities were intimately involved in social and political reform movements. *Jane Addams* (1860-1935), who founded Hull House, a settlement house for immigrants, was among them. She worked ceaselessly for women's rights and for peace, winning the Nobel Prize for Peace in 1935. Many sociological reformers of this era, it should be noted, were biased by their rural, Protestant backgrounds (Mills, 1951). During the nineteenth century and well into the twentieth, the numerous contributions of women and ethnic-minority sociologists were overlooked. Please be sure to read Box 2.3 on W.E. B. DuBois, a famous early American sociologist.

--- **BOX 2.3** ---

W.E.B. DuBois: An American Sociologist

Historians of sociological thought often overlook the contributions of African Americans. One of the most notable early American sociologists is **William Edward Burghardt DuBois** (1868-1963). Born in Great Barrington, Massachusetts, on February 23, 1868, DuBois was an outstanding student from an early age. He became rigorously educated in ancient Greek philosophy while still a youth. By age 16, he already had mastered Latin and Greek. DuBois entered Fisk University in Nashville, Tennessee, where received his first undergraduate degree in 1888. He then earned his second undergraduate degree from Harvard University, graduating *cum laude* from Harvard in 1890. DuBois then enrolled in the Ph.D. program at Harvard. His doctoral dissertation is entitled *The Suppression of the African Slave Trade to the United States of America 1638-1870.* DuBois is the first African-American to receive a Ph.D. from Harvard (1895).

DuBois' postgraduate studies were completed in Germany under the famous German sociologist, Max Weber, at the University of Berlin. Back in America, DuBois devoted his sociological career to understanding and changing the dire conditions of many African Americans. He wrote no fewer than nineteen monographs concerning all aspects of black life in America, including music, art, heath, religion, crime, family, and economics. Many of his "published studies investigated certain areas for the first time and are still authoritative" (Chapman, 1991: 96). DuBois worked for social justice. He espoused a theory of the "Talented Tenth." This viewpoint held that privileged African Americans had a responsibility to support the other ninety-percent of less privileged African Americans. In the political realm he insisted that sound social policy had to be based on an accurate perception of facts.

DuBois was one of the first to apply the positivist approach to the study of race relations in the United States. His book, *The Philadelphia Negro* (1899) is a sociological investigation of the economic and social conditions of the 45,000 blacks living in Philadelphia at the close of the nineteenth century. His studies were conducted by going door-to-door to collect information on the social, religious, economic, and family life of African Americans in Philadelphia.; making on-site observations, and interviewing people. The "sociological methods of DuBois were adapted by Park and Burgess at the University of Chicago" (Gonzales, 1990:2).

One of DuBois' most famous works is *Souls of Black Folk* (1903), wherein he cogently argues that the experience of slavery and of racism in America has created a "double consciousness" for African Americans. Blacks in America live in two worlds, two cultures, both of which inform African Americans' interpretation of reality. DuBois argued for "gentle readers" of his book to understand the "strange meaning of being black here at the dawning of Twentieth Century; for the problem of the Twentieth Century is the problem of the color line." The verdict in the O.J. Simpson criminal trial suggests that the experiences of African Americans and of white Americans still differ significantly in this country at the dawning of the twenty-first century.

DuBois founded the Niagra Movement in 1905, which sought equal rights for African Americans, and the National Association for the Advancement of Colored People (NAACP) in 1909. The NAACP called for equal educational opportunities, the enforcement of the Fourteenth and Fifteenth Amendments of the U.S. Constitution, the abolition of racial segregation, and for the right to vote (Gonzales, 1990: 85). From 1910 to the early 1930s he edited the NAACP's monthly journal, *The Crisis.*

DuBois brought sociology to black colleges. He also held many teaching positions. He taught sociology at the University of Pennsylvania (1896-1897) as well as economics and history at Atlanta University (1897-1910). At the age of 66, when many people already have retired, he became chair of the sociology department at Atlanta University (Chapman, 1991:96). He served there as department chair for over a decade, during which time he also founded the journal, *Phy-*

lon, and he continued to conduct research.

By the 1950s, DuBois had left Atlanta University. His politics had moved far to the left. At the age of 82 he ran unsuccessfully for the U.S. Senate. During the McCarthy era, he was arrested as an "agent of a foreign government" for his left-wing activities. He was dismissed from the NAACP. He lost faith in the idea of racial integration and supported the self-segregation of African Americans. He became disillusioned with American society, which becomes understandable when one recalls the blatant racism of the time, which at that time manifested itself in numerous lynchings and other acts of violence perpetrated against blacks. He joined the American Communist Party.

In October 1961, he rejected

the racist policies of American society by engaging in self-imposed exile to the Republic of Ghana. His long-time friend, President Kwame Nkrumah, had invited him to Ghana. President Nkrumah appointed DuBois as Director of the Encyclopedia Africana project. DuBois died in Accra, Ghana, on August 27, 1963 on the eve the massive Civil Rights March on Washington, D.C.

DuBois had a strong influence on other African-American sociologists that can be seen in E. Franklin Frazier's books *The Negro Family in Chicago* (1932), the *Negro in the United States* (1957), and *Black Bourgeoisie: the Rise of a New Middle Class in the United States* (1957) and in William Julius Wilson's *The Truly Disadvantaged: the Inner City, the Under Class, and Public Policy* (1987).

Between World War I and World War II, and continuing through the McCarthy era of the 1950s, the zeal for reform gave way to an effort to develop sociology as an impartial science that utilizes and relies on value-neutral "objective" methodological procedures and quantitative techniques of data analysis. **Quantitative data** are data in numerical form. Then in 1954 the U. S. Supreme Court rendered its *Brown v. Topeka* decision which declared racial segregation of public facilities unconstitutional. Subsequently, the civil-rights movement, sparked by Rosa Parks and led by Dr. Martin Luther King, Jr., began its historical march. As a result, many American sociologists rethought and discarded the ethos of value neutrality. They embarked on an intimate involvement with social and political reform. The reform emphasis in American sociology intensified during the strife-torn years of U.S. military involvement in Southeast Asia. It has shown no indication since then of ebbing. To the contrary, during the past few decades the applied reform emphasis in American sociology has grown and diversified. Its impact on social policy remains substantial as

the United States prepares to enter the next millennium.

The Chicago School

The first department of sociology in the United States was established at the University of Chicago in 1892. The American Sociological Association was established a little more than a decade later. At the University of Chicago, sociologists like Robert E. *Park* (1864-1944), Ernest W. *Burgess* (1886-1966), Louis *Wirth* (1897-1952), and F.M. *Thrasher,* along with *William Isaac Thomas* (1863- 1947) and Polish sociologist Florian *Znaniecki* researched the phenomena of juvenile delinquency, gangs, and the cultural adaptations of immigrants (Wirth, 1938; Thrasher, 1936; Thomas and Znaniecki, 1918).

Particularly between the two world wars, the University of Chicago dominated American sociology. The University of Chicago produced a prodigious amount of sociological research. Many persons who earned their Ph.D. in sociology at the University of Chicago went on to teach in, and to be departmental chairs of, departments of sociology across the breadth and width of the nation.

The distinctive approach known as **the Chicago school** or as "Chicago sociology" still exists today as an approach to sociological analysis. Chicago sociology is referred to as "a school" because its research, particularly that conducted during the interwar years has several common characteristics, among which are the following four.

- First, it is heavily influenced by the theories of German sociologists Ferdinand Toennies (1855-1936) and Georg Simmel (1858-1918). You will get to know their ideas in this textbook.
- Second, this research is concerned with the problems or challenges of community and of urbanization.
- Third, this research utilizes a particular research method, ethnography, which relies on detailed personal observations of the daily lives of the people being studied.
- Fourth, this research is characterized by the symbolic interactionist approach. The University of Chicago is known for its important role in the development of the symbolic interactionist approach, to which we now turn our attention.

Symbolic Interactionism

The foundations of symbolic interactionism were laid by the economist and social psychologist Charles Horton Cooley (1864-1929) of the University of Michigan and by the philosopher and social psychologist George Herbert Mead (1863-1931) of the University of Chicago. Mead himself published little. His books actually are compilations of his lectures published by his students after Mead's death. Prime among them is *Mind, Self, and Society* (1934). Mead's students also coined the term **symbolic interactionism** after his death to describe Charles Horton Cooley and Mead's approach to understanding the social world. Both Mead and Cooley emphasize that human nature is socially constructed and, more specifically, that the individual's sense of self is socially constructed. As a way of knowing, this approach stresses the importance of language, gesture (gestural communication), and role taking in the formation of the mind, the self, and

society. This approach is uniquely important in sociology because it provides the theoretical basis for labeling theory, and because it is a critique of positivism. As a way of knowing, symbolic interactionism stresses that the subjective or inner life of the individual is an important source of social behavior and of social action.

Cooley uses the concept of **looking-glass self** (1902) to refer to the process whereby an individual develops an identity or self concept (self). According to this view, we come to know or to define ourselves through the process of internalizing the responses of others to us. Just as we know what our physical self looks like by gazing into a mirror, so too, we know what our "self" is like by using the responses of others to us as a guide. In Cooley's view, we become that which we are addressed: If people who are important to us keep telling us that we are stupid, awkward, and ugly, we will come to have a conception of self as an ugly, stupid, awkward person. In other words, we come to adopt or to accept as our own the perceptions we have of the responses of others to us. It is the individual's conception of the responses of others to her or him, rather than the actual responses of others, that is viewed by Cooley as crucial in the process of self development. Cooley views this process as particularly important in the early years of childhood.

A familiarity with the meaning of several concepts makes it easier for us to understand Mead's contributions to symbolic interactionism. As used by Mead, a **gesture** is any physical movement or vocalization that conveys meaning and that also evokes a response in one or more persons. A **sign** is any cue or stimulus—an object, an event, a sound, a sight, a smell, a word, etc.—that is associated with, or that evokes a response to, something else which is not physically present at the time. A **symbol** is a sign that evokes a uniform social response from one or more audiences. A flag, a number, an engagement or wedding ring, the Fourth of July, and the year 1066 are examples of symbols. Sociologists stress that the *meaning* of a symbol is arbitrary, in the sense that it is not inherent in the object, sound, or sight, itself but is derived from the consensus of the people who use it in communication. To right-wing militia groups in the United States, "Ruby

Ridge" and "Waco" have a meaning very different than they do to agents of the Federal Bureau of Investigation and of the Alcohol, Tobacco, and Firearms Bureau. "Ruby Ridge" and "Waco" are symbols. **Role taking** refers to taking the point of view, attitudes, or behaviors of another person by imaginatively perceiving oneself *as* the other person, in order to be able to anticipate that person's actual or likely behavior. For instance, a husband who has fallen in love with a cute little fluffy puppy, that he has just found abandoned by the side of the road, might say to himself: "Knowing my wife and her attitudes and sensibilities, and putting myself in *her* place, what would *I* do if my beloved spouse brought home a new puppy as a potential member of our household?"

Mead emphasizes that the self emerges through the process of social interaction with others. Mead stresses that language, gestural communication, and role-taking are important bases of social life. Language makes available shared symbols through which a child achieves a fully human mind. In Chapter 6 (Socialization: Internalizing Relationships That Make a World) we compare Mead's theory with others about the formation of self. For now, it is enough to know that, according to Mead, the child takes on the role of another person at first in play. Mead calls this *the play stage.* Initially, the child takes on the role of a *specific other*—Mommy, Daddy, Aunt Flora, or Grandfather Lewis, etc. Eventually, the child achieves sufficient cognitive sophistication that the child can take on the role of **the generalized other,** the attitudes and expectations of behavior held by a larger social group (the community, the society, and so forth). Mead calls this **the game stage** of the development of self. We explore these stages in greater depth in Chapter 6 (Socialization: Internalizing Relationships That Make a World).

Mead also distinguishes two parts of the self: the **"I"** refers to the spontaneous, self-interested, unsocialized part of the self; and the **"me"** refers to the socialized self that has internalized the community's notions of appropriate behavior. What Mead refers to as the "I," Sigmund Freud (1869-1939), would call the "id"—our innate sexual and aggressive drives. What Mead refers to as the "me," Freud would call the "superego" (conscience). Mead, then,

looks at the psychological construct of conscience as being developed in a social context.

In his writings, Mead stresses that society has an objective existence. He stresses that society does not consist solely of arbitrary meanings given to it by its individual members (subjective awareness). There are two basic schools of symbolic interactionist thought that springboard off of symbolic interaction as viewed by Mead. Some symbolic interactionists ignore this part of Mead's work and consequently sometimes ignore the effects of society's structural constraints on human social action. These interactionists view society as emerging out of the subjective awareness and interactions of the participants. From their viewpoint society is defined by the arbitrary meanings that participants attach to it. Other sociologists, however, combine an appreciation of social structure with symbolic interactionism. For instance:

■ Lyn Lofland, of the University of California, Davis, has conducted a cross-cultural and historical analysis of order and action in urban public space (1973). She analyzes both the pre-industrial city (that emerged roughly 4,000 years ago in Mesopotamia and Sumer) as well as the modern industrial city. Using both macro and micro sociological methods, she both asks and presents answers to the question: How is it possible to live in a world of strangers? Her analyses are theoretically grounded as well as substantively rich and insightful.

■ Elliot Liebow's award-winning book, *Tally's Corner* (1967), is a case study of a type of social order that German sociologist *Ferdinand Toennies* (1855-1936) calls **Gesellschaft** (1988/1887). According to Toennies, Gesellschaft (e.g., modern industrial society) is founded on **artificial will,** which means that human relationships are founded on rational calculation rather than on spontaneous attraction. Others are seen not as ends in themselves, but as means to ends outside the relationship. You say hello to Patty because you want to borrow her textbook. These also are *segmental* relationships, wherein one relates just to part of a person rather than relating to the entire person. You know Mr. Mohammed Jabal, who lives next door to you, but you know him in only a few of the various roles he occupies. Gesellschaft frequently is translated into English as "society."

In contrast, the term **Gemeinschaft** (e.g., hunting and gathering society) is founded on what Toennies calls **natural will,** which means that relationships are founded on spontaneous attraction: Relationships are warm, personal, direct, and *diffuse* (in that they are founded on contact between whole people rather than on contact between just parts of people). That is to say, in a Gemeinschaft, you know people in all their different roles. In a Gemeinschaft you also relate to people as ends in themselves, not as means to an end. Thus, you say hello to Patty because you like her, because she is a community member, not because you want to borrow her textbook or a cup of sugar. You relate to other people because the interaction is meaningful in itself; it is a positive end or purpose for you. Gemeinschaft frequently is translated into English as "community."

Toennies goes on to argue that there has been an evolutionary trend, whereby urbanization and industrialization are breaking down the fabric of solidarity, of Gemeinschaft, and are turning the world into an emotionally bleak Gesellschaft. Toennies argues that society is coming to be an entity founded on brute force and material interest, whereas in Gemeinschaft, society had been founded on warm personal fellow feeling. Toennies argues that at most in a Gesellschaft, there are small, isolated, unstable solidary groups. There are groups, to be sure, that are tied together by emotional attractions. But these groups have no support from a larger social order. They do not tie into, are not articulated with, the fabric of the larger social order in any meaningful way; and hence, they are isolated and they are unstable.

■ One of the best modern depiction's of Gesellschaft is an account of relationships among poor, inner-city, African-American males on the street corners of Washington, D.C. Elliot Liebow chronicles their activities in *Tally's Corner* (1967), a case study of Gesellschaft. It describes a set of men who spend a great deal of time on street corners, working only occasionally; having no real opportunity to get a good job that would tie them to the larger society in meaningful ways; lacking effective political participation; their lives, accordingly, revolving around the street corners and the things that happen on street corners.

The lives of these men are not bereft of emotional content. These men constantly form and end close relationships with each other. They refer to having one of these close relationships as being "uptight" or as "going for brothers." It is noteworthy that although the "uptight" relationship is emotionally penetrating and deep, it is also transient and unstable. Why transient and unstable? Because there is nothing in the larger social order to maintain it. As a consequence, these men tend to live a volatile emotional existence in which they are up-tight one day, and the next day they are sworn enemies. Because Liebow attempts to relate this pattern of instability and volatility in interpersonal relationships to the lack of bases for solidary organization within this particular segment of society, this book is a penetrating study of the concept of Gesellschaft.

■ Sociologist Norman K. Denzin (1992) also combines an interest in social structure and symbolic interactionism. Denzin focuses on communication technology and its structural and individual-level effects. How do those in power *create*, not just report on, "news"? What are the individual-level and structural effects of watching television? Many American children spend more combined time watching television and watching violence on television and at day-care centers than they spend interacting with their families. Denzin argues that many American children are more influenced in their **socialization** by mass-media agents than they are by their own families.

Socialization refers to the process whereby we learn roles and norms, develop a capacity to conform to them, and develop a conception of self. It is a process that takes place across the life-span: tiny babies do not have a corner on the socialization market. Many sociological paradigms are useful in studying socialization, including symbolic interactionism. We focus on socialization in Chapter 6 (Socialization: Internalizing Relationships That Make a World).

In terms of methodology, symbolic interactionists favor the **case study** method, wherein the researchers participate in an intensive, long-term study of a single case or "unit." For instance, researchers study a single street corner society, or a particular gang in a particular city. Examples of actual research include an analysis of daily life in a karate dojo (Fritschner, 1977), a deviant youth gang (Thrasher, 1936), and an alcoholics" rehabilitation group (Donovan, 1984); life in a mental hospital in general (Goffman, 1961) and life in a mental hospital as perceived by a patient (Rosenhahn, 1973); the social organization of the work stetting in a hospital (Ashley, 1977), federal bureaucracy (Blau, 1964) or a multinational corporation (Kanter, 1977; Peters and Waterman, 1982); and the study of the meanings of violent street crime as perceived by the perpetrators (Katz, 1988).

In the United States in the 1970s, symbolic interactionism was viewed as an alternative paradigm to functionalism (sometimes referred to as structural-functionalism; consensus theory; order theory; or as social systems theory, particularly as developed by Talcott Parsons). Functionalism, which became increasingly more influential after World War I, became the dominant school of thought in American sociology shortly after the end of World War II. From that time until the mid or late 1960s, functionalist sociologists and functionalism dominated American academic sociology. We turn now to an examination of this sociological paradigm.

Structural Functionalism

As a sociological way of knowing, structural functionalism was introduced to American sociology by Talcott Parsons in the late 1930s (1937). In its American sociological form, this paradigm is heavily influenced by the European sociologists Emile Durkheim and Max Weber. It dominated American sociology throughout the 1950s up to the late 1960s. It remains one of the major theoretical perspectives in American sociology today.

What does it mean to take a **structural view** of society? It means two things. First,

society is viewed as consisting of "parts." Some of these parts, for instance, are roles, statuses, groups, norms, and institutions (bundles or complexes of norms). Second, the parts are perceived as interconnected; this interconnectedness of the parts is called *interdependence.* Hence, if one part of society changes, it has repercussions on other parts, and hence on society as a whole.

Structural functionalism is a macro structural view that focuses on large-scale structures. It differs from conflict theory with respect to which "part" of society is viewed as most important. *Society as a whole* tends to be the focus for functionalists. Functionalists believe that in terms of understanding human social behavior it makes sense to speak in terms of "society as a whole" or of "the community as a whole." Hence, if a functionalist wants to understand a particular social behavior or institution, the question that tends to be asked is: How does this practice help the society as a whole to persist across time? A well-known functionalist explanation of why structured inequality, to some degree, is found in virtually all human societies maintains that structured social inequality helps (1) to fill social positions and (2) to motivate the incumbents to fulfill the rights, duties, and obligations attached to those positions with at least some minimally acceptable amount of diligence and competence (Davis and Moore, 1945).

Another classic example of a functionalist approach to understanding social behavior is Kingsley Davis' famous analysis of prostitution (1937). Davis notes that human societies tend to have an approach-avoidance relationship with prostitution. It is found in many agrarian and industrial societies, where it is both condemned as well as tolerated (although not necessarily by the same audiences). Davis concludes that prostitution serves important latent functions: it is a safety-valve of sorts, providing a sexual outlet for many disfigured, old, ugly, not socially-skilled people who otherwise might not be able to secure a willing sexual partner. It helps keep marriages together: Many husbands still can have a sexual outlet, even for culturally despised forms of sexual expression, even if their spouses are unwilling to participate in these activities. Prostitution, by helping to keep families intact, helps keep the institution of the family viable. The family, among its other functions, is a primary agent of informal social control. So, by keeping the family as institution intact, Davis views prostitution as performing a vital function that enables societies to continue to exist across time.

So, if a functionalist were to ask the question, "Who benefits? Who or what part of society benefits by the existence of a particular social behavior or social institution?" the answer tends to be "Society as a whole." For instance, sociologist Linda Marie Fritschner, of University of Indiana at South Bend, in a sociological ethnographic analysis of karate as a leisure-time activity (1977), finds that, although karate has widespread appeal, it is primarily working-class males, most of whom hold dead-end jobs, who stick to the rigors of the training program. She finds that karate, and its offer of indomitable power, "function to make and [to] maintain a class of underdogs by offering a system of vertical mobility [that] is parallel to the system of stratification by economic rank. The result is the structural preservation of idealized American values of diligence, hard work, suffering, and honesty in a class of potential malcontents." (Fritschner, 1977: 3)

Functionalism gives us some interesting insights into everyday life. Robert K. Merton, in his book **Social Theory and Social Structure** (1968: 105), asserts that an important aspect of the functionalist way of knowing is the ability to perceive, and to perceive the difference between, two types of functions. **Manifest functions** are the purposive and intended outcomes of a social institution. **Latent functions** are the often-time hidden, unrecognized, and unintended consequences of a social institution. For example, a manifest function of work is to give you an income (and, perhaps, some type of meaning in your life). The unintended outcomes are that work also becomes a place where you make friends, meet future marriage partners, and develop networks of colleagues. Its unintended consequences are the relationships and interactions that make a world.

Structural functionalism maintains that society by its very nature has an *imperative need* for order and that members of society have a *need for solidarity*, a need for solidary order, a need to belong (Ridgeway, 1992). One of the aspects of making a world is solidary order. Functionalism views society as a social system

of interdependent relationships and interactions. Functionalism maintains that the main institutions of society perform **imperative functions,** functions which, in the final analysis, contribute to the well-being and overall functioning of the entire social system. These institutions include the family, religion, social stratification, government, and the economy (Parsons, 1977). From the point of view of functionalism, if we want to arrive at a sociological understanding of a problem in one of the institutions of society, we cannot view that problem in isolation. We cannot focus only on the problem if we want to understand it. Because all parts of the social system are interrelated, we need to focus on them, also, in order to understand a problem in one of its parts.

Functionalism uses the term **function** (or positive function, eufunction) to refer to those instances wherein one or more parts of society (or of another system, such as a small group) operate in such a way that they contribute to the survival and stability of the system. For instance, the function of gift-giving is to re-enforce the solidary order (Hagstrom, 1966). The adjectival form of "function," of course, is *functional.* Functional relationships are those that contribute to the well being of society. Thus, Emile Durkheim believed that many forms of deviance (norm violation) are functional for society: the condemnatory responses of others to the deviant and to the deviant act re-assert the importance of the norm in the face of its violation. In contrast, functionalism uses the term **dysfunction** to refer to those instances wherein one or more parts of society (or of another system, such as a community, city, and town) operate in such a way that they disturb, hinder, or threaten the integration, adjustment, or stability of the system. Thus, incest is a dysfunction; it threatens the authority and solidary structures of the family. The adjectival form of "dysfunction" is *dysfunctional.* Of course, what may be perceived as dysfunctional for one part of a system may be viewed as functional for some other part. For example, in a particular social-class system, the widespread existence of a certain belief ("The working classes are dirty and they smell bad") may be functional for the upper class but dysfunctional for the lower class. Thus, W. Somerset Maugham, English man of letters, talks about how such a belief among the English gentry and nobility served to create and to sustain social distance, which is one part of a social class system:

> . . . in the West we are divided from our fellows by our sense of smell. The working man . . . stinks: none can wonder at it, for a bath in the dawn when you have to hurry to your work before the factory bell rings is no pleasant thing, nor does heavy labour tend to sweetness; . . . I do not blame the working man because he stinks, but stink he does. It makes social intercourse difficult . . . The matutinal tub divides the classes more effectually than birth, wealth, or education. . . . It is responsible for class hatred more than the monopoly of capital in the hands of the few. (1977: 142, 143)

Social Conflict Theory

Social conflict refers to conscious struggle between groups (or social categories, social aggregates, institutions, etc.) over resources. The resource may be any number of things: a goal, value, meaning, class, status, power, income, property, and so forth. Social conflict occurs within, between, and among collectivities. The collectivities engaged in social conflict may be of any size. The smallest group is a dyad, which consists of two persons.

Theorizing about social conflict undoubtedly is ancient. Social thinkers in many countries—including China, India, Greece, Italy, France, and Arabia—theorized about war and revolution before Karl Marx. In England, Thomas Hobbes (1588-1679), Adam Smith (1723-1790), and Thomas Robert Malthus (1766-1834) added a materialist or scientific basis to the study of social conflict (Hobbes, 1651; Smith, 1776; Malthus, 1798).

In the United States in the mid to late 1960s, social conflict theory was viewed as an alternative to functionalism as a way of knowing human social behavior. Much of this theory drew on the insights of Karl Marx, and hence is termed neo-Marxian. "Neo" means "new."

Neo-Marxian theory in the United States developed during the turbulent days of the civil-rights movement, the Vietnam War, urban riots, and concern about poverty in the cities and in the countryside. Neo-Marxian theory posed a theoretical and political challenge to structural functionalism. Once again, social, intellectual, political, and cultural turmoil manifested itself in the emergence of a perceived need freshly to understand *the things that make a world.* Once again, it was time to toss out old ways of knowing in favor of new ones. Rapid social change and social movements concerning gender inequality, racism, and poverty called for new ways of looking at, and of understanding, the world. It was time to take a fresh look at the elephant of human social action.

Neo-Marxist sociologists established a scholarly sociological journal, *The Insurgent Sociologist,* now named *Critical Sociology.* Sociologists who view the world through the lenses of Marxian sociological theory publish their works on labor, class, gender, work, race, and the logic of imperialism in this journal. Following in the tradition of American sociologist C. Wright Mills (1956), these sociologists analyze networks of power and changing class formations and relations in the United States and abroad (Wright, 1985, 1987; Szymanski, 1978, 1983; Burris, 1979, 1987; Levine and Lembcke, 1987).

Following the lead of Karl Marx, neo-Marxians view the economic order as the primary causal agent of social life and of social order, social change, and history. Social class, they stress, is a viable concept for explaining social behavior, social action, and life outcomes. They stress that relationships to the means of production are primary among all relationships that make a world. Whether you marry; whom you marry; the number of friends you have; whether you attend college or university, and, if you do, which particular college or university you attend; the occupation you attain; even the values you possess, all these and more, from this point of view, are products of social class. Unlike functionalism that stresses cohesion and order, Neo-Marxism asks: "*Whose* cohesion, and *whose* order? *Who* (i.e., *which social class*) makes the rules (norms), has the power, and actually governs the society? *Who benefits?*" Their answer is that those who own the means of production rule, it is they who have the power, it is they who actually govern. They impose power on the rest of us. *They* benefit at *our* expense.

Neo-Marxianism is but one variety of social

conflict theory. Feminism has its own versions of social conflict theory, which collectively are called *feminist theory* (e.g., de Beauvoir, 1949; Millett, 1969; Greer, 1970; Gilligan, 1982; Daly and Chesney-Lind, 1988; Wharton, 1991; Rineharz, 1992; Anderson, 1993; Hippensteele and Chesney-Lind, 1995). These theories also ask the question, "Who benefits?" Their answer, "Males; males benefit at the expense of females." **Patriarchy** is a term from feminist theory that refers to male supraordination. On the variables of class, status, and power, males tend to rank higher than do females. If Marxians and neo-Marxians want to overthrow capitalism, it is patriarchy that feminists want overthrown (e.g., Firestone, 1970). Patriarchy is the substructure, if you will, from this theoretical viewpoint. Art, literature, government, language, the family, the economy, and so forth are the superstructure. If one wants changes in the suprastructure, the substructure must be changed. In feminist theory, this means that patriarchy must be swept aside and gender-equal relations established in all spheres of social life and of social action. In other words, from a feminist theoretical perspective, it would be possible, theoretically, to put the means of production in the hands of the proletariat, and yet very little would change for females. Why? Because the means of production actually would be in the hands of *male* proletarians, *not* in the hands of female proletarians, and not equally in the hands of either sexes or genders.

There are other varieties of social conflict theory. Some American sociologists interested in racial and ethnic dynamics, for instance, perceive race as a variable that is not to be subsumed under economics (e.g., Memmi, 1965; Blauner, 1972; Bonilla-Silva, 1997; Bonilla-Silva and Lewis, 1997). From this framework, for instance, it would be possible, theoretically, for the means of production to be in the hands of the proletariat, and yet very little would change for, say, persons of color. Why? Because the means of production actually would be in the hands of white proletarians, not equally in the hands of proletarians of all races and of all ethnicities.

Another version of social conflict theory is *controlology* (Goode, 1997). Controlology refers to the view that social control is state or state-like control. From this point of view, in order to understand social order, social behavior, and social action, it is necessary to understand how the state and its allies (henchpeople) control populations they perceive as troublesome (Scull, 1988; Cohen, 1985; Foucault, 1967, 1979). One problem for controlology as a way of knowing, of course, is that the state is a relatively new institution in human societies. It did not exist throughout 99.99 percent of human existence on this planet; so, by focusing on the state as the primary cause of human social behavior, they ignore most of human history.

Sociology Today

Sociology is a multi-paradigmatic way of knowing that reflects the cultural diversity of its proponents. Within the past thirty years, sociology as a profession has become more diverse in terms of the gender, race, ethnicity, sexual orientation, physical disability, and other attributes of its practitioners. These attributes influence *the lives* that these practitioners live, their *perceptions of human social behavior and social action*, the *questions* they ask, and hence, the research *methods* and *theories* they employ as a way of knowing human social behavior and social action (Bonilla-Silva, 1997, Bonilla-Silva and Lewis, 1997). There are numerous schools of sociological thought in the world today, and not one of them is dominant in American sociology at the present time.

One pragmatic school of thought that is worth noting is **applied sociology,** which utilizes a variety of sociological perspectives, principles and research methods to solve social problems. These sociologists are employed by government agencies to collect data and information that allow for informed social policies. Some applied sociologists are university and college professors who consult for the public and private sector; they tend to use research grant money provided by both government and non-profit foundations to conduct their research. Other applied sociologists work for major corporations as marketing researchers; others work for a variety of agencies that work for social change and reform (e.g., labor unions, gay-rights non-profit agencies, the American Association of Retired Persons). Included in applied sociology are those who engage in what is termed *clinical sociology,* the application of sociological skills and methods in therapeutic practice with individuals and groups. Its emphasis is on direct intervention by the clinical sociologist, based on existing knowledge. Areas in which clinical sociologists practice include marriage and family counseling, drug and alcohol rehabilitation, corrections and probation, and law enforcement. This way of knowing assumes that research findings are public information that should be used for the improvement of society, even if it proceeds by increments of one individual, family, or meso-level group (e.g., youth gang) at a time.

The various ways of knowing in sociology are not mutually exclusive. Some sociologists use a variety of perspectives, while others subscribe only to one. As indicated previously, one should guard against assuming that one way of knowing is right and another is wrong. Each way of knowing has advantages and disadvantages. Each is "right" according to its own domain assumptions. A particular theory and a particular method are tools that allow us to focus on particular aspects of social reality and social action to the exclusion of others.

As the authors of this textbook, we are not here to advocate any particular sociological way of knowing as the "truth." If you are looking for "magic bullets" (instant answers) you are bound to be disappointed, because you will not find them here. Our position is that the variety of sociological ways of knowing, together, allows us to perceive and to understand the multi-dimensional nature of *relationships that make a world.* All of these positions are ultimately linked anyway.

As we discuss throughout this textbook

there are imperative forces to maintain social order (functionalist perspective), and there are social forces that undermine and cause society to change (conflict perspective, neo-Marxist perspective). In seeking to understand social behavior and social action, it is imperative to understand how people attribute meaning, what the meanings are that they attribute, how people are socialized, through what agents of socialization, and in what cultural context (symbolic interaction). Furthermore, the social order is made up, at least in part, of exchange relations; and both *personal and political power* are socially organized (*imperative order*). Social order also is made up, at least in part, of *solidary order* (e.g., a perceived need to belong) and of rules (norms) of various sorts (*normative order*). There are many relationships that make a world. Different theories and different methods are the tools that sociologists use in their attempt to understand the relationships that make a world. Once more to apply our metaphor: various theories and research methods are the tools that sociologists use to understand the "elephant" of social behavior and social action.

Throughout this text, we use the above-mentioned paradigms to introduce you to sociology. We also use any and all scientific information, method, theory, and data that allow us to attain a clearer understanding of things that make a world. In short, we use whatever it takes to introduce to you *relationships that make a world.* Our aim is to assist you in developing and in adopting a powerful sociological imagination that you can then use in your efforts to contribute to and to participate fully in the modern world.

Key Concepts

administrative system
alienation
altruistic suicide
anarchy
anomic suicide
anomie
antithesis
applied sociology
artificial will
Auguste Comte
authority
autokinetic effect
base-rate information
bourgeoisie
case study
causal reasoning
class
common errors in everyday
  inquiry
conspecific
definition of the situation
dialectic
dysfunction
economic means of production
egoistic suicide
Elliot Liebow
Emile Durkheim
ethnography
exuvial magic
feminist theory
Ferdinand Toennies
function
functionalism
gemeinschaft
generalized other
gesellschaft
gesture
group

group-serving bias (ultimate
  attribution error)
historical materialism
hypothesis
imperative order
institution
Karl Marx
latent function
longitudinal data
looking-glass self (Charles
  Horton Cooley)
magic
manifest function
Max Weber
mirror-image perceptions
natural will
patriarchy
patrimonial rule
peer group
pluralism
positivism
power
pragmatism
primary group
probabilistic reasoning
proletariat
rationalism
rationalization
reference group
role
role taking
science
scientific method
secondary group
self-serving bias
sign
social aggregate
social category

social conflict
social conflict theory
social dynamics
social fact
social statics
social structure
socialization
status
steps in the scientific method
structural view
substructure
superstructure
supportive social system
supraordination
symbol
symbolic interactionism
synthesis
Tally's Corner
the "I"
the "me"
the Chicago school
the economic order
the economy
the Enlightenment
the game stage
the play stage
the political order
The Protestant Ethic and the
  Spirit of Capitalism
the ways we know
the Yanomamo
theodicy
thesis
variable
verstehen
W.E.B. DuBois

Internet Resources

http://ezinfo.ucs.indiana.edu/~jgreen/home16.html
  Document: W.E.B. DuBois

gopher://wiretap.spies.com/00/Library/Classic/manifesto.txt
  Document: *The Communist Manifesto*

http://csf.colorado.edu/psn/marx
  Document: the Marx-Engels Archives, by Cyber-Marx International

http://www.asanet.org/

Document: the Home Page of the American Sociological Association (ASA)

You will find information regarding ASA student competitions, ASA activities and meetings, recent publications of interest to sociologists, and links to sociological resources on the internet, and more.

http://www.runet.edu/~lridener/DSS/DEADSOC.HTML

Note: the symbol after ~ is lower-case letter "L."

Document: Dead Sociologists' Society

You find many classical sociological theorists here, including Comte, Martineau, Marx, Spencer, Durkheim, Simmel, Weber, Addams, and more. For each one, there is a photo depiction, a section devoted to the theorist (The Person), a Summary of Ideas, and the Original Work. There also is a series of sociological links by topics—criminal deviance, age inequality, culture, the family, social class, poverty, medicine and health, and many more.

Suggested Readings

Berger, Peter, *Invitation to Sociology* (New York, NY: Doubleday, 1963).

Charon, Joel M., *Symbolic Interactionism: An Introduction, An Interpretation, An Integration* (Sixth edition) (Upper Saddle River, NJ: Prentice Hall, 1998)

Collins, Randall, *Four Sociological Traditions* (New York, NY: Oxford University Press, 1994).

Mills, C. Wright, *The Sociological Imagination* (New York, NY: Oxford University Press, 1959).

Ritzer, George, *Modern Sociological Theory* (Fourth Edition) (New York, NY: McGraw-Hill, 1996).

Rogers, Mary F., *Multicultural Experiences: Multicultural Theories* (New York, NY: McGraw-Hill, 1996).

Learning Exercises

The learning objective of this chapter is for you to appreciate how beliefs, values, and behavior are molded or created by the groups to which we belong. In the writing assignments below, you are to follow the directions and to write a response to the questions or issues indicated. Your answers to the written assignments are to be typed, double-spaced, and stapled in the upper-left hand corner.

Learning Exercise 2.1

Writing Assignment

Answer the following questions in an essay in which you use some of the key concepts from this chapter. Your essay is to be typed, double-spaced, and stapled in the upper-left hand corner. Your essay will be no shorter than three full pages in length.

1. Briefly describe and distinguish among and between the different perspectives in sociology. How does American sociology differ from European sociology?
2. W.E.B. DuBois is an African-American sociologist. How did his background influence his view of the world? What do think female sociologists study? Why?
3. List some of the benefits of having a sociological perspective.

■ ■ ■

Learning Exercise 2.2

Writing Assignment

Answer the following seven questions in an essay in which you use some of the key concepts from this chapter. Your essay is to be typed, double-spaced, and stapled in the upper-left hand corner. Your essay will be no shorter than three pages in length.

1. How was the author's father's childhood important for his adult life? Describe those experiences in a sentence or two. What was the importance of the year his father was born for his values and beliefs? Do you know anyone in your family or anyone else from your community who experienced this or something similar to this? If so, how do they describe their childhood and adult life? What was it like for them to grow up in a rural area or in an urban area in America? What attitude did the author's father have concerning African Americans? Why?
2. The author's father became a Protestant minister. The author's father was not necessarily a religious person before his conversion. Why do you think he changed? What is the importance of having a "perspective?" Do you have a perspective? Please describe this perspective in a sentence or two.
3. List some of the events and things that changed in the 89 years that the author's father lived. Are these events and things important for a person's perspective? Why?
4. What is a sociological conception regarding "human nature"? How is this conception different from a religious one? Are individuals adaptable and malleable? What does the author suggest about the pervasive influence of groups and social structure on values, attitudes, and social behavior? Do you believe it? Why?
5. Do you have a best friend? Did your best friend influence you? How? Give examples. Are your peers important to you in what you think, believe, and feel?

6. In his autokinetic-effect research, Sherif is making the point that individuals conform to group rules (norms). Do you think individuals carry within them the group's "definition of the situation?" Do you conform to the rules of group(s) to which you belong? Why?
7. Mr. O.J. Simpson's criminal trial and acquittal have created a great deal of controversy in American society. How does the author suggest we should understand and explain the differences between white and African-American attitudes towards the O.J. Simpson criminal trial and verdict? Are there other explanations?

■ ■ ■

Learning Exercise 2.3
Writing Assignment

Answer the following questions in an essay in which you use some of the key concepts from this chapter. Your essay is to be typed, double-spaced, and stapled in the upper-left hand corner. Your essay will be no shorter than three full pages in length.

1. Study "the ways we know." Which ones do you think are most useful for developing an accurate view of the social world? Why is knowing the domain assumptions of the ways we know important? What ways do you use to know about the world around you? How do your friends know the world around them?
2. Describe to the reader "common sense." How is it different than sociology?

■ ■ ■

Learning Exercise 2.4
Writing Assignment

Answer the following questions in an essay in which you use some of the key concepts from this chapter. Your essay is to be typed, double-spaced, and stapled in the upper-left hand corner. Your essay will be no shorter than three full pages in length.

1. You probably have seen individuals like "Mac" in large cities. Do you know anything like what the author describes? In reference to Mac, what is the author's view of human nature and his ideal of social life? If Mac were your father or best friend, how would you view him differently? Why?
2. You may have known someone who committed suicide. How does integration into a social system of support prevent suicide? Does the example of suicide raise questions about "the good life" in American society? Why?
3. Divorce rates in American society are high. How would knowledge about divorce in American society help you de-personalize its impact on you?

■ ■ ■

Applying Sociological Analysis to the World

For those who may not want to respond to the above exercises, you may choose instead to view one of the following video tapes and to write a short typed, doubled-spaced paper (stapled in the upper-left corner) integrating concepts you have learned in class lecture, discussion, and your readings. Your essay will be no shorter than two full pages in length. You must obtain the videos on your own at your own expense.

- Milgram Experiments
- Malcom X
- Philip Zimbardo's Stanford Prison Guard Experiment

Have you ever experienced something like the Stanford-Prison-Guard experiment in your own life? That is, have you ever found yourself in a position where another person or persons have had a lot of power relative to you and your life and you have had very little? Tell us about it.

■ ■ ■

Learning Exercise 2.6

Engaging in Sociological Research

For those who may not want to watch videotapes or to view a movie, you may get together in groups of two or three persons. Use this group to engage in *one* of the following three activities that one or all of you may present in class.

1. Interview individuals who are over 65 years of age and ask them what it was like growing up in (insert name of the state in which your college or university is located). Present your findings to the class.
2. Repeat Sherif's experiment and present your findings to the class.
3. Ask members of your group to discuss examples of individuals projecting "definitions of situations" or images of themselves in one situation. You may want to perform a skit for the class.

■ ■ ■

Learning Exercise 2.7

Sociology and the Internet

In this learning exercise you are to answer *three* of the following four questions. Follow the directions. Your answers are to be typed, double-spaced, and stapled in the upper left corner.

1. Select a search engine for the internet (e.g., Yahoo, InfoSeek, Web Crawler, Alta Vista, Lycos, and so forth.). Here are the "addresses" (URLs) for some of the highly popular search engines:

http://www.altavista.digital.com/
http://www2.infoseek.com/
http://webcrawler.com/

http://www.excite.com/
http://www.lycos.com/
http://www.yahoo.com/

Enter a sociological theorist's full name, someone other than W.E.B. DuBois (e.g., Emile Durkheim, Max Weber, Karl Marx, Jane Addams). Using a search engine, run a search. Browse through three of the sites. In a two-hundred-and-fifty word essay, please characterize and summarize the portrayal of the theorist you have selected that is communicated to you on these web sites. In your essay, please identify (a) the theorist on whom you performed a search, (b) the search engine that you utilized, and (c) the URLs of the sites you have accessed. Also, please (d) indicate the ways in which the web-site portrayal of the theorist is similar to, and different than, that conveyed to you in this chapter of your textbook.

2. Here is an internet addresses on W.E.B. Du Bois:

http://ezinfo.ucs.indiana.edu/~jgreen/home16.html

Document: W.E.B. DuBois

This site provides information on W.E.B. DuBois. Read it. This site also provides links to a biographical sketch of DuBois from Encyclopedia Britanica and to the W.E.B. DuBois Institute at Harvard University. Explore these links. Then, please do the following:

(a) In a two-hundred-and-fifty word essay, please summarize the portrayal of DuBois that is communicated by these sites, indicating the ways in which the portrayal is similar to and different than that you gathered from reading this chapter in your textbook.

(b) Using a search engine of your choice, run a search for W.E.B. DuBois. Access two of the web sites (other than those listed above). Browse through those two sites. What did you learn about DuBois and about his influence on sociology, social science, social policy, and social action that you didn't previously know? Please tell us about it. In your answer, please indicate the name of the search engine that you utilized, and the URL and name of the web sites you accessed.

3. Below are some internet addresses on secure-housing units (SHUs) in the United States. Each of these web sites can be accessed through the search engine Web Crawler. Secure-housing units are part of the correctional system of the federal government and of some state governments in this country.

http://www.wco.com/%7Eaerick/twelve.htm

Document: "The Department of Corrections Dirty Dozen," by Paul Wright

http://www.wco.com/%7Eaerick/cor.htm

Document: "Justice for Prisoners from Corcoran State Prison," by Corey Weinstein

http://www.sonic.net/~doretk/Issues/96-10%20OCT/theycallthem.html

Document: "They Call Them 'Control Units,'" by Dan Pens

http://www.sonic.net/~doretk/Issues/96-08%20AUG/indeterminate.html

Document: "Challenging the Indeterminate SHU Term," by Steve Castillo and Graham Noyes

gopher://gopher.igc.apc.org:7020/00/pubs/pb-ex/Pelican%20Bay%20Express%20V.2%233

Document: Pelican Bay Express V.2#3

Please access *two* of the above web sites and read and reflect upon the material found there. Please write an essay of not less than two typed pages in length in which you use sociological terms and concepts to analyze what you have read about secure housing units. Sociologically speaking, which theoretical perspective or perspectives inform the two articles you have read? Support your position with logical reasoning and with concrete examples.

http://szocio.tgi.bme.hu/replika/hozzaszol2.html

Document: Acquired Immune Deficiency Syndrome in Social Science in Eastern Europe: the Colonization of Eastern Europe Social Science

Please access this 22-page document and read it. Summarize this article in 100 words. From what theoretical perspective is this article written? Support your position with logical reasoning and with concrete examples. Select a different theoretical perspective. *From that theoretical perspective,* write a 50-word characterization of the phenomenon discussed. Then, please reflect in writing on this analysis opportunity. Was it difficult or awkward for you to write about the phenomenon from a perspective other than the one you had just read? Why do you think this is the case? Then, define the concept "rationalization" as used by Max Weber. Is the point of view of the authors of this article similar to, or different than, Weber's perspective on rationalization? Explain, supporting your position with examples and with logical argument.

■　■　·　■

Multiple-Choice and True-False Test

1. Social structure refers to _____.
   A. attitudes and beliefs
   B. definitions of the situation
   C. stable patterns of social relations
   D. unconscious motives

2. _____ is the scientific study of how and why we form groups, live together in small ones and in larger ones and it encompasses the functioning of whole societies and the social, economic, cultural, political, and technological relationships within, between, and among societies.
   A. Political Science
   B. Anthropology
   C. History
   D. Sociology
   E. Social Work

3. The term "sociology" was coined by _____.
   A. Max Weber
   B. Emile Durkheim
   C. Auguste Comte
   D. Bill Clinton

4. Lee Robins' study of Vietnam veterans showed _____.
   A. that once an addict always an addict
   B. that a major influence in becoming an addict was group membership
   C. that veterans were able to stay free of addictive drugs after they changed their environments
   D. both (B) and (C)

5. Michael Argyle showed that non-aggressive caregivers _____.
   A. are less effective in child rearing
   B. create environments that increase intelligence and emotional bonding
   C. create children who have achievement motivation and are able problem solvers
   D. both (B) and (C)

6. Primary group refers to _____.
   A. our family
   B. our friends
   C. groups in which we have close intimate relationships
   D. all of the above

7. Polls on O.J. Simpson's criminal trial showed _____.
   A. O.J. was guilty
   B. O.J. was innocent
   C. peoples' perceptions were influenced by ethnic-group or racial affiliation
   D. O.J. was a victim of the mass media

8. The example of describing the elephant by four blind-folded persons showed how wrong each person was in trying to understand the elephant.
   A. True   B. False

9. Tradition as a way of knowing can be detrimental for us.
   A. True   B. False

10. Sociological research demonstrates that people perform random acts of kindness.
    A. True   B. False

11. Mac lay dead for hours because _____.
    A. people were callous
    B. Mac looked grubby
    C. his friends were not around
    D. people by their nature are apathetic
    E. people by their nature are pathetic

12. A sociologist studying suicide would _____.
    A. look at clinical depression
    B. discover psychological reasons
    C. want to know the method of suicide
    D. look the rate of integration in society

13. Divorce in American society is caused by poor communication skills.
    A. True   B. False

14. Sociology does not have any likeness to other social sciences.
    A. True   B. False

15. The means of production refers to _____.
    A. business peoples' ability to help workers find jobs.
    B. the working classes' ability to find work
    C. ownership of property necessary for economic production
    D. patriarchy
    E. the superstructure

16. Alienation refers to _____.
    A. normlessness
    B. helplessness
    C. hopelessness
    D. powerlessness
    E. anomie

17. Solidarity refers to _____.
    A. lack of norms
    B. powerlessness
    C. hopelessness
    D. feelings of we-ness in a group

18. Norms _____.
    A. are rules for behavior
    B. have positive and negative sanctions
    C. are our values
    D. both (A) and (B)

19. Anomie refers to _____.
    A. lack of spirituality
    B. powerlessness
    C. normlessness
    D. alienation

20. Rationalism _____.
    A. refers to the philosophical doctrine that reason and logical thinking are the only basis of valid knowledge
    B. refers to the substitution of explicit formal, written rules and procedures for earlier spontaneous, arbitrary, capricious, erratic approaches
    C. is the same thing as rationalization
    D. anomie
    E. Gemeinschaft

21. Rationalization _____.
    A. refers to the philosophical doctrine that reason and logical thinking are the only basis of valid knowledge
    B. refers to the substitution of explicit formal, written rules and procedures for earlier spontaneous, arbitrary, capricious, erratic approaches
    C. is the same thing as rationalism
    D. both (A) and (C)
    E. Gemeinschaft

22. Verstehen means _____.
    A. objective understanding
    B. subjective understanding
    C. cost efficiency
    D. purposive behavior
    E. frotteurism

23. The development of American sociology _____.
    A. was influenced by pragmatism
    B. was more individually oriented than European sociology
    C. began in 1950
    D. all of the above
    E. both (A) and (B)

24. The first official department of sociology in the United States was established at
    _____.
    A. Harvard
    B. Princeton
    C. Yale
    D. the University of Chicago

25. An early American sociologist _____.
    A. Karl Marx
    B. Rita Levi-Montalcini
    C. Ferdinand Toennies
    D. William E. B. DuBois

26. DuBois' life was distinguished by which of the following?
    A. the first black to graduate from Harvard with a Ph.D.
    B. one the founders of the NAACP
    C. drawing attention to the problems of racism in American society
    D. all of the above

27. DuBois' self-imposed exile was in _____.
    A. South Africa
    B. Ghana
    C. Philadelphia
    D. Mozambique
    E. Yale

28. Anomie is a synonym for anarchy.
    A. True B. False

29. Gemeinschaft is founded on _____.
    A. natural will
    B. artificial will

30. Gesellschaft is founded on _____.
    A. natural will
    B. artificial will

31. Which of the following is/are (a) relationship(s) that make a world?
    A. normative order
    B. imperative order
    C. exchange order
    D. solidary order
    E. all of the above

32. According to Karl Marx, those who own the means of production are _____.
    A. proletariat
    B. bourgeoisie
    C. bureaucrats
    D. anomic
    E. anarchic

33. According to Karl Marx, those who sell their labor to the bourgeoisie are _____.
    A. proletariat
    B. bourgeoisie
    C. bureaucrats
    D. anomic
    E. anarchic

34. This concept expresses the view that social change (history) depends on the clash of contradictions.
    A. dialectic
    B. anomie
    C. Gemeinschaft
    D. Herrschaft
    E. exuviae

35. _____ refers to the often-time hidden, unrecognized, and unintended consequences of a social institution, behavior, event or policy.
    A. Manifest function
    B. Latent function

36. Male supraordination is referred to by feminists as _____.
    A. alienation
    B. patriarchy
    C. heterosexism
    D. androgyny
    E. Herrschaft

37. Parts of social structure that provide individuals with social support and that positively integrate individuals into communities and into their society are referred to as _____ by Emile Durkheim.
    A. dysfunctions
    B. anomie
    C. synthesis
    D. photosynthesis
    E. supportive social systems

3

Social Structure as Patterns of Solidarity and Conflict

Conflict is a form of sociation . . . a certain amount of discord,
inner divergence and outer controversy, is organically tied up with
the very elements that ultimately hold the group together.

Georg Simmel, *Conflict: The Web of Group Affiliations*

■ ■ ■

Solidarity—Ties That Bind

What makes for lasting friendships? Why were the friendships among Mac and his buddies enduring and stable, while those among the men studied by Elliot Liebow on the street corners of Washington, D.C., fleeting and brittle?

A sociologist might explain this difference in durability in terms of the ways in which the two networks are connected to the larger social structure. Those connections are virtually *absent* among the Tally's-Corner men while both are *present* and reasonably *robust* in the case of Mac and his friends.

The men on the street corners of Washington, D.C. have no enduring ties of employment, of political participation, or of exchange with the larger social structure. The affiliative ties between and among the men, without crosscutting or overlapping social circles to infuse them with strength and durability, simply fall apart. Sociologist S. N. Eisenstadt, who has worn well Weber's mantle in assessing the

objective and subjective dynamics of change, corroborates that solidarity is both a crucial and *fragile* dimension of any social order (1995).

In contrast, enduring, robust, informal ties of exchange (*exchange order*) connect Mac and each of his buddies not only to each other but to the larger social structure as well. If one of the fellows were to break with the group, this fellow would lose more than friendship. He also no longer would have a place to sleep unmolested at night (in the doorways of the merchants' expensive shops); he no longer would have good meals and medical attention over the weekends; he no longer would have a steady, dependable supply of cheap wine to drink during the week. It is important to note that the reciprocal informal relationships Mac and his friends have with the merchants (sleeping space in exchange for keeping an eye on the store) and municipal police (informing about potential burglars in exchange for a nice place to sleep, good food, and free health care on weekends) reveal the presence of crosscutting or overlapping social circles that both (a) tie the friendship group together and (b) tie each of its members to the conventional and larger social structure.

It is also important to appreciate that the municipal police are part of the *imperative order* of the larger social structure. They are obligated to enforce the laws. In connection with the duties attached to that position in the social structure, the municipal police have the right to issue certain commands to citizens, and citizens have the duty to obey them (domination). Their enduring and reciprocal informal relations with Mac and his friends give strength to the friendships among the men. Any one of the men had a lot to lose other than friendship by breaking with Mac's small band of men. Please complete the following exercise before reading the remainder of the chapter.

Learning Exercise 3.1

Before you read this chapter, please take a few minutes to write your responses to "Who Am I?" Please start at "1" and continue through "20," putting only one answer on each line. Your responses are from the point of view of you looking at yourself.

Who Am I?

01. _____
02. _____
03. _____
04. _____
05. _____
06. _____
07. _____
08. _____
09. _____
10. _____
11. _____
12. _____
13. _____
14. _____
15. _____
16. _____
17. _____
18. _____
19. _____
20. _____

When we view these two contrasting situations from the vantage point of relationships that make a world, we see, to use a metaphor, that the friendships among the men in Mac's group endured because they were infused with the "social-structural glue" (crosscutting or overlapping social circles) that bound them together. The enduring ties between each man and the *imperative order* and between each man and *exchange order* of the larger social order buttressed and gave muscle to the friendship ties among themselves. *Without the strength provided by overlapping social circles, friendships simply collapse.* So, even friendship is not solely a personal matter.

Solidarity is one of the relationships that makes a world (Silverstein and Bengtson, 1997). In this chapter, we identify and discuss various forms of solidarity in human societies. Then we examine the bases or forms of solidarity and the intricate relationship between solidarity and conflict. We conclude this chapter with an examination of the effects of solidarity and its absence both for individuals and collectivities.

Forms of Solidarity

The terms social solidarity, **solidarity**, cohesion, and social cohesion are used interchangeably and synonymously by sociologists. Sociologists informally define solidarity as the sense of "we-ness" in a group or collectivity—the sense among members of a collectivity that those persons who are members of the collectivity are different, for better or for worse, than persons who are not members of that particular collectivity.

There are many ways to categorize the forms of "we-ness" found in human social organizations. It is not that one conceptual framework is right and another is wrong. Conceptual frameworks illuminate certain aspects of the world and direct our attention towards those things, thus deflecting our attention from other aspects of the world. They are thus handy, useful tools for bringing order out of chaos.

It is somewhat arbitrarily, then, that we select as a conceptual scheme one presented by American sociologist Leon Mayhew (1971: 74-75). Mayhew identifies four types of solidarity,

which he terms **attraction**, **loyalty**, **identification**, and **association**. Those terms are *neologisms*. If you look up neologism in the dictionary, you find that it has two main meanings. One meaning is the creation of a brand new word out of whole cloth. Sometimes this is called "word-smithing." Thus, *Sandra Bem,* a social scientist interested in gender roles, was a word smith when she invented the word **androgyny** out of two Greek roots—"andro," meaning male and "gyny," meaning female—to refer to gender roles characterized by equal amounts of traditionally "masculine" and "feminine" personality traits (Bem, 1975). A second meaning of neologism is to use an already existing word and to ascribe to it a new, different, particular meaning. It is in this second sense that attraction, loyalty, identification, and association as forms of solidarity are neologisms. Let us now look in turn at each of these forms of solidarity.

Attraction

Attraction refers to positive affective attachment to another person (Stimson, 1992). This concept is straight forward, and it refers, for instance, to the ideal relationship in the United States between husband and wife, or to the relationship between best friends, girlfriend-boyfriend, mother-child, and father-child. We now turn our attention to scientific research findings regarding the importance for a child's behavior and orientation to the world of attraction, which in some research traditions is referred to as *attachment*.

Researchers both observe and document the importance of attachment on a child's adjustment (Ainsworth, 1982; Kagan, 1985: 79-89). Sociologists *Robert B. Cairns and Beverley D. Cairns* (1994) use longitudinal data to study children and adolescents at risk in the southeastern United States, youth who either engage in or are victims of aggression and violence, youth who drop out of school, bear children at an early age, run away from home, and so forth. The authors find that friendships with conventional adults are a "life line" that enables many youth to turn their lives around. The youth could turn their lives around "because they did not stand alone . . . [they experienced] the commitment of a responsible and supportive adult (Cairns and Cairns, 1994: 237). Hazan and Hutt (1993) also find that youth who had poor relationships with their parents but who managed to construct a warm, supportive relationship during childhood with an adult have more favorable life trajectories than youth utterly bereft of positive affective relationships with adults in the conventional social order. Similarly, in a longitudinal study of an entire **birth cohort** (i.e., all persons born in a given year) in a racially diverse area in the United States, *Emmy Werner*, of the University of California, Davis, finds that the ability to seek out a helping adult is crucial to being able to thrive despite hardship (Werner, 1987; Werner and Smith, 1989). Her carefully-crafted study documents that those youth who thrive despite having parents who use drugs, who are convicted felons, and who suffer severe acute and chronic mental disease; who thrive despite being victims of physical abuse, sexual abuse, psychological abuse, and parental neglect were relentless in their efforts to construct, to maintain, and, when necessary, to replace friendships with responsible, caring adults.

Dr. *Mary Ainsworth* observes three styles of attachment in her laboratory studies of babies between the ages of one and two (1982). She finds that the styles of attachment are a product of the way the caregivers had treated the infants in the preceding months. When caregivers respond promptly and warmly to their infants' entreaties for contact and comfort, the infants tend to form secure attachments. *Securely-attached* babies use their mothers as a secure pad or base from which to explore their environment and from which to operate when playing. When mother leaves the room, these babies show distress; but when she returns, they are reassured, after which they again explore their environment and play. In Ainsworth's view, these infants had learned that they could count on their caregivers to be responsive, which "gave them the confidence they needed for exploration" of unfamiliar territory (Hazan, 1995: 42). These toddlers, when older, have fewer disciplinary problems than those who had been either insecurely or avoidantly attached.

Some caregivers are not as responsive. Some caregivers are inconsistent in responding to their infants. Sometimes they are warmly

responsive; at other times, they are variously neglectful or intrusive. Their infants tend to form insecure attachments. *Insecurely-attached* babies appear extremely distressed when their mothers leave the room. When she returns, the infants seek contact during the reunion, but also appear angry and have difficulty settling. Later, they tend to stay close to the mother rather than venturing off to play. When they do play, they seem too anxious to enjoy the toys, even when the mother is present. Ainsworth views this behavior as a way of coping with inconsistent caregivers. Their caregivers' unpredictability left them feeling insecure and made them angry.

A third type of attachment Ainsworth notes is avoidant. This form of attachment is associated with fairly consistent rejection on the part of the caregivers. Instead of responding warmly or inconsistently to their infants' bids for contact, these caregivers regularly rebuff the infants. The caregivers seem to avoid close contact with their own infants. In the play situation, the *avoidantly-attached* babies seem to focus on the toys and to avoid their mothers when the mothers are in the room, and they display no interest in her comings or goings. Ainsworth views this behavior as indicating that the infants had learned that it is futile to seek comfort from the caregivers and adapt by keeping their distance.

Longitudinal studies on attachment indicate to many researchers that one of the long-term results of failure to form a secure attachment between the main nurturing figure and infant is an inability to establish intimate ties with another person even as an adult. Researchers have studied the relationship between attachment to a nurturing figure at a young age and its effects on other behaviors (Argyle, 1994; Ainsworth, 1989; Sroufe, 1984; Erikson, Sroufe, and Egeland, 1985; Schneider-Rosen et. al., 1985; Miyake, Chen, and Campos, 1985; Haigler, Day, and Marshall, 1995). Those securely attached to their mothers at age six months or younger are more likely to do the following:

■ *at two years of age:* seek their mothers' help when performing difficult tasks. The ability to seek help from a competent source is a valuable asset, a trait or orientation to the world that significantly increases the probability that one will persist at a difficult task instead of giving up and going on to something else instead. Persistence at a task, in turn, is positively correlated with successful completion of a difficult task. *Have you, or anyone you know, ever tried to accomplish a task—to ride a bike, to learn to use a computer for data analysis or for word processing, to learn a foreign language, to learn to water ski or to cross-country or down-hill ski, to sew, to repair your car, for instance—and, had you not asked for assistance, would have given up? Tell us about it.*

- *at five years of age:* are more resourceful in adapting to changing circumstances and more persistent in coping with tasks (Wilson and Herrnstein, 1985; Bowlby, 1982; Bersheid, 1985; Lewis et. al., 1984). In contrast, those who had been insecurely or avoidantly-attached at age six months or earlier, at age five fall apart—become angry, distressed, contrary—when faced with a difficult task.

Weak attachment, these researchers conclude, does not so much lead to a particular form of misconduct—nose picking, or being a bully, or being insolent, or being lazy—as it does to misconduct quite generally. Thus, one child, whom we call Jack, was liked by his teachers because he so obviously craved attention. The other children avoided him because he was highly manipulative, uncooperative, and could not tolerate the slightest frustration. Another boy, whom we call Denzel, was hostile, devious, manipulative, and sadistic. His teachers didn't like the boy, but several of Denzel's classmates, noting his superb skill in controlling others, were drawn to him.

Similarly, Emmy Werner's longitudinal study finds that secure attachment to the main nurturing figure by age one is strongly related to being slow to anger and to tolerating frustration well in a disorderly household at two years of age; to being cheerful and enthusiastic, seeking help from adults effectively, and being flexible and persistent at age 3 ½; to being able to distance oneself from emotional turmoil, to seeking out and finding adults for guidance and help when parents falter in childhood; and

to planning rather than acting on impulse as a teen (Werner, 1987; Werner and Smith, 1989).

Loyalty

As a form of solidarity, **loyalty** refers to attraction to groups as groups (Scharr, 1968). Once again, "loyalty," as used here is a neologism. The distinction being made between loyalty and attraction is that loyalty refers to direct, positive affect to a group as a group, whereas attraction refers to direct positive affect to another individual as an individual. The distinction rests on whether the objects of attachment are persons (individuals) or established groups, such as gangs, work groups, military units, sororities, fraternities, cell blocks, deaths row, age sets, villages, and so forth (Nagel, 1994; Bakalian, 1993). U.S. Navy SEAL Commander Richard Marcinko is talking about loyalty when he writes the following concerning his first command of a SEAL team in wartime:

> What you learn very quickly is that your men—your unit—are everything. Like a mafioso, you take an oath of blood with your men. You cherish them, nurture them, protect them. You keep their foibles to yourself. You must be completely loyal to them—and they will be the same to you. (Marcinko and Weisman, 1992: 106)

Marcinko appreciates that members of a group may change, they may come and go, yet people continue to feel loyalty to the group, because their loyalty is not so much to any particular member or members within the group as it is to the group itself. Thus, students probably already have graduated, and hopefully will continue to graduate, from the university or college you now are attending. Students obviously graduated from the high schools that many of you attended. The particular members come and go, yet many persons continue to feel attachment to their high school and to the university or college they attended. Likewise, the particular individuals who worship or who collectively participate in communal rituals at your mosque, synagogue, or church, may come and go; nonetheless, many persons, and perhaps you, yourself, continue to feel attachment to, loyalty to, the religion or religious body symbolized by a synagogue, church, or mosque. These are all examples of positive affective attachment to a collectivity; they are all examples of a form of solidarity known as loyalty (Hurtado, Gurin, and Peng, 1994).

Rich bodies of observational and experimental evidence suggest that attraction to groups as groups (loyalty) probably is as primordial as attraction to another person and that it fulfills certain felt human needs, such as those called "safety" and "belongingness" by Abraham Maslow (Maslow, 1954; Heslin and Patterson, 1982; Rodin, 1985; Forsyth, 1990; Lenski, 1995). Had you been a participant in *Stanley Schachter*'s classic experiment (1959), you would have volunteered to be a research subject in an experiment being conducted at a prestigious university you are attending. Upon showing up at the appointed place and time to participate, you would be informed that, as a participant, you would receive a series of electric shocks. In one condition, the shocks are described as intense and as extremely painful. In a comparison condition, the shocks are described as very mild and as resembling "a tickle or a tingle" (Schachter, 1968: 545). You are then told that you have to wait for the experiment to begin. You get to choose between waiting alone by yourself or waiting with others who are strangers to you but who also will be participating in the same experiment that day. *Which would you choose?* If you are anything like the research subjects in either the original experiment or in a number of subsequent similar experiments, the more anxious or fearful the condition ("intense and extremely painful shocks"), the more likely you are to choose to wait with people. If you think the experiment is going to be a cakewalk, you don't mind waiting by yourself. There seems to be something calming, soothing about being in a group when one is anxious or fearful. *Have you, or anyone you know, ever been in a state of fear or anxiety and have found it soothing to be around others, even if you did not know the other people who constituted the collectivity in which you sought refuge? Tell us about it.*

Differences Between Highly Cohesive Groups and Other Groups

Empirical, field-based research within sociology indicates that groups that are highly cohesive are different in several respects, including their organizational consequences, than groups that are not highly cohesive (e.g., Roethlisberger and Dixon, 1939; Janis, 1982). While research has generated many findings, we now bring four of them to your attention (Collins, 1992; Ridgeway, 1992). *First*, highly-cohesive groups demand more conformity from their members than lowly-cohesive groups. *Second*, a highly cohesive group tends to punish nonconformity to the norms of that particular group more than lowly-cohesive groups. *Third*, the more cohesive a group, the more likely it is that the conformity it demands is conformity to the norms of that particular group and not conformity to the norms of the larger social structure in which that group is situated, located, or embedded. *Fourth*, the more cohesive a task group, the more important it is to structure the group in certain ways if you want to guard against a desire for group harmony getting in the way of and interfering with effective problem solving (e.g., Janis, 1982). We address this fourth point under the heading of "Group Polarization and Groupthink in Formal Organizations" in Chapter 12 (Groups, Organizations, Bureaucracy, and Work: Relationships of Power and Exchange That Make a World).

Because these four points are somewhat abstract, we want to make them clearer and more concrete for you. While we address the fourth point in a later chapter of this textbook, we now turn our attention to the others by means of examining a classic empirical research study about **work-restriction norms** (Roethlisberger and Dixon, 1939), a study which gave birth to the specialty area of *industrial sociology*. Work-restriction norms are informal rules-of-the-game that workers develop that seem to help them to cope in the face of the difficulties encountered on the job. You will not find any of these informal rules in an official rules-and-procedures manual of any firm or factory. They are informal ways of coping that workers develop over time that, from their point of view, seem to help them accomplish their task in the face of all the obstacles they encounter in their particular day-to-day work situation.

The field of industrial sociology is a particularly American specialty that dates from the studies conducted by *Elton Mayo* and a Harvard University research team at the Western Electric Company's Hawthorne Works in Chicago from 1924 to 1932. These studies are known as **the Hawthorne studies.** Twenty thousand workers were involved in them. The research originally was done to determine the relationship among employee working conditions and employee productivity and satisfaction. Such variables as the amount of light, temperature, level of humidity, length and number of work breaks were varied to ascertain the effects of each on worker morale and productivity.

The major findings of the Hawthorne studies are that human factors are more important than environmental ones as determinants of both worker productivity and worker morale (Filtzer, 1994). The informal work group developed norms of their own, norms that were contrary to the expressed goals of management. Management wanted to increase worker productivity. Management instituted a wage-incentive plan in an attempt to raise employee productivity. Each individual worker's total wage was determined to a certain extent by the level of group output. This incentive plan was not effective.

The workers had their own ideas regarding the amount of work appropriate during a work day (group norm), and their idea was significantly *lower* than what management wanted. The informal work groups enforced their group norms and effectively restricted output. If a worker worked too fast or produced more than the group thought appropriate, he would be ridiculed as "a rate buster" or as a "speed king." If a worker produced too little, he would be ridiculed as a "chisler." Another sanction was what the workers called "binging." One worker would walk up to a worker whom he thought was breaking the informal norms of the work group and would hit him smartly on the upper arm. It wouldn't break the worker's arm, but it would hurt. It was supposed to hurt.

In other words, cohesive groups develop norms of their own, they demand conformity to these norms, and they punish nonconformance to these norms. A group within a larger organization can develop norms that run counter to the norms of the larger organization in which it is situated. A sociologist might rephrase this by noting that patterns of identification with and loyalty to smaller groups within a larger-scale organization affect not only the individual members within the smaller groups, but also the capacity of the larger-scale organization to meet its larger-scale goals and to solve its larger-scale organizational problems.

The remaining forms of solidarity are based not on direct emotional attachment but on a sense of belonging, of membership or inclusion in a group.

Identification

We speak of **identification** when part of one's identity, part of one's sense of self derives from one's membership in a group or groups. *How did you complete the "Who Am I" exercise at the beginning of this chapter?* Even if you have been reared in a western industrialized culture that stresses an ethic of rugged individualism, the first few responses probably refer to your social connections and group affiliations. "I am Muslim," "I am a Roman Catholic," "I am African -American," "I am female," "I am Hispanic," "I am Irish," "I am a college student," "I am a sports fan," are examples of group affiliations. After these first few collectivist or group identifiers, you may well have described yourself in terms of individual traits—for instance as tall, friendly, shy, polite, courteous, fun-to-be-with, intelligent, funny, fat, short, blonde, etc. In cultures native to South America, Asia, Africa, and South and Central America, identity is even more heavily defined in relation to collectivities. This is recognized by referring to the sense of self in these cultures as *interdependent,* a concept emphasizing that the sense of self is heavily embedded in group affiliations. Thus, the Japanese are more likely than people in the United States, and Malaysians more likely than people from Britain, to complete the "Who Am I" statement with group identities (Markus and Kitayama, 1991; Bochner, 1994).

My friend, whom I'll call Alex, is an apt example of a person in an individualistic culture who nonetheless has his identity rooted in group affiliations. Part of Alex's identity is bound up with being a "sociologist." Particularly in the first couple of years after his doctor-ate had been awarded, he would say of himself with pride, "I am a brand new Ph.D." That statement reveals that his sense of self was largely bound up in being a "sociologist." Unfortunately, Alex then had a narrow, restrictive conception of what this thing called a "sociologist" is. To him, a sociologist is someone who has earned a Ph.D. in sociology, who teaches sociology courses at a University, and who conducts and publishes scholarly works that enhance our understanding of social conduct. Alex enjoyed doing all those things, and he was delighted at his good fortune to be paid for doing the things he loved.

One day Alex discovered that he was being let go from the academic position in the university at which he had been teaching for several years. Alex was amazed, aghast at how he felt. He felt as though the center of his being had been removed, sucked out. Upon reflecting from whence that horrible feeling came, Alex realized that his very sense of who he was, of "Who am I?," was threatened in a fundamental fashion by unemployment. After all, a big chunk, possibly the biggest chunk of his sense of self was bound up in that single aspect of self. If he didn't fit his definition of a sociologist, then he was not a sociologist. Delete "sociologist" from his sense of self and what was left? In his case, not much. There were then few other aspects of self on which he then hung his identity. No wonder he felt resonantly empty.

In the United States in the late 1970s and 1980s many women who had their identity bound up in being "wives and mothers" felt uneasy. They felt that the core of their sense of self was being devalued and denigrated by the "women's liberation" movement. The career woman, not the devoted wife or homemaker, then seemed to hold the limelight of the national media; it was she who was the media darling, the model to which females were encouraged to aspire.

Many women in this country had grown up with "wife and mother" as *the* ideal role cluster for females. The heroines, the models to be emulated and to which they had been encouraged to aspire could be summed up in three words, as "wife and mother" or in two words, as "home maker." Many females had interna-

lized these as core aspirations, as core identities. Many wives and mothers who sincerely wanted to be wives and mothers and who had no desire to "dress for success," or to "have power lunches," or to get on "a fast track" in the extra-familial labor force, now found the value, the worth of core aspects of their identity being called into question and found wanting by salient audiences. At the level of the individual, one result was that many of these women experienced anxiety—a feeling of uneasiness, of malaise, which eventually crystallized itself into what American feminists in later years would term a "backlash" (Faludi, 1992).

Just as the anti-feminist backlash movement ricocheted off of the Women's Liberation Movement, so a raid made by police on a gay bar known as the Stone Wall Inn brought about a very unexpected outcome. According to American sociologist **Erich Goode**, homosexual behavior in this country tended to be clandestine and furtive until the late 1960s. Then, one summer's night in 1969, the police raided a gay bar in Greenwich Village, New York, called the Stonewall Inn. While in the past, municipal police across the nation had been able to raid gay bars without resistance, on this particular night, the gays in this particular bar resisted arrest, which touched off a riot. The riot, now known as the Stonewall riot, in turn touched off a gay civil-rights movement. One outcome of the Stonewall riot of 1969, then, was the formation of an identity group that pursued "an active, open, gay civil rights movement" (Goode, 1994: 272).

A careful and sensitive reader might note from the examples we have presented that identifications frequently refer to broader groups than do attractions or loyalties (Gaskell and Smith, 1986). Thus, a Californian need not know, need not even like all other Californians to recognize a common fate with them and to experience identity as a Californian. An American female need not know, need not even like all other females in the United States in order to recognize a common fate with other American females and to experience identity as a female. So, too, with African Americans, fat people, the spinal-cord injured, and the severely mentally challenged, to cite just a few examples. Each of these examples represents a social movement and an **identity group** that can be understood sociologically, at least in part, as an attempt by a collectivity to construct an alternative basis for inclusion in the national life as "an organized, autonomous, and culturally distinct group" (Mayhew, 1971: 90). "Established, institutionally defined groups that have this sense of membership will be termed **identity groups**. Identity groups range in scope from a few members to whole nations" (Mayhew, 1971: 74; emphasis added).

Primordial and Nonprimordial Groups

Five additional points about identity groups deserve attention. First, in modern societies, many identity groups are also nonprimordial groups (Gusfield, 1996). American sociologist *Edward Shils* makes a distinction between **primordial** and **nonprimordial**

groups (1957). Primordial groups are those that come first in our experience, like our families, territorial groups, communities, and so forth. If a group is not primordial, it is nonprimordial. An example of a nonprimordial group is my Introduction to Sociology class. The students enrolled in it didn't know each other before they walked into that class a few short weeks ago. It's a new, nonprimordial group. Another example is boot camp in the military. The people who go through boot camp together do not know each other beforehand. They are strangers before they find themselves together in boot camp. At the beginning of boot camp, they are a new group, a new nonprimordial group. Be sure to read nearby Box 3.1 on nonprimordial rescue behavior during the Holocaust.

── Box 3.1 ──

Nonprimordial Rescue Behavior During the Holocaust

That identification can be a powerful and enduring source of attachment to *nonprimordial groups* is vividly illustrated by the research of sociologists *Samuel P. and Pearl M. Oliner* (1988). Samuel P. Oliner was a young child when his entire family was murdered by the Nazis in Poland. Thanks to help from a Polish Christian woman, he found a place to hide and thereby managed to survive while ninety percent of Lithuanian and Polish Jewry, fifty percent of Rumanian Jewry, and eighty percent of the Jews who remained in Germany after the emigration between 1933 and 1941, died (Oliner and Oliner, 1988).

His experience left him with a fundamental sense of wonder at what had led the kindly woman—and 50,000 to 500,00 non-Jews like her—to help Jews to survive and to flee the Reich, without material rewards of any kind, at a time when to do so meant certain death both for the rescuers and

for their families as well as confiscation of all their property by the state should they be caught by the Nazis.

To answer this question, the Oliners interviewed almost seven hundred people—406 *rescuers*, 150 survivors, and 126 *nonrescuers* who had been living in Germany and in Nazi-occupied Europe during the Second World War. Those designated as rescuers were identified as such by the Israeli Yad Vashem, whose charge it is, at least in part, to authenticate and to honor those who risked their lives (without remuneration) to rescue Jews.

One distinguishing characteristic of Holocaust rescue activity is its duration: for most rescuers, the activity continued from two to five years. Another is that help was extended to a group that differed from themselves in religion, culture, and ethnicity (Oliner and Oliner, 1988: 6). Why did the rescuers rescue Jews? What led them to help? What differentiated them

from the nonrescuers? the Oliners' data indicate that social class, however you want to measure it, is *not* an important determinant of rescue activity. Age, sex, religious affiliation, and intensity of religious commitments also fail to differentiate rescuers from nonrescuers.

Extensivity is the key. Extensivity refers to an orientation to the world that focuses outward towards others and that emphasizes both the common humanity of all persons as well as an ethical obligation to help all persons in need. Rescuers have this orientation while nonrescuers do not. Nonrescuers instead are characterized by **constrictedness**: more centered "on themselves and their own needs, they pay scant attention to others. At best, they reserve their sense of obligation to a small circle from which [most] others are excluded" (Oliner & Oliner, 1988: 251).

Applying the terms we have learned in our textbook,

we could rephrase the Oliners' findings and say that the rescuers have a sense of *identity* that is broad and inclusive; it encompasses all of humanity; it extends to those to whom they are not bound by primordial ties. In contrast, nonrescuers have a narrow sense of identity; it excludes most people and those to whom they are not bound by primordial ties.

The rescuers, the Oliners' research informs us, *are quite ordinary people, people cut from the same bolt of cloth as you or I.* What may differentiate them from you or me, and what differentiates them from the nonrescuers, is that they had learned from their parents an inclusive view of humanity as well as an ethical obligation to help those in need (socialization). Their parents taught them these orientations through their own actions of caring for others while the rescuers were growing up.

The Oliners' research suggests that extensivity and constrictedness are abiding, enduring orientations to the world. During the year preceding their participation in the research project, which was roughly forty years after the Holocaust rescue activity had ended, far more rescuers than nonrescuers had engaged in many and varied activities involving helping nonprimordial others in need, such as attending to the sick or the aged.

The second point is that many actors in an open modern industrial society have numerous, as well as a wide range of, identities and identifications; other actors have few, as well as a narrow or short range of, identities and identifications. Third, because entire segments of our identity are bound up in, are rooted in, and stem from group membership, we tend to support and to protect those identity groups in order to protect and to enhance our sense of self. The more important a particular identity is to us, and the more strongly attached we feel to an identity group, the more likely we are to sacrifice ourselves and others for that collectivity. Thus, Croatian, Serb, Slovenian, and Rwandan represent identities for which people are prepared to commit genocide (Gourevitch, 1995; Gusfield, 1996). Fourth, attachment to nonprimordial groups is always problematic (Blau, 1987; Popielarz and McPherson, 1995; Holy, 1996). Identification is one source of attachment to nonprimordial groups; association is another. Fifth, a social definition of who we are in terms of the groups in which our identity is rooted or embedded—e.g., our race, religion, sex, academic major, occupation, political party affiliation—implies a definition of who we are not. The circle that includes me and "us" excludes "them" (Gamson, 1995).

In-Group—Out-Group

Sociologists capture this dimension of identification as a form of solidarity with the distinction between *in-group* and *out-group* (Gamson, 1995; Davies, et. al., 1981; Ellis, 1981; Doty, 1995; Hippensteele and Chesney-Lind, 1995). The *Modern Dictionary of Sociology* defines **in-group** as any group "whose membership has a strong sense of identification and loyalty, and a feeling of exclusiveness toward nonmembers" (Theodorson and Theodorson, 1969: 203). In contrast, an **out-group** refers to (1) all nonmembers of an in-group; and to (2) a group "whose members are considered to be in opposition, or to be in some way alien, to an IN-GROUP" (Theodorson and Theodorson, 1969: 289).

In-Group Bias and Perception

There is a tendency, termed **in-group bias**, for people who belong to an in-group to favor their own group (Platz and Hosch, 1988; Mullen, Brown, and Smith, 1992; Myers, 1993: 389; Roy, 1994; Gamson, 1995). This tendency occurs even among groups that, in worldly terms, rank lower in terms of power and status than other groups. Members of groups that rank lower on these dimensions can deal with it in a number of ways. Several types of definitions of the situation are possible (Argyle, 1991: 229). These include discovering dimensions to use for comparative purposes on which the in-group ranks higher; deciding that certain dimensions that the in-group possesses and which out-groups disparage in fact are admirable (e.g. "Black is beautiful," "We're here and we're queer: get used to it!"); and selecting different out-groups to use as evaluative reference groups. An example is that South African Hindus see themselves as superior to whites in spiritual, social, and practical spheres, even though whites no doubt view the Hindus as inferior in wealth and social status (Mann, 1963).

There also is a tendency termed *out-group favoritism* that takes place on dimensions that are unimportant to the in-group, but important to the out-group, and on which the latter are superior (Mummendey and Simon, 1989). As a careful reader may have noticed, what both in-group bias and out-group favoritism have in common is a tendency for in-group members, on dimensions that are important to the in-group, to have a higher estimation of those groups to which they belong than do people who are not members of those groups. If you are a member of a particular sorority at your University, you probably hold that group in higher estimation than do those who are not members. The in-group bias occurs among both males and females, among persons of diverse ages and nationalities (Turner, 1984; Myers, 1993: 389; Hraba, Dunham, and Tumanov, and Hagendoorn, 1997), although particularly among people from individualist cultures (Gudykunst, 1989). In-group bias also is more likely if the in-group is small relative to the out-group (Mullen, 1991). In comparison with those whose in-group is the majority, to be a woman at a conference attended mostly by men, to be a Native American student on a campus attended mainly by white students of Anglo-Saxon Protestant descent, or to be a sixty-year old freshman is to feel one's social identity and in-group membership more keenly.

Because part of our self-evaluation, of our self-estimation, is based on our group memberships, seeing our own groups as superior or as better aids us in feeling good about ourselves. Having a sense of "we-ness" based on group memberships, then, *"feels* good" (Myers, 1993: 390; emphasis in original). So much so, report Charles Perdue and fellow researchers, that merely pairing a nonsense syllable such as *yof* with words like "us "and "we" makes the syllable seem more pleasant than those paired with "they" or "them" (1990).

It is notable how little it can take to create in-groups, out-groups, and in-group bias. This is illustrated in "Let That Be Your Last Battlefield," an episode of the original *Star Trek*

television series, a series that became a force in popular culture in this country. This particular episode features a genocidal rivalry between two alien species, one pigmented black on the right side and white on the left side, and the other, in whom these colors are reversed. The crew of the United Federation of Planets' Starship, *Enterprise*, are out-group members from the vantage point of each of the warring species. The *Enterprise* crew initially detect no differences between the two species and in fact perceive them as similar, a perception sharply at odds with the perceptions of the members of the contending species themselves. They perceive crucial, glaring differences between each other. Those pigmented in one fashion feel unity with one another and distance from those whose colors are reversed (Donovan, 1993).

Another example of how seemingly easy it is to create in-groups and out-groups is provided in the traditionally popular musical, "My Fair Lady" by Professor Higgins, a famous dialectician and grammarian, who observes that "An Englishman's way of speaking absolutely classifies him. The moment he talks, he makes some other Englishman despise him." In other words, even minor differences in the way a single language is spoken can serve as a basis for the formation of in-groups, out-groups and in-group bias. Even dividing people into categories on a virtually random basis—say, forming groups "A" and "B" with the flip of a coin; if heads comes up, you're assigned to group "A," and if tails comes up, you're assigned to group "B"—is sufficient to produce some in-group bias (e.g., Billig and Tajfel, 1973; Tajfel and Turner, 1986).

Max Weber wrote about the formation of in-groups, out-groups, and in-group bias as resulting simply because people ate together at the same soup-kitchen. In order to appreciate Weber's insights, it helps to know that a **caste** is a type of group defined by means of entrée and egress. The way one gets into a caste is to be born into it and the way one gets out of a caste is to die. In *The Religion of India* (1958), Weber notes that in **the great famine of 1866** in Bengal, India, the British rulers opened public soup kitchens accessible to persons of all castes. In their dire need, impoverished persons of all castes visited, and communally ate within sight of each other, in these soup kitchens, even though it was strictly forbidden by caste rules to eat within the sight of persons not belonging to one's caste. As the result of having broken caste regulations, a separate lower caste, *the Kallars,* arose and continued from thence onward among the people who had infracted the ritual and dietary laws during the famine (Weber, 1958).

The example of the birth of a new caste illustrates that, from the point of view of out-groups, it seemingly can take very little to give rise to in-groups, out-groups, and to solidary identification groups (e.g., Goode, 1963: 203-269; Morris, 1973: 218-248). Once these groups are formed they can have profound, if subtle, effects. One of these is the *tendency for members to underestimate differences within categories and to overestimate differences between categories* (e.g., Myers, 1993:4). The sentiment "Women (or Men, Whites, African Americans, etc.) are all alike" expresses these tendencies. "Boys will be boys, and girls will be girls," also expresses the sentiment or perception that significant differences within a group do not exist and neither does any overlap between the categories specified. Similarly, "They (e.g., Whites, Chinese Americans, old people, Mexican Americans, etc.) all look alike" is a verbal manifestation of a perception far more likely to be made with regard to out-group members (Anthony et. al., 1992; Bothwell et. al., 1989; Brigham and Malpass, 1985; Chance, 1985). A tendency in the national press in this country to refer to someone as a *prolocutor* (spokesperson) of, say, the African-American community or of women's groups likewise expresses a sentiment that African Americans (or women) are all alike. On the other hand, it's almost unheard of for a white member of the national press in this country to refer to someone as a prolocutor of white America.

Association

The oldest form of association is the primordial kinship group. The smallest part of a kinship structure is a family, which in its elementary form consists of parents and their dependent children. The family is the nucleus of any society.

A **band** is a territorially based community that is smaller than a tribe. It is "the most elementary form of community and is often found among nomadic and semi-nomadic peoples" (Theodorson and Theodorson, 1969: 26). A **tribe** is a preliterate community or collection of communities occupying a common geographical area and having a similar language and culture (Theodorson and Theodorson, 1969: 443).

In early societies known as *band societies,* kinship relations were the basic "atoms" of society (Sahlins, 1972; Lenski, Nolan, and Lenski, 1995). As bands differentiate into kinship groups they came to be known as tribes. Tribes, in turn, form alliances with each other, which the members or leaders of the alliance "cement" (i.e., reinforce or strengthen) through marriage. *Pantribal associations* are formed when individuals in each band and tribe meet together on a regular basis to trade information (gossip, information about watering holes, etc.) and other valuable resources (e.g., salt for hides). For example, shamen form pantribal associations to share information concerning herbs, roots, and other "tricks of the trade." Chiefs and headpeople (who frequently are men) form pantribal associations to solve problems and to arrange marriages; they even strike political alliances with each other. Modern forms of pantribal associations are diverse and include quilt-making groups, support groups, alliances among voluntary militia groups, alliances among religious groups, stamp-collecting groups, and so forth. **Association**s are two or more groups whose memberships crosscut or overlap; these groups, by virtue of their overlapping memberships, are characterized by what are termed *crosscutting circles* or *overlapping social circles, crosscutting solidarity,* or *overlapping solidarity.* The terms are used interchangeably and synonymously. Associations, then, are an elementary basis of solidarity.

Voluntary Association

Voluntary association is a nonprimordial form of solidarity that refers to reaching out beyond a primordial membership to establish common cause with others. Alexis de Tocqueville (1805-1859), a French aristocrat who wrote perceptively on comparative political systems and who visited the United States in 1831-1832 to examine our prisons, was struck by the extent and diversity of voluntary associations in the United States. He referred to voluntary associations in our country as networks of democracy and of participation. Examples of voluntary associations today include the National Rifle Association, Mothers Against Drunk Drivers, Alcoholics Anonymous, Boy Scouts, Girl Scouts, PETA (People for the Ethical Treatment of Animals), the American Sociological Association, the Ku Klux Klan, the NAACP (National Association for the Advancement of Colored People), the Republican Party, the Democratic Party, the American Civil Liberties Union, the Red Cross, the American Communist Party, and Overeaters Anonymous.

Voluntary association is one process that creates *social circles* (solidarities) that *crosscut* or *overlap* already existing groups and identities such as primordial memberships. This is a very important process in human societies, the forging, creating, and maintaining of solidarities that crosscut already existing groups and identities (Blau, 1987). Be sure to read nearby Box 3.2 entitled "Crosscutting Social Circles Among the Nuer." The ties of cooperation, of cohesion, and of trust created by association are as important a part of human societies as the more immediate ties of attraction and loyalty, although the former may be more brittle and more difficult to institutionalize (Popielarz and McPherson, 1995; Blau, 1984; Singerman, 1995).

What sociologists like Edward Shils (1957), Rosabeth Moss Kanter (1972), Marjorie Donovan (1984) and Peter Blau (1984, 1987, 1994) point out is that groups formed by reaching out beyond a primordial membership to establish common cause can function very much like primordial, primary groups, uniting members because they assert that they have a sense of common interest.

Box 3.2

Crosscutting Social Circles Among the Nuer

The Nuer, as studied by Evans-Pritchard (1940, 1951), are a nomadic people living in what used to be Anglo-Egyptian Sudan. Numbering about a million people, they live by herding cattle, making dairy products, fishing, hunting, and by engaging in some horticulture. Primarily, they raise cattle. They live in small communities, and they are stateless. Traditionally, that is to say, there is no chief, no king, no President, no Prime Minister, no House of Representatives, no Senate.

How can a large group of people who are spread out live without a state? The answer is that *they have an almost perfectly balanced system of crosscutting social circles* that is built into the very warp and woof (social structure) of their society, that is built into the basic categories of membership in their social order. There are four bases of cross-cutting social circles among the Nuer: the local community, the maternal kin, the paternal kin, and the age-structuring of the community. Let us address each of these in turn.

One solidary group is the *local community*, the local community where you live, the people who herd cattle with you, the people who work with you, and so forth. As Evans-Pritchard phrases this:

Just how strong is village sentiment may be gathered from the fact that sometimes men who intend to leave the village of their birth to settle permanently in another village, take with them some earth of their old village and drink it in a solution of water, slowly adding to each dose a greater amount of soil from their new village, thus gently breaking mystical ties with the old and building up mystical ties with the new. I

was told that were a man to fail to do this, he might die (1940:120).

The people living in a village need each other. One reason they need each other is the lion problem. Lions pose a serious menace to the herds and are a perceived threat to individuals. Then, too, a single individual, even a single family or household could not protect and herd their cattle alone, and the cohesion of the village is to be understood in light of these facts (Evans-Pritchard, 1940).

Another solidary group consists of those people who are related to you through your father, that is, your *paternal kin*. You are bound to your paternal kin by ties of loyalty that neither derive from nor depend upon mutual affection. In fact, there is a tendency for paternal kin *not* to like each other very much. This is manifested in a number of ways, one of which is the institution called *leng*, the conventionalized exchange of obscenities among paternal kin. To indicate to you of what this consists, let us quote Evans-Pritchard:

A man says to a paternal kin "bang leng," "Let's have a slanging game." Then they abuse each other in turn, prefacing each epithet with the exclamation *awai yah!* the exchange often develops into a contest to see which of the two can continue the longest without repeating himself. As Nuer are practiced and have a fertile imagination in such matters, the duel may be kept up for several minutes before one of the men cannot think of an obscenity he has not already used, and thus loses the duel. The obscenities, which are the most extravagant I have ever heard, cover, with many elaborations, every possible kind of sexual act, the sodomy motif being the most prominent, and refer to the partners to the duel themselves and their fathers, others, sisters, paternal and maternal aunts and uncles, grandparents, and sweethearts, though only terms of relationship and not proper names are used. The partners also call one another Dinka, witches, spongers, bastards, gluttons, and so forth. (1951: 160)

You do have obligations and commitments to your paternal kin. Providing **bride wealth** in the form of cattle is one of these. Bride wealth refers to a sum of money or property brought to a marriage by the family of the groom at specific times during the marriage process; to whom it is given varies (Goode, 1982: 58). If a male relative is getting mar-

ried, you have to give him some cattle from your herd as bride wealth. Among the Nuer, this amounts to about two or three cattle per each marriage, if you're an uncle. The number of cattle you must provide varies by kin relationship; and, yes, the Nuer are polygynous. **Polygyny** is a form of marriage in which a male is permitted more than one wife simultaneously. Of course, your male relatives, in turn, would do as much for you, when you get married.

You are also obligated to support your paternal kin through ritual warfare, dispute settlement, and blood revenge. For instance, if you perceive that someone is violating your rights and you want them punished, the way you mobilize collective authority is to go to your paternal kin—to your cousins, brothers, uncles, to anyone of a common male ancestor. You go to your collective kin and you say: "So-and-so really took me, and we have to go and get him and rip him limb from limb." Your paternal kin will have to help you.

Another solidary group are your *maternal kin*, people related to you through your mother. You don't have any obligations to these people: you don't owe them cattle at marriage, you don't owe them dispute resolution or blood revenge. These are people for whom you have particularly tender feelings. You really like them, and you can be utterly at your ease in their company.

Another solidary group are members of your *age set*, your peers of the same age and gender as yourself. Members of an age set go through a painful, rigorous gender-specific initiation ceremony together either in the same season or they all go through it together as a

group. Members of the same age set are on terms of equality with each other; there is a brotherly, easy going camaraderie among members of the same age set. You don't stand on ceremony with your age mates; you joke with them, you associate at work with them, you play with them, you are at your ease when around them.

What happens when a dispute arises? What happens if, for instance, you think that someone has violated your rights and you want that person punished? You go to your paternal kin, and you say to them: "Alex and Fred really took me, and we have to go and get them." Now, who are these people you want them "to get?" They are likely to be people who live in the same territorial community as you or to be one of your age mates. Just as (or even more) importantly, they are likely to be age mates or territorial-community mates of the very people you want to act as your dispute-resolution squad. In other words, *it is difficult to mobilize the punishment machinery in any but the most serious cases*, because the potential punishers are people who have overlapping loyalties and who, therefore, would much rather say: "Listen, I've got a much better idea than tearing Alex and Fred limb from limb. Why don't you, they, and I get together, and we'll talk about this." There's *strong motivation for reconciliation by virtue of the fact that potential cleavages that are activated tend to be bound together by a series of crosscutting or overlapping social circles.* The numerous bases of overlapping solidarity among the Nuer constitute a type of overlapping web for cohesion of the group.

There are numerous forms of voluntary association. We briefly discuss three: *alliance, prolocutorship,* and *influence.* In **alliance,** persons in different positions reach out to form an association based on mutual benefit. An example would be labor unions. Thus, let us say that you, I, Chinua, Zeus, and Sally are instructors at the University of the Coast. In terms of rank, let us assume that you are a Full Professor, Chinua is an Associate Professor, Zeus and I are Assistant Professors, and Sally is an Instructor. The University administration fires all its instructors at will and then hires other persons as instructors for a lower salary. There is no apparatus internal to this University for appeal of the fairness of these actions. When approached about setting up an apparatus for review of the fairness of firing decisions, the University flatly refuses, and tells us that if we don't like the way things are done at this University, we should leave and work somewhere else instead. Let us further assume that Sally, a young, white, single, female Roman Catholic, is sick and tired of this situation. She approaches Zeus, and says, "Hey, Zeus, have you noticed how arbitrarily the University fires its faculty? Henry got cut loose last week. It could be you or me next week. Let's form a Union. All we have to loose are our chains of oppression, huh?. . . . A guy named Karl once said something like that." Zeus replies: "Karl . . . Karl. . . . I never heard of a guy named Karl working here. Anyway, why should I help form a union?" Sally replies, "Why? Because it's in *our interest* to do so!" Well, that was news to Zeus, a late middle-aged, African-American Muslim, married father of four children, a person who previously never had considered that he and Sally had much of anything in common. When he reflected upon it, however, he could see that he and Sally did have an interest in common in terms of forming a union; he could see that they did form a "we," something of which he previously hadn't been aware.

According to American sociologist *Talcott Parsons* (1967: 366-378), we may interpret the process of exercising this type of association as a process of influence, and we may view the process of influence as a way of establishing solidarities. In the Parsonian paradigm, *influence* consists of affecting another's behavior by

pointing out that what is wanted of that person is in her or his own interests, as well as being in "our" best interests. "The subject and object of influence create a new solidarity for . . . [one] who influences creates a 'we' by saying, 'Let's do this for it is in our interests'" (Mayhew, 1971: 75). Parsons, Mayhew, and Blau (Blau, 1984, 1987) say that when Freddie goes up to Samantha and says, "Hey, I want you to do such-and-such,' and Samantha says, "Why?" and Freddie says, "I want you to do such and such, because *it's in our interest* that you do such-and-such," that what Freddie is doing is asserting a solidarity. Freddie, right there, is attempting to stake out or to manufacture a solidarity, a crosscutting social circle, by asserting a "we" that the other person may never have thought of before.

In short, what voluntary association, alliance, influence and even **prolocutorship** have in common is a reaching out beyond primordial ties to manufacture, to construct a "we," a nonprimordial solidarity. In prolocutorship, a person assumes the position of spokesperson for an alleged common interest. A prolocutor is not necessarily an appointed or elected official of a formal organization, although such a person may also be a prolocutor, as when, say, the President or Chairman of the Board of General Motors speaks on behalf of automobile manufacturers in the United States. A person is a prolocutor if she or he alleges a solidarity by presuming to speak for a "we." In this sense, then, a leader of an emergent social movement, a journalist, a person who views her- or himself as a leader of any somewhat heterogeneous group is a prolocutor.

For example, before the publication of *The Feminine Mystique* (1963), *Betty Friedan's* name was not known in households across the United States; essentially, she was an unknown entity. In that book, she assumed the position of prolocutor. Betty Friedan wrote on behalf of females in the United States who felt uneasy, who felt a malaise and couldn't figure out why they were unhappy. In this seminal work, which was a popular success, Friedan identifies the source of their malaise as due to gender oppression, and, according to many, thereby kicked off the modern women's movement.

The "we" formed in the processes of association, prolocutorship, influence, or alliance are tenuous, tentative, and fragile. Hence, the probability that an association, alliance, prolocutorship, and influence can survive across time is enhanced if they are ratified or stabilized or strengthened by the formation of new identities that cement the newly emerging ties. A sociologist might rephrase this by saying that old identities are transcended in order to form new, more inclusive ones (Mayhew, 1971; Kanter, 1972; Donovan, 1984). This transcending process in always problematic in open, flexible social orders.

Patterns of Solidarity and of Conflict

Social Conflict and Overlapping Social Circles

In open, pluralistic societies, many persons above the bottom of the social structure are loyal to, and identify with, many voluntary associations. Most people, in other words, move within a network of loyalties and of crosscutting social circles—their primary groups of family and close friends, their political party, their religious group, their occupational group, service organizations, clubs of various sorts, and so forth (Scott, 1985; Singerman, 1995; Erikson, 1996). These networks of overlapping memberships and of identifications and of loyalties have implications for social conflict.

Partial, segmental, particularistic loyalties are many in loosely structured groups and in open, pluralistic societies. These are not viewed as incompatible with loyalty to a larger community (such as to a city, county, state, nation, or larger political community). In fact, these crosscutting social circles of loyalty and of identification and of voluntary association are viewed by pluralist theorists as the "glue" that holds the larger community together (e.g., Simmel, 1908; Grodzins, 1956; Dahrendorf, 1959; Coser, 1968; Blau, 1984, 1987; Collins, 1992). This view shares Edmund Burke's (1729-1797) "insistence that what holds society together and gives it meaning and richness is the multiplicity of its 'little platoons,' its primary associations of individuals" (Scharr, 1968: 485).

American sociologist Lewis A. Coser argues that a multiplicity of memberships produces

crosscutting conflicts (which also are known as *overlapping conflicts*), in which a person who is an ally in one dispute is an opponent in another (1968). This patterning of conflict prevents conflicts, although varying in intensity, from falling along one axis and dividing the community along dichotomous or multiple lines. German sociologist *Ralf Dahrendorf* likewise concludes that in open, pluralistic societies voluntary memberships overlap, and hence conflicts also overlap and do not reinforce each other (1959). As among the Nuer with their multiple primordial crosscutting or overlapping social circles, so, too in loosely structured groups and in open, pluralistic societies whose members have a diversity of non-primordial segmental memberships: when disputes arise, the greater the probability that the members to the conflict will chose means that will not permanently menace their common bonds. In other words, there is a lower probability that the parties to the conflict will engage in violence (Coser, 1968; Collins, 1992).

The situation is different in rigid social structures and in closed groups. Such groups tend to inhibit both (1) a multiplicity of crosscutting memberships, and (2) the open acting-out of disagreement or hostility. Closed, rigid groups, whether large or small, tend to absorb their members jealously (Kanter, 1972; Collins, 1992; Yang, 1994). They are jealous of their members' affiliation with other groups and want to monopolize their loyalty and identification. The resulting deep involvement of the members in the group is likely to lead to a "great deal of hostility and ambivalence, a hostility, however, to which the group denies legitimate outlets" (Coser, 1968). Such groups fear the disruptive effects of hostility and conflict. If conflict does break out, it is likely to be *intense* for two reasons. First, the deep personality absorption of the individual in such groups tends to mobilize and focus the psychic energies in the conduct of the struggle. Secondly, the conflicts, once loosed, are not likely to remain limited to the issue at hand but tend to spill over to relieve grievances that long have been denied expression (Coser, 1968: 233-234; Collins, 1988, 1992). In short, the lack of multiplicity of segmental, crosscutting social circles and the lack of multiple allegiances that crosscut each other, intensify those conflicts that do break out, and the division of society into hostile groups or classes, as envisioned by Marx, is a far higher probability.

Violence is one means for carrying out a social conflict. The more integrated into mainstream society the groups to the conflict, the less likely that conflict between them will be violent. Instead, less militant means, that do not permanently menace the common bonds, tend to be utilized, including peaceful noncompliance with the law, sit-in demonstrations, general strikes, political marches, institutionalized strikes, ritualized contests, and so forth. The less integrated into mainstream society the groups to the conflict, the more likely that violence between them will be violent.

American sociologist *Randall Collins* (1975, 1992) perceives that the differences among stratified groups are due to daily micro-level interactions that occur along two dimensions—power and solidarity. These interactions have consequences for *identifications, associations, loyalties,* and *social conflict.* Collins points out that *persons who give orders* have *identifications* and *loyalties* that differ from *persons who take orders.*

Our appreciation of Collins' insights will be enhanced if we are familiar with a couple of symbolic-interactionist concepts and if we know what a ritual is and how sociologists view the relation between ritual and solidarity. We turn now to these matters, after which we resume our discussion of the relation among power, identifications, loyalties, group structure, solidarity, and conflict.

American sociologist *Erving Goffman* (1922-1982), a 1953 University of Chicago Ph.D., developed what has come to be known as the "dramaturgical" approach in American symbolic interactionism. In this approach, the metaphor of the stage, of drama is used heavily. Life is a "drama, " persons are "actors," there are different "audiences," and so forth (Goffman, 1959, 1961, 1963). Goffman distinguishes between "frontstage" and "backstage" behaviors. **Frontstage** behaviors refer to those behaviors in which actors seek to put on a definite "performance" for a specific audience. For instance, when the authors of this textbook present a lecture to an Introduction to Sociology class, the authors as "actors" wear "costumes" (e.g., suit and tie), use "props"

(overhead projector, blackboard, computer-generated images, etc.), and formal language (as opposed to colloquialisms) in their "scripts" (lectures) to the audience. Those are their frontstage behaviors. In contrast, **backstage** behavior refers to those behaviors in which the actors rest from their performances, de-brief, discuss and analyze their performances, and plan future ones. For example, after class, when in the backstage region (e.g., in their offices with doors closed) professors may loosen their ties or kick off their pumps, use colloquial language in analyzing the response of the audience to their performance, laugh about having ad-libbed their "lines," and so forth.

The terms **ritual** and *rite* often are used interchangeably by sociologists. A ritual refers to a "culturally standardized set of actions with symbolic significance performed on occasions [and by persons] prescribed by tradition. The acts and words that comprise a ritual are precisely defined and vary . . . little if at all from one occasion to another" (Theodorson and Theodorson, 1969: 351).

The *functions of ritual* are several (Theodorson and Theodorson, 1969: 351). *First*, according to Durkheim rituals are important in the creation and maintenance of social solidarity (Kertzer, 1988; Edelman, 1988; Berezin, 1994). *Second*, rituals are believed, by the participants and by the persons conducting them, to have the power in themselves to produce certain results. For instance, this is the case with certain religious rituals and quite generally with rituals associated with exuvial magic. *Third*, rituals are a means of relieving feelings of anxiety in times of crisis. *Fourth*, rituals are important as symbols: they usually symbolize a basic belief and are intended to induce a feeling of reverence and awe.

Persons who give orders tend to hold leadership positions (imperative order) in rituals. It is they who perform the rituals. *They* also *identify with their frontstage* behaviors and frontstage selves. They identify with the official symbols of the organizations they control or of the means of production that they own. For instance, if the mascot of your college or university is, say, a Tiger named "Gus," the administrators (Chancellor, Vice-Chancellor, Deans, Department Chairs) are likely to pay homage to Gus, to display posters in or near their offices featuring Gus and the university logo, to wear shirts with the college and university logo on them, to have license-plate holders on their cars that display the university's name or logo, and so forth. They likely will respond negatively to those who disparage Gus and who deface their college or university's logo (Collins, 1975, 1992). In fact, individuals who *give orders and who belong to tightly enclosed, localized groups* (Collins, 1988; 1992: 290) tend to do the following:

- emphasize and enforce conformity to the group's traditions,
- be suspicious of strangers (out-group members), and
- react strenuously and emotionally against in-group members who are disrespectful of the group's symbols.

In contrast, **persons who take orders** (Collins, 1975, 1988, 1992) tend to be alienated from official rituals. They tend to identify with their backstage behaviors and selves. Loosely organized networks of multiple, segmental, overlapping social circles have less solidarity and they exert less pressure for **conformity** (Ridgeway, 1992).

Conformity refers to a change in an individual's behavior or beliefs as a result of real or perceived group influence or pressure (Myers, 1993; Ridgeway, 1992). Two types of conformity are **compliance** and **acceptance.** Compliance refers to conformity that is merely public rather than private as well. In compliance, one publicly acts in accordance with the norm, even though one privately disagrees. Sam may think the corporation he works for is corrupt and a polluter of water tables and he may have private contempt for it, yet he wears the corporation's logo on the shirts he wears at work. In acceptance, one both publicly and privately agrees with the norm.

Conflicting interests may exist for a long time without sparking social conflict. Karl Marx appreciated that several factors increase the probability that a group will mobilize itself for social conflict: (1) physical concentration of members, (2) sharing a common culture, and (3) the material resources for communicating among themselves. In general, elite classes are more mobilized than the lower classes, and

frequently social struggles for power take place among different segments of the higher classes. In contrast, the lower classes tend to be more fragmented into localized groups and are more readily mobilized when they are a homogeneous racial, ethnic, or religious group concentrated in one place.

Overt social conflict tends to increase the solidarity of the contending groups (Klein, 1971; Driscoll, Davis, and Lipitz, 1972; Cialdini, 1984; Collins, 1992) and motivates the contending sides to seek allies (Coser, 1956; Collins, 1992). The polarization of society into contending camps is deflected when there is a widespread segmental multiplicity of memberships in the population. In these cases there are many crosscutting social circles; class, racial, ethnic, religious, regional, familial, occupational, political, and tribal lines overlap. In these cases, then, mobilization of one of these domains in conflict (e.g., class conflict) tends to put a strain on other identifications and loyalties (e.g., race, ethnicity). There is a tremendous motivation to resolve disputes and disagreements peacefully (Glassman, 1986; Lawler and Bacharach, 1987). Due to these dialectical dynamics, Lewis Coser observes that "conflicts may be said to sew pluralistic society together" (1968: 233).

Reinforced Cleavage

The opposite of overlapping social circles is **reinforced cleavage.** This term refers to the superimposition of multiple lines of group membership (Collins, 1992; Mayhew, 1971). When multiple lines of group membership are superimposed, conflicts are more extreme (Marsden, 1992; Collins, 1992; Thompson, 1995). The polarization of society into contending camps is far more likely when multiple lines of membership are superimposed. In these cases there is an absence of crosscutting social circles. Class, racial, ethnic, religious, linguistic, regional, familial, occupational, political, and tribal lines do not overlap. They are separate.

Apartheid in South Africa is a classic example of reinforced cleavage. The racial caste system known as apartheid divided the population into four groups or castes, each of which was internally stratified along class lines.

Please see Table 3.1. These castes are the whites, who constitute little more than ten percent of the population but who have accrued over half of the total personal income; the Coloureds, persons officially viewed as being of mixed race, who constitute about 8 percent of the population; Indians, descendants of persons from India, who originally came to South Africa in the latter part of the nineteenth century to work as indentured servants on the sugarcane plantations, and who constitute about 3 percent of the population; and the African population (blacks, called Bantu by white South Africans), the caste most oppressed under apartheid who constitute fully 76 percent of the population. The latter three groups were referred to as persons of color, as non-whites, or as non-Europeans by white South Africans.

TABLE 3.1. Population of South Africa: Selected Population Statistics, by Race _____

Racial Group	Percent of Population, 1993	Infant Mortality Rate, 1990*	Percent of Total Personal Income, 1988
White	13	8.9	54
African	76	65.0	34
Coloured	8	36.0	9
Indian	3	13.7	4

Source: Leonard Thompson, 1995: 278,279, 290.
* Rate per 1,000 live births.

Under apartheid, the criteria of internal class stratification differed across these four groups (van den Berghe, 1965, 1978; Thompson, 1995). Major cultural and institutional variations also distinguished each caste. Each caste could live only in specific, and restricted, parts of the country. Political participation by law varied across caste lines. The white government effectively pursued a policy of *tertius gaudens* (divide and conquer) for four decades. The struggle to end apartheid was protracted, violent, intense, and bloody.

Reinforced cleavages abound today in many countries in the world. The creation and maintenance of nonprimordial overlapping social circles in these societies, and in any diverse country, is always problematic (Blau, 1987, 1994; Cerulo, 1993; Popielarz et. al., 1995; Walder, 1995; Gamson, 1995; Kupferberg, 1996; Gusfield, 1996).

Further Bases of Solidarity

In *The Division of Labor in Society*, Durkheim makes a distinction between two types of "glue" that hold society together (1895). He terms these mechanical and organic solidarity. Durkheim views the former as characteristic of what we will come to know as *folk societies* (Redfield, 1947) and the latter as more prevalent in highly differentiated and heterogeneous social orders.

Societies characterized by subsistence-level existence, nomadicism, little economic surplus, and considerable homogeneity—including considerable homogeneity on the variables of class, status, and power—tend to be held together by **mechanical solidarity**. It is in these types of societies that humans have spent most of their existence. Anthropologist *Robert Redfield* describes them as *folk societies*, and Toennies calls them Gemeinschaft. In this type of society, what you believe, I believe, we all believe. While there is a lot of variation across these societies, within each there is considerable homogeneity of beliefs, attitudes, and values. Durkheim phrased this by saying that such societies are characterized by a **common conscience.** In these societies, people are held together by their similarities, by things they have in common.

In contrast more highly differentiated societies, such as modern industrial societies, are characterized by considerable economic surplus; and by considerable heterogeneity on the variables of class, status, and power; and by a division of labor based on more than age, sex and ritual. The division of labor is highly developed. Among the constituent groups that comprise such a society, there tends to be considerable variation in language, religion, occupation, values, attitudes, family forms, cultural beliefs, cultural content, and so forth. Durkheim states that these societies are held together by **organic solidarity**, that is, by the division of labor and the interdependence of their members. The members need each other; they are held together by their interdependencies (their complementary needs and interests). For instance, let us say that you are conversant in the healing arts. You know which herbs are good for relieving muscle aches and tooth aches and infections; you're knowledgeable about how to ease the pains of labor in the birthing process; you know how to treat various forms of rash. I know nothing or next to nothing about those things, but I am knowledgeable about how to construct a dwelling, about which you know next to nothing. Elmer knows how to make shoes, about which you and I know nothing. Chinua doesn't know how to do any of these things, but he knows how to build a sea-worthy canoe, about which the rest of us haven't a clue. In this fictitious example, Elmer, you, Chinua, and I need each other; we are, to use the Durkheimian language, *interdependent*. It is this type of interdependence that can bind the members in highly differentiated populations together.

In *The Division of Labor in Society*, Durkheim stresses that organic and mechanical solidarity are neither mutually exclusive nor antagonistic. They may and do co-exist in the same society; the presence of one does not preclude the other. Nonetheless, Durkheim, like Toennies, argues that there has been a long-term trend whereby in more highly differentiated social orders, mechanical solidarity tends to give way to organic solidarity. A point that Durkheim was trying to make is not that industrialization and urbanization destroy solidarity but that new forms of solidarity develop.

Thus far we have examined numerous possible bases and forms of solidarity in human societies. The following list reminds us of some of these (Shotola, 1992):

artificial will	influence
association	interdependence
attraction	loyalty
common conscience	prolocutorship
identification	voluntary association

Other Effects of Solidarity

While high cohesiveness of groups frequently is perceived as a sign of "health," it actually is more accurate and precise to say that high cohesiveness heightens members' susceptibility to influences present in the group (Myers, 1993). Thus, as you recall from the Hawthorne studies, the influence of informal friendship structures was to decrease worker productivity. Let us look at how a sociological appreciation of solidarity can help us to understand various aspects of collective action as it applies to the world in which we live. One possible effect of solidary groups on their members that we as yet have not discussed is **de-individuation** (Gamson, 1995: 10). De-individuation refers to a loss of self-consciousness and of evaluation apprehension (Harré and Lamb, 1986: 74; Myers, 1993: 316-322; Gamson, 1995: 10). De-individuation can be elicited or generated in a number of ways, including via communal participation in rituals.

Group singing, shouting, chanting, clapping, dancing, prancing, and the wearing of uniforms that mask individuality can increase solidarity. These activities also can have the effect of de-individuating those engaging in the activities. In a scholarly cross-cultural study, *Robert Watson* documents that warriors wearing de-individuating face paint or masks are more brutal to their victims than other warriors (1973). A vivid example from film and literature is provided by *Lord of the Flies*, the movie version of *William Golding*'s novel bearing the same title (1959).

The novel and the movie are about young, pre-adolescent boys marooned on an island in the South Pacific after their plane crashes. No *compos mentis* adult survives the crash. A highly-manipulative youth named Jack, who is a master at leadership, organizes some of the boys into a tightly-knit band of hunters by (1) stripping them of their school uniforms that symbolized loyalty to a different group, (2) painting the lads and himself with the blood from their successful hunts in designs that symbolized ferocity as hunters and loyalty to himself as leader, and (3) devising and having all the boys of his band participate communally in shouting, dancing, singing, chanting, and using group slogans. These processes de-individualized the boys to such an extent that on one occasion, under the cover of darkness, they communally kill a gentle, wise boy named Simon, mistaking him for a monster.

One of their chants was "*Kill the pig. Cut his throat. Spill his blood.*" This chant was a favorite before hunting. They were chanting it while dancing on the night that they killed Simon. As William Golding describes it, under the cover of darkness, a

> circling movement developed and a chant . . . "*Kill the pig!. Cut his throat! Spill his blood!*" the movement became regular while the chant . . . began to beat like a steady pulse . . . Some of the littluns started a ring on their own; and the complementary circles went round and round . . . There was the throb and stamp of a single organism (1959: 140).

On a separate occasion of de-individuation, they set fire to the island while hunting the last remaining boy who refused to join their band. Cloaked in de-individuating face and body paint, and aroused by their fire-setting activities and by the thrill of the hunt, they were about to kill him when an outsider, an armed member of the military who was attracted to the island by the fire visible many miles away, intervened.

Circumstances that diminish self-awareness tend to increase de-individuation. It is noteworthy that the beating of unarmed Rodney King by four police officers, while over twenty other police officers watched and did not intervene, occurred under the cover of darkness. After a high-speed car chase, police officers apprehended King. Emotions were volatile. The uniformed officers enjoyed each other's companionship and camaraderie, unaware that outsiders would be privy to their actions. The cover of night gave the police officers the perception of being anonymous, and their evaluation apprehension plummeted.

Leon Mann, in an analysis of 21 instances in which crowds were present as someone threatened to jump from a building or a bridge, also found that when the cover of night or even the size of the crowd gave people the perception of anonymity, the crowd usually baited and jeered the would-be jumper, encouraging her or him to take the fatal leap (1981). For instance, David Myers (1993: 316), reports that in "a 1967 incident, 200 University of Oklahoma students gathered to watch a disturbed fellow student threatening to jump from a tower. They began to chant 'Jump. Jump. . . .' The student jumped to his death."

TABLE 3.2. Happiness of the Married, Single, and Divorced, Percent "Very Happy"

Marital Status	Gender of Respondents	
	Men	Women
Married	35.0	41.5
Single	18.5	25.5
Divorced	18.5	15.5

Source: Veroff, Douvan, and Kulka, 1981.

A sociological appreciation of solidarity can help us understand not only police beatings of citizens of a different race than themselves and certain aspects of de-individuation, it can also help us understand something as seemingly ordinary as the perception of the availability of baby sitters. Thus, the American sociologist *Robert K. Merton* (1957) studied a small suburban community in the United States given the pseudonym Craftown. Merton finds that parents, although living in a suburb with relatively few baby sitters, nonetheless perceive that there are *more* of them than there had been in their previous urban residences. In actuality, in an absolute sense, there had been more potential baby sitters in the urban areas. The Craftown suburbanites felt more at ease and trusted teenagers more than they did when they had lived in the city. Thus, as Merton suggests, the perception of the number of baby-sitters apparently does not depend entirely on their actual number as it does on trust. Craftown, unlike the former urban neighborhoods, is a comparatively cohesive community characterized by intimate contact with others. Consequently, as cohesion increases, so too does the perception of the number of potential baby sitters.

Integration into social groups also helps us to cope with crisis (Lin and Ensel, 1989; Dean et. al., 1990;) and it helps to prevent perceptions of loneliness and of isolation (Stokes and Levin, 1986; Hobfoll, 1988). Social interaction with females is found to do more to relieve loneliness, both for males and for females: Both sexes perceive interactions with females as pleasanter, more meaningful, and more intimate than those with men (Wheeler, et. al., 1983).

Being enmeshed in overlapping circles of social support also helps people get jobs, not only in the United States (Lin et. al., 1981), but in other countries as well (Walder, 1995; Bian, 1997). Dense networks of social support have been shown to lead to a lower incidence of cancer and of arthritis and cholesterol among workers who have lost their jobs (Argyle, 1992: 237) and to have positive effects on blood pressure, mental health, pregnancy, and other physical conditions that involve stress (Johnson, 1992: 1978). Absence of social networks is associated with relatively poor mental and physical health throughout the life course (Kraus et. al., 1993). When social support is given willingly and with regard for the recipient's perceptions, there is a relationship between social support and reduced morbidity (illness) and mortality (Blazer, 1982; Rook, 1984; Pagel, Erdly, and Becker, 1987).

A famous longitudinal study in California follows 6,900 people in the San Francisco bay area for over nine years (Berkman and Syme, 1979) and finds massive differences in mortality rates among those who at the beginning of

the study have dense verses weak support networks. For men in their fifties, of those with the strongest networks, 9.6% had died, compared with 30.8% for those with the weakest networks. Many other studies also document this effect, including Schwarzer and Leppin's meta-analysis of 55 studies that involve over 32,000 people (1989).

With regard to gender, men's friendship groups in Australia, the USA, Japan, and Korea tend to me more cohesive than women's friendship groups (Stokes and Levin, 1986). A woman's friends tend not to be friends to each other, while a man's friends tend to be so (or at least, so to perceive each other). This could be due, at least in part, to the social fact that men's friendship groups tend to include more nonprimordial others, co-workers, than is the case with women, whose friendship networks contain more primordial others (family members) (Moore, 1991, 1992). Developmental studies also suggest that while girls tend to interact in dyads, boys tend to interact more in larger groups (Kashima, et. al., 1995). It might be inferred that this differential socialization provides boys with interactional experience with nonprimordial others at a young age, so that in later years, they feel comfortable interacting in larger, nonprimordial groups in the workplace.

Key Concepts

acceptance
androgyny
apartheid in South Africa
association
attraction (attachment)
avoidantly-attached babies
backstage behavior
band
bases of solidarity among the Nuer
birth cohort
bride wealth
caste
cohesion
common conscience
compliance
conformity
constrictedness

crosscutting conflicts
crosscutting social circles
de-individuation
Edward Shils
Evans-Pritchard
extensivity
frontstage behavior
functions of ritual
identification
identity groups
in-group
in-group bias
insecurely-attached babies
interdependence
loyalty
Mary Ainsworth
mechanical solidarity
nonprimordial group

organic solidarity
out-group
out-group favoritism
overlapping conflicts
pantribal associations
polygyny
primordial group
prolocutorship
Randall Collins on
    identifications and loyalties
    among (a) persons who give
    orders and among (b)
    persons who take orders
reinforced cleavage
ritual
Robert K. Merton on the
    relationship between
    community cohesiveness and

perception of number of
available baby sitters
Samuel P. and Pearl Oliner
Sandra Bem
securely-attached babies
social cohesion
social conflict and overlapping
social circles

social conflict and reinforced
cleavage
social solidarity
solidarity
Talcott Parsons on influence
the dramaturgical approach
(Erving Goffman)

the Hawthorne studies
the Kallars
The Nuer
the Stonewall riot
tribe
voluntary association
work-restriction norms

Internet Resources

http://www.unhcr.ch/

Document: Home Page of United Nations High Commissioner on Refugees

This site provides text-based access to country-specific information on all aspects relating to refugees and displaced persons, "including their countries of origin, legal instruments, human rights, minorities, situations of conflict, and conflict resolution."

http://usa.ilo.org/ilowbo/index.html

Document: International Labor Organization Home Page, Washington Branch Office

A United Nations agency, the International Labor Organization seeks to promote social justice and to establish internationally-recognized standards of human labor and of labor rights. It issues press releases that focus on equality for women, child labor, underemployment and unemployment, and other issues.

http://www.ilo.org/public/english/90ipec/index.htm

Document: International Programme on the Elimination of Child Labor (IPEC)

http://www.oneworld.org

Document: Amnesty International On-Line

http://www.state.gov/

Document: U.S. Department of State Official Web Site

Suggested Readings

Argyle, Michael, *Cooperation: the Basis of Sociability* (New York: Routledge, 1991).

Bakalian, Anny, *Armenian-Americans: From Being to Feeling Armenian* (New Brunswick, NJ: *Transaction*, 1993).

Gonzales, Juan L. Jr., *The Lives of Ethnic Americans* (Third edition) (Dubuque, Iowa: Kendall-Hunt Publishing Company, 1998).

Gourevitch, Philip, "Letter from Rwanda: After the Genocide," *The New Yorker*, December 8, 1995, pp. 78-94.

Gusfield, Joseph R., "Primordialism and Nationality," *Transaction*, Vol. 33, No. 2 (January/February) 1996: 53-57.

Holy, Ladislav, *The Little Czech and the Great Czech Nation: National Identity and the Post-Communist Transformation of Society* (New York: Cambridge University Press, 1996).

Nagel, Joane, "Constructing Ethnicity: Creating and Recreating Ethnic Identity and Culture," *Social Problems*, Vol. 41, 1994: 1562-176.

Roy, Beth, *Some Trouble with Cows: Making Sense of Social Conflict* (Berkeley: University of California Press, 1994).

Learning Exercises:

The learning objective of this chapter is for you to begin to appreciate that solidarity is one of the relationships that makes a world. In the writing assignments below, you are to follow the directions and write a response to the questions or issues indicated. Your answes are to be typed, double-spaced, and stapled in the upper left-hand corner.

Learning Exercise 3.2

Writing Assignment

Answer the following questions in an essay in which you use some of the key concepts from this chapter. Your essay is to be typed, double-spaced, and stapled in the upper left-hand corner. Your essay will be no shorter than two full pages in length.

1. Briefly define attraction, loyalty, identification, and association as forms of solidarity. Describe how each of these forms is manifest in your life today.
2. Samuel P. Oliner is a sociologist. How did Samuel P. Oliner's background influence his choice of questions or issues to investigate sociologically? What is the Oliners' explanation of nonprimordial rescue behavior during the Holocaust?
3. Have you, or anyone you know, ever tried to accomplish a task—to ride a bike, to learn to use a computer for word-processing or for data-analysis, to write an essay, etc.--and, had you not asked for assistance, would have given up? Tell us about it. What is the relationship between persistence at a task and attachment?
4. Social conflict, far from always being a "negative thing" that always tears apart or that always tears down, may contribute in many ways to the maintenance of personal friendships, of groups, and of larger collectivities. Explain, citing examples from your own life or from your observations of the world in support of the points you make.

■ ■ ■

Learning Exercise 3.3

Writing Assignment

Answer the following six questions in an essay in which you use some of the key concepts from this chapter. Your essay is to be typed, double-spaced, and stapled in the upper left-hand corner. Your essay will be no shorter than three pages in length.

1. Have you, or anyone you know, ever been in a state of fear or anxiety and have found it soothing to be around others, even if you did not know the other people who constituted the collectivity in which you sought refuge? Tell us about it. How does this experience relate to the findings of Stanley Schachter's classic experiment that is described in Chapter 3?
2. Differentiate between the concepts "primordial group" and "nonprimordial group." List and briefly describe your primordial group memberships. List and describe your nonprimordial group memberships.
3. Differentiate between the concepts of "in-group" and "out-group." List and briefly discuss your "in-group" memberships and the relationships and experiences you have with out-groups. Do you observe any overlap between your primordial relationships and your "in-

group" memberships? Explain. What is "in-group bias?" Have you ever experienced it in one or more of your own "in-groups?" Give a couple of examples.

4. Explain the concept "overlapping social circles." What is a pantribal association? Do you belong to any? List them and briefly describe one of them. List and describe the overlapping social circles in your own life. Would you describe your network of overlapping social circles as sparse, as dense, or as something else? How do you account for that?

5. Sociologist Randall Collins suggests that people who give orders have identifications and loyalties different than those who take orders. Explain. Do you see this in your own life or in the life of someone you know? Do you identify with your frontstage behaviors and your frontstage selves? Do you identify with your backstage behaviors and your backstage selves? Briefly describe and give a few examples.

6. Why were the friendships among Mac and his friends enduring and stable while those among the men studied by Elliot Liebow on the street corners of Washington D.C. fleeting and unstable? Have you observed anything like this in your own life or in the life of someone you know? Explain. What does a sociologist mean when she or he makes the sociological observation that friendship is not solely a personal matter? Do you agree with this observation? Please explain why or why not.

■ ■ ■

Learning Exercise 3.4

Writing Assignment

Answer the following six questions in an essay in which you use some of the key concepts from this chapter. Your essay is to be typed, double-spaced, and stapled in the upper left-hand corner. Your essay will be no shorter than three full pages in length.

1. Define conformity, compliance, and acceptance. Give a couple of examples of each from your own life. Why do you think you engage in conformity? Why do you think you engage in compliance?

2. Define reinforced cleavage. Give an example. Discuss the implications of reinforced cleavage for social conflict. Define overlapping solidarity. Discuss the implications of overlapping solidarity for social conflict. Can you think of some examples of overlapping solidarity and social conflict from your own life? Please describe and then share an example with us. Can you think of some examples of reinforced cleavage and social conflict from your own life? Please describe and share an example with us.

3. What is ritual? Describe a ritual or two of some groups to which you belong. What are the functions of ritual? List and describe the manifest and latent functions of the rituals you have described.

4. What is de-individuation? Can you think of instances of de-individuation that you yourself have experienced? Briefly describe a couple of examples.

5. Research indicates that integration into groups can have beneficial effects on physical and mental health. Can you think of some examples of this from your own life, or from the lives of people you know?

6. What does Emile Durkheim mean by the concept of mechanical solidarity? Have you ever been a member of such a group? Describe and explain. What does Emile Durkheim mean by the concept of organic solidarity? Have you ever been a member of such a group? Describe and explain.

■ ■ ■

Learning Exercise 3.5

Applying Sociological Analysis to the World

For those who may not want to respond to the above exercises, you may choose instead to view one of the following video tapes and to write a short typed, doubled-spaced paper (stapled in the upper left corner) integrating concepts you have learned in class lecture, discussion, and your readings. Your essay will be no shorter than three full pages in length. You must obtain the videos on your own at your own expense.

- The Gods Must Be Crazy I
- Who Framed Roger Rabbit
- Independence Day
- The Hunt for Red October

■   ■   ■

Learning Exercise 3.6

Engaging in Sociological Research

For those who may not want to watch videotapes or to view a movie, you may get together in groups of two or three persons. Use this group to engage in *one* of the following three activities that one or all of you may present in class.

1. Ask the members of your group to discuss: Are you, or have you ever been, a member of a group that some audiences might define as being of lower status and power? Give some examples. Discuss the definitions of the situation that members of the group used that enabled them to favor their own group (in-group bias) and relate this to the reading and concepts of our class. In conjunction with your class report, you may also want to present a skit to the class.
2. Repeat Schachter's experiment and present your findings to the class.
3. Interview individuals from a culture or from a subculture very different than your own and ask them ask them to describe their friendship circles (how many people are in it? are they family members? are they similar to themselves in certain respects? which respects—gender, country of origin, age?; what types of activities do they engage in when they get together?; do they tend to get together at each other's homes, or elsewhere, such as at a park, or at restaurant, or at a pub? Are there any rituals that are important in their lives, perhaps rituals associated with special holidays? Which holidays? Ask them to explain why this holiday is important to them, what meaning it has to them and their family and friends. What are the rituals like? Describe them and the meanings they have for the people participating. Present your findings to the class.

■   ■   ■

Sociology and the Internet

1. The Committee to End the Marion Lockdown (CEML) was founded in 1985 to fight against perceived injustices at Marion Federal Penitentiary. Go to the following Web site:

   http://www-unix.oit.umass.edu/~kastor/ceml_articles/cu_in_us.html

   > Document: "Control Unit Prisons in the U.S.: From Alcatraz to Marion to Florence— Control Unit Prisons in the United States," by CEML

   Read and reflect upon this article. Then, write an essay of not less than three typed pages in length in which you indicate the defining characteristics of a "control unit" (otherwise known as a secure-housing unit), discuss the functions of control units, and discuss the proliferation of control units in this country. Then, explain from which theoretical perspective(s) this article was written. Base your position on logical reasoning and give some examples to support your position. Then, use a different theoretical perspective to analyze the phenomenon of "control units." Which alternate theoretical perspective do you chose? Tell us. Then, describe what control units look like from that theoretical point of view. Which of these two theoretical perspective makes more sense to you, and why?

2. To access the 1996 U.S. Department of State *Country Reports on Human Rights Practices*, please do the following: (1) Go to the U.S. Department of State official Web site at **http://www.state.gov/** (2) Then conduct a search. Double click on "Search." In the search box, simply enter **human rights practices** and then click on "Search." This procedure will get you to the Country Reports on Human Rights Practices whose URL is

   http://www.state.gov/www/global/human_rights/1997_hrp_report/97hrp_report_toc.html

   From this URL you can easily access information on human rights practices in many countries of the world, including, but not limited to Egypt, Russia, Turkey, Colombia, Guatemala, Peru, Brazil, Tunisia, Nigeria, Cuba, Mexico, the Occupied Territories, China (Peoples Republic), Algeria, Philippines, Kenya, Uzbekistan, Sri Lanka, Honduras, Indonesia, Poland, Croatia, Cambodia, Morocco, Bosnia and Herzegovina, Albania, Pakistan, Venezuela, Bangladesh, Serbia, Montenegro, and so forth.

   For each of the countries, this site contains the U.S. Department of State's assessment of the political situation and of human-rights abuses, among other things. Please browse at this web site for a while. Then, select a country *other than the United States*. Read about the political situation in that country and about the specific human-rights abuses in that country. Write an essay of not less than two typed pages in which you relate the findings regarding specific human-rights abuses in that country to its political situation.

■　■　■

Multiple-Choice and True-False Test

1. Sociologists tend to use the terms solidarity, cohesion, social solidarity, and social cohesion, synonymously and interchangeably.
   A. True   B. False

2. _____ refers to positive affective attachment to another person.
   A. Commitment
   B. Anomie
   C. Alienation
   D. Loyalty
   E. Attachment

3. _____ babies use their mothers as a secure pad or base from which to explore their environment and from which to operate while playing.
   A. Securely-attached
   B. Avoidantly-attached
   C. Insecurely-attached

4. Caregivers of these babies responded promptly and warmly to their infants' entreaties for contact and comfort.
   A. Securely-attached
   B. Avoidantly-attached
   C. Insecurely-attached

5. Caregivers of these babies were inconsistent in responding to their babies. Sometimes they were warmly responsive; other times they were neglectful or intrusive.
   A. Securely-attached
   B. Avoidantly-attached
   C. Insecurely-attached

6. Caregivers of these babies tended to be consistently rejecting of their babies' bids for contact and for comfort.
   A. Securely-attached
   B. Avoidantly-attached
   C. Insecurely-attached

7. As discussed in the textbook, research indicates that infants securely-attached to their mothers at age six months or younger _____.
   A. acted differently at age six months than those who were not securely attached to their mothers at age six months.
   B. acted differently later than those who were not securely attached to their mothers at age six months.
   C. both of the above
   D. none of the above

8. Emmy Werner's longitudinal study finds that secure attachment to the mother (nurturing figure) by age one is strongly related to _____.
   A. being able to distance oneself from emotional turmoil in later childhood
   B. being able to seek out and to find adults for guidance and help when parents faltered in childhood
   C. planning rather than acting on impulse as a teen
   D. all of the above
   E. none of the above

9. _____ refers to attachment to a group as a group.
   A. Attachment
   B. Loyalty
   C. Anomie
   D. Alienation
   E. Verstehen

10. As indicated in the textbook, _____ conducted experiments that demonstrated that there appears to be something calming and soothing about being in the company of others when one is anxious or afraid.
    A. Stanley Schachter
    B. Max Weber
    C. Karl Marx
    D. Irving Janis

11. The field of industrial sociology was born in _____.
    A. Stanley Schachter's classic experiments on groups
    B. research studies conducted by Elton Mayo and Harvard researchers at the Western Electric Company's Hawthorne Works in Chicago
    C. Mary Ainsworth's studies on being sane in insane places
    D. Elizabeth Kuebler Ross' classic studies on men and women of the international corporate complex in Tokyo, Japan, in the 1880s
    E. Harry Harlow's classic studies on cyberphobia during the McCarthy era

12. We speak of _____ when part of one's identity (sense of self) derives from one's sense of membership in a group or groups.
    A. attachment
    B. identification
    C. loyalty
    D. association

13. The Stonewall riot sparked _____ in the United States.
    A. the civil-rights movement
    B. the women's movement
    C. the gay-rights movement
    D. the animal rights movement
    E. campaign-spending reform movement

14. _____ groups are those that come first in our experience, like the family, territorial groups, and community.
    A. Primordial
    B. Nonprimordial

15. The Oliners' research on rescuing Jews during the Holocaust is an example of helping _____.
    A. members of one's primordial group
    B. nonprimordial-group members

16. An orientation to the world that focuses outward towards others and that emphasizes both the common humanity of all persons as well as an ethical obligation to help all persons in need.
    A. constrictedness
    B. extensivity
    C. anomie
    D. attraction
    E. alienation

17. A tendency for people who belong to an in-group to favor their own group.
    A. fundamental attribution error
    B. frotteurism
    C. constrictedness
    D. in-group bias
    E. retreatism

18. One gets into this by being born into it and gets out of it by dying.
    A. class
    B. status
    C. estate
    D. caste

19. A **band** is a territorially based community that is larger than a tribe.
    A. True   B. False

20. According to American sociologist Talcott Parsons we may interpret the process of influence as a way of establishing solidarities.
    A. True   B. False

21. Paternal kin, maternal kin, the local community, and age peers are bases of _____ among the Nuer.
    A. reinforced cleavage
    B. overlapping social circles

22. In loosely structured groups and in open, pluralistic societies, partial, segmental, particular-istic loyalties _____ viewed as incompatible with loyalty to the larger political community.
    A. are
    B. are not

23. In this type of conflict, a person who is an ally in one dispute in an opponent in another.
    A. reinforced cleavage
    B. crosscutting or overlapping conflicts

24. _____ tend to inhibit a multiplicity of crosscutting memberships and the open acting out of disagreement or hostility.
    A. Loosely structured groups and open, pluralistic societies
    B. Rigid social structures and closed groups

25. According to Randall Collins, _____ tend to identify with their frontstage behaviors and frontstage selves; they identify with the official symbols of the organizations they control or of the means of production that they own.
    A. persons who give orders
    B. persons who take orders

26. According to Randall Collins, individuals who give orders and who belong to tightly enclosed, localized groups tend to _____.
    A. emphasize and enforce conformity to the group's traditions
    B. be suspicious of strangers (out-group members)
    C. react strenuously and emotionally against in-group members who are disrespectful of the group's symbols
    D. all of the above
    E. none of the above

27. Compliance and acceptance are two forms of conformity.
    A. True   B. False

28. In _____ one publicly acts in accordance with a norm but privately disagrees.
    A. acceptance
    B. compliance
    C. in loco parentis
    D. mens rea
    E. restitutive law

29. According to Durkheim, these societies are held together by a common conscience.
    A. Gesellschaft
    B. organic
    C. mechanical

30. According to Durkheim, these societies are held together by a division of labor and by interdependence.
    A. Gesellschaft
    B. organic
    C. mechanical

31. As indicated in Robert K. Merton's study, the perception of the number of baby sitters depends _____.
    A. how many persons there are between the ages of 14-55 years of age in the two-mile radius around where you live
    B. on trust

32. According to Sandra Bem, in _____ one has equal amounts of traditionally feminine and traditionally masculine gender-role traits.
    A. androgyny
    B. anomie
    C. lex salica
    D. actus reas

33. Who are the Kallars?
    A. neighbors of Sigmund Freud
    B. neighbors of Max Weber
    C. a caste in India, formed in Bengal after persons of diverse castes broke caste obligations together in the great famine of 1866
    D. early telecommunication workers in Detroit

34. Highly cohesive groups demand more conformity from their members than lowly-cohesive groups.
    A. True   B. False

35. The more cohesive a group, the more likely it is that the conformity it demands is conformity to the norms of that particular group and not conformity to the norms of the larger social structure in which that group is situated, located, or embedded.
    A. True   B. False

36. Work-restriction norms _____.
    A. are norms that you will find in the official rules-and-procedures manuals of any firm or factory
    B. are informal rules-of-the-game that workers develop that seem to help them cope in the face of the various difficulties encountered on the job

37. In-group bias is more likely if the in-group is small relative to the out-group.
    A. True   B. False

CHA**4**TER

CHAPTER

Human Inquiry and Research Methods

The truth is arrived at only by the painstaking process of eliminating the untrue.

Sherlock Holmes, "Dressed to Kill"

■ ■ ■

The Intensive Care Unit (ICU) at the University of Kansas Medical Center (KUMC) is a curiously quiet place. Doctors, medical students, and nurses whisper as they confer over what to do with an unconscious teenager who came to them from the emergency room with severe gun shot wounds to the head, stomach, and legs. Let us name this teenager Wesley. An array of tubes connect vital-signs monitoring equipment and life-support machines to Wesley's arms, head, and chest. Other than hushed whispers, all that is heard is chirping from a monitor that connects Wesley's chest to a respirator. All that is seen are the blinking lights of these new marvels of medical technology.

Suddenly, the predictable chirps turn into a long scream, and the attending physicians concentrate on keeping Wesley alive. After all attempts fail, Wesley, who came to them an hour or so ago, expires without regaining consciousness. It is the junior attending physician's turn to inform relatives, who are waiting just outside the ICU, of the death of their son and grandson.

The next task in this teaching and research institution is to establish cause of death. In the cold environment of the autopsy room, the pathologist and second-year medical students

use the *tools of research* to discover the foundation of death: suffocation caused by internal bleeding into the lungs, complicated by damage to the cortex of the brain. Medical science could not stanch the blood flowing from Wesley's wounds. In lay person's terms, Wesley suffocated in his own blood, due to gun shot wounds.

Other tests later reveal a .9 percent alcohol content, enough legally to establish that the teenager had been drunk when he was shot. Traces of crack-cocaine and of heroin were also present in his blood. Another test revealed, days later, that Wesley had been HIV-positive, indicating he was infected with the AIDS virus.

Wesley's remains are released to his mother and to his maternal grandmother. The hospital social worker writes a report indicating that the mother, age 32, and grandmother, age 64, knew about the boy's gang activity but had been unable, despite numerous attempts, to prevent Wesley from dropping out of high school and joining a gang. His father left Wesley's mother before Wesley was born.

Neither the alcohol level nor the drug content of Wesley's blood surprised his mother and grandmother. However, they are startled by the HIV-AIDS test results. A social worker as-

103

signed to help the family cope with the tragedy reports that mother and grandmother are bitter towards the police in Kansas City, Kansas. "Why couldn't they protect the neighborhood better?" they ask.

The police report Wesley's death as a murder. The police report shows that the sixteen-year-old teenager has a history of fighting with other male teenagers in his neighborhood and that he has a record of arrest for burglary, attempted rape, and drug dealing. Young Wesley already had served six months in a residential youth center by the order of the court. At the residential youth center Wesley had been given an IQ test which indicated he was of normal intelligence and a standardized self-esteem test that indicated he had low self-esteem. Treatment for self-esteem is addressed in the residential youth center via group therapy, the most cost-efficient approach. After his release, Wesley is required to report monthly to a parole officer.

Wesley is survived by his mother, maternal grandmother, and by a six-month-old baby girl born of his live-in girlfriend, Marion, aged 17. Marion is receiving Aid for Dependent Children, ADC, from the Department of Social and Rehabilitative Services (SRS) of the state of Kansas. The drive-by shooting was caused by Wesley's attempt to settle grievances with another gang member who had made offending remarks about Marion. The weapon that caused Wesley's death was a semi-automatic rifle, stolen from a local pawnshop in Kansas City, Missouri. In Kansas City, Kansas, he was the 123rd victim of gang violence within the past several years and 35th murder victim this year. It is only March.

The data on Wesley's death are entered automatically into the Federal Bureau of Investigation's (FBI) *Uniform Crime Reports* (UCR). Municipal police departments, including those of Kansas City, Kansas, send their data to the state-level FBI every six months. The FBI then uses the data on Wesley's death and other crimes known to the police throughout the entire nation to compile Uniform Crime Reports (UCR). The UCRs are published annually by the FBI and distributed to municipal, county, and state police agencies.

The costs associated with Wesley's medical treatment and autopsy—the costs of being transported to the emergency room; of emergency-room services; of the ICU; of blood, plasma, bandages, tubes, x-rays, syringes, and antibiotics; of laboratory tests; of physician fees for reading the x-rays; and of physician fees for treating Wesley—total $15,000. The hospital administrator, a kind man in his late 40s, confers with Wesley's mother and discovers that she does not have hospital insurance, nor does she qualify for Medicaid. She has not graduated from high school and has not earned a GED. She has no fewer than three part-time jobs, all of which pay minimum wage and none of which provides health-care coverage. The hospital administrator works out a monthly-payments schedule but knows that the costs reflected in this bill probably either will be passed along to other patients in the form of higher rates for services, or they will be paid by the people of the state of Kansas whose taxes support KUMC.

Common Sense

Many readers of this apocryphal story may not be alarmed. In fact, the story might confirm what some readers already believe about large-city life, teenagers, medical science, hospitals, single-parent families, medical costs, the police, and welfare. Some readers might conclude that Wesley was the cause of his own demise. As unfair as it may seem to some, many readers might conclude that the mother and grandmother were the cause of Wesley's death: had they correctly reared him, he would not have had a police record and would not have joined a gang, both of which increase the probability of an early demise through violent means. Many Americans are outraged by a perceived lack of police control of violence in the inner city. As taxpayers, they also disapprove of a welfare system that apparently perpetuates illegitimate births. Some of these same taxpayers may even support the "right to life" as an alternative to abortion. Marion may even have HIV-AIDS herself; or, even worse, she may have passed it on to her baby. It is conceivable that many people view this case as one more indicator of the failure of a welfare state to solve social problems.

Common-sense explanations are cultural traditions or folk knowledge that form a body of shared and somewhat standardized attributions (explanations) of a variety of phenomena and that contain "solutions" for everyday problems ("Just say 'No' to drugs") (Theodorson and Theodorson, 1969: 61). Some of these common-sense explanations may be strongly held beliefs or even viewpoints that are perceived as "politically correct." Common-sense explanations may be accurate or inaccurate from the vantage point of **the way of knowing** called the scientific method. (Please review Chapter 2.) In other words, some common-sense explanations may be true, while others are mere twaddle. How do we distinguish the accurate from the mere twaddle?

Research Methodology in Sociology

Research methods, sometimes called *research methodology,* allow us to discern when common sense is accurate and when it is not. As a way of knowing, the scientific method requires that we use research methodology instead of common sense. **Research** refers to the following elements:

- a systematic and reasonably objective study of a problem for the purpose of deriving general principles (Theodorson and Theodorson, 1969: 347)
- the investigation is guided by, or responds to, previously collected data
- one aim of research is to add to the body of knowledge on a subject

Methodology refers to the logic of science as a way of knowing. As it applies to sociology, methodology includes the following:

- the analysis of the basic assumptions of science in general
- the analysis of basic assumptions of sociology
- the process of **theory** construction
- the relationship of theory and research
- the procedures of empirical investigation

Methodology, then, is concerned with the logical, conceptual, research procedures by means of which substantive knowledge is built. To use a metaphor, we might conceive of methodology as a tool chest, whose tools, when appropriately selected and used within the framework of the steps of the scientific method, allow us to gain knowledge in a particular way—the way of knowing called the scientific method.

A sensitive, careful reader might notice that research methods as here defined do *not* refer to going to the library, looking up a topic, copying down some notes, and then writing or typing it up in a paper. Call *that* process information transferal, fact transferal, a library exercise, an indoor exercise, or a partial review of selected literature, but do not confuse it with the systematic process known as research.

The Uses of Theory in Social Science Research

Theory is one aspect of methodology. Theory refers to a set of interrelated principles and definitions that conceptually organize selected aspects of the empirical world in a systematic fashion. Theory is indispensable to the scientific way of knowing. As you recall from Chapter 2, in our search for knowledge and for explanations we social scientists are interested in discovering patterns of behavior, recurring events and characteristics. Sociology is interested in the development of generalized principles of human relations. *A specific event is of sociological significance only to the extent that it can be related to patterns of events that yield such principles.* So, unlike a pathologist who "explains" the cause of Wesley's death as due to suffocation, and unlike a police officer who reports and records pertinent information and data, sociologists, in their roles as scientists, endeavor to understand a drive-by shooting as it relates to patterns of events that yield generalized principles of human relations. Some sociologists are interested in using the results of social-science research to design social policies to ameliorate social problems. Theory is indispensable to this process. Theory guides research: it is the locomotive that pulls the research train. Hoover and Donovan list the four particular uses of theory in social-science thinking that follow (1994: 35):

1. Theory provides patterns for the interpretation of data. Theory tells us what data "mean" or signify.

2. Theory links one study with another.
3. Theory supplies frameworks within which concepts and variables acquire special significance.
4. Theory allows us to interpret the larger meaning of our findings for others and ourselves.

In the social sciences there are many types of theories. There is *micro theory* that attempts to *describe, explain,* and *predict* behavioral patterns in small social settings and institutions, such as in the family, peer group, classroom, youth gang, prison gang, and case study. Many psychologists, for example, study the interaction of small groups in their efforts to discover mechanisms that affect personality, self-esteem, and self-control. Anthropologists study single groups of individuals within a cultural context to discover and to understand kinship patterns, hierarchy, reciprocity, and the social control of human sexual expression. Sociologists engage in case studies to determine how the social environment affects behavior, values, and attitudes (Leary, Nezlek, Downs, Radford-Daveport, Martin, and McMullen, 1994; Otnes, Kyungseung, and Kim, 1994; Aron, Paris, Aron, 1995; Schütz, 1995; Tice, Butler, Muraven, Stillwell, 1995; Walens, 1997). Symbolic interactionism is an example of micro theory.

Another type of theory is *macro theory*. Macro theories focus on the larger social structure, which includes structured gender and racial inequality, social class, and social change (Bernhardt and Handcock, 1995; Downey, 1995; Fisher, 1995; Gerber and Hout, 1995; Kadushin, 1995; Ishida, Müller, Ridge, 1995; Quillan, 1995; Sakamoto and Powers, 1995; Sorensen and Trapp, 1995; Wright, Baxter, and Birkelund, 1995). Conflict theory and functionalism are examples of macro theory. Macro theories are often at odds with each other since they make different basic assumptions. Their basic assumptions may differ, for instance, with regard to the nature of human nature, what variables are important in causing social change, the relationship between gender and economic inequality, and the relationship between race and economic inequality.

Conceptualization and Logical Models of Theory Construction

The foundation of theory is a set of assumptions and **axiom**s. An axiom is a statement whose truth is either so well established that it is both unquestioned and virtually accepted universally in a scientific community, or it is self-evident. Of course, what is "self-evident" today may not be tomorrow; and what is accepted unquestioningly at one point in time (Newtonian physics) may not be at another point in time. If the foundations of a theory are rejected according to the steps of the scientific method, the validity of that theory collapses. In other words, the axioms and assumptions that underlie a theory are important. Discredit them effectively and you discredit the theory. At least in part, perhaps this is the reason that people who adhere to a particular theory seem to become uneasy when a scientist questions the assumptions and axioms on which their pet theory rests.

There are two logical models by means of which theory is constructed, induction and deduction,. We now discuss each of these. **Deduction** is the logical model in which specific hypotheses are developed on the basis of general principles. The traditional model of science uses this logical model. Sometimes deduction is described as reasoning from the general to the particular or as applying a theory to a particular case. This logical model is difficult for some undergraduate sociology students to grasp and to use. Practice makes progress; if at first the process of deduction is difficult for you to grasp and to put to use, keep trying.

Marjorie Donovan's doctoral dissertation exemplifies the process of deduction (Donovan, 1977). This research examines the relationship between the expansion of high schools and the structure of the labor force in the United States during the era from the end of the Civil War to the beginning of the First World War. Structural-functional theory holds that schools expanded to provide the growing number of white-collar workers needed in the occupational structure (e.g. Trow, 1961, 1962). If this were true, the higher the proportion of the labor force engaged in white-collar work, the higher the proportion of the appropriate age grade enrolled in high schools. The author uses existing historical records to investigate this relationship in 1870, 1880, 1890, 1900, and 1910. The data fail to support the hypothesis. As a result, the author suggests a theoretical framework that better fits the historical data: ascribe if you can and let who must achieve. The data indicate that between 1870-1910, white, native-born males did not need a high school education in order to secure a white-collar job. Conversely, for the foreign born, a high-school education was a necessary but not a sufficient condition of white-collar employment. They needed a high school education in order to be in the running for a white-collar job, but it guaranteed them nothing. For them, a high school education was not much of a "union card" during this particular era.

Induction refers to the logical model in which general principles are developed from specific observations. Sometimes induction is described as reasoning from particular instances to the general, or as arguing from facts to theory. In this model, one starts from observed data and develops a generalization, which explains the relationships between the objects observed. Sherlock Holmes uses this method. For instance, he might notice that one has a Chinese coin as a decoration on a pocketwatch chain, that one's right hand is a half-size larger than the left, that one has a tattoo of a certain shape and color, that one's right cuff is frayed and that the left-elbow of one's jacket is shinier than the right elbow. From this he inducts that one had been a manual laborer at some point (one hand is larger than the other), had been to China (the coin and the tattoo), and that one had done a great deal of writing lately (the shiny right cuff and left-elbow of the jacket). Within sociology, *grounded theory*, sometimes used in field work, uses this method (Glaser and Straus, 1967). Grounded theory is addressed below, in our exploration of field research.

Some researchers prefer one of these logical models to the other. It is important to appreciate, however, that these logical models are not mutually exclusive and one model is not "better" than the other. Many researchers move from induction to deduction and back to induction, and so forth, over the course of a research project, which is indicated in Figure 4.1, "Theory and Research."

Many sociologists and social scientists believe that scientific knowledge is generated largely by induction (Glaser and Straus, 1967). For instance, after observing many politicians, a theory might state that "most politicians are crooks." Although this theory is based on many observations in many locations over a considerable number of years, its empirical verification requires observing a probability sample of politicians at the local, state, and national levels. To falsify a theory would require finding a substantial proportion of politicians who are not crooks. In other words, a scientific hypothesis must have the characteristic of being *falsifiable*, by finding events or classes of events that do not support the theory (Popper, 1959; Stinchcombe, 1987; Derksen and Gartrell, 1992).

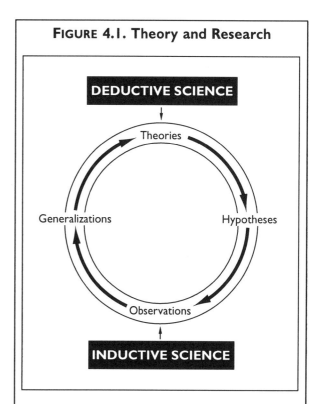

FIGURE 4.1. Theory and Research

Researchers may start or stop at any point. Observations begin when researchers examine the social world.

Adapted from: Walter Wallace, The Logic of Science in Sociology (New York: Adline de Gruyer, 1971).

Several steps are involved in testing scientific theories. The theory, or hypotheses derived from it, must be stated in abstract, verbal terms called constructs. A **construct** is an abstract mental concept—words or sets of words that express the general nature of something or the relationship among things from a particular point of view. Social class, status, power, influence, race, ethnicity, religiosity, the family, delinquency, and patriotism are examples of concepts. Concepts are the building blocks of theory (Turner, 1991: 6). Concepts are rich, abstract descriptions of an entity to be studied. Concepts often provide a category for classifying phenomena. Concepts are central to the process of generalizing and focus our attention on certain aspects of social phenomena to the exclusion of others. Concepts help us make large and small distinctions among events. To use a simile, concepts are like fishing nets, insofar as they capture certain aspects of reality and let others go by. Concepts are not viewed as "right" or "wrong" but instead are a means of bringing order out of chaos, of attributing meaning to things.

Through a process of trial and error, humans learn to name things. When we name things, we assign things a *nominal* definition. Concepts have nominal definitions. Thus, each of us who reads this book is able to conceptualize what a family is and what it is not. Each of us is able to conceptualize who is a member of our family and who is not. Sociologists conceptualize these relationships as kinship. In the story that opened this chapter, we used the concepts of live-in girlfriend, child, daughter, mother, grandmother, son, and grandson in describing age and kinship relations.

We may define a **variable** as a concept that is precisely defined, with measurable traits that vary. A concept that has different degrees of magnitude or different categories is a variable. Thus, sex or gender is a concept and a variable, whose categories, also called *attributes,* are male and female. Likewise, education is a concept and a variable: a person may have different amounts of it. *Age* is both a variable and a concept. In the story that opened this chapter, Wesley was described as a *teenager.* We may somewhat arbitrarily define a person's age by how old that person was as of her or his most recent birthday.

Quantification of Variables and Levels of Measurement

Accurate and precise measurement of phenomena is crucial to scientific explanation and to the way of knowing called the scientific method. For instance, "teenager" is a concept that refers to the classification of age. We may somewhat arbitrarily define persons who are older than 19 years of age and younger than 25 as *young adults*, and a *teenager* as someone who is at least 13 years of age and less than twenty years of age. Persons below the age of thirteen but older than nine years of age may be categorized as *pre-adolescents.*

The assignment of symbols, usually numbers, to the properties of objects or events is called **measurement. Quantitative data** are data in numerical form. They are gathered through measurement and enumeration. **Quantitative analysis**—also termed *quantitative research* or *quantitative methodology*—refers to analysis, research, or methodology that is based on precise measurement and enumeration. A few moments ago, we *quantified* the concept of age—we *operationalized* the concept of age—by assigning specified age groups nominal definitions.

Operationalization is a set of instructions for how a researcher measures concepts and variables. These instructions are sufficiently precise and detailed so that the same results will be achieved by any competent person who uses them (Blalock, 1979; Derksen and Gartrell, 1992:1714). For instance, we could operationalize the variable education by using self-report data of respondents. We could rank-order the amount of education for each respondent by assigning a code of 1 = less than 8 years of schooling, 2 = some high school, 3 = high school graduate, 4 = less than two years of college, 5 = two years of college, 6 = graduated from college with a Bachelor of Science or Bachelor of Arts degree, 7 = Master's of Arts or Master's of Science degree, 8 = Ph.D. or M.D. or D.V.M. or D.D.S., 9 = Other (Please Specify: _____), −5 = No Response. In this example we have operationalized the variable education in a quantitative manner. The categories or attributes of this variable are mutually exclusive and all inclusive. In the story that opened this chapter, both Wesley and his mother had dropped out of high school. If they were respondents in our study, each would be coded as a 2 = some high school on the variable of education.

How would you operationalize the concept of "crook," in the hypothesis: "All politicians are crooks"? How would you operationalize the concept of "politician?" Tell us about it.

Two principles guide the researcher in assigning attributes (or categories) to a variable: *mutual exclusiveness* and *exhaustiveness*. Variable attributes should be **exhaustive**: the attributes should include all possible categories of the variable, so that the observer is able to classify every observation in terms of one of the attributes that compose the variable. Thus, for the variable of sex or gender, every person is categorizable either as female or as male. Because these attributes cover all possibilities, they possess the characteristic of exhaustiveness. At the same time, these attributes are **mutually exclusive**: it is possible to define sex in such a way that every person can be classified in terms of one and only one of the attributes. Every person is capable of being classified as male *or* female, not as both at the same time.

Levels of Measurement: Nominal, Ordinal, Interval, Ratio

Characteristics of the attributes that compose a variable are used by scientists to categorize and to define levels of measurement. There are four levels of measurement. From least complex to most complex these are **nominal, ordinal, interval,** and **ratio.** *Each level of measurement has all of the attributes of the level immediately preceding it, plus something else.* We now examine the levels of measurement, after which we indicate their practical implications.

1. **Nominal measures** are variables whose attributes have only the characteristics of mutual exclusiveness and exhaustiveness. When we name something we give it a nominal definition. Your favorite movie, the brands of shampoo you most recently

used, and the state in which you reside exemplify this type of variable, a variable with a nominal level of measurement. Here are some other examples of nominal variables and their attributes:

- religious affiliation: Protestant, Catholic, Jew, Mormon, Other: (Please specify: _____), None
- sex: Female, Male
- eye color: Blue, Brown, Hazel, Green, Other: (Please specify: _____).
- hair color: Blonde, Black, Brown, Red, Gray, Other: (Please specify: _____).
- ethnicity: African-American, Hispanic, Native American, Irish-American, Italian-American, Chinese-American, Japanese-American, Other (Please specify: _____).

There is no *rank order* inherent in the attributes of these variables. One attribute is not higher or lower than another. One attribute is not more or less than another. There is no inherent rank order to the attributes of nominal variables, even when they are designated arbitrarily by numbers in the coding process. In the coding process, we arbitrarily assign numbers to the attributes of a variable. For instance, we assign a code of 1 = Female, 2 = Male. These code numbers have no quantitative meaning.

When we statistically analyze nominal-level data, we cannot calculate the mean or median. It would make no sense to speak of the mean eye color or mean ethnicity. Our analysis is restricted to speaking about the mode and enumeration. We could speak about the modal eye color (mode) of respondents and we could calculate how many people are in various categories or attributes (enumeration): 500 brown-eyed people, 250 hazel-eyed people, 100 blue-eyed people, 75 other-eye-colored people, etc.

2. **Ordinal measures** have all the characteristics of nominal variables (mutual exclusiveness, exhaustiveness), *and* they may be logically rank ordered from smaller to larger, lower to higher, younger to older, thinner to fatter, and so forth. Sometimes the only thing a researcher wants to do is to

order social classes (or people, or events, or objects, or whatever) from the one possessing the least of the characteristic—say, obesity—to the one possessing the most. The numbers used to code, to indicate, ordered position are usually assigned, such that 1 goes to the person with the least amount of the characteristic, 2 goes to the person with the second least amount, and so forth. The numbers indicating ordered position are termed **ranks.** Ranks indicate an ordinal level of measurement. For each ordinal variable, the attributes represent relatively more or less of the variable. Here are some examples of ordinal variables with their attributes:

- military rank: private, corporal, sergeant, lieutenant, captain, major, lieutenant colonel, colonel, general
- college academic degrees: A.A., B.A., M.A., Ph.D.
- hardness of rocks in the physical sciences: talc, feldspar, quartz, diamond

The perceptive reader will note that the distance between these attributes is *not* equal. There is *no* implication of a uniform rate of increase or decrease between categories. It may be three times as difficult to earn a Master's degree as a Bachelor's degree, and 37 times as difficult to earn a Ph.D. as a Master's degree.

Ordinal measures are used frequently in the social sciences in general and within sociology in particular. You find them everywhere. A Likert scale ("Strongly Agree," "Agree," "No Opinion," "Disagree," "Strongly Disagree") is an example of an ordinal measure. Social class is measured as an ordinal variable (Lower-Lower Class, Lower-Middle Class, Middle Class, Upper-Middle Class, Lower-Upper Class, Upper-Upper Class). Most attitude scales are ordinal scales.

3. **Interval measures** have all of the characteristics of ordinal-level measures (mutual-exclusiveness, exhaustiveness, rank order) *and* the actual distance separating the attributes is equal. To repeat: in interval-level measures, the distance between each of the attributes is equal. A ruler, and a tempera-

ture thermometer are interval-level measures.

In physical science, in the Fahrenheit or Celsius scales, the distance between 70° and 80° , (10), is the same as the distance between 10° and 20°, (10). *However,* 50° is *not* twice as hot as 25°. Why? Because *in interval–level measurement there is no true zero; instead, there is an arbitrary zero.*

In the example that opened this chapter, we learned that Wesley had been administered an IQ test while he was committed to a secure facility and that he had a normal IQ. An IQ test, such as the Stanford-Binet test, is the most widely used interval-level instrument in social scientific research. The national average in the U.S. on the Stanford-Binet IQ test is 100. Social scientists tend to refer to standardized IQ scores of 79 or lower as, say, "Developmentally Disabled," of 80 - 90 as "Low," of 91 - 100 as "Normal," of 101 - 114 as "High," and 115 or higher as "Genius." These are categories for applying meaning to the interval-level Stanford-Binet test. This instrument is interval level because there are equal intervals between the points on the instrument. The interval separating scores of 145 and 120, 25 points may be regarded as the same as that separating a score, of 100 and one of 75. But, there is no true zero on this instrument. A score of zero is theoretically possible. Yet a score of zero would not indicate an absence of intelligence. Why? The zero in this instrument is arbitrary. As a result, a score of 75 does *not* signify that this person is half as intelligent as someone is with a score of 150.

4. **Ratio measures** have all the characteristics of interval-level measures (mutual-exclusiveness, exhaustiveness, rank-order, equal distance between attributes) *plus* a true or absolute zero. The Kelvin temperature scale is a ratio measure. Also, age, length of residence in a particular place, the number of organizations to which a person belongs, the number of times a person attended church or synagogue or temple during the past year, the number of times a person has been married, the number of Arab friends one has are all examples of

ratio-level measures. If I have 4 Arab friends, I have twice as many of them as someone who has 2 Arab friends.

The Practical Implications of Levels of Measurement

The implications of levels of measurement pertain primarily to the analysis of data. These implications should be taken into consideration when you structure your research project. A research project typically involves many variables. Some of the variables may be measured at the nominal level (e.g., sex), others at the ordinal level (e.g., social class), still others at the ratio level (Please indicate your age at your last birthday: _____), and so forth. As you will learn in greater detail when you take statistics and research-methods courses, certain statistical procedures require that variables meet certain minimum levels of measurement. The mode can be used with nominal-level data. The mean, however, requires ratio-level data. Specific measures of association require that variables meet certain minimum levels of measurement.

You should also keep in mind that *a variable representing a certain level of measurement*—say, age measured at the ratio level—*may be treated as representing a lower level of measurement*—say, ordinal. Thus, in your research project, let us say that you collect ratio-level data on the age of respondents. In your research report, you may find it useful to treat age as an ordinal-level variable. For example, you could breakdown the ratio-level data into ordinal categories, such as the following: less than 20 years of age, 20-35 years of age, 36-51 years of age, 52-67 years of age, and 68 years of age or older. However, you *cannot* convert a lower-level measurement to a higher-level one. Commit this to your memory. The practical implication? *Collect data at the highest level of measurement possible.*

Purposes of Research

The careful and attentive reader recalls that the scientific method as a way of knowing has *prediction* as its ultimate goal. Sociological research often serves other additional purposes as well. Three of the most common purposes of research are exploration (exploratory research), description (descriptive research), and explanation (explanatory research, also known as causal research) (Rubin and Babbie, 1993). A research project may, and usually does, have more than one purpose.

Whether you are conducting exploratory, descriptive, or explanatory research, it is important that you are aware of what the units of analysis are in the study being conducted. In the social sciences there exists a big range in the "what" or "whom" being studied. Some studies have the individual as the *unit of analysis;* others have groups, social aggregates, or social artifacts as the units of analysis. The term *social artifacts* refers to the products of human beings or their behavior. This "umbrella" term includes such things as editorials, novels, movies, poems, economic depressions, songs, jokes, and new technologies. You want to collect data on the unit of analysis that you are interested in. You want to understand, and perhaps even to predict, this particular unit of analysis. Unless you keep the unit of analysis constantly in mind, it is possible that you could collect data on the wrong unit of analysis, i.e., one in which you are *not* interested. For example, you want to avoid collecting data on one unit of analysis (crime) and making conclusions about another unit of analysis (criminals).

Now let us examine each of these three types of research separately. The purpose of research has important implications for various aspects of the research design.

Exploration: Exploratory Research

Sometimes you are interested in a topic about which you and everyone else know practically nothing. You decide to engage in research to provide a beginning familiarity with the topic. Such research is termed *exploratory.* As an example, let us say that you are interested in impersonal sex in public restrooms, which is referred to as tearoom trade (Humphreys, 1970). You are curious as to what types of people engage in it. You do a literature search and find that nobody knows anything about it. You decide to engage in exploratory research to find out who is engaging in it. You do this by going to public bathrooms located in public parks in a large city, and you volunteer at each place to be a *watchqueen*—somebody who keeps an eye out for police. If you notice the approach of a police officer, you warn the people inside who are engaging in quick, anonymous, same-sex sexual encounters, so that they can stop doing whatever it is that they are doing. From an *exchange theory* point of view, the active participants are not suspicious of your offer to serve as watchqueen, because they simply assume that your payoff or reward is the opportunity to observe the sexual action in the public toilet. Some persons derive sexual satisfaction from observing the sexual actions of others.

You notice that many of the men who come to the public toilet drive there in cars. You jot down the license-plate number of each of these cars. You know someone who has access to information contained in the motor vehicles' department of the state in which your study is located. You ask this person to look up the name and address of each of these license plates, and your friend complies. Then, you disguise yourself so that the participants in tearoom trade would not recognize you, and you go to each of the addresses that your friend has supplied.

Your mission now is to gather basic demographic data on the household—occupational/income level, marital status, number of children, etc. You do not reveal the true purpose for being there; instead, you give a bogus reason. For instance, let us pretend that you say something like the following: "Hello, I am Samuel Spade of Spade and Archer Enterprises, and we are conducting a survey on levels of consumer satisfaction with the perceived safety and usefulness of various domestic products. Would you please give me just a couple of minutes of your time so that American manufacturers may produce products that are safer and that better meet the preferences of the American buying public?"

Through the use of such ruses Laud Humphreys discovered that those who engage in impersonal sex in public bathrooms frequently are married, middle-class males who have children, a spouse, a nice job, and are well-respected members of their communities (Humphreys, 1970). Humphreys' research methods and findings shocked many people.

Every form and method of research has advantages and disadvantages. An advantage of exploratory research is its very purpose: it gives us a beginning familiarity with a topic about which there previously had been no scientific information. To use a metaphor: it gives us hints regarding the "lay of the land" in a scientifically unexplored territory. Exploratory research is therefore valuable whenever we break new ground, whenever we "go where no one has gone before." Exploratory research also is a vehicle for generating hypotheses on which further research can be based. Also, exploratory research may attune us to variables that might be of interest for further study and it may provide insight into useful ways to operationalize variables important for further study.

The major limitation of exploratory research is a product of its very nature: lack of generalizability of research results. Thus, we cannot generalize the findings of Laud Humphreys' study to tearoom trade in other cities, in other countries, in other regions of the same country, or to anonymous, quick, same-sex sexual encounters in other settings, such as in bath houses. In other words, this study tells us something, but what it tells us is quite limited.

Description: Descriptive Research

In *descriptive research*, a researcher observes deliberately and carefully and then describes what is observed. Field research and survey research are descriptive methods appropriate for many research problems.

The United States Census is an example of descriptive research. The Constitution of the United States mandates that this particular census be taken every ten years. It is a survey whose goal is an accurate, precise description of a wide variety of characteristics of the entire population of the United States. The *Uniform Crime Reports* (UCR), published annually by the Federal Bureau of Investigation (FBI), is another example of descriptive research. The most widely cited source of crime data in this country, the UCR provides information on the amount of violent and property crime in the nation, based on crimes reported to the police. A Gallup Poll on the attitudes of the American population is another example of descriptive research. If a survey is properly constructed and implemented, and if its results are properly analyzed, a survey can describe a population while making appropriate allowances for the degree of error that exists. Descriptive research is useful for answering the "What" variety of questions: What is the leading cause of death among people aged 13-26 in the United States? What are the voting intentions of the electorate in the upcoming presidential election? What are the age, sex, gender, and racial characteristics of the college population in the United States? What is the average age at which people first marry in this country?

Descriptive and exploratory research, however, are not designed to answer "Why" questions, which include the following: Why is the age of first marriage what it is? Why are poor youth more likely to join a gang than affluent youth? Why do gang members engage in drive-by shootings? Why does genocide happen in the modern world while major news media in the United States say nothing about it? Why do young females bear children out of wedlock? Why do people rob banks? Why do serial murderers kill people? If we want answers to such questions, we engage in explanatory research.

Explanation: Explanatory Research

Reporting the number of gangs in a city at a given point in time is descriptive research. Reporting why some cities have more gangs and more violent gang activity than others, and reporting why some cities have more violent gang activity at one point in time than at another are matters of *explanatory research.* A researcher has an explanatory purpose if she or he wants to explain why someone who is battered remains with the battering spouse, why the unemployment rate is a certain level, why salary levels for workers are not higher, why delinquency occurs, why administrators at a particular university have salary levels that are 113% of the national average while their faculty have salaries that are only 85% of the national average, and why certain forms of behavior and certain conditions are perceived as deviant by particular audiences.

When one answers "why" questions, one is, in essence, arguing cause and effect. One is making an argument that variable X causes variable Y. A variable that is considered as the cause is termed the **independent variable** and

a variable that is considered as the effect or result is termed the **dependent variable.** Independent and dependent variables are just two types of variables. There are many types of variables.

The status as an independent or dependent variable is not inherent in the entity itself (e.g., facial blemishes, hamburgers), but is a function of the research question. Thus, in the statement "Hamburgers and fries cause facial blemishes," the independent variable is hamburgers and fries, and the dependent variable is facial blemishes. In the statement, "Hamburger consumption varies by social class," the independent variable is social class and the dependent variable is hamburger consumption. In the statement, "Facial blemishes cause young persons embarrassment," the independent variable is facial blemishes, and embarrassment is the dependent variable. In other words X causes Y.

Causal Argument

Every time you want to argue that X causes Y, it is necessary to demonstrate three things (Lazarsfeld, 1959; Babbie, 1995). While each sounds simple and straightforward at first glance, actually accomplishing or executing each step may require the investment of considerable effort, time, and attention.

Criteria for Inferring Causality

1. *Temporal Order* The first requirement for a causal relationship is that the cause precedes the effect. This sometimes is referred to as temporal order: the independent variable must precede the dependent variable in time. While this sounds simple and straightforward, it often causes problems. As you will become aware while engaging in a thorough literature review, the causal order often is not clear. *With an unclear time order, one cannot convincingly make a causal argument.* Simply because you may not be aware that the causal order is not clear does not alter the fact that, to salient audiences, the causal order cannot be clearly discerned.

Suppose, for example, that research reveals, as in fact it does in the United States, that poor people are more likely than affluent people to suffer from schizophrenia, a serious, treatable, chronic form of mental illness wherein one suffers a break with reality. Whatever "reality" is, people suffering from schizophrenia experience a break with it. They hear voices the rest of us do not hear and see things that the rest of us do not see; they have delusions of grandiosity (think they own the University you are attending, that they are Hitler's grandson or Lenin's granddaughter and so forth). The research question is—which comes first, the mental illness or class position? Does mental illness cause lowered class position? Or is it the other way around—the stresses of being poor actually bring on, or cause, mental illness?

2. *Correlation* The second requirement for a causal relationship is that there is a correlation between the independent and dependent variables. With regard to quantitative variables, sociologists use the terms relationship, correlation, and association interchangeably. A correlation between two (or more) quantitative variables refers to a relationship wherein an increase or decrease in the magnitude of one variable is associated with the magnitude of the other(s). When two variables are highly correlated, it is possible to predict the magnitude of one variable from a knowledge of the magnitude of the other.

Measures of association or of correlation tell us whether two or more variables are related and the *strength* of the relationship. When you take a course in statistics, you learn many measures of association (measures of correlation) and the conditions under which their use is appropriate. Using measures of association, it is possible to describe a relationship between two or more variables as weak, medium, or strong.

Relationships between variables also may be described as positive or negative. Please see Table 4.1. A correlation is termed **direct** (or **positive**) if as one variable increases in size or magnitude, the other increases in size or magnitude; as one variable decreases in size or magnitude, the other decreases in size or magnitude. For instance, there is a direct (also known as a positive) relationship between education and income in the United States: as education increases, income increases; as education decreases, income decreases. Relationships may be described as **negative** (or **inverse**): as one variable decreases in size or magnitude, the other increases in size or magnitude; as one variable increases in size or magnitude, the other decreases. For example, there is an inverse relationship in the United States today between social class and cigarette smoking: as social class increases, the percent of people who smoke decreases; as social class decreases, the percent of people who smoke increases. There also is an inverse relationship in the United States today between social class and obesity: the higher the social class, the lower the percent of persons who are obese; the lower the social class, the higher the percent of persons who are obese.

Relationships may be described as *linear*, which is the simplest form of relationship, or as *curvilinear*. Positive and negative relationships

TABLE 4.1. Examples of Positive and Negative Relationships _____

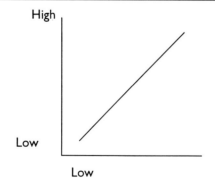

Positive Relationship

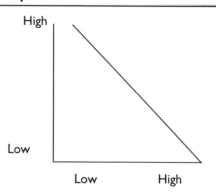

Negative Relationship

are examples of linear relationships. In a curvilinear relationship, as variable X increases in size or magnitude, variable Y increases (or decreases) in size or magnitude up to a certain point, and then as X continues to increase in size or magnitude, Y decreases (or increases) in size or magnitude. For instance, one theory posits that the relationship between test performance (as measured by grade on test) and arousal (as measured by extent of evaluation apprehension, rate of respiration, heart rate) is curvilinear. This theory predicts that low levels of arousal lead to poor test performance (as measured by grade on test), a medium amount of arousal increases test performance, and very high arousal again causes poor test performance. Please see Table 4.2. If drawn on a graph, this curve would be an *upside down* U.

Another example of a curvilinear correlation is the relationship between family form and type of society (Goode, 1963). Please see Table 4.3. Let us use the term **conjugal family** to refer to a family that consists of husband, wife, and their dependent children and that has loose relations with other family members (in-laws, cousins, grandparents, etc.). Let us use the term **urban-agrarian** to refer to a type of society in which no more than roughly ten percent of the total population lives in cities and in which the great majority of the population are agricultural laborers tied to and dominated by an urban elite. These are the most unequal societies known to sociologists and to other social scientists. On whatever dimension of social inequality in which you are interested—class, status, power, gender, and so forth, these societies are characterized by the most inequality. Table 4.3 indicates that the relationship between family form and type of society is curvilinear. If drawn on a graph, the curve would be approximately a *right-side-up* U-shape (Goode, 1963).

3. *Checking for Spuriousness* The third requirement for a causal relationship is that the relationship between two variables cannot be explained away as being due to *the influence of a third variable that is the cause of them both.* This is sometimes referred to as the issue of spuriousness.

A relationship between two variables is considered as **spurious** when it is actually accounted for by the relationship of the two variables to a third variable. For example, a relationship is observed between the size of a person's social support network and health status: People with larger social-support networks tend to be healthier than persons with smaller (or no) social-support networks. Let us assume that we know, which we do not, that the size of social support networks is antecedent to health status. Before we may legitimately conclude that size of social support networks is the cause of health status, we must check for spuriousness. (When you take a statistics course, you learn how to do this.) It is possible that a third variable, such as age, accounts for both variables. As people age, their friends and family members (aunts, uncles, parents, cousins, etc.) die; this can shrink the size of social-support

TABLE 4.2. Curvilinear Relationship Between Arousal Level and Test _____

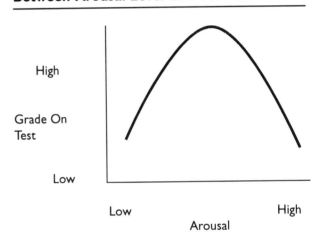

TABLE 4.3. Curvilinear Relationship Between Type of Society and Family Form _

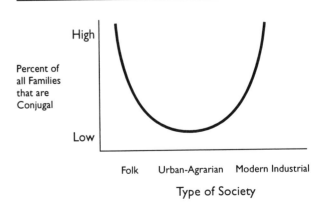

networks. As people age, their bodies fall apart—even if they jog, even if they eat their vegetables and fruits. This manifests itself in increased **morbidity** (illness). In other words, age may account both for size of social-support network and health status. This is an empirical question, and it can be answered empirically. Were it the case that age accounts both for size of social-support network and for health status, we would say that the original relationship between size of social-support group and health status is **spurious.**

To review, most sociologists consider two variables as causally related when it has been demonstrated that (1) the cause precedes the effect in time, (2) there is an association between the two variables, and (3) no likely third variable is the cause of them both. Any relationship between two variables that satisfies these three criteria is causal. If even one of these criteria is not met, the relationship is not causal. Satisfying two out of three criteria does not win you a silver medal or support a causal argument.

Reliability and Validity

Our appreciation of research methods and causal inference is enhanced by understanding the concepts of reliability and validity. Each of these terms has several meanings. We first address the generic meaning of each and then look at more specialized forms when and as appropriate.

Validity refers to the correspondence between what a measuring instrument is supposed to measure and what it actually measures. To the extent that a measuring instrument measures what it is supposed to measure, to that extent it has validity. For example, Hindelang, Hirschi, and Weis have found that self-report delinquency is differentially valid by race by sex (1981); that is, African-American males fail to report the lion's share of their serious crime. The self-reports of African-American males about their delinquent acts are invalid. Perhaps an additional example will help to clarify the concept of validity for you. When a student laments about a test she or he has taken, "I really knew the material covered on the test and yet I got a bad grade on it! That exam might have measured how much I could write in fifty minutes; it might

have measured how many multiple-choice questions I could read in a short period of time, but it surely did not measure the extent of my knowledge about _____" (fill in the blank with the name of your favorite class)." That student is raising the question of the validity of the test.

In contrast, **reliability** refers to the extent to which the same or similar results are obtained when a researcher uses the same measurement instrument on the same or similar sample or population of subjects. There are many types of reliability. For instance, if you are conducting a study that involves judgments made by an observer, then it is necessary to use more than one judge (observer, rater) and to assess the extent of agreement or consistency between or among observers or raters. This is called *inter-rater* or *inter-judge reliability.* The use of inter-rater reliability is illustrated in a study of the pictorial representation of males and females in premier science journals (Donovan, 1992) conducted by one of the authors of this textbook. This study uses a measure of facial prominence called the face-ism or facial-prominence score (Archer et al, 1983). It consists of an index, whose numerator is the distance in a depiction (in a picture of a person) from the top of the head to the lowest point of the chin, and whose denominator is the distance in a depiction from the top of the head to the lowest visible part of the subject's body. The limits of this index range from 0.00 (only part or all of the subject's body, but no face is shown) to 1.00 (the picture shows the face only, and no other parts of the subject's body are visible). Archer and colleagues report that this facial prominence index is highly reliable across judges (Archer et, al., 1983). Ninety-nine times out of 100 the measurements of the two judges are in agreement. This method of measurement, in other words, is highly reliable across judges.

Using this index, the author finds that in 1990, there is a pronounced tendency to represent men with their faces and women with their bodies in *Science,* the weekly publication of the American Association for the Advancement of Science which is the most highly cited general science journal in the world. The mean face-ism score for the pictures of men is .59. This indicates that approximately sixty percent of each picture is devoted to a man's face. The corresponding figure for women is .482. Less than half of each picture is devoted to a woman's face. This difference easily reaches *statistical significance* (p.< .002). Statistical significance is a measure that tells us what the probability is that the results are due to sampling error, or chance, alone. In the present example, there are fewer than two chances out of 1,000 that these gender differences are due to sampling error or chance alone.

These gender discrepancies in facial prominence are similar to those found in other media, including newspapers, weekly news magazines, and *Ms. Magazine* (Archer et. al., 1983). The greater prominence given to women's bodies and to men's faces is noteworthy because people whose faces are prominent are perceived as more intelligent, ambitious, and attractive (Archer et. al., 1983). An implicit, latent-function message being transmitted from the top of the scientific community in the United States, then, is that women scientists, when they are visible at all, are less intelligent, less attractive, and less ambitious than their male counterparts (Donovan, 1992).

It is possible for an instrument that lacks validity to be a reliable measure. Please see Figure 4.2, "An Analogy to Validity and Reliability." Thus, let us say that according to his bathroom scale Hugh weighs 145 pounds. Hugh gets on the scale in the morning, in the evening, and in the afternoon, and it says that he weighs 145 pounds. Next week, it says he weighs 145 pounds. The scale is giving highly reliable (i.e., consistent) readings. Its readings, in this particular case, lack (criterion) validity. Hugh actually weighs 185 pounds, and he has weighed 185 pounds for several months. Ac-

cording to the scale at his health club (the criterion), and according to the scale at his physician's office (the criterion), Hugh weighs 185 pounds.

There are many varieties of validity. Please be sure to read nearby Box 4.1 entitled "Varieties of Validity" in which some of the common forms of validity are defined and illustrated. Another important form of validity is **internal validity,** which refers to the extent to which the results of a study accurately depict whether one variable is or is not a cause of another (Rubin and Babbie, 1993; Babbie, 1995). Ascertaining the internal validity of a study is done on the basis of how well the study has controlled for various threats to internal validity. Campbell and Stanley (1963), Cook and Campbell (1979), Rubin and Babbie (1993), and Babbie (1995) point to several threats to internal validity. Here are nine:

Threats to Internal Validity

1. *History.* We are using "history" as a neologism to refer to extraneous events that coincide in time with the manipulation of the independent variable. These events may confound the results of a study. For instance, suppose that one aspect of a study is a questionnaire that elicits perceptions regarding sexual harassment on the job. A couple of weeks after you mail the questionnaires, a major scandal breaks regarding heterosexual sexual harassment of troops in the American military. It is possible that the dialogue resulting from this scandal serves to change (to increase) the consciousness of females regarding what constitutes sexual harassment. One result

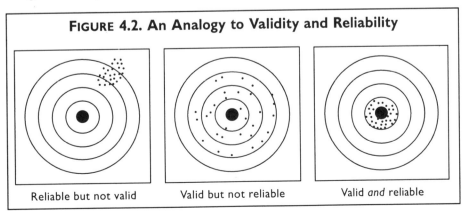

FIGURE 4.2. An Analogy to Validity and Reliability

Reliable but not valid   Valid but not reliable   Valid *and* reliable

BOX 4.1

Varieties of Validity

Some common forms of validity are defined and illustrated below. *Since a measure may be valid by one of these standards and invalid by another, it can be misleading to speak of validity without specifying the criterion by which validity is being assessed.* The implication? When assessing the validity of an instrument *specify* the types of validity a measurement instrument possesses or that it lacks, but do not merely say "It lacks validity" or "It has validity." Be more specific in your assessment by noting, for instance, "While it lacks construct validity, content validity, and criterion-related validity, it has face validity."

construct validity: The extent to which a measure relates to other variables as predicted by a theory is termed construct validity. Operationalizing the concept "delinquency" as someone below the age of majority who uses illegitimate means to attain a legitimate goal has construct validity from the point of view of Robert K. Merton's theory of anomie. It has construct validity.

content validity: The extent to which a measure covers the range of meanings included in a concept is termed content validity. The greater the extent to which a measure covers the range of meanings included in a concept, the greater its content validity. Operationalizing the concept "delinquent" as a person below the age of majority who commits a behavior that would not be criminal if that person were an adult lacks content validity. It fails adequately to cover the range of meanings included within the concept. Thus, in addition to the particular meaning indicated in the proposed operational definition, the concept also commonly refers to persons below the age of majority who are deemed by the juvenile court (1) to be in need of care, (2) to have been neglected, or (3) to have committed acts that would be criminal if the perpetrator were an adult.

criterion-related validity: The extent to which a measure is correlated with an external criterion is its criterion-related validity. The greater the extent to which a measure relates to an external criterion the greater its criterion-related validity. The validity of the Graduate Record Exam and of the Scholastic Aptitude Test is demonstrated by the ability of the test to predict college success of students.

face validity: If a measure makes sense as an indicator of a concept, it has face validity. Face validity sometimes is called **logical validity.** Using income as an indicator of social class seems to made sense "on the face of it" without a great deal of explanation. It has face validity.

---

of this dialogue is that respondents answering the questionnaire *after* the scandal becomes public perceive *more* sexual harassment in their lives than those who answered the questionnaire before the scandal broke.

As another example, let us suppose that you are presenting an argument that the reason the wages of males have declined in the past twenty years in the United States is because women have been entering the labor force. A student in an Introduction to Sociology class actually made this argument recently. His technique was more akin to dogmatic assertion than to the scientific method, and he was unaware that his methodology was funda-

mentally flawed. The pertinent question in terms of history and internal validity is: *What else was going on in the last twenty years that might account for declining wages?* There are a number of likely candidates, and each must be investigated and either accepted or rejected as a source of spuriousness. In statistics class you can learn how to perform the series of empirical and statistical investigations known collectively as "checking for spuriousness." Some factors other than X (competition by females in the job market) that could cause Y (a decline in male wages) follow:

■ The loss of world-market share in key areas of the U.S. economy (steel, automobiles, consumer goods, manufacture of aircraft, ship building, defense, and aerospace) immediately springs to mind as a likely candidate.

- The increasing concentration of ownership in important industries (e.g. publishing, print communications, video communications, defense) is another.

- The effects of the General Agreement on Trade and Tariffs (GATT) and of the North American Fair Trade Agreement (NAFTA).

The point is that according to the scientific way of knowing, in order to argue effectively that a decline in male wages is due to competition posed by women in the job market, one must control for (i.e., statistically and empirically investigate and then reject with known probabilities of error) each of the many other variables that could account for Y other than X.

2. *Maturation effects.* People are continually changing and maturing, whether or not they are part of a research study, and these changes affect the results of a research study. For instance, suppose a study evaluates the effectiveness of a particular intervention in reducing the amount of official delinquency, that is, delinquency known to the police. You design a longitudinal study, one that follows the same subjects across time. You randomly assign youth to one of two programs. In one (the control group) the youth receive the usual services for juvenile probationers in your county. In the other condition (experimental group), you manipulate the independent variable. You expose the subjects to intensive supervision and intensive services (school tutoring, mentoring, counseling, self-esteem enhancement, drug rehabilitation, etc.) Ten years later, you compare official offending rates during the tenth year for both samples of youth. Simply due to maturation, we would expect lowered rates of offending, even if youth received no services whatsoever. This phenomenon is called aging out or the maturation effect. The passage of time can account for reduced rates of offending.

3. *Beware the extremes: regression to the mean.* Sometimes subjects are included in a research study because of their extreme scores. For instance, a neighborhood might be included in a study because its mortality rate due to death by hand guns is five times the city average; a particular intervention designed to lower recidivism is pilot tested among twice-convicted felons. *From a clinical sociological viewpoint*, it makes sense to select as subjects those who appear to be most in need of intervention. *From a methodological viewpoint*, selecting only subjects with extreme scores as research subjects is not sound procedure due to the statistical tendency known as **regression to the mean.** Over time, extreme scores tend to regress to the mean, to the average, even without any intervention. This tendency can confound the interpretation of research results. It would be a serious error to attribute a lowering of extreme pretest scores on the posttest to an intervention (the independent variable), when it actually was a mere statistical artifact of regression to the mean.

Murray and Cox's study of the deterrence effect of two state training schools in Illinois is a good example (1979). In the juvenile-justice system in the United States, a *state training school* is the analogue of a medium- to high-security prison in the adult criminal-justice system. Placement in a state training school is the most severe disposition (sentence) in the juvenile-justice system in this country. In juvenile- and criminal-justice, *deterrence* refers to abstention from crime due to fear of punishment. There are two varieties of deterrence, *specific* (sometimes-called *special*) and *general. Specific deterrence* refers to punishing ego to prevent ego from committing crime. Thus, Fred steals money from a store. Fred is punished to prevent Fred from stealing money from a store again. That is an example of using punishment as a specific deterrent. *General deterrence* refers to punishing ego to prevent others who are law-abiding from committing crime. In the above example of Fred stealing money from a store, punishing Fred to prevent law-abiding Sally, Chinua, and Sam from stealing money from a store is an example of using punishment as a general deterrent.

Murray and Cox (1979) analyze the specific-deterrent effect of two state training schools in Illinois. The rehabilitative services (referred to by the juvenile-justice system and by the courts as *programming*) available in these institutions include basic schooling, (group) counseling, and regimentation. In other words, these youth are not "coddled." They receive the minimum programming acceptable to the U.S. Supreme Court. Murray and Cox find that in the youth released from these two training schools, crime is suppressed by 68%. The "average number of arrests during the 12 months prior to placement was 6.3 per youth but only 2.0 during the year after release" (Whitehead and Lab, 1996: 293). Murray and Cox conclude that traditional state training schools achieve specific deterrence.

Lundmann (1993) rightly criticizes the Murray and Cox study on the grounds of internal invalidity. Murray and Cox (1979) do not consider or control for the confounding effects of maturation, regression to the mean, and rehabilitation. *Maturation* as an alternate cause of desistence from crime indicates that time spent in the state training school is a time of personal development, which in itself might account for a decline in offending. *Rehabilitation* as an alternate cause of desistence from crime refers to the effect of programming in the state training schools. It is possible that the programming in the state training schools changed (i.e. reformed, saved) the youth from crime. Likewise, if a youth had been committing crime at a high rate and gets petitioned to the juvenile court, after release from state training school she or he most likely reverts back to her or his true mean or average, which is lower than the rate at which she or he had been offending immediately prior to being taken into custody and sent to a training school. This decline in rate of offending is simply *regression to the mean* and is not due to any intervention effect.

4. *The Hawthorne effect.* The Hawthorne effect refers to the confounding effects on research outcomes due to research subjects' responses to being studied. The term

derives from the series of studies conducted at the Western Electric Company's Hawthorne works between 1924 to 1932. Several of these studies find that each change by the researchers in employees' working conditions, even seemingly adverse ones like decreasing lighting by 50 to 70 percent, results in increased worker productivity. Although the specific causal elements are not well understood, the confounding effects of the research process on research results is termed **the Hawthorne effect** (Lang, 1992). The mere fact of engaging in research may enhance or degrade performance of research subjects, without any corresponding actual change in the underlying construct being measured.

5. *Instrumentation effects.* Some research designs call for testing research subjects both before (pretest) and after (posttest) the manipulation of the independent variable. If we use a different instrument to measure the dependent variable at $time_2$, it is imperative that we make sure that the two measures are comparable. If they are not, it is possible that the scores at $time_2$ were different merely because the test was different at $time_2$ than at $time_1$, even if there were no change in the underlying construct. If we use the same measurement instrument at both points in time, it is possible that the research subjects merely remember their answers to the questions at $time_1$ and give a different answer at $time_2$. **Instrumentation effects** refer to the confounding effects that repeated measures of the dependent variable have on research outcomes.

6. *Noncomparable groups.* Results do not have any meaning unless we have something with which to compare them. Comparisons do not have any meaning unless the two groups being compared are actually comparable. For instance, suppose we want to see if Native Americans living on reservations have similar cultural perceptions about a specific genre of movies as Native Americans who do not live on reservations (Shively, 1992). To find out, we ask for volunteers. We show a sample of Native Americans who have less than a high-school education, who hold working-

class jobs, and who live on a reservation a particular John Wayne cowboy-and-Indian movie. They fill out a questionnaire immediately after viewing the film. We show the same movie to a sample of Native Americans who are living in a middle-class suburb in a different region of the nation. They fill out the same questionnaire immediately after viewing the film. The problem here is that these two groups are not comparable, and lack of comparability poses a serious threat to internal validity. The differences in occupational level, in regional culture, and in educational level each could account for any observed differences in the responses to the questionnaire. If you use comparable groups in a study, it is not enough for you to say that the two groups are comparable. You must document their comparability.

7. *Diffusion or imitation of treatments.* If a research study involves an experimental group (that gets exposed to the independent variable), a control or comparison group (that does not get exposed to the independent variable), and an independent variable, it is possible that the independent variable has become diffused into mainstream culture. In that event, the subjects in the control or comparison group actually have been exposed to the experimental stimulus, and they do not constitute a real control or comparison group. This sometimes is referred to as the "contamination" of the control group.

For instance, let us say you want to compare the effects on mother-infant bonding of traditional hospital birthing practices verses more holistic birthing processes wherein the mother is supported by friends and family during the birthing process and wherein the mother receives no chemicals (painkillers, sedatives). You have selected as a sample ten women who plan on having a hospital birth and ten women who plan on using a midwife and having at-home births. In your comparison, you have not taken into account that many hospitals have birthing rooms that look very much like rooms at home. Family members and close friends are welcome in

these rooms during the birthing process. Medical personnel are sympathetic to and willing to practice "natural" birthing practices wherein no painkillers or other chemicals are used. The point is that many of the traditional advantages of birthing at home with a midwife have been incorporated into the birthing options offered by many hospitals. In this case, the control group in fact has been contaminated, which undermines the internal validity of the study.

8. *Mortality.* The term mortality refers to research subjects dropping out of a study. In a longitudinal study, mortality can be especially problematic for the accurate interpretation of research results. For instance, a mortality rate of two percent per year does not sound very serious, does it? Nonetheless, over a twenty-five year study, this means that 50% of the original sample has dropped out of the study. **Experimental mortality** poses a serious threat to internal validity.

9. *Ambiguity regarding causal time order.* There is a possibility that the causal time-order is not clear. Whenever this occurs, a research conclusion that the independent variable caused the dependent variable can be challenged by the explanation that the dependent variable actually caused changes in the independent variable.

The preceding nine factors that pose a challenge to internal validity do no exhaust the possibilities. *Can you think of additional factors that pose challenges to the internal validity of a research study? Tell us about them. (If you came up blank, please see Earl Babbie, 1995: 243–244 for some ideas.)*

Ethics of Research with Human Subjects

An **ethic** is a principle of right or of good conduct. *Ethics* refers to the study of the general nature of morals and of concrete moral choices. Whenever we engage in research involving human subjects, it is necessary that we follow the ethical guidelines that prevail in sociology (American Sociological Association, 1989) and in allied disciplines. These ethical guidelines include the following eight:

1. *Voluntary participation.* The research subjects need to be informed that their participation in the study is strictly voluntary and that they may withdraw without penalty at any time they choose and that they may expect no rewards for participation (e.g., early release from prison, custody of their children).

2. *Informed consent.* Before they are included in a study, all subjects must be fully informed about the consequences of participation—psychological, emotional, economic, physical, and so forth. In participating, subjects sometimes are asked to confront aspects of themselves or of their lives that may be particularly painful. Subjects need to be informed of this ahead of time. Please see anonymity and confidentiality below.

3. *Do no harm.* Just as physicians take an oath to do no harm, so, too, social researchers must do no harm to the subjects in a research project. As researchers, we must not embarrass them, degrade them, endanger their friendships or relationships with family members or with employers, lower their self-esteem, and so forth.

   For instance, if we are conducting research in a small community, and if we include direct quotations from respondents, it is possible that a respondent or other members of the community may be able to recognize a response as having been made by a particular individual. That may cause a person embarrassment or worse. Similarly, research subjects might request a copy of the research report, and the research report may be published as a popular book. Research subjects may be able to identify themselves in various tables in the report and might find themselves characterized as highly authoritarian, homophobic, racist, and anti-democratic. Some of the characterizations are likely to threaten their sense of self worth. Thus, while doing no harm to subjects is easy to accept in the abstract, it is sometimes difficult to execute in particular situations.

4. *Anonymity.* The researcher protects the identity of all research subjects. By doing this, the researcher helps to protect them from harm. When a researcher promises **anonymity,** the researcher is unable to identify a particular response with a particular respondent.

5. *Confidentiality.* When a researcher promises **confidentiality,** the researcher *is* able to identify a particular response with a particular respondent but promises not to do so publicly. If a subject's participation is confidential but not anonymous, the researcher has an ethical obligation to make this known to the subject as part of informed consent.

6. *No deception.* It is unethical to deceive research subjects. Deception, if used in sociological or social-science research, needs to be justified and outweighed by compelling scientific or administrative concerns. Even then, the ethics remain arguable, questionable. For instance, when I conducted research on gender, situation, and perception of threat, I informed the research subjects (students in social science classes) that I was interested in their responses to certain stimuli. I told the students that the stimuli were pictures and that there were no right or wrong answers. I did not tell them that the pictures were Thematic Apperception Tests (TATs) from Harvard University. I did not lie to the students, but I did not spell out exactly what I was looking for either. TATs are well known "projective tests," and, informing the research subjects of the precise identity of the pictures may have resulted in eliciting from them responses prototypically consistent with this research tradition. This concern is called the problem of demand characteristics. **Demand characteristics** are cues that signal to the research subjects what behavior is expected of them. The researcher must avoid using demand characteristics.

7. *Analysis.* As a researcher, you have ethical obligations to your colleagues in the scientific community. You have the ethical obligation to be straightforward about the findings, shortcomings, and failures of your study. Avoid the temptation to make findings sound like the result of a well-planned study when they are not. Many findings in science are serendipitous.

Learning Exercise 4.1

Application of Sociological Concepts

Write an essay in which you analyze Laud Humphreys' research on tearoom trade In light of the guidelines for research involving human subjects, indicating which guidelines are followed and which are violated. Give examples to support the points you are making.

_____

_____

_____

_____

_____

_____

_____

_____

_____

_____

■   ■   ■

8. *Reporting.* If there are findings that undermine the point you are making, you have the ethical obligation to report them and to discuss their implications for the findings of your study. If you have findings that are surprising or anomalous, you have the ethical obligation to report them as such.

Thus, during one fall and spring semester I collected data from students enrolled in social-science courses at a Midwestern state university for the purpose of studying the relationship among gender, situation, and the perception of threat. To that end, subjects were administered several Thematic Apperception Tests (TAT), some of which used pictorial cues and others of which used verbal cues. During the reading and scoring of those protocols, I was impressed by what seemed a barrage of negative portrayals of the women depicted as holding scientific positions in the TATs. These negative portrayals included those of scientists as "mad"/insane; as traitors; as illicit drug manufacturers, dealers, or users; and as persons whose relational lives were in shambles. This anomalous finding served as a stimulus for me to engage in the previously discussed analysis of gender-based perceptions of women in science (Donovan, 1990).

It's a Matter of Perspective

Let us see how several disciplines in the social sciences might formulate a *statement of the problem*, with miscellaneous intervention techniques and social policies:

TABLE 4.4. Academic Disciplines, Problem Statement, and Social Interventions or Policies

Academic Discipline	Statement of Problem	Intervention or Social Policy
Psychology	Individuals with low self-esteem place themselves in situations that they could avoid if they had better conventional-living and decision-making skills. This teenager's self-esteem is low due to his interactions with peers in his socio-economic group who make decisions to commit acts of violence. They are at high risk for being victims of acts of violence, including murder. Records indicate Wesley's behavior includes patterns of violence and of acting-out. Intervention techniques for six months were ineffective. Diagnosis: DSM IV Oppositional Defiant Conduct Disorder.	Teenagers who are committed by the juvenile court to secure confinement and who have low self-esteem should participate in both one-on-one therapy and peer-group therapy, so that they can improve their self-esteem. This will facilitate their reintegration into the community. Implement ongoing treatment in the community through one-on-one therapy. Wesley should be counseled about alcohol and drug abuse through established community programs. HIV/AIDS education should be implemented. Violent outbursts could be controlled through the use of psychotropic drugs.
Social Work	This teenager comes from a dysfunctional home. Mother reports that she had no control over the teenager's dropping out of school or joining a gang. State should have placed this teenager under court custody and separated him from his family of origin and placed him either in foster care or in a residential group home. A reintegration plan should have included parenting-skills classes for Wesley, his mother, and the grandmother. Wesley has very low self-esteem.	Create community-based outreach programs for juveniles, such as mentoring programs (Big Brother, Big Sister), dispute-resolution workshops, and night basketball games organized by local mental-health organizations (Anderson, 1994; Becker, 1994; Grossman and Garry, 1997). This would facilitate intervention regarding youth-gang influences. Create community-based job-training programs oriented towards obtaining GED and towards integration into the labor market. Institute effective parenting workshops for Wesley, the mother, and the grandmother.

Police and
Law Enforcement

Police are understaffed, underpaid, and overworked. Calls to police in low-income areas of the city are at an all-time high. Youth gangs have more sophisticated weapons than do police. Laws concerning search and seizure hinder police efforts to control crime in these areas. The courts and criminal-justice system do not act as deterrents to juvenile crime (Torbet, 1997). Judges are too "soft" on perpetrators giving them reduced sentences. Thus, the penal system allows dangerous teenagers back on the streets where they continue to commit more crime. Police officers' role as enforcers of law has been expanded. Police officers are not equipped to handle family and teenage types of problems, especially the problems faced by single-parent families.

Hire and train more police. Adjust salaries of police officers so that salaries of police officers are proportional to their qualifications, including educational qualifications, and to the comparable worth of their profession. This should help to reduce police "burn-out."

Require all police officers to obtain and to sustain helping and counseling skills. This would facilitate better relations with their communities. Police should have regular walking "beats" where they get to know, and become integrated into, the community. Construct and staff local police stations in these communities so there is a police presence. Institute community policing (Cox, 1996). This facilitates better relations with the community. Amend laws so that police can arrest known trouble makers, drug dealers, and gang members. Construct more youth detention centers. Create more "boot camps" for juveniles. Pass legislation so that violent youthful offenders can be prosecuted and sentenced as adults. Pass legislation so that there are stiff mandatory sentences for violent youthful offenders and so that violent youth serve the maximum sentence without possibility of parole. Extend the "three times and you are out" law for felony crime to include violent youth with a history of vicious criminal behavior. Accomplish this by passing violent predator statutes similar to the sexual predator statutes, so that it is possible to place youth in secure mental-health facilities after they have finished serving their sentences in secure facilities. Create mandatory sentencing guidelines for juvenile court.

Increase family-preservation services, so that single-parent household can learn the skills of effective parenting and of household maintenance. Prosecute, fine, and jail landlords who do not maintain their rental properties. Enact legislation that mandates, on pain of felony prosecution, that the landlord live in one of her/his rental properties until all of her/his rental properties are brought up to code.

Increase opportunity structures in mainstream society to decrease drift into the cultures of violence and crime. Increase the number of drug and alcohol detoxification centers. Increase job-training opportunities through local community colleges and through local business schools. Eliminate huge housing projects, which, under current conditions, are unsafe (high rates of crime victimization). Replace huge housing projects with homes. For the able bodied and for those not otherwise employed, these homes

Sociology

Historically, in American society, youth gangs have been an integral part of the urban landscape. Each immigrant population developed gangs as a response to cultural assimilation. Youth gangs are part of a subterranean youth culture. Liebow (1967) and Whyte (1988/1943) suggest that youth gangs are highly organized with structures of power, respect, and authority. Youth gangs function to supplement an underground economy, to provide a social system of support, and to help young people integrate themselves into the larger community (Bloch and Niederhoffer, 1958).

The apparent recent proliferation of youth gangs in economically underdeveloped urban areas is not something new or novel (Butterfield, 1994; Moore, 1997). Modern youth gangs are mere extensions of old gang structures; they closely resemble tribes with chiefs as leaders. The increase in violence of these gangs is caused by a deterioration of informal social control and by participation in illicit drugs. Single-parent households often are unable adequately to socialize and socially to control their youth. Single-parent households have increased dramatically as economic conditions have deteriorated in the inner cities.

Many landlords do not maintain their rental properties adequately, so that children get removed from homes that are unsafe due to broken windows, bad plumbing, peeling paint on the walls, holes in the floor and walls that allow the entry of rats and other vermin.

In the 1980s the legitimate opportunity structures—well paying manually skilled and semi-skilled jobs in the conventional labor force—by means of which these youth could integrate themselves into conventional mainstream American society, declined. Poor minority inner-city youth created an alternative and illegitimate opportunity structure: illicit drug sales (Merton, 1938). Many single parents lack the skills and resources by means of which they could adequately socialize their own children. These children do not learn to obey parents and to say "No" to drugs.

As economic structures deteriorate in urban areas, as social-support services to poor families get cut back even further, we should expect more teenagers to be attracted to the "magic bullet" of youth gangs that appear to promise short-term profits and high status. A "culture of violence" will develop in the void of inadequate informal social control.

The problem of rising health costs is endemic to the health- care delivery system in the USA. There have been few incentives to keep costs down. Private insurance companies have an incentive to insure only healthy individuals. The de-industrialization of the 1980s left many families without adequate health insurance. Many individuals and families turn to emergency-room service, the most expensive care, as their only primary-care agency. In a fee-for-service health-care system, the uninsured poor cannot receive care elsewhere. There are incentives for medical-school students to go into specialized medicine, leaving lower-status and lower-paid family physicians caring for the majority of the population. Many physicians are located in urban areas, leaving rural populations under served.

should be constructed by those who will occupy them. The federal government should regulate mortgage rates, so that prohibitively high interest rates are not charged. Provide incentives for maintaining these homes in good condition while acting as informal agents of social control.

Provide free licensed daycare to allow parents to gain and to retain employment. Employment integrates adults into mainstream conventional society.

Males and females should not be given incentives to bear children out of wedlock. Instead, the female should receive allowances for one child, with adequate access to health-care and to birth control. The father of the child should be mandated to pay child support. Abortion should be available upon request during the first trimester of pregnancy. Any hospital that does not receive federal funds does not need to provide access to abortion services for members of the community.

Health care (including dental, eye-care, and hearing), paid for by a health-care tax, should be available to all persons. Private hospitals should recognize that they cannot provide all services while keeping costs manageable. Instead, regional hospitals could be a key component of a unified system of care. Increase the number of primary-care physicians available for family practice. Emphasize preventive medicine: incentives should be instituted for preventing serious diseases and illnesses. Prevention decreases health-care costs.

We can see that each discipline makes different assumptions about what variables are important in interpreting the teenager's final plight. Moreover, each perspective recommends different interventions and social policies.

Psychologists view the teenager's behavior as due to deficits of "self-esteem." Therapeutic techniques are viewed as the solution for violent acting out and for "oppositional behavior disorder." Little or no recognition is given to environmental, social, or political issues, other than helping Wesley to achieve higher self-esteem so that he can cope with the environment. Based on the psychological view, we could formulate the following hypotheses:

- Increasing decision-making skills increases self-esteem.
- Increasing conventional living skills leads to increases in self-esteem.
- Increases in self-esteem lead to decreases in acts of violence.

Each of these hypotheses can be operationalized. Each of these hypotheses can be tested using a pretest-posttest quasi-experimental research design. Once this particular study is begun, it will take six months to collect the data.

In the pretest condition, 200 youth diagnosed with oppositional behavior disorder are measured on level of self-esteem. Youth are then randomly assigned to the experimental or to the control group.

In the control group, termed regular probation, youth send a postcard to their probation officer once a month. This procedure is not uncommon for property offenders in large urban counties. This procedure or something very much like it, might even be recommended by sociologists who adhere to "labeling theory."

In the experimental group, youth participate three or four times each week in workshops and in clinical counseling sessions that stress reality-therapy, a therapeutic modality designed to assist the youth to assist themselves in improving both their conventional decision-making and conventional-living skills.

After three months of participating in these conditions, all 200 youth are measured on level of self-esteem. After another three months, all 200 youths are measured on the number of violent acts they committed within the preceding three months. The hypotheses lead us to expect that increases in decision-making skills and conventional-living skills are associated with increases in self-esteem. *How would you operationalize the concept, "conventional-living skills"? How would you operationalize the concept "conventional decision-making skills"?* Also, increases in self-esteem should be associated with a decrease in the number of acts of violence. In operationalizing the concept "acts of violence," both self-report measures and official measures could be used. Five self-report measures of the concept "acts of violence" are the following:

Activity Response

	Yes	No

Have you ever attacked or threatened anyone in any of the following ways within the past three months?

1. With a weapon, for instance with a gun or knife?
2. With anything like a baseball bat, frying pan, scissors, or stick?
3. By throwing something, like a bottle or a rock?
4. By grabbing, punching, or choking?
5. Any attack or threat or use of force?
   Please mention it even if you are not certain that it was a crime.

The social-work perspective incorporates more environmental factors in its explanation and understanding of the teenager's final plight. Dysfunctional families are those whose role boundaries are not clearly defined. As a result, individuals in subordinate positions assume the roles of supraordinates and norms of appropriate behavior are not socialized and appropriated. The conventional socialization process is disrupted. Normal bonding among members is not accomplished. As a result, mechanisms of informal social control are not established.

From the social-work formulation, we could formulate the following hypotheses:

- Increased self-esteem leads to better conventional living skills (wears clean clothes, bathes regularly, brushes teeth a couple of times each day, attends school, does homework on time, performs chores at home, reduction in number of violent acts, engages in non-violent dispute resolution).
- Increased self-esteem leads to decreased school drop-out rates.
- Participating in family-preservation services leads to increases in social control of children.
- Participation in family-preservation services leads to decreases in violent acting-out behaviors of children.
- Participation in family-preservation services leads to increased self-esteem of children.
- Participation in mentoring programs increases self-esteem of children.

A researcher could test these hypotheses with a pretest-posttest quasi-experimental research design. For instance, in the pretest, two hundred youth about to be released from a residential group home are tested on level of self-esteem. Then, 200 youth released from a residential group home are randomly assigned either to a control group or to an experimental group.

The control group receives regular aftercare (parole), wherein the youth sends the parole officer a postcard once each month. The experimental group receives family-preservation services and mentoring. In family-preservation services, one specially trained social worker is available twenty-four hours a day, seven days a

week, for a six-week period. (After that, the social worker also is available on an as-needed basis.) The social worker is available to help the family to help itself to learn to function as a healthy, cohesive family unit. Also, Wesley participates once each two weeks in a 3 to 4 hour mentoring program.

After six weeks, all 200 youth are measured on self-esteem. Six months later, all 200 youths are measured for dropping out of school, the number of acting-out behaviors within the past six months, the number of violent behaviors within the past six months, the number of times the youth was taken into custody or referred to the juvenile (or criminal) court. The families of the two hundred youths also are measured for the extent of being a "functional" family.

We would expect that families that successfully completed the family-preservation services would be more functional. We could have "blind" raters evaluate the families in terms of extent of being "functional." We would expect that youth who participated in family preservation services would have higher rates of school retention, higher levels of self-esteem, and lower rates of violent acting out, lower rates of being taken into custody, and lower rates of arrest than the controls. We would expect youth that participated in mentoring programs to have higher self-esteem than the controls.

The police and penology perspective also is very testable. In its formulation this perspective points out that police officers are ill prepared to handle modern domestic issues. Police are trained to enforce the law, to investigate, to arrest, to fingerprint, and to interrogate. In many jurisdictions, however, they are *not* educated in how to handle family problems. Examples of family problems are parents, children, and other relatives who act out violently and who use drugs. The teaching of counseling skills as a required part of an on-going in-service training program required of all police officers might allow police better to intervene in volatile domestic situations. Moreover, as police have more presence as community counselors and as community problem solvers, there is an increase in the likelihood both of police officers becoming more effective as agents of social control and of being perceived by community members as allies of all who live in the community rather than as their enemy.

From the police and penology perspective we could formulate the following hypotheses:

- In-service training of police officers in family counseling skills makes police officers more effective in responding to domestic crimes.
- In-service training of police officers in family counseling skills improves police-community relations.
- Police walking beats reduces fear of crime.
- Community policing strategies improve community-police relations.
- Increasing police wages and community-policing strategies lead to lower rates of police burnout.

A researcher could test these hypotheses with a pretest posttest quasi-experimental research design. For instance, in the pretest, a random sample of community members fills out a questionnaire designed to assess the extent of the fear of crime and the quality of community-police relations. Also, as part of the pretest, the police officers fill out an anonymous and confidential questionnaire regarding their perceptions about the level of stress and burnout in their jobs. As part of the pretest, a random sample of family members who had experienced police intervention within the past six months are interviewed to find out their perceptions regarding their level of satisfaction with police interactions in those domestic contacts. Community policing policies are then begun. Researchers survey the community to find out, from the point of view of community members, what the police can do for the community and what the priorities of community members are in terms of police services. The police then target their resources toward fulfilling those perceived needs. Police also begin walking regular "beats" in parts of town where fear of crime is the highest. Police officers also begin participating in an ongoing series of workshops designed to impart family-counseling skills.

One year after the initiation of these changes, researchers posttest a random sample of community members on the extent of their fear of crime and on the extent of community-police relations. Also, part of the posttest consists of a random sample of police officers filling out an

anonymous and confidential questionnaire to ascertain their perceptions regarding the current levels of stress and burnout they are experiencing in their jobs. Also, in the posttest, researchers interview a random sample of family members who had experienced police intervention in a domestic situation within the past six months. The goal is to obtain respondents' perceptions regarding their level of satisfaction with police interactions in those domestic contacts.

Our hypotheses lead us to expect lowered levels of police burnout, a reduction the level of fear of crime in neighborhoods where police walk regular "beats," improved police-community relations, and increased levels of satisfaction with police officers who had responded to domestic problems.

The sociological perspective on urban violence is macro theoretical and structural in its formulation. By placing violence in an historical frame of reference, sociologists often are able to offer insight into the nature of urban violence, youth gangs, delinquency, and crime. Social historians document that in England, France, Italy, and the Netherlands, homicide rates were extraordinarily high in during the Middle Ages. Then, in the 16th and 17th centuries, an increase in state power helped to curb impulsive, violent behavior, and murder rates declined. For instance, the homicide rate in Amsterdam dropped from 47 per 100,000 people in the mid 15th century to 1.5 per 100,000 in the early years of the nineteenth century (Butterfield, 1994). The murder rate in medieval England was 10 times higher than that of twentieth-century England; and a study of the university town of Oxford by social historian Lawrence Stone of Princeton University indicates that in the 1340s Oxford's murder rate was 110 per 100,000 people per year. Studies of London in the first half of the fourteenth century indicate that the homicide rate varied from 36 to 52 per 100,000 people per year. These rates far exceed the 1993 homicide rate of New York City, 25.9 per 100,000 population, and the 1996 rate for the United States, which preliminary figures place at 7.3 per 100,000 population per year (Butterfield, 1997). So, in the late 16th and 17th centuries an increase in state power reduced the rates of violent behavior, including murder. This decline continued until the 1960s, at which time around the world homicide rates did an about face. Why this about face?

The sociological perspective provides theoretically based explanations that direct our attention to structural reasons for violent youth behavior from the 1960s through the 1990s. For instance, by suggesting that youth gangs now are a culture of violence conditioned by a vacuum of informal familial social control, by limited opportunity structures, and by the objective socio-economic position of many youth in the inner cities, the sociological view suggests that the important independent variables are structural in nature. From these theories we could formulate the following sociological hypotheses:

- As economic structures deteriorate in urban areas, youth gang membership increases.
- As legitimate opportunity structures increase in urban areas, youth gang membership declines.

One way to test these hypotheses is by engaging in secondary analysis of official data. For instance, we could construct measures of "economic opportunity structures" for several large cities in the United States. Also, we could locate survey data on the extent of gang membership for those large cities, and we could locate data on the age-structure of those cities from the U.S. Census or from *Current Population Reports,* both of which are published by the federal government. For the large cities we have selected, we could locate data on the extent of youth crime from the F.B.I.'s annual *Uniform Crime Reports.* These hypotheses are readily testable.

Summary

Whether we want to formulate a research question from a sociological or social science point of view, it is possible to construct valid and reliable measures of the independent and dependent variables. In the social sciences, we assume that *everything social can be measured and tested.* Conceptualization, measurement, and testing simply require scientific thinking about ordinary problems.

Procedures of Empirical Investigation: Transparent Methodology

An essential part of any research report is a clear, detailed, and complete exposition of the research procedures on which the study is based. Please read and study Figure 4.3, "Transparent Methodology." Researchers report all aspects of the methods used in the study.

One way of expressing this aspect of a research report is to say that the methodology is *transparent.* Nothing is hidden, all is clearly, precisely described. After reading the research report, other scientists would know how to conduct the same study on the same or on a similar population or sample.

Field Research: Qualitative Methodology

Qualitative methodology (also called *qualitative analysis*) refers to analysis or methodology that is not based on precise measurement and quantitative claims or statements. For instance, if our goal is to acquire a subjective understanding of a particular group of people, we might make observations of their daily lives without counting instances of particular behaviors. Such research could be described as *qualitative.*

Field research refers to a way of knowing "that results from deep involvement in, or intimate familiarity with, the settings, activities, and persons studied" (Holstein and Gubrium, 1992: 711). Field research examines people as they go about their everyday lives. Any and all research that has this characteristic—that takes place "in the field"—may be referred to as field research. Field researchers avoid as much as possible any alterations of or artificial interference with the settings and persons studied. They conduct formal and informal interviews. They make observations of activities, interactions, events, and settings. They interact with and talk with people in naturalistic settings. They inspect formal documents (an organization's mission statement, grant proposals) and informal documents (e.g., unpublished diaries, letters).

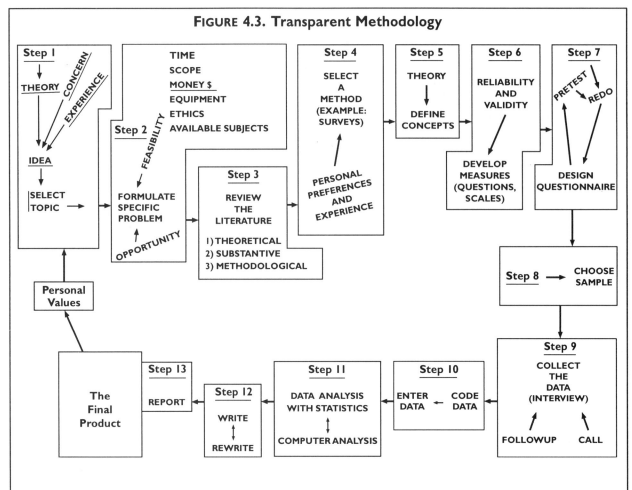

FIGURE 4.3. Transparent Methodology

TRANSPARENT METHODOLOGY = "The complete exposition of the process of doing research, reporting all aspects of the methods and experiences involved in a project.—Making methodology and the research process public."
"There are two worlds in which we live: one we experience and from which we learn—another we live."

The ultimate goal of field research is the development of theoretical insights about social life. A more immediate goal is to produce an **ethnography**—an empirically based analytical description of social life. There are many approaches to the analysis of field data. Many have in common the goal of producing theoretical generalizations based on field observations. An example of this inductive approach is Barney Glaser and Anselm Strauss's **grounded theory** (1967). Glaser and Strauss coined the term *grounded theory* to refer to the inductive method of observing social life and then developing theory through observation.

Listening and seeing are skills we must acquire if we want to engage successfully in field research. We can learn and hone these skills with practice. Listening skills are impera-

tive in field research. To be listened to by another is to be understood and to be respected. Listening also is an effective way to generate reliable data. A field researcher must learn to listen quietly and to take very careful field notes *into which she or he does not interject personal opinions without labeling them as such.* The trained observer is patient and unobtrusive.

Engaging in field observation is not a one-time experience. It is conducted on more than one occasion, over a period of time. Ideally, field observations should be conducted when one is not under time constraint, stress, or emotional duress. Human beings have limited attentional resources. If we are thinking about the meeting we must attend in twenty minutes, or about our hot date tomorrow night, or about the fight we had with our significant other last night, we have few, if any, attentional resources to devote to field observations. Emotions and moods influence perception.

The field researcher dresses appropriately. In this regard, there is a learning curve. Dressing appropriately means that the researcher is aware of the participants' definition of appropriate attire. It takes time to discover and to learn these definitions. Thus, a sociologist friend of mine was interviewing working-class dockworkers, and he dressed like a dockworker. The dockworkers were offended. They knew he was a college professor *pretending* to be one of them. Dressing appropriately means understanding the definition of the situation from the point of view of the participants.

Field observers need to take precise field notes. Why? Memory is fragile and it degrades quickly. Memory fails us. Learn to discipline yourself so that you record all observations immediately after observations are made. Be sure to record day, date, year, time, exact location, and confidential names of those being observed.

For social workers, psychologists, and others in the helping or human-service professions, making and keeping precise field records is especially important. In court, professionals may be questioned about the precise location, the specific persons who were present, the year, month, date, time of day, and so forth. It is not good enough to say, "I am not sure, but I *think* it happened this day,' or "I think he said this or that." Remember: those in helping professions may be called as expert witnesses in court. They may be called to testify in court (in delinquency hearings, in child-custody hearings, in child-abuse investigations, in spousal-abuse cases, etc.). *They have a great deal of power over the lives of others.* Logging daily reports may be tedious, it may be time-consuming, and it may be difficult to acquire the discipline to do it, but if you do not like doing it, do not engage in field research. Also, please remember that you are professionally responsible for your field notes. Do not leave them out in plain sight where others—your roommates, the custodial personnel, or passersby—may read them. You do not want to violate the confidentiality or anonymity of those you observe.

In field research, we should take notes about, and draw diagrams of, props and gateways of communication. Props include telephones, desks, signs on desks (that say "Dr. Donovan," or "Susan Beach, Attorney at Law"), briefcases, laptop computers, skirted suits, suits and ties, etc. Gateways of communication include windows up to which customers step in order to talk with the receptionist, a door on which students knock to speak with a professor, etc. We also always should be attentive to body language. Communication is 90% nonverbal. Does the clerk look at you with unfocused eyes, point a finger at your nose, use an unnecessarily loud voice to converse with clients? Field research skills can be honed through practice.

In **participant observation** the researcher joins and participates in a group, culture, or subculture, and over time, investigates, in great detail, the group's attitudes, values, norms, and views of the world from that group's perspective. This method is commonly used by sociologists and anthropologists to investigate a particular group, culture, or subculture. In this approach researchers must decide the roles they will occupy in the setting—complete observer, participant as observer, observer as participant, or complete participant, among others. The ethics of covert field research are debated by sociologists and by other field researchers (Denzin, 1989). In participant observation the researcher exists in two worlds—the one of the investigator and the other of the participant.

With this approach one is able to discover the myths, norms, symbols, nonverbal communications, leadership structures, cliques, hierarchy, rituals, and kinship patterns of the group. Good examples of research utilizing participant observation as a data-gathering methodology include Elliot Liebow's *Tally's Corner* (1967), William Foote Whyte's *Street Corner Society* (1955), Spradley and Mann's *The Cocktail Waitress* (1976), Napoleon Chagnon's *The Yanomamo* (1983), Kai T. Erikson's *All in Its Path* (1976), and Howard Becker's *Boys in White* (1961) and *The Outsider* (1963). This research strategy is often important in initial contact with groups about which little or no scientific knowledge is available. One can use this method to develop a better conceptual understanding. In some instances, data that are collected via participant observation by cultural anthropologists are later compiled by other social scientists into a data archive. These data archives then are used by researchers to discover overall patterns of cultural social organization in particular types of societies or in particular types of social groups (Lenski, Nolan, and Lenski, 1995). Thus anthropologist George Peter Murdock located hundreds of ethnographic studies and placed the data in an archive known as the Human Relations Area File. Sociologists Gerhard and Jean Lenski engaged in secondary analysis of these data and thereby empirically constructed a theory of social stratification (Lenski, 1966).

Survey Research: Quantitative Methodology

One variety of quantitative analysis is survey research. **Survey research** refers to the systematic gathering of data about individuals and collectivities through use of the interview or questionnaire, analyzing the resulting data through statistical analyses, and interpreting the results. Survey research is widely cited as the most frequently used data-gathering technique used by sociologists.

The purpose of survey research may be descriptive (e.g., the U.S. Census), exploratory, or even causal. Descriptive research relies heavily on descriptive statistics. Descriptive surveys mainly analyze the data in percentage frequency counts and report it in tabular form. For instance, in a general election in the U.S. the percent of women, of African-Americans, and of Hispanics who vote for a particular political party's presidential candidate may be compared with comparable results from previous years. Or the percent of women in the U.S. who favor U.S. military intervention in Bosnia-Herzegovina is compared with the percent of men who favor such intervention.

If one's purpose is to test theoretical hypotheses or to argue cause and effect, one uses other statistical techniques, techniques learned when you take statistics courses and research-methods courses, particularly at the graduate student level. These techniques include causal modeling and multivariate statistical analyses, such as regression analyses with dummy varia-

bles. The point is that the purpose of research influences the research design, including the design of surveys. A survey may be described as consisting of three parts—sampling, questioning, and data analysis. We now examine each of these.

Sampling

Probability Sampling

In statistics, a distinction is made between a *sample* and a population. A **population** is **the** total number of cases with a given characteristic or characteristics, or all members of a given class or set. Thus, we may speak of the population of females in the United States, or the population of white males in Kansas, or the population of convicted felons in the United States. A **sample** is part of a population.

To people unfamiliar with the theory of probability and with the theory of sampling, it seems mysterious that a sample of 1500 persons could represent the voting intentions of people aged 21 years or older in the United States. It also seems bewildering that those 1500 persons can be used to estimate, within known degrees of error, the extent to which values calculated from it (say, the percent who say they would vote for a particular candidate for President) are likely to deviate from the values that would have been obtained had the entire population of persons aged 21 or older been surveyed. The estimate of that error is known as *sampling error.*

Estimates of (the amount of) sampling error can only be made legitimately if one is using probability sampling. A sample is a **probability sample** if it has been drawn in accord with *probability theory*. Probability theory is part of mathematics, but it is heavily relied upon by social scientists. You can learn more about probability theory and about probability sampling in statistics and research-methods courses. For now, let us point out that in probability sampling, some mechanism of random sampling is used to select respondents. A **random sample** is one in which every case in the population has an equal probability of being selected. For instance, in a random sample of adults aged 21 years or older in the

United States, every person aged 21 or older in the U.S. would have the same chance of being selected. In a random sample of households, each household has the same chance of being selected. Examples of probability sampling techniques include area probability sampling, simple random sampling, stratified sampling, and systematic sampling. Please read Box 4.3 entitled "Some Varieties of Probability Samples." When we use probability-sampling techniques, we may legitimately generalize the results from our sample to a larger population.

Of course, it is one thing to draw a sample according to the scientific principles of probability sampling. It is altogether another thing to approach each of these people and to secure their voluntary full participation in a social survey. People may not cooperate. Not to cooperate in a social survey is their right and their option. To the extent that intended respondents do not participate, the scientific character of the survey is jeopardized. This is *the problem of non-response.* Probability theory assumes a 100% response rate. "The degree of jeopardy (technically termed 'bias') is a function of both the amount of nonresponse and the extent to which the nonrespondents differ from those who do respond" (Schuman, 1992: 2120). If, as is the case in the United States, young African-American and Hispanic males are more likely than other categories of persons to be missed in social surveys, the results of the surveys do not adequately represent the entire population. The U.S. census perennially struggles with the problem of bias. One marker of scientifically adequate survey is the information provided concerning nonresponse (Schuman, 1992).

Non-Probability Sampling

A sample is a **non-probability sample** if it is *not* possible to determine the probability—the statistical chance—that each case in the population has of being included in the sample. The proverbial "person on the street" interview is an example of a non-probability sample. Examples of non-probability samples include samples of convenience (sometimes called accidental sampling), purposive sampling (sometimes called judgmental sampling), snowball sampling, and quota sampling. Please read Box 4.4 entitled "Some Varieties of Non-Probability Samples."

As consumers of survey information, we all need to remember that when we use nonprobability sampling techniques, we *cannot* legitimately generalize the results from the sample to a larger population. Non-probability sampling approaches lack justification for estimating sampling error and for generalizing results to a larger population. Consumers of survey information—which is all of us—need to be aware of the vast differences that exist in the quality of sampling. All sampling techniques are not equal. The results of all sampling techniques should not be given equal credence. As sociologist Howard Schuman phrases this (1992: 2120), "It is definitely not the case . . . that all published results deserve equal confidence." As you study, learn, and apply the materials in this research-methods chapter to the evaluation of information, you will become a more discerning consumer of information.

Questioning

Asking people questions as a way of gathering information for analysis and interpretation is often used in survey research, in field work, and even in experiments. There are various modes of question administration. An interviewer in an interview may ask the questions. The interview may take place face-to-face or over the telephone. The questions may be written down. If written down, a researcher might give or mail the questions to the respondents who are asked to complete them. This procedure is termed *self-administration.* Whatever the mode of administration, we may refer to the sets of questions as *questionnaires.* When an interviewer asks the questions, we may refer to the questionnaire as an *interview schedule.* When the questions are written down and given or mailed to respondents to complete, we may refer to the questionnaires as self-administered questionnaires (Rubin and Babbie, 1993).

In designing questions, a researcher must decide whether to ask *open-ended questions,* to which the respondents provide answers of their own design. For instance, community members might be asked, "What do you feel is the most important problem facing your community today with regard to which the police could be of service?" An interviewer could write down the exact response of the respondent, or a space

BOX 4.3

Some Varieties of Probability Samples

Area sampling: This is a type of sample wherein the participants are selected on the basis of geographical location. The total area to be sampled is divided up into geographical areas, from which a random sample is selected. These, in turn, are divided into areas, from which a random sample is selected. From these areas, a randomly chosen set of cases is studied. (Sometimes called **multi-stage cluster sampling.**)

For instance, let us say you live in a city and you want to interview 100 households in this city. There are 1,000 blocks in this city. You have taken some research-methods classes, and you know that you want to interview 5 households per city block. In stage 1, you identify each of the 1,000 blocks in the city, you give each one a code number, and you randomly select 20 blocks. In stage 2, for each of the twenty randomly selected blocks, you list all households by their address for each block. In stage 3, you select a random number between one and ten, for each block. You will use that number as your "starting number" for each block. Thus, for the first block, let us say that its random starting number is 3 and that that there are 21 households on this block. From the list for this block, you select #3 and every 4th household after that. (You select household #3, #7, #11, #16, and #19 from this block.) You repeat the process on each of the 19 remaining blocks.

You already have a randomly selected "starting" number between 1 and 10 for each of the blocks. So, for each of the re- maining blocks, you construct a list of each of the households on the block. The number of house- holds divided by 5 = the sam- pling **interval** —the standard- ized distance between elements (households) selected from a population for a sample. You start with your random start number as the first household, and then select every Xth (Xth = sampling interval) household.

Simple random sample: Every element in the population has an equal chance of being se- lected in the sample. This is a useful sample design for a fairly homogeneous population.

Let us say that you want to select a simple random sample of students enrolled at your col- lege or university. You define what you mean by "stu- dent"—Does it include every person who takes as much as 1 credit hour? Or, are you refer- ring only to "full-time" stu- dents (e.g., 12 credit hours per semester for undergraduates, 9 credit hours for graduate stu- dents). Do "extension" courses count? You have to operational- ize what you mean by "stu- dent."

Your college has 6,000 stu- dents and you decide to sample 300 of them.

Let us say that your college or university has a list of every person, by name and address, by the number of credit hours per semester that they are tak- ing, and that you have legiti- mate access to this list for the purpose of drawing a sample. The list of all students is called a **sampling frame**, that is, a list of all elements or units in a population; from this list a sam- ple is drawn.

You assign a number to each element in the list. A table of random numbers is then used to randomly to select 300 peo- ple for the sample. You can also enter the sampling frame and the code numbers into a com- puter file and have the comput- er select a random sample. The computer does electronically what human beings do; it num- bers the elements in the sam- pling frame, generates a series of random numbers, and gives you a list of the 300 elements selected randomly. You then in- terview each of the 300 people.

Systematic sample: Every Kth element in the sampling frame is chosen for inclusion in the sample. If the list, as in the above example, includes 6,000 students, and you want to have a sample of 300, then 6,000 divided by 300 = 20. You select every 20th element for inclu- sion in your sample.

It is a good idea to get a random start. So, pick a random number from 1 to ten. Use that number as the first case, and then select every 20th person following it. This method tech- nically is termed a *systematic sample with a random start.*

Stratified sample: This is a use- ful method of sampling a popu- lation with great diversity, pro- viding that you have access to sampling frames for each of the subgroups in the population. The purpose of stratified sam- pling is to divide the population into homogeneous subsets, and then within each subset ran- domly to select appropriate numbers of elements. In diverse populations, this sampling method obtains a greater degree of representativeness.

_____ BOX 4.4 _____

Some Varieties of Non-Probability Samples

Convenience sample This is also known as an *accidental sample* or as an incidental *sample.* Sampling on a catch-as-catch-can basis. Interviewing the first 20 people to walk through the main entrance of the Student Center on a Monday morning in order to find out what students at your college or university feel about a particular issue is an example of convenience sampling, accidental sampling, incidental sampling.

Purposive sample This is also known as a *judgmental sample.* The researcher selects cases to be included in the sample on the basis of her/his own *judgment* about which ones will be most representative or useful. A *focus-group* could be used to generate a menu of cases to be selected as a sample.

Quota sample The researcher selects cases to be included in the sample on the basis of characteristics specified in advance

(e.g., age, sex, ethnicity, social class, political-party affiliation), so that the total sample will have the same distribution of characteristics as is presumed to exist in the target population. Please read Figure 4.4, "Quota Sample."

Snowball sample Each person interviewed is asked to suggest a few other people for interviewing. Often used in field-research.

---

could be provided for the respondent to write her or his response.

In contrast, in *closed-ended questions,* the respondent is asked to select an answer from a menu of possible responses provided by the researcher. For instance, respondents might be provided with the following statement: "Illegal drugs are the biggest problem faced by our community today" and be asked if they "Strongly Agree," "Agree," have "No Opinion," "Disagree," or "Strongly Disagree." This procedure, named after Rensis Likert who developed it, is known as a Likert scale. Likert-scale questions can be used profitably in questionnaires.

Two principles guide the researcher in designing closed-ended questions: *mutual exclusiveness* and *exhaustiveness.* Response cate-

gories should be exhaustive: they should include all possible responses. Often, researchers insure this by adding "Don't Know," "No Opinion," or "Other: Please specify: _____." Thus, a researcher wants to know where respondents were born. The researcher asks respondents: "In which of the following states were you born?" and lists the names of the fifty states in the U.S. as response options. The design of the question is flawed. The response options are not exhaustive. Some respondents may have been born in another country, for which there is no response option. The question, as constructed, violates the principle of exhaustiveness.

Response categories should be mutually exclusive; the categories should not overlap, and the respondent should not feel internally

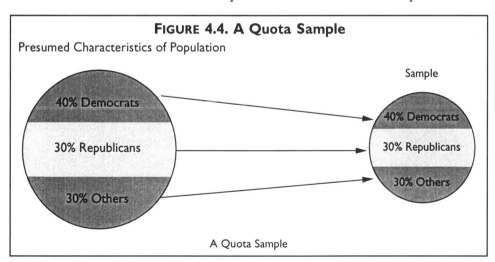

FIGURE 4.4. A Quota Sample

Presumed Characteristics of Population

Sample

40% Democrats → 40% Democrats

30% Republicans → 30% Republicans

30% Others → 30% Others

A Quota Sample

compelled to select more than one response option. Let us suppose that a researcher were interested in religious affiliation as a variable. The researcher gives instructions that respondents should answer each of the questions, and that they should select the *one* best answer to each question. One of the questions is: "What do you feel is your religious affiliation?" The menu of response options is "Protestant, Catholic, Jew, Episcopalian, Baptist, Other: Please specify: _____." The response options are flawed. Episcopalians are Protestants, and Baptists are Protestants. The response options violate the principle of mutual exclusiveness.

Principles Guiding Question Construction

Several principles guide researchers in designing questions. Six of these principles follow (Rubin and Babbie, 1995):

1. *Make items clear.* Do not ask "What do you think about the proposed 'half-way-in' house in this community?" Respondents may not know what a "half-way-in house" is, they may not know that one is planned for their community, and they may not know where in their community it is likely to be situated. Questions and statements should be clear and unambiguous.

2. *Use single-barreled questions and statements.* A question or statement has a single barrel if it asks one question or makes one statement. A question is double-barreled if it asks two questions as one question. "Do you approve of President Clinton's Supreme Court nominations and of his balanced-budget proposal for 1998?" is double-barreled. If the researcher actually were interested in peoples' attitudes with regard to both issues, the simplest solution would be to create two questions and to ask each of them. As a general rule, if you see the words "and" or "or" in a question/statement, it is double-barreled. Do not use or construct questions/statements with more than one barrel.

3. *Use short items.* Respondents should be able to read, process, and respond to the questions/statements quickly. If the questions are long, complex, and require a great

deal of cognitive processing to understand, respondents are likely to get frustrated and, as a result, tend not to respond to questions that have these characteristics, or they fail to complete the questionnaire and consign it instead to the proverbial "file thirteen," the waste-paper basket or dust bin.

4. *Use positives.* In mathematics and in English grammar, two negatives sometimes make a positive. In survey research, one negative makes for a poorly constructed question; two negatives in the same question or statement are even worse. "Police should not carry no weapons" is a statement containing a double negative. If respondents were asked to agree or to disagree with that statement, there could be a great deal of confusion. Why?

Double negatives require substantial cognitive processing, more than the typical respondent is willing to invest. As a result, double-negative constructions increase both the nonresponse rate and raise the issue of reliability. Respondents who read the question quickly—and, as a researcher, you should assume that they *will* both read and respond quickly—may miss the double negative altogether. If they misconstrue the question, the responses are unreliable. Even a single negative in a question or statement requires a lot of cognitive processing. For instance the question "Do you feel that homosexuals should not be permitted to teach in elementary schools?" with the response options of "Yes," "No," and "Don't Know" could create a lot of confusion. There are a number of better ways to ask this question. One possibility is to ask respondents whether they "Strongly Agree," "Agree," have "No Opinion," "Disagree," or "Strongly Disagree" that "I am willing to have homosexuals as teachers in the elementary schools." Whenever possible, then, be sure to frame questions and statements as positives and to avoid using negatives in constructing questionnaire statements and questions.

5. *Use only unbiased items and terms.* As you recall, there is a tendency for people to think well of themselves (self-serving bias), and hence to say or to do things that make

them or their reference groups or their identity groups look good. One implication for question construction is that we need to avoid constructing questions that encourage respondents to answer in a particular way. For instance, we would not want to ask "Do you agree with Charlie Vale, this community's most revered humanitarian, that . . ." Likewise, we would *not* want to ask "Don't you agree with Senator _____ (fill in the space with the most senior senator in your state) that . . ."

6. *Respondents must be competent to answer.* In asking respondents to provide information, we should continually ask ourselves whether they could do so reliably. If a researcher were to ask respondents one or more questions about a particular bill scheduled for a vote in their state legislature or in the House of Representatives or in the U.S. Senate, many people may not know anything about it. If a researcher were to ask respondents how many cents per mile driven they pay annually on the combined repair of, and gasoline for, their motor vehicle (automobile/van/truck), many people who own or lease a motor vehicle would not have the faintest idea. They may not know with any accuracy how many miles they drive each year, how much money they spend on gasoline or diesel fuel, and how much they spend for repairs. They even may not know how to compute per-mile costs.

Pilot Test

An important principle of questionnaire construction is pilot testing. A *pilot test* or *pilot study* is research designed to evaluate the feasibility of a larger study (Lachmann, 1991: 218). In experimental research, pilot studies are conducted to find out whether the experimental manipulations are operating as planned. In survey research, they are conducted to determine whether the questions one proposes for a larger study are understandable to the respondents for whom they are targeted, whether the questions designed to tap particular variables actually do so, and how much time it takes respondents to complete the questionnaire.

The respondents used for a pilot test are similar to, but not the same people as, those who will be in your sample. *Focus groups*, discussed below, can be used to pilot test or to pretest questionnaires.

Pilot testing is crucial. Why? Because, as the couple of examples, which we shortly examine, illustrate, not even the most seasoned researcher can foresee all the difficulties and ambiguities a set of questions potentially holds for respondents. This is particularly true when a population is as diverse as that of the United States. Thus, sociologist Howard Schuman found that "a frequently used question about whether the 'lot of the average man is getting worse' turns out on close examination to confuse respondents about the meaning of 'lot'—some taking it to refer to housing lots" (Schumann, 1992: 2122). Another example is provided by a sociologist who interviewed respondents in rural and small-town Appalachia:

> Many of the questions on the interview schedule were Likert-type items ranging from "very much" to "very little" or "very good" to "very poor." The problem was that in the colloquial language of the region, the word "very" apparently has an idiomatic usage which is closer to what we mean by "fairly" or even "poorly." For instance, if you inquired about someone's health and they responded that they were doing "very well," they do not mean that their health is excellent, but quite the contrary, that they are just getting along.
>
> One assumption of a survey, which seems so obvious that it is usually ignored, is that the researcher and the respondent are speaking the same language. In this case, the sponsors of the survey . . . refused to consider the difference in language usage: they told their interviewers to code "very well" if that was what the respondent said. In other words, in many cases the coded response was quite likely the exact opposite of the respondent's opinion. (Crew, 1993)

The results of a pilot test indicate whether research procedures, the questions asked, or the order in which they are asked should be revised. Researchers who fail to heed the results of pilot tests jeopardize the scientific integrity of their survey.

Analysis of Data

After data are gathered, they normally are entered into a computer file for statistical analysis. This process is called *data entry*. Data usually are *coded* in numerical form. Thus, the gender of the respondents might be coded as 1 = Female, 2 = Male, -5 = No Response. If open-ended questions have been used, an intermediate step is necessary. For each question, the researcher first must devise mutually exclusive and all-inclusive categories and then must code the answers of each respondent. For instance, a question that asks "What is the most important problem facing our community today with regard to which your community police can be of assistance?" might yield categories of gang violence, drugs, dogs, parking, property crime, domestic disputes, noisy neighbors, prostitution, and so forth, even though the exact words used by respondents may differ. The researcher, of course, must provide verification of the reliability of the coding procedure. This could be accomplished by both training and using more than one coder. The extent of inter-rater reliability is then measured, and this information is presented in the final research report. The perceptive reader will note from this discussion that it is possible to engage in quantitative analysis of qualitative data.

Data are analyzed in terms of sociological theory, logical analysis, sociological analysis, tabular presentation, and statistical measures, which provide the basis for a final report. The general principle, which is contrary to common sense, is that *the answers people give to questions* do *not speak for themselves.* This is the case even with closed-ended questions, and even if the questions are both well constructed and based on a national probability sample of adequate size. *Answers take meaning when they are compared to something.* The comparison may be across time. For instance, you compare the answers of a probability sample to a particular question this year with the answers to the same question from a comparable probability sample of the same population four years ago. Comparisons may be across social categories (e.g., age, gender, race, ethnicity, years of education, marital status, religious affiliation, and so forth) or across other classifications (e.g., geographical region, rural-urban, city size).

Beware of Generalizing the Results of Responses to a Single Question

Another important principle with regard to understanding survey data is to *beware of generalizing the results of responses to a single question*, even if the responses are based on a well constructed question and a national probability sample of adequate size. The results to surveys frequently are presented as simple percentages. For example, let us pretend that 45 percent "Strongly Agree," 20 percent "Agree," 5 percent have "No Opinion," 20 percent "Disagree," and 10 percent "Strongly Disagree" that "City police should intervene in violent domestic disputes between spouses by arresting the violent spouse who must then spend the night in jail." There are several reasons why one should be careful not to overgeneralize from the percentage distributions of responses to a single question. Here are five of them (Schuman, 1992: 2122-2123).

First, any important issue (e.g., abortion) actually consists of a cluster of constituent issues, sub-issues, or parts (e.g., a woman's right to control her own body, state intervention in the intimate lives of people, the issue of what is "life," the issue of when does "life" begin, etc.). No single question can capture the range of constituent issues involved. Each of the parts may be asked about. Each part, however, may yield dramatically different distributions of results. Thus, in the United States, responses to the issue of gun control vary a lot depending on the proposed method of control, the amount of control, and the type of weapon to which reference is made. Because the distributions of responses across sub-issues can vary greatly, and because a number of sub-issues may be involved, care must be taken not to overgeneralize from the results of a single question. Had a different question been selected, the conclusions drawn could have differed greatly

Second, even minor differences in the wording of questions can alter the percentage results greatly. Thus, researchers Elizabeth Loftus and Guido Zanni (1975) find that using the word "the" instead of "a" in a question can make a

BOX 4.5

All Averages Are Not the Same: Measures of Central Tendency

MEAN: The mean of a data set is the sum of the measures in the data set divided by the number of measures in the data set. Data must be measured at the interval-level or higher in order to calculate the mean. *Note well:* The *mean is misleading* as a summary measure of a data set if the data are not normally distributed, i.e., *if the data set is skewed.* If a data set departs significantly from that of a normal distribution, it is skewed.

It is convention to represent the mean of a sample by the figure $\overline{X}$ (which is pronounced as X-bar).

Example: Here is a data set: 1, 6, 7, 8, 11, 80. Calculate the mean.
Solution:
$1+6+7+8+11+80 = 113$
$113 \div 6 = 18.9$ or 19 is the mean.
MEDIAN: The median is the middle value in a set of numbers that has been arranged from lowest to highest. *Note well:* The median is a good measure of central tendency when the data set is skewed. It may be calculated on ordinal-level and interval-level data.

How to calculate the median:
(1) *In a data set that has an odd number of items:*

Solution:
✔ rank order the items from lowest to highest
✔ position of median = $\underline{N + 1}$
Where N = the number of items in the data set.
Example: Here is a data set: 25, 11, 13, 12, 16 17, 20 Calculate the median.
Solution:
✔ rank order the items from lowest to highest

raw number:		rank order:
11	←	1
12	←	2
13	←	3
16	←	4
17	←	5
20	←	6
25	←	7

formula: $(7 + 1) / 2 = 8 / 2 = 4$
Thus, the position of the median is in the forth slot according to rank order. Thus, the median is 16.
(2) *In a data set that has an even number of items: The median is the mean of the middle two ranks.*
Example: Here is a data set: 26 11 25 12 13 21 17 16. Calculate the median.
Solution:
✔ rank order the items from lowest to highest

✔ compute the mean of the middle two ranks

raw number:		rank order:
11	←	1
12	←	2
13	←	3
16	←	4
17	←	5
21	←	6
25	←	7
26	←	8

Mean of the middle two ranks = $(16 + 17) / 2 = 33 / 2 = 16.5$
Thus, the value of the mean is **16.5**
MODE: The mode is the most frequent value in a distribution. Some distributions have no mode: all values appear with equal frequency. Some distributions have more than one mode. For instance, in the following data distribution—11,14, 17,17, 18,18, 20, 25,29, 37—there are two modes (17, 18). Each of these values appears twice and no value appears more than twice. Appropriate levels of measurement include nominal, ordinal, and interval. The word "mode" is a noun. The word "modal" is the adjectival form of the noun, mode.

dramatic difference. The question "Did you see the broken headlight?" triggers twice as many "memories" of a nonexistent event as does the question "Did you see a broken headlight?" The percent of respondents who answer "Don't Know" to a question varies by 25 percent or more, depending on the extent to which the researcher legitimates it as a response option by mentioning it—"Yes," "No," "Don't Know"—along with other alternatives or omitting it (Schuman and Presser, 1981; Schuman, 1992: 2123).

Third, even if the wording of a question remains the same, the order in which questions are asked significantly effects responses. For example, a widely-used question about allowing legalized abortion in the case of a married woman who wants no more children produces significantly different answers depending entirely on its placement before or after another question about abortion in the case of a defective fetus (Schuman: 1992: 2123).

Fourth, the interpretation of a percentage distribution tends to involve an implicit comparison with some other distribution, real or imagined. To report that 65 percent of Americans are satisfied with the Chief Justice of the U.S. Supreme Court could be grounds for joy or for consternation. What the "65 percent are satisfied" *signifies* depends on the average level of satisfaction typical for the same leader, on the level of satisfaction with the same leader last year or four years ago, or on the level of satisfaction with persons in comparable leadership positions. As the careful and attentive reader recalls, answers have no meaning unless they are compared to something. *People construct meaning, at least in part, by means of comparisons.* It is for this reason, that whenever possible, sociological research contains explicit comparisons of survey data.

Fifth, if an interviewer is used to administer a questionnaire, either in the face-to-face situation or in telephone surveys, the perceived demographic characteristics of the interviewer—including perceived race, ethnicity, and gender, can dramatically effect the answers (e.g., Hyman, 1954; Nandi, 1982; Eichler, 1988; Rubin and Babbie, 1993). These considerations need to be addressed in the research design, questionnaire construction, pilot test, administration of the instrument, and in the analysis and interpretation of the results.

Advantages of Survey Research

There are several advantages of survey research as a method of gathering data. It is a useful method for gathering information about large populations. Survey research enables researchers to use a relatively small sample of individuals, who are carriers of information about themselves and about their culture, to learn about a society's class structure, economic structure, political structure, solidary order, exchange order, and so forth.

Moreover, surveys also conform to major requirements of a way of knowing called the scientific method:

- Surveys allow a considerable degree of *objectivity.* In science, objectivity has at least two important meanings. The first meaning is agreement among observers regarding what they have observed (e.g., inter-rater reliability). For observation to be objective in this sense, (1) agreed-upon procedures

must be followed; (2) the observation must be replicable, which means that the study must be repeated by other researchers to see how the results compare; and (3) the same or similar results must occur regardless of which competent person administers the instrument to the same or similar population or probability sample. If I am a creationist, and you are a firm believer in evolution, and we both follow the same research procedures and administer the same instrument to the same or similar probability sample of the same population, we should get similar results. This type of objectivity is termed *intersubjectivity,* and it is crucial to scientific explanation as a way of knowing.

- A second meaning of the term objectivity is "value free," which means that the values, attitudes, and interests of the researcher should not influence the type of knowledge produced. Objectivity in this sense is hotly debated (e.g., Weber, 1949; Acker, Berry, and Esseveld, 1983; Brown and Tandon, 1983; Whyte, 1989; Cancian and Armstead, 1992).
- Surveys allow for tests of the reliability of the information gathered.
- Surveys allow for tests of the validity of the information gathered.
- If a *probability sample* is used, surveys allow for the calculation, within known degrees of error, of the extent to which the sample of results deviate from the values that would have been obtained had the entire population been surveyed. In other words, this method allows for generalizability of the results to a larger population, with known degrees of error, called *sampling error* because it is due to having surveyed a sample instead of the entire population.

Disadvantages of Survey Research

There are also disadvantages of survey research. The survey-research method has been criticized from within sociology on several grounds. First, sociologists concerned with more subjective understanding perceive that the survey sacrifices depth and richness of understanding for the sake of acquiring measures that are more amenable to quantitative analysis. Sociologists committed to the analysis of larger social systems criticize survey research as focusing too much on the individual and on the characteristics and perceptions of the individual, neglecting the relationship among powerful institutions. Sociologists from the hermeneutic or interpretive perspective and from the post-modern perspective take issue with the positivist assumptions on which survey research rests. They do not accept the assumption that the concepts and methods used to describe the physical world are applicable to understanding social life (Cancian and Armstead, 1992).

Focus Group Research

Focus group research is the means by which social scientists select a special group, through convenience sampling, to investigate a single topic. In this approach the researcher may select a random sample from a larger population or the researcher may select a *cohort* and then—through the process of discussion, debate and dialogue—discover how this group understands topical issues. In this strategy the researcher takes careful notes of what participants say. Then the researcher performs a content analysis, to discover the dominant themes revealed in the discussions. Researchers may allow participants to write responses to open-ended questions and then allow discussion of these responses to focus the group on the issue. These open-ended responses may be analyzed using *content analysis* to discover themes.

Simple percentages can be used to classify and analyze these data. This strategy is being used by many political scientists directing political campaigns to get at the issues their candidates should address. Moreover, focus group research can be used to develop questions for larger survey research projects. Again only limited generalization can be made from focus group research that is based on nonprobability samples. However, their findings are helpful to researchers in constructing both surveys and interview schedules.

Secondary Analysis

Secondary analysis of data refers to the use of an available data resource by a researcher to study a problem different than that for which the data originally were collected (Parcel, 1992). Sociologists, social workers, and

social geographers use diaries, public archives, medical records, and other written sources to construct a client's or a collectivity's social history. This is well exemplified in sociologist Catherine Clinton's book, *Plantation Mistress: Woman's World in the Old South* (1982). Clinton utilizes letters, household inventories, physicians' records, wills, and the unpublished diaries and memoirs of plantation wives in the seven seaboard states during the first fifty-five years following the American Revolution (1780-1835). She thereby reconstructs both the inner and daily lives of these elite women whom history and sociology previously had either ignored or misconstrued (1982).

Clinton documents that elite women in the North and the South had comparable educational opportunities during the early years of the Republic. One regional difference is that in the South, legislative restrictions prevented women's independent administration of plantations. Clinton's careful analyses make it clear that white elite women were not mere window dressing on southern plantations. They performed complex and essential functions within both the planter **ideology** and the cotton economy. An ideology is an idea or set of ideas held by a social group (or groups or a society) that reflects, defends, justifies, and rationalizes the institutional commitments and interests of that collectivity. The value of their contributions *increased* during the post-Revolutionary cotton boom, a situation sharply in contrast to the position of bourgeois women in the New England and Middle Atlantic States. Northern bourgeois women suffered a decline in status, closely linked to the decline in importance of the household economy in the industrializing Middle Atlantic and New England states. Clinton clearly documents important regional variations in the status of women during the formative years of this nation.

Advantages of Secondary Analysis

The advantages of secondary analysis of data are many. *First*, the researcher does not have to develop and to pretest questions. Frequently the questions have been developed and field-tested by large survey-research enterprises, of whose expertise researchers may avail themselves. Large, competent survey-research enterprises are many. They produce numerous surveys of fine quality. These include the National Longitudinal Surveys of Labor Market Experience (NLS). These surveys are produced by the Center for Human Resource Research (CHRR) at Ohio State University. An *NLS Handbook* is produced each year by CHRR. These surveys, the details of which you may read about in the most current *NLS Handbook*, contain a wealth of data on five cohorts. The data pertain to the respondents' work history, earnings, employment status, education, training, marital status, fertility, and household composition. The surveys also contain background material on respondents' parents.

The NLS data sets are produced with the cooperation of the U.S. Bureau of the Census, CHRR, and the National Opinion Research Center (NORC) of the University of Chicago. NORC handles the sample design, CHRR is responsible for questionnaire construction, and the U.S. Bureau of the Census has the responsibility for the field work and data reduction.

Second, the researcher is able to take advantage of a national sample of respondents or even of data produced on national populations. The numbers of cases available in secondary analysis often surpass what an individual researcher could afford to produce. *Third*, large sample sizes and random sampling techniques enhance the precision of parameter estimates and make possible statistical analyses that smaller non-random samples preclude. *Fourth, compared to conducting comparable research from scratch*, secondary analysis is not time consuming. Of course, analyzing your secondary data may take you a lot of time, and figuring out what those data mean or signify may take even longer. *Fifth, compared to conducting comparable research from scratch*, secondary analysis is inexpensive. The researcher needs to have access to the data, to a well-equipped personal computer or to a mainframe computer, to an appropriate statistical package, and to a printer with paper. The researcher enters the data into the computer, analyzes the data with the statistical package, prints the results, and interprets them in terms of theory, past research, and the problem being investigated. To the extent that time is money, much time is spent on reflecting on the implications of the data for theory and for the problem under investigation and on writing up the findings; but in comparison with engaging

in large-scale survey research, the expenses are minor.

Disadvantages of Secondary Analysis

The disadvantages or shortcomings of secondary analysis are inherent in its advantages. *First*, the secondary data may not be well connected to the phenomena the researcher desires to study. In the research design, the researcher should take special care to point out this limitation. *Second*, because many secondary analyses are conducted on survey data, effective use of secondary data depends on a thorough knowledge of both research methods and statistics. Effective use of secondary data frequently presumes that the researcher is knowledgeable regarding reliability issues, validity issues, sample design, question wording, questionnaire construction, levels of measurement, and measurement techniques. *Third*, making sense out of survey results presumes that one is familiar with a broad range of sociological theory.

Unobtrusive Methods

Unobtrusive methods are those methods that do not intrude on the phenomena being studied. Archaeologists and physical anthropologists conduct unobtrusive research when they explore the remains of previous life. Other people's trash becomes important information about diet, social structure and daily life.

Police utilize unobtrusive methods in the examination of evidence left at a crime scene. Finger prints, clothes, foot prints, blood, letters, and so on are data which give the keen observer information untainted by the observer's presence.

Social workers utilize unobtrusive methods in much of their investigations of child abuse. Bruises, broken bones, x-rays, and emergency room reports are unaffected by the observer's presence. They are compelling evidence in any court case, especially when researchers have documented their findings in a systematic manner.

Hospital social workers often use unobtrusive methods in investigating many of the confused elderly clients who wonder into the emergency rooms or are taken there by friends and relatives. Often the examining physician misdiagnoses these patients with senile dementia. By examining the client's residence they discover many things. Looking in the refrigerator for food that was consumed in the last 48 hours and in the medicine cabinet for medications, which might have been misused, may be valuable information to the physician for proper diagnosis and accurate treatment. Elderly patients often have poor eyesight and may improperly use medications.

Experimental Methods

An **experiment** is an investigation in which there is controlled manipulation of the independent variable by the investigator and precise observation and measurement both of the variables and of the results. It is a research method well suited to investigating relationships of cause and effect.

There are many types of experiments. Please study Figure 4.5, "Diagram of *Elements of Classical Experimental Design.*" The **classical experimental design** is characterized by **random assignment** of research subjects to one of two experimental conditions. Research subjects randomly assigned to the experimental **group** receive exposure to the independent variable by the researcher. Research subjects randomly assigned to the **control group** are not exposed to the independent variable by the researcher.

Random assignment is a critical element in the classical experimental design. Why? Because random assignment is viewed as making the research subjects virtually *equivalent, except for exposure by the researcher to the independent variable.* In other words, if random assignment is utilized, the fat, the young, the skinny, the old, the sick, the racist, the altruistic, the tall, the short, the rich, the poor, the politically liberal and the politically conservative, as well as those with efficient and inefficient immune systems, those who rank high on authoritarianism and those who rank low on it are equally likely to be assigned to the experimental and control groups. The only way the research subjects in the two groups differ significantly is in exposure by the experimenter to the independent variable.

If an element of the classical experimental design is absent, the experimental design is termed *quasi-experimental, pseudo-experimental, or semi-experimental.* If random as-

signment is not used to assign subjects to one of two experimental conditions, the term **comparison group** is used to designate those subjects not exposed to the experimental stimulus. There are many types of quasi-experimental designs. Quasi-, pseudo-, semi-, and classical-experimental designs collectively are referred to as *experimental methods.*

There are many reasons, including ethical concerns, why a researcher might want to utilize a research method other than the classical experimental design, even if she or he were interested in investigating cause and effect relationships. There are practical concerns, including considerations of cost and of time constraints. The classical experimental design may be too expensive and too time-consuming, given the resources at your disposal. Ethical concerns may rule out the method. For instance, you may decide that the use of random assignment violates your professional code of ethics. For example, let us say that you are interested in the efficacy of a particular pharmaceutical intervention in the treatment of AIDS. This new pharmaceutical intervention promises significantly to lengthen the number of years people with AIDS can expect to live reasonably healthy lives. Ethically, you cannot bring yourself to assign human subjects to the control-group condition. To do so, you feel, would be to shorten their lives. In other words, while strictly *scientific* considerations may suggest the usefulness of the classical experimental design, you may opt for another research method for *ethical* reasons.

Psychologists, social psychologists, and social workers often use experimental methods. Although experiments comprise a minority of all sociological research, and although sociologists use experimental methods less frequently than some other social scientists, their use by sociologists is still quite common (Marwell, 1992:616). *Field experiments* are prominent in program-evaluation research, especially in applied areas. Applied areas are many and include education, public health, and proposed social-policy initiatives such as guaranteed minimum-income proposals (e.g., Rosenthal and Jacobson, 1968; Slavin and Darweit, 1985; Rowe, 1974a, 1974b; Jones, 1981; Hannan, Tuma, and Groenveld, 1977). Also, there are field experiments in the areas of juvenile and criminal justice (e.g., McCord and McCord,

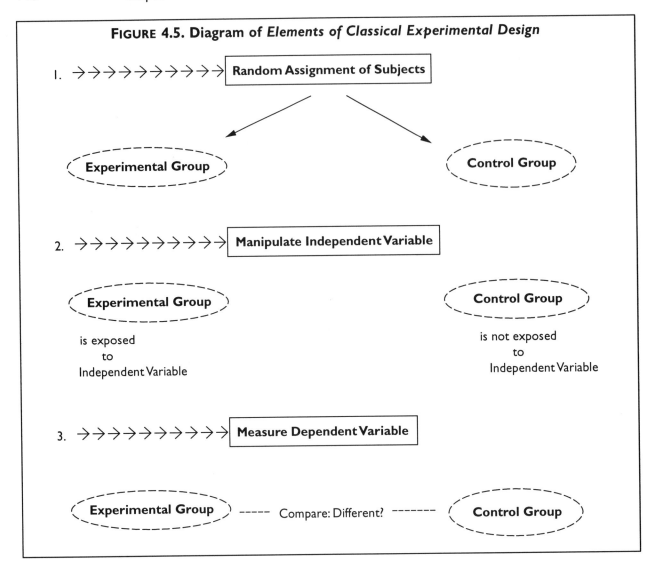

FIGURE 4.5. Diagram of *Elements of Classical Experimental Design*

1. →→→→→→→→→→ **Random Assignment of Subjects**

   Experimental Group   **Control Group**

2. →→→→→→→→→→ **Manipulate Independent Variable**

   Experimental Group   **Control Group**

   is exposed   is not exposed
   to   to
   Independent Variable   Independent Variable

3. →→→→→→→→→→ **Measure Dependent Variable**

   Experimental Group ----- Compare: Different? ------- **Control Group**

1959a, 1959b; Rossi, Berk, and Lenihan, 1980; Zeisel, 1982; Frihart, Humphries, and Cameron, 1990). Questionnaire experiments test methodological issues and vignette experiments are used to study attitudes (e.g., Marwell, 1992: 616; Schuman and Presser, 1981; Rossi and Nock, 1982).

Frihart, Humphries, and Cameron (1990) utilized a semi-experimental design to measure the effects of teaching law-enforcement officers counseling skills to see if this allowed them be effective as drug-abuse education counselors to teenagers in southeast Kansas. In this study, the researchers developed a questionnaire to measure the attitudes of law-enforcement officers toward children. Pretest results indicate that law-enforcement officers perceive themselves as authoritarian in their role as police officers and that they believe that children

should be respectful toward authority. Previous research indicates that an authoritarian style interferes with counselor-client efficacy among drug-abuse counselors. Posttest results of the Frihart, et al. study indicate that counseling-skills training leads to a statistically significant reduction in authoritarian styles of presentation of drug information to children by police officers. Follow-up research (Cameron and Donovan, 1998) indicates that after six months, these law-enforcement officers returned to high authoritarian styles. This indicates that counseling-skills training has only short term effects. The researchers postulate that law-enforcement officers belong to an occupational sub-culture that reinforces authoritarianism, and that ongoing in-service training programs are necessary to sustain a reduction of authoritarian traits.

TABLE 4.5. Strengths and Weaknesses of Research Methodologies in the Social Sciences

Research Method	Strengths	Weaknesses
Field Research Observation Participant Observation	Opportunity to study insider's view. Inexpensive.	Cannot generalize beyond one case. Difficult to establish causal relationship. Lack of accurate measures. Non-probability sample. Data qualitative—difficult to quantify reliably and validly without sufficient knowledge of research methods.
Focus Group Research	Focus on topical issues. Helpful in constructing and in pretesting questionnaires and interview schedules.	Cannot generalize beyond one single group.
Survey Research Questionnaires Interviews	The ability to describe large populations, using probability sampling techniques. Ability to establish causality.	Expensive and time consuming. May not be able to provide an insider's view.
Secondary Analysis Content Analysis Unobtrusive methods	Inexpensive and readily available. Use of media and other sources. Possibility of longitudinal study.	Others' data and question may not be relevant or precise for one's research question.
Experimental Methods Semi-experimental Methods	Ability to isolate variables. Replication of study possible. Ability to establish causality. Used in field research for intervention studies.	Conducted in artificial environment. May not be generalizable to larger population. Difficulty in obtaining volunteers.

Quasi-experimental research designs are especially relevant for sociologists in clinical practice and for social-service workers whose practice includes intervention programs for dysfunctional families, for juvenile-delinquency prevention and treatment, for living-skills programs for foster children, for parenting-skills programs for parents at risk of losing custody of their children, and so on. Quasi-experimental research helps answer questions such questions as the following ones: How *effective is your intervention in changing behavior? How effective is your intervention in changing attitudes so that clients increase their probability of becoming contributing, positively functioning adults in the modern world?* Many funding sources—including many federal and state funding agencies—require that grant applications provide a research-design to evaluate program effectiveness. In order to receive a grant to begin a social-intervention program or to continue an already-existing one, grant proposals increasingly require a quasi-experimental research design for effective program evaluation.

Regardless of the area of your vocational choice, understanding, comprehending, and mastering the tools of research are important for your success. Either as consumers of research or as producers of it, you will be required to make judgments about a body of information and/or knowledge. Research methods are agreed-upon procedures used to observe and to measure reality.

Reading and Constructing Tables

Sometimes a picture is worth a thousand words. Tables are visual devices (pictures) for presenting data to audiences. A well-constructed table is helpful to audiences; a poorly and inappropriately constructed one is not. While you will learn much more about table construction and interpretation when you take research-methods and statistics courses, we now review what tables mean in the explanatory process and what the conventional guidelines are both for constructing and for reading tables. Scientists and other salient audiences who read the reports that you write assume that you are conversant with these guidelines. So, if you want you report to be intelligible to employers, to grant-proposal review boards, and to other consumers of research, you need to follow these guidelines in your report.

Tables do not mean much in the explanatory process unless they compare the target group with something. For instance, a table may compare the target group with the control group or with a comparison group, or the table may focus on within-group differences.

Constructing and reading tables requires *attention to detail.* If attention to detail does not come readily to you, please remember that practice can strengthen your abilities in this domain. Practice makes progress.

Review of Basic Concepts

Statistical tables may be described as consisting, at least in part, of cells, rows, and columns. Table 4.6 presents hypothetical data on variations in editorial content (dependent variable) by city size (the independent variable). In a statistical table, a **cell** is the place for each entry of data. The cells provide for all possible combinations of the rows (horizontal) and columns (vertical) of the table. In a statistical table, a **row** refers to the horizontal listing of data in a series of categories, all of which have a common classification. In Table 4.6, the categories "Favorable," "Unfavorable," and "Neutral" have in common that they are the categories of the variable Editorial Policy. A **row caption** or **row heading** is a title that

describes the common classification of the data listed in the rows. In Table 4.6, the row caption is "Editorial Policy."

In a statistical table, a **column** refers to the vertical listing of data in a series of categories, all of which have a common classification. In Table 4.6, the categories "Cities Under 100,000 Population" and "Cities Over 100,000 Population" have in common that they are the categories of the variable, City Size. A **column heading** or **column caption** is a title that describes the common classification of the data listed in the columns. In Table 4.6, the column heading is "City Size."

It is customary to use the columns of a statistical table for the categories of the *independent variable* (cause) and the rows for those of the *dependent variable* (effect). In Table 4.6, the categories of the independent variable (city size) are located in the columns and those of the dependent variable (editorial content) are located in the rows.

This convention is helpful to someone who reads a table. For instance, let us say that you are reading a table and that you are temporarily confused: you can't tell what is the independent variable and what is the dependent variable. A partial solution presents itself as you remember that you can get a hint by looking at the table. *The physical location of variables on a table tells you something:* the independent varia-

TABLE 4.6. Crosstabulation of Hypothetical Data on City Size and Editorial Policy Regarding Legalization of Marijuana, 1998

EDITORIAL POLICY	Cities Under 100,000 Population	Cities Over 100,000 Population	Total
Favorable	14 / 11%	140 / 32%	154 / 27%
Unfavorable	37 / 29%	175 / 40%	212 / 38%
Neutral	76 / 60%	123 / 28%	199 / 35%
Total	127 / 22.5%	438 / 77.5%	565 / 100%

Row Marginals (row totals); Total Sample Size; Column Marginals (column totals)

Source: Hypothetical data

ble is located in the columns and the dependent variable is located in the rows. In Table 4.6, city size is the independent variable and its categories are located in the columns. City size is broken down into two categories: cities under 100,000 population and cities of more than 100,000 population. The dependent variable, editorial policy regarding the legalization of marijuana, is located in the rows. The dependent variable is broken down into three categories: favorable, unfavorable, and neutral.

The term **frequency** refers to the number of occurrences of a particular value or category of a variable in a data set. A **frequency distribution** is a classification of data showing the raw or absolute number of occurrences of each subdivision, category, attribute, or value of a variable. A frequency distribution provides a basic ordering of the data in a data set. It is frequently the first step in statistical analysis. A frequency distribution may be displayed in a number of ways: in a table, a pie chart, or a bar chart, for instance. For example, in Table 4.6, in cities under 100,000 population, 11% of the newspaper editorials favor the legalization of marijuana, 29% are unfavorable, and 60% are neutral. In contrast, in cities of more than 100,000 population, virtually *one-third* of the editorials favor the legalization of marijuana. The larger the city size, the greater the support for legalization of marijuana.

A score is termed raw and is called a **raw score,** or **absolute score,** if it reveals how much of the characteristic of interest is possessed by an individual (or by an event, object, and so forth). A raw score (raw number, absolute number) refers to any datum that provides an absolute, not relative, assessment of one's position on a quantitative variable (Huck and Cormer, 1996: 62). Raw scores provide a more precise form of measurement than do ranks. Whereas ranks are data that indicate relative position, raw scores indicate absolute position and provide information for absolute comparisons. To say that Tony earned 93 points out of 100 possible on an exam, while Alfred earned 72 points on it is to make an absolute comparison. To say that Tony earned the second highest score while Alfred earned the second lowest score is to make a relative comparison.

A table may present data on just one variable, in which case it is referred to as a *univari-*

ate distribution. A table displaying data on three or more variables is a *multivariate distribution.* A table presenting data on two variables is a *bivariate distribution.* More precisely, a bivariate frequency distribution refers to the joint presentation of the frequency distribution of two variables, both for the same sample or population of subjects. In a bivariate distribution, each category of one variable is combined with each possible category of the other variable, and the raw number and percent of cases in each possible combination of categories is displayed.

Table 4.6 is a bivariate table or a bivariate distribution. In a bivariate frequency distribution, the cases are analyzed according to the attributes of the independent variable (city size), to discover differences on the dimensions of the dependent variable (editorial policy or stance regarding legalization of marijuana). In Table 4.6, in cities over 100,000 population, 32% of editorials favor the legalization of marijuana, 40% are unfavorable, and 28% are neutral.

A bivariate table sometimes is referred to as a **contingency table** or as a **cross-tabulation table** (or **cross-tab** for short). A contingency table or cross-tabulation table is a method of ordering and of displaying data so that a cross-classification of two or more variables is presented. The table presents the raw number of cases and the percent of cases falling in each combination of categories of the two or more variables.

The raw and percent frequency distributions of each variable, separately, can be found along the edges or margins of the table. Their physical locations are indicated in their names: **row marginals** and **column marginals.** These totals are called **marginal distributions.** In Table 4.6, the right margin provides a raw frequency and a percent distribution for editorial policies. Of the 565 editorials in this study, 154 (or 27%) are favorable to the legalization of marijuana, 212 (38%) are unfavorable, and 199 (35%) are neutral. Similarly, the marginal distribution of city size is found in the bottom margin of the cross-tab. These raw frequencies and percents for cities under 100,000 population and for cities over 100,000 population are the column totals, since city size is the variable heading the columns. Let us call cities under

100,000 population "small cities" and cities over 100,000 population "large cities." Thus, of the 565 editorials in the study, 127 (or 22.5%) came from small cities, and 438 (77.5%) are from large cities. The percentages in the marginals sometimes are called **total percents** because they are derived by dividing each frequency by the total sample size and multiplying the result by 100.

Contingency or cross-tabulation tables are the "bread and butter" of social research. You find them everywhere—in newspapers, in marketing research, in journal articles, in the *Uniform Crime Reports,* in the *National Crime Victimization Surveys,* and so on. With a little practice, cross-tabulations or contingency tables are easy to construct, to read, and to understand. We now look at the conventional guidelines for constructing and for presenting data in the form of contingency tables (cross-tabulation tables). Each time you construct a table, you should follow each of these guidelines.

Principles of Table Construction

1. *All tables should be numbered.*
2. *All tables should have a title* that indicates what variables are contained in the table.
3. *All tables should include column headings and row headings*.
4. *The original raw data* (sometimes called "hard" or "absolute" data) of the variables *should be present in the table.* Traditionally the letter n or N is used to refer to the number of cases in a cell. In a cross-tab, present the raw number and percent of cases for each cell and for the row and column marginals.

   Please note: If one is analyzing the responses to a question in a questionnaire or survey, it is crucial that you always present the exact wording of the original question or item being examined. Place this material either below the title of the table or below the table number.

5. *Use no abbreviations* in the table. Thus, if you are using states, spell out the name of each state. Write California instead of CA; write total percents, *not* total %.
6. *Report all missing data* in the table.
7. *Easy to read and interpret.* Tables are presented for the reporting or analysis of information. They should be designed so that they are easy to read and uncomplicated to interpret.
8. *Cite your sources fully.* Beneath each table, give full bibliographic information regarding the source of the data in the table.

Conclusion

There is no place for sloppy and irrational thinking in the research process; it only produces sloppy, illogical results. All research is in some way connected to real-life events. If concepts are not clearly and precisely defined and measured, the results are invalid and it's back-to-the-drawing-board time, thus producing a waste of valuable time and other resources.

Mastering the fundamentals of human inquiry, which is both exciting in itself and intrinsically worthwhile, is also important in any career or endeavor. Many careers, including those in business, communications, human-resource management, journalism, correctional systems, law-enforcement, human services, and communications utilize and analyze social-science research. Employers are looking for these critical-thinking skills. In your job, you might be asked to conduct surveys, program evaluations, and interventions. Even as consumers, we need to know how to evaluate data and how to read tables if we want to understand and to contribute to the changing world of today and tomorrow. Thus mastering these skills directly benefits you both personally and professionally.

Key Concepts

absolute score
anonymity
association
bivariate
causality
cell
classical experimental design
column
column caption
column heading
column marginals
common sense
concept
confidentiality
conjugal family
construct validity
content validity
contingency table
control group
convenience sampling
correlation
criterion-related validity
cross tabulation
datum, data
deductive logic
demand characteristic
demand characteristics
dependent variable
ethnography
experiment
experimental group
face validity
field research

focus group
frequency
frequency distribution
generalization
hypothesis
independent variable
inductive logic
informed consent
instrumentation effects
internal validity
interval level
linear relationship
longitudinal study
mean
measurement
median
methodology
mode
morbidity
negative relationship
nominal
non-probability sample
operationalization
ordinal
participant observation
population
positive relationship
probability
probability sample
purposive sample
quantitative analysis
quantitative data
quota sample

random sample
ratio level of measurement
raw score
regression to the mean
reliability
research
research design
row
row caption
row heading
row marginals
sample
sampling error
sampling frame
sampling interval
science
secondary analysis
simple random sample
snowball sample
spurious correlation
statistical significance
stratified sample
survey
systematic sample
theory
total percents
transparent methodology
univariate
unobtrusive methods
urban-agrarian society
validity
variable
voluntary participation

Internet Resources

http://www.lib.berkeley.edu/GSSI/sociolog.html

Document: Sociology

Government and Social Science Information. This site is the Sociology web site of the library of University of California, Berkeley. It provides links to data archives and to journals of interest to sociologists and to students of sociology.

http://odwin.ucsd.edu/jj/idata

Document: Data on the Net

This site is maintained by University of California, San Diego. It contains descriptions and links to (a) over 800 Web sites with numeric data ready to download to your own personal computer, (b) over 100 social-science gateways to resources of interest to sociologists and other social scientists, and (c) over 60 data archives.

http:/www.census.gov/

Document: United States Census

Here you may search the U.S. Census. Simply use the *search* option to find information on the population group of your selection.

http://www.ojp.usdoj.gov/bjs/

Document: The U.S. Bureau of Justice Statistics web site

The Bureau of Justice Statistics (BJS) is the statistical agency of the U.S. Department of Justice. A special report, written in September 1997, on gender differences in violent victimization in the United States in 1994, is available at this web site. This special report is based on National Crime Victimization (NCVS) data for 1994. The NCVS obtains information about crimes, including incidents not reported to the police, from a nationally representative sample of households in the United States every six months. The special report data, and supporting documentation, are available through the BJS Website. When you are at the BJS web site, simply search for data set ICPSR 6406.

http://www.whitehouse.gov/fsbr/ssbr.html

Document: Social Statistics Briefing Room (SSBR)

This site provides access to recent federal social statistics on a wide variety of topics, including crime statistics, demographic statistics, education statistics, and health statistics. Here you can access recent data, for instance, on income by race, literacy rates, and leading causes of death. At this site you will find links to information provided by several federal agencies, including the Federal Bureau of Investigation, the U.S. Census Bureau, and many more.

http://www.soc.surrey.ac.uk/socresonline/

Document: *Sociological Research Online*

The latest issue of *Sociological Research Online* is available at this Web site. In this cyberspace sociological journal you will find "high quality applied sociology, focusing on theoretical, empirical, and methodological discussions which engage with current political, cultural, and intellectual topics and debates."

Suggested Readings

Babbie, Earl, *Observing Ourselves: Essays in Social Research* (Belmont, CA: Wadsworth Publishing Company, 1986).

Gibbs, Leonard E., *Scientific Reasoning for Social Workers: Bridging the Gap Between Research and Practice* (New York: Macmillan Publishing Company, 1991).

Hoover, Kenneth, and Donovan, Todd, *The Elements of Social Scientific Thinking* (Sixth Edition) (New York: St. Martin's Press, 1994).

Maples, William R., and Browning, Michael, *Dead Men Do Tell Tales: The Strange and Fascinating Cases of a Forensic Anthropologist* (New York: Doubleday, 1994).

Walens, Susann, *War Stories: An Oral History of Life Behind Bars* (Westport, CT: Praeger Publishers, Praeger Series in Criminology and Crime Control Policy, 1997).

Learning Exercise 4.2
Applying Research Methods

The learning objective of this chapter is for you to learn how critically to assess, to consume, and to use research methods. The main theme in utilizing the hypothetical teenager, Wesley, is for you to separate common sense understanding from scientific reasoning. Research methods enable you to discover patterns of behavior, reoccurring events, and characteristics. Common sense understanding refers to your personal opinions, which may be full of errors and illogical reasoning. Scientific investigation attempts to obtain information that is both reliable and valid. Science, then, is a way of thinking and of knowing.

In the questions that follow, please be sure to use the concepts of this chapter in framing your responses. For instance, remember the elements of the classical experimental design—random assignment of subjects, experimental group, and control group. Remember that data do not speak for themselves and that they gain meaning only when compared with something, whether with the expectation of theory, the results of a comparison or control group, etc.

Many Russians believe that drinking ice water gives them a sore throat. This is common sense in their culture. Russians wrap their throats with fur and wool scarves so the cold does not give them a sore throat. The germ theory of disease, so prevalent in the thinking of many persons in the United States, has little room in their explanations of sore throats.

1. How could we test the hypothesis that drinking ice water gives one a sore throat?
2. What are the Russians' basic assumptions?

Many Americans believe that poor people do not want to work. This is common sense for many Americans.
3. How could we test this hypothesis?
4. What are the basic assumptions behind such a statement?

■ ■ ■

Learning Exercise 4.3
Applying Research Methods

The basic elements of social scientific thinking are theories, concepts, variables, measures, and hypotheses. Scientists agree that the goal of science is prediction based on the collection of data. Scientific reasoning includes deductive and inductive logic. Deductive logic goes from the general to the specific. Inductive logic goes from the specific to the general. If we go from the general to the specific we have begun the process of defining our concepts, giving them meaning through operationalization; we have stated an hypothesis or hypotheses in operationalized form, and in so doing, we have both identified and created our independent and dependent variables.

Inductive logic involves going from the specific observation to making some type of generalization or conclusion concerning a theory. In this chapter we reviewed how different disciplines and perspectives might look at the same problem.

1. Take one concept, like self-esteem, and attempt to define and to develop measures for it.
2. What are other ways of measuring the concept?

The following resource might be available in your college or university's library, perhaps in the Reference Department or area: John P. Robinson and Philip Shaver (Eds.), *Measures of Social Psychological Attitudes* (Revised Edition) (Ann Arbor, Michigan: Survey Research Center, Institute of Social Research, 1973). Chapter 3 is entitled "The Measurement of Self-Esteem and Related Constructs," by Rick Crandall. This chapter lists 31 instruments that measure self-esteem and related constructs. Also included are reliability and validity information for each instrument. Chapter 2 focuses on life satisfaction. It lists several instruments that measure various aspects of life satisfaction. It gives you information on for whom (children, adults, the mentally challenged, etc.) each instrument was developed, and the sample(s) on which each instrument was developed and devised. Also included are reliability and validity information for each instrument.

The following resource might be available in your library (or you might consider getting it via inter-library loan if your library does not have it in its collection): J.P. Robinson, P.R. Shaver, and L.S. Wrightsman (Eds.), *Measures of Personality and Social Psychological Attitudes* (San Diego, CA: Academic Press, 1991). J. Blascovich and J. Tomaka, "Measures of Self Esteem," on pages 115 - 160 of this book contains instruments that measure self-esteem and related constructs.

■ ■ ■

Learning Exercise 4.4
Applying Research Methods

The tools of research include access to a library and its resources, understanding the techniques of observation (experiments, surveys, unobtrusive research and so on), the knowledge of and use of appropriate statistics, the knowledge of and access to a computer and applicable software for analyzing data, and proficiency in language, including foreign languages if necessary.

The research design is a plan for how one going to conduct research. In the research design you must be concerned with the unit of analysis and a time frame.

1. How would you conduct research utilizing the concept that you defined and operationalized in Learning Exercise 4.3?
2. What type of sampling procedure would you utilize: random, convenience, stratified, or what?
3. Why is the sampling procedure important? What are the implications of the sampling procedure you have selected for the extent to which you may generalize the findings of your study?
4. How are you going to analyze your data and organize your tables?
5. How are you going to communicate your findings to your audience in a convincing manner?

■ ■ ■

Sociological Analysis of a Medical Setting: Passive Observation Exercise

The following is a passive observational assignment. It is passive because you will not intrude or be obtrusive in your observation of individuals. Select an appropriate setting to observe for about 10 hours. The purpose of this exercise is to hone your observational skills and to become aware of the empirical phenomenon that social realities are not what they appear to be. Specifically, we want you to learn to see the different in the familiar.

1. Focus on the symbolic interaction between medical professionals and their clients. This relationship may include such role relationships as receptionist-client, secretaries-client, bookkeeper-client, doctor-client, nurse-client, or another professional-client types of relationships. This is your focus, your observational frame.
2. In your analysis you are to make a sketch of the site, describing how the furniture and other "props" are arranged. In your analysis you should analyze the "front stage" and "back stage" regions and performances. You should take into account the audience and how props and other factors are used to direct the interaction.
3. Focus on an observational encounter. How do professionals and practitioner-clients interact? How do status differences influence the interaction? How are symbols manipulated? What are the symbols of status? What are the symbols of deference? How are props and symbols employed to create a performance?
4. Remember, it is always the obvious that seems to elude us. Our eyes, ears and all other sensory equipment are inadequate. Our minds have to be trained to listen and to observe. Thus, you should be aware of your moods, the day, the month, the time of day and so on. You should be aware of: how you dress, what your facial expressions are, what your body language is, the presentation of your "self." You should observe it the same time each day. You should be awake and aware. You should take careful notes. Be systematic. *Take field notes right after each observational encounter. These notes will be attached to your report.*
5. In writing this assignment, do not write merely a description of events. Make inferences based on your observations.

■ ■ ■

Applying Research Methods

1. Your group may want to conduct systematic observations on campus. Select a site and length of time you want to observe. For example, you may want to observe group life in the dormitory or how students present themselves to each other at social gatherings.
2. Take Marx's concept of alienation and operationalize it. How would you measure alienation?
3. Operationalize Durkheim's concept of anomie. How could anomie be defined and measured? Are surveys appropriate? How else could anomie be measured?

The following resource might be available in your college or university's library, perhaps in the Reference Department or area: John P. Robinson and Philip Shaver (Eds.), *Measures of Social Psychological Attitudes* (Revised Edition) (Ann Arbor, Michigan: Survey Research Center, Institute of Social Research, 1973). Chapter 5, entitled "Alienation and Anomie," by John Robinson, lists 14 instruments that measure alienation or anomie and gives you information on for whom (children, adults, the mentally challenged, etc.) each instrument was developed, and the sample(s) on which each instrument was developed and devised. Also included are reliability and validity information for each instrument.

■   ■   ■

Learning Exercise 4.7

Library Exercise

In this exercise, you are to go to the library and locate the following journals: *American Sociological Review, American Journal of Sociology*, and *Sex Roles.* In one of these journals, find an article that has been written within the past year, one in which you are interested, and one which you can understand. Read the article. Write a 500-word synopsis of it. Do not copy anything verbatim. Do not merely restate the abstract of the article. Then, write a 100-word summary of it. Then, relate the article to something—to a theory, to an occurrence in the world, etc. Include with your paper a Xerox copy of the *entire* article.

■   ■   ■

Learning Exercise 4.8

Application of Sociological Analysis to Social Life

Develop well thought-out answers to the following questions. Answers are to be typed, double-spaced, and stapled in the upper left-hand corner.

1. Explicate the scientific method. What are the basic elements of scientific thinking? How is science different from common-sense inquiry? How can science be applied to understanding everyday life? Illustrate to the reader the usefulness of scientific thinking. What is the importance of a random sample?
2. Describe to the reader the strengths and weaknesses of observational techniques in the social sciences. What is the basic importance of reliability and validity? What do social scientists mean by statistical significance?
3. Develop a research design to study alcohol-related problems at _____ (insert the name of the college or university you are attending). What are the many ways a researcher may understand and discover the problems concerning alcoholism and related problems?

■   ■   ■

Learning Exercise 4.9

Sociology and the Internet

1. The Society for the Study of Symbolic Interaction (SSSI) has a Web site that provides links to papers posted by the SSSI as representative of good research from a symbolic interactionist perspective. This Web site is found at

   http://sun.soci.niu.edu/~sssi/papers/papers.html

   > Go to the SSSI Web site and investigate several of the papers for which links are provided. Then select *one* of the articles. Give us full bibliographical information on the article (author, title of article, journal, volume number, year, pages; URL). Then write an essay of not less than three hundred and fifty words—1½ typed pages—wherein you explain why the article you selected is a good example of solid research from a symbolic interactionist perspective.

2. Go to the Web site of *Sociological Research Online* at

   http://www.soc.surrey.ac.uk/socresonline/

   > Please provide full bibliographic reference for the issue that is on-line when you do this learning exercise. Explore the contents of this issue of *Sociological Research Online*. What types of topics are found there? What types of topics are not found there? What theoretical approaches are represented in the various articles? Give specific examples. Is one theoretical orientation more heavily represented than others are? If so, which one? Which theoretical orientations are not found in this issue?

■ ■ ■

Multiple-Choice and True-False Test

1. A logical system that bases knowledge on direct systematic observation is called
   _____.
   A. personal opinion
   B. faith
   C. consensus
   D. science

2. The logical model in which specific hypotheses are developed on the basis of general principles.
   A. deduction
   B. induction

3. Common sense and science are the same.
   A. True   B. False

4. _____ includes the analysis of the basic assumptions of science in general and of sociology in particular, the process of theory construction, the relationship of theory and research, and the procedures of empirical investigation.
   A. Science
   B. Methodology
   C. Common sense
   D. Ethics
   E. Research

5. A logical model in which general principles are developed from specific observations.
   A. induction
   B. deduction

6. A statement whose truth is either so well established that it is unquestioned and virtually accepted in a scientific community or it is self evident is termed a(n) _____.
   A. theory
   B. concept
   C. hypothesis
   D. relationship
   E. axiom

7. _____ is the term for the quality of the *consistency* of a measurement?
   A. Reliability
   B. Predictability
   C. Validity
   D. Repeatability

8. A set of interrelated principles and definitions that conceptually organize selected aspects of the empirical world in a systematic fashion.
   A. theory
   B. concept
   C. hypothesis
   D. relationship
   E. axiom

9. What is the term for a measuring instrument measuring precisely what it is intended to measure?
   A. reliability
   B. validity
   C. predictability
   D. repeatability

10. A tentative testable statement about the relationship between two or more variables is termed a(n) _____.
    A. theory
    B. concept
    C. hypothesis
    D. relationship
    E. axiom

11. *Random selection* of subjects means that sociologists stand in the Student Center and select the first fifty people who walk through the door.
    A. True   B. False

12. A *cross-sectional* research design is a study in which data are collected at only one point in time.
    A. True   B. False

13. The *control group is* exposed to the experimental stimulus (independent variable).
    A. True   B. False

14. This type of research has as its goal or purpose providing a beginning familiarity with a topic.
    A. exploratory
    B. explanatory

15. This type of research has as its goal or purpose the answering of "Why?" questions.
    A. exploratory
    B. descriptive
    C. explanatory

16. One of the principles in the code of ethics for conducting research with human subjects is confidentiality.
    A. True   B. False

17. Which observation technique investigates cause and effect relationships under a highly controlled condition?
    A. survey
    B. experiment
    C. interview
    D. questionnaire

18. *Longitudinal* studies are studies of the same research subjects over a period of time.
    A. True   B. False

19. Studying people in their natural environments is called _____.
    A. experimental research
    B. survey research
    C. field research
    D. unobtrusive research

20. Research where the sociologist studies the remains or things left behind is called

    _____.
    A. unobtrusive research
    B. the Hawthorne effect

21. A research strategy often used in large populations is called _____.
    A. unobtrusive research
    B. survey research
    C. in loco parentis
    D. field experiments

22. In a contingency table, the raw and percent frequency distributions of each variable, separately, can be found along the edges or margins of the table. These raw and percent frequency distributions are the _____.
    A. marginal distributions
    B. cells
    C. column headings
    D. row headings
    E. column captions

23. This type of research has as its goal or purpose the answering of "What?" questions.
    A. descriptive
    B. explanatory

24. The strategy where a researcher utilizes questions and data collected by another researcher is called _____.
    A. experimental research
    B. survey or quantitative research
    C. secondary analysis
    D. field experiments
    E. primary research

25. In the statement "Carelessness causes forest fires" the *dependent variable* is _____.
    A. forest fires
    B. carelessness
    C. Unable to determine from the information given.

26. Semi-experimental design allows researchers _____.
    A. to conduct research in the field
    B. to evaluate intervention programs
    C. not to have a control group
    D. all of the above

26. The *experimental group* is *not* exposed to the experimental stimulus (independent variable).
    A. True   B. False

27. In the statement "Carelessness causes forest fires" the *independent variable* is _____.
    A. forest fires
    B. carelessness
    C. unable to determine from the information given.

28. Fred has to write a paper in which he argues cause and effect. He knows you are taking introduction to sociology, so he asks you what he must demonstrate to make a causal argument. You tell him _____.
    A. Cause must precede effect in time
    B. There must be an association or correlation between the variables
    C. The relationship between the variables cannot be explained away as being due to the influence of a third variable that is the cause of them both.
    D. all of the above
    E. none of the above

29. *Internal validity* refers to the extent to which a measuring instrument secures consistent readings of the underlying construct.
    A. True   B. False

30. Elizabeth is conducting a program evaluation. She selects as the subjects in her study those who show extremely high scores on the pretest. She tells you about her research project. You inform her that _____ is a threat to the internal validity of her study.
    A. reliability
    B. in loco parentis
    C. regression to the mean
    D. anarchy
    E. the classical experimental design

31. This level of measurement has a true or absolute zero.
    A. nominal
    B. ordinal
    C. interval
    D. ratio

32. _____ data are data in numerical form.
    A. Qualitative
    B. Quantitative

33. The research procedure changes the behaviors being observed. This is called _____.
    A. NAFTA
    B. GATT
    C. UCR
    D. the Hawthorne effect
    E. all of the above

34. If a measure makes sense as an indicator of a concept it has _____ validity.
    A. face validity
    B. content validity
    C. criterion-related validity
    D. construct validity

35. _____ refers to the confounding effects that repeated measures of the _____ variable has on research outcomes.
    A. Instrumentation effects; independent
    B. Internal validity; intervening
    C. Instrumentation effects; dependent
    D. External validity; independent

36. The term *experimental mortality* signifies that the principle researcher died during the course of the study.
    A. True   B. False

37. When we name something we assign that thing a _____ definition.
    A. nominal
    B. ordinal
    C. interval
    D. ratio

38. A relationship between two variables is considered as _____ when it is actually accounted for by the relationship of the two variables to a third variable.
    A. direct
    B. inverse
    C. spurious

39. The extent to which a measure relates to other variables as predicted by a theory.
    A. face validity
    B. content validity
    C. criterion-related validity
    D. construct validity

40. The extent to which a measure covers the range of meanings included in a concept.
    A. face validity
    B. content validity
    C. criterion-related validity
    D. construct validity

41. Snowball, convenience, quota, and purposive are examples of _____ sampling.
    A. probability
    B. non-probability

42. Area and systematic sampling are examples of _____ sampling.
    A. probability
    B. non-probability

43. A type of sample selected on the basis of geographical location. The total area to be sampled is divided up into geographical areas, from which a random sample is selected. These, in turn, are divided into areas, from which a random sample is selected. From these areas, a randomly chosen set of cases is studied.
    A. area sample
    B. simple random
    C. snowball
    D. convenience

44. This measure of central tendency is useful when the data set is skewed.
    A. mean
    B. median

45. The most frequently occurring datum in a data set is the _____.
    A. mean
    B. median
    C. mode

CHAPTER 5

Culture

Cultural Relations That Make a World

Culture may even be defined simply as that which makes life worth
living.

T.S. Eliot, *Notes Towards the Definition of Culture*

■ ■ ■

Culture lies at the heart of world development. Technical progress,
bureaucratization, capitalistic organization, states, and markets are
embedded in cultural models of the "nature of things" and the
"purposes of action." These cultural conceptions do more than
orient action; they also constitute actors.

John Boli and George M. Thomas, "World Culture in the World Polity"

■ ■ ■

It is now two days since an American Fulbright Scholar arrived, alone, in the Russian Federation. He is a sociologist whose first name is Harry. Harry is in the city of Kazan, the capitol of the state of Tatarstan. He knows barely a dozen Russian words. Initially euphoric at being in this country, he quickly discovers that his ten-month stay here is going be challenging.

Harry has consumed all the food he brought. He is hungry and he is thirsty. There are no public drinking fountains in this large city. Food shopping, he soon discovers, is a modern form of "hunting and gathering," and he hasn't a clue about the norms governing this form of social interaction in Kazan.

Arriving at one of the local state stores, he observes that all essential food, including things to drink, are carefully secured behind thick glass counters. No sales associate approaches him to inquire if he is in need of assistance. He does spy a woman whom he (correctly) assumes is a clerk. She is sitting in a chair, chatting quietly with a friend. He assumes that, once she notices him, she will politely and promptly wait on him. He is wrong.

The sales associate continues to talk with her friend. Ten minutes pass. Harry, suffering from thirst, finally musters enough courage to ask her for assistance. He wants to buy orange juice. She rapidly says the price, speaking in Russian. Not understanding a word she said, Harry asks her to say it again, please, more slowly. The elderly sales associate turns up the volume of her voice. She screams the price so loudly that everyone in the store can hear how much orange juice costs. He meekly pulls out rubles to pay for the orange juice, thinking it will be mere seconds before he can quench his tremendous thirst. He discovers, however, that to pay for the orange juice he must first stand in a long line. Then, he must stand in another line to pick it up. This is the double-barreled process that he must execute for each item he purchases. Because he has not brought a sack with him, and because there are no grocery carts or grocery baskets at the store, he must purchase a sack so that he can carry his purchases around in the store and then transport them to his home. Sacks are not free. There is no choice as to which type of sack to purchase. There is but one. He buys one.

There is a large, half-naked woman printed on the sack. No matter how he holds the sack, the naked woman is (to him) painfully visible. After having spent a total of four hours on this first grocery-shopping adventure, he now must carry this sack, with his precious groceries in it and a naked woman on its exterior, for blocks, and he is deeply embarrassed.

He becomes disoriented in the maze of the colossal collective housing projects. Evening approaches. Finally, he recognizes that he has been walking in circles. Now in total darkness, he locates the twelve-story building on whose third floor his flat is situated. There is no light in the foyer or in the stairwells. He cautiously ambulates over to the elevator, which is "out of order." He stumbles upstairs, with both hands full of groceries, to his third-floor flat. Finally he arrives at his flat and firmly secures three locks on its steel front door.

Psychologically and physically exhausted, he wants to take a warm, comfortable bath. (There is no shower.) Turning on the hot-water faucet, he hears a sucking sound that he later learns to associate with "no hot water today." It is still summer, the beginning of August. The collective's hot water is not turned on for another seven or eight weeks, in late September. If he wants a hot-water bath at home before then, he must heat water in pots on the gas stove, a time-consuming process for those unaccustomed to it.

It is an hour's journey on public transportation from Harry's flat to the University where he works. This city's inhabitants shove, push, scramble and squeeze in and out of trams and buses at every stop. They grate, growl and curse everyone nearby. Elderly women use their elbows to assert a rightful place on the overcrowded buses.

This is Harry's first trip on the tram, and soon he is terrorized. He cannot discern at what stop he should disembark. He is apprehensive to ask because he knows so little of their language, and he perceives no one as sympathetic to a stranger in need. The bus makes a round trip and he ends up getting off where he got on. He is back where he began.

During his first few days in Kazan, Harry is invited to have dinner with an ordinary Russian family. Upon arriving, Harry presents the host and hostess a gift, an act which is in keeping with their traditions. The hostess is very nice and kind. According to Russian norms of hospitality, she treats the American visitor to each dish three or more times—sour milk, carrots, apples and cheese, rice and beef, fish and potatoes, pancakes and raspberries. Harry, not knowing the local norms and not wanting to offend the hostess, accepts each of her gracious offers. He becomes "stuffed," literally unable to eat another morsel.

At the end of the meal, after several copious glasses of locally produced vodka, homemade wines, and cognac, the host and hostess walk our American sociologist, arm in arm, to the nearby bus stop. They linger with him until they are certain he is on the proper bus for the pilgrimage back to his flat. If they had not enjoyed his company, he later finds out, they would not have strolled with him to the bus stop. He also later learns that in order to politely refuse any more to drink or to eat, he merely must respond "no, no, no" (i.e., "no" three times) to a request.

Culture and Society

Conventionally sociologists make a distinction between the concepts of **culture** and **society**. Society refers to group of people with a common culture who occupy a particular territorial area, have a sense of unity, and who regard themselves as different than nonmembers. While there is no agreed-upon definition of **culture** in sociology, quite generally it refers to a group's human made environment, including all material and nonmaterial products of group life that are transmitted across generational lines (Theodorson and Theodorson, 1979: 95; Gilmore, 1992; Abercrombie, Hill, and Turner, 1994: 98-99). The original anthropological definition of this concept was written by Edward B. Tylor and published in 1871. Taylor defines culture as "that complex whole which includes knowledge, behavior, art, morals, law, custom, and any other capabilities and habits acquired" by humans as members of society (1871: 1).

Because the concept is broad, a distinction is made between material and nonmaterial culture. **Nonmaterial culture,** sometimes called *symbolic culture,* is an umbrella term referring to all human made intangibles that are passed from generation to generation—norms, symbols, social structure, folklore, ideas, beliefs, values, habits, customs, traditions, rituals, language, knowledge, and so forth. **Material culture** refers to all human made tangible objects—paper, the Leaning Tower of Pisa, toothpicks, condoms, footballs, nuclear weapons, the clock, bubble gum, and so forth that are transmitted from one generation to another.

The Study of Culture in Sociology and the Social Sciences

Many social sciences are involved in the study and analysis of the creation, consumption, transmission, and change of culture. Primary among these are physical anthropology, social anthropology, linguistic anthropology, archaeology, psychology, developmental psychology, social psychology, social work, political science, economics, and sociology.

Within sociology, the study of culture has flourished (e.g., Peterson, 1990; Gilmore, 1992) during the last third of the twentieth century. The Culture Section has become one of the largest, and remains one of the fastest growing, of all scholarly sections at the American Sociological Association's (ASA) annual meetings. Additionally, the number of scholarly journals and articles devoted to cultural analyses has increased significantly (Berger, 1997). In sociological research during this period, the concept of culture tends to be used primarily in one of two ways. The first, which is indebted to the anthropological tradition, views culture as "conduct embedded in or constitutive of social life" (Peterson, 1990: 498). The study of the

genesis, spread, consumption, and change in values, norms, habits, customs, rituals, and social structure is part of this approach. The second approach, heavily indebted to the symbolic interactionist tradition, views culture as the "symbolic products of group activity" (Jaeger and Selznick, 1964; Peterson, 1990: 498).

Culture and Meaning Attribution

It is a sociological axiom that culture makes the world a predictable, orderly, coherent place in which to live. Let us illustrate this point by relating to you an experiment conducted some years ago by sociologist *Harold Garfinkel.* Garfinkel is the founder of **ethnomethodology,** a school of sociology devoted to the study of how people construct meanings and make sense out of their own activities in everyday life. The prefix "ethno" and "ethn-" stem from the Greek *ethnos,* which translates into English as "people." The suffix "-logy" stems from the Greek *logos* and translates into English as "the study of." The root "methodo-" refers to the system of procedures, principles, and practices applied to a branch of knowledge (Morris, 1969). Hence, the emphasis "in ethnomethodology is on meanings as understood by the social actors themselves" (Frank, 1991). A classic example of how people construct meanings is found in an experiment that could be called The Magical Therapy Machine.

The Magical Therapy Machine

The research subjects in this experiment are undergraduates at a public university in the United States. Garfinkel is a professor at that university. He explains to the research subjects that the university and its staff want to help undergraduates solve the problems they experience. All students experience problems, and these problems can potentially interfere with success in their studies. The way he and his associates are going to help is by asking them, one at a time, to go to this nice comfortable room down the hall. There they can construct a series of questions, questions that can be answered by a simple "Yes" or "No," questions, which, if answered, would help them, solve their problems. The students, in privacy and with confidentiality, then ask each of their questions, via intercom, to a perceptive, attentive, experienced, and expert therapist seated in the next room. The intercom is connected to these two rooms only. The therapist is not able to see them, and they are not able to see the therapist, so there is no need for any embarrassment in this situation. The student asks a question, and the amiable therapist gives an answer.

Actually, there is no therapist in the next room. There is a machine, with a random series of "Yes" and "No" answers on it. What happens in this situation is something like this:

QUESTION: "Am I studying enough?"
ANSWER:"No."
QUESTION: "Should I study more?"
ANSWER:"No."

After the experiment, the students are asked if they had been helped. Their response? Overwhelmingly, "Yes." When asked, "What do you think the therapist had in mind when she/he said . . . ," the students give original, inventive, explanations for any apparent inconsistencies in the therapist's responses. For instance, a student might say something like this: "Oh, there's no inconsistency there. You see, one of my problems *is* that I'm not studying enough. I don't need to study *more*, I merely need to study in a *more focused way*. The *quantity* of my studying is fine; it's the *quality* that I need to improve."

Constructing Order Out of Chaos

Garfinkel's experiment underscores the following sociological insight about culture: *it is culture that makes life seem orderly, coherent, and meaningful.* The answers the students receive from the "therapist" are, quite literally, random chaos—a series of random "Yes"'s and "No"'s. However, the students define this experience as orderly, coherent, meaningful, and helpful. How does this come about? Their culture informs them that "therapists" and "counselors" are (a) experts in the field of understanding human behavior and (b) that their mission is to *help* people, not to trick them or to deceive them, or to hurt them. Drawing on the "cultural definitions of the situation," students "laid meaning on the random, chaotic experience and thereby gave meaning, order, and coherence to this piece of their existence" (Donovan, 1995: 25).

An examination of cultural variability in food habits also vividly makes the point that humans routinely attribute meanings to things that have no inherent meaning. Simply put—*what we consider as edible and as a "delicacy" is taught to us by our culture and has little if anything to do with the physical properties of the item.* Thus, the Eskimos studied by Edward M. Weyer (1962) loved to eat the following as delicacies:

- eggs in any stage of incubation or of deterioration, discarding only the eyes of the embryos;
- a paste made from mashed fish heads that had been buried and allowed to decay until the bones acquire the same consistency as the flesh;
- the raw intestines of fish and birds, swallowed whole;
- live fish, gulped down head first and whole; and
- deer droppings, munched like berries.

There is immense variability, then, in how people define material and nonmaterial cultural elements. A sociological study of culture tells us something important about human malleability and about *the symbolic nature of "human nature."* Humans respond not so much to material and nonmaterial elements per se, but to their *socially constructed* and *socially acquired meanings and contexts.* We perceive material and nonmaterial elements through layers of meaning that we learn from our culture. Culture makes the world predictable by providing gestures, meanings, interpretations, a shared set of expectations, a pallet for interpreting events, a view of the world that we learn in the socialization process. Without this predictability, life would be miserable.

When people are "bashed" in their cars—deliberately and repeatedly smashed into by an automobile driven by a stranger who typically flees before the authorities arrive—their intense, initial fear of driving again in public places stems from the knowledge, forged in the fire of experience, that driving in public space is *unpredictable.* They *know* that at any moment a stranger may "come out of nowhere" and "smash" into them, leaving them to die if they are not discovered by altruistic others. Now, if *all* social situations were similarly unpredictable, life would be hell.

Thomas Stearns Eliot, whose quote opens this chapter, appreciates that culture makes life predictable. The way he phrases it is that "Culture may even be defined simply as that which makes life worth living" (1949: 26). He is saying that it is precisely because most people the majority of the time accepts shared cultural meanings, definitions, and expectations that orderly, meaningful, predictable social life is possible.

Culture Shock

When we find ourselves outside of our familiar culture and in a culture we perceive as significantly different than our own—as happened to the American Fulbright scholar, Harry, in the story that opens this chapter—we tend to experience a disorientation known as **culture shock.** Life is perceived as unpredictable, different, complex, cumbersome, and difficult. We no longer know the repertoire of cultural gestures and symbolic cues that make meaningful and accurate communication possible. We no longer know what to expect or how to make our needs and wants known to others. We do not understand the gestures that other people use. In addition to cultural shock we tend to experience **ethnocentrism:** we perceive the norms, values, institutions, gestures, and other material and nonmaterial components of our culture as "right" and as preferable to those of other cultures.

People do not have to live abroad to experience culture shock. People may temporarily experience it if they travel abroad as a tourist, if

they engage in missionary work abroad, or if they perform National Guard duty in another country. Please read and study Tables 5.1 through 5.7 on some aspects of cultural diversity within the United States. In a country as diverse as the United States, people may experience culture shock when they move to, or move about in, a part of the country—or of their own city—with which they are unfamiliar. *Have you, or anyone you know, ever-experienced culture shock? Please tell us about it.*

TABLE 5.1. Religious Affiliation of U.S. Population.

Church, Sect, Denomination:	Percent
Protestant	53.80
Roman Catholics	38.60
Jew	4.0
Orthodox (Eastern Rite) Catholic	2.70
Buddhist	0.01
Atheist and Others	0.10
Total₁	**100%**

Source: U.S. Bureau of the Census, 1992.
1. May not add to 100 due to rounding.

TABLE 5.2. Race and Ethnic Affiliation of U.S. Population.

Race and Ethnic Affiliation:	Percent
White European	75.90
African American	12.10
Hispanic	2.90
Native American	0.08
Total₁	**100%**

Source: U.S. Bureau of the Census, 1993.
1. May not add to 100 due to rounding.

TABLE 5.3. Top 25 American Indian Tribes for the U. S.: 1990 and 1980 _____

Tribe	1990 Census		1980 Census		
	Number	Percent	Number Percent		Percent
All American Indians	1,937,391	100	1,478,523		1000
Cherokee	369,035	19.6	232,080		15.7
Navajo	225,298	11.6	158,633		10.7
Sioux	107,321	5.5	78,608		5.3
Chippewa	105,988	5.5	73,602		5.0
Choctaw	86,231	4.5	50,220		3.4
Pueblo₂	55,330	2.9	42,552		2.9
Apache	53,300	2.8	35,861		2.4
Iroquois₃	52,557	2.7	38,218		2.6
Lumbee₄	50,888	2.6	28,631		1.9
Creek	45,872	2.4	28,278		1.9
Blackfoot₂	37,992	2.0	21,964		
Canadian & Latin American	27,179	1.4	7,804		0.5
Chickasaw	21,522	1.1	10,317		0.17
Tohono O'Odham	16,876	0.19	13,297		0.9
Potawatomi	16,719	0.9	9,715		0.7
Seminole₂	15,564	0.8	10,363		0.7
Pima	15,074	0.8	11,722		0.8
Tlingit	14,417	0.7	9,509		0.6
Alaskan Athabaskans.	14,198	0.7	10,136		0.7
Cheyenne	11,809	0.6	9,918		0.7
Comanche	11,437	0.6	9,037		0.6
Paiute₂	11,369	0.6	9,523		0.6
Osage	10,430	0.5	6,884		0.5
Puget Sound Salish	10,387	0.5	6,591		0.4
Yaqui	9,838	0.5	5,197		0.4

Source: U.S. Bureau of the Census, Release date: August 1995. (Data are based on a sample)
1 Any entry with the spelling 'Siouan' in the 1990 census was miscoded to Sioux in North Carolina.
2 Reporting and/or processing problems in the 1980 census have affected the data for this tribe.
3 Reporting and/or processing problems in the 1990 census have affected the data for this tribe.
4 Miscoding of entries in the 1980 census for 'Lummee,' 'Lummi,' 'Lumbee,' or 'Lumbi' have affected the data for this tribe.

TABLE 5.4. Detailed Language Spoken at Home and Ability to Speak English for Persons 5 Years and Over—50 Languages with Greatest Number of Speakers. Ranked by Total Number of speakers, United States, 1990

RANKED LANGUAGE	TOTAL SPEAKERS	English Ability VERY WELL	WELL	NOT WELL	NOT AT ALL
UNITED STATES	230,445,777				
ENGLISH ONLY	198,600,798				
TOTAL NON-ENGLISH	31,844,979	17,862,477	7,310,301	4,826,958	1,845,243
1. SPANISH	17,339,172	9,033,407	3,804,792	3,040,828	1,460,145
2. FRENCH	1,702,176	1,226,043	318,409	149,505	8,219
3. GERMAN	1,547,099	1,161,127	284,809	96,804	4,359
4. ITALIAN	1,308,648	874,032	283,354	134,114	17,148
5. CHINESE	1,249,213	496,277	379,720	264,240	108,976
6. TAGALOG	843,251	556,252	223,971	58,320	4,708
7. POLISH	723,483	455,551	169,548	852,988	13,086
8. KOREAN	626,478	242,939	195,120	154,617	33,802
9. VIETNAMESE	507,069	186,207	177,689	118,180	24,993
10. PORTUGUESE	429,860	235,283	96,243	71,305	27,029
11. JAPANESE	427,657	203,197	133,364	83,276	7,820
12. GREEK	388,260	266,072	78,153	38,799	5,236
13. ARABIC	355,150	235,509	82,149	31,596	5,896
14. HINDI (URDU)	331,484	234,705	67,276	24,365	5,138
15. RUSSIAN	241,798	110,368	66,126	50,365	14,939
16. YIDDISH	213,064	151,377	44,213	15,431	2,043
17. THAI (LAOTIAN)	206,266	78,246	70,177	47,374	10,469
18. PERSIAN	201,865	125,135	51,517	19,749	5,464
19. FRENCH CREOLE	187,658	89,056	56,730	35,710	6,162
20. ARMENIAN	149,694	74,586	36,408	25,401	13,299
21. NAVAHO	148,530	82,261	44,481	14,172	7,616
22. HUNGARIAN	147,902	96,200	37,875	12,691	1,136
23. HEBREW	144,292	110,440	26,685	6,471	696
24. DUTCH	142,684	108,936	27,888	5,470	390
25. MON-KHMER (CAMBODIAN)	127,441	33,996	38,782	40,921	13,742
26. GUJARATHI	102,418	67,704	22,657	8,998	3,059
27. UKRAINIAN	96,568	60,949	22,515	11,870	1,234
28. CZECH	92,485	65,336	21,435	5,422	292
29. PENNSYLVANIA DUTCH	83,525	47,402	31,310	4,112	701
30. MIAO (HMONG)	81,877	18,328	25,645	26,505	11,399
31. NORWEGIAN	80,723	63,681	12,706	4,174	162
32. SLOVAK	80,388	58,311	16,322	5,503	252
33. SWEDISH	77,511	62,724	11,364	3,234	189
34. SERBOCROATIAN	70,964	43,303	18,149	8,365	1,147
35. KRU	65,848	53,563	10,630	1,511	144
36. RUMANIAN	65,265	33,552	20,332	8,922	2,459
37. LITHUANIAN	55,781	38,775	11,930	4,820	256
38. FINNISH	54,350	40,996	10,230	3,001	123
39. PANJABI	50,005	31,837	10,448	5,616	2,104
40. FORMOSAN	46,044	20,791	15,562	7,712	1,979
41. CROATIAN	45,206	29,989	10,964	3,912	341
42. TURKISH	41,876	25,684	10,515	4,653	1,024
43. ILOCANO	41,131	18,197	14,770	7,354	810
44. BENGALI	38,101	25,417	9,808	2,578	298
45. DANISH	35,639	29,665	4,771	1,135	68

46. SYRIAC	35,146	20,636	9,106	3,956	1,448
47. SAMOAN	34,914	23,660	7,712	3,129	413
48. MALAYALAM	33,949	21,131	10,093	2,006	719
49. CAJUN	33,670	23,834	7,577	2,073	186
50. AMHARIC	31,505	18,643	9,359	3,078	425

NOTE: 1990 Census language questions: 'Does this person speak a language other than English at home?' 'What is this language?' 'How well does this person speak English–very will, well, not at all?'
Source: U.S. Bureau of the Census, 1990 Census of Population, CPHL - 133

TABLE 5.5. Persons and Families in Poverty in U.S., by Race and Ethnicity, in Numbers (in Thousands) and Percents, 1996

Characteristic	Number (in Thousands)	Percent
PERSONS₁:		
Total	36,529	13.7
White	24,650	11.2
Non-Hispanic White	16,462	**8.6**
Black	9,694	**28.4**
Asian and Pacific Islander	1,454	14.5
Hispanic Origin₂	8,697	**29.4**
FAMILIES₁:		
Total	7,708	11.0
White	5,059	8.6
Non-Hispanic White	3,433	**6.5**
Black	2,206	**26.1**
Asian and Pacific Islander	284	12.7
Hispanic Origin₂	1,748	**26.4**

Source: U.S. Bureau of the Census, March 1997, Current Population Survey. http://www.census.gov/
1. Data for American Indian, Eskimos, and Aluets are not shown separately.
2. Persons of Hispanic origin may be of any race.

TABLE 5.6. Median Net Worth₁ of Households in U.S., by Race and Ethnicity, 1993

Median CHARACTERISTIC OF HOUSEHOLDERS	Net Worth₁
Total	$ 37,587 (+/- $1250)
White	$ 45,740 (+/-$1307)
African-American	$ 4,418 (+/- $697)
Hispanic-origin	$ 4,656 (+/- $681)

Source: U.S. Census Bureau, September 1995.
1. Measured net worth is defined as the sum of measured assets less measured liabilities, such as bank loans, credit card or store bills, and other unsecured debts. All figures are in 1993 U.S. dollars.

Culture as a Group Attribute

The sociological viewpoint informs us that culture is a group attribute. (Please read nearby Box 5.1, "Cinco de Mayo.") It is something that all human groups possess—inner-city gangs (Hunt, Joe, and Waldorf, 1997), monks in a monastery, nuns in a convent, restaurant workers (Fine, 1996), middle-class gangs (Chambliss, 1973), the poor (Lewis, 1966; Galbraith, 1979), financial elites, hunting-and-gathering societies (Redfield, 1947; Sjoberg, 1952), IBM and other large corporations, feudal or urban-agrarian societies (Sjoberg, 1955, 1960), modern industrial societies, prison guards, opera

────── **BOX 5.I** ──────

Cinco de Mayo

Cinco de Mayo, the 5th day of the month of May, is celebrated with much fanfare by Latinos in the United States. It is one of two Mexican Independence days. Here is some background on this important cultural element.

Miguel Hidalgo y Costilla was an important leader in Mexico's revolt against the imperial might of Spain. He is sometimes called the father of Mexican independence. Hidalgo abandoned academic life in the late eighteenth century and served as pastor of several parishes in Mexico. Under his guidance, many of these parishes came to flourish as centers of cultural life and independent economic enterprise, even though the law of Spain prohibited economic enterprise that competed with her industry. As pastor of the town of Dolores in Guanajuato, he and others conspired to wrest independence from Spain. When their plans were discovered, they proclaimed rebellion—el Grito de Dolores (the cry of Dolores)—on September 16, 1810. It is this day that is celebrated in Mexico as Mexican Independence Day.

Mexico was eventually conquered by France. The Mexican army later defeated the French on May 5, 1862, at the Battle of Puebla in Mexico. It is this day that the Cinco de Mayo celebrates.

fans, outlaw motorcyclists, vegetarians, gays and lesbians (Murray, 1996), people on deaths row, mushroomers (Fine, 1997), and so on.

Basic Components of Culture

Sign

A **sign** is a cue or stimulus that is associated with, or that evokes, a response to something else that is not physically present at the time. As you sit in your study, you hear the footsteps of your significant other—your boyfriend, girlfriend, spouse—on the hallway floor, and you smile in anticipation of seeing her or him. The sound of the footsteps is a cue (stimulus) that is associated with your loved one who is not physically present with you. The sound of the footsteps is a sign. A sign may be perceived or experienced through any of the senses—sight, smell, sound, touch, or taste. Signs may be simple (the sound of footsteps) or they may be complex (language).

Symbol

A **symbol** is an arbitrary sign. Paul Revere's "One if by land and two if by sea" is an example of the use of symbolism. In his community, it was agreed that the use of lantern light would signal how the British, the enemy, were approaching. The light of *one* lantern signified that the British were coming by land, and the light from *two* lanterns signified that they were coming by sea. Other examples of symbols include the following:

- Officers in the British Army used a white feather to signify cowardice.
- In the United States, if one is "blue," one is depressed.
- In Germany, if one is "blue," one is inebriated, intoxicated, not depressed.

The meaning of a symbol, then, is not inherent in the object—in the feather, the lantern, or the color—itself. Each particular meaning of the color "blue" is arbitrary. The *meaning of a symbol derives from* common learning and *the consensus of the people who use it in communication.* Please read Box 5.2, "Kwanzaa: An African-American Cultural Festival," and Box 5.3, "Seven Guiding Principles (Nguzo Saba) Infuse Kwanzaa" to learn about the symbols that infuse this celebration with meaning.

I was once surprised to learn that an American friend of mine, during her first few weeks of living and studying in Dublin, Ireland, was mistaken for a prostitute. Men were approaching her on the street and asking "How much?" for various sexual services, as if she were a sexual gas station and they were potential clients wanting so many gallons of petrol for their tanks. It did not matter what part of the city she was in, men approached her in this manner. She found this peculiar. Upon discussing these encounters with local university students, she learned that the culprit was the boots she wore. White patent-leather boots. On a female these *symbolized,* in this particular location (Dublin) at this particular historical moment, *a prostitute plying her trade.* She stopped wearing the boots and received no more unwanted solicitations. A symbol, then, is a sign that evokes a uniform social response form one or more audiences; it is anything that stands for or represents something else.

Gesture

A **gesture,** according to George Herbert Mead, is any vocalization or physical movement that conveys meaning and that evokes a response in one or more persons. A baby cries, and the caregiver picks up baby. The cry is a gesture. In the United States, if a person extends the middle finger of the hand while the thumb and other fingers are clenched and points it at someone, doing so is a gesture, a particular type of insult. In Germany, if one wants to communicate that another person is crazy, one waves one's hand back and forth in front of one's face. In the United States, one twirls one's index finger in circles around one's ear to signify the same thing.

Gesture is an important part of communication. Charles Darwin published a famous book about it over 125 years ago, *The Expression of Emotions in Man and Animals* (1872). He documents that across many cultures, certain facial expressions convey similar emotional states. Social anthropologist Edward T. Hall (1959, 1966), social scientist Nancy Henley (1977) and others (e.g., Efron, 1972) have conducted pioneering analyses of the use of gesture—the use of eyes, arms, hands, legs, and so forth—in human communication in various cultures. In the United States, hands on hips (akimbo) are perceived as a bossy, imperious, defiant, unyielding gesture. Arms crossed signify stubbornness, opposition, or "I am not listening to you." Arms extended, palms open, indicate that "I am open to you," "I am listening to what you say." *Steepling,* that is, touching the fingertips together in a raised position, is a gesture that exudes confidence. It tends to be performed by the dominant person in an encounter. This is the confident, pontifical, egoistic, proud gesture used by Sherlock Holmes when he is raising the consciousness of his devoted sidekick, Dr. Watson.

In the United States, in Anglo-Saxon cultures, eyes up signifies that "I am thinking," while lowering of the eyes signifies submission or sadness. Rolling one's eyes indicates disapproval or derision. Staring is a gesture of aggression, a threat display. In Anglo-Saxon cultures, looking one's conversational partner in the eye signifies interest and honesty. In many Native American Indian cultures, however, eye contact with a conversational partner of higher status is a sign of disrespect. Dilated pupils of the eyes signify interest, and unfocused eyes signify disinterest and boredom.

Language

Language is a universal form of human behavior involving symbolic communication through a culturally accepted system of sound and gesture patterns that have standardized meanings. Some cultures use a **gesture** or pantomime **language** in specific ritualistic occasions. The Aranda of Australia, for instance, use a gesture language when communicating long distances, when greeting members of other tribes, and when custom forbids the use of verbal communication, as during the first year after the death of one's spouse. Gesture languages are also used today among hearing- and speaking-impaired people who have learned at least one of several gesture-languages that are ubiquitously available.

In most human societies today, gesture language is not the only means of communication. It accompanies verbal communication. Cultures vary not only in the meanings they attribute to a given gesture but in the quantity of gesturing that accompanies language. There are "high" and "low" gesturing cultures. For example, studies indicate that during a one-hour conversation, Puerto Ricans use gestures about 180 times, the French about 110 times, Italians 80 times, British, 0 times, Anglo-Saxon whites in the United States, 2 times, and Finns only once (Efron, 1972; Jourad, 1966). In Finnish and British culture, and even in U.S. Anglo-Saxon culture, "speaking with hands" in ordinary daily discourse is perceived as inappropriate behavior, while *not* speaking with the hands is perceived as inappropriate in Italian or Puerto Rican communities.

Sociolinguistics is the study of how language varies by social contexts—for instance, by social class, geographical region, or subculture. A **subculture** refers to the more or less different folkways, mores, material and non-material cultural traits developed by a group within a society. In a particular study, a **cultural trait** (also called a *cultural element*) is the simplest identifiable and significant unit of a culture. Examples of subcultures are the Amish, skin-heads, hunters, vegetarians, feminists, gays and lesbians, juvenile delinquents, writers, quilters, students of karate, body builders, motorcyclists, and so forth.

Studies by William Labov define social class in terms of income, occupation, and education and indicate that variations in social class in New York City have a direct bearing on a speaker's pronunciation of certain consonants and vowels. These differences in pronunciation vary by the interactional situation, whether formal or informal (1973). Other stud-

ies indicate that social *labeling* (social definition) occurs on the basis of these language variations. For instance, the verbalization of people in lower social classes are more likely to be marked by grammatical (e.g., no subject-verb agreement) and phonological speech characteristics (e.g., a "twang"), causing people from higher social classes both to perceive and label them negatively. In contrast, middle, upper-middle, and upper-class speakers are identifiable, not by the presence of "prestige factors" in their language, but by the absence of the *stigmatized* ones (Siiter, 1991).

A **stigma** is an attribution, a social definition, that is discrediting for a person or group. There are stigmas of speech (stuttering, saying "uhh" a lot), of the body (blemishes, scars, disfigurement), of character (untrustworthiness, cowardice, untruthfulness), and of collectivities (what Weber would call *pariah groups*).

Values and Norms

A **value** is a nonmaterial cultural element—an abstract, generalized conception of what is desirable to which members of a group feel a strong, positively-toned commitment and which serves as a standard for selecting and evaluating concrete means, goals, rules, and actions. In short, a value is a concept of what is desirable and what is undesirable. Examples of values are freedom, fraternity, unity, liberty, individualism, patriotism, romantic love, equality, the pursuit of happiness, and justice. Because values guide choices and evaluations of means, goals, rules, and actions, the sociological study of values involves the study of attitudes, behaviors, norms, institutions, social interaction, and social structure.

Values provide generalized standards of behavior that are expressed in more concrete form in other nonmaterial and material cultural elements. For example, values receive expression in *attitudes* and *norms,* which are nonmaterial cultural elements. The value of liberty receives expression in the Statue of Liberty, a material cultural element. Values also find expression in *institutions.* Sociologists use the analytical concept **institution** to refer to an interrelated system of roles and norms organized around meeting important social needs or

BOX 5.3

Seven Guiding Principles (*Nguzo Saba*) Infuse Kwanzaa

1. *Umoja (Unity)* The first principle celebrates the importance of unity in the family, community, nation, and race. This value is expressed in an African saying sometimes translated as, "I am because We are."
2. *Kujichagulia (Self-Determination)* to define ourselves, to name ourselves, to speak for ourselves, and to create for ourselves. This principle encourages people to perceive, to focus on, and to act upon their common interests. People are celebrated for making decisions that are in the best interests of their families and communities.
3. *Ujima (Collective Work and Responsibility)* to build and maintain our community together and to make our sister's and brother's problems our own and to solve them. This principle affirms that people have a role in the family, community, race, and nation.
4. *Ujamaa (Cooperative Economics)* to build and to maintain our own stores,

shops, and other businesses together. This principle affirms the importance of meeting common needs through mutual support.
5. *Nia (Purpose) to* make our collective calling the building of our community to restore our people to greatness. This principle affirms the importance of setting personal goals that benefit the community.
6. *Kuumba (Creativity) to* leave our community more beautiful and beneficial than we inherited it. This principle affirms the importance of using creative energies to build and to sustain a vibrant, hardy community.
7. *Imani (Faith) to* believe with our hearts in our people, our parents, our leaders, our teachers, and the ability of people to succeed and to triumph in righteous struggle.

Important Symbols:
- Colors
  - ✔ Black: for unity, for the face of our people

  - ✔ Red: for the blood shed by our people
  - ✔ Green: for hope and for the color of the motherland
- Nguzo Saba (the seven principles)
- Mishumaa Saba (seven candles, that symbolize the seven principles and the seven days of celebration)
- Kinara (candle holder, that holds the seven candles)
- Umoja (unity, the back center candle)
- Zawadi (gifts)
- Karamu (the feast)
- Kikombe Cha Umoja (unity cup)
- Mazao (fruits, ground provision, vegetables)
- Mkeka (mat, usually made of straw)

A Couple of the Rituals
- The black candle (unity) is placed in the center of the Kinara. Three green candles are placed on the left and three red candles are placed on the right. Candles are then lit each day, alternately from left to right.
- The Kinara is placed atop the Mkeka.

tasks. Examples of institutions are the economy, the family, education, the political order, the military, and religion. The value of capitalism finds expression in the economy of the United States.

Technology

Technology refers to that segment of culture, including tools and knowledge, that embraces all forms of productive technique used by humans and by some non-human primates

(Goodall, 1968, 1971, 1986) to manipulate the physical environment in order to attain a desired practical result (Lachmann, 1991: 297-298). Examples of technology in different types of societies are a digging stick in hunting and gathering societies, the plow in urban-agrarian (feudal) societies; the steam engine, in early industrial societies; and the personal computer in post-industrial societies. Sociologists study the relations among technology and other aspects of social structure.

Cultural Universals and Cultural Variation

Groups that persist across time regularly transmit from one generation to the next the elements of culture—signs, symbols, gestures, language, values, technology, and norms. In this sense, there exists consensus among social scientists that **cultural universals**—cultural elements that are found in virtually all societies—exist. American cultural anthropologist *Ralph Linton* is credited, at least by some, with having coined the term over sixty years ago (1936).

Consensus among social scientists in general, and among sociologists in particular, tends to break down when greater specificity is exacted regarding which specific cultural elements are found universally or ubiquitously in human societies. British anthropologist *George Murdock,* on the basis of extensive cross-cultural analysis, observes that the following are among the cultural elements found in virtually all human societies—courtship, marriage, the family, cooking, a gendered division of labor, an age-based division of labor, a ritualistically-based division of labor, funereal rites, humor, games, myths, incest taboos, and norms regarding dispute resolution (1945, 1949). Murdock stresses that there is immense variation in the expression of cultural universals. For example, with regard to funereal rites, one culture may specify that the deceased is placed in a certain geographic location so that birds may dispose of the flesh; in another, the body is wrapped, rituals are performed, and the wrapped body is placed in the ground; in another the body is burned on a big pyre; and in yet in another the body is prepared in accordance with specific guidelines, is then placed in a particular type of container, which in turn is placed somewhere—in the ground or in a specific above ground structure (mausoleum, pyramid, etc.).

Brown's Universal Norm

Roger Brown observes that basic patterns of social structure are reflected in (a) terms of address and in (b) the initiation of change in intimacy among status unequals. Brown terms this ubiquitous patterning in social interaction

Brown's universal norm (Brown, 1965). Let us briefly look at each part of this norm.

The first part states that if a particular form of address is used to speak with social subordinates, it also is used with intimates; and the form of address used with social superiors or supraordinates is used with strangers (Brown, 1965: 92). Thus many languages have two forms of address, the formal and informal. For instance, in German, the formal word for "you' is "Sie" (sounds like *Zee*), and the informal is "du." Thus, the formal German form of the question "Can you help me?" is "Koennen *Sie* mir helfen?" The informal form is "Kannst *du* mir helfen?" Germans addresses their boss at work as "Sie," even if they have been working together for years. Germans also addresses a stranger as "Sie," for instance when asking for directions, for the time of day, or for assistance. The *informal* mode of address is used with social subordinates (e.g., young children) and intimates (e.g., spouses, sweethearts). Likewise, many other highly inflected languages also utilize two similar forms for the word "you," with the formal form used both with strangers and social superiors and the informal with intimates and social subordinates.

The second part of Brown's universal norm states that when a clear status difference exists between two or more persons, the right to initiate change to more intimate forms of relationship—such as using first names or familiar forms of address—belongs to the person occupying the socially supraordinate status. A boss may say to an employee, "Just call me Janet." A boss invites an employee and her or his significant other home to dinner before the employee would invite the boss. In a heterosexual dating relationship, usually the male is the first to place his arm around the female or to initiate handholding. *Please reflect on your own social interactions. Can you think of instances of Brown's universal norm from your own life? Please tell us about them.*

Cultural Variation within a Society

Cultures may be large or small. In a society that is diverse in terms of geography, region, climate, age, sex or gender, social class, race, ethnicity, religion, occupation, education, and language, sociologists expect culture to vary across individuals and groups. Below are some examples, drawn from the U.S. and elsewhere, of cultural variation within a society with respect to cuisine, neighborliness, voting behavior, perceptions of school climate, surviving the holidays, and access to and use of personal computers.

- *cuisine:* The cuisine of the heartland (Midwest) is heavier—containing more fats, red meat, sugars, starches and fewer fresh vegetables and fruits—than the cuisine of the West Coast.
- *neighborliness:* Neighbors in the Midwest routinely keep an eye out for each other, noting who goes into, and parks outside of, each other's homes (a type of informal Neighborhood Watch). On the East and West Coasts these behaviors are perceived as inappropriately invasive.
- *voting behavior:* Among white voters in the United States, Catholics and Jews long "have provided bedrock support for the Democratic Party," and "mainline Protestant sects generally [have] remained solidly Republican in their preferences during and after the New Deal era." African Americans, many of whom are members of doctrinally conservative fundamentalist Protestant churches, have been aligned with the Democratic Party since 1960 (Manza and Brooks, 1997: 39).
- *school climate:* In high-poverty urban schools, African-American elementary school children view child-teacher relations as the most important dimension of school climate. For them, caring teachers who acknowledge a student's best efforts, listen to children, and are available to help and to comfort those who experience school and personal problems are the most important dimension of school climate (Epps, 1992; Lee and Slaughter-Defoe, 1995; Slaughter-Defoe and Carlson, 1997). In contrast, Latino elementary school children tend to find others things, which might be referred to by the umbrella-term "moral order," as the most important dimension of school climate ("How many kids in class try hard to learn? How many kids share with each other? How comfortable are you when meeting new people at your school?") (Slaughter-Defoe and Carlson, 1997).
- *surviving the holidays:* Sociologists *Ofra Anson* and *Jon Anson* of Ben-Gurion Uni-

versity of the Negev recently concluded a study of subcultural gender differences in surviving the holidays (1997). The research subjects were male and female Moslems in Israel. *Ramadan* is one of two original festivals of Islam. It is a time of atonement and forgiveness. Ramadan lasts a month, during which food, fluid, and other substances should be avoided from sunrise to sunset. At sunset, the fast is broken by a festive meal that is served by females to male family members, male invited relatives, and male poor persons of the community (Esposito, 1990). The fasting of Ramadan is the fourth pillar of Islam and is considered as an important religious duty by Moslems. Men are expected to spend the fasting time in prayer and in reading of the Koran, and women are expected to spend the days fasting and preparing the evening meal whose menu they are expected to change each day of the month.

Robert Handy, executive director of the World Trade Association, reminds us that "In the Middle East, you don't insist on the wife sitting down with the group. . . . Women do not eat with the men. As much as you don't like that, it is true" (CIA World Fact Book, 1995). What this cultural division of gendered labor means within the context of Ramadan, the Ansons point out, is that males are the officiants and participants in the series of ritualized actions that indicate the transition from the profane to the sacred. These important rituals enhance and strengthen social integration and reduce egoism among the men. "Women, by contrast, are required to shoulder the burden of creating the transition to festive sacredness" (Anson and Anson, 1997: 383). Using mortality data for the period 1983-1992, the Ansons document that Ramadan is associated with a *reduction* or postponement *of mortality* among *the men* and an *increase in mortality among the women,* which reflects their different roles in the preparation and celebration of the holy day rites.

- *Computer access and use:* Please read and study Table 5.7, "Level of Access to and Use of Computers in USA, by Race and Ethnicity," which addresses some aspects of subcultural variation in utilization of and access to

TABLE 5.7. Level of Access to and Use of Computers in USA, by Race and Ethnicity, 1984 and 1993, in Percents

	1984	1993
ALL RACES		
Access to a computer: Age 3 to 17 years	15.3	31.9
Access to a computer: 18 years and older	9.1	25.6
Use computer at work₁	24.6	45.8
WHITE		
Access to a computer: Age 3 to 17 years	17.1	35.8
Access to a computer: 18 years and older	9.6	26.9
Use computer at work₁	19.0	37.5
BLACK		
Access to a computer: Age 3 to 17 years	6.1	13.0
Access to a computer: 18 years and older	4.4	13.8
Use computer at work₁	18.3	36.1
HISPANIC₂		
Access to a computer: Age 3 to 17 years	4.6	12.1
Access to a computer: 18 years and older	4.1	12.9
Use computer at work₁	16.44	29.3

Source: Data were collected in October, 1993 in the Current Population Survey, Education and Social Stratification Branch, Population Division, U.S. Bureau of the Census.
1. Use computer at work based on persons with a job.
2. Persons of Hispanic origin may be of any race

an important technology in the United States today. The Current Population Survey of the U.S. Bureau of the Census indicates that of children 3 to 17 years of age, relatively three times as many white (36%) as Black (13%) and Hispanic (12%) children have access to a personal computer (1993). Social Scientist Sherry Turkle's studies support the observation that when children learn to "play" with a computer at a young age, computer proficiency becomes "second nature," part of their sense of who they are (Turkle, 1984, 1995). In our society, computer literacy is becoming an increasingly important component of a liberally educated individual (Shapiro and Hughes, 1996; U.S. Bureau of Labor Statistics, 1997). *Do you feel comfortable using a personal computer for word processing? For analyzing data? Do you have access to the Internet at home? At school? Have you "surfed" the Net? Have you used the Internet to access information useful to you in your university or college studies? If you are working, do you use a computer in your work? Please tell us about it.*

Cultural Capital

Some individuals and groups accept the elements of the dominant culture more than others. The term **cultural capital** (Bourdieu, 1973) refers to the extent to which an individual or a group has absorbed the dominant culture. The greater the extent to which an individual or group has absorbed the dominant culture, the greater its cultural capital (Bourdieu, 1973). The level of an individual or a group's cultural capital influences its life experiences in important ways (e.g., Aschaffenburg and Maas, 1997; Blankston III, Caldas, and Zhou, 1997).

Counterculture

Since the 1960s, American sociologists have used the term **counterculture** to refer to a subculture that rejects key norms and values of the conventional society in which it is situated. In this sense, the Europeans who came to North America would, from the viewpoint of various indigenous groups, have constituted a counterculture. Because much sociology traditionally has been written by persons belonging to more privileged groups, it has been customary for the term counterculture to be used by them when referring to subcultures whose members reject their key values and norms. Examples of countercultures in this country are the Shaker communities (1787-); the old-order Amish; Brook Farm (1841-1847); the Oneida Community of up-state New York (1848-1881) (Kanter, 1972); the Bruderhof or Society of Brothers, founded in the United States in 1953; the "beatniks" of the 1950s; the "flower children" and "hippies" of the 1960s; and present day Aryan Nations, Christian Identity and other white-supremacist militias that view the federal government as an intrusive evil force that they intend to overthrow through violent means (Flyn and Gerhardt, 1990).

Please read Box 5.4 on the "Oneida Community (1848-1881)."

BOX 5.4

The Oneida Community (1848-1881)

John Humphrey Noyes, a preacher and graduate of Yale Theological Seminary, conducted a Bible class in his home in Putney, Vermont. He lost his license to preach there because of his unconventional teachings. Undeterred, he founded the Perfectionists, a group that believed that people could achieve perfection here on earth. In 1848 he founded the Oneida Community about four miles from Oneida, New York. Branches of Oneida also were formed in Wallingford, Connecticut, and in Brooklyn, New York. These communities were structured according to the five following principles.

1. *Economic communism:* All members signed a document transferring money and major possessions to the community. Communal ownership of property was the norm, even when it came to clothes. The community manufactured steel traps, for which they gained patent rights. The traps became the standard brand in the United States and Canada. Oneida was organized around economic communism at a time when the rest of Anglo-Saxon America was organized around the principle of laissez faire capitalism. Oneida was immensely successful economically. Other Oneida industries included the manufacture of silverware. Jobs were rotated from year to year, and in the eyes of the community, all jobs were equally honorable. Men and women shared all labor in the field and in the factory as equally as possible. The sharing of work extended even to the children, who worked from one to three hours a day, six days per week, making the chains for the steel traps. Children needed to produce a minimum quantity and quality of work before being allowed to play.

2. *Communal living:* Communal labor, where the community worked as a group, was used whenever feasible. Communal focus permeated all aspects of social life. The members of the community ate together in one large dining hall and lived in one house. The community convened each evening in a meeting house for prayer and discussion meetings. The members of Oneida viewed all members as forming one big family. In recreation, the most enjoyed activities were those that brought the whole community together—operettas, plays, concerts by the community musicians, and dancing.

3. *Communal child rearing:* Once children were born, they were raised communally in a wing of the house devoted to children. In this wing were three sections or departments: one devoted to a nursery for children up to the age of four, a kindergarten up to the age of six, and another for children up to the age of 12 or 14. The heads of the children's departments or wings were called "papa" and "mother." An excess of affection from the biological parents was viewed as inappropriate because it was viewed as interfering with communally-wide solidarity. Even friendships between children were censured if they excluded others. Children found to be partial could be separated from each

other for a while. An hour in the early evening—6 PM to 7 PM—was "the children's hour." All the children congregated in one room to play games and the adults convened to watch them. Even here, group games, including card games, were encouraged.

4. *Complex marriage:* A distinction was made in Oneida between sexual relations and the bearing of children. All adults had sexual access to every other consenting adult of the opposite sex, and access was sought through a third party. Sexual relations were supervised and regulated by the community. Exclusive relationships were strongly discouraged. If sexual couples formed, they would be broken up; one member could be sent to another branch of Oneida, or the couple could be expelled.

Because it was believed that the young (and hence less spiritually advanced) should learn from the older, more spiritually advanced members, sexual contacts also generally proceeded along these lines. A male's first intercourse would be with a post-menopausal woman, and visa versa.

The Oneidans refrained from child bearing from 1849 to 1869. Child bearing was strictly regulated by the community. All mature females were encouraged to be fruitful and to multiply, and all

men were allowed to have one child. Having more than one child was allowed only to the more spiritually advanced men (called "stirps"). John Humphrey Noyes, as founder of the community, was viewed as the most spiritually advanced male.

In order to have sexual relations for reproductive purposes, members made applications to a committee whose members assessed their "fitness." This process was called *stirpiculture.* If a member of a petitioning pair was considered spiritually unfit, a replacement would be recommended. Of 58 children thus conceived at Oneida, nine were fathered by Noyes himself.

5. *Government and social control through mutual criticism:* Spiritual enhancement was the goal of Oneida. To this end, all members, adults and children alike, were encouraged to report each others misbehaviors. Sinners, after all, should be corrected as soon as possible. At the evening meetings each day of the week, general as well as individual problems and transgressions were communally discussed. Additionally, from time to time members submitted to criticism by a committee of six to twelve community members who served as "judges." In extremely serious cases, the whole community convened to act as judges. The community member was expected to

submit to this criticism in silence and to confess transgressions in writing. The judges pointed out the member's good points as well as his or her weaknesses and gave suggestions as to how the member could best engage in upward spiritual mobility. This was a powerful weapon in the armory of social control. There was no matter too private for mutual criticism.

Oneida viewed the outside world as corrupt, filthy, and sinful. In Oneidans' eyes, it was they themselves who set the example for "the good life." The members of the community had as little contact as possible with the outside world. Members underwent purification rituals to cleanse themselves after having had contact with outsiders. Children were forbidden to speak to outsiders. After outsiders visited the community, Oneidans engaged in communal cleansing of the premises, to erase every trace of the "filthy invaders." Oneidans viewed the outside world as a counterculture, as deviant.

In 1881, the Oneida community dissolved into the Oneida joint-stock company. At that time, it gave up communal childrearing, complex marriage, and much of their communal living arrangements. They continued to manufacture silverware. *(Source: Kanter, 1972: 4-18.)*

Culture in the United States

The General Social Survey

The United States is a large, vastly diverse society. *The National Data Program for the Social Sciences,* more generally known as *the General Social Survey (GSS),* gives us a highly reliable and valid window on various aspects of its social landscape. The goal of the GSS is to make scientifically reliable and valid data available to the social-science community. The basic purposes of the GSS are to gather data on American society in order:

1. to explain constants and trends in behaviors, attributes, and behaviors;
2. to examine the functioning and structure of society as well as the role played by various groups within it;
3. to compare the United States with other highly industrialized societies; and
4. to make high quality data readily available to students, policy makers, and others.

From gender and racial attitudes, to questions of national identity and economic concerns, to the number of Americans who grow vegetables and flowers in a garden, to sexual practices, to musical preferences over the life course, the GSS measures trends in Americans' concerns, attitudes, practices, and experiences.

The General Social Survey is the largest sociology project funded by the *National Science Foundation* (NSF). The General Social Survey is a regular, ongoing personal-interview survey of households in the United States. The personal interviews last about 90 minutes in length and are conducted by the *National Opinion Research Center (NORC).*

The first survey took place in 1972. Between then and now, over 35,000 respondents have answered almost 3,000 different questions. Because some questions are asked in several years, the total number of questions answered by respondents easily exceeds 3,000. Since 1972 the GSS has conducted over 20 independent cross-sectional studies, based on national probability samples of the noninstitutionalized adult population of the United States. Response rates are a respectable 75% or better. Once performed as an annual survey, the GSS was changed to a biennial survey in 1994. It was fielded for the 21st time in 1996. These surveys, regarded as a national treasure, have been disseminated and analyzed widely. Sociologists use data from the U.S. census more than data from the GSS. After the U.S. census data, however, the next most widely used source of data for sociologists are the GSS data. To date, the National Opinion Research Center has documented the publication of over 4,000 articles containing GSS data. Additionally, GSS data are used widely in undergraduate and graduate-level college classes and the news media make continual use of them in stories that cover a wide range of topics.

We use GSS data in this chapter and throughout this textbook because they provide us with a picture window of the United States today and over time. For example, one trend the GSS has noted is a dramatic increase over the past three decades in support for civil liberties. On a lighter note, the GSS finds that the music we prefer when we are teens remains our favorite for the rest of our lives.

Please indicate your preference in music as a teenager: ——————————————————.

Values in the United States

American sociologist Robin M. Williams identifies the following ten values as particularly important to people in the U.S. (1970):

1. *Individualism* Americans view people as responsible for their own successes and failures. When asked from 1983 through 1994 in the General Social Survey, "If you had to choose, which one thing . . . would you pick as the most important for a child to learn to prepare him or her for life?," roughly 70% of American respondents consistently say that *to be able to think for oneself* is either the first or second thing that a person needs to know in order to be prepared for life. That's individualism.
2. *Achievement and success* Americans highly value attaining success through competition with others and tend negatively to value those who are less successful.
3. *Activity and work* Americans prize industriousness and hard work and disparage people who lack these attributes. Stephen

M. Petterson of the Department of Sociology of the University of Virginia recently completed an empirical study of the folk wisdom that young Black men in the United States experience more joblessness than their White counterparts because they price themselves out of the market; that is, they are less willing to seek out low-paying jobs (1997). According to survey data, a growing number of white Americans believe that discrimination is no longer an important issue. Please read Table 5.8, Perception of Discrimination Against African Americans in Jobs, Income, and Housing in U.S. for Selected Years, 1972-1994. Rather than perceiving the worse jobs, income, and housing of African Americans as being due to discrimination, many Americans perceive that the persistence of racial inequality is self-created and that their perceived idleness is voluntary (Mead, 1992; Kluegel, 1990). However, based on data covering almost a decade that are drawn from the National Longitudinal Survey of Youth, Petterson finds *no* differences in wages sought by White and African-American young persons between the ages of 14 and 21 years of age.

4. *Equality* Americans positively value equality *of opportunity. Everyone* should have an equal chance to achieve success and to pursue happiness.

5. *Freedom* Individual freedoms and liberties cherished by Americans include those of religion, speech, privacy, and expression; the freedom to assemble, to dissent, to date and to marry whomever they wish, to own private property and to engage in free enterprise; to be free from taxation without representation and to be free from unwarranted search and seizure.

6. *Democracy* Americans believe that people have a right to be heard, to express their opinions, and to give their input in decision-making processes. According to the value of democracy, imperative order—whether in business, politics, or other domains—best occurs with the consent, in-put, and representation of the people.

7. *Progress and material comfort* Americans believe in progress; the belief is that, with time, things get "better," more just, more affluent, more successful. Americans expect and positively cherish material comfort across domains of behavior, including housing, food, healthcare, personal transportation (automobiles, trucks, motorcycles, bicycles, etc.), recreation and games.

8. *Efficiency and practicality* Efficiency refers to production with the least amount of waste (Lachmann, 1991: 102). Americans positively value efficiency and constantly strive to increase it.

9. *Humanitarianism* Americans positively value personal kindness, helpfulness, and generosity, especially following natural disasters (floods, tornadoes, hurricanes, earthquakes, fires, draughts, etc.).

10. *Racism and group superiority* People tend to value their own group—whether a racial, ethnic, or some other type of cultural group—above others. This is ethnocentrism. Many Americans even feel

TABLE 5.8. Perception of Discrimination Against African Americans in Jobs, Income, and Housing in U.S. for Selected Years, 1972-1994

"On the average (Negroes/Blacks/African-Americans) have worse jobs, income, and housing than white people. Do you think these differences are mainly due to discrimination?

	Year				
	1972-82	1983-87	1988-91	1993	1994
YES	39 %	43 %	40 %	41 %	41 %
NO	56	53	54	54	54
DON'T KNOW OR NO ANSWER	5	4	6	5	5
Total₁	100 %	100 %	100 %	100 %	100 %

*Source: **General Social Survey**, 1994.*
1. May not total to 100 due to rounding.

this way about their high school, college, hometown, and their country—that the United States is "best." The 1993 General Social Survey asked: "Do you feel the quality of life is better in America than in most other advanced industrial countries, about the same, or do you feel that people are better off in most other advanced industrial countries than they are in the United States?" Fully 78% of Americans reply that things are better in America, 15% think things are about the same, and only 4% think things are better in other advanced industrial countries.

Although we explore issues of racism in Chapter 10 (Race and Ethnicity), let us now note that, as used by sociologists, **racism** refers to an individual's or a group's (1) prejudicial attitudes and discriminatory behaviors towards people because of their racial-group affiliation; or (2) institutional practices that subordinate people on the basis of race. Generally speaking, racism is less overt in this country than it was, say, thirty years ago. However, it is by no means absent (Farley, 1997). For instance, a recent content analysis of the portrayal of athletes in advertisements in *Sports Illustrated* from 1985 to 1994 by Mikaela Dufur of Ohio State University reveals that black athletes are more likely to be portrayed as violent, angry, or hypersexual (1997). Black athletes also are more likely to be portrayed as succeeding because of innate physical prowess. White athletes, in contrast, are more often portrayed as succeeding because of leadership qualities, hard work, and intelligence, attributes highly valued both in the business world and in the larger society.

These ten values are some of the core American values. *Can you think of others? Please tell us about them.* For instance, **sexism** is at least as abiding a cultural value in this country as racism. Although we explore issues of sexism elsewhere in this textbook, let us now note that as used by sociologists sexism refers to an individual's or a group's (1) prejudicial attitudes and discriminatory behaviors towards people because of their sex or gender; or (2) institutional practices that subordinate people on the basis of sex or gender. In the United

States legislative and judicial efforts have been made throughout the past few decades towards reducing sexist attitudes and behaviors with moderate success. Realistically speaking, however, sexism is still readily found in many areas of modern American life.

Cultural Values and Inconsistency

Sociologists use the term *value inconsistency* to refer to the conflict between or among two or more simultaneously held values. The attentive reader may have noticed that some core American values conflict with each other. Racism and sexism conflict with the values of equality, freedom, and democracy. Efficiency conflicts with the value of democracy. It takes *time*, effort, patience, tolerance, and perseverance for people to give input, to listen to and to consider the recommendations of others, and to arrive at consensus. Democracy is often an affront to efficiency. The value of justice, an important core value, sometimes conflicts with the value of efficiency. Lynching is efficient but it undermines the values democracy, justice and due process before the law, all core values in the United States.

Many social processes of interest to sociologists revolve around value inconsistencies. *Can you think of one or more current social controversies that involve a conflict or clash of cherished values? Please tell us about it.*

Cultural Values and Personality

Cultural values shape and form personality (Kohn et. al, 1990; Kohn, Slomczynski, and Schoenbach, 1990; Kohn, Slomczynski, Janicka, Khmelko, et. al., 1997). Previously we outlined Max Weber's thesis concerning the Protestant ethic and the spirit of capitalism. It is Weber's thesis that the values of hard sustained work and calculated efficiency legitimized the economic activities necessary for the functioning of capitalism. It is no surprise, then, that in the capitalist United States a majority of people positively value these attributes. All the major institutions—the family, politics, education, and the work place, to volunteer and religious organizations—disseminate and affirm those who possess these values.

Social Relations and Cultural Pluralism: An Emerging American Value

The United States is a mosaic of cultures. **Cultural pluralism** is a perspective and an approach to social relations that holds that cultural heterogeneity is a goal that should be pursued and attained by society. As one of the authors of our textbook points out elsewhere, cultural pluralism allows for cultural differences so long as these differences do not interfere with the principal values and mores of the dominant society (Gonzales, 1990: 56-57). Those who pursue this vision of cultural relations believe that cultural diversity is good for society, that it should be encouraged, and that it is possible for diverse groups to live in social harmony and to experience mutual understanding and respect. Adherents of social pluralism maintain that these should be the goals of society, not a "blending" or a "melting" of groups, not the domination of one group by the other, and not the independent and isolated existence of each group separate from the others.

In the United States today we see more and more signs of the diffusion and acceptability of cultural pluralism. People from various cultural groups practice many of their cultural group's traditions. Please examine nearby Box 5.5 about practices and traditions regarding burial, bereavement, and memorial services among Chinese-, Japanese-, Vietnamese- and Filipino Americans (Braun and Nichols, 1997). In the public and private educational system these days many children, adolescents, and adults are exposed to cultural diversity in a positive environment. This engenders mutual understanding and respect for people who are culturally different. In the 1994 General Social Survey, Americans were asked the following question: "Now, I would like to ask whether you have ever felt the following ways about blacks and their families. For each of the feelings that I ask you about, please tell me whether you have felt that way very often, fairly often, not too often or never. How often have you felt admiration for blacks?" Fully 57% of Americans say they feel that way very often or fairly often and only 7% say they never have felt that way.

BOX 5.5

A Summary Comparison of Bereavement, Memorial Services, and Burial in Four Asian-American Cultures

Chinese Americans

- Do not move the body of the deceased for 8 hours after death.
- Burn symbolic money, mattresses, furnishings, transportation, servants, and so forth for the deceased's use in the next life.
- Traditionally, the Chinese like to be buried with jewelry, particularly jade. A pearl may be place in the mouth of a dead woman, a coin in the mouth of a dead man, to keep them from talking.
- Open caskets are common.
- Mourners wear white, except if the deceased is an old person. In that case, a bright

color, even red, is worn. Red is a symbol of celebration. An old person's funeral is a celebration of the deceased's long life.
- It is important to rearrange the furnishings and decorations of the house of the deceased. It is bad luck to leave them intact in the place where the deceased lived. The family will not use the deceased's personal belongings, and they are given away.
- Memorial services are held every 7 days for 49 days.
- Ancestors are honored annually at Ching Ming Festival

- Mourning time varies according to the relationship between the deceased and the survivor. Generally, 100 days should pass before survivors engage in any form of entertainment (weddings, celebrations, parties, etc.). Commonly, there is a 3-year period of mourning following the death of a child or of a parent, and a 1-year period following the death of a spouse.

Japanese Americans

- It is important for the family to gather at the deathbed immediately after death while a minister chants the *mukurago,* or *pillow sutra.* This sutra expresses the deceased's gratitude toward both life and death, and it contains a number of *gata* (verses) that are chanted by those in attendance and that are soothing to those who chant them. Traditionally, this sutra is read at the bedside of the dying person, so that her or his last thoughts will be of peace and of gratitude. More often these days, it is chanted at the bedside of the deceased, so that her or his spirit is helped to find a "right" direction as it moves away from the physical body.

- Cremation is preferred over burial.
- White is worn to funerals.
- Memorial services are held every 7th day for 49 days, which allows relatives to comfort one another, to get to know one another better. Memorial services are also held after 100 days and at the 1-,3-,7-,17-, 25-, 33-, and 50-year anniversaries of the death.
- **Obon** is an annual Buddhist cultural event celebrating the lives of those who have died. During Obon season, people participate in traditional dances under lantern-filled courtyards at the Buddhist temple.

Vietnamese Americans

- Relatives should not cry out or show emotion at the moment of their beloved's death, because to do so might jeopardize the deceased's soul from being reborn.
- Consult a monk or a priest for an auspicious day and for a time of day for the burial.
- Place coffee and tea in casket to keep deceased's body fresh.
- Deceased is buried with a piece of rice or a tiny piece of gold in her or his mouth.
- Eldest son makes funeral arrangements.
- Dress the deceased in beautiful clothing.
- Place lighted candles at the four corners of the casket to ward off ghosts.
- White, a sad color, is worn to funerals.
- A blessing is held before burial or before cremation. In Viet Nam the custom is to bury the dead. In the U.S. it has become acceptable to cremate the deceased and to bring the ashes home or to place them in the temple.
- It is important for nonfamily to attend the funeral, to comfort and support the family of the deceased.
- A white headband is worn at memorial services which are held every 7 days for 7 weeks and then again after 100 days.
- Annually, ancestors are remembered in the third lunar month during a ceremony called **Thanh Minh.** Family members come to the cemetery to tend the grave. Also, annually in the seventh lunar month, the ritual of **Vu Lan** is observed. Family members go to the temple to pray for the souls of their ancestors to be liberated.
- Mourning can last up to 3 years. During mourning survivors wear only white or attach a piece of black fabric to their clothing.

Filipino Americans

- A 9-day novena is held. Prayer services are held each night. During this time, family members customarily take turns watching over the body. If the deceased is a husband, the widow must not go out unaccompanied during this time.
- On the 9th night, an **atang** (feast containing the favorite foods of the deceased) is held during which the deceased may appear to say good-bye). A place is set at table for the deceased, so she or he may also eat. It is customary for personal belongings to be buried with the deceased, so the deceased will not come back and request these items (e.g., soap, glasses, razor, etc.) Paper and writing implements may be placed with the deceased, so that the deceased may write messages rather than return to relay them in person.
- When a child dies, white is worn, because children are considered to be with the angels after death, and angels do not wear black. Black is worn by family members when an adult dies. A combination of white and black is worn by family members when a younger person dies.

Source: Braun and Nichols, 1997.

Another indication of the extent of cultural pluralism comes from an analysis of responses to two questions regarding self identity that appear for the first time in the 1993 General Social Survey. Please read Tables 5.9 and 5.10 on American Self-Identity. These tables reveal that when asked: "When you think of social and political issues, do you think of yourself mainly as a member of a particular ethnic, racial, or nationality group or do you think of yourself mainly as just an American?," *between 89-91% of Americans think of themselves as "just an American" on most or all issues even as they practice cultural diversity.*

Strain and Conflict Amid Cultural Diversity

We must not over state the amount of agreement among cultural groups in the United States. We have not yet achieved the goal of cultural pluralism. From 1989-1991 and again in 1994, the General Social Survey asks people to respond to the following: "There is a lot of discussion today about whether Americans are divided or united. Some say that Americans are united and in agreement about the most important values. Others think that Americans are greatly divided when it comes to the most important values. What is your view about

this?" Most Americans, 63% in 1988-1991 and 55% in 1994, say that we are greatly divided when it comes to the most important values. At both time periods only one American in three—32% in 1988-1991 and 39% in 1994—says that we are united and in agreement about the most important values.

There also is evidence of strain and a potential basis for conflict in perceptions regarding fair access to schooling and jobs in this country. There is a decline in popular support for government intervention to help improve the living standards of African Americans. Please read Table 5.11, "American Attitudes on Government Help and Race, 1972-1994." Since 1972, the General Social Survey has asked Americans the following question: "Some people think that (Blacks/Negroes/African-Americans) have been discriminated against for so long that the government has a special obligation to help improve their living standards. Others believe that the government should not be giving special treatment to (Blacks/Negroes/African-Americans). Where would you place yourself on this scale, or haven't you made up your mind on this?" American support for government help declined from less than 24% in 1972 to 15% in 1994. Many Americans experience value inconsistency and agree with both sides of the issue.

TABLE 5.9. American Self-Identity, I _____

"When you think of social and political issues, do you think of yourself mainly as a member of a particular ethnic, racial, or nationality group or do you think of yourself mainly as just an American?

	YEAR 1993
Just an American	89.0%
Some particular ethnic, racial, or nationality group	7.3
Two or more ethnic, racial, or nationality groups	0.2
Just an American and one or more particular ethnic, racial, or nationality groups	1.3
It depends	0.8
Don't know or no answer	1.0
Total₁	100%

*Source: **General Social Survey**, 1993.*
1. May not total to 100 due to rounding.

TABLE 5.10. American Self-Identity, II _____

"When you think of social and political issues, do you think of yourself mainly as a member or a particular ethnic, racial, or nationality group or do you think of yourself mainly as just an American?"

"Do you think of yourself as "just as an American" on all issues, or just a few issues?"

	YEAR 1993
All issues	60%
Most issues	31
Some issues	6
Just a few issues	2
Don't know or no answer	1
Total	100%

Source: General Social Survey, 1993.

TABLE 5.11. American Attitudes on Government Help and Race, 1972-1994 _____

"Some people think that (Blacks/Negroes/African-Americans) have been discriminated against for so long that the government has a special obligation to help improve their living standards. Others believe that the government should not be giving special treatment to (Blacks/Negroes/African Americans). Where do you place yourself on this scale, or haven't you made up your mind on this?"

```
        |----------------------------------------|
        I        2        3        4        5
```

1 and 2 = I Strongly Agree the Government Is obligated to Help Blacks
3 and 4 = I Agree with Both Answers
    5 = I Don't Know or No Answer

	YEAR				
	1972-1982	1983-1987	1988-1991	1993	1994
RESPONSE:					
Government help	**24**%	18%	19%	17%	**15**%
Agree with both	33	46	47	52	52
No special treatment	**40**	32	30	27	**29**
Don't know or no answer	3	4	4	4	4
Total	100%	100%	100%	100%	100%

Source: *General Social Survey*, 1994.

Evidence of strain and of the potential for conflict may be found in perceptions of equal access to schooling and jobs. Please read nearby Tables 5.12 and 5.13. A majority of Americans (67%) perceive that it is either "very likely" or "somewhat likely" that a white person won't get admitted to a college or university program while a less qualified black person gets admitted instead (General Social Survey, 1994). And throughout the period from 1988 to 1994, which is the most recent period for which we have data, the majority of Americans (67%)

likewise perceive that it is either "very likely" or "somewhat likely" that these days a white person won't get a job or promotion while an equally or less qualified black person gets one instead (General Social Survey, 1994). When asked what the chances are these days that *you or anyone in your family* won't get a job or a promotion while an equally or less qualified (White/Black/African American) employee receives one instead, the percentage who think this "very likely" or "somewhat likely" drops to 46%.

TABLE 5.12. College _____

"What do you think the chances are these days that a white person won't get admitted to a college or university program while a less qualified black person gets admitted instead? Would you say: very likely, somewhat likely, or not likely."

	YEAR 1994
very likely	27%
somewhat likely	40
not likely	27
don't know or no answer	6
Total	100%

Source: *General Social Survey*, 1994

TABLE 5.13. Jobs _____

"What do you think the chances are these days that a white person won't get a job or promotion while an equally or less qualified black person gets one instead? Is this very likely, somewhat likely, or not very likely to happen these days?"

	YEAR	
	1988-1991	1988-1991
very likely	25%	25%
somewhat likely	39	39
not very likely	34	34
don't know or no answer	2	2
Total	100%	100%

Source: *General Social Survey*, 1994

Sociological Imagination Enhances Our Understanding of Cultural Conflict

A sociological imagination helps us to make sense out of these data. Many Americans seem to be expressing anxiety about unfair access to scarce yet widely valued goods and services—access to college and access to jobs. Even the expressed fear regarding access to a college education could be interpreted as a marker for anxiety about access to jobs. Many Americans view a college education mainly as a means to the end of a well-paying job.

What *else* besides competition from other workers could be causing a perception of scarcity in the number of jobs in America, especially of well-paying, secure jobs? The attentive reader recognizes this as a question of internal validity. Other than competition (whether fair or unfair) from other workers, what could cause a perception of a decline in the number of available well-paying jobs?

A decline in the number of manufacturing jobs is one factor. It is also a manifestation of *major changes in the occupational structure* that have been occurring in the United States over the past several decades. The manufacturing sector of the economy was once a treasure-trove of highly unionized and well paying jobs. The U.S. has lost world-market share in steel production, automobile manufacturing, and shipbuilding. As a result many well-paying and secure jobs have disappeared from our communities. This process is sometimes referred to as *the deindustrialization* of America.

Consolidation or concentration has been occurring within industries. One company buys out another, lays off workers, and becomes an economically more competitive organization. It then repeats the process, again and again. Many Americans have lost their well-paying jobs due to these processes.

Moving companies off-shore This practice has proliferated. Instead of paying workers the relatively high wages and fringe benefits (health care, retirement benefits, sick leave, disability insurance, etc.) that many American workers are accustomed to earning, a company moves its business to another country where wages are a mere fraction of what they are in the United States and fringe benefits are next to nonexistent. The company's profit margins increase, its stockholders are happy, and many people in this country are without work. A variation on this theme is to have the *parts* manufactured in another country and then to assemble the final product in this country. Once again, many jobs are lost. *The North American Free Trade Agreement* (NAFTA) and the *General Agreement on Tariffs and Trade* (GATT) have accelerated these trends. Those who manage to keep their jobs are more tractable employees. They are less likely to make demands on their employers because they are afraid of losing their jobs, and they know jobs are scarce.

White majority–group Americans have lost far more jobs because of these structural changes than they have to fair or unfair competition from fellow workers, whether these workers are white, black, male, female, disabled, able-bodied, native-born or immigrants

However, it is far easier for many Americans to "see" a person whose physical and cultural appearance differs from their own than it is for them to "see" these larger-scale meso- and macro-level factors. Your growing sociological imagination helps you to (1) look for, (2) to perceive, and (3) to understand the importance of these larger factors in shaping the landscape of our daily lives. We find answers where we look.

Marxian conflict theorists would observe that people who fail to look for larger-scale causes of the perception of job scarcity are suffering from false consciousness. Persons with **false consciousness** fail to perceive two things: (1) that they have interests in common with all others whose relation to the economic means of production is the same as theirs and (2) that their common interests are both different than and opposite to those who own the economic means of production. In the Marxian paradigm, people with false consciousness fail to perceive that the objective economic interests of the owners of the economic means of production are different than, and opposite to, the interests of those who sell their labor. *Functionalist* or *consensus theorists* might point out that by "blaming" and fighting amongst each other, people from different cultural traditions are *not looking elsewhere* for causes of perceived job scarcity, a situation which, while rough on each other, works to the advantage of those already privileged economically.

This phenomenon is called tertius gaudens. In **tertius gaudens** already existing cleavages both between and among the constituent groups in a population are reinforced and accentuated, thereby making it decidedly more likely that the various groups would fight among themselves rather than against those who actually are dominating and exploiting them. "Tertius" is Latin for "third" and "gaudens" is Latin for "joy of." Although the common translation is "divide and conquer," the literal translation into English as "joy of the third" captures the point that a third group (C) benefits by two other groups (A, B) fighting among themselves. The third and joyous group is left alone in peace, while the other two groups fight and kill each other.

Culture in Other Societies

A central and perhaps the most-researched dimension along which cultures vary is individualism-collectivism (Hofstede, 1990; Cousins, 1989; Singelis, Triandis, Bhawuk, and Gelfand, 1995; Aaker and Maheswaran, 1997). Please read Table 5.14, "Individualism-Collectivism: A Comparison of Attitudes and Behaviors." **Individualism** is a concept that gives priority to defining self in terms of personal attributes and to one's own goals over the goals of the group (Myers, 1993:213). Members from individualistic cultures such as the United States, Canada, Great Britain, and Australia tend to develop a view of the self that emphasizes separateness, internal attributions ("I made that happen"), and the uniqueness of individuals. Individualism tends to flourish when the kinship structure or government no longer controls the individual's access to scarce and widely valued goods and services.

TABLE 5.14. Individualism-Collectivism: A Comparison of Attitudes and Behaviors _____

Social or Cultural Element	Type of Culture	
	Individualism	**Collectivism**
SELF	Defined more in terms of individual attributes (red hair, tall, athletic)	Defined more in terms of important others and of group affiliations (family, kin, ethnicity, race, religion, village, community, etc.) The self is adequate, whole, and fulfilled to the extent that it lives up to and contributes to attaining the goals of the community.
ROLE OF OTHERS	Others are useful for self-evaluation ("How well am I doing?" Oh, I'm definitely doing better than Alfred and Susie. I'm doing OK.)	Others are more important in self-definition. Social relationships (family, kin, clan, ethnic group, village, etc.) crucial in self-definition.
VALUES	Emphasis is on self, individuality, separateness.	Emphasis is on interconnectedness, inter relatedness, relationships.
BEHAVIOR	Individual reflects on ego, on what ego's wants and desires are. In this sense, ego is introspective. One "does one's own thing."	The individual is outward looking, focused more on groups outside of self. In this sense, ego is mortified and transcended. Individual does the community's thing and thinks that it and his or her own thing are one and the same.

Source: Adapted from Aaker and Maheswaran, 1997: Table 1, p.316.

In contrast, **collectivism** is a concept that gives priority to defining self in terms of group affiliations and gives priority to the goals of the group over one's own personal goals (Myers, 1993: 213). Goals of the clan, the village, and the family are given priority over one's own wants and desires. Collectivist cultures include Taiwan, Japan, Peoples Republic of China, the former Soviet Union, and aborigines in Australia (Fogarty and White, 1994). People there tend to develop a view of the self as *interdependent.* This view emphasizes that one lives in a social context enmeshed in a web of connectedness. Collectivism tends to flourish where families are large, people face shared threats (e.g., tigers and lions, marauders, famine, harsh climate), and where the mode of life requires a great deal of coordinated effort (as when building or maintaining canals and irrigation systems).

World Culture

For a century and more, the world has been conceptualized as a unitary social system, increasingly bound together by overlapping social circles of economic exchange, cooperation, and competition (Boli and Thomas, 1997:172). World culture was created after the end of the Second World War. At this time, the United Nations and related bodies (e.g., the General Agreement on Tariffs, the International Monetary Fund, and the World Bank) established agendas of concern for world society. These include a focus on individual rights; egalitarian justice; participatory representation; economic development; scientific, medical, educational development; and environmental protection and reclamation (Jones, 1992). A wide range of social domains became eligible for international scrutiny and discussion.

Sociologists John Boli of Emory University and George M. Thomas of Arizona State University remind us that culture is increasingly global (1997; Featherstone, 1990; Robertson, 1992). As happens in all cultures, "world culture becomes imbedded in social organization," particularly in organizations operating at the global level (Boli and Thomas, 1997: 172). Most of these organizations are international non-governmental organizations (INGOs). While these organizations traditionally are referred to by the acronym NGO, Meyer, Boli,

Thomas, and others use the acronym INGO, which better stresses their *international* focus. John Boli and George Thomas (1997) and sociologists John W. Myer and Francisco O. Ramirez, both of Stanford University, directly identify and explore the basic elements of world culture through an analysis of the basic structures, goals, and operations of INGOs (1997). We now outline some of the results of their analysis of world culture.

International Non-Governmental Organizations (INGOs)

Since 1850 more than 25,000 INGOs have debuted on the world stage (Meyer, Boli, Thomas, and Ramirez, 1997: 174). These include the International Sociological Association, International Catholic Child of the World, International Labor Organization, the United Nations Children's Fund (UNICEF), Commission for the Geological Map of the World, the Pan American Association of Ophthalmology, and the International Tin Council. Only a few, such as the International Red Cross, the International Olympic Committee, Amnesty International, Greenpeace, and the World Wildlife Fund, are widely known. *Using a search engine, enter the name of an INGO and go to its Home Page. Access its mission statement and its goals statement.*

INGOs' Goals

INGOs originate and continue through the voluntary actions of individual social actors. INGOs have explicit, rationalized goals. They operate in accordance with strong norms of participatory democracy and of open membership. They seek, in a general sense, to disseminate "progress" throughout the world by encouraging more efficient and safer technical systems,

■ more powerful knowledge systems,
■ friendly competition, and
■ better care of the human body.

To achieve these goals, they emphasize individual commitment, consensual values, democratic decision making, communication, knowledge, and rationalization in the Weberian sense (Boli and Thomas, 1997: 180).

Categories of INGOs

Table 5.15, Percentage Distribution of INGOs active in 1988, by Categories, documents that INGOs cover a broad range of activities. The distribution of these activities reveals a couple of important points. First, INGOs, and the world culture they champion are heavily "economic." They are concerned with economic and business development. Twenty-five percent of all active INGOs are based on industry, trade, and tertiary (service) organizations. Second, many INGOs are concerned with scientific and technical knowledge, along with the communication of that knowledge. They account for slightly over one-third of all INGOs. In total, *nearly 60% of INGOs focus on technical rationalization* or economic concerns.

It is also noteworthy that more than 200 sports are organized at the world level. Sports activities serve as a major source of identity and of solidarity (Boli and Thomas, 1997: 183). Sports and leisure, while providing avenues of personal fulfillment ("Leisure provides what work denies"), also have become highly rationalized. In sports organized at the world level, INGOs centralize and standardize rules, measurement procedures, and training methods. That's rationalization. What once was based on insight and "by the seat of your pants" becomes highly regularized and predictable.

Individual rights and welfare INGOs promote universal group rights (for minorities,

TABLE 5.15. Percentage Distribution of INGOs Active in 1988, by Categories

Category	Percent
Industry/trade/industrial groups	17.6 %
Medicine/health care	14.9
Sciences/mathematics/space	11.6
Sports/hobbies/leisure	8.0
Technical/infrastructure/communications	7.4
Tertiary economic/finance/tourism	7.2
Individual rights/welfare	6.3
World-polity	6.2
Religion/family/cultural identity	6.1
Labor/professions/public administration	6.0
Education/students	4.2
Humanities/arts/philosophy	3.9
Political ideologies/parties	0.6
Total	100 %

Source: Boli and Thomas, 1997: Adapted from Figure 2, p. 183.

women, the disabled, indigenous peoples, children, refugees, and so forth). The world-polity INGOs promote international law, human rights, world peace, and environmental preservation. These latter two sectors or categories contain the most widely known organizations and jointly account for about 6% of the INGO population.

Those INGOs promoting primordial ties—to family, religion, ethnic or cultural identity—account for about 6% of INGOs. These, along with Labor/Professions/Public Administration and Political Ideologies/Parties (the smallest sector), are sectors whose shares of the total INGO population have declined (Boli and Thomas, 1997). The relative decline of these *particularistic* sectors indicates that the value of individualism has become stronger since the early part of the twentieth century, at which time the particularistic sectors had their largest share of the INGO population

Particularism refers to the orientation of one individual (or social actor) to another on the basis of the special nature of their relationship to each other (for instance,, membership in the same group or category—they both have blue eyes). If a judge sentences a person leniently because the person is her or his nephew, the judge is applying *particularistic* standards. The opposite of particularism is universalism. **Universalism** refers to the orientation of one individual (or social actor) to another on the basis of generalized standards or principles of behavior rather than on any special relationship that may exist between them. If a special relationship exists between persons in a situation defined as appropriately universalistic, the persons are expected to ignore this relationship. If a nephew appears before a judge for sentencing, and the person is the judge's nephew, the principle of universalism requires that the judge apply the same standards to him as to others. In some societies, people are expected to practice the principle of universalism, while in other societies they are not.

Manifest Functions of INGOs

INGOs serve several manifest functions (Meyer, Boli, Thomas, and Ramirez, 1997; Boli and Thomas, 1997). They provide access to the following inventory of cultural assets: (1)

leading-edge ideas and technologies; (2) models of organization and of policy construction and implementation; (3) consultants who give hands-on assistance; (4) training programs that assist a country's elite in learning the cultural principles of the INGOs. INGOs also provide the following as assistance:

1. help countries develop economically
2. collect data helpful in assessing a country's population—its health, health-care needs, level of literacy, political status, language distribution, labor force characteristics
3. provide models of data analysis and of interpretation

Also, many INGOs have a "missionary" or "social-movement character" (Meyer, Boli, Thomas, and Ramirez, 1997:164). They actively champion a cause (human rights, consumers' rights, the rain forests, endangered species, and wildlife). They decry abuses in particular locales and demand their correction. Through these functions, then, INGOs *redefine the society in fully rationalized terms* as a fitting candidate for modernity. Eventually, social actors know enough to push this rationalizing process along themselves.

Latent Functions of INGOs: Individual and Collective Identity Construction

In a quote that opens this chapter sociologists John Boli of Emory University and George M. Thomas of Arizona State University remind us that the *cultural principles of INGOs* do more than merely orient human action. They *define the self* (1997). In the next chapter (Socialization: Internalizing Relationships That Make a World) we examine several social-science perspectives of human development. The sociological view is that *we draw on cultural principles in constructing our sense of self*, in constructing a sense of "who we are." INGOs provide a particular menu of options for telling us who we are. People draw on these world cultural elements or principles in order to achieve the following:

■ Construct a sense of self.
■ Construct social identities.

■ Construct roles and statuses by means of which we may pursue our interests.
■ Define collective identities and interests (business firms, nations).
■ Define the organizational form (rationalized bureaucracy) to be adopted by us as citizens of the world.

Elements of World Culture Embodied in and Disseminated by INGOs

Five basic world-cultural elements are embodied in and spread by INGOs: individualism, universalism, rational voluntaristic authority, rationalization (in the Weberian sense), and world citizenship (Boli and Thomas, 1997; Meyer, Boli, Thomas, and Ramirez, 1997). Let us examine each in turn.

1. *Individualism* Most INGOs only accept individuals as members or associations of individuals (e.g., the International Sociological Association). The big exceptions are trade and industry groups. Individualism is evident in their democratic decision-making procedures of one person/one vote. In the worldview (*Zeitgeist*) of INGOs individuals are the only real social actors. INGOs, in other words, engage in the fiction that collectivities are mere assemblages of individuals.
2. *Universalism* The view of human nature that informs INGOs is that all humans have free will, the same needs and desires, and are able to act in accordance with common principles regarding authority. All humans also, according to INGOs, have the same goals. Any interested person may become a member of an INGO. Anyone, anywhere, is a beneficiary of INGO activity. INGOs commonly and habitually invoke "the good of humanity" as a goal. They view themselves as occupying a moral high ground.
3. *Rational voluntaristic authority* INGOs embody a particular cultural model when they organize, debate principles and models, recommend policies and so forth. In this model, rational individuals acting collectively by means of rational and democratic procedures are able to determine

cultural rules that are efficient, just, and equitable. Moreover, no external authority is required for their legitimization.

This, at first glance, appears remarkable to some observers. Why? INGOs have little sanctioning power (little imperative order). Yet they make rules (normative order) and expect them to be followed. They plead their views to the international community and to transnational corporations (solidary order). They issue policies, guidelines, and rules. If these are not followed, they issue moral condemnation.

Sociologists note that their authority is *informal*. Its basis of legitimization is cultural, not organizational (rational-legal), not traditional (rooted in ancient custom or tradition), and not rooted in the followers' belief in the extraordinary character of their leader (charismatic authority). The authority of INGOs is rooted in "the diffuse principles of world culture" (Boli and Thomas, 1997: 181).

As we later learn in Chapter 12 (Groups, Organizations, Bureaucracy, and Work), it is *not* unusual, sociologically, for authority to be based on the shared consensus of a community of social actors. Sociologists are merely unaccustomed to observing it being played out in this form at the *global* level. Sociologists, like yourselves, are just learning about *global* culture.

4. *Weberian rationalization* INGOs are rational structures. This is evident in their purposive mission and goals statements and in their attention to procedures. Some INGOs—those in science, AMA-style western medicine, and technical fields—are engaged in "purely rationalized and rationalizing activity" (Boli and Thomas, 1997: 181). Most of the other INGOs rely on science, professionalization, and expertise in their programs and operations. Rational progress is what INGOs seek; and, at all levels—individual, corporate, society, and world—progress is viewed as due to rationalization. In INGOs, almost all domains and aspects of social life are eligible for discussion, debate, and rationalization, including political structure, family life, religious doctrines, economic structure, education, organization, sexuality, and hu-

man reproduction. All these are expected to conform to world cultural principles.

5. *World citizenship* The other four principles come together in the construct of world citizenship. According to INGO's viewpoint, every person is endowed with certain rights and obligations. Everyone is capable of free will. Everyone seeks a rational solution to social problems. Therefore, "everyone is a citizen of the world" (Boli and Thomas, 1997: 182).

As viewed by INGOs, world citizenship is highly egalitarian. Humans differ in capacities, gifts, resources, and so forth, but what really counts is that all have the same obligations and rights. It is further held that democratic governance structures, and no others, are fully compatible with world citizenship. This viewpoint is codified in *The Universal Declaration of Human Rights*, which was ratified on December 10, 1948, by the General Assembly of the United Nations. (The URL of a Web site that contains both a summary and the full text of The Universal Declaration of Human Rights is listed as an Internet Resource at the end of this chapter.) Following this historic act, the General Assembly called upon all member countries to publicize the text of the Declaration and "to cause it to be disseminated, displayed, read and expounded principally in schools and other educational institutions, without distinction based on the political status of countries or territories."

Strain, Conflict, and World Culture

Many of the principles of world culture are contested and generate conflict. World culture is a hotbed of conflict and of internal contradictions. For instance, the value of individualism conflicts with values cherished in more authoritarian societies, such as those of the former Soviet Union and the Peoples Republic of China. Then, too, there is value inconsistency inherent in world cultural values themselves—equality versus liberty, diversity versus standardization, individuality versus efficiency, and so forth. Actors contest and disagree about the level of state regulation; too much may inhibit economic development; not enough may lead to the lack of a rationalized legal system, which in turn makes economic development precarious; a lack of state regulation may lead to an "excessive" level of social inequality. Too much nationalism may lead to genocide (or *ethnic cleansing*, as it is often termed in the 1990s); too little to anomie.

In short, world culture is not static. It is dynamic, changing, evolving. World culture increases the bases for solidarity and cohesion and it also increases the bases for conflict. For instance, a dialectic or tension operates between the concepts of rationality and irrationality. The effect of this dialectic is to strengthen both (Thomas, 1989; Boli and Thomas, 1997: 181). The apparent failure of actors to behave rationally leads to theorizing about the irrational self and about irrational culture. Rationalized actors are thus culturally defined as possessing an irrationality that is more primordial than their rationalized selves (Gusfield, 1996) and that represents their true selves. The irrational, à la Nietzsche or à la Freud, thus becomes an arena of authenticity (Katz, 1988).

Social movements arise to counter rationalization, movements claiming to be anti-science, post-modern, anti-Western, and so on. Rationalized western social science rides roughshod over the cultural contributions and worth of peoples of color. The colonization of the New World is rampant Eurocentric imperialism that destroys what it touches. Capitalism is an evil dehumanizing force that must be resisted by all authentic persons to maintain their true humanity, liberty, and irrationality. In this dialectical process, irrationality itself is rationalized and channeled into rationalized forms (e.g., UFO cults). Yoga becomes a technique to lower blood pressure. Extra-sensory perception becomes a technique for apprehending criminals. Many social processes may be examined and understood sociologically in terms of world-cultural social dynamics and dialectics.

Please read Box 5.5, "A.K.D., World Culture, and You."

BOX 5.6

A.K.D., World Culture, and You

Alpha Kappa Delta (A.K.D.) is an international sociological honor society. It began in 1920 when American sociologist Emory S. Bogardus suggested to sociology students at University of Southern California (USC) that they form a society in which students could become acquainted with each other's research projects.

Devised by Professor Bogardus and adopted by the members of the USC chapter of A.K.D., the name Alpha Kappa Delta represents the first letters of three Greek words. The "A" is for "anthropon" which translates into English as "humankind." The "K" is for "katamanthaneion, "which translates variously as "to conduct research" or as "thoroughly to investigate." The "D" is for "diakonesein," which translates

into English as "for the purpose of service." Thus, the name of the sociology honor society implies conducting research for the purpose of serving humankind.

Today there are 60,000 of members of A.K.D. in over 400 chapters throughout the world (Maurer and Sheets, 1998: 2379). Many countries have A.K.D. chapters, including the United States, the Peoples Republic of China, Canada, Taiwan, and the Philippines. Perhaps you may become a member one day.

A suggested initiation of new members into A.K.D. includes the following ritual which we quote directly from **The 1995-1996 Handbook of the United Chapters of Alpha Kappa Delta,** pp. 26-28:

President[of local A.K.D. chapter] speaking:

Initiates to Alpha Kappa Delta:. . . Because of your superior scholarship and your serious interest in sociology, you have been invited to become members of Alpha Kappa Delta, the International Honor Society in Sociology. Mr./Ms. _____, our Initiating Officer, will now instruct in the history, organization, aims, and ideal of Alpha Kappa Delta.

Initiating Officer speaking:

Candidates for Initiation:

In the fall of 1920, under the direction of Dr. E.S. Bogardus, 14 graduate students and members of the sociology staff of the University of Southern California organized a society for those who were vitally interested in, and who were doing outstanding work in, the field of sociology. The society grew out of the feeling that there was a need for both faculty and students to get together regularly to discus the sociological projects that they were undertaking.. The society was named Alpha Kappa Delta. During the following year, Dr. Bogardus, Chair . . . of the Department of Sociology, invited other sociology departments to establish similar honor societies.

At that time, there were many sociology clubs in many schools, as there still are, but Alpha Kappa Delta thought it desirable to limit membership in Alpha Kappa Delta to those students with superior scholarship and serious interest in sociology. Thus, superior undergraduates were united with graduates students and faculty members in an organization which was both an honor society and working group of able people all devoted to the science of sociology.

In 1922, the second chapter was founded at the University of Wisconsin, and in December, 1924, at the annual meeting of the American Sociological Association in Chicago, sociology representatives from the University of Southern California, Wisconsin, Northwestern, and Kansas organized the United Chapters of Alpha Kappa Delta. Thereafter, the roster grew rapidly until there are now chapters in all parts of the United States and several other countries. Chapters in each state are named according to the Greek alphabet in the order of their founding. The chapters in this state are the Alpha _____, founded in 19 _____, at _____ University; Beta _____, 19_____ at _____ University, etc.

To be eligible for a chapter, an institution's sociology department must have at least two full-time teachers of sociology, and it must offer 30 semester hours of standard courses of sociology exclusive of summer sessions and extension teaching offerings. New chapters must be approved by three-fourths of the Council.

Alpha Kappa Delta derives its name from the first letters of the three Greek words, "anthropon" (humankind), "katamanthanein" (to investigate thoroughly), and "diakonesein" (for the purpose of service). When this phrase is translated freely, it expresses both the goal and the method of Alpha Kappa Delta: "To study humankind for the purpose of service." In the last analysis, the purpose of all science is to improve people's adjustments to their physical, sociological, and cultural environments. The purpose of Alpha Kappa Delta is to promote human welfare through the association of a fellowship group interested in developing scientific knowledge that may be applied to the solution of social problems.

We believe that social phenomena are natural phenomena and can be studied by the same methods which have been so successful in the physical and biological sciences, and by other methods that sociologists have devised. Therefore, we believe in the whole-minded acceptance of the scientific point of view and the rigorous application of scientific method to all human problems. Alpha Kappa Delta thus stands for the achievements of the GOOD LIFE by the methods of social science.

Since social science deals with a changing world of unlimited and unknown possibilities, it must continuously change its techniques, theories, and conclusions. We believe that social, like physical and biological occurrences, are natural phenomena; that in all the universal flux and change, there is sufficient degree of relatively stable and repetitive uniformity to make useful provision and prediction possible within carefully delimited frames of reference. In short, we believe that human choice, intelligence, and effort are susceptible to some as yet undetermined degree of rational organization and control. We believe that humankind, personally and societally, can achieve rational, integrated, creative and democratic social relationships.

Our ideal is to help create a world-wise culture in which all people cooperate for the good of all; to apply an ever-increasing fund of scientific knowledge and reasonable inference there from; to renounce self-pity, irrational hopes, and fears, and all animistic falsifications of reality; to master the physical, biological, and cultural factors which menace life and health, confuse the mind and threaten the welfare of the human race.

We hope all of you will attain responsible leadership in your chosen fields and that you will discharge your duties with modesty and intelligence, with dignity and efficiency, with democratic respect for the rights and privileges of others. We hope you will have the gift of working, plying, learning, and loving with joy and enthusiasm as long as you shall live. No matter what authority and fame you may attain, we hope you always will be most notable for your simplicity, sincerity, tolerance, courage, honesty, kindness, humor, democratic respect for human personality and your devotion to the scientific habit of mind and way of life. Alpha Kappa Delta is a democratic, non-secret organization dedicated to the scientific study of social phenomena for the promotion of human welfare. Election to Alpha Kappa Delta has always been and will continue to be without regard to race, creed, or national origin. Therefore, we require no oaths, vows, or pledges, but as you receive the Certificate of Membership, we hope this simple act and this simple initiation will help you to make the ideals of Alpha Kappa Delta your own.

Now you have attained full membership in Alpha Kappa Delta. On behalf of _____ (letter) of _____ (state), I welcome you to our fellowship.

Each year in the United States, undergraduate students who are very similar to yourselves take part in this ritual. This ritual acknowledges all the hard work they have invested in their studies and in the life of the mind. This ritual honors them and indicts them into AKD. This ritual, which is part of the culture of college-student life, also is heavily infused with world-cultural values.

Key Concepts

access to and use of computers in the United States, by race and ethnicity
achievement and success
activity and work
Alpha Kappa Delta (A.K.D.)
atang
Brown's universal norm
Cinco de Mayo
collectivism
complex marriage
components of culture
consensus theory
counterculture
cultural capital
cultural pluralism
cultural trait or element
cultural universal
cultural values and personality
cultural variation in burial and bereavement practices in the U.S.
culture
culture shock
democracy
efficiency and practicality
equality
ethnic cleansing

ethnocentrism
ethnomethodology
false consciousness
freedom
functionalist theory
General Social Survey (GSS)
George Murdock
gesture
gesture language
institution
international non-governmental organization (INGO)
material culture
median net worth of households in U.S. by race and ethnicity
Miguel Hidalgo y Costilla
National Data Program for the Social Sciences
National Science Foundation (NSF)
nonmaterial culture
norms
obon
Oneida
pariah group
pariah group
particularism

progress and material comfort
racism
Ralph Linton
Ramadan
rationalization (Weber)
sexism
sign
society
sociolinguistics
steepling
stigma
stirpiculture
subculture
surviving the holidays and culture
sutra
symbol
symbolic culture
technology
tertius gaudens
the cultural elements of Oneida
the General Social Survey
Universal Declaration of Rights
universalism
value
values in the United States
world culture

Internet Resources

http://members.aol.com/toyeh/anairhpg.htm

Document: Osiyo! Welcome to The Alliance for Native American Indian Rights Web Site

http://ccme-mac4.bsd.uchicago.edu/DSADocs/UniHRts

Document: The Universal Declaration of Human Rights

This site contains both a summary and the full text of The Universal Declaration of Human Rights

http://leb.net/fchp/FC-MNFM.HTML

Document: The Fertile Crescent Home Page

http://www.inform.umd.edu/EdRes/Topic/Disability/Journals/News/Rag/vol13n03-rag

Document: The Disability Rag

http://www.washington-report.org/resource.htm

Document: The Washington Report's Resources Page

Suggested Readings

Back, Les, *New Ethnicities and Urban Culture: Racism and Multiculture in Young Lives* (New York: St. Martin's Press, 1996).

Chagnon, Napoleon A., *Yanomamo, The Fierce People* (Third edition) (New York: Holt, Rinehart and Winston, 1983).

Harris, Marvin, *Cannibals and Kings: The Origins of Cultures* (New York: Random House, 1977).

Harris, Marvin, *Cows, Pigs, Wars, and Witches: The Riddles of Culture* (New York: Vintage Books, 1975).

Harris, Marvin, *Cultural Materialism: The Struggle for a Science of Culture* (New York: Random House, 1979).

Kephart, William M., and Zellner, William W., *Extraordinary Groups: An Examination of Unconventional Lifestyles* (New York: St. Martin's Press, 1998).

Levin, Jack and McDevitt, Jack, *Hate Crimes: The Rising Tide of Bigotry and Bloodshed* (New York: Plenum Press, 1993).

Ritzer, George, *The McDonalization of Society* (Revised edition) (Thousand Oaks, CA: Pine Forge Press, 1996).

Sniderman, Paul, Fletcher, Joseph F., Russell, Peter H., and Tetlock, Philip E., *The Clash of Rights: Liberty, Equality, and Legitimacy in Pluralist Democracy* (New Haven, CT: Yale University Press, 1996).

Turkle, Sherry, *Life on the Screen: Identity in the Age of the Internet* (New York: Simon and Schuster, 1995).

Zukin, Sharon, *The Culture of Cities* (Cambridge, MA: Blackwell Publishers, 1995).

Learning Exercises

The learning objective of this chapter is for you to understand the concept of culture. The problem we have in understanding our own culture is similar to a fish being in water. (At least I am assuming that) Fish take for granted the water that keeps them alive. So, too, in our everyday lives we tend to take our own culture and its elements for granted. They are, if you will, "invisible" to us. Your growing sociological imagination will enable you to perceive these elements and to understand where and how they "fit" in the larger social landscape.

One of the ways we can come to understand our own culture is to be out of our familiar surroundings. We experience culture shock when we cannot understand and when we are aware that we misunderstand the behavior and/or ideas of others.

In the writing assignments below, you are to follow the directions and to write a response to the questions or issues indicated. Your answers are to be typed, double-spaced, and stapled in the upper left hand corner.

Learning Exercise 5.1

Writing Assignment

1. Many students come from backgrounds where their exposure to cultures other than their own is minimal. They may perceive themselves as not having been exposed to one or more cultures different than their own. In your own words, please describe to the reader the social interactions you have experienced with people from ethnic groups other than your own. These interactions include social interactions as a family member, or as a family friend, childhood friend, teenage friend, college-friend, church/synagogue/mosque/temple friend, coworker, current friend, or current neighbor. Do you consider your life to be multicultural? How could a sociological perspective help you to understand the culture of others?

2. People tend to evaluate the behavior, morality, values, attitudes, and beliefs of others. We have defined ethnocentrism as the tendency to view the norms, values, and institutions of one's culture as right and as preferable to those of other cultures. When we are immersed in another culture, we become aware of our ethnocentrism. In your own words, please describe to the reader an uncomfortable situation or instance where you asserted that your family's way (or your group's way) is the way it should be. Can you see that culture is learned? Have you observed how it is learned? Please describe.

3. We define culture as the language, norms, values, beliefs, material and nonmaterial elements that are shared and passed from one generation to the next. What are some examples of material culture? Give the reader some examples of nonmaterial culture.

■ ■ ■

Learning Exercise 5.2

Writing Assignment

1. You have read about cultural diversity. Please describe to the reader how some aspect of American social life is normative with respect to some cultural tradition while it may be perceived as deviant (norm violating) in terms of another cultural tradition.

2. To what subcultures do you belong? How can you tell if you are a member of a subculture? Can you identify any countercultures in _____ (Please write in the blank space the name of the city or town where you go to college) ? Give the reader some examples of your own experiences of countercultures. Explain why Oneida is a counterculture.

3. You have read about American cultural values. Can you see those values in your own life? Which ones, if any, are absent?

4. How does world culture differ from the culture in which you live in your daily life? Can you see any world-cultural principles at work in your life? Please tell the reader about it.

5. What world-cultural values are present in, and absent from, the ritual that inducts students into A.K.D?

■   ■   ■

Learning Exercise 5.3

In-Class Learning Exercise

In your group play the following game. Read the following story. "Once upon a time there were five people. Alma and John are in love. They want to get married right away. However, Alma is separated from John by a river that is deep and 15-miles wide. The only way Alma can cross the river is by a boat owned by Tom. Tom charges $2,000 to cross the river one way. Alma has only $200. Alma's neighbor, Betty, is rich and is willing to loan the rest to Alma, but she would charge her 25% interest. Tom has a friend, Edward, who says he would pay her way if she would "spend time with him."

Below, you will see the name of each person in our story. To the immediate right of each name is a short line. Individually, *without consulting with each other*, please write on each line a number from 1 to 5. *Each number must be used once and no more than once.* Each character must receive one of the numbers. Each number represents how much you sympathize with that character. 1 indicates that you have the least sympathy for that character, and 5 indicates that you feel the most sympathy. In other words, you are rank ordering how sympathetic you feel towards each character in the story.

How Much Sympathy I Feel for Each of the Characters in the Story

1	2	3	4	5

I feel least
sympathetic

I feel most
sympathetic

Alma: _____

John: _____

Tom: _____

Betty: _____

Edward: _____

After each of you has rated the characters, as a group talk about why each of you rank-ordered as you did. On a piece of paper, each member of your group is to write down groups of people toward whom you know you have negative feelings. Explain to the group why you have these feelings and where you leaned about the nature of these groups you have negative feelings about. For example, did you receive personal hurt from a member of that group? Do you have knowledge of the group's evil goals or characteristics? Did you hear your parents talking about this group while you were growing up? Did you learn about this group from TV? Was it from information you learned at school? Was violence done to your group by a member of the group in the past (even centuries ago)? Have you heard rumors that the group has hostile feelings toward a group you belong to? Are your negative feelings due to no apparent cause; you just have a feeling they are different, strange, and threatening?

In the text you read about ethnocentrism and racism. Explain to the group how these concepts may play into your negative feelings. Phobia is defined as an irrational fear. Xenophobia is the irrational fear of foreigners. How may you increase your comfort zone with people from other cultures?

■   ■   ■

Learning Exercise 5.4

Sociology and the Internet

1. Go to **http://aspe.os.dhhs.gov/**
    Document: Department of Health and Human Services, Office of the Assistant Secretary for Planning and Evaluation (ASPE)
    Scroll down to **Poverty Guidelines, Research, and Measurement**
    Click on it. This brings you to **THE HHS POVERTY GUIDELINES.**
    Scroll down to **1997 HHS Poverty Guidelines.** Using this information, what is the official 1997 operant definition of poverty for a family of 4 living in the following areas?
    - within the 48 contiguous states and the District of Columbia? _____
    - in Alaska? _____
    - in Hawaii? _____
    - Scroll down to the data on individuals. Using that data, what is the official 1997 definition of poverty for *one person* living in the 48 contiguous states and the District of Columbia? _____

2. Using AltaVista as a search engine, go to the following URL:

    http://members.aol.com/toyeh/anairhpg.htm

    Document: Osiyo! Welcome to The Alliance for Native American Indian Rights Web Site
    - **Click on The Alliance for Native American Indian Rights**

    This brings you to The Alliance for Native American Indian Rights
    Read this material and answer these questions:

    - Who are they?
    - Why do they exist?
    - What do they do?

    Then, scroll to the end of this document and click on **RETURN TO ALLIANCE HOME PAGE**

    - At this site you will find, among other things, case-study materials relating to efforts to protect Native-American burial grounds and other culturally significant places. Write an essay in which you tell the reader about *two* of these efforts that are covered in this web site.

3. Go to **http://leb.net/fchp/FC-MNFM.HTML**

    Document: The Fertile Crescent Home Page (FCHP)

    - You are to read this material so that you can answer the following questions:
    - What is the Fertile Crescent?
    - Where is the Fertile Crescent?
    - What is the Fertile Crescent Home Page?
    - What are its goals?

    ■   ■   ■

Multiple-Choice and True-False Test

1. _____ refers to a group of people with a common culture who occupy a particular territorial area, have a sense of unity, and who regard themselves as different than nonmembers.
   A. Culture
   B. Society

2. _____ is an umbrella term referring to all human-made intangibles that are passed from generation to generation—norms, symbols, social structure, folklore, ideas, beliefs, values, habits, customs, traditions, rituals, language, knowledge, and so forth.
   A. Material culture
   B. Non-material culture
   C. Magic

3. _____ refers to all human-made tangible objects—paper, the Leaning Tower of Pisa, toothpicks, condoms, footballs, nuclear weapons, the clock, bubble gum, and so forth that are transmitted from one generation to another.
   A. Material culture
   B. Non-material culture
   C. Magic

4. _____ is a school of sociology devoted to the study of how people construct meanings and make sense out of their own activities in everyday life.
   A. Anarchy
   B. Epistemology
   C. Epidemiology
   D. Ethnomethodology

5. As indicated in our textbook, which of the following affiliations accounts for the highest percentage of religious affiliation in the U.S. population?
   A. Protestant
   B. Roman Catholics
   C. Jew
   D. Islam

6. As indicated in our textbook, the largest American Indian tribe in the U.S. in the 1990 census is _____.
   A. Blackfoot
   B. Sioux
   C. Cherokee
   D. Iroquois
   E. Apache

7. As indicated in our textbook, in terms of absolute numbers of people, which of the following has the largest number of officially poor people in the United States?
   A. White
   B. Non-Hispanic white
   C. Black
   D. Asian and Pacific Islander
   E. Hispanic origin

8. In order to experience culture shock, you have to live in another country.
    A. True   B. False

9. When we find ourselves outside of our familiar culture and we are in a culture we perceive as significantly different than our own, we tend to experience a disorientation known as _____.
    A. anomie
    B. tertius gaudens
    C. culture shock
    D. counterculture

10. The components of culture include _____.
    A. sign, gesture, values
    B. symbol, language, norms
    C. technology
    D. all of the above
    E. (A) and (B)

11. _____ is an African-American cultural festival.
    A. Thanh Minh
    B. Ramadan
    C. Kwanzaa
    D. Oneida

12. _____ is an Islamic festival.
    A. Thanh Minh
    B. Ramadan
    C. Kwanzaa
    D. Oneida

13. Nguzo Saba, Umoja, Kujichagulia, Ujima, Nia, and Ujamaa are nonmaterial cultural elements important in _____.
    A. Thanh Minh
    B. Ramadan
    C. Kwanzaa
    D. Oneida

14. **Technology** refers to that segment of culture, including tools and knowledge, that embraces all forms of productive technique used by humans and by some non-human primates to manipulate the physical environment in order to attain a desired practical result.
    A. True   B. False

15. _____ is variously translated into English as "first," "first fruit," and "first fruits of the harvest."
    A. Thanh Minh
    B. Ramadan
    C. Kwanzaa
    D. Oneida

16. Cultural universals refer to cultural elements that are found in virtually all societies.
    A. True   B. False

17. According to British anthropologist George Murdock, which of the following is/are cultural universals?
    A. gift giving
    B. humor
    C. a gendered division of labor
    D. marriage, the family, myths
    E. all of the above

18. According to Brown's universal norm, if a particular form of address is used to speak with social subordinates, it is also used with _____.
    A. strangers
    B. intimates
    C. nobody else
    D. everybody else

19. According to _____, the initiation of change in intimacy among status unequals belongs to the person holding the person holding the socially _____ status.
    A. Brown's universal norm; supraordinate
    B. Brown's universal norm; subordinate
    C. Weber's concept of pariah group; stigmatized

20. Data on the median net worth of households in the United States in 1993 indicatesthat the median net worth of whites is roughly _____ of _____ households.
    A. equal to that; African American
    B. half that; African American
    C. ten times that; Hispanic-origin
    D. ten times that; African American
    E. both (C) and (D)

21. In the United States, the cuisine of the Midwest is *lighter* than the cuisine of the west coast; Midwestern cuisine contains fewer red meats, fats, sugars, and starches.
    A. True   B. False

22. _____ lasts a month.
    A. Quanzaa
    B. Ramadan
    C. stirpiculture

23. Stirpiculture and complex marriage are nonmaterial cultural elements of _____.
    A. Quanzaa
    B. Islam
    C. Oneida

24. In high-poverty urban schools in the United States, the sociological research of Epps, Lee, and Slaughter-Defoe indicates that _____ elementary school children view child-teacher relations as the most important dimension of school climate.
    A. African-American
    B. Latino
    C. all
    D. no

25. Sociologists Ofra Anson and Jon Anson of Ben-Gurion University of the Negev recently concluded a study of surviving the holidays. Their research focuses on Ramadan. Their study finds _____.
    A. no evidence of subcultural differences in surviving the holidays
    B. gender differences in surviving the holidays
    C. that Ramadan is associated with a reduction or postponement of mortality among Islamic men and an increase in mortality among Islamic women
    D. both (B) and (C)

26. According to data in the 1993 Current Population Survey of the U.S. Census, of children 3 to 17 years if age in the U.S., _____.
    A. there are no significant racial/ethnic differences in levels of access to computers
    B. whites are relatively three times as likely as Blacks and Hispanics to have access to a computer
    C. whites are about three times less likely than Blacks and Hispanics to have access to a computer

27. **Cultural capital** refers to the extent to which an individual or a group has absorbed the dominant culture.
    A. True   B. False

28. **Counterculture** refers to a subculture that rejects key norms and values of the conventional society in which it is situated.
    A. True   B. False

29. Oneida was not much of a success economically.
    A. True   B. False

30. The General Social Survey is based on a sample of convenience.
    A. True   B. False

31. The basic purposes of the General Social Survey are to collect data on U.S. society in order to _____.
    A. compare the U.S. with other highly industrialized societies
    B. to make high-quality data readily available to students, policy makers, and others
    C. explain constants and trends in behaviors, attributes, and behaviors
    D. all of the above
    E. none of the above

32. According to sociologist Robin M. Williams, the following values are particularly important to people in the U.S.:
    A. humanitarianism
    B. efficiency
    C. individualism
    D. racism
    E. all of the above

33. In the United States, people of white, Anglo-Saxon heritage tend to wear the color black to funerals. The color black is worn by mourners in all cultures; it is one of George Murdock's cultural universals.
    A. True   B. False

34. Burial (in the ground, in a pyramid, in a mausoleum, etc.) is preferred to cremation in all cultures; it is one of George Murdock's cultural universals.
    A. True   B. False

35. **Value inconsistency** refers to a conflict between two or more simultaneously held values.
    A. True   B. False

36. In the U.S. when adults think of social and political issues, most tend to think of themselves mainly as _____.
    A. some particular ethnic, racial, or nationality group
    B. just an American
    C. two or more ethnic, racial, or nationality groups
    D. just an American and one or more particular ethnic, racial, or nationality groups

37. **Cultural pluralism** is a perspective and an approach to social relations that _____.
    A. holds that cultural heterogeneity is a goal that should be pursued and attained by society
    B. allows for cultural differences as long as these differences do not interfere with the principle values and mores of the dominant society
    C. both of the above
    D. none of the above

38. In the United States, there has been a decline in popular support for government intervention to help improve the living standards of African Americans.
    A. True   B. False

39. Most Americans say that Americans are united and in agreement about the most important values.
    A. True   B. False

40. _____ is a concept that gives priority to defining self in terms of personal attributes.
    A. Collectivism
    B. Individualism
    C. Both of the above

41. These days, in total, nearly 60% of INGOs focus on technical rationalization or economic concerns.
    A. True   B. False

42. _____ refers to the orientation of one social actor to another on the basis of the special nature of their relationship to each other (for instance, they are cousins).
    A. Universalism
    B. Particularism

43. _____ refers to the orientation of one social actor to another on the basis of generalized principles of behavior rather than on any special relationship that may exist between them.
    A. Universalism
    B. Particularism

44. One striking aspect about INGOs is that hardly any of them actively champion a cause (human rights, environmental protection, etc.).
    A. True   B. False

45. As envisioned by INGOs, the concept of world citizenship is highly egalitarian.
    A. True   B. False

46. False consciousness is a term from which theoretical approach?
    A. conflict theory
    B. consensus theory
    C. symbolic interactionism

C H A P T E R 6

Socialization

Internalization of Relationships That Make a World

> All armies impose some sort of oath on their recruits. . . . The
> Roman legionary swore an oath to the state and, until 216 BC, to
> his comrades as well. The form of the Roman military oath, with its
> emphasis upon public affirmation of allegiance and pledge of brave
> conduct, has proved remarkably durable. . . . This type of oath has
> survived in . . . armies to the present day.
>
> Richard Holmes, *Acts of War: The Behavior of Men in Battle*

■ ■ ■

On a frigid and icy day in Kazan, Tatarstan, Russia, an old woman, waiting for a bus, confronts an elderly man with his three-year-old grandson. Pointing her fingers and raising her voice, she reproaches the old man, lamenting, "The young boy has no fur to keep him warm. He is standing in the street while you ignore him." She accompanies the young boy to the shelter afforded by the nearby bus station, and again she criticizes the elderly man for being careless about the boy's health and safekeeping. She tenaciously stands beside the lad, holding his hand until the bus arrives, insuring that he does not run out into the busy and dangerous street. The elderly man defers to her authority.

Imagine that you volunteer to participate in an experiment at your college or university. You arrive at the room designated for this purpose, and the experimenter requests that you sit at a table and turn wooden knobs for the next hour. You comply, even though you find it

a boring, repetitive task (Festinger and Carlsmith, 1959; Osberg, 1993; Hom, Jr., 1994).

At the end of the hour, the experimenter informs you that this is an experiment concerning the effects of subjects' expectations on their performance. The next research subject is waiting outside and must be led to expect that this is an engrossing, interesting experience. The problem is that the assistant who usually creates this expectation is unable to make the next session, and, hence, the experimenter is in a bind. "Could you please help out and take the usual assistant's place?" By doing so you would be helping to generate scientific knowledge, and, besides, you'd be paid. You'd be paid right now.

After being paid either $1 or $20 to be an assistant, you tell the research subject, who unbeknownst to you actually is the experimenter's real assistant, that this is a really interesting experiment. "Oh? A friend of mine participated in this experiment a few days ago. She told me it was really *boring.*" "Oh, no," you respond. "This is a really delightful experience. You even get some exercise while turning the wooden knobs. I'm highly confident that you'll enjoy it."

Finally, after you complete your task, someone else who is studying the experiences of undergraduate students participating in experiments, asks you privately to complete a questionnaire that asks you how much you actually enjoyed turning the wooden knobs. *Under which condition, being paid $1 or $20, do you believe that your actual enjoyment rating of the knob-turning tasks would be higher?* Please write your response here ——————.

Socialization and the Social Sciences

The vignettes that open this chapter are instructive examples of socialization. The first raises, and the second helps us to answer, the question: How *do we learn the norms and values that guide our behavior in everyday life?* Socialization.

This chapter explores various explanations of and insights into socialization. We first examine the place of socialization in the social sciences and in the history of social and intellectual thought, within whose contexts a sociological understanding of socialization emerged and develops. Then we gain an insight into the importance of **primary socialization,** the socialization that comes first in our lives, by examining the insights into this process offered by Sigmund Freud (1865-1939), George Herbert Mead (1863-1931), Erik Erikson (1902-1994), Lawrence Kohlberg (1927-1987), Jean Piaget (1896-1980) and their critics. We will then focus on various contexts within which socialization typically occurs. We analyze socialization in the family, paying particular attention to the process of internalization and to the latent effects of several approaches to child rearing. We will also examine related areas such as peers, the mass media, and schools as contexts of socialization. We conclude with observations regarding adult socialization and re-socialization. In short, in this chapter, we examine socialization across the life course from a number of perspectives.

In its most general and common usage, **socialization** refers to the processes of interaction whereby a person (a novice) acquires the norms, language, beliefs, values, and attitudes of her or his group (Gecas, 1992: 1863). The sociological view maintains that in the course of acquiring these cultural elements, the individual acquires a self and a personality. From the classical sociological perspective, the self and personality are social constructs, and we appropriate culture through the socialization process. The babushka in the vignette that opens this chapter, then, is able successfully to chastise the elderly man for taking inadequate care of his three-year-old grandson, because in traditional societies it is a cultural norm that the entire community, not just the immediate family, is responsible for rearing children. In traditional Tatarstan, as in traditional African societies, it is a proverb that "It takes a whole village to raise a child." As part of that village, it is the babushka's obligation to look out for the boy. The babushka is a legitimate agent of informal social control in this setting. She and the elderly man had learned these norms as part of their socialization experience. Within sociology, then, socialization addresses two important issues in social life: the issue of human development and the issue of societal continuity (social and cultural reproduction) across generational lines (Gecas, 1992).

Several academic disciplines claim socialization as a central process. Different academic disciplines tend to focus on different aspects of socialization. Political science focuses on the processes by which political attitudes and political orientations are formed and shaped (Gecas, 1992: 1864). Anthropology tends to view socialization as cultural transmission across generational lines. This emphasis manifests itself in a tendency to substitute the term *enculturation* for socialization. In the 1920s and 1930s a "culture and personality" orientation emerged in anthropology, and it helped to shape the anthropological approach to socialization. Examples of field work during this period include American anthropologist Margaret Mead's *Coming of Age in Samoa* (1928), British anthropologist Bronislaw Malinowski's *Sex and Repression in Savage Society* (1927), and American anthropologist Ruth Benedict's

Patterns of Culture (1934). Much of the work in the culture and personality field was influenced by the work of Sigmund Freud, particularly in the United States.

Rather than emphasizing the transmission of culture, psychology is more likely to emphasize various aspects of an individual's, or of human, development (e.g., Maslow, 1954; Piaget, 1926; Kagan, 1978). There is considerable diversity within psychology regarding the aspect of socialization studied. For behavioral psychologists, socialization is viewed as learning behavior through the application of rewards and punishments (e.g., Watson, 1924; Skinner, 1938, 1953, 1974). For developmental psychologists influenced by Jean Piaget, socialization is equivalent to cognitive development, which usually is viewed as influenced by maturation and social influences (e.g., Piaget, 1926). Socialization is tantamount to child-rearing practices for many psychologists interested in child development (e.g., Baumrind, 1978, 1980; Clausen, 1968). Clinical psychologists and personality theorists tend to equate socialization with the establishment of character traits, usually within the context of early childhood experiences.

Socialization and Sociology

Two main orientations to socialization have characterized sociology. The first views socialization primarily as the learning and internalization of roles, norms, values, and statuses of the groups to which an individual belongs. **Internalization** refers to the process whereby social rules, norms, and statuses become internal to the individual, part of the individual's sense of self. This perspective has been present from the birth of sociology and is most closely associated with the structural functionalist paradigm (Gecas, 1992: 1864).

A second sociological perspective views socialization as self-concept (identity) formation, the process whereby we develop a sense of self. The development of a sense of self within the context of social interaction is considered to be the essence of socialization in this perspective. This view is closely associated with symbolic interactionism, whose ideas we initially examined in Chapter 2. (Please review Chapter 2.) As you recall, George Herbert Mead, a sociologist at the University of Chica-

go, and Charles Horton Cooley of the University of Michigan developed a view of the self as a thoroughly social and reflexive construct that emerges through social and symbolic interaction. In role taking, the individual views herself or himself through the eyes of another person. This is a basis of *reflexivity*, the ability to view (to reflect upon) one's self and one's situations through the eyes of another. Mead called the reflexive part of the self "the me."

In the sociological view, then, socialization is the process whereby we learn roles and norms, develop the capacity to conform to them, and develop a sense of self. In the sociological view, socialization is a lifelong process. In the sociological view, a person or institution engaging in socialization is referred to as an **agent of socialization.** An agent of socialization may be a person, such as a parent or daycare attendant. An agent of socialization may be a group, such as a youth group or youth gang, or even an institution, such as a school, a family court, or the media.

Sociology uses the term *primary* to refer to the socialization that comes first in our lives. Primary socialization takes place during the first few years of life. In **primary socialization** we learn basic conceptions of self (e.g., "I am female," "I am male"), basic values, norms, beliefs, and motivations. This initial or primary socialization of the young child usually takes place within the context of our families. However, babies do not have a corner on the socialization market. **Secondary socialization** occurs after the first few years of life. Secondary socialization may take place within any number of contexts, both familial and extra-familial. Extra-familial contexts include the school, the peer group, the mass media, the work place, or the health club. During your life course, many of you who now are reading this textbook will learn to think of yourselves as (identity, self-concept), and to behave as (roles) college students, spouses, parents, grandparents, great grandparents, workers, friends or close relatives of someone who has AIDS, members of the armed forces, inmates in prison, friends or close family members of a person in prison, widows or widowers, and so forth. Secondary socialization may entail significant identity transformation. Socialization is a lifelong process.

Social Darwinism, Evolutionary Theory, Social Behaviorism, and the Women's Movement: Changing Ideas Regarding Biology as Destiny

A movement of social thought based on applying *Charles Darwin*'s ideas of evolution to provide an understanding of human social action, human development, and social change emerged in Western Europe and England between 1850-1880 (Harré and Lamb, 1986: 70). This movement is known as *Spencerism, social evolutionism, evolutionary theory*, or *social Darwinism*. Between 1880 and the end of the First World War it reached its initial peak of scientific, political, social, and ideological influence in the United States and Western Europe.

Its origins can be traced to two distinct traditions at the beginning of the nineteenth century. One of these is *Malthusian theory*. Thomas Robert Malthus' *Essay on the Principle of Population* (1798) was instrumental in shaping both Herbert Spencer's theory of social evolution and Charles Darwin's theory of natural selection. In his *Essay on the Principle of Population* Malthus endeavored to refute the theories of progress popularized by the French Enlightenment philosophers like Condorcet and Diderot who speculated on the perfectibility of humans and of society. According to Malthus' understanding of population dynamics, progress through political revolution, reform, and education were doomed by a fundamental imbalance between the rate of population increase and the rate of increase in the food supply. This imbalance is sometimes called *the Malthusian dilemma*. The dilemma that dooms perfectibility, according to Malthus, is that the food supply increases at an arithmetic rate (1, 2, 3, 4, 5, 6, 7) while population increases at a geometric rate (1, 2, 4, 8, 16, 32, 64). In short, population growth outstrips the food supply.

Darwin attributes his discovery of the principle of natural selection to his reading of Malthus' *Essay* (Harré and Lamb, 1986: 70). Unlike *Malthus*, however, Darwin optimistically emphasizes the goodness of the struggle for life that results from the imbalance between population and food supply posited by Malthus. The inevitability of progress that he foresees is phrased in terms of a law of nature, which he terms natural selection (Darwin, 1859: 86, 449).

The second tradition that informs evolutionary theory is well represented in the works of Comte, Hegel, and Saint-Simon in the early nineteenth century. (Please review Chapter 2). *Herbert Spencer* (1820-1903), a British philosopher, developed a general theory of the evolution of social systems that used the concepts of competition, struggle for existence, and adaptation. Spencer argues that social systems adapt to their environments and that there has been an evolutionary progress of societies from simple homogeneity in "militant" societies to greater complexity in industrial society. In *The Proper Sphere of Government* (1842) and in *Social Statics* (1850), Spencer attempts to find a solution to the Malthusian dilemma in a theory of the inverse relationship between fertility and intelligence (i.e., the higher the intelligence, the lower the birth rate; the lower the intelligence, the higher the birth rate). Spencer is responsible for coining the concept "survival of the fittest," and he bases that concept on the idea of a struggle for existence. He "had popularized the term 'evolution' by 1857" (Harré and Lamb, 1986: 70) and welcomed the publication of *Origin of Species* (1859) as a confirmation of his own published ideas regarding social evolution.

From the early 1870s to the mid 1890s, economic deflation of crisis proportions wracked the industrialized world (Harré and Lamb, 1986: 71). The elites of these countries attempted to alleviate the situation through a variety of strategies and policies characterized by racism and sexism, including imperialism and economic *laissez-faire*, governmental non-interference in the workings of the economy. New markets were ruthlessly opened and conquered. Increased production was achieved through the unbridled exploitation of both environmental and human resources. Protective economic tariffs, primarily benefiting the more affluent, were erected and strengthened. Under the cloak of social Darwinism, British, European, and U.S. policy makers, imperialists, and economic elites came to view economically poor people and persons of color, particularly those possessing less-advanced technology, as inferior and as less fit. Persons of color were labeled by the elites as a "white man's burden," and hence as fit to be exploited and colonized. It is worth noting that in this era, forms of governmental economic interference that benefited the economic elites were viewed as appropriate and as desirable by those elites. It was the use of governmental interference to further the interests of the average person or of the person at or below the subsistence level of existence that was labeled by the elites as improper, as working against the survival of the fittest.

Evolutionary theory—a perspective for understanding social behavior that gives great explanatory power to the concepts of competition, struggle for existence, adaptation, and survival of the fittest—had a significant impact on, and actually came to dominate, many of the natural and social sciences in England, Germany, Austria, France, other European countries, and the United States from 1870 to the end of the 1920s (Harré and Lamb, 1986: 71). In Italy, Cesare Lombroso explained crime and deviance in terms of biology as destiny. In his view of the empirical evidence, persons who commit crimes are not as highly evolved as their law-abiding counterparts (1899). In France, *Gustave Le Bon* (1903, 1910) and *Gabriel Tarde* (1903) used Darwinistic ideas to understand crowd and mass behavior. Tarde himself viewed the dynamics of crowd behavior as a substantial threat to democratic rule (1903, 1910), and his writings enabled others to appreciate crowd phenomena as a basic element of social life and of social action. Dictatorial political leaders, such as Adolph Hitler (1889-1945; 1933-1945) in the German Reich and Benito Mussolini (1883-1945; 1922-1943) in Italy, effectively availed themselves of Le Bon's insights. Mussolini used them skillfully to intimidate opponents through manipulating crowd violence, and Hitler used them to construct large public ritualistic occasions wherein ordinary citizens publicly participate in activities that served to generate, heighten, and sustain commitment to the political regime and to him as its supreme leader (van Ginneken, 1992). The dynamics that Tarde and Le Bon elucidated almost a century ago have been both admissi-

ble and effective as legal defense against the criminal charge of homicide and manslaughter in times of riot both in South Africa and the United States during the last twenty years of this century.

In the United States, social Darwinist ideas inform and dominate much of early American sociology. This fact is manifest in the works of many early Chicago School sociologists, including those of Lester Ward, Edward B. Taylor, and William Graham Sumner. For example, American sociologist Don Martindale quotes William Graham Sumner (1840-1910) as saying that life is about "root, hog or die" (1988: 167). This was , Sumner's vivid way of saying that, in his view of nature, only the fittest survive. Sumner also opposed social policies that would financially assist the poor. Why? Because in his view, the "elimination of widows and orphans" was a "first step in maintaining the quality of the race" (Martindale, 1988: 167).

Social Darwinistic ideas became part of the popular white, Anglo-Saxon Protestant culture in the United States. A widely held assumption in these circles was that differences in status, wealth, deviance, and criminality between established and immigrants groups, and between whites and nonwhites, were essentially biological in nature; biology was viewed as destiny. Concern about the proliferation of less advantaged groups, via in-immigration and a high birthrate, spread. It manifested itself in national legislation restricting immigration and "a national conference on race betterment in 1914. One year later, twelve states had passed sterilization laws" (Kagan, 1989: 70). The belief that differences in social status and intelligence were due to biological factors was strengthened when intelligence tests administered to U.S. military recruits during World War I revealed substantially lower scores among African Americans and immigrants than among native-born whites.

Not until the mid 1960s, with the re-emergence of the women's rights movement, did social Darwinistic explanations for *gendered* behavior come under sustained attack in the social sciences and in the larger society. By the mid-1970s, a paradigm shift was underway in the social sciences with reference to understanding, and as a way of knowing, gendered behavior and gendered social action. With regard to other domains of behavior, however, social Darwinistic explanations fell out of favor far sooner. Gendered stratification—unequal access to scarce yet widely valued goods and service on the basis of sex or gender—appears far more resistant to efforts to reduce or to eliminate it than many other forms of domination.

In the 1920s and 1930s, with regard to racial and ethnic minorities and majority males, social Darwinistic explanations for social behavior and for social status came under effective attack by many forces, including the development of social behaviorism and the Great Depression. The Great Depression, when more than 30 percent of Americans were unemployed, coincided with the popularization of social behaviorism and structural sociological theories of inequality. Social Darwinism did not appear to offer compelling explanations of this trauma. Many Americans were unwilling to accept as reasonable that over 30 percent of the U.S. population was either sufficiently inferior or so morally flawed as to be unable to work. It was time for a paradigm shift.

Social Behaviorism

Social behaviorism arose during the period of 1890-1910, at a time when psychology was trying to define itself as an empirical, experimental science, distinct from philosophy and biology. In 1902 Russian psychologist and behaviorist Ivan Petrovich *Pavlov* (1849-1936) formulated his law of reinforcement, or learning by conditioning. He demonstrated that a dog who is fed at the same time as a bell is rung soon learns to salivate at the sound of the bell even when no food is present. Pavlov's work was elegant, empirical, experimental, and scientific. Other scientists replicated his findings. Pavlov's work, which was popularized by *James B. Watson* (1878-1958), emphasized the role of experience and of learning, not biology, in shaping behavior and in promoting both stability and change in behavior. By the late 1920s, a paradigm shift was clearly in the making. Learning by conditioning had replaced biology as a key independent variable in explaining human behavior. Learning by conditioning was a key mechanism in human

development in virtually all newly published textbooks (Kagan, 1989: 73). With this change came more attention to the importance of social experience in shaping social action, with special attention given to experience in the family, especially in the early years of life.

Ethnographic studies of culture indicate that there is a relationship among childhood experiences, culture, and personality (Mead, 1935, 1965; Chagnon, 1983; Werner, 1989; Argyle, 1994). As we review in this chapter, early childhood socialization shapes the foundation upon which healthy self-esteem is established (Argyle, 1994).

Abandonment and Isolation: Effects on Human and Nonhuman Primates

Nonhuman Primates

Terry-Cloth "Mothers," Trust and Attachment. Research with nonhuman primates demonstrates the importance of early learning experiences for later development. A series of classic experiments with rhesus monkeys by primatologists *Harry* and *Margaret Harlow* of the University of Wisconsin Primate Laboratory (e.g., Harlow, 1962; Harlow and Harlow, 1962) underscore the extent to which, among primates, becoming an adequately functioning social actor is dependent upon interaction with others.

The Harlows artificially inseminated female rhesus monkeys, and reared the resulting offspring in isolation. In the now famous cloth-mother and wire-mother experiments, isolate-reared rhesus monkey infants had access to soft terry-cloth mothers who gave no milk and to lactating wire-surrogates. The infant monkeys spent only a few minutes each day nursing from the wire surrogate and virtually the rest of the time clinging ventrally to the cloth surrogate mother. Monkeys need something soft and warm to cling to in order to feel comfortable, reassured, and calm. Correspondingly, basic trust is the first of Erikson's eight human developmental crises (Erikson, 1950), and prolonged ventral clinging to a warm, soft terry-cloth mother instilled a basic sense of security and trust in these infants (Harlow and Zimmerman, 1959).

While the monkeys developed a strong attachment to the cloth mother and little or none to the wire mother, regardless of which one gave milk, in almost all other respects, the monkeys had failed to develop into adequately functioning social actors by the time of adolescence and adulthood.

Parenting and Reproduction. For instance, when the baby female monkeys who had cloth-surrogate mothers grew up, they themselves were artificially inseminated. After giving birth, they did not engage in parenting behaviors with any minimally acceptable amount of competence or diligence. They rejected their young and would not let them nurse. They abused their babies. They would crush their child's face into the floor, chew off its fingers and feet, or even put the infant's head in their mouths and crush it like an eggshell. In primates, then, it appears that parenting has largely learned components.

The isolate-reared monkeys of both sexes also failed to learn to copulate. Harlow (1962) reports on his efforts to "re-educate" male and female rhesus monkeys who had grown up in isolation in his laboratory. He paired the isolate-reared mature females with his "most experienced, patient, and gentle males," whom he refers to as *sophisticated males* (1962: 7); and he paired the isolate-reared males with his "most eager, amiable, and successful breeding females," whom he refers to as *sophisticated females* (1962:7). The results?

■ *For females:*
When the . . . [isolate-reared] females were smaller than the sophisticated males, the girls would back away and look appealingly at these would-be consorts. Their hearts were in the right place, but nothing else was. When the females were larger than the males, we can only hope that they misunderstood the males' intentions, for after a brief period of courtship, they would attack and maul the ill-fated male. (Harlow, 1962:7)
The re-education program for the males fared no better.

■ *For males:*
[The isolate-reared males] approached the females with a blind enthusiasm, but it was a misdirected enthusiasm. Frequently the males would grasp the females by the side of the body and thrust laterally, leaving themselves working at cross-purposes with reality. Even the most persistent attempts by these females to set the boys straight came to naught. Finally, these females either stared at the males with complete contempt or attacked them in utter frustration. (Harlow, 1962:7)

Assessment. Among primates, then, there are learned components to behaviors as fundamental as parenting and copulation. While early attachment and trust are important to further development, they do not suffice as a foundation for normal primate development. What else is needed?

Harlow's research documents that peer relations are crucial to the development of the young. If infants with terry-cloth mothers get to play for twenty minutes each day with fellow isolate-reared infants in a playroom supplied with equipment for climbing and swinging, they develop normally in every respect. If deprived of intimate interactions with peers, the young fail to develop normally.

Harlow's research indicates that the effects on monkeys isolated for the first three months of life are reversible. This is equivalent to about the first six months of life for a human infant. However, baby monkeys isolated for the first six months of life are impaired permanently both emotionally and behaviorally.

Human Primates: Isolation and Development in Human Infants

Research on the effects of isolation on human infants shows strikingly similar results. From time to time the media and scholarly literature report on children who, in one way or another, have been isolated for years—locked in a closet, garage, or cellar; chained to a bed in a spare room, and so forth (Itard, 1932; Davis, 1940, 1948; Curtiss, 1977; Rymer, 1994). Deprived of all but the most trivial and fleeting human contact, these extremely neglected children have only their genetic resources upon which to draw in order to become human, and they are starkly impaired behaviorally and emotionally as a result. When found, these children lack language ability and merely make grunting-like sounds. They are indifferent to their surroundings. They make no efforts to control bowl and bladder functions. Much like Harlow's isolate-reared monkeys, these children often spend a lot of time rocking rhythmically back and forth on their heels.

These extremely isolated children are sometimes referred to as **feral.** Most precisely, the term feral refers to persons who, according to legend, have been reared by animals, apart from humans. The Roman legend of Romulus and Remus is an example. Romulus and Remus are twins who were reared and nursed by a she-wolf. These boys are feral children. They founded the city of Rome, and the city is named after Romulus. The legend of Tarzan provides another example of a feral child.

Isolation in Orphanages

In a well-known study, *René Spitz* (1945, 1947) compares 130 infants reared for the first year of life either in a Belgian orphanage or with their mothers in a prison. The prison infants were looked after much of the time by their mothers. They got lots of hugging and cuddling. The mothers spoke to them a lot. At the end of a year, these infants were robustly healthy, highly curious about their environment, and displayed great motor skills. They vocalized freely, and some actually spoke a word or two. They all understood the significance of simple social gestures. By two years of age, most of these infants could feed themselves with a spoon; they understood commands and obeyed them; they ran playfully around the room; they played lively social games with each other; and they had made substantial progress in toilet training. Over a period of two years, not a single child died.

In the orphanage, the hygienic and medical care were good, as was the food. But, in sharp contrast to their prison counterparts, each of these infants had to share her or his caretaker, a busy nurse, with seven other infants. These infants, as a result, were largely isolated and spent most of their time alone in their cots. The result? These children, from the third month of life onward, showed extreme susceptibility to infection and illness. They were sick a lot. Their mortality rate also was extremely high. More

than 37% died in a period of two years. Their motor skills were severely impaired. Fully 24% were incapable of any locomotion, and only 14% could sit up unassisted. By the age of two, hardly any of them could eat alone, even with a spoon, and hardly any were toilet trained. Very few could dress themselves or say even a couple of words. They were incapable of social play with peers. They displayed bizarre, stereotyped motor patterns. They would grab their heads between their hands and rock rhythmically back and forth, distinctly reminiscent of the isolate-reared monkeys in Harlow's studies and of autistic youth.

Assessment. What these and similar cases show is that to become an adequately functioning human requires a social process of intensive face-to-face interaction between the developing infant and other people. The evidence supports the position that there may be a critical period during which interaction is essential for subsequent normal development. Although the human is a resilient life form, research suggests that there may well be a limit to the length of isolation that a primate, including human primates, can sustain in the first years of life without resulting in developmental disturbances—including a reduced capacity for learning language and other social skills—that are remarkably resistant to reduction or elimination by normal measures and by known therapeutic techniques.

Theoretical Perspectives on the Socialization Process

The process and consequences of socialization are important and complex. We now examine the process of primary socialization as it is illuminated by some of the most influential social scientists of this century.

Sigmund Freud

Sigmund Freud (1856-1939) lived in Vienna, Austria, during the same turbulent times as Weber, Durkheim, and Marx. Like other social theorists whose ideas we have examined, Freud's thought was influenced by the currents of social change. He was trained as physician at the University of Vienna. His interests turned to the origins of civilization. Civilization, claims Freud, is made possible by turning our innate sexual and aggressive drives to ends no longer sexual and no longer aggressive, a process he terms **sublimation** (1930).

Freud's theory of the relationship among the personality, the individual, and society is the story of socialization. It is a story of contradictions, conflict, and often of pain and suffering. Suffering characterized the bloody First World War where he served as a medical doctor. Freud systematically observed the effects of soldiers loosing fingers, arms, and legs. He observed grown men calling out for their mothers in grueling agony. He observed soldiers imagining that their body parts, which had been blown away or surgically amputated, were intact. Freud observed the psychological effects of prolonged stress and fatigue on soldiers, effects which social scientists today term as delayed stress syndrome.

We can understand how uncontrollable disasters such as earthquakes, hurricanes, floods, and tornadoes wreck our lives. Out of this rubble we start again afresh. But how do we understand envy, jealousy, love, hatred, lack of ability to forgive, guilt, rejection, pity, and acts of kindness and of violence? The Freudian paradigm provides a template for answering these questions.

The force of life for Freud is the **libido,** which is Latin for desire or lust. The aim of libido is the satisfaction of instinctual drives towards survival, pleasure, and pain avoidance. Libido is expressed in the part of our personality known as the **id.** The id is our basic needs, innate sexual and aggressive drives, desires, and pleasures. Id is impulsive, unconscious and covert. Id is petty, selfish, and self-centered. Id in raw form has no rational logic or sense of time. It is the infant's screaming in the middle of church service while the minister calls upon her or his congregation to be saved. Id is a direct cause of caregivers' sleepless nights when newborns cry and demand food and comfort. Id is demonstrated when tots are at peace, calm and smiling, while danger is all around them. A baby's id is satisfied when its need to feel warm and secure is met by the loving arms of babushka. Libido pushes for wish fulfillment, which Freud calls *the pleasure principle.* Libido is in constant tension or conflict with the part of the personality known as

the **ego.** The function of the ego is to regulate our actions in accordance with reason and logic, otherwise known as *the reality principle.* The reality principle of the ego (e.g., You have a Chemistry 101 exam at 8 AM Monday morning, and you have yet to study and to read three chapters of the textbook) often conflicts with the pleasure principle of the libido (e.g., There is a party you really want to go to on Friday night). The frustration of libidinal energy underlies anxiety.

Ego, a Latin word for "I,' is the part of the personality we present to others. Ego is largely conscious, aware of itself. Ego's basic function is appropriately to balance id's demands with the requirements of society, which are expressed in the part of our personality known as the **superego.** Ego is what we put on the line when we request that our needs be fulfilled. Ego is punched, made fun of, pinched, poked, and even battered. Ego protects us and defends us from the unpleasantness of life's disappointments. Ego is largely overt. Ego develops defenses, known as ego defenses, to unpleasant events and thoughts. Please read Box 6.1, "Some Common Ego Defenses."

Superego is our conscience, the norms, values, notions of right and wrong that we have internalized from significant others who live within a particular historical period and within a specific culture. The activity of the superego is often unconscious. According to psychoanalytic theory, the severity of the superego's pressure reflects the strengths of a person's own aggressive impulses and does not reflect only the actual severity of parents. Superego is the guilt we feel when we eat the last cookie on the plate. Superego urges us to help others in need. Superego respects authority. Superego is the shame we feel when mom disapproves. Superego is society within us.

We may conceive of the id, ego, and superego as representing different drives or desires within us. The id says: "I want it, I want it." The superego says, "You can't have it; it's bad for you." The ego, as mediator or umpire, says, "Well, you can have a little bit of it, later." According to Freud, the battle among ego, id, and superego is ceaseless.

Freud generalizes his concept of libidinal energy in his theory of *psycho-sexual development. Psycho* is a root that means breath, life,

--- **BOX 6.1** ---

Some Common Ego Defenses

In psychoanalytic theory, a **defense mechanism**—also known as an *ego defense* or as an *ego defense mechanism*—is a technique used by the ego to defend itself from anxiety. The aim of a defense mechanism is to divert anxiety away from the consciousness of the ego. In psychoanalytic theory, there are three sources of anxiety: (1) when an impulse in the id is pushing for gratification; (2) when the superego does its job—exerts moral pressure against a wish, desire, idea, or intention; (3) when there is actual danger of injury or pain.

In psychoanalytic theory, there are a number of defense mechanisms, which include the following:

■ **Repression** One prevents a mental element—an idea, wish, anxiety, impulse, or image—from becoming conscious; and rejecting a mental element from consciousness to unconsciousness.

■ **Projection** One attributes to another a property of oneself. One thereby can blame the other person instead of feeling *guilty* oneself; guilt is a type of anxiety.

■ **Reaction formation** One's anxiety about something (e.g., being attracted romantically to someone who has spurned you) is kept at bay by overtly assuming the opposite (e.g., "I dislike/ hate/am indifferent to that person."). This is a brittle, fragile defense unless buttressed with a lot of supports.

■ **Identification** The threat of an aggressor or of a more powerful person or group is neutralized by adopting the characteristics of the ag-

gressor (e.g., **the Stockholm syndrome,** wherein hostages identify with, or experience feelings of empathy toward, the hostage takers and displace their frustration and aggression toward the authorities).

■ **Sublimation** One directs the energies of the id to ends no longer sexual and no longer aggressive. In psychoanalytic theory, sublimation is the major defense mechanism of the genital (most mature) stage of psychosexual development.

■ **Rationalization** One intellectually rationalizes or excuses what was a freely chosen action.

■ **Self-handicapping** One creates a ready excuse for failure, which serves the function of protecting one's self-image.

---

soul, spirit, and indicates the mind, personality, or mental processes (Morris, 1969: 1055). Psycho-sexual development indicates that the development of mind, personality, and sexuality are inextricably intertwined; one cannot understand the development of the mind and personality without understanding the simultaneous development of sexuality and visa versa. In the normal course of human development, according to Freud, the individual gets instinctual satisfaction from different parts of the body because libidinal energy is associated with different orifices of the body at different age levels. Libidinal satisfaction or frustration at each stage of development is accompanied by particular emotions. Those emotions that are particularly intense or preponderant become consolidated as chronic dispositions, according to Freud. Too much satisfaction or frustration of libido at any stage of development can result in libido becoming fixated at

that stage. **Fixation** means that a disproportionate amount of libidinal energy is invested in a particular bodily orifice, personality is dominated by the traits associated with that level of development, and psycho-sexual maturity is not attained

The Stages of Psycho-Sexual Development According to Freud

According to Freud, there are five stages of psycho-sexual development. Because the content of the first two stages is the same for males and females, it is said that an initial stage of homosexuality underlies all human development in the Freudian paradigm.

1. *Oral Stage.* In the newborn infant, and until about two years of age, libido is associated with the mouth, and hence this stage is known as the oral stage. The baby's emotional gratification now centers on oral

activities, like sucking and swallowing, biting and spitting. Sucking and swallowing are conducive to an attitude of basic trust, and help the infant to develop attitudes of pleasure, acceptance, affection, and security. According to Freud, biting and spitting express rejection, hurtfulness, and destructiveness, which are characteristic of mistrust. The traits viewed by Freud as emerging from oral satisfaction include optimism, tolerance, and generosity. Traits viewed by Freud as emerging from oral frustration include jealousy, hostility, and impatience. Those fixated at the oral stage of psychosexual development are expected later in life to be compulsive talkers, eaters, smokers, and so forth.

2. *Anal Stage.* From roughly age two to three years of age, libidinal energy is associated with the anal orifice, and hence this stage is known as the anal stage. The baby now derives pleasure from the process and products of its own excretions. These pleasures tend to be opposed by the caretakers who socialize the baby. Hence, this is commonly the age at which toilet training occurs. Those fixated at this stage of psychosexual development are expected later in life to develop problems with relationships to authority and to lack self-control.

According to Freud, the anal stage is important for ego development and for emotional development. It is with toilet training that the infant is first confronted with libidinal frustration (i.e., not defecating when she or he is not supposed to, even if her or his body is telling the infant that she/he really "has to go") in exchange for social respectability. Defecation must be confined to certain places and to certain times. This learning of impulse control is important for ego development. The issues confronted by the infant at this time, according to Freud, include giving-withholding, tension-reduction, retention-release, obstinacy-flexibility, mess-cleanliness, and approval-shame.

3. *Phallic Stage.* After the anal stage is the **phallic stage,** which begins at three to four years of age and which is completed by five or six years of age. This stage sometimes is

called the *Oedipal period* or *Oedipal complex (Oedipus complex)*, particularly for boys, after a Greek legend in which King Oedipus inadvertently kills his father and marries his mother. For girls, this stage sometimes is called the *Elektra complex,* after a Greek legend in which Elektra avenges the murder of her father by assisting in the murder of her mother. Libidinal energy now is associated with the penis in boys and with the clitoris in girls. The child shows sexual curiosity and engages in specifically sexual play. The child's attachment to the opposite-sex parent becomes sexualized. Subconsciously the child wishes to possess the opposite-sex parent sexually and sees the same-sex parent as a rival.

The boy fears that his biggest rival, his father, will cut off his penis, which has given the boy much pleasure. This fear is termed *castration anxiety,* and it is a powerful motivator. The boy who successfully resolves the Oedipal complex deals with this anxiety by "identifying" with his powerful father, internalizing his notions of right and wrong, prime among which is that the son give up sexual desires for Mom. At this point, the boy successfully has resolved the phallic stage. In the Freudian paradigm, then, *castration anxiety is the basis for the formation of the boy's* primitive *superego.* Due to castration anxiety, boys develop a robust conscience (superego).

Girls are not as fortunate. According to Freud, from a girl's point of view, the worst already has happened. She has no penis. It must have been cut off and she knows who must have done *that*—the major rival for her father, the mother. The girl who sexually desires her father does not have the powerful force of castration anxiety to motivate her. She already has lost a penis and has only, in the Freudian view, an inferior clitoris. Lack of a penis is a wound to her narcissism; she wants a penis. She has *penis envy.* Maybe the powerful father will be able to give her one. When it dawns on her that the powerful father can do many things, but, alas, even he cannot give her a penis of her own, she identifies with the mother. She internalizes the mother's notions of right and wrong, prime among which is that the daughter gives up sexual desires for Dad.

She may not be able to have a penis of her own, now; but *she can* eventually *give birth to one* (i.e., give birth to a boy child). At this point the young girl, motivated by *penis envy,* successfully has resolved the phallic stage.

For Freud, the phallic stage is a crucial period of development for both boys and girls, and for the men and women they later will become. Many anxieties and conflicts need to be dealt with at this stage, and Freud claims that much of our later personality is determined by the ways in which we resolve this stage of development.

4. *Latency.* The fourth stage of development is latency, the calm after the storm of the phallic stage. Sexual and aggressive fantasies now are relatively dormant. The latency stage begins after the end of the phallic stage and continues until the onset of puberty, which marks the onset of the final stage of psycho-sexual development, the **adult genital stage.**

5. *Adult Genital Stage.* This stage is characterized by a move away from a focus on self-pleasure toward a reciprocal pleasure-giving relationship with a person, with reproduction as a goal. Manifestations of the genital stage of psycho-sexual development include social awareness, constructive projects (such as work), and participating in group activities. In short, Freud believes that healthy individuals now put their libidinal energies into family and work, both of which are important for the reproduction of culture and society.

The first revision of his theory was a result of the currents of social change in which he lived. The major concepts of his system—libido, id, ego, superego, the pleasure principle, and so forth—did not allow him to explain why soldiers who returned from battle in the First World War and who were well removed from combat still experienced recurrent nightmares of the hell of war. In *Beyond the Pleasure Principle,* Freud concludes that there is a compulsion to repeat. This compulsion to repeat is viewed as primordial as the pleasure principle. However, the compulsion to repeat is viewed as in the service of a general destructive force or motive. Freud calls this general destructive force or motive

Thantos, the death instinct (Freud, 1920, *Standard Edition,* Vol. 18). A group of constructive motives, which he collectively terms *Eros,* or the life instinct, contend against *Thantos.*

Assessment

No doubt some of Freud's positions sound bizarre at the dawn of the twenty-first century. His paradigm has been criticized on many grounds. Please note some of these in the following list.

■ Many Christian religions have been highly critical of Freud's ideas, since he maintained that religion is an illusion that helps the helpless to identify with a powerful male god (Freud, 1927). Freud holds that healthy humans should attempt to live their lives without illusions; people should squarely face their anxieties.

■ Feminists claim that Freud's theory is inherently sexist in that it is excessively biological and focuses on the role of father and father-like figures. Some feminists maintain that there are and were female-centered societies.

■ Anthropologists criticize Freud's theory as ethnocentric. **Ethnocentrism** refers to the tendency to view the norms, values, and institutions of one's culture as right and as preferable to those of other cultures. Not all societies share Freud's views of socialization and of the role of the father. In some societies, the biological father is excluded from the family life of the children.

■ Methodological criticisms stress the lack of objective, reliable measures of many key concepts, the lack of objectivity in observation, and the difficulty of deriving testable hypotheses from the theory.

■ Behaviorists are critical of abstract concepts like id, ego, superego, sublimation, and so forth that cannot directly be observed and measured. They prefer to explain personality development in terms of the rewards and punishments that the individual receives. For behaviorists, behavior is learned, and the mechanisms involved in the process of conditioning suffice to explain differences in competence, motivation, and emotional adjustment. From this point of view, focusing on the past is fruitless. For example, Albert

Ellis maintains that thinking is learned, and only by changing thinking can the individual change the emotional response and thereby move on to appropriate behavior (1973, 1976, 1977).

■ Freud's theory also has been criticized as too deterministic and as not giving sufficient weight to social processes in the formation of self. Freud "saw personality as fully developed" or at least as "determined by about the age of four years" (Harré and Lamb, 1986: 247), a position that many social scientists reject. Some social scientists reject Freud's emphasis on sexual drives and pay more attention to social and interpersonal aspects of development. For instance, Erik Erikson, an influential theorist of the psychoanalytic school, stresses interpersonal relationships across the individual's life span as heavily influencing the capacity for development and personal adjustment (Erikson, 1963).

George Herbert Mead

As you recall, George Herbert Mead (1863-1931) is an American philosopher and sociologist, one of the founders of symbolic interactionism. As a social theorist, Mead represents and extends the view of social behaviorism we examined with respect to Pavlov and John B. Watson. Much of Mead's work is a reaction against the biological determinism of social Darwinism.

Unlike Freud who focuses largely on the unconscious mind, Mead's concern is with consciousness. Unlike Watson who concentrates on behavior, Mead's starting point is with conscious mind activity.

The Stages of Human Development According to Mead

1. *The Imitation Stage.* For Mead there are three stages in the process of socialization (Mead, 1934). The first occurs from birth to about three years of age and is called the *imitation stage.* Like Watson and modern behaviorists, Mead generally believes that infants know the world only from imitating those around them and from their social experiences. From receiving rewards from their environment, infants learn to identify certain sounds that they make as being important in satisfying their needs. Baby cries and mother responds by picking up, cuddling, and nursing baby. With a different type of cry, baby notices that the caregiver responds by coming to baby and changing baby's diapers. In other words, *gesture language* is the first language babies learn. (Please review Chapter 2). Babies can squint their eyes, snort their noses, blow bubbles out of their mouths, smile, cry, shriek, and wail—all gestures by means of which they can communicate their subjective experiences (e.g., hunger, thirst, need for affiliation).

Around the age of two, the baby develops the cognitive ability to use language. From the Meadian view, this is a significant milestone in the developmental process, because language opens many avenues of socialization. Eventually, the baby makes a vocalization, which significant others interpret as a significant symbol, say, as "Mom" or "Dad." They reward the baby with praise. Baby thereby learns to use these words.

2. *The Play Stage.* In order to be able to communicate effectively, baby needs to be able imaginatively to construct how she or he looks to others. In the Meadian view, the self emerges in play as we learn to imagine how we appear to others. More specifically, we develop a self as we perceive ourselves through the responses of others to us. Play is important in the development of self.

In the *play stage,* roughly from three to five years of age, children learn to use language and, in play, to take on the roles of others, one "other" at a time. Imagination leads children to act out some of the many others they encounter in their lives. A clear example of this is playing "dress up." In this game, common in the United States, a child puts on, say, Mommy's or Daddy's shoes or clothes, which are termed *props* by symbolic interactionists. The child, in play, actually *becomes,* say, Mommy or Daddy. Taking the role of the other is a difficult, elaborate, sophisticated mental operation for the young child. The props, talking out loud, and engaging in actions typical of the child's view of that person help the child to accomplish this cognitive feat.

By taking the role of the significant other, children learn the attitudes, values, and beliefs of that significant other. From play, the child learns that there are rules that she or he is expected to follow in a particular situation ("Wash you hands before dinner;" "Look *both ways* before crossing the street"). Children come to view themselves as a significant other views them. Let us share with you one parent's observations in this regard:

> I recall an argument I had with my son when he was three. He was sent to his room, and for the next half-hour I heard our argument continuing with my son playing both parts. Not only did he get rid of some anger this way, but he also produced in his own mind a clearer image of my expectations (however unreasonable they might have been). He was learning to see himself as I saw him. (Luhman, 1989: 211)

Can you recall similar or analogous observations with regard to someone you know? Can you think of one or more instances of a young child learning the role of the significant other? Did you, or anyone you know, ever play "dress up" as a young child? Please tell us about it

3. *The Game Stage.* The play stage is transformed into the **game stage** when the child gains and develops the cognitive capacity to understand a rule, to play accordingly, and to view a game from a number of different points of view simultaneously. In the Meadian view, a game is a form of social interaction that requires more cognitive sophistication than does mere play. Games have several characteristics that mere play lacks. First, games tend to be *competitive* (e.g., a score is kept and there are winners and losers). Second, playing a game (such as baseball, soccer, football, school band, or orchestra) requires that a member *cooperates* and *coordinates* her or his efforts with those of team mates. Third, games are structured according to *agreed upon rules*. In engaging in game behavior, a child learns to bring her or his behavior in accord with these agreed upon rules. In

short, games require that a child view a common activity from numerous points of view simultaneously, which Mead refers to as the ability to construct a **generalized other.**

The generalized other is a composite of all the other players in the game and of the rules of the game. It is a normative order. It is "the moral system that the individual internalizes, makes his or her own" (Charon, 1998: 180). It is a set of rules that guides our thinking and our **self-control,** the ability to take others into consideration and actively directing ourselves in relation to those others. A generalized other helps to make self-control possible. Social "interaction depends on individuals who *share* a generalized other," who share a set of rules (norms) to some extent so that **cooperation**—making one's actions consistent with what others are doing—is possible (Charon, 1998: 180; italics in original). As sociologist Joel M. Charon observes, "We can afford to act alone without a generalized other when our actions do not need to be coordinated with anyone else's; however, once others are needed for cooperation a generalized other needs to enter into what we do" (Charon, 1998: 180). In a game, a sophisticated form of play, our actions need to be coordinated with those of the other players. We need a generalized other in order to be able to play a game. Our "generalized others are guides to how we deal with situations—they set our limits, they inform us as to how best to deal with problems" (Charon, 1998: 180). Mead uses the game of baseball to illustrate the generalized other.

In a baseball game, a player physically plays only one position. Mentally, however, she or he plays every position. In other words, a member bases his/her actions on the rules of the game and the imaginative construction of all the other players' actions. For example, your team already has two "outs." This is your team's last inning to have batters at the plate; the bases are loaded, your team is down by one point, and it is your turn at bat. You imagine yourself as the batter and you take on that perspective. You simultaneously imagine yourself as the players who are on first, second, and third base. As batter, you want to hit the ball so that you can make it to first base, and so that the person on third base can run home safely and thereby score, thus tying the game. You know that the person currently on first base needs to make it to second base, and that the person currently on second base needs to make it safely to third base. You know that the other team is winning the game, and that if they get you, or any of your team mates currently on base, out, they win the game. You imagine what you would do if you were in each of the other positions, both on your team and on the other team, simultaneously. You are able to take the role of the generalized other. You understand, in other words, how to play the game.

Erik Erikson

Erik Erikson is an important theorist whose ideas on human development bridge a gap between the works of Freud and those of George Herbert Mead and Charles Horton Cooley. Unlike Mead, Erikson stresses that socialization is a lifelong process. Erikson's ideas are heavily influenced by Freudian thought. He borrows some elements from the Freudian paradigm, including the importance of ego and of identification, while rejecting others. Erikson rejects Freud's views of personality development as fixed in the first few years of life and of the primacy of sexuality in human development (Erikson, 1963, 1980). Instead, Erikson stresses the importance for human development of *social relations across the life span*. Because of this emphasis, his theory sometimes is referred to as a *psycho-social perspective*, a concept that emphasizes that we cannot understand the development of the self (psyche) without understanding the social relations we have with significant others, and visa versa. Figure 6.1 compares the stages in Erikson's theory with the Freudian equivalent.

Erikson envisions human development as consisting of eight stages. These stages span from birth to later adulthood. Each stage lays the foundation for the next stage. Each stage has a particular crisis or task, which is conceived of as a polarity and which emerges out of physiological changes and the changing social situation. If the individual leaves a task unresolved, then the individual moves on to the next stage, only to revert back to the incomplete stage whenever the individual confronts the developmental issues characteristic of that stage in the course of social interaction. Failure to complete the task characteristic of a given stage of development can produce an individual who is unable to engage others in satisfying relationships and who is unable successfully to meet the challenges of the next stage. Through the successful resolution of each stage, the individual achieves a sense of well-being and of balance. Moreover, Erikson views human development, the self, and even social structure itself as emerging out of, and as shaped by, the way we resolve each task. Let us now explore Erikson's eight stages of human development.

Erikson's Stages of Human Development

1. *Basic Trust vs. Mistrust.* From the time of birth through the first year of life, the major task facing the infant is trust versus mistrust. The infant is born helpless and dependent, and without caretakers to meet its basic needs, the infant will languish and die. The feelings/emotions of the infant develop according to the quality of response the infant receives or elicits from basic caregivers. For illustration, let us compare the following two situations:

    Say a two-month old baby wakes up at 3 AM and starts crying. Her mother comes in and, for the next half-hour, the baby contentedly nurses in her mother's arms while her mother gazes at her affectionately, telling her that she's happy to see her, even in the middle of the night. The baby, content in her mother's love, drifts back to sleep.

    Now say another two-month-old baby, who also awoke crying in the wee hours, is met instead by a mother who is tense and irritable, having fallen asleep just an hour before after a fight with her husband. The baby starts to tense up the moment his mother abruptly picks him up, telling him, "Just be quiet—I can't stand one more thing! Come on, let's get this over with." As the baby nurses his mother stares stonily ahead, not looking at him, reviewing her fight with his father, getting more agitated

FIGURE 6.1. Erikson's Stages, Age, and the Freudian Equivalents _____

Erikson's Stage	Age	Freudian Equivalent
1. Basic Trust vs. Mistrust	Infancy	Oral
2. Autonomy vs. Shame and Doubt	Toddler	Anal
3. Initiative vs. Guilt	Pre-school	Phallic (Oedipal, Elektra)
4. Industry vs. Inferiority	School Age	Latency
6. Intimacy vs. Isolation	Young Adulthood	Genital
7. Generativity vs. Stagnation	Middle Adulthood	None
8. Ego Integrity vs. Despair	Later Adulthood	None

herself as she mulls it over. The baby, sensing her tension, squirms, stiffens, and stops nursing. "That's all you want?" his mother says. "Then don't eat." With the same abruptness she puts him back in his crib and stalks out, letting him cry until he falls back to sleep, exhausted. (Goleman, 1995: 194-195)

These two different interactions, if repeated over and over, instill very different emotions in a toddler about him- or herself and about close relationships. When the infant signals through crying and other gestures that she/he is afraid, or hungry, or lonely, do the caregivers respond consistently and promptly by coming to the infant and picking her/him up, cuddling, caressing, reassuring her/him and making her/him comfortable? If so, the infant is learning that people can be trusted to notice her/his needs. People can be counted on to help. She herself or he himself is effective in getting help. As a result, this toddler is learning that she/hi is a master of her/his own fate. Such toddlers develop a trusting, hopeful attitude towards others and towards life. They thereby lay the foundation for a healthy ego and sense of self. In contrast, when the infant signals that she/he is hungry, afraid, and lonely, are the caregivers undependable, inconsistent, and rejecting? If so, the infant responds with suspiciousness, anxiety, fear, rage, cautiousness, feelings of inadequacy, despair, and eventually, with withdrawal. The infant learns not to trust himself/herself or others. The infant learns that she/he is impotent in getting help.

2. *Autonomy vs. Shame and Doubt.* Between two to three years of age, the toddler is learning to talk, to walk, and to engage in bowl and bladder control. Once again, the

toddler's emotions and feelings develop as a response to the actions of caregivers. Are the toddler's efforts at mastery consistently met with firm reassurance and encouragement? Is the toddler encouraged to develop a sense of mastery over self and the environment? If a toddler is having trouble with a puzzle and asks a busy Mom for help, is the toddler's request met with undisguised delight? If so, the toddler learns one set of lessons. The toddler learns persistence at a task and that she/he is a capable person. However, if the toddler's request is met with indifference or with a rebuff—"Don't bother me. I've got important work to do"—very different lessons are learned, particularly when such encounters are typical of caregiver and toddler. This toddler learns shame and feels ridiculed (Goleman, 1995: 195). The toddler learns to doubt her/his own ability to accomplish a task and to influence the world.

3. *Initiative vs. Guilt.* The next stage, from around four to five years of age, involves the issues of initiative versus guilt. As children develop their motor and language skills, as they learn in play to take on the roles of specific others, they develop feelings of efficacy, that is, of self worth. Ridicule and disinterest in the child's activities may lead to feelings of guilt. Encouragement in exploration leads to a well-developed sense of personal initiative. Nothing succeeds like early success.

4. *Industry vs. Inferiority.* In the middle childhood years, from age six until the beginning of adolescence, the developmental task is industry versus inferiority.

School, peers, and community increase in importance for children, as does recognition of their abilities by extra-familial institutions. Recognition is attained by striving for and by attaining success in mental skills (e.g., winning a "spelling bee," getting honorable mention in a science fair), physical skills (e.g., track and field, baseball, football, tennis, swimming, basketball), and through producing things. In contrast, disparagement because of one's race/ethnicity, religion, gender, perceived sexual orientation, and inability to achieve may be social experiences that lead to feelings of inadequacy and inferiority.

5. *Identity vs. Role Confusion.* The fifth stage of development is adolescence, roughly from twelve to eighteen years of age. Peers are very important in this phase of development. The task the individual faces is to forge an ego identity that can form a bridge across the tumultuous time of puberty to adulthood.

Identity is a central concern for Erikson (1968). In his paradigm *identity* refers to an ability to achieve a sense of self-continuity about one's past, present, and future. If one is unable to construct an identity that takes into account the many and varied roles one has occupied, is occupying, and is likely to occupy in the future, the result is *role confusion.* In the grip of role confusion, individuals have no clear direction in their lives and they drift without purpose.

Erikson maintains that role diffusion occurs when individuals feel apathetic because they have not internalized the expectations of the larger society. These individuals have not integrated their personal abilities as unique individuals with a core identity. *Premature closure of identity* occurs when an individual leaves the fifth stage unresolved, which sometimes occurs in response to the demands of others. (What do you want to "be" when you grow up? What is your academic major?) Sometimes it occurs because an individual has low tolerance for ambiguity. For instance, for many people with a low tolerance for ambiguity, selecting an academic major—any academic major—is preferable to not having one. Yet, because they selected in haste, they may not have chosen

well. Yet, they may be reluctant to change academic majors, for any number of reasons and so they stay with their original selection. Thus, it should not surprise us that people who engage in identity closure prematurely often do not feel authentic in what they pursue.

6. *Intimacy vs. Isolation.* The first stage of adult development is called young adulthood, and it spans from about nineteen through thirty-five years of age. The crisis at this stage is intimacy versus isolation. In the Eriksonian paradigm, only with a clear sense of ego identity and an ability to trust can the individual avoid isolation. Intimacy—friendship, marriage, a committed intimate relationship—requires facing the possibility of rebuff, rejection, and betrayal. A willingness to face the risk of "being hurt" is part of the price of intimacy.

At the beginning of this stage, many adolescents in this country leave home to go to college or to begin an occupational career. Home ties are no longer enough, and one reaches out beyond primordial ties to establish intimate relations with nonprimordial others. During this stage many people begin marriage or some other form of committed intimate relationship with a significant other. Erikson envisions the alternative as consisting of a deep sense of lonely isolation, which may manifest itself in competitiveness and combativeness with others that serve to protect a "fearful" self who pushes away from those who could have nurtured the self. Healthful solitude has little place in the Eriksonian paradigm. (For an alternative view, please read Storr, 1988.) For Erikson, to love and to work are twin capacities that mark successful adulthood.

7. *Generativity vs. Stagnation.* The crisis the individual faces in the middle stage of adulthood, from 35 to about 50 years of age, is generativity versus stagnation. *Generativity,* being productive and creative to the benefit of others, manifests itself in establishing relationships and in guiding the next generation. Thus, adults make a meaningful contribution by rearing children and by engaging in creative works. Work itself may consist of creative endeav-

ors and be as important as family or even an alternative to it. Perceptions by the individual of life as inherently boring, dull, and painful, and "early invalidism, physical or psychological" are indicators that the individual has found stagnation and self-absorption rather than generativity (Erikson, 1968:267).

8. *Ego Integrity vs. Despair.* The final stage of human development begins in later adulthood at about fifty years of age. It concerns the crisis of ego integrity versus despair. *Integrity* involves coming to terms with life and death. If the individual views her or his life as a series of opportunities missed and feels that the time to start afresh is past and cannot be reclaimed, the individual has found *despair.* If, upon reviewing her or his life, the individual feels that, all things considered, she or he has contributed more to life than she or he has detracted from it, life has been worth living. The things she or he has wanted to accomplish and the relationships she or he has wanted to establish can no longer be put off, and she or he does not fear death, the individual has found ego integrity.

Please look at your own life (or the life of someone you know) from the perspective of Erikson's eight stages of development. At what stage are you now? At what stage is your best friend? At what stage is your significant other or spouse? At what stage are your parents? Can you see Erikson's stages of development in your own life or in the life of someone you know? What did the family contribute at each of these various stages? Peers? Please tell us about it.

Assessment: Issues of Love, Gender, and Culture

Erikson's theory of human development resembles those of Mead, Freud, and Kohlberg by viewing the process of socialization as consisting of stages and by viewing the process by which the individual handles each stage as having repercussions for later development. Please read the Box 6.2, Lawrence Kohlberg's Social Learning Perspective on the Stages of Human Development, for an exploration of

Lawrence Kohlberg's insights into the socialization process. Erikson's viewpoint also resembles those of Mary Ainsworth (1982, 1989), John Bowlby (1982), René Spitz (1945, 1947), and Harry Harlow and colleagues by assuming that higher-order primates, including humans, possess a physiologically based need to love and to be loved and that this need is shaped by early interactions with caregivers. These assumptions are basic to Freud's hypothesis regarding the transformation of libidinal energy from infancy to adulthood, at the core of [Mary Ainsworth's and] John Bowlby's ideas on the consequences of secure and insecure attachments, and central to Erik Erikson's suggestion that an infant's trust of its mother will eventually become the adult's ability to love another. (Kagan, 1989:10). However, not all students of human development share these assumptions (e.g., Kagan, 1989: 10-12; Storr, 1988).

Some social scientists criticize the paradigms of Kohlberg and Erikson as gender bound. While these perspectives provide valuable insight into the process of *male* socialization, they inadequately explain the socialization process, experiences, and effects for females (e.g., Gilligan, 1982, 1987, 1988; Clinchy, 1989; Archer, 1992; Matteson, 1993; Knight, Elfenbein, and Messina, 1995; Lytle et. al., 1997). Thus, **Carol Gilligan** of Harvard University stresses that female socialization engenders a perspective of *care and responsibility* towards others and towards situations (Brown and Gilligan, 1992; Taylor, Gilligan, and Sullivan, 1995). In contrast, male socialization tends to engender a perspective more concerned with formal rules as the appropriate criterion for reaching decisions regarding right and wrong. Gilligan terms this particular way of viewing others and situations *a justice perspective.*

For instance, social science research reveals that boys and girls tend to have different play and game experiences in childhood (e.g., Piaget, 1932: 83; Lever, 1976, 1978; Maccoby and Jacklin, 1987; Goleman, 1995; Funk and Buchman, 1996; Colley, et. al., 1996). Sociologist *Janet Lever* studied over 180 fifth-grade, middle-class white ten and eleven year olds. She observed these children while they played at recess and during physical-education class at elementary school. She also kept diaries of these children's self-reports regarding how

BOX 6.2

Lawrence Kohlberg's Social Learning Perspective on the Stages of Human Development

Lawrence Kohlberg views socialization as a social-learning experience (Kohlberg, 1969; Kohlberg, Levine, and Hewer, 1983) that consists of three stages. According to Kohlberg, it is the child's social environment that is important in the acquisition of values and norms, not the child's current physiological or cognitive state of development. Because Kohlberg stresses the importance of the social environment and discounts as unimportant physiological and cognitive aspects of development, his theory and ones similar to it, sometimes are termed *social-learning theories.* From the point of view of social-learning theory, parents (and significant others quite generally) easily can teach children to internalize values and norms that are characteristic of a higher level of development than that at which children currently find themselves.

The **pre-conventional stage.** From birth to about eight or ten years of age, most children experience the world in terms of pain and pleasure. At this point, *what is right* is perceived as *what feels good to me.* "If it feels good, go for it" is an apt motto for this stage of development.

The **conventional stage.** At this stage, which characterizes most adolescents and adults, individuals have internalized and largely conform to the social norms of the conventional social order (Figurski, 1992). The individual now defines *what is right* in terms of Mead's generalized individual's desire (libido), the individual is able to refrain from acting on the basis of the pleasure principle and is capable of following through with the moral course of action.

The **postconventional stage.** This state of development is reached by very few persons, according to Kohlberg. In this stage, people move beyond the norms of their society to ponder their ethical and moral worth. *'This is the norm of my group. But, in terms of a larger ethical system, is it right? Is it moral?"* At this stage, people (like Mahatma Gandhi, Rosa Parks, Malcolm X, Martin Luther King, Jr.) ponder the norms and laws of their society. They ponder the meaning of abstract concepts like justice, equality, fairness, freedom, and equal justice before the law. They may be critical of their own society because they perceive that their existing laws *are not right.*

they spent their out-of-school time. Lever reports significant gender differences in socialization experiences. The gender differences of children in play observed by Janet Lever also have been recorded by Jean Piaget (1932:83) and others (Hughes, 1988; Howes, 1988; Swadener et. al., 1989; Boulton, 1996). What are these durable gender differences in play?

Boys tend to play outdoors more than girls do, to play in larger groups, and to engage in games that are competitive and rule-bound, games like football, soccer, baseball, basketball, football, and so forth. What happens when a player getting hurt disrupts a game? The boy is expected to get out of the way so the game can continue. What happens if a quarrel erupts? During the course of her study, "boys were seen quarreling all the time, but not once was a game terminated because of a quarrel and no game was interrupted for more than seven minutes" (Lever, 1976: 482). The gravest disputes were inevitably settled according to the official rules, by repeating the play. These experiences, repeated over and over again, help to instill in boys *a justice approach* to others and to situations.

In contrast, disputes tend to end girls' games. Girls' games tend to occur in more intimate, smaller groups. Traditional girls' games, like hop-scotch, jump rope, "Mother may I?," and "hide and seek" are turn-taking games that maximize cooperation and minimize direct competition. One person's success does not signal another's failure. What happens when a game is disrupted by a player getting hurt? *The game stops.* The girls gather around their hurt playmate to help her feel better. Girls thereby learn to view themselves as situated in a web of connectedness and they learn to experience empathy. These experiences, repeated over and over again, help to instill in girls an ethic of *care and of responsibility.*

Other social scientists criticize Erikson and Kohlberg's theories by pointing out that we need to take culture and history into account in understanding human development. The content of socialization may vary by gender, race, and religion. The stages themselves may also vary by culture and history. For example, childhood as an identifiable stage of social life is a relatively recent social invention in Western societies. It emerged first in late seventeenth and early eighteenth centuries in Western Europe, first among the nobility and upper classes, and first with regard to males. There were male children well before there were female children. Only later did this concept spread to females and to other social classes (Aries, 1960). Adolescence is an even more recent social invention (Musgrove, 1965). The number of stages one observes over the life course, then, varies by culture and historical period (Gecas, 1992).

Jean Piaget

Swiss-born social psychologist Jean Piaget is an impressive student of early childhood development. He spent more than thirty years observing and studying the development of children of varying ages. Piaget perceived that children are active participants in their own development.

Piaget conceives of development in terms that differ significantly from those of Freud, Erikson, the behaviorists, and social-learning theorists. Piaget views development as an "ability to reason abstractly, to think about hypothetical situations in a logical way, and to organize rules . . . into [increasingly] complex" structures (Eshleman, 1978:543). Piaget envisions human development as consisting of four stages. Each stage lays the foundation for the next.

Stages of Human Development According to Piaget

1. *The sensorimotor stage* lasts roughly from birth through the first eighteen months of life. At birth, the infant can suck, and squirm, and clinch her or his fists in response to internal states. Later in this stage, the infant engages in these activities with the intent to have the caregivers respond to the infant's needs. A lot of development in motor ability occurs. Awareness of gender

differences is evident at this stage, even before children have a clear sense of their own gender permanence (Maccoby and Jacklin, 1987; Martin, Wood, and Little, 1990; Cann and Vann, 1995). A major cognitive development during this stage is the emergence of *object permanence.* A ball or rattle that is under the blanket has not disappeared from the world. A caretaker who is not in the baby's line of vision has not vanished or dissolved permanently. A cat cannot become a dog; a girl cannot become a boy, and visa versa.

2. *The preoperational stage* lasts roughly from age two through age six. The child has difficulty in separating self from nonself and in taking the role of the other, whether of a child or of an adult. The child learns language and, with language competence, the ability to manipulate symbols. A doll may be a baby; a stuffed toy, may be a bear.

3. *The concrete operational stage* lasts from about age seven to age eleven. Children learn to consider viewpoints other than their own, to classify objects, to differentiate between dreams and reality, and to understand the concepts of cause and effect. Children during this stage acquire the ability, in the Meadian sense, to take the role of the generalized other. Children also learn *conservation of mass.* For instance, a lump of playdough three inches square has the same mass if you take it in your hands, place it on a table, and roll it into a long rope shape. The shapes are different, but the mass is the same. A child who has finished the concrete operational stage can comprehend this, but a child in the preoperational stage cannot.

The child also learns *conservation of measure.* To illustrate this concept, let us suppose that you volunteer to participate in an experiment regarding conservation of measure. The experiment involves you as the experimenter and two children. Two children will participate, one at a time, in this experiment with you. One of the children is of preoperational age—say, age three or four. The other is of concrete operational age—say, age eight or nine. You and one of the children enter a room that contains a table on which are three clear glass containers and a pitcher of red liquid. You ask the child to sit in a chair at the table. Directly in front of the child are the three clear glass containers, two of which are tall and skinny. The third glass is short and squat.

You ask the child to fill the two tall skinny glasses half-full with the red liquid. You then ask the child if the amount of liquid in the two glasses is the same or different. The child answers that the amount is the same. You then ask the child to pour the contents from one of those glasses into the short squat glass. You ask the child if the amount of liquid in the two glasses is the same or different.

The result? The child at the concrete operational stage will be able to do this exercise correctly. The child's response will be something like, "Of course, the amount of liquid in the two containers is the same. This is dumb and boring. Are we going to do anything fun?" In contrast, the child at the preoperational stage of development will give you the wrong answer. She or he will be sure that the amount of fluid has changed.

While the majority of people successfully complete this stage of development, many people do not reach, let alone successfully complete, the next stage.

4. *The formal operational period.* This stage begins around age 12. During this period people develop a competence in abstract thinking. People use and develop their capacity to think in terms of abstract concepts (e.g., social class, stratification, domination, honor), theories (e.g., functionalism, social Darwinism, behaviorism, conflict theory, symbolic interactionism, feminism), and general principles (e.g., gravity, equity). People learn to derive testable hypotheses from theory and learn to test these hypotheses. A focus on thought, on the life of the mind, is a hallmark of this stage of development. When universities across this nation stress critical thinking, they are endeavoring to assist students in developing their formal-operational skills, in the Piagetian sense.

Assessment

Piaget's insights into cognitive development are path breaking, and have had tremendous influence in numerous fields, including computer science, artificial intelligence, child development, and education, to name but a few. His viewpoint sometimes is construed as a critique of behaviorism and even of social-learning theory. Why? Because Piaget's extensive empirical research leads him to the conclusion that moving from one developmental stage to another is based, at least in part, on the physical and cognitive maturation of the individual. Just as a child must physiologically mature in order to engage in bowel and bladder control, so, too, must the individual mature in order to develop sensorimotor skills and to learn conservation of measure. Before this maturation occurs, no re-enforcement schedule will suffice to teach children the cognitive skills that are at a higher level of cognitive development than that in which the children currently find themselves. For instance, regardless of the re-enforcement schedule, one cannot successfully teach three-year-olds conservation of measure.

The ages for moving from one stage to another are not fixed, and there is a significant range of variation across individuals. Some individuals move from one stage to another before or after the years specified. Also, cultural differences can be significant (e.g., Kabagarama, 1993). We cannot assume that the process of thought is the same in all cultures. Cultural anthropologist Dorothy Lee, for instance, demonstrates that the people of the Trobriand Islands apprehend reality in a nonlineal way that is in sharp contrast to our own lineal mode of codifying reality (1950).

Contexts of Socialization

Much sociological research on socialization concerns the aspects of an individual's development as influenced by contexts and agents of socialization. The family is the context in which much primary socialization occurs. We will now examine this important institution as an agent of socialization.

Family Gender Socialization

Parental Warmth and Parenting Styles

Parental warmth and *parenting styles* are among the most robust variables in the literature on the family as primary socialization agent (Gecas, 1992). Other terms used for the dimension of *parental warmth* include parental support, parental love and support (Argyle, 1994), and a nurturing relationship between an adult and child. *Parenting style* refers to the manner by which, and the degree to which, parents attempt to place restraints on a child's behavior. Other terms for this parenting dimension include parental control, discipline, training, supervision, strictness, monitoring, punishment, and permissiveness.

Researchers distinguish different styles or types of parental discipline. The different styles are important because they have different short-term and longer-term consequences for the child and for the adult the child will become (Barnett, 1987; Dekovic´ and Geeris, 1992; Simons, Johnson, and Conger, 1994; Chassin and De Lucia, 1996; Hawkins et. al., 1997; McCord, 1997; Smith and Stern, 1997). A series of studies by Marian Radke-Yarrow and Carolyn Zahn-Waxler of the National Institute of Health demonstrates, for instance, that parenting style influence whether empathetic concern develops in very young children (1984). Empathetic two-and-a-half-year olds have parents whose discipline consistently calls strong attention to how their misbehavior emotionally distresses someone else. Responding to misbehavior by saying "Look how sad you've made Susie feel" instead of with "You were naughty," or "Wait until Daddy hears about this" goes a long way toward instilling empathy. Young children also learn empathetic responses by seeing it modeled by their peers (Radke-Yarrow and Zahn-Waxler, 1984) in day to day interactions. By imitating what they see, children develop a menu of emphatic response options useful in helping others that are distressed.

Styles of Parental Control

An important distinction is made by *Diana Baumrind* of the University of California, Berkeley, between **authoritarian** and **authoritative** control (1978). Rollins and Thomas refer to these differences, respectively, as coercive and **inductive** (1979).

1. **Authoritarian** or **coercive control** refers to discipline based on threat, force, or physical punishment. This style is more frequent among working-class parents than among the more educated and more affluent. Authoritarian parents are aloof and cold and control their children closely. Authoritarian parenting also is more prevalent among parents who are closely supervised at work and who are expected to follow orders (Kohn, 1977; Kohn et. al., 1990; Harrison et. al., 1990; Argyle, 1994). Authoritarian parents compare their children or adolescents' behavior against an absolute set of standards. They emphasize to their children the importance of obedience, conformity, and respect for authority. They use physical punishment and also discourage verbal give-and-take with their children. Studies indicate that in the U.S. authoritarian methods tend not to be perceived as good and reasonable by working-class adolescents and lead them to feel unwanted (e.g., Elder, 1962). Parental coldness or neglect in combination with inconsistent and excessively harsh punishment tend to be found in families whose children are chronically delinquent (Hirschi, 1969; West and Farrington, 1973; Wilson and Herrnstein, 1985; Simons, Johnson, and Conger, 1994; Fendrich, et. al., 1997; Lawrence, 1998).

2. **Authoritative** or **inductive control** refers to discipline based on logical reasoning and explanation. These parents use far less physical punishment than their authoritarian counterparts. Authoritative parents base discipline on appeals to reason, guilt, isolation (e.g., a child is sent to her or his room as punishment), and appeals involving the threat of loss of love. (Their small children thereby learn to use these methods *on their parents*. "I hate you!" is a taunt hurled by a child to a parent the child is trying to discipline.) This style is more frequent among the middle and professional classes, whose members have more freedom from close supervision, flexibility, and creativity

in their occupations. Authoritative parents encourage verbal give-and-take with their children and explain the reasons behind discipline. While they encourage conformity to adult expectations, they also stress the importance of self-direction and independence (Alwin, 1990). They set standards for behavior and enforce them. In short, a warm and affectionate bond between caregivers and children, plus consistent and judicious discipline in combination with explanations for the reasons for various rules are found among families whose children tend to be self-reliant, cooperative, sociable, educationally successful, and without a record of official delinquency (Clark, 1983; Dornbusch et. al., 1987; Wilson, 1993; Sokol-Katz, Dunham, and Zimmerman, 1997).

3. **Permissive control** refers to consistently lax control, whereby parents indulge the child's impulses and use little control or punishment. They are affectionate to their children and yet they make few demands for the children to accept responsibility as members of the household (e.g., the children are responsible for few or no "chores"). They allow the child to regulate his or her own activities. For instance, even on school nights, the child does not need to go to bed by a certain time. These children tend to lack self-control.

Internalization

The Process of Internalization

By way of exploring the process of internalization let us tell you something about Piaget's early work with very young children and an attractive toy—a toy parrot. Piaget would get a child interested in a toy parrot, so that the child really likes to play with it. Then Piaget takes the parrot away. The child attempts to recover the parrot.

Piaget takes the parrot away in a number of ways. First, he puts the parrot under a *blue* blanket and teaches the child that if she or he pulls the blue blanket away, the parrot is there. This becomes a "peek-a-boo" type game of finding the parrot. After the child learns to do this, Piaget takes the same parrot and puts it

under *red* blanket, *with the blue blanket still there.* What happens?

Some children continue looking under the *blue* blanket, even though they just saw Piaget put it under the red blanket. Others pick up the red blanket and find the parrot. It's largely a matter of *age,* i.e., of *maturation of cognitive ability.* A quite young child is unable to understand that the parrot is underneath a different blanket, the red blanket, even though she or he just watched you put it under that red blanket. The quite young child already had learned, via stimulus-response learning, that you placed the parrot under the *blue* blanket. The young child learned that in much the same way as one of Pavlov's dogs learns to salivate at the sound of the bell, and in much the same way as a lab rat learns a maze. Stimulus-response learning is a less sophisticated form of learning than is *the ability imaginatively to construct the parrot in the absence of its physical presence.* That's what the older children accomplish, the children who pick up the red blanket and find the parrot. The younger child cannot do that; she or he can only, by trial and error, experiment with different magical means of attempting to make the parrot reappear. In contrast, the *older child, through thought and reasoning, can imaginatively construct the parrot in the physical absence of the parrot and guide her or his behavior accordingly.*

This cognitive feat is not as peculiar as it might at first glance appear. Most of us who now are reading this text do it all the time when, say, we enter a dark room that we never before had entered. What do *you* do when you enter a pitch-black room? Reach for a light switch. You imaginatively construct the arrangement of the room in your mind, and you say to yourself in an internal dialogue: "The probable location of the light switch is somewhere around the door." You then reach around, feeling around for a light switch, not at random, mind you, but *in accordance with your mental image of the likely location of the light switch.* That image guides and directs your conduct.

As with light switches and toy parrots, so, too with the self. The sociological tradition of Mead and Cooley informs us that one of the objects that we can internalize, in addition to parrots and light switches, is the self. According to Cooley, we become that which we are addressed. According to Mead, we learn to take the role of a specific other, and later we learn to take the role of the generalized other. We use these elaborately constructed images of ourselves to guide and to direct our actions.

Conditions Favoring Internalization

Research indicates that some conditions trigger internalization, while others produce mere compliance. If you want to produce internalization, what conditions would you employ?

1. Consistent application of rewards and punishments

If internalization is a goal, it is important to employ inducements consistently. By way of addressing this point, let us suppose that a parent wants a child to internalize a certain rule (e.g., that there is a right and a wrong time for eating candy; no whining or sniveling; do not make a scene in public). Let us also suppose that the child wants something (e.g., candy at the supermarket) that the mother perceives as inappropriate. The mother usually ignores the request, while occasionally saying yes, and occasionally slapping the child for pestering her. The child cannot internalize the rule from this pattern of interaction. What a child *does* learn from this pattern of interaction is that the child is in a "lottery in which he sometimes wins big (free candy), sometimes loses (the slap), but usually is ignored. The best strategy for playing this lottery is to nag his mother all of the time" (Wilson, 1993: 149). *Erratic use of rewards and penalties produces misconduct.*

It widely has been found that capricious, severe discipline is a good recipe for creating bullies of both genders (Olweus, 1986; Patterson, 1986; Lerner, et. al., 1988; Argyle, 1992). For instance, over 600 children from upstate New York were studied from the time they were eight years old until they were thirty (Huesmann et.al,1987). What similarities in parenting characterize those who, as children, were the quickest to start fights and whose preferred mode of dispute resolution was force? When these people were children, parental discipline was arbitrary and harshly punitive. If their parents were in a bad mood, they

would receive severe punishment, even if they had done nothing to warrant punishment. If their parents were in a good mood, they could get away with anything with impunity. The probability of punishment had more to do with the mood of the parent than the behavior of the children. While they punished the children with noteworthy severity, otherwise they ignored or took little interest in them. They displayed little interest in the day-to-day lives of the children and shared few activities together. (Please see Warr, 1993, for similar findings that are based on a longitudinal study of a national probability sample of people aged 11 to 17 years of age in the United States.) As a result, the children felt hopeless, worthless, and helpless. They had low self-esteem and an external locus of control. They felt that threats were everywhere and could strike at any time, which, under the circumstances, were fairly accurate perceptions of their home environments. Their posture to the external world was combative, aggressive, and defiant. They were the children most at risk both for dropping out of school and for having an official record of violent crime by the age of thirty.

2. Beware of large sanctions

The mighty power of small inducements is illustrated in a classic experiment conducted by Jonathan Freedman (1965). He appreciates that internalization is reflected in what we do when we think no one is looking. Freedman introduced elementary school children to an attractive toy and requested that they not play with it when he was out of the room. Freedman used a mild threat with half the children and a severe one with the others. Both sufficed to deter the children. A couple of weeks later, another researcher, with no apparent connection to the previous events, leaves the same children in the same room with the same toys. Of the children who had received the severe threat from Freedman, fully 78% now played with the forbidden toy. In contrast, fully two-thirds of those who had received a mild deterrent played with other toys and still refrained from playing with the forbidden toy. Having made a decision not to play with the forbidden toy, the mildly deterred children apparently *internalized* their decision. Their decision became part of their

Internalization: The Insufficient Justification Effect

The tendency to engage in internalization when the external inducement is small and, as a result, we perceive that our actions are freely chosen is demonstrated in the results to the knob-turning experiment that opens this chapter. Please refer back to *your* answer to the following question: *Under which condition, $1 or $20, do you think your actual enjoyment rating of the knob-turning task would be higher?* What was your answer?: Please write it here: _____. Most of us who answered this question probably did so on the basis of what we supposed was "true" or "false." When American social scientist Timothy Osberg (1993) recently asked a question like this to students enrolled in his undergraduate courses, they overwhelmingly voted for the $20 payment. They apparently accepted as true the common wisdom that big rewards produce big enjoyment. *Is your answer similar to theirs?*

The scientific results run counter to common wisdom here. *Festinger* and *Carlsmith* (1959) find that those receiving one dollar rated the task as far more enjoyable than those paid $20. Why? When our actions (telling a lie) are not fully explained by external rewards (One dollar is insufficient justification) or by coercion ("Do this or I will knock your block off"), we experience unpleasant arousal. We can reduce this unpleasant arousal by coming to believe what we have done ("Maybe the experiment was sort of interesting"). Many studies indicate that if we want someone to internalize a rule (or meanings, values, norms, etc.), encouragement and inducement should be *large enough to elicit the desired behavior but small enough so that the person feels that her or his actions are freely chosen.*

The tendency to internalize a request (or values, norms, meanings, etc.) when we perceive that our actions are freely chosen and when the external inducement is small is known as **the insufficient justification effect** (Festinger and Carlsmith, 1959). If Mommy or Daddy says; "Clean your room, Samuel, or else

I will give your favorite bicycle to your cousin who lives in Alaska," Samuel does not need internally to justify the action of cleaning his room. The external threat (loss of his favorite bike) is justification enough.

Whereas behaviorism focuses attention on the effectiveness of rewards and punishments in eliciting compliance, internalization focuses our attention on acceptance, on outwardly complying *and* inwardly agreeing with the rule. For this reason, conflict theorists tend to view internalization (socialization to identity) as a stealth bomber of social control. If Samuel has internalized the rule, he will say, "I am cleaning my room because I am a person who wants a clean room," rather than, "I am cleaning my room because my folks will kill me if I don't." Internalization gets us to engage in actions not to gain external rewards and to avoid external punishments, but because engaging in the action *is part of who we are, part of our very identity.* This internalization reproduces society.

As we internalize norms, identities, values, beliefs, statuses, and roles, *we transform social control into self-control* (Gecas, 1992). Sociologist Viktor Gecas makes the following observations about this process: Self-control

> is largely accomplished through the development of identities, the various labels and characteristics attributed to the self. Commitment to identities (such as son, mother, professor, honest person) is a source of motivation for individuals to act in accordance with the values and norms implied by these identities . . . The focus on identity also emphasizes the membership component of socialization: To be socialized is to belong, via idealification with one's group (1992: 1864).

Gender Socialization

Socialization to gender begins at birth if not before. One of the first question friends and relatives ask parents about a newborn concerns the baby's gender (Intons-Peterson and Reddel, 1984). Even the newborn's reception varies by its gender. In traditional Hindu India, communities welcome the news of the birth of a male child with rituals of joy and celebration. Village women slam the wooden bolts of their doors back and forth and grind coconut shells in a mortar, all to express joy and praise. This hullabaloo is absent upon the birth of a female child, whose family members are said to look as if in mourning. In the United States, congratulations cards sent to parents typically are gender coded, with different colors, messages, and activities conveyed on the basis of the newborn's gender (Bridges, 1993). Parents frequently provide the infant with bedroom decor, toys (Pomerleau, Bolduc, Malcuit, and Cossette, 1990), and clothes that reliably convey the infant's gender to others (Shakin et. al., 1985).

In the United States, parents perceive their newborns in ways that have more to do with the gender-stereotypes held by the parents than with the physical characteristics of the newborns. Both mothers and fathers perceive their newborn females as "finer featured," as "more delicate," and as "less strong" than newborn boys (Karraker, Vogel, and Lake, 1995). Parents also engage in more rough and tumble play with boys. They lift boys high into the air and swirl them around. They bounce boy infants vigorously on their knees. Parents are more gentle with girls (Eccles, Jacobs, and Harold, 1990). Parents give girls lots of hugs and kisses, a form of interaction not showered upon males. Mothers talk to and touch their daughters more than their sons, and they keep their daughters closer to them (Goldberg and Lewis, 1969). By the time they are thirteen months old, girls stay closer to their mothers while playing, and return to them sooner, than do boys (Goldberg and Lewis, 1969). Preschool boys are allowed to roam further away from home than are females (Munroe and Munroe, 1971; Nerlove et. al., 1971) and they engage in more unsupervised play (Edwards, 1991). From preschool age through early adolescence, children play largely in sex-segregated groups and have different play and game experiences (e.g., Bloch, 1989; Carpenter, Houston, and Serpa, 1989). Their reading materials also convey different visions of the good life. In Caldecott Award children's books during the last half century, boys are five times more often shown using production tools (e.g., pitchfork, plow), and girls are four times more often shown using domestic implements such as pots and pans, a broom, and a sewing needle (Crabb and Bielawski, 1994). A study of thirty Caldecott Medal and "honors" books for the period

1984-1994 reveals that a greater number of males than females are depicted both in titles and pictures and that males are described as more potent and active (Turner-Bowker, 1996). The result? The social reproduction of traditional gender roles. Women are the primary providers of socio-emotional support in the home (Rossi and Rossi, 1991). The United Nations reports that ubiquitously cooking and washing dishes are the least shared household tasks (1991).

When mothers play with their daughters, they display a wider range of emotions. When conversing with their children, parents' references to emotion are more frequent and varied, and they mention sadness and dislike more often, with daughters than with sons (Adams, Kuebli, Boyle, and Fivush, 1995). Parents also discuss emotions, except for anger, more with daughters. When mothers talk to daughters about feelings, they discuss in more detail the emotional state itself than is the case with sons (Brody and Hall, 1993). Even when parents make-up stories to tell their preschool children, the stories told to girls contain more emotion words than the stories told to boys. Not too surprisingly, by age two, girls converse more about their feelings than do similarly aged boys (Dunn, 1987, 1988), and they continue to do so as they mature (Adams, Kuebli, Boyle, and Fivush, 1995). Young girls even express more affection in their letters to Santa Claus than do boys (Otnes, Kim, and Kin, 1994), and as adolescents they are more likely than males to express both responsibility and concern for the well-being of others (Beutel and Marini, 1995).

One result of maturation and of socialization is the emergence of **gender identity,** a fundamental sense of self as "I am male" or "I am female." Gender identity emerges and then becomes permanently established between 3 to 6 years of age (Lachmann, 1991: 122). There is some controversy regarding the forces that shape gender identity, and different theoretical positions proffer different explanations regarding the forces that influence its emergence and permanence. John Money and associates at Johns Hopkins University have found, among the children in their professional practice, that gender identity is firmly established by age three (Money and Wiedeking, 1980).

Some Other Effects: Friendship, Loneliness, Definition of Encounters as Violent in Intimate Cross-Gender Dyads, and Misperceptions of Sexual Interest

Gendered socialization fosters the development of different social skills and orientations to social life (Nurius, et. al., 1996; Range and Stringer, 1996). In other words, **gender role** socialization is a basic part of the socialization process. Gender roles, also known as sex roles, refer to expectations of behavior (roles) that are attached to one's perceived sexual status of male or female.

Friendship

From roughly age two until age eleven, boys and girls play mainly in gender homogeneous groups. Boys' playgroups are larger and more hierarchical than are girls' groups (Knight and Chao, 1989; Grotpeter and Crick, 1996). From a young age, females become more attuned to interpersonal connections, and boys to formal rules; girls become more attuned to noticing, deciphering, and responding in a sensitive way to someone else's subjective feelings as revealed in facial expression, tone of voice, and other nonverbal cues (Brody and Hall, 1993). Not too surprisingly, males value friendships that focus on shared interests and activities (e.g., hunting, football, karate), whereas females place greater value on trust and self-disclosure (Richey and Richey, 1980; Davis, Franzoi, and Wellinger, 1985).

Loneliness

Male and females also tend to experience **loneliness,** a painful perception that our relationships with others are less meaningful or numerous than we desire, under different circumstances (David Myers, 1996: 177; Boivin and Hymel, 1997). Males experience loneliness when deprived of *group contact* that focuses on shared activities, and females experience loneliness when deprived of *close one-on-one relationships that focus on understanding and emotion-*

al support (Douvan and Adelson, 1966; Stokes and Levin, 1986).

Adolescent and adult males who are both less attuned to and less adept at reading emotional content, are (1) less likely than females to define a cross-sexual dyadic encounter as violent in nature (Browning and Dutton, 1986; Demaris, Pugh, and Harman, 1992); and (2) more likely than females to construe friendliness on the part of a person of the opposite sex as sexual interest (Abbey, 1987, 1991a, 1991b; Kowalski, 1993). Please read Box 6.3, "Stranger Invitations: How Would *You* RSVP?"

Definition of Encounters as Violent in Intimate Cross-Gender Dyads

Research using couple-level data consistently reveals considerable discrepancies when both members of a dating or marital couple are questioned about the incidence of physical violence in their relationship. The general pattern that emerges is that females are far more likely than their male partners to report violent acts, whether perpetrated by themselves or by their partners, in their relationship (Jouriles and O'Leary, 1985; Edleson and Brygger, 1986; De Maris, Pugh, and Harman, 1992; Szinovacz and Egly, 1995; Anderson, 1997). Males fail to define encounters as violent in nature that are perceived as violent by their female partners.

Misreading of Emotional Warmth as Sexual Interest

The misreading of emotional warmth as sexual interest leads to behavior that females perceive as sexual harassment (Saal, Johnson, and Weber, 1989; Johnson, Stockdale, and Saal, 1991). It may also help explain why eight times as many American females say they have been forced into unwanted sexual behavior as the 3 percent of American males who admit that they ever have forced a female into a sexual encounter (Laumann et. al., 1994). Social scientists are not the only ones to notice that sexual fantasies express this difference in orientation. Humorist Dave Barry makes the following observation:

Women can be fascinated by a four-hour movie with subtitles wherein the entire plot consists of a man and a woman yearning to have, but never actually having a relationship . . .

BOX 6.3

Stranger *Invitations: How Would You RSVP?*

In an experiment conducted by Elaine Hatfield and Russell D. Clark, male and female college students were the research subjects (Clark and Hatfield, 1981; Hatfield and Sprecher, 1986: 136-137). They varied in physical attractiveness from "slightly unattractive" to "moderately attractive." They approached attractive males and females of the opposite sex and said: "I have noticed you around campus and I find you very attractive." They then asked them one of three questions: (1) "Would you go out with me tonight?," (2) "Would you come over to my apartment tonight?," and (3) Would you go to bed with me tonight?" Re-sults? Somewhat surprisingly, slightly over half of both genders agreed to go out on a date with a complete stranger. (Perhaps this reflects a rudimentary trust of one member of a campus community for another.) However, as the requests increased in intimacy, the proportion of males agreeing to the encounter *increased*, while the proportion of compliant fe-males *decreased*. Fully 69% of the males agreed to come over to the woman's apartment and fully 75% agreed to go to bed with her. In contrast, only 6% of the females agreed to go over to the male's apartment and *none* would go to bed with him (Hatfield and Sprecher, 1986: 137). Equally revealing were the verbal responses to the requests. The males made comments such as "Why do we have to wait until tonight?" or "I can't to-night, but tomorrow would be fine." In contrast, the females responded with "You've got to be kidding" or "What is wrong with you?" (Hatfield and Sprecher, 1986: 137).

This experiment demon-strates that males are far more willing to engage in an intimate sexual encounter without a pre-viously existing relationship than are females, a finding cor-roborated by large-scale survey research (Laumann, Gagnon, Michael, and Michaels, 1994).

Men HATE that. Men can take maybe 45 seconds of yearning, and they want everybody to get naked. Followed by a car chase. (Barry, 1995, as cited in Myers, 1996: 201)

Media

Mass media. An increasingly important agent of socialization within families is televi-sion, a form of **mass media**. The mass media refer to the organized transmission of a mes-sage to a vast audience. The vastness of the audience varies from relatively small for spe-cialized magazines to very large for prime-time television broadcasts. The mass media include television, radio, the press (magazines, news-papers, books), and movies (Brabant and Mooney, 1997; Leppard, Ogletree, and Wallen, 1993). The sociological study of mass media includes the intra- and inter-societal structure of mass media; audience characteristics and measurement; the processes and technologies of persuasion; and the social, political, and cultural effects of the mass media on individu-als and collectivities.

Magazines. In Japan, magazine reading is the number one media source for teens, and hence magazines are an important agent of socialization (White, 1994). Even in the United States, magazines aimed at teens are a signifi-cant source of socialization. What images of gender are portrayed in teen magazines in this country? Sociologist Kate Pierce (1993) wanted to find out. She has analyzed all the fiction stories for the years 1987-1991 that appeared in *Seventeen* and *Teen*, magazines with a circula-tion of more than 1 million nationally. Occupa-tions were more severely sex typed than the actual situation in the U.S. labor force. In all but 2 of the 44 occupations mentioned in the stories, occupation was stereotypically depict-ed. For instance, males were portrayed as busi-ness owners, security guards, bankers, veteri-narians, and police officers, while females were fortune tellers, secretaries, social workers, and salespersons. In more than half of the stories, the main female character does not solve her own problems. She depends on someone else to do it for her.

Television. The role of television as a socia-lizing agent in the U.S. is increasing, at least in part, by default (Gecas, 1992: 1867). Various social forces, including the percent of working mothers with children, the professionalization of childcare, and the percent of dual-career families have decreased the amount of parent-child interaction. In the United States, the average white parents spend ten fewer hours per week with their children than they did in 1960, and the decline is even greater for African-American parents (Fuchs, 1988). Many children spend as much time watching television as they do at school (Gecas, 1992). The average U.S. household has at least one television "on" for almost seven hours each day (Signorielli and Lears, 1992). The estimates of average per-person per-week viewing time for television is slightly lower in Britain (27 hours) and significantly lower in western European countries (e.g., 16 hours per week in Germany and France) (Gunter and Svennevig, 1987). Data are clear that for U.S. teens and children, television is the number one media source (White, 1994).

In industrialized countries there is an inverse relationship between number of hours spent viewing television and social class. Lower social classes view more television than the more educated and more affluent (Bianchi and Robinson, 1997).

The manifest function of most television programs aimed at children and adolescents is to entertain and to sell products. A good deal else is likely to occur, from shaping perceptions of reality (Larson, 1996), to modeling behaviors appropriate to gender, race, and other social locations (Press, 1993; Mwangi, 1996; Gerbner, 1996). Heavy viewers of television tend to believe that the real world is like the world shown on television programs (Gerbner, Gross, Morgan, and Signorielli, 1994). Please read Box 6.4 regarding what adolescents learn about single motherhood from watching soap operas.

Gender socialization and television. Research indicates that television provides a limited, distorted view of gender. For instance, a study examining women in eighty prime time television programs concludes that adolescent girls are portrayed as being primarily interested in just two things—clothes and boys (Barricklow, 1992). Studies examining the roles of women in television programs and in advertisements report similar findings in the USA, Britain, Canada, Australia, Kenya, and Italy (Mwangi, 1996; Furnham and Bitar, 1993; Mazella, Durkin, Cerini, and Buralli, 1992). Fe-

males are significantly underrepresented and tend to be portrayed in traditionally female sex roles across television networks, including cable networks. Public broadcasting stations (PBS), funded in part through federal income-tax revenues, have the lowest representation of females (Kubey, Shifflet, Weerakkody, and Ukeiley, 1995). Males outnumber females 2 to 1 in MTV videos (Somners-Flanagan et. al., 1993). Of commercials having voice-overs, the percent having males as narrators ranges from 85% to 95%, a situation that depicts men as more credible and authoritative (Brett and Cantor, 1988; Furnham and Bitar, 1993; Mwangi, 1996).

School

The school has in common with the family a mandate to socialize children. In contrast to the family, the manifest function of the school is to develop cognitive skills via formal instruction. In this sense, the school is less involved in primary socialization and is more involved in secondary socialization. The latent functions of the school include the socialization of values, norms, and attitudes. In fact, sociologists Samuel Bowles and Herbert Gintis contend that schools expanded in this country in order to prepare a docile, tractable labor force. Learning punctuality, neatness, respect for the private ownership of property, and nonviolent modes of dispute resolution are but some of the values instilled in children by schools in capitalist America (Bowles and Gintis, 1975). Conflict theorists, then, view schools as serving the needs the elites, not the needs of the children or of the poor.

Teachers' Expectations, Labeling, and Self Concept. Many of the activities associated with schools have implications for the child's self-concept. When children enter school, their performance is evaluated by non-primordial others, teachers. Success, particularly early success, in performance evaluation is good for one's self concept, and it builds confidence in one's abilities. One possible consequence of failure, however, is that the student is "labeled" as a "slow learner," "dumb," "under achiever," "learning disabled," or as "cognitively challenged." Labels, whether positive or negative, influence the way others respond to the child. These responses, in turn, influence

---
BOX 6.4

Single Motherhood:
Television Soap Opera Reality vs. Real Life in the United States

Television is a medium with potential for socializing viewers about important issues and social problems, such as single parenthood in the United States. In this country, single parents and their children are at high risk for poverty and poor physical health. The children of single parents are at high risk for official juvenile delinquency, illicit drug use, dropping out of school, and low wages (Whitehead, 1993).

The United States has the highest rates of teen pregnancy and childbirth in the industrialized world (Wattleton, 1989). There has been a large increase in single motherhood within the past few years. In Minnesota, for instance, births to girls under age 15 increased 100% from 1980 to 1993 (Larson, 1996).

Social scientist **Mary Strom Larson** of Northern Illinois University wanted to discover what messages about single motherhood are being portrayed on daytime soap operas, a form of programming particularly popular among adolescent females (Williams, 1992). From the summer of 1991 to the spring of 1993, Larson taped soap operas that featured single mothers—*Days of Our Lives, All My Children, Santa Barbara,* and

the *Bold and the Beautiful.* She and her colleagues then content-analyzed these videotapes (Larson, 1996).

Larson's analysis yields the following comparison of single motherhood according to soap opera reality and according to real life.

TV Soap Opera Reality

- Most single mothers appear to be upper-middle class and white. They wear designer dresses and well-tailored skirted suits. Babies are not even fussy, let alone ill.
- These mothers hold professional jobs (e.g., magazine editor, board member of a major corporation, child therapist in a hospital)
- These mothers are highly educated, judging from their professional careers.
- These mothers live in well-furnished homes whose tables are bedecked with freshly-cut flowers. These mothers do not talk of concerns about money, because money is not a concern.
- These mothers have an active social live which includes two or three adult male friends. Babies actually seem to enhance these women's social lives. These

babies are welcome at adult parties and at dinners in fine restaurants.
- Most of these mothers have handsome men with well-paying careers in their lives. These men are ready and eager to nurture baby. These men stop by mother's house in mid-afternoon to take care of baby so that mother may have some time for herself.

Real Life

- 45% of female-headed households live in poverty; because of inadequate prenatal care, babies are frequently ill.
- Children in female-headed households are six times as likely to be poor as those in two-parent families.
- Half of teen mothers do not finish high school.
- Teen mothers realize half the lifetime earnings of those who delay motherhood to age 20 or older.
- Teen mothers report having virtually no free time to themselves and no social life.
- Single mothers receive little or no help from the baby's father.

and shape the child in the labeled direction. This process is termed a **self-fulfilling prophecy** by Robert K. Merton (Merton, 1957).

Are teachers' evaluations ever a cause of student performance? How could we investigate this question experimentally?

We could inform a teacher that several students—whom, unbeknownst to the teacher,

we actually select *at random* from the students in his or her classroom—are unusually talented and are about to experience a great spurt of intellectual growth. Will the teacher act differently toward these students and actually elicit from them the very growth the teacher expects? In a now famous study, *Robert Rosenthal* and *Lenore Jacobson* report precisely that (1968).

Experimenters gave students in an elementary school in San Francisco a paper and pencil test. After analyzing the results of the test, the experimenters informed the teachers that several students—say, Beth, Arnold, Elijah, and Manuel—were about to experience a significant intellectual growth spurt. Several months later, when the experimenters again retested the children, Beth, Arnold, Elijah, and Manuel (whom the experimenters had selected at random) in fact had made significant cognitive gains. When a teacher had been led to believe that a student would be a slow learner, the student was more likely to do poorly in class. Expectancy and labeling effects occur in most socializing contexts and have important consequences for self-concept development (Gecas, 1992: 1867). *Have you (or anyone you know) ever experienced expectancy and labeling effects in your school experience? Please tell us about it.*

Later studies indicate that the teacher-expectations' effect is not as powerful or as reliable as the Rosenthal and Jacobson experiment suggests (Thorndike, 1968). For instance, Rosenthal's own count (1991) reveals that in only 39% of the over 400 published experiments do teachers' expectations significantly influence performance. Still, in roughly four out of ten studies, teacher expectations matter. Why do teachers' expectations matter?

Rosenthal and colleagues report that teachers smile, look, and nod more at "high potential" students (Babad, Bernieri, and Rosenthal, 1991). Teachers may also set higher goals for students for whom they hold high expectations, call on them more, and give them more time to answer (Rowe, 1974a, 1974b; Harris and Rosenthal, 1986; Jussim, 1989).

Striving for Success and Avoiding Failure. Sociologists Covington and Beery (1976) and others (Ornstein and Levine, 1989; Ogbu, 1989, 1990; Anderson, 1990; Reyes and Jackson, 1993) propose that two fundamentally different patterns emerge among students as a result of labeling and expectancy effects. One is a striving toward success, and the other is avoiding failure.

The ***striving-for-success strategy*** is exemplified by Vietnamese American students. Sociologists Carl Bankston III of University of Southwestern Louisiana, Stephen J. Caldas of University of Southern Illinois, and Min Zhou

of University of California at Los Angeles (1997) propose that peer relations among Vietnamese American students promote advantageous attitudes toward education as inherently valuable and as a means of upward mobility. Other sociologists similarly attribute the scholastic success of Mexican-American students (Matute-Bianchi, 1986), of Punjabi students in California (Gibson, 1989), and of children of Indochinese refugees in this country (Caplan, Whitmore, and Choy, 1992) to a strong identification with their ethnic communities. These identities nurture and promote striving for success via education.

In contrast, ***failure-avoidance strategies*** work against school success (Covington and Beery, 1976; Ogbu, 1989, 1990). These strategies encompass a variety of specific behaviors, such as not showing up when you had committed to give an oral report in class, putting off working on an assignment until the last minute, and investing little effort into school work. These are attempts to distance one's performance from one's self-worth and ability. We can attribute failure to something specific, temporary, or external ("I had the flue," "I didn't spend much time on the project," "I had dress rehearsals and three performances in the school play," "My child was sick," "I had to work overtime because the boss got sick") instead of to a lack of talent or ability. As David Myers observes, "If we fail while working under a handicap, we can cling to a sense of competence; if we succeed under such conditions, it can only boost our self image" (1996: 67). If our self worth is tied up with performance, it can be more threatening to try and to fail than to have a handy excuse. For some youth, failure avoidance strategies are an unintended consequence of socialization in the classroom, in the peer group, or in the community. These strategies are not optimal adaptations because they increase the probability of dropping out of school and hence of having dramatically lower lifetime earnings (Gecas, 1992).

Sociologist ***John Ogbu*** argues that failure-avoidance strategies are particularly likely to be adopted by youth of caste-like groups. These youths are at high risk for developing identities and peer relations that undermine the probability of academic success (Ogbu, 1989, 1990).

Due to shared experiences of racism and of institutionalized discrimination, these youths share a view of the concrete benefits available to them through education as limited and slim. These youths do not view education as a means of upward mobility in a society they perceive as inherently racist. Hence, they spend little effort on schoolwork. Their shared attitudes toward schooling are not conducive to academic success.

Marxian conflict theorists view these adaptation strategies as *alienated*, because they create a distance between one's self and the products of one's labor. Many other sociologists view these behaviors as forms of *role-distancing*, "the separation of self from the behavior required of a role occupant" (Gecas, 1992: 1868).

Please reflect upon your own life course, reflecting on various roles you have occupied. Can you think of examples of role distancing from your own life? Please tell us about one or two instances of role distancing from your own life.

Peers

Peer group as a context of socialization. The peer group is an important context of socialization of children, particularly during adolescence (Giordano, Cernkovich, and De Maris, 1993; Quigley and Marlatt, 1996). There are five characteristics of the peer group as a context of socialization that are important (Gecas, 1992). These features differentiate the peer group from the family and school and help to explain why attachment to it may be even stronger than attachment to family, particularly during adolescence. *First*, the peer group is a voluntary association. *Second*, by definition, the peer group is an association among status equals. This means that the relationships among members are based on equality, shared interests, mutual tolerance and concern and not on hierarchical authority relationships. *Third*, the peer group provides a domain free of parental control. As such, it is a context fostering the development and expression of social action, values, beliefs, and norms that are independent of, and that conflict with, those of adults (e.g., Davis, 1940). *Fourth*, the peer group provides an alternate reference group as well as an alternate source of identity

and self-esteem for children and adolescents. *Fifth*, children's peer groups in the United States and in many other societies are gender homogeneous. For instance, one study of children's friendships finds that three-year olds say that roughly half their friends are of the other gender. By five years of age, the percent of other-gender friends has dropped to 20 percent. By age seven, virtually no boys or girls say they have a best friend of the opposite sex (Gottman, 1986). Another study finds that play with same-gender peers increases almost fourfold between four and six years of age (Maccoby, Jacklin, and Nagy, 1987). Studies also document that during childhood peers implement harsh sanctions against members who cross the gender divide (Sroufe, Bennett, Englund, Urban, and Shulman, 1993; Thorne, 1993) and have cross-gender playmates or friends. *Can you think of instances from your own life, or from the life of some one you know, of negative sanctioning from peers for associating with cross-gendered persons? Please tell us about it.*

Peers and delinquency. Sociological research indicates that peers are important in promoting or preventing delinquent behavior (Barnes and Farrell, 1992; Aseltine, 1995; Coughlin and Vuchinich, 1996; O'Callaghan et. al., 1997). In the United States *juvenile delinquency* is a concept that has at least three possible meanings. A **juvenile delinquent** is a person below the legal age of majority (juvenile) (1) who is dependent, neglected, or abandoned; or (2) who commits an act that would be legal if she or he were an adult but which is prohibited because she or he is below the age of majority; or (3) who commits an act that would be a crime if she or he were an adult. For our present purposes, let us use the latter as our definition of delinquency—committing an act that would be a crime if one were an adult. Let us measure this concept by means of the self-report method. The time frame for which we ask respondents to provide us information is "from Christmas a year ago to the Christmas just passed." As researchers, we promise respondents anonymity and confidentiality, and ask them in which, if any, of a menu of behaviors they themselves have engaged. We also ask them to indicate how many, if any, of their friends have engaged in each of those behaviors. We also ask our respondents to fill out a paper and pencil test to measure level of school attachment. Our measure of school attachment includes such Likert-scale items as "How important is school work to you?," "How important to you is a high grade point average?," "How do your teachers think you are doing in school?," and "How important is it to you that teachers think of you as a good student?"

This is precisely how sociologist *Richard Lawrence* (1991, 1998) of St. Cloud State University in Minnesota investigated the relationship among school attachment, peers, and delinquency, using self-report data from a national survey. This research finds that *peer relationships have a greater influence on delinquent behavior than does attachment to school.* The more delinquent friends one has the higher the number of delinquent acts one reports, even among those with higher school attachment. "Youth who had fewer friends who had committed delinquent acts reported less delinquent involvement themselves, regardless of high or low school attachment" (Lawrence, 1998: 50). The highest rates of self-reported delinquency in this study are among those with lower school attachment and more delinquent friends. These findings indicate that the nature of peer relationships is important in explaining the probability of delinquent behavior.

Racial and Ethnic Socialization

Racial and ethnic groups. In addition to gender socialization, we experience and participate in racial and ethnic socialization during our lives. A **racial group** is an anthropological concept that implies "that basic biological differences exist" or are imputed to exist "among various groups" or aggregates (Gonzales, 1990: 6). Commonly observed physical characteristics that are used by anthropologists and others to define racial groups include facial features, skin color, the color and texture of the hair, and body shape and size. An **ethnic group** "is an anthropological concept that is based on the distinctive cultural characteristics of a particular group" (Gonzales, 1990:7) or aggregate. Common cultural characteristics that are used by anthropologists and others to define a n ethnic group include language, social customs, religion, community traditions, manner of

dress, choice of foods, and historical origins (Gonzales, 1990:7).

Peer choice and race/ethnicity. In a study of nine to ten-year olds attending a publicly funded school in a large city in England, Michael J. Boulton observed British Asian and British white children of both genders on the playground during recess in order to observe their spontaneous peer preferences. All four groups—Asian males, Asian females, white males, white females—exhibited a highly significant tendency to play with own-race and own-gender peers more than with any other type of peer (Boulton and Smith, 1993; Boulton, 1996). Preferences for own-race over other-race peers are evident from both verbal self-reports (Boulton and Smith, 1996) and observational data (Urberg and Kaplan, 1989). These preferences emerge during the preschool stage of development and persist until early adolescence (Finkelstein and Haskins, 1983).

Early development of own-race awareness. Scholars find that own-race and other-race awareness, and ethnic and racial attitudes and values are apparent in very young children (Goodman, 1964; Marger, 1994). Using a systematic progression of experiments, Lawrence Hirschfeld (1996) proposes that very young children do not form beliefs about race from simple observation of surface cues (color of skin, hair texture). Instead, we seem to pick up the idea of race from our discursive environment—from hearing talk (Hirschfeld, 1996: 193). Young children "initially do not *see* race; they *hear* it" (Hirschfeld, 1996: 195; italics in original). This position is consistent with other research. Branch and Newcomb find that parents are an important source of influence regarding racial attitudes among children below 8 years of age (1986).

Socialization to race in children's literature in the United States. Several studies of race relations in children's books reveal that persons of color largely have been underrepresented, and when depicted at all, tend to be depicted in roles subservient to whites (e.g., Larrick, 1965; Masden, 1980; Klein, 1985; Pescosolido, Grauerholz, and Milkie, 1997). Literature is important. It is a powerful vehicle of socialization, of assimilating one's cultural heritage (Bettelheim, 1977). What is the picture of race relations that young children read and are read to by their parents and other caretakers?

Egalitarian cross-racial peer relations (whether among children or adults) and the portrayal of African-American adults as focal characters are rare in children's literature, as measured by a content analysis of award-winning children's books published from 1937 to 1993. African-Americans have been "ignored, stereotyped, or demeaned" according to an historical study of race relations in this form of literature by Bernice Pescosolido of Indiana University, Elizabeth Grauerholz of Purdue University, and Melissa Milkie of University of Maryland (1997). This study also provides an interesting analysis of the rise and fall of persons of color in children's literature in the United States. From the late 1930s through the 1950s, African Americans were peripheral and largely subordinate characters in award-winning children's books. The period from the late 1950s through the first half of the 1960s was a time of racial conflict in this country, as measured by the numbers of legal actions, protests, and conflicts. Virtually no African Americans appear in children's picture books published between 1958-1964, "indicating indecision or unwillingness to portray racial contact in new (and at the time, radical) ways" (Pescosolido, Grauerholz, and Milkie, 1997: 460). As racial harmony is reconstructed and restored in the wider society during the decade spanning the mid-1960s through the mid-1970s, the percent of children's books depicting Black characters rises. Their depictions of race relations are considerably improved over the earlier stereotyped portrayals. Nonetheless, Black characters "reappear . . . in 'safe,' distant images." The increase in the representation of Blacks, either alone or with other races, ceases in 1975 and pretty much stabilizes at new, higher levels. From 1975 to 1993, about 20 to 30 percent of all newly published children's books, and from 30 to 50 percent of those featuring humans, portray Blacks as characters. Nonetheless, even in this most recent period, children's books rarely depict mutual, egalitarian cross-racial relationships that are central to the story line (Pescosolido, Grauerholz, and Milkie, 1997: 443, 452-455)

Perceptions of physical beauty. Sociological research indicates that the level of satisfaction with physical appearance varies across racial/ethnic groups and that peers are an important source of satisfaction level. Thomas Cash of Old Dominion University in Norfolk, Virginia, and Patricia Henry of University College in North Wales conducted a national probability survey in the United States in 1993 of the body images of over 1900 women, ranging in age from 18 to 70 years (1995). Their national sample is representative of adult women in the U.S. in terms of age, race, education, income, and geographical region based on the 1990 census data. Across all ages, African American females are significantly more satisfied with their global body image, weight and specific body areas than are either white or Hispanic females. These findings are consistent with studies of perceptions of physical attractiveness based on college-student samples (Rucker and Cash, 1992).

Research on perceptions of physical attractiveness in the United States consistently demonstrates that white females prefer a thin body for themselves and an average body for own-race males (Polivy et. al., 1986). White males prefer an average body for themselves and express an equal preference for either an average or thin body for own-race females (Furnham, Hester, and Weir, 1990). African-American females prefer a larger body size for themselves than do white women (Kemper et. al., 1994; Parnell et. al., 1996). African-American males share this preference for larger-bodied own-race females (Thompson, Sargent, and Kemper, 1996).

The cultural context clearly influences what is perceived as "beautiful" or as "sexy." The folk wisdom that "You can't be too thin" does not adequately describe the perception of physical beauty for all groups. For instance, research indicates that point of view in the United States is a white point of view to which African Americans by and large do not subscribe (Jackson and McGill, 1996). While white females report that they find obese same-race males unattractive, African-American females are far more likely to associate "sexiness" with same-race obese males. Likewise, although white males associate negative characteristics (e.g., lazy, uneducated) with obese same-race females, African-American males are far more likely to associate positive characteristics with same-race obese females and to perceive them as "attractive." White respondents of both sexes perceive obesity as "unsexy;' African-American respondents of both genders perceive it as "sexy" (Jackson and McGill, 1996). A recent study of a stratified random sample of almost five hundred white and black high-school-aged males by Sharon Thompson of Coastal Carolina University, Roger Sargent of University of South Carolina, and Karen Kemper of Clemson University also indicates a preference among African-American males for larger-bodied same-race females (1996). African-American males are 1.9 times more likely to prefer significantly larger hip/buttocks and 1.7 times more likely to prefer a significantly larger thigh size in same-race females than are white males. Beauty is in the eye of the beholder.

Adult Socialization

The socialization experience of adults generally builds upon the socialization experiences of childhood and of adolescence, and in this sense is secondary. Much of it is also role-specific (e.g., wife, husband, parenthood, occupational role in extra-familial labor force, nursing-home resident), and many people have engaged earlier in life in **anticipatory socialization** for some particular role. Anticipatory socialization is a term introduced by Robert K. Merton and Alice S. Kitt (1950), and it refers to learning the rights, duties, obligations, values, attitudes and outlook typical of a particular social role *before* one occupies it. For instance, when little girls play "house" and occupy the role of "Mommy," they are engaging in anticipatory socialization for motherhood, years before they actually occupy that status. *Can you think of examples of anticipatory socialization from your own life? Please tell us about it.*

Many adults in modern industrial societies work in the extra-familial labor force. For this reason work is an important context of socialization for many adults. Part of this socialization entails learning the skills and knowledge necessary for the performance of their jobs. There tend to be other effects as well, particularly on values, attitudes, and personality (Gecas, 1992: 1868). Research indicates that people who oc-

cupy order-taking positions in jobs that are closely supervised and whose tasks are routine and lacking in complexity tend to value conformity (Kohn and Schooler, 1983). In contrast, people who work in jobs that place a premium on creativity and whose tasks are complex tend to encourage the development of the values of independence, self-direction, and autonomy. A prevalent theme in sociological literature, particularly that written by conflict theorists, concerns the alienating consequences of work in capitalist societies.

Resocialization

Numerous other contexts are socializing arenas for adults—the family, religious organizations, political organizations, the local public-welfare agency, the country club, and the unemployment office, to name just a few. Much of the socialization that takes place in these contexts builds upon, and is an extension of, prior socialization and in this sense may be conceptualized as developmental in nature. In contrast, **resocialization** represents a break with the past and its aim is radically to change in the person, to tear down the individual's old world view, beliefs, values, and conceptions of self, and to replace them with new ones. Typically this is accomplished through intense interaction in small groups within a setting whose physical, social, technological, and symbolic environments are finely and extensively controlled by the agents of socialization. Sociologists term institutions of this type **total institutions.** In a total institution, the participants' activities and actions are highly regimented, and the participants are socially, physically, psychologically, and symbolically insulated from the outside world. Examples are military boot camps, prisoner-of-war camps, mental hospitals, high-security prisons, some therapeutic communities, political-indoctrination camps, some religious-conversion settings, and some religious communities. Resocialization is an experience that usually entails considerable stress and pain for the individual undergoing the experience (Schneider and Schneider, 1992). Let us briefly examine military boot camp as a context of resocialization.

Resocialization: Military Boot Camp

Military inductees sign on the dotted line and take the military oath. It is easy to dismiss a military oath as a hollow gesture, as a meaningless charade that has little practical value. To do so, however, is to underestimate the importance and the effects of public ritual (Feise, Hooker, Kotary, and Schwager, 1993; Aafke and Vollebergh, 1997). Even in the Vietnam era, when young Americans seemed to set less store by ritualistic formalities than previous generations had, the oath still had an important symbolic effect even on some of those who were unenthusiastic at the prospect of military service. A black GI, David Parks, recalled:

'The officer told us to step right foot forward, raise our right hand and take the oath. It was all over in about a minute. I felt trapped.' (Holmes, 1985:33-34)

A physical metamorphosis directly follows the rite of passage represented by taking the public oath. Another well-known landmark of military induction is alteration of the new recruits' hair. In many modern armies, the hair either is cut uniformly short or the heads are shaved. In addition to whatever practical effects the almost obligatory haircut may have in modern armies (e.g., control of head lice), it also serves two latent functions: (1) it produces a uniformity of appearance that helps to strip away, or at least to submerge, the new recruit's previous individual identity, and (2) it outwardly symbolizes "the inner transformation produced by the oath" (Holmes, 1985: 34). The recruits also remove their comfortable and familiar civilian clothes and exchange them for an often strange and seemingly ill fitting uniform. Female recruits are deprived of their makeup. Male and female recruits are deprived of their mementos. Privacy and individuality are largely things of the past.

Not familiar with how to put on the uniform or even to assemble the new equipment, the recruit is keenly aware of the boots that need breaking in and of the change in status. Even learning "the myriad of dodges which have always been associated with uniform since it came into general use in the seventeenth century" in western Europe "is an important part of the process of socialization into the ways of the army" (Holmes, 1985: 35).

The new recruits live in open squad bays. Their new uniforms are arranged in their lockers in a militarily ordained fashion. They even are told how to fold their underwear that is kept in the locker. They are rigidly scheduled regarding when to sleep, change clothes, eat, shower, talk, walk, and run. They share a bathroom, the latrine, with a lot of other people. They work with other men and women whose likes they had never seen before.

Basic training instills physical conditioning, military customs, military history, self-control, precision, teamwork, and basic competence in such things as weapons handling and minor tactics. It also serves to inculcate the military ethos into the recruits, and to replace the individual values that prevail in many civilian societies with group loyalties and group spirit. Repetitive training and drill are used to inculcate the habit of automatic obedience. Close-order drill makes people *look* like soldiers and *feel* like soldiers. It also has an important ritualistic and morale-building role: it binds a unit together.

The firm-but-fair instructor is an image that recurs regularly and constantly in memoirs and interviews of former soldiers. Instruction during basic training is carried out largely by noncommissioned officers (NCO), drill instructors (DIs), who are known in some services as training instructors (TIs). The separateness of the instructor from the recruits tends to be emphasized by dress (e.g., the broad-brimmed hat worn by drill sergeants in the U.S. Army), by their impeccable appearance, and by their language.

Language is important. Instructors are renowned for their profanity. There are few soldiers in the English speaking world who have not been called the basest of profanities by their instructors. The intense psychological attack that such language represents functions to destabilize an individual's sense of self, to instill self-control, and to promote the creation of a new military identity. Even one's civilian patterns of speech are renounced (Ofshe, 1992: 213). Says one soldier:

I had a problem with saying 'ma'am,' because to me 'ma'ams' were grandmothers. They said, 'Yes, what?' I says, 'Yes, I agree.' So I had to go to the latrine. I had to go in each stall and say

'Yes, ma'am' ten times. After that I said 'ma'am' after everything. (Schneider and Schneider, 1992: 26)

Even college graduates are reduced "under the taunts of sarcastic drill sergeants to a vocabulary of monosyllabic conformity interspersed with obscenities adopted from their mentors" (Bourne, 1970).

Alongside a language of derogation is the language of encouragement in a situation of shared privation. There is a harshness about basic training that sometimes becomes brutality. Spartan accommodation, long working days, little sleep, and collective punishments for individual transgressions help to construct group identity in an atmosphere of shared hardship.

The hardship and pain of basic training bear a direct relationship to the level of group cohesiveness that emerges from it. Experimental research confirms observations from the field that those who undergo a severe initiation value their membership more and display greater affection for their group members than do those whose initiation is mild (Freedman, 1965). This process is most marked in the basic training carried out by specialists like U.S. Marines, parachutists, and U.S. Navy SEALS. The rigorous training for such units, the high failure rate, and an emphasis on mental toughness and physical fitness weld persons from diverse backgrounds together into cohesive and highly-motivated fighting forces. These fighting units think of themselves not only as different than, but as better than, the remainder of the armed forces. Military historian Richard Holmes terms their socialization "a process of cultural pseudospeciation" that is marked by appearance as well as by language. For instance, "British parachutists look upon anyone not fortunate enough to wear the red beret as a 'craphat'" (Holmes, 1985: 48). This bond among in-group members is reinforced if aggression is directed against a common, if imaginary, enemy. Almost anyone outside the in-group suffices. This helps to make understandable the chequered disciplinary record (brawls with regular soldiers and with civilians in various contexts) enjoyed by many of these elite fighting groups.

After the Gulf War, Dorothy and Carl Schneider interviewed women from the United States Army, Navy, Air Force, and Marines. What they discovered about women in the military was that as the weeks remaining of basic training grew shorter, the fifty women in the flight started working together as a team. They turned to each other for emotional support and coordinated their efforts to help one another master the skills needed successfully to complete basic training. For instance, all new recruits had to be able to run a mile and a half in order to complete basic training successfully. One member, who had gotten out of shape physically because of a bout with pneumonia, didn't know if she was going to make it. About ten of the other women ran with her, day in and day out, even though they didn't have to, in order to get her in fit condition. It was an overwhelming feeling for her to see fifty women from very different backgrounds, who hadn't as much as known each other a few short weeks ago, work together as a team. She remembers that in her unit there were women who "were brought up in the rough parts of town and [they] wanted to fight" the other members of their unit at the beginning of basic training, because when they were civilians, they "figured fighting was their way up. They just set that aside and decided that teamwork was what it was all about" (Schneider and Schneider, 1992: 28-29).

Through a process of intensive symbolic interaction during basic training, the fifty once-green recruits internalized the relationships that make a world. They internalized a military generalized other, a *normative order*. They became willing and able to use its expectations of behavior as their own guidelines for social action. As a result they now have self-control: the individuals consider others and actively direct themselves in relation to those others. The once green recruits now *share a perspective*. They are able to engage cooperatively in problem solving and to achieve collective goals. They have appropriated military culture. Those possessing skills assist other members in acquiring those skills, and receive admiration in return (*exchange order*). The recruits acknowledge their superior officers' right to give them orders which they have the obligation to obey (*imperative order*). The fifty have become one (*solidary order*).

Conclusion

The learning objective of this chapter is for you to come to an understanding of how we learn roles and norms, develop a capacity to conform to them, and develop a sense of self. This process is called socialization. It is the process by which we appropriate culture and internalize the relationships that make a world. Socialization is a lifelong process without which social life among higher-order primates would not be possible.

This is exemplified by instances in which the relationships that make a world do not emerge in social interaction. For instance, sociologist *Tamotsu Shibutani*, in *The Derelicts of Company K: A Sociological Study of Demoralization* (1978) writes about a group that has fallen apart and whose members are unable to engage in cooperative problem solving. The relationships that make a world, no longer were found in Company K, a unit stationed in Minneapolis, Minnesota, at the end of the Second World War. The members of Company K are not committed to a military generalized other (no normative order). They fail to acknowledge the right of their superior officers to give orders which they must obey (no imperative order). They experience no solidarity with the larger organization in which they are situated (breakdown of solidary order). They lack self-discipline with regard to accomplishing goals as set for them by the official chain-of-command. The exchange order between members of their unit and the larger organization had broken down as well. Here is a brief description of the social organization that had fallen apart.

> Company K had all the symptoms of a demoralized group. The most common form of resistance was evasion of duties, but opposition went well beyond mere recalcitrance. Shouting obscenities and insults from ranks was commonplace. Violence erupted, and a brief reign of terror developed. Local officials, though held personally accountable for the accomplishment of military objectives, found it impossible to maintain order; at times the men became so unruly that the officers simply left them to their own resources. (Shibutani, 1978: 8)

Shibutani describes soldiers walking off work details, refusing to salute, fighting with and embarrassing superior officers, and going absent without leave (AWOL). One officer who was particularly disliked by the men of Company K ended a lecture by saying: "You must obey orders regardless of how stupid or absurd they may seem." The entire company burst out laughing (Shibutani, 1978:123).

Relationships that make a world are always problematic to establish and to maintain. As human beings, we are not robots. While we are socialized to accept our culture, in our actions we may turn on those who socialize us and act as we choose. Tamotsu Shibutani reminds us of this in *The Derelicts of Company K*. Those soldiers rebelled against an authority they perceived as unjust and refused to obey any orders they perceived as not in their best interests (Shibutani, 1978). Rosa Parks had grown up in a system of *de jure* (by law) racial segregation. Nonetheless, by refusing to sit at the back of a Montgomery, Alabama, bus, she ignited a civil-rights movement in this country. Timothy McVeigh had been socialized as a child to respect his country and to be loyal to it. He even served his country honorably in the Gulf War. A few years later he blew up the Oklahoma City federal building, a symbol of a government he had come to hate and to view as unjust. In that bombing he killed over 170 people, including nineteen children, and injured many others. A sociological view thus informs us that freedom as well as constraint, justice as well as tyranny arises from social processes.

Key Concepts

adult genital sexuality

agents (contexts) of
socialization

an ethic of care and
responsibility

anal stage

anticipatory socialization

authoritarian (coercive)

authoritative (inductive)

Autonomy vs. shame and doubt

Behaviorism: James B. Watson

Carol Gilligan

castration anxiety

Charles Darwin, Origin of
Species

children's literature and
socialization to gender

concrete operational stage

conditions favoring
internalization

conservation of mass and
measure

conventional stage of human
development (Piaget)

cooperation

ego

ego defense

ego defenses (defense
mechanisms)

ego integrity vs. despair

Elaine Hatfield and Russell
Clark's experiment: asking a
stranger for a date

initiative vs. guilt

internalization

isolation and human
development

Jean Piaget

latency

Lawrence Kohlberg: social
learning perspective on
human development

libido

loneliness and gender

magazines and gender
socialization

mass media and socialization

object permanence

oral stage

parental warmth

parenting styles

penis envy

permissive

phallic (Oedipal, Elektra) stage

post conventional stage

pre-conventional stage

premature closure of identity

primary socialization

projection

props

Psycho-sexual development

Psycho-social perspective

race in the U.S.: perceptions of
physical beauty

racial group

rationalization

reaction formation

René Spitz: isolation in
orphanages

repression

resocialization

Robert Malthus, Essay on the
Principle of Population

role diffusion

role distancing

Erik Erikson

eros

ethnic group

ethnocentrism

evolutionary theory

feral children

fixation

formal operational stage

Gabriel Tarde

gender identity

gender role

gender socialization

generalized other

generativity vs. stagnation

George Herbert Mead

gesture language

Gustave Le Bon

Harry Harlow's experiments:
the effects of isolation on
rhesus-monkey development

Herbert Spencer

id

identification

identity vs. role confusion

imitation stage

industry vs. inferiority

school: striving for success or
avoiding failure

secondary socialization

self-control

self-fulfilling prophecy (Robert
K. Merton)

self-handicapping

Sigmund Freud

single motherhood: TV reality
vs. real life

social Darwinism

social Darwinism in the United
States

social evolutionism

socialization

socialization to race and
children's literature

Spencerism

stages of human development

stages of psycho-sexual
development

sublimation

sublimation

superego

television and socialization

thantos

the game stage

the insufficient justification
effect

the Malthusian dilemma

the play stage

the pleasure principle

the reality principle

the sensorimotor stage

the Stockholm syndrome

total institution

trust vs. mistrust

William Graham Sumner: root,
hog, or die

Internet Resources

http://socserv2.mcmaster.ca/~econ/ugcm/3ll3/malthus/popu.txt

Document: Thomas Robert Malthus, *An Essay on the Principle of Population*

http://etext.lib.virginia.edu/cgibin/toccer?id=BonCro&tag=public&images=images/mode
ng&data=/lv1/Archive/eng-parsed&part=O

Document: Gustave Le Bon, *The Crowd: A Study of the Popular Mind*

http://www.literature.org/works/Charles-Darwin/origin

Document: Charles Darwin, *Origin of Species*

http://www.cs.cmu.edu/books.html

Document: The On-Line Books Page

This site indexes over 6,000 on-line books. You may browse by author or title. Some books are in languages other than English. Books can be listed here only if someone has put them on-line. The three books listed above (by Le Bon, Darwin, and Malthus) are listed at this Web site, as are many others of interest to sociologists and to students of sociology.

http://www.ncjrs.org

Document: The Justice Information Center

The National Criminal Justice Reference Service (NCJRS) Information Center World Wide Web site. The National Criminal Justice Reference Service, created by the National Institute of Justice in 1972, is one of the most extensive sources of information on criminal justice in the world. NCJRS provides publications and a wealth of other information on-line. You will find links to Corrections, Courts, Crime Prevention, Criminal Justice Statistics, Drugs and Crime, New This Week, International, Juvenile Justice, Law Enforcement, Research and Evaluation, Victims, and more.

Suggested Readings

Anderson, Elijah, *Streetwise: Race, Class, and Change in an Urban Community* (Chicago: The University of Chicago Press, 1990).

Cash, T.F., *What Do You See When You Look in the Mirror? Helping Yourself to a Positive Body Image* (NY: Bantam, 1995).

Cash, T.F., and Pruzinsky, T. (Eds.), *Body Images: Development, Deviance, and Change* (New York: Guilford Press, 1990).

Dines, Gail, and Humez, Jean M. (Eds.), *Gender, Race, and Class in Media* (Newbury Park, CA: Sage Publications, 1995).

Fleisher, Mark, *Beggars and Thieves* (Madison: University of Wisconsin Press, 1995).

Gibson, M.A., *Accommodation without Assimilation: Sikh Immigrants in an American High School* (Ithica, NY: Cornell University Press, 1989).

Goffman, Erving, *Asylums* (New York: Anchor Books, 1961).

Mead, George Herbert, *Mind, Self and Society* (Chicago: University of Chicago Press, 1934).

Rodin, Judith, *Body Traps* (New York: Morrow, 1992).

Schneider, Dorothy, and Schneider, Carl J., *Sound Off! American Military Women Speak Out* (New York: Paragon House, 1992).

Wolf, N., *The Beauty Myth: How Images of Beauty are Used Against Women* (New York: Morrow, 1991).

Wright, Kevin N., and Wright, Karen E., *Family Life, Delinquency, and Crime: A Policymaker's Guide* (Washington, D.C.: Office of Juvenile Justice and Delinquency Prevention, 1994).

Zborowski, Mark, "Cultural Components in Responses to Pain," *Journal of Social Issues*, Vol. 8, 1952: 16-30.

Learning Exercises:

The learning objective of this chapter is for you to appreciate that socialization is a process whereby we learn roles and norms, develop a capacity to conform to them, and develop a sense of self. Socialization also is the process whereby we appropriate (internalize or learn to comply with) the expectations of our culture. It is a lifelong process.

In the writing assignments below, you are to follow the directions and to write a response to the questions or issues indicated. Your answers to the written assignments are to be typed, double-spaced, and stapled in the upper left hand corner.

Learning Exercise 6.1

Writing Assignment

Answer the following questions in an essay in which you use some of the key concepts from this chapter. Your essay is to be typed, double-spaced, and stapled in the upper left hand corner. Your essay will be no shorter than four full pages in length.

This chapter introduces you to some early pioneers in American and European sociology who wrote about socialization: Freud, Watson, and Mead. Some of their ideas were directed at Social Darwinism.

1. What is social Darwinism? How would a social Darwinist view the socialization process? Discuss the implications of the ideas of (a) Freud, (b) Watson, and (c) Mead for a social Darwinistic view of socialization (human development).
2. Describe to the reader your childhood experiences. How would you characterize the style of parental control under which you grew up (authoritarian/coercive, authoritative/inductive, permissive, or what? Is corporal (physical) punishment necessary?
3. The authors introduce you to several theoretical perspectives concerning the socialization process—Freudian, social behaviorism, Meadian, Piagetian, Eriksonian, and social-learning (Kohlberg) theories. Reflecting upon your own life and childhood experiences, which theory or theories do you think best explains the socialization process, and why?.
4. In a previous chapter, the authors explain what Max Weber means by the concept of *rationalization*. In this chapter, you learn what Sigmund Freud means by the concept of *rationalization*. Compare and contrast Weber and Freud's conception of *rationalization*.

■ ■ ■

Learning Exercise 6.2

Writing Assignment

Answer the following questions in an essay in which you use some of the key concepts from this chapter. Your essay is to be typed, double-spaced, and stapled in the upper left hand corner. Your essay will be no shorter than three full pages in length.

1. In this chapter, the authors familiarize you with *defense mechanism* as a concept and with seven common defense mechanisms—sublimation, self-handicapping, identification, repression, projection, rationalization, and reaction formation. Please reflect on your own life, and then provide an example of an instance where you have used these defense mechanisms. Please select *four* defense mechanisms. For each one, describe an instance in which you have used it.

    George Herbert Mead stresses that in order to be able to communicate effectively, baby needs to learn to be able imaginatively to construct how she or he looks to others. In the play stage, children learn to take on the roles of others, one "other" at a time. A good example of this is playing "dress up" (or playing "school," "house," "army," "cops and robbers," "sports hero," "church," "superman," or "dancing school," and so forth). By taking the role of a significant other, children learn the attitudes, values, and beliefs of that significant other. From play, the child learns that there are rules that he or she is expected to follow in a particular situation.

2. Can you recall an instance from your own life—or from the life of someone you know—of a young child learning the role of the significant other? Did you (or anyone you know) ever play "dress up" or ("school," "house," "dance class" "cops and robbers" or an analogous game as a young child? Please tell us about it and what you think you learned from the experiences.

3. Please look at your own life, or at the life of someone you know, from the perspective of Erikson's eight stages of development. At what stage are you now? At what stage is your best friend? At what stage is your significant other or spouse? At what stage are your parents? Can you see Erikson's stages of development in your own life or in the life of someone you know? What did the family contribute at each of these various stages? Peers? Please tell us about it.

■ ■ ■

Learning Exercise 6.3

Writing Assignment

Answer the following questions in an essay in which you use some of the key concepts from this chapter. Your essay is to be typed, double-spaced, and stapled in the upper left hand corner. Your essay will be no shorter than three full pages in length.

1. Describe to the reader your *gendered* socialization from birth through childhood, paying attention to your experiences with regard to the major contexts of socialization, including family, media, peers, and school. Can you think of instances from your own life, or from the life of someone you know, of negative sanctioning from peers for associating with cross-gendered persons?

2. Are teachers' evaluations ever a cause of student performance? Have you or anyone you know ever experienced expectancy and labeling effects in your school experience? In your work experience? Please tell us about it.

3. Discuss the importance of schooling and peers as agents of socialization. Did your schooling prepare you for a university education? Why or why not? What were some of the shortcomings of your schooling? How important were your peers in you decision to get a college education? Did your best friend have an influence on you? Is your family supportive of your educational process (e.g., On a regular and consistent basis, do they give you the unfettered time, free of other distractions, that you need to read, to study, to write your term papers)? Does schooling prepare you for the world of work? Explain.

4. Please reflect upon your own life course and the various roles you have occupied. Can you think of instances wherein you engaged in *role distancing*? Please tell us about two or three instances of role distancing from your own life.

■ ■ ■

Learning Exercise 6.4

Writing Assignment

Answer the following questions in an essay in which you use some of the key concepts from this chapter. Your essay is to be typed, double-spaced, and stapled in the upper left hand corner. Your essay will be no shorter than three full pages in length.

1. Describe to the reader your socialization to race or ethnicity from birth through childhood, to the stage of life where you are today, paying attention to your experiences with regard to the major contexts of socialization, including family, media, peers, school, and work. Can you think of instances from your own life, or from the life of someone you know, of negative sanctioning from peers for associating with cross-race or cross-ethnic-group peers? Please tell us about it. How would you characterize your particular strategy in elementary school, in high school, in college, and in work (if applicable)—as striving for success, or as failure avoidance? How do you account for adopting the strategy that you chose?

2. Please reflect on your own life course with regard to the concept of anticipatory socialization. Please tell us about a couple of instances of anticipatory socialization from your own life.

3. Please reflect on you own life course with regard to the concept of resocialization. Have you, or anyone you know, experienced resocialization? Please describe the process of resocialization itself, the social setting(s) in which it took place, the length of time of the process, its short-term and longer-term effects on you, and the changes you perceive in your attitudes, beliefs, values, world view, and conceptions of self as a result of the experience. Would you characterize at least part of the resocialization experience as uncomfortable or as painful? Resocialization experiences need not occur within the context of a total institution. Would you characterize the setting(s) in which this resocialization took place as a total institution?

■ ■ ■

Learning Exercise 6.5

Sociology and the Internet

Barbara Tatem Kelley, Terence P. Thornberry, and Carolyn A. Smith, all of the Office of Juvenile Justice and Delinquency Prevention (OJJDP), are the authors of *In the Wake of Childhood*

Maltreatment, a study published in 1997 and available (without a fee) electronically from the federal government. The item number of this 16-page report is *NCJ 165257*. The number might be helpful if you were looking for a hard copy of this article in a government-documents section of a library. To gain access to this item electronically, please do the following: (1) Go to the Office of Juvenile Justice and Delinquency Prevention's Home Page at **http://www.ncjrs.org/ojjhome.htm** Once you are there, (2) click on **Publications.** Once you are there, click on **OJJDP and Other Publications: Juvenile Justice/Justice Information Center.** This will bring you to a **Juvenile Justice** page. Once there, click on **Violence and Victimization.** Then, scroll to **In the Wake of Childhood Maltreatment,** which you may read online, save it to disk, or download it as an ASCII text file or as an Adobe Acrobat File. (The number of pages in the online versions may differ from the number of pages in the hard copy of the NCJ 165257 document. Do not worry about this discrepancy.)

In any case, read the report. The report explores the connections between maltreatment as a child and problem behavior as a teen, drawing on the Rochester Youth Development Study (RYDS).

In a paper no shorter than two typed pages in length, you are to describe the research methods on which this study is based. Do the researchers use a control group, a comparison group, or what? Is there random assignment of research subjects to a control and experimental condition? Are the youth in the study scientifically representative of some larger sample or population, or are they merely a sample of convenience? What are the study's major findings? Of the theories of human development that you have studied in this chapter, which help you the most in making sociological sense of these findings? Explain. In light of the insights into conducting scientific inquiry that you have gained by studying this chapter of our textbook, what limitations or shortcomings of this study do you detect?

■   ■   ■

Multiple-Choice and True-False Test

1. Socialization includes which of the following?
   A. learning roles and norms
   B. developing the capacity to conform to roles and norms
   C. developing a sense of self
   D. all of the above
   E. both (A) and (B)

2. The socialization that comes first in our lives.
   A. primary
   B. secondary
   C. tertiary
   D. anomic

3. Socialization addresses the issues of ———————————.
   A. human development
   B. societal continuity across generational lines
   C. both of the above
   D. none of the above

4. Which of the following academic disciplines claim(s) socialization as a central process?
   A. political science
   B. anthropology
   C. psychology
   D. sociology
   E. all of the above

5. The main orientations to socialization within sociology include ———————————.
   A. the learning and internalization of roles, norms, values, and statuses of the groups to which an individual belongs
   B. self-concept (identity) formation
   C. both of the above
   D. none of the above

6. ———————————— viewed the self as a thoroughly social and reflexive construct that emerges through social and symbolic interactions.
   A. Freud
   B. Piaget
   C. Erikson
   D. George Herbert Mead and Charles Horton Cooley

7. Mead called the reflexive part of the self the ———————————.
   A. I
   B. me
   C. you
   D. he
   E. she

8. _____ wrote *Essay on the Principle of Population* (1798).
   A. Thomas Robert Malthus
   B. Karl Marx
   C. Davis and Moore
   D. Thomas Moore
   E. James Dewey

9. The observation that population increases at a(n) _____ rate while the food supply increases at a(n) _____ rate is called the _____.
   A. arithmetic; geometric; capitalistic dilemma
   B. fast; even faster; storage dilemma
   C. geometric; arithmetic; Malthusian dilemma

10. _____ coined the term "survival of the fittest."
    A. Herbert Spencer
    B. Karl Marx
    C. Charles Darwin
    D. Thomas Robert Malthus
    E. Charles Horton Cooley

11. Charles Darwin's *Origin of Species* was published in what year?
    A. 1798
    B. 1859
    C. 1945
    D. 1968

12. Social Darwinism reached its peak of scientific, political, and ideological influence _____.
    A. in the fourteenth century
    B. the signing of the Declaration of Independence and the Jacksonian era
    C. between 1880 and the end of the First World War
    D. between the end of the Second World War and the Korean War

13. _____ theory had a significant impact on, and actually came to dominate many of the natural and social sciences in England, Germany, Austria, France, and the United States from 1870 to the end of the 1920s.
    A. Evolutionary
    B. Freudian
    C. Social behaviorism
    D. Piagetian learning
    E. Eriksonian

14. Gustave Le Bon and Gabriel Tarde _____.
    A. applied Freudian insights to the development of award-winning children's picture books
    B. conducted research on college campuses in the United States in order to investigate gender differences in accepting an invitation for a date from a total stranger
    C. used Darwinistic ideas to understand crowd and mass behavior
    D. are Chicago-school sociologists who studied the formation of self in very young children in the inner city
    E. are Freudian child psychologists who popularized Freud's ideas among Swiss school teachers in the 1980s

254

15. In the United States, _____ ideas inform and dominate much early American sociology.
    A. social Darwinistic
    B. Freudian
    C. Lawrence Kohlberg's
    D. Karl Marx's

16. "Root, hog, or die" is associated with _____.
    A. William Graham Sumner's view that only the fittest survive
    B. gestural language, according to René Spitz
    C. James Watson
    D. token economies
    E. the game stage of development, according to Carol Gilligan

17. Social behaviorism arose during _____.
    A. the Enlightenment
    B. 1890-1910
    C. the 1930s
    D. the 1960s

18. James B. Watson is most closely associated with what intellectual tradition?
    A. behaviorism
    B. Freudian theory
    C. conflict theory
    D. feminist theory
    E. Piagetian developmental theory

19. Basic trust is the first of _____ eight stages of human development.
    A. Sigmund Freud's
    B. Erik Erikson's
    C. Lawrence Kohlberg's
    D. Carol Gilligan's
    E. George Herbert Mead's

20. Harry and Margaret Harlow et. al.'s research on isolate-reared rhesus monkeys shows that _____.
    A. rhesus monkeys need something soft and warm to cling to in order to feel comfortable, reassured, and calm.
    B. peer relations are crucial to the development of the young.
    C. the effects on monkeys isolated for the first three months of life are reversible.
    D. baby monkeys isolated for the first six month s of life are impaired permanently both emotionally and behaviorally
    E. All of the above.

21. Research on the effects of isolation and abandonment on human infants shows results strikingly similar to those of the Harlow et. al.'s research.
    A. True   B. False

22. Feral children are _____.
    A. children who have not successfully resolved the oral stage of human development
    B. children who have successfully attained the fifth stage of development in the Erik-sonian paradigm
    C. children who successfully complete the game stage of Meadian development
    D. extremely isolated children who, according to legend, have been reared by animals, apart from humans.

23. René Spitz's research on isolation in orphanages shows that _____.
    A. If orphanages are clean and antiseptic, the children tend to be healthy, are hardly ever sick, and there is a low mortality rate
    B. the infants spent most of their time alone in their beds
    C. the infants were extremely susceptible to infection and illness, and the ortality rate was extremely high
    D. by the age of two, hardly any of the children could eat alone, even with a spoon, and hardly any of them were toilet trained
    E. (B), (C), and (D)

24. Libido is the force of life according to _____.
    A. James B. Watson
    B. B.F. Skinner
    C. Sigmund Freud
    D. George Herbert Mead
    E. Carol Gilligan

25. Research on perceptions of physical attractiveness in the United States demonstrates that
    _____.
    A. African American females are significantly more satisfied with their global body image, weight, and specific body areas than are either white or Hispanic females
    B. white females are significantly more satisfied with their global body image, weight, and specific body areas than are either African-American or Hispanic females
    C. there are no differences across white, Hispanic, and African-American women with regard to level of satisfaction with their global body image, weight, and specific body areas

26. Freud's term for the conscience: _____.
    A. id
    B. ego
    C. superego

27. According to Freud, the ego operates on the basis of _____.
    A. the reality principle
    B. the pleasure principle

28. Libido operates on the basis of _____.
    A. the reality principle
    B. the pleasure principle

29. In the Freudian paradigm, fixation means that _____.
    A. psycho-sexual maturity is not attained
    B. a disproportionate amount of libidinal energy is invested in a particular bodily orifice
    C. personality is dominated by the traits associated with the traits associated with the level of development at which fixation occurred
    D. all of the above
    E. none of the above

30. The stages of psycho-sexual development in the Freudian paradigm occur in which order?
    A. trust vs. mistrust, autonomy vs. shame and guilt, industry vs. inferiority, identity vs. role confusion, intimacy vs. isolation, generativity vs. stagnation, ego integrity vs. despair
    B. oral, anal, phallic, latency, adult genital
    C. anal, oral, latency, phallic, adult genital
    D. oral, anal, latency, phallic, adult genital
    E. trust vs. mistrust, identity, latency, adult genital

31. This person developed a psycho-social theory of human development.
    A. Sigmund Freud
    B. Erik Erikson
    C. James B. Watson
    D. Jean Piaget

32. In Erik Erikson's paradigm of human development, this stage encompasses adolescence.
    A. Initiative vs. guilt
    B. Industry vs. guilt
    C. Identity vs. role confusion
    D. Intimacy vs. isolation
    E. Ego integrity vs. despair

33. Erikson's theory of human development resembles those of Mead, Freud, and Kohlberg in which of the following ways?
    A. viewing the process of socialization as consisting of stages
    B. viewing the process by which people handle each stage as having repercussions for later development
    C. both of the above
    D. none of the above

34. Lawrence Kohlberg's social-learning perspective on socialization includes which of the following stages?
    A. the pre-conventional stage
    B. the post-conventional stage
    C. the conventional stage
    D. all of the above
    E. both (A) and (C)

35. According to Lawrence Kohlberg, the _____ stage is reached by very few people.
    A. the pre-conventional stage
    B. the conventional stage
    C. the post-conventional stage

36. According to Lawrence Kohlberg, at this stage of development people ponder the meaning of abstract concepts like justice, equality, fairness, and equal justice before the law.
    A. the pre-conventional stage
    B. the conventional stage
    C. the post-conventional stage

37. According to Carol Gilligan of Harvard University, in the United States female socialization tends to engender a(n) _____ and male socialization tends to engender _____.
    A. an ethic of care and responsibility; an ethic of care and responsibility
    B. an ethic of care and responsibility; a justice perspective
    C. a justice perspective; a justice perspective
    D. a justice perspective; an ethic of care and responsibility

38. According to Carol Gilligan of Harvard University, if we view ourselves as situated in a web of connectedness and experience empathy we are manifesting _____.
    A. an ethic of care and responsibility
    B. a justice perspective

39. Which of the following statements is more accurate?
    A. In all societies in all historical periods, social scientists find that there is an identifiable stage of social life known as childhood.
    B. Childhood as an identifiable stage of social life is a relatively recent social invention in Western societies.

40. The first stage of development according to Jean Piaget.
    A. the concrete operational stage
    B. the sensorimotor stage
    C. the formal operational period
    D. the pre-operational stage

41. Conservation of mass and of measure emerge during this stage of development according to Jean Piaget.
    A. the concrete operational stage
    B. the sensorimotor stage
    C. the formal operational period
    D. the pre-operational stage

42. According to Jean Piaget, In this stage of development, people use and develop their capacity to think in terms of abstract concepts and general principles; people learn to derive testable hypotheses from theory and learn to test these hypotheses.
    A. the concrete operational stage
    B. the sensorimotor stage
    C. the formal operational period
    D. the pre-operational stage

43. Parenting styles influence whether empathetic concern develops in young (e.g., two-and-a-half year old) children.
    A. True   B. False

44. _____ refers to parental discipline based on threat, force, or physical punishment.
   A. Authoritarian control
   B. Authoritative control
   C. Permissive control

45. _____ refers to parental discipline based on logical reasoning and explanation.
   A. Authoritarian control
   B. Authoritative control
   C. Permissive control

46. The conditions favoring internalization include _____.
   A. using powerful, large sanctions (e.g., physical punishment)
   B. being inconsistent in the application of rewards and punishments
   C. both of the above
   D. none of the above

47. The Huesmann et. al. longitudinal study of over 600 children from upstate New York reveals that capricious, severe discipline is a good recipe for _____.
   A. creating bullies of both genders
   B. creating empathetic people sensitive to the needs of others
   C. creating children who feel hopeless, worthless, and helpless
   D. creating people whose posture to the external world is combative, aggressive, defiant
   E. (A), (C), and (D)

48. Jonathan Freedman introduced elementary-school children to an attractive toy and requested that they not play with it when he was out of the room. Freedman used a mild threat with half the children and a severe one with the others Those children were most likely to internalize the rule who _____.
   A. had been given a mild sanction
   B. had been given a severe threat

49. In the United States, research indicates that from a young preschool age until early adolescence, children play in largely _____ groups.
   A. gender integrated
   B. gender homogeneous

50. Which of the following is/are true regarding gender socialization in the United States?
   A. Mothers and fathers perceive their newborn females as finer featured, more delicate and as less strong than their newborn boys.
   B. Parents engage in more rough-and-tumble play with boys.
   C. Mothers talk to and touch their daughters more than their sons
   D. Preschool boys are allowed to roam further away from home than are females
   E. All of the above

51. A recent study of Caldecott children's books that _____.
   A. a greater number of males than females are depicted in titles
   B. males are described as more potent and active
   C. girls are more often shown using pots and pans, broom and sewing needle than are boys
   D. all of the above

52. Which of the following is/are true regarding gender socialization in the United States? When conversing with their children, _____.
   A. parents' references to emotion are more frequent and varied with daughters than with sons
   B. parents discuss emotions, except for anger, more with daughters
   C. when parents make-up stories to tell their preschool children, the stories told to girls contain more emotion words than the stories told to boys
   D. when mothers talk to daughters about feelings, they discuss in more detail the emotional state itself than is the case with sons
   E. all of the above

53. Research reveals that males value friendships that focus on _____, and females _____.
   A. shared interests and activities; place just as much value on shared interests and activities as a basis for friendship as do males
   B. trust and self-disclosure; place just as much value on shared interests and activities as a basis for friendship as do males
   C. shared interests and activities; place greater value on trust and self-disclosure

54. Elaine Hatfield and Russell D. Clark conducted an experiment wherein college males and females approached attractive members of the opposite sex and asked one of three things: "Would you go out with me tonight?," "Would you come over to my apartment tonight," or "Would you go to bed with me tonight?" The results demonstrate that _____.
   A. the more intimate the request, the higher the percent of males who said "Yes"
   B. the more intimate the request, the lower the percent of females who said "Yes"
   C. about half of males and of females agreed to the least intimate request
   D. both (A) and (B)
   E. (A), (B), and (C)

55. Research indicates that in the United States _____.
   A. male and females tend to experience loneliness under the same circumstances
   B. males tend to experience loneliness when deprived of groups focusing on shared activities
   C. females tend to experience loneliness when deprived of close one-on-one relationships focusing on understanding and emotional support
   D. both (B) and (C)

56. Adolescent and adult males are _____ females to construe friendliness on the part of a person of the opposite sex as sexual interest.
   A. just as likely as
   B. more likely than
   C. less likely than

57. In Japan, magazine reading is the number-one media source for teens, and hence magazines are an important agent of socialization.
   A. True   B. False

58. For U.S. teens, the number-one media source is television.
   A. True   B. False

59. In the United States, the average white parents and the average black parents spend _____ hours per week interacting with their children as/than they did in 1960.
   A. just as many
   B. a lot more
   C. at least ten fewer

60. In the United States, in real life, most single mothers have which of the following characteristics?
   A. They are upper-middle class in terms of social status.
   B. They hold professional jobs and they are highly educated.
   C. They receive a lot of help with baby from the father of the baby or from other male friends
   D. all of the above
   E. none of the above

61. In the United States, in TV soap operas, most single mothers have which of the following characteristics?
   A. They are upper-middle class in terms of social status.
   B. They hold professional jobs and they are highly educated.
   C. They receive a lot of help with baby from the father of the baby or from other male friends
   D. all of the above
   E. none of the above

62. In television, of those commercials having voice-overs, the percent having males as narrators _____.
   A. is equal to the percent having females as narrators
   B. is far less than the percent having females as narrators
   C. ranges from 85% to 95%, a situation that depicts men as more credible and authoritative

63. A study examining gender roles in prime time television programs concludes that adolescent girls are portrayed as being interested primarily in two things:
   A. their studies and their families
   B. their families and their jobs
   C. clothes and boys

64. Agents of socialization include _____.
   A. family
   B. peers
   C. school
   D. the mass media
   E. all of the above

65. Samuel Bowles and Herbert Gintis contend that schools expanded in this country in order to prepare a docile, tractable labor force.
   A. True   B. False

66. Four out of ten studies that attempt to replicate the now-famous Rosenthal and Jacobson study of teacher-expectancy effects indicate that teacher expectations have an influence on student performance. Which of the following might explain these results?
    A. Teachers smile, look, and nod more at "high potential" students
    B. Teachers may set higher goals for students for whom they hold high expectations
    C. Teachers may call on "high potential" students more, and give them more time to answer
    D. all of the above

67. The insufficient justification effect refers to _____.
    A. social Darwinism
    B. social behaviorism
    C. the tendency to internalize a norm, value, or meaning, etc., when we perceive that our actions are freely chosen and when the external inducement is small

68. Sociologists Covington and Beery propose that two fundamentally different patterns emerge among students as a result of labeling and expectancy effects. One is a striving for success and the other is avoiding failure. The striving for success strategy is exemplified by _____.
    A. not showing up for class on the day your oral report to the class is due
    B. putting off working on an assignment until the last minute
    C. investing little effort in school work
    D. all of the above
    E. none of the above

69. The avoiding failure strategy is exemplified by _____.
    A. not showing up for class on the day your oral report to the class is due
    B. putting off working on an assignment until the last minute
    C. investing little effort in school work
    D. all of the above
    E. none of the above

70. *Role distancing* behavior refers to separating the self from the behavior required of a role occupant.
    A. True   B. False

71. The peer group has which of the following characteristics?
    A. It is not a voluntary association.
    B. It is an association among status equals.
    C. It provides a domain free of parental control.
    D. All of the above.
    E. Both (B) and (C)

72. Sociological research indicates that peers are important in promoting or preventing delinquency.
    A. True   B. False

73. In a study of 9- to 10-year olds attending a publicly funded school in a large city in England, Michael J. Boulton observed British Asian and British white children of both genders on the playground during recess in order to observe their spontaneous peer preferences. This study indicates that all four groups—Asian males, Asian females, white males, white females—exhibit _____.
    A. a highly significant tendency to play with own-race peers
    B. a highly significant tendency to play with own-gender peers
    C. both of the above
    D. a highly significant tendency to play with cross-sex peers and with cross-race peers
    E. a highly significant tendency to play with same-sex peers and with cross-race peers

74. Pescosolido, Grauerholz and Milkie have conducted an historical study of race relations in award-winning children's books published from 1937 to 1993. Their content analyses reveal that _____.
    A. the portrayal of African-American adults as focal characters are a high percentage of all characters throughout the period
    B. during periods of racial strife (as measured by the number of riots, protests, and legal actions), many African Americans appear as interacting with white characters as status equals in children's books, indicating a decision or willingness to portray racial contact in new ways
    C. mutual, egalitarian cross-racial relationships that are central to the story line comprise a high proportion of all relationships, particularly after 1975
    D. all of the above
    E. none of the above

75. Research on perceptions of physical attractiveness in the United States consistently demonstrates that _____.
    A. there are no racial differences in perceptions of preferred body size
    B. white females prefer a thin body for themselves
    C. African-American females prefer a body for themselves that is just as thin as that desired by white females
    D. both (B) and (C)

76. Anticipatory socialization refers to learning the rights, duties, obligations, values, attitudes and outlook typical of a particular role *before* one occupies it.
    A. True   B. False

77. The hardship and pain of military basic training bear no relationship to the level of group cohesiveness that emerges from it.
    A. True   B. False

78. Resocialization represents a break with one's past and its aim is radically to change the person, to tear down the individual's old world view, beliefs, values, and conceptions of self, and to replace them with new ones.
    A. True   B. False

79. From a sociological perspective, the military oath is a meaningless charade.
    A. True   B. False

80. From a sociological perspective, self-control is a social construct.
    A. True   B. False

CHAPTER 7

Gender and Society

'[T]ens of thousands of Eritrean women . . . played an active and often a combat role in the war against Ethiopia for at least twenty years. Eritrean women . . . see it as their duty both to fight (and if needed die) for the nation . . ."

Roy Pateman, *"The Legacy of Eritrea's National Question"*

■ ■ ■

Maxine Hong Kingston's (1989) critically acclaimed autobiography begins with the story of the "no-name woman" (1989). The woman is her paternal aunt.

In the year 1924, in rural China, Maxine Hong Kingston's aunt was married to a man who was leaving for the Gold Mountain (California) the next day. She only knew him for a day. After he had been gone for a long time, she became pregnant by a man other than her husband. The villagers also noticed that she was pregnant and knew it to be an illegitimate child. On the day she was to deliver the baby, they stormed her family home, killed the domestic animals and broke the house, all the while cursing her. That night the "no-name woman" gave birth to her baby in the pigsty, as was the custom to fool jealous gods. In the morning, she committed suicide by throwing herself and the baby in the family's drinking well. She never revealed the identity of the father of her child, and took the secret to her watery grave. Maxine Hong Kingston suspects the baby was a girl because there may have been some "forgiveness" for a boy.

Subsequently, the family conspired by participating in **the silence,** by never mentioning the aunt. It was as though she had never existed. Since her existence was denied, Maxine Hong Kingston never learned her name or any other details about the incident. Her mother narrated this story when Kingston reached puberty. The story came with a taboo; it was never to be repeated to anyone. The mother's motive for telling Kingston the story was to warn her. If Kingston should ever dishonor the family, she too would be disowned and forgotten like the "no-name woman."

What is the impact of the no-name woman's silence? The "no-name woman's" silence perpetuates oppression and injustice. Not only do we not know her name, but we also do not know what really transpired between her and the man whose baby she bore. Had the no-name woman been raped? Had she been in love with the father of her child? Did he threaten her and order her to keep quiet? And did she comply because she was accustomed to obeying male authority? Did he, or his kin on his behalf, lead the raid against her? Was he part of the mob?

The above episode occurred in the first quarter of the twentieth century in China. Some observers of our own country during the last decade of the twentieth century maintain that we are not very far removed from the social dynamics portrayed in the story of the "no-name woman." Consider for a moment *the confirmation hearings of Clarence Thomas* in October of 1991. Clarence Thomas was the President's nominee for a seat on the United States Supreme Court. During his confirmation hearings, Anita Hill testified against Clarence Thomas. Bravely, she broke the silence and publicly accused him of sexual harassment. Thereby she challenged his competence to occupy one of the highest positions in the nation.

The latent function or long-term impact of Anita Hill-Clarence Thomas hearings is to reaffirm to many women that it is better to keep quiet and to suffer rather than risk public humiliation. For Anita Hill personally, she would never be the same person again. These hearings had transformed her life irrevocably and she can never return to her private life as a small town professor in Norman, Oklahoma. The hearings were a public degradation ceremony for Anita Hill. However, feminist scholars point out that *she had spoken,* and by that act, she had recovered the power that Clarence Thomas had taken from her. Observers from another theoretical framework might phrase this as: She regained an *internal locus of control.* Additionally, she made women's struggle a little easier. In many people's eyes, Clarence Thomas's reputation was "irrevocably tarnished." By them, he will never be trusted completely again. The hearings, in the short run, also had the sad effect of dividing the African American community. Many African Americans felt that Hill had betrayed the cause of racial unity and that she had collaborated with the "enemy" (McKay, 1992). However, one of the greatest accomplishments of the hearings was that sexual harassment laws were enacted to protect women (Martin 1995).

The Study of Gender and Society

The scholarly study of gender and society is interdisciplinary. Many of the liberal arts and social sciences—including anthropology, English, psychology, history, social work, political science, archaeology, women's studies, and so-

ciology—now have specialty areas devoted to the study of gender.

Women's studies is interdisciplinary and places women at the center of analysis. In this study, *women's subjective experiences,* which have been silenced throughout history, *are seen as significant.* Silencing women is a means of controlling women. For instance, if women do not know that females fight in combat roles in armed struggle, they may not demand access to similar positions in the armed services of their own countries. Maxine Hong Kingston's "no-name woman" was silent and we never learn her side of the story. Women's studies challenges past scholarship by readjusting the focus for understanding women's lives. Feminist scholarship makes women's contributions visible.

The term **feminism** originated in France in the early 1900s. The first wave of feminism began in the nineteenth century and reached its peak when the nineteenth amendment granted women the right to vote in 1920. After this period, the word feminism fell into disrepute. It became associated with radical feminism, which was said to be led by lesbians. In the 1960s, a new generation revived the struggle and called it Women's Liberation or the women's movement. Their slogan was **The Personal is Political.** The second wave was successful in focusing public attention on violence against women. The movement also addressed structural issues and demanded women's position in the family as well as the labor force be corrected.

Women's studies is critical to the production process of knowledge, called the feminist dialect. The **feminist dialect** asserts that knowledge is always biased in societies where females are subordinate to males. The interests of the dominant group (males) are viewed as influencing the production and dissemination of knowledge. Hence, the production and dissemination of knowledge in societies with gender inequalities are often manipulated and therefore inauthentic. Feminist scholarship argues that the only way to validate the reality of a situation is to achieve a system of discourse that permits an "egalitarian exchange of views in which all parties openly acknowledge both the partialness and the interest-based character of their views." Therefore the feminist agenda is to acknowledge and "explore the situated perceptions of reality held by" women in different economic positions as well as by women of differing racial and ethnic backgrounds and sexual orientations (Langermann and Niebrugge-Brantley 1990).

Some feminist scholars view the production and dissemination of knowledge from the time of the Enlightenment until the Second World War as having their basis in the Judeo-Christian tradition. That is, knowledge was western in origin. This viewpoint maintains that during this era, knowledge largely was produced by and for male consumption. In this tradition, knowledge was defined as that which had the characteristics of being scientific, objective, and rational (Seidman, 1994). Women, in this view, were marginal because of their proclivity to be excessively irrational. Women could not control the urge to be emotional. Emotionality was inherent in their biological makeup. This, it was posited, was due to the fact that women were subject to monthly hormonal imbalances (Hubbard 1995). At any given point in the life course, women were deemed beyond the pale of reason in young adulthood she experienced monthly menstrual (hormonal) cycles (pre-menstrual syndrome); at menopause, the hormonal damage to reason was, if anything, even more severe; and after menopause, the woman was beyond reason.

Subjectivity

Women's scholarship has focused on the subjective aspects of women's experiences. **Subjectivity** in this form of scholarship refers to women's personal experiences and to how women see and interpret their situations and lives. Women's subjectivity traditionally has been denied in scholarly writings on gender and society. Therefore, this chapter is written in the spirit of citing women's autobiographies and incidents from their lives. In the past, women's history has not been considered significant enough to be recorded in writing and was not presented, by and large, through the ages in publications widely read by the general public or by the intellectual classes. Writing was viewed as the medium of expressing reason (Gates 1992). This narrow view of textual

history excluded a generous portion of women's and other minority groups' experiences (Saldivar 1991). Women's unrecorded-unwritten history celebrates life and living through stories, parables, folk tales, and the supernatural phenomena. For instance, this world is transmitted through the oral tradition (word of mouth) from one generation of women to the next.

The Distinction Between Sex and Gender

The sociological study of males and females distinguishes between sex and gender. The word sex refers to physical differences between males and females. Examples would be primary sexual characteristics, such as testes and ovaries. Secondary sexual characteristics would include hormonal balances, fat to muscle ratio, body size, the amount and placement of body hair, and so forth. Other physical differences between males and females (e.g., chromosomes) also are included under the concept of sex. The term **gender,** on the other hand, refers to social, psychological, and cultural differences between males and females. Gender, in other words, is a social construction. **Social construction** is a social process that subordinates women on the basis of sex. We can see this construction in the primary socialization experiences of males and females which we analyzed in an earlier chapter.

Sexism is a pervasive bias against a person on the basis of sex, gender, or sexual orientation. Sexism is manifest when one looks at the history of the gay world. Lesbians are conspicuously absent in literature until the end of the nineteenth century. They are mentioned only when they return to wage labor (Adam 1996). Historically, then, homosexuality is seen as a male propensity. When lesbians do make an appearance, they are stereotyped as masculine (Weeks, 1996). In 1885, England's male homosexuals were targets of laws (Greenberg and Bystryn, 1996).

Social life in the United States is characterized by capitalist patriarchy. The term **capitalist patriarchy** refers to a society where males are in-control of all the important societal processes, especially the economy. In this type of society, females are in subordinated positions in the political realm, the economic realm, the occupational realm, and many more. Some scholars argue that females are subordinate to men in this type of society primarily because they are home makers and men are bread winners. Whatever the case in that regard, women's work at home tends to be taken for granted or ignored. Even those women who work outside the home, return home to do domestic chores. Hochschild (1989) calls this unpaid labor *the second shift*. Second shift labor not only is unpaid, but it is also trivialized and viewed as non-essential. Even those males who make the choice to be the house husband while the wife works outside the home tend to be ridiculed by salient audiences. It doesn't seem to matter which gender does this labor; the labor itself is demeaned. In contemporary America, most are perceived as working for wages while second shift work—even if performed full time and hence is first shift labor—is viewed as being done *out of love for their families* (Hoffnung, 1995). Love is free and therefore second shift labor is devalued.

When most American men do work around the house, there is a division of labor. Men tend to do tasks such as mowing the lawn, repairing appliances or taking the garbage out. Women, on the other hand, are involved in the cooking and cleaning tasks that are both monotonous and repetitive. A man can postpone mowing the lawn until the next day or even the next week. A woman cannot tell her baby that she will change its diaper tomorrow or the next week. Thus, there is an immediacy and urgency to tasks that tend to be delegated to females (Steil, 1995).

Please reflect on the gendered division of labor in your family while you were growing up. What tasks did your dad tend to do? What tasks did your mom tend to do? If you had siblings of both genders—brothers and sisters—and if any of you had "chores" as part of your family responsibilities, what types of tasks tended to be delegated to the sons and which to the daughters? How did you feel about this division of labor as a child? How do you feel about it now? Was the division of labor similar in the homes of your childhood friends? Do you want
a similar division of labor in your own home when or if you are married? Why or why not? Please tell us about it in the spaces below.

Gender: A Biological or Cultural Construct? Or a Combination of Both?

As we prepare to enter the next millennium, scholars and scientists in a variety of disciplines are still debating the issue of whether differences between the sexes are inherently biological or cultural. Hubbard (1995) charges that the scientific construction of biology is not authentic. Gender and the importance of sex are, in fact, largely socially and politically constructed. For many persons in industrial societies, no one in the pregnant female's family needs to hunt or gather food from dawn until dusk; no one needs to protect her, or the small children, from lions and tigers. A division of gendered labor that may have made "sense" in such circumstances is not necessarily a viable model under radically different circumstances. For many categories of labor, there are no significant differences in the capacity of women and men to do similar work. Some scholars argue that the only difference is in the procreation process.

What Causes Gendered Differences?

Role of Socialization

During early socialization, little girls are conditioned to be sympathetic and co-operative. This, in part, is accomplished by the little girl's connecting to the mother. On the other hand, little boys' socialization is markedly different; it encourages them to be strong individuals through separation from the mother (Chodorow, 1978). Being female and being male, in other words, have large cultural components that are learned during early socialization. The large extent of cultural determination gives the unwary observer the impression that being one gender or the other is natural (Butler, 1990).

Division of Labor in My Childhood Family

_____

_____

_____

_____

_____

_____

_____

_____

■   ■   ■

BOX 7.1.

Gendered Values, Attitudes, and Expectations

Let us look at the relative values, attitudes, and expectations attached to women and men's behavior.

- When a man has several affairs and sleeps with many women, he is macho, while a woman pursuing a similar activity is a whore or a slut.
- When a man is aggressive, he is being assertive, while a woman similarly engaged is pushy and aggressive.
- When a man is talking on the phone, he is conducting business, while a woman is merely gossiping.
- Please look around you in the class and observe how women and men sit. A man tends to occupy more space and sits more sprawled out. A woman tends to sit with her legs together (even if crossed) and occupies little space.
- Men's social worth frequently is measured in terms of how much money they make. A woman's social worth tends to be based on her physical appearance. Recall the number of fat, bald, paunchy men you see with slender, beautiful women holding onto their arms.
- Facial hair on men is manly while on women it is undesirable and unfeminine.
- Male students occasionally touch young female faculty members while talking. If the female instructor were to touch the male student, it would be seen as a sexual advance or as inappropriate behavior.
- Women are usually in subordinate positions in the work place. They are more often nurses than doctors, secretaries rather than managers.
- To sharpen the differences among infants, we distinguish among them by their apparel. Baby girls wear pink and baby boys wear blue.

BOX 7.2.

Cultural Lag, Gender, and the Mass Media: The Case of *Seventeen* Magazine

Studies of the print media reveal that "magazines such as *Seventeen, Sports Illustrated, Teen, Time, Ebony, Young Miss, Jet, Newsweek,* and *Vogue*" account for "more than half of all reported reading" by adolescents in the United States (Strasburger, 1995:46). One may well wonder what images of gender relations are conveyed by the print media as an agent of socialization. Sociologists Jennifer Schlenker, Sandra L. Caron and William Halteman of the University of Maine recently conducted research on this matter (1998). What follows is a summary of their research.

The Women's Movement

The women's movement, sometimes called the feminist movement, has been viewed by some analysts as consisting of three major periods or waves that have risen since the past century. The first arose from the abolitionist movement of the nineteenth century and focused on gaining the women the right to vote in political elections. The second emerged from the Civil Rights movement of the 1960s and early 1970s. Following a backlash (Faludi, 1992) in the 1980s, a third wave has emerged during the 1990s and it focuses on topics that include day care, abortion, and comparable pay.

Seventeen Magazine is the teen magazine with the longest publication and largest circulation records. First published in 1944, this monthly magazine now sports a circulation of 1.8 million. The inside cover of each issue describes the magazine as "(t)ailored for young women in their teens and early twenties," and as covering "fashion, beauty, health, fitness, food, cars, college, careers, talent, entertainment, fiction, . . . [and] crucial personal and global issues."

Research Methods

Schlenker, Caron and Halteman performed a content analysis of all articles and regular features, with the exceptions noted below, in all 12 issues of *Seventeen* for the years 1945, 1955, 1965, 1975, 1985, and 1995 to determine the content of the magazine and to ascertain whether the content changed across time. The regular features not included in their analyses are all advertisements, letters to the editor, "Horoscope," and the movie and music reviews. The authors utilized conceptual categories developed in prior research by other scholars.

The authors coded the content of all articles as containing either a feminist or traditional message. *Traditional messages* emphasized (1) appearance—fashion trends, hairstyles, makeup, beauty products, how one looks to others; (2) male-female relations—fictional romantic-love stories, advice about relationships, how to find a boyfriend, how to please a boyfriend, feature articles on male entertainers; (3) home—cooking, decorating, sewing, crafts, playing gracious hostess. *Feminist messages* emphasized (1) self-development—health and wellness, hobbies, relations with persons other than boyfriends; (2) political and world issues—the environment, education in other countries, politics, international and military issues; (3) career development—college, famous females, careers.

Coding Reliability

When two judges independently read four sample articles, the judges (coders) agreed on 88% of the categorizations.

Findings

Two findings are worth noting. *First*, there is a relationship between the content of *Seventeen* Magazine and events in the larger society such as the women's movement. Higher percentages of feminist messages are found in 1945 (the Second World War mobilization effort during which many women held high paying jobs), 1975 (the social reform movements of the late 1960s and early 1970s), and 1995 (during the most recent wave of the women's movement). The 1980s in the United States were years of feminist backlash (Faludi, 1992), and the percent of articles with feminist content fell from 40% in 1975 to 35% in 1985%.

Second, the changes in article content are slight and do not adequately reflect the various roles that teen females occupy and to which many of them aspire. The content of the articles thus lags behind changes in the social structure. This is an example of cultural lag. Feminist scholars and conflict sociologists generally might make the observation that the content of *Seventeen* Magazine serves the latent function of oppressing females, by emphasizing traditional roles and aspirations and by underemphasizing the opportunities for changing the institutional practices that have kept females in subservient positions in the social structure. From these viewpoints, the mass media may be characterized as opiates of the masses.

Source: Adapted from Schlenker, Caron and Halteman, 1998.

Capitalist Development

Gerstel and Gross (1995) analyze the structural factors that make family units a function of economic dependency. Popular myth has it that people stay together for reasons of love. Their historical analysis focuses on the evolution of the family since the colonial period. In their study, they find that colonial families were not self-sufficient units because they relied on neighbors and kin for exchange of domestic goods and work.

The father was the head of the family and controlled the family's estate until his death. The family was a unit of production, sharing in what they needed. Although women's and men's work was distinct, they both welcomed and reared children together. Children offered their labor to the family and were viewed as providing security to aging parents.

However, in the late 1700s and early 1800s, the family was transformed with the advent of factories under industrial capitalism. The new economic arrangement undermined the family economy. Land became difficult to procure and production moved out of the home. The changing economic landscape also transformed the ideas about home and work by compartmentalizing the two domains as separate but interrelated institutions. Home now became a place of refuge and recreation. Men were engaged in productive labor that paid them money wages. A sharp demarcation between women's and men's lives took place in the nineteenth century that came to be known as the cult of true womanhood. **The cult of true womanhood** is a Victorian idea-defining women as fragile and helpless. It also emphasizes that women's place is at home and that their primary responsibility is to raise children and to look after the house.

TABLE 7.1. Content Analysis of Seventeen, 1945-1995. _____

Category of Article	Percent of Articles, by Year₁					
	1945	1955	1965	1975	1985	1995
TRADITIONAL						
Appearance	23	43	48	35	42	45
Male-Female Relations	17	14	13	06	13	14
Home	08	17	13	19	10	01
TOTAL TRADITIONAL₁	**48**	**74**	**74**	**60**	**65**	**60**
FEMINIST						
Self-Development	32	15	17	29	23	24
Career Development	13	10	8	10	12	14
Political and Global Issues	07	01	01	01	01	02
TOTAL FEMINIST₁	**52**	**26**	**26**	**40**	**35**	**40**
TOTAL PERCENT₁	**100**	**100**	**100**	**100**	**100**	**100**

Source: Adapted from Schlenker, Caron and Halteman, 1998: Table 1, p. 1. May not total to 100 due to rounding.
1. May not total to 100 due to rounding.

This idea first developed among the urban elite. The proper place for the wife, according to the cult of true womanhood, is the home, and the wife's primary responsibility is taking care of the house and rearing children.

During the colonial period, children were welcomed for their labor. They had duties that included helping on the farm and taking care of younger siblings. With the arrival of the capitalist economy, urban middle-class children became economically worthless. During this period, both fertility and infant mortality rates declined sharply.

By the 1800s, boys were being socialized to play competitive games and girls played house. Children learned that women's family work was really play. Children were now viewed as emotionally priceless. Father's were now presumed (and were) too busy being the breadwinners to participate in child rearing. Since the father was seldom home, women had to be self-sacrificing and remain in the home for the sake of the children. The father returned home in the evening after a hard day's work, to his loving family. Thus was born the ideological concept of love. However, that marriage still remained an economic necessity is shown by the fact that women who were economically independent, opted to remain single. (Please read Table 7.2, "The Percent of Women Entering Marriage Before Age 20 by the Woman's Level of Education in Selected Countries, 1992." This Table indicates that economically independent women still do postpone marriage far longer than their poorer counterparts.) Men continued to depend on the unpaid labor of their wives. Men, then, worked for wages and women worked out of love for their families; working for love was not real work.

TABLE 7.2. The Percent of Women Entering Marriage Before Age 20, by the Woman's Level of Education, for Selected Countries, 1992. _____

Country	Percent Of Women Entering Marriage Before Age 20		
	No Education	Primary Education	Higher Education
Botswana	35	30	14
Brazil	56	46	14
Guatemala	72	62	27
Egypt	77	59	13
Kenya	78	69	36
Thailand	63	49	14

Source: Adapted from Riley, 1997: 23.

Since well-to-do women could afford to stay at home and cultivate the cult of true womanhood, life became very difficult for poor and minority women because they did not have the option of remaining at home pursuing leisure activities. There developed a middle-class, Victorian bias that women who worked did so for pin-money or to pass their time while waiting to marry. A man received a family wage to support a wife and children. Single men also received a lower wage until they married.

Women's labor continues to receive a lower

value because of the historical practice where it was believed that women did not really need the job. Silicon Valley, the high-tech mecca of the world, hires poor Asian and Latina immigrant women who cannot speak English and therefore will not organize. The poor immigrant women are paid low wages for jobs that are unsafe, monotonous, uncomfortable, and unsteady. The logic that employers advance for exploiting immigrant women are based on immigrant logic that the women manage quite well. The justification is that they are better off in the United States than in their own countries and immigrants remit money back. These savings are substantial in their home countries. The gender logic for underpaying women is by far the most unjust. It states that women can afford to work for less because it is assumed the women are attached to male workers who earn more than the women. Data reveal that eighty percent of the women were the main wage earners in their families (Hossfield 1994).

This myth persists in spite of the fact that current data on families reveal that fully 36.2 percent of all female-headed households live below the official poverty line. A family of four living on $15,141 per annum is the official poverty line. The percentage of female-headed families jumps higher when one controls for ethnicity. Thus, 51.7 percent of Hispanic and 47.5 percent of African American female-headed families live below the poverty line as compared to 29.1 percent of white families. Asian female-headed families have a higher rate of families living in poverty as compared to men. However, Asians are a heterogeneous group and recent refugee families such as the Laotian and Cambodian families have 61.5 percent of their families in poverty (Andersen 1997).

Motherhood: The Current Dilemma

Increasingly, women do not have a choice to work outside the home or stay at home because women's income is required for survival. However, the ideal woman remains first and foremost a mother. Numbers show, married women with children have increased threefold in the labor force since 1960 (Andersen 1997) out of economic necessity.

As stated earlier, motherhood was socially constructed in the mid-nineteenth century. Prior to that time period, children were integrated as part of women's work. Older siblings were responsible for the care of their younger sisters and brothers. Indeed, children were expected to do their share of work in the family. Since the creation of the mystique of motherhood, the dominant ideology has taken strong roots and conditions women's responses. Women attempt to have both a family and a career but have to choose one over the other once they have children.

Women's career strategies reflect flexibility to accommodate their primary responsibility as wives and mothers. Women take on part-time work or take extended maternity leave. Essentially, *most women readjust work schedules* that frequently leave them jobless. The cost women incur is extremely high, both in terms of material and psychological well being (Hoffnung 1995).

Isolation

Caring for a child is a full-time, demanding job. It transforms her life, leaving a woman in the company of an infant. She loses her self-confidence, becoming increasingly dependent on her husband for financial support and on the children for psychological support. She is dependent on the very people she serves. When mothering is over (in eighteen or twenty years), she finds she does not have the skills to return to the labor force. If women work, they feel guilty for leaving the child behind or in some one else's care. They are always pressed for time rushing to work and then rushing home with little time for themselves. However, mothers who are employed are better adjusted than women "without multiple key roles" (Hoffnung 1995).

TABLE 7.3. Maternity Benefits in Various Countries in the 1990s _____

Country	Weeks of Leave (Approximate)	Specific Provisions	Percent of Wages Covered	Provider of Wage Coverage
AFRICA				
Cameroon	14	—	100	social security
Egypt	7	50 days	100	social security and employer
Ethiopia	13	90 days	100	employer
LATIN AMERICA				
Brazil	17	120 days	100	social insurance
Costa Rica	17	1 month before and 3 months after delivery	100	social security and employer
ASIA				
Bangladesh	52	6 months before; 6 months	100	employer
China	8	56 days	100	—
India	12	—	national average daily	social security and employer
Philippines	14	10 weeks before; 4 weeks after delivery	100 for first 60 days	social security

Source: Adapted from Riley, 1997: Table 11, p. 41.
—Data not available.

_____ **BOX 7.3.** _____

Women and HIV/AIDS, 1997

In 1997 about 6,000 females became infected each day with HIV/AIDS. Globally, females account for 41 percent of adults who are living with HIV/AIDS. Of course, the percent of HIV-infected adults who are female varies by world region. In Sub-Saharan Africa, HIV is spread mainly via *heterosexual* sexual intercourse. Females there account for fully one-half of the nearly 20 million adults who are living with HIV infection. In most other regions of the planet, women constitute 20 to 30 percent of all HIV-infected adults. Since the beginning of the HIV/AIDS epidemic, females account for 4 million of the 11.7 million persons (34 percent of those) who have died of AIDS.

Source: Adapted from Population Reference Bureau, 1998: 5.

Violence and Social Control

Universally, women are subject to violence as a form of social control. For many women, safety is a primary concern (Anzaldua, 1987). Please read Box 7.4, "Homeless Women."

Rape

Rape is a form of violence against women and it is highly under-reported to the police, even in the late 1990s in the United States. It has been estimated that there are approximately 310,000 rapes or attempted rapes per annum in this country and that only one in four rapes is reported. There is another problem, that of classification. In this country, rapes that are reported to the police and that also end in murder are reported as homicides in the Uniform Crime Reports, the most frequently cited source of data on crime in America (Andersen, 1997).

Women: A Cross-Cultural Perspective

Cross-culturally, acceptable forms of violence and social control that target women masquerade under the guise of tradition or religious requirement. These practices treat women as objects of little value that may be replaced at the whim of their husbands.

The Dowry in India

Female infanticide is quite common, even today in many countries of the world. One variant of it, sati, was practiced legally in India,

---

BOX 7.4.

Homeless Women

Shadow Women by Marjorie Bard (1990) is an insightful book that describes the plight of homeless women, abandoned by men. Bard, herself, had been homeless for a period in her life. The book illustrates the tragic outcome of women dependent on marriage. Most of the women in the book become homeless as a result of divorce, marital separation, or death of a husband. Some women lose their jobs as secretaries because younger women replace them. Women tell awful tales of violence, incest and an unresponsive social system. *Most of the women had livea d middle to upper class existence prior to becoming homeless.* Most of the women are middle-aged and Caucasian.

These women are invisible in society, partly because they are powerless and not organized. Secondly, these women pursue a variety of strategies to remain undetected because their survival depends on anonymity. The number one concern for homeless women (as also for women in general) is safety. Therefore, they take extraordinary precautions to protect themselves and remain hidden for discovery may lead to a loss of their temporary residence. Part of protecting themselves is to not look homeless by looking their best. That is one of the reasons why it is difficult to detect a homeless woman.

Homeless women are unable to find a job because they do not have an address, phone number or references which perpetuates the continuation of their vulnerable positions. State agencies, designed to aid them, do not provide assistance because these women are not informed of their rights. Legal systems, whose responsibility it is to help women in that situation, have prerequisites. For instance, legal aid is not provided to a married woman unless she is divorced and has a child custody problem. There are tremendous inconsistencies in requirements regarding the social welfare system. The aid procedures and applications are extremely frustrating and demeaning and are not considered worth the effort. The social security system deliberately misinforms homeless women regarding their eligibility. Many homeless women try the legal channels before resorting to illegal means to survive.

Homeless women's experiences with an unresponsive system bring a realization that the system is against them because they are poor and powerless. Disillusioned, they survive by pursuing several strategies, which do not alter their condition in the long run. As a consequence of living an unpredictable life, several of the women suffer "psychological deterioration," which is never addressed. Agencies and individuals that they come in contact with believe they know what is best for these women. No one asks them for self-evaluation. Everyone silences the victims.

until the middle of the nineteenth century. **Sati** refers to the customary practice whereby women sacrificed themselves on their deceased husband's funeral pyre. It must be kept in mind that at this time in India, the practice of *child marriage* was common. This means that the widow might be a young child. The Hindu religion cremates the dead body. It is for this reason that the living widow was expected to use this particular means of killing herself. The practice was legally abolished by the British colonial government with the support of liberal Indian reformers (Heimsath, 1964). However, the tradition of wife burning has been revived as dowry deaths.

When marriages of upper caste girls are arranged by family members in contemporary India, they are required to pay a dowry to the bridegroom's family. A **dowry** is a sum of money or property which is brought to the marriage by the family of the bride. To whom it is given varies across cultures. In traditional India, it went to the family of the groom.

The Brahmins are the highest caste in India. The parents of a Brahmin son could demand, and receive, a large dowry. The dowry might be very difficult for the family of the bride to pay. They save for it for years.

The dowry also is an occasion for demonstrating one's status through lavish gift giving. Dowry includes cash, jewelry, clothes, gifts for all the members of the bridegroom's family and relatives, a car, and/or expensive household appliances. A house or apartment may also be part of the bargain. In addition, the bride's family pays for all the expenses associated with the ceremony and of the wedding (Chandra, 1998).

The salaried middle-class and lower-class families with daughters are particularly vulnerable to the demands for dowry from the bridegroom's family. They cannot afford to give extravagant dowries, although they often agree to pay the amount later. The new bride is not permitted to forget that she did not bring an adequate dowry. She is constantly harassed by her husband and his extended family members (Fernandez, 1997).

The bride cannot return to her family as it would involve a loss of prestige and ideologically she *belongs* to her husband's family. However, the women are frequently sent back.

Generally, the parents take their daughter back when they fear her life may be in danger. These women shuttle back and forth between their parents' home and their marital home with intervention from the police or **caste panchayats,** the local governing bodies of the village or sect (Fernandez, 1997). When women are killed because of an inadequate dowry, the preferred method is to douse her with kerosene before setting her on fire. Fernandez (1997) documents the threat issued to a returning daughter-in-law where the intermediary is warned that the husband's family should not be held responsible if the daughter-in-law sets herself on fire.

The historical connection with sati and dowry death is symbolic. Both have fire as an important element. Fire is said to be the most purifying of all agencies in the Hindu religion. Historically, a newly widowed woman was cremated with the dead husband because she had no status without him. In the modern version, the departure from tradition occurs when the young bride is actually murdered by her husband or his family. There is absolutely no legal sanction for the act.

Dowry is a woman's share (which goes to the family of the man she marries) of her father's property. By **customary law**—according to traditional practices as they are carried out in the present day—she and only she can dispose of it. However, an Indian woman, whose life is sheltered and her marriage is arranged, has few rights, in reality, if her husband does not support her. It must be pointed out that dowry deaths are not a pervasive phenomenon in India. It is regional in nature, mainly confined to parts of northern and western India. Not all Indian families kill their daughters-in-law, but a segment of the aspiring middle-class does so.

Foot Binding in Traditional China

In China, the custom of binding women's feet was culturally sanctioned as a sign of beauty. Peasant women did not have their feet bound because they had to work in the fields. Older women bound the feet of young girls. The tradition tied the feet of five-year-old girls by twisting the toes under their arches (Saltzberg and Chrisler, 1995).

TABLE 7.4. Women's Share of Political Offices, in Selected Countries, 1994.

	Percent Filled by Women		
Country	Seats in Parliament	Ministerial Level	Subministerial Level
AFRICA			
Cameroon	12	3	5
Egypt	2	4	0
Kenya	3	0	4
Sudan	15	0	0
ASIA			
Bangladesh	10	8	2
China	21	6	4
India	7	3	7
South Korea	1	4	0
Philippines	11	8	11
LATIN AMERICA			
Brazil	6	5	11
Costa Rica	14	10	9
Mexico	8	5	5

Source: Adapted from Riley, 1997: Table 4, p. 13.

TABLE 7.5. Percent Illiterate, by Sex and Age Categories, for Various Countries in the 1990s.

	Percent Illiterate			
	Ages 15-24		Ages 25+	
Country	Women	Men	Women	Men
AFRICA				
Cameroon	29	15	68	43
Egypt	46	29	78	50
Ethiopia	69	51	89	74
Kenya	14	8	54	26
Sudan	61	41	88	63
ASIA				
Bangladesh	73	55	87	63
China	13	4	54	23
India	60	34	81	50
Malaysia	17	10	62	30
Philippines	4	4	9	7
LATIN AMERICA				
Brazil	10	15	25	22
Costa Rica	2	3	10	10
Mexico	5	4	20	13

Source: Adapted from Riley, 1997: Table 1, p. 7.

Piercy (1995) compares the cultivation of the bonsai tree to femininity. The bonsai tree is pruned carefully every day. The gardener whittles back the branches as he mumbles about the nature of the tree to be small. He also informs the bonsai tree about its good fortune because it has its very own pot to grow in. Distorted notions of femininity are similar to the bonsai tree where, like the tree, women's feet are bound and the brains are crippled. The sole reason for the practice is to be decorative like the bonsai tree.

Female Circumcision

The term **female circumcision** or **female genital mutilation** (FGM) refers to at least three practices that are embedded deeply in the culture of many ethnic groups around the world. Please read Table 7.6, "Prevalence of Female Genital Mutilation Among Women Aged 15-49 in Selected Countries, 1990-1996." One practice, common in Egypt, is called **Sunna circumcision,** after the Arabic word for tradition. In this procedure, the clitoral foreskin (or prepuce) is removed. Sometimes all or part of the clitoris also is removed. A second practice involves the removal of the clitoris along with the labia minora. A third practice, called **infibulation** or **pharonic circumcision** is the most severe. Infibulation is common in Africa. It involves the removal of the clitoris, the labia minora, most of the labia majora, and the sewing together of the raw surfaces of the labia majora, leaving only an opening large enough for the passage of menses and of urine.

TABLE 7.6. Prevalence of Female Genital Mutilation Among Women Aged 15-49 in Selected Countries, 1990-1996

Country	Percent Of Women Aged 15-49 Who Are Genitally Mutilated
Tanzania	18
Côte d'Ivoire	43
Northern Sudan	89
Mali	94
Eritrea	95
Egypt	97

Source: Adapted from Kate Chalkley, 1997: 5.

There are short-term and longer-term health consequences of FGM (Chalkley, 1997; Carr, 1997). In the short term, shock, hemorrhage, infection, and even death can result from the procedures which often are performed under non-sterile conditions. Longer term consequences include chronic reproductive tract infections, chronic pelvic pain, and painful sexual intercourse. The infibulated female must be cut open in order to have sexual relations with her husband, and she may be sewn up again if he leaves home for an extended period of time, as on a business trip abroad. The infibulated female must be cut open further if she is to give birth vaginally. After birth, the woman often will be again infibulated. Then, she will be cut open in order to have sexual relations with her husband. These repeated procedures over time can lead to a build up of scar tissue, leading to urinary and menstrual complications.

FGM is most common in parts of the Arab peninsula and in sub-Saharan Africa. The World Health Organization has documented FGM among some groups in Asia as well as among Arab and African immigrants in North America, Australia, and Europe. The Centers for Disease Control in Atlanta, Georgia now estimates that more than 150,000 girls currently residing in the United States either have experienced FGM or risk having the operation this year. In 1997, a new law took effect in that criminalizes FGM (Chalkley, 1997: 4). This law requires

- federal authorities to inform new immigrants from the Middle Easy and Africa, where FGM is prevalent, that they face up to five years in prison if they perform the procedure or arrange it to be performed on their daughters.
- United States representatives to international financial institutions (e.g., the World Bank, the International Monetary Fund) to oppose aid to countries whose governments fail to enact educational programs that combat FGM.
- The United States Department of Health and Human Services educate Arab and African immigrant communities in the United States on the psychological and physical health consequences of FGM. It is worth noting, however, that *no funding has been allocated for these services.*

In Northern Sudan, young girls are circumcised and infibulated. The genital mutilation is

an effective way of controlling the sexuality of women. The practice is commonly associated with the Islamic faith in Africa, Malaysia, and Indonesia. Some Middle eastern countries that follow the Islamic faith do not circumcise their women. The practice is said to be dictated by tradition where the holy text of Islam, the **Koran** is cited as justification. However, many scholars can find no place in the Koran where female genital mutilation is mandated.

The story of Aman, a young Sudanese girl, is the story of one female's coming to terms with FGM. In Aman's culture, older men marry younger women. A man is permitted to take several wives and conflicts among co-wives occur, although a system of informal authority among the wives helps to keep conflicts in abeyance. Women and the young do most of the hard-physical labor, which requires them to be out in public. A herding life-style makes a division between the sexes difficult because these people need to be flexible and mobile. Divorce is common and women wield some influence in the system.

Aman is circumcised before she reaches puberty. An older woman performs the circumcision. When she marries, she is very afraid of the process of being **disvirgined**—a term used by Aman in referring to the first time she is to have sexual relations with her husband. Aman's husband locks her up and makes preparations to cut her open with a razor. She runs away. Subsequently, she uses intercourse as an economic transaction. Aman's early experience with circumcision has a far-reaching impact on her development as a woman. Throughout her autobiography, the reader is aware of the fear that lurks in Aman's existence. Early in the narrative her fear that she may be killed because she is fond of an Italian boy, is very real (Barnes and Boddy, 1995).

What is common in all three societies—India, Somalia, and traditional China? All three societies use religion or tradition to justify the oppression of women. In all three societies, marriages are arranged by the parents, and male and female children are used to seal alliances between families (and sometimes between countries). In all three societies, the honor of the family depends on the compliance of their children. Women, as bearers of tradition can betray family honor by becoming pregnant by someone other than her husband, as was the case of the no-name woman. Women's fertility is prized because it ensures the continuation of the lineage. However, it has to be strictly controlled and monitored. Women are seen as inferior, less-valued beings, who need to be controlled. In all three societies, younger women are abused by older women who police the system (Walker and Parmar, 1993; Daly, 1979).

Sex and Gender in the United States

Sex and gender influence our life experiences in all known human societies, both past and present. There is tremendous variation across types of societies in the specific ways that sex and gender influence social life. Even within a particular type of society—hunting and gathering, feudal, modern industrial, post-industrial—there is significant variation in the ways that sex and gender influence the experience and structuring of social life.

This complexity and variation make it difficult to study sex and gender reliably and validly. Nonetheless, we now examine various aspects of sex and gender among various cultural and ethnic groups in the United States.

Native American Women

Economic Independence and Desirability: The Case of the Osage Women

Native American women are the earliest known inhabitants of the United States. Like their African American sisters, Native American women have a high rate of teen pregnan-

cies and female-headed households. Although there are several variations in the pattern of family life within the group, men still control the lives of women. Like the society in Aman's tribe, Native American women have been involved in intensive labor (Gonzales, 1994).

Even though two-thirds of the Native American tribes were based on matrilineal descent and matrilocal residence, Native American women are conspicuously absent in existing literature. Wilson's (1994) study on the Osage women, analyzes the changes that occurred within the community from 1870-1980. These changes were triggered by contact with western intruders and interfering government policies, which were governed by a civilizing mission to educate and convert the heathens.

In 1897, oil was discovered on the Osage reservation, which generated unwanted publicity. Anglo suitors became interested in marrying Osage women because of their new-found wealth. However, Osage women within the tribe had to struggle to acquire political power. The Osage men objected to granting power to women because they were afraid that the women's white husbands would gain access and influence through their Osage wives.

Hale, a long time resident of Osage County, had a nephew, Ernest Burkhart, who had married an Osage woman. The uncle and nephew hatched a plot to murder the female relatives of the Osage woman, thereby acquiring all the head rights and properties. The killings lasted from 1921-1926 and Ernest was the loudest in his proclamation of outrage at the murders. Eventually Hale and Ernest were caught.

TABLE 7.7.   Age-Adjusted Mortality Rates Due to Various Causes of Death per 100,000 Persons in the United States, By Sex, Race and Ethnicity, 1995

RACE OR ETHNICITY	Homicides		Motor Vehicle Accidents		Suicides	
	Male	Female	Male	Female	Male	Female
African American	70.7	13.4	25.3	08.5	12.9	02.1
Hispanic	28.4	04.8	25.2	08.2	12.6	02.1
Non-Hispanic Whites	05.6	02.6	21.6	09.7	20.2	04.8

Source: Adapted from Banks, 1998: Table 2, p. 280.

─── **BOX 7.5.** ───

Domestic Chores Still Primarily Women's Responsibility

Have you heard the rumor that husbands in the United States are doing more housework compared to a decade ago? For example, about a decade ago married mothers performed two-thirds of the household chores, compared to 85 percent in the mid 1960s. Recent studies indicate that "men have *not* increased the hours they spend doing domestic chores during the past decade" in the United States. The apparent increase in husbands' share of housework "reflects the fact that *women have been doing less housework, rather than men picking up more of the slack.*"

Source: Adapted from Bianchi and Spain, 1997: 2. Italics added.

The litigation and murder trial led to the enactment of a new federal law protecting the women of the tribe and their wealth from unscrupulous suitors. The law explicitly stated that only those individuals who had half or more Indian blood could inherit a deceased Osage member's estate.

What is significant to note is, once Osage women acquired economic wealth, male suitors emerged to marry them. However, today, women in the United States earn about 30 percent less than men (Andersen 1995) and that makes men more attractive. Exchange theorists argue that women want to marry the men who are financially well off. The exchange is that the woman gets something she wants (economic position) and the man gets something he wants (beautiful young wife). *What would happen to this exchange structure if females earned just as much as males?*

African American Women

The Black Woman as Seductress

In the United States, sexuality has been defined by race and ethnicity. Thus, a racist and sexist stereotype is that Asian women are exotic, erotic, and "submissive domestic goddesses," while Asian men are either sexless or rapists (Walsh, 1990).

African American women and men are also subject to out-group sexual stereotyping. This sexist and racist stereotyping was underpinned by an ideology—an idea or set of ideas held by a social group (or groups or society) that reflects, defends, justifies and rationalizes the institutional commitments and interests of that collectivity. Historically, this ideology held that the sexuality of African Americans was menacing to the social order and needed to be kept in check constantly. Historically, African Americans have been controlled by the threat of sexual violence (rape of the women and castration of the men). Black women were raped with impunity and the myth stated it was her "morally obtuse" and "openly licentious" promiscuity that was responsible for the black male rapist. The black male had to be over sexed to satisfy "such hot natured" women. In 1892, there were 255 recorded lynchings in the South. **Lynching** was legally defined in many jurisdictions in this country as three or more people getting together to kill a man. This mode of murder—death by hanging—was an extreme measure of informal social control used by whites in the American South against African American males. Black men were lynched, allegedly for attempting to rape, or actually raping, white women. *Ida B. Wells's anti-lynching campaign* challenged sexual notions about black women and men. She called the community to unite against the injustice of racial and sexual violence. Wells documented inter-racial liaisons in the South. She also provided an example of a lynch victim who had been trying to avoid the advances of his boss's daughter by going so far as to leave his job. However, the girl continued to pursue him and they were apprehended together. The girl charged the black man with rape.

When these findings were published, Wells was out of town. Her office was burned to the ground and she was warned never to return to Memphis or she would be lynched herself (Giddings, 1984).

However, the images of black women's

sexuality and of the lynching of black men are alive and well. This was clearly demonstrated during the confirmation hearings of Clarence Thomas in October 1991 (Painter 1992). Thomas used the metaphor of lynching to his advantage. Over the years, the image of lynch victims has been reworked. Lynch victims are now seen as black men who were wrongly accused and murdered for raping or attempting to rape white women. Thomas likened the hearings to the lynch mob of yesteryear, even though there were glaring dis-similarities between the poor vulnerable lynch mob victims of the past and his own position, of a highly, educated man of status who had worked his way up from humble beginnings to be considered for one of the nation's highest offices, that of a Justice of the United States Supreme Court.

Anita Hill, on the other hand, appeared unreal as a highly educated, dignified, black female. Painter (1992) argues that both black and white audiences were unable to connect with the image. Typically, *the white American stereotypes of black women* have fallen into three categories, the Mammy, the Welfare Queen, and the Sexy Jezebel. Anita Hill fit none of these stereotypes. The stereotypes are these:

- *The Mammy* This stereotype is from the slavery era in this country. The term mammy refers to African American women who worked as domestics in the plantation house and who served as a nanny for the master's children. The mammy was depicted as fat and jolly. However, she was a strict matriarch when it came to her own family.
- *The Welfare Queen* This is a stereotype that says that African American and other minority women have children so that they can live on welfare. The condition allegedly is passed on from generation to generation from mother to daughter. Studies show this is not true.
- *The Sexy Jezebel* This stereotype portrays African American women as seductresses who can never be raped because they are always ready for sex.

In these stereotyped images, black women are denigrated in a variety of ways and portrayed as being traitors to their race. The black woman who was regularly raped during the period of slavery thus stood accused of an even bigger racial crime that of being mother and lovers of whites. Clarence Thomas evoked these old stereotypes by implying, through the lynching metaphor, that Anita Hill had joined the white lynch mob (who were white senators bent on confirming him because he was a black with Republican leanings).

Clarence Thomas' ploy is a good, if sad, example of the intersection of race and gender. In this particular combination of race and gender, black women are not supposed to speak out against black men. Black women should engage in the silence, either in the interest of racial unity, or because to speak out would embarrass the modesty and sensibilities of many Americans of many ethnicities, or because it is not proper for a black woman to try to bring down a black man. Anita Hill not only broke the silence, but she also violated an important norm of the African American community — that of speaking publicly against a black man and revealing the internal fissures within the community (Painter 1992).

Beauty: The Elusive Ideal

Dominant ideas of feminine beauty vary with time and place. What is common to all notions of beauty is the physical discomfort and mental anguish accompanying the pursuit of the ideal. The ideal's motto might be: "No Pain, No Gain." The thousand year old Chinese practice of binding little girls' feet, or the tight corsets of European women, or breast implants, or starvation and exercise to sculpt the female body, or plastic surgery on the face and neck—all these cultural impositions leave women both physically and mentally crippled. Besides, to attain the ideal is also expensive and time consuming. The practices are elite in that they are best able to be pursued effectively by persons with copious amounts of two scarce and widely valued resources: money and time. They render racial minorities, the poor, and the disabled as invisible. The secret that is never revealed after spending all the time and energy on beautification is that it leaves women ambivalent and unhappy with the results. In spite of achieving a physical semblance close to the beauty ideal, even the most beautiful women feel insecure because they are painfully aware of the transitory nature of beauty (Saltzberg and Chrisler, 1995).

A structural cause for the persistence of beauty myths is big business. The health food and beauty/body products industries are highly profitable industries. The pursuit of the beauty myths leads people to purchase many expensive products. It serves these businesses' interests to keep females dissatisfied with their appearances. The marketing of new beauty enhancing products depends on the unhappiness of women. Parts of women's bodies, like their breasts, are regularly on display in the latest fashions. Revealing women's bodies makes them feel vulnerable. The parts that show should meet the standards of the beauty myths. Fashion does not display the bodies of males in a similar and consistent fashion. Male fantasies of women's bodies help to maintain the boundary between male and female. Women talk about their "ugly" or unsatisfactory body parts, like other people talk about rotten vegetables at the market. But the ugly body parts problem is far more serious. Women are not ashamed about a mealy apple or a shriveled potato in the food bin. However, women talk about their "ugly" body parts—including the breasts, thighs, buttocks, and bellies—in hushed whispers and with shame. These are the very same body parts that are mutilated by male sex offenders or that are battered by abusive men (Wolfe, 1995).

Global Interdependence: Gender and Objectification

As part of the objectification of women, global interdependence takes on new meaning when sex tourism is analyzed. Women become objects when they are bought as prostitutes. Men become objects (in the eyes of the service provider) whey they buy the services of prostitutes. The role of the United States and Japan—and of the United States and the newly emerging states of Central and Eastern Europe—in perpetuating sexual slavery by exploiting Asian, Central European, and Eastern European women has been documented. In this section we focus on the United States and Asian countries.

In the Philippines, former "hospitality girls" and "comfort women" are suing the United States Navy, demanding justice for their children and themselves so that they may live a life of dignity that has been denied them so far (Coronel and Rosca, 1993). The description and analysis below demonstrates the manner in which women become commodities to be bought and sold to any bidder in the market place.

Kim (1984) demonstrates the pattern of the sex tourism industry by identifying four interrelated structural components. The structural components are as follows:

1. Unequal relations between and among nations
2. Unequal relations between men and women
3. The active collusion between the elites in those countries that supply women (the host society) and those in nations that are consumers of sex tourism
4. The vulnerability of poor, uneducated, and unskilled women of Asia

Rich nations, such as the United States and Japan, use poor Asian women as a tourist attraction for their countrymen. These women are used as prostitutes. The hierarchy among nations enables this exploitative practice. Asian countries, strapped for foreign exchange, offer their women as objects for male consumers.

Traditionally, unequal relations occur in human societies quite generally. The inequality of gender relations tends to be *least* in hunting and gathering societies, *most severe* in urban agrarian (feudal) societies, and intermediate in advanced industrial societies. That is, the relations between men and women in industrial societies tend to be less equal than those in hunting and gathering societies (folk societies), but they tend to be far more equal than those characteristic of feudal societies.

Those persons controlling the prostitution and sex tourism industries benefit handsomely from the miserable labor of women. Prostitution is a multinational industry.

Like any trade under capitalism, the sex industry seeks cheaper and cheaper sources of women. In the process, they move operations to different Asian nations to ensure profitability. Japanese women are expensive in Japan, therefore for reasons of affordability, the trade was conducted in Taiwan. One night with a woman costs between $48-$120, the hotel was not included. After 1972, relations between Taiwan and Japan soured because Japan normalized relations with China, Taiwan's arch enemy.

The Japanese soon found a new location, South Korea. South Korea provided better economic deals. $615 could fetch a round trip package for four days and three nights, including women, hotel and airfare. Similarly, the Philippines is considered a cheap location for sex tourism. In 1980, a woman could be rented for $12.50 a night in Thailand or a man could receive a volume discount on a weekly rate of $50. Prostitutes in the Philippines makes $60 but actually receive between $4.25 to $5.75. The rest is distributed to men who own the hotels and clubs, tour guides, and to pay off the police. Deductions are also levied on the women in the form of fines, for alleged infractions.

The women are controlled by the fact that prostitution is illegal in these countries. However, Kim provides evidence of state sponsorship in the trade. Even international agencies provide support for sex tourism by providing financial aid in the form of loans to actively develop tourism in developing countries. The women who are involved in the sex industry are poor and uneducated with few marketable skills. They could work in Japanese owned factories, but the prevailing wages are pitiable compared to the lure of fast money in prostitution. Few women can resist the money given their desperate condition of poverty. Most of the women remit money to their families in rural areas.

Current Position: The Feminist Movement

Currently, a great challenge facing the feminist movement are schisms of class and race. Women of color are disappointed by the feminist movement. They view it as white, middle-class oriented, and as not addressing working-class concerns, such as those pertaining to child care, health care, and so forth (Garcia, 1994; Bard, 1990; Hooks, 1989; Anzaldua, 1983). Bard (1990) wrote a scathing indictment

of the feminist movement because it had failed the cause of homeless women.

Apart from fighting racism externally, women of color also have to contend with sexist behavior from within their ethnic community. Male dominated civil rights movements in ethnic communities accuse women of betraying the common cause of racial oppression. Feminists are seen as aping white women and abandoning their traditional roles supportive of men and families. Women of color are triply oppressed by the intersection of race, class, and gender.

Some Proposed Solutions

There are many solutions proposed to end unequal treatment on the basis of sex, gender, and sexual orientation. Here are but a few of them, viewed largely from one way of knowing. Weisstein's (1995) seminal article on male scientific authority constructing women challenges the scientific nature of science in defining women. Her research supports the finding that the bias of the researcher will influence the results: we tend to find answers where we look. For Weisstein the social context is very important. She suggests that society should have the same expectations for both women and men.

For Hoffnung (1995), changing social values is important. She argues for structural change whereby women's economic independence would give them power over their own lives.

Saltzberg and Chrisler (1995) suggest women's wasted energy on beautifying themselves could be utilized more productively in creative ways. The result would be akin to a nuclear explosion. The quality and meaning of women's lives would be transformed in a positive direction if it was not "dependent on the silence of bodily shame."

Please select three different theoretical orientations (other than the one just presented). From each of those viewpoints, please generate four proposals regarding ending the inequity of unequal treatment on the basis of sex, gender, and sexual orientation. Which of these viewpoints makes the most sense to you, and why? The least sense to you, and why? What is your vision of gender relations in American society fifty years from now? How do we get from here to there? Please tell the reader about it.

Key Concepts

beauty myths

capitalist development and gender roles

caste panchayats

content analysis of *Seventeen* Magazine

criminalization of FGM in the United States

customary law

disvirgined

domestic chores and gender (USA)

dowry

education and age at marriage

female circumcision

female genital mutilation (FGM)

feminism

feminist dialect

foot binding in China

gender

gender and HIV/AIDS

the second shift

the Sexy Jezebel

the silence

homeless women

Ida B. Wells and lynching in the American South

infibulation

lynching

pharonic circumcision

racist and sexist stereotypes of the African American woman in the United States

sati

sex

sex tourism

sexism

social construction

subjectivity

the confirmation hearings of Clarence Thomas

the cult of true womanhood

the effect of the "silence"

the mammy

the Osage Women

The Personal is Political

the story of Aman

the structural components of the sex tourism industry

the Welfare Queen

Internet Resources

http://info-sys.home.vix.com/men/index.html

Document: The Men's Issues Page

The Men's Issues Page maintains up-to-date information on men's groups and movements. This web site links readers to men's groups and organizations and to other links that deal with male issues such as fathering, paternity, etc.

http://www.now.org/

Document: National Organization For Women (NOW)

NOW's home page contains many different resources on women's issues, including the latest legislative updates. Sign up for NOW's e-mail action list and receive regular "action alert" announcements.

http://www.igc.org/igc/womensnet/

Document: WomensNet

WomensNet is an international resource page for women. This page lists various international women's organizations and offers many links to a variety of women's issues such as health and reproductive rights, activism, women of color links, and other directories.

http://www-leland.stanford.edu/~slg/

Document: Chicana Feminist Homepage

This site offers information on Chicana feminist theory. It also contains suggested reading lists, and many links to other Chicana and ethnic women web sites.

http://www.umiacs.umd.edu:80/users/sawweb/sawnet/

Document: Sawnet (South Asian Women's NETwork)

Sawnet covers South Asian women's issues and links readers to legal issues, women's organizations, books, entertainment, etc. This web site provides a mailing list for women to discuss female issues related to South Asian women.

Suggested Readings

Anderson, M.L., *Thinking About Women* (Fourth edition) (Boston, MA: Allyn and Bacon, 1997).

Bard, M., *Shadow Women* (Kansas City, KS: Sheed and Ward, 1990).

Butler, J., *Gender Troubles: Feminism and the Subversion of Identity* (London: Routledge,1990).

Chesney-Lind, Meda, and Sheldon, Randall G., *Girls, Delinquency, and Juvenile Justice* (Second edition) (Belmont, CA: West/Wadsworth, 1997).

Jones, Richard Glyn, *The Mammoth Book of Killer Women* (New York, NY : Carrol and Craf Publishers, Inc., 1993).

Kates, Gary, *Monsieur d'Eon Is a Woman: A Tale of Political Intrigue and Sexual Masquerade* (Boulder CO: Basic Books, 1996).

Kesselman, A.; McNair, L.D.; and Schniedewind, N. (Eds.), *Women: Images and Reality* (Mt. View, CA: Mayfield Publishing Company, 1995).

Kingston, Maxine Hong, *Woman Warrior: Memoirs of a Girlhood Among Ghosts* (New York, NY: Vintage Books, 1989).

Moscos, Charles C., and Butler, John Sibley, *All That We Can Be: Black Leadership and Racial Integration—The Army Way* (Boulder, CO: Basic Books, 1997).

Rotundo, E. Anthony, *American Manhood: Transformations in Masculinity from the Evolution to the Modern Era* (Boulder, CO: Basic Books, 1994).

Stack, Carol B., *All Our Kin: Strategies for Survival in a Black Community* (Boulder, CO: Basic Books, 1997).

Learning Exercises

The learning objective of this chapter is for you to rethink women's roles and positions both in our society and the world we live in. In the writing assignments below, please follow the directions and write a response to the questions or issues as indicated. Please type your answers, double spaced, and staple in the upper-left hand corner.

Learning Exercise 7.1

Writing Assignment

Answer the following questions in an essay in which you use some of the key concepts from the chapter. Please type your essay, double-spaced, and staple in the upper left-hand corner. The essay should be at least three full-length pages.

1. What is the impact of the "no-name woman's" silence? Provide other examples wherein women have been silenced. How do you interpret silence in your culture?
2. Do you think Anita Hill was sexually harassed? Provide reasons for your answer. How did these hearings transform Hill's life? What impact did they have on the women's movement?
3. In what ways is women's work invisible? When a woman stays at home, we frequently hear the phrase, "She does not work. She is a home maker." Is it true that women who do not work outside the home, do not work in the home? Explain.
4. In your opinion, is gender a biological construct? a social construct? Are women and men inherently different? Why do we not understand each other? Do women and men communicate differently? Do we have similar interests? How do you account for gender differences and similarities?

■   ■   ■

Learning Exercise 7.2

Writing Assignment

Answer the following questions in an essay in which you use some of the key concepts from the chapter. Please type your essay, double-spaced, and staple in the upper left-hand corner. The essay should be at least three full-length pages.

1. How do your friends and family view the women's movement? Do you think women are in a subordinate position?
2. Make a list of the similarities and differences between men and women. Why do you think they are similar? Why are they different? What accounts for the differences?
3. How do Gerstel and Gross explain the development of capitalism and its connection to the changes in the relations between women and men? How do you view these explanations? Why?
4. Sex tourism and the objectification of women are common in Asia. How are women turned into commodities in the United States? Write your answer within the context of Bard's book on homeless women. Why do men discard their middle aged wives for younger women? Are they treating their wives like commodities? Is a human being the same as an old shoe to be discarded once it is old?

5. What are the common factors in the stories from China, India, and Somalia regarding traditional practices? What purpose do these practices serve in the subordination of women?
6. What is the dilemma for the working mother? Do women have a choice to pursue the cult of true womanhood? If you could afford to do so, would you want to do so? How do women deal with work, child care and taking care of the home? Who works harder, women or the men?

■ ■ ■

Learning Exercise 7.3

Writing Assignment

Answer the following questions in an essay in which you use some of the key concepts from the chapter. Please type your essay, double-spaced, and staple in the upper left-hand corner. The essay should be at least three full pages in length. Please answer these questions by thinking about current issues and how they connect.

1. Define the concepts of silence, subjectivity and isolation. Provide an example of each one from the life of your mother or from the life of any female relative. Are all women silenced? Why or why not? Can you think of other categories of persons who also are silenced? How do you account for the similarities?
2. There are a number of bad marriages yet many women remain in them. Why do they stay? Would the children be happier with a single parent and with peace in the house? Does having only one spouse in the house necessarily guarantee that there will be peace in the house? Why or why not?
3. When we talk about other cultures and the manner in which they subordinate women, do we see a similar pattern in the US? How do you see the myth of the ideal woman? Is the beauty image easy to achieve? Is it a form of violence against women?
4. How are rape and domestic violence connected? What are the common features in violence against women and children? How do you account for the rise in crime rates against children?
5. Why were the Osage women attractive and desirable to men? What did you learn from this episode? Do you think women and men are located in niches that make men more attractive as partners because they make more money? How is sex tourism a trade? How are the four structural variables listed by Kim related?

■ ■ ■

Learning Exercise 7.4

Engaging in Research

Answer the following questions in an essay in which you use some of the key concepts from the chapter. Please type your essay, double-spaced, and staple in the upper left-hand corner. The essay should be at least 8 full pages in length. Please answer these questions by thinking about current issues and how they connect.

1. Have you ever been in a position where you were afraid for your safety? Please answer this question with reference to rape, incest, domestic abuse, and verbal abuse.

2. How do the media portray women? men? What are the images that you see on MTV? Are they real? Analyze three songs from an MTV video and see how they portray women, men, and their relations to each other. (Please tell the reader the name of the singer or group and the name of the song.)
3. Pick up any 5 magazines and look at the images of women that are portrayed. How have they changed? Are they still supporting the cult of motherhood? Are advertising companies still portraying women in a traditional image? Do you see beauty myths manifested in these magazines. Tell the reader about it.
4. How do you see the pattern of behavior towards women of color or towards poor women? towards poor men? Do you think women are treated with respect in the United States? Do you think men are treated with respect in the United States? State your reasons.
5. Is it okay for women and men to be paid different wages for the same job? How are divorce and poverty linked? Are women doing well in the economy? Can we hope to have a woman as President any time soon?

■   ■   ■

Learning Exercise 7.5

In-Class Small Group Discussion

Think about these issues for a few minutes in silence before the class breaks into your small groups. It is important that each group has a fairly balanced number of males and females in it. Engage in a discussion with the members of your small group. How do each of you see these issues?

- Why is sex tourism in Asia thriving?
- How are images of Asian women in the United States seen as exotic and erotic?
- Why do Asian women marry Caucasian men?
- Why do white women marry successful black men?
- How do societies justify differential behavior accorded to women and men?
- Discuss some of the basis for explaining inequality:
  ✔ Is there any truth to the belief that women have hormonal swings and are irrational?
  ✔ What about men in this regard?
  ✔ What in your opinion will create an equitable distribution of rewards in society?
    ✔ Why do you think that in some domains (e.g., President of the United States, Chief Justice of the United States Supreme Court, Chair of the Joint Chiefs of Staff, Presidents of Universities, of Prisons, Deans of Colleges in American Universities, Chiefs of Police, and so forth) women have been unable to achieve parity with men?
- What are your suggestions for making this a better world?
- Do women abuse other women?
  ✔ What causes them to engage in such un-sisterly acts?
  ✔ Do women steal other women's husbands and boyfriends?

Small Group Discussion on Gender and Society

After you have completed the above small group discussion, please take a few minutes to address the following question. *Who is doing most of the talking in the group? Why do you think this person has taken on the leadership role? Who appointed her/him the group leader?*

_____

_____

_____

_____

_____

_____

_____

_____

_____

_____

_____

_____

_____

_____

_____

_____

_____

■   ■   ■

Multiple Choice and True/False Test

1. The "no-name woman" was Maxine Hong Kingston's _____.
   A. grandmother
   B. aunt
   C. mother

2. The Hill-Thomas hearings divided the African American community. Many felt
   _____.
   A. Hill was unreal
   B. Hill helped the poor women's cause by testifying
   C. she was lying

3. According to the **feminist dialect,** knowledge in societies in which women are oppressed
   _____.
   A. is only accurate when viewed from women's perspective
   B. is unbiased
   C. should be egalitarian and take into account all participants' situated reality

4. In women's scholarship, the concept of "subjectivity" deals with _____.
   A. the social life of men
   B. women's irrational urges
   C. women's biological processes
   D. personal accounts of women's lives

5. A manifestation that women are a minority group is that _____.
   A. they are paid more than men
   B. they are paid less than men
   C. there is no wage gap between the sexes

6. In the United States little boys are socialized to be _____.
   A. sympathetic and co-operative
   B. independent

7. The Osage woman attracted many suitors _____.
   A. after oil was discovered on the Osage reservation
   B. after her feet were bound
   C. after her feet were unbound
   D. after she won a foot race in the community

8. According to Gerstel and Gross, the real demarcation in women's and men's roles occurred
   because of the development of _____.
   A. industrial capitalism
   B. television
   C. the personal computer
   D. antibiotics

9. In countries like Brazil, Egypt, Kenya, Thailand, Guatemala, and Botswana, what is the relationship, if any, between the woman's level of education and the percent of women marrying before age 20?
   A. There is no relationship between these variables.
   B. Economically independent women—those with more education—postpone marriage far longer than their poorer and less educated counterparts.
   C. The relationship is direct—the higher the educational attainment, the higher the percentage of women who marry before age 20.

10. Examination of illiteracy rates in the 1990s in developing countries like Cameroon, Egypt, Kenya, India, Bangladesh, and Costa Rica indicates that _____.
    A. there are no gender differences in illiteracy
    B. there are significant gender differences, and a lower percent of males tend to be illiterate than is true for females
    C. more males tend to be illiterate than females

11. The **cult of true womanhood** _____.
    A. developed first among the urban elite
    B. maintained that the proper place for woman was the home
    C. maintained that the woman's primary responsibility was taking care of the house and rearing children.
    D. all of the above
    E. none of the above

12. Two-thirds of Native American tribes were based on patrilocal residence.
    A. True   B. False

13. In the United States, the Asian groups with the highest percentage of women living below the poverty line are _____.
    A. Chinese and Japanese
    B. Koreans and Filipinos
    C. Laotians and Cambodians
    D. Indonesians and Malay

14. As cited in this chapter, in the United States the official poverty line for a family of four per annum is _____.
    A. $8,127
    B. $11,149
    C. $15,141
    D. $19,461

15. In the United States, motherhood poses a dilemma for many married women with children. Their strategy to cope with this is to _____.
    A. advance in their career
    B. put their children in a good day care center
    C. readjust work schedules
    D. stop working and be full time mothers

16. Two thirds of the Native American tribes were based on matrilineal descent.
    A. True   B. False

17. _____ is one of the most highly under-reported crimes.
    A. Murder
    B. Automobile theft
    C. Rape

18. In the United States, a problem in classifying rape is compounded by _____.
    A. women's reluctance to report
    B. rapes that end in death are reported as homicides
    C. is not clear if a woman provokes the attack

19. To what does the traditional practice of **sati** in India refer?
    A. woman being drowned
    B. women killed in infancy
    C. the wife has to marry her deceased husband's brother
    D. self-immolation of a woman on her husband's funeral pyre

20. **Dowry** in India is given to the _____.
    A. bride's family
    B. bridegroom's family
    C. to the head priest
    D. to the community

21. Much violence against women in India is connected to the dowry.
    A. True   B. False

22. When women are killed because of an inadequate dowry, the preferred method in India is to _____.
    A. beat her to death
    B. douse her with kerosene and set her on fire
    C. drown her
    D. push her from a skyscraper
    E. hire a hit man (assassin)

23. The practice of foot binding was a custom in _____.
    A. Africa
    B. India
    C. America
    D. China

24. The popular justification for binding women's feet was to _____.
    A. enhance their beauty
    B. make them work better
    C. reduce their height

25. Female circumcision is the mutilation of girls' _____.
    A. hands and feet
    B. genital organs
    C. facial features
    D. feet
    E. ears

26. The justification for female circumcision is said to be part of the _____.
    A. Hindu faith
    B. Christian faith
    C. Islamic faith
    D. Buddhist faith
    E. Taoist

27. In India, China and Somalia, traditional practices have a common theme which states women in these cultures must be strictly controlled and monitored.
    A. True   B. False

28. Married women in the United States currently are performing a lower percent of the household chores than their counterparts in the mid 1960s. Research has shown _____.
    A. that men have increased the hours they spend doing domestic chores during the past decade
    B. that the apparent increase in husbands' share of housework actually reflects the fact that women have been doing less housework, rather than men doing more housework
    C. that once a week fully one household in three now hires at least two people to do the housework

29. Hale and Burkhart hoped to become rich by _____.
    A. making patents for scientific equipment needed by the pharmaceutical industry
    B. murdering the men of the community
    C. murdering the female relatives of Burkhart's Osage wife
    D. adopting Osage children

30. After the murder trial of Hale and Burkhart, a new federal law was enacted stating that only those individuals could inherit Osage property if they had _____.
    A. one quarter Indian blood
    B. three quarter Indian blood
    C. full Indian blood
    D. half or more Indian blood

31. In American society, Asian women's sexuality is viewed as _____.
    A. aggressive
    B. exotic
    C. assertive
    D. masochistic

32. During his confirmation hearings, Clarence Thomas evoked the image of _____.
    A. lynchings
    B. lazy women

33. Ida B. Wells is famous for being _____.
    A. a singer
    B. an outspoken critic of lynching
    C. an actress
    D. a famous chef
    E. a signer of the Declaration of Independence

34. In the United States, the suicide rate (mortality due to suicide) is _____.
    A. higher among males than females
    B. higher among females than males
    C. does not vary by gender/sex

35. An explanation for the persistence of the beauty myth is _____.
    A. the profit they generate for business
    B. women's inherent psychological make-up
    C. women's inherent biological make-up

36. The primary consumer nations of sex tourism are _____.
    A. India and China
    B. United States and France
    C. Ireland and Greece
    D. United States and Japan

37. Schlenker, Caron, and Halteman's content analysis of *Seventeen* Magazine _____.
    A. lacked inter-coder reliability
    B. found a relationship between the content of Seventeen Magazine and events in the larger society
    C. found that changes in article content are slight and do not adequately reflect the various roles that teen females occupy and to which many of them aspire
    D. all of the above
    E. both (B) and (C)

38. In Sub-Saharan Africa, HIV is spread mainly via _____.
    A. heterosexual sexual intercourse
    B. homosexual sexual intercourse
    C. intravenous drug use

39. Women of color are disappointed by the feminist movement because _____.
    A. it is white and middle-class oriented
    B. it is too theoretical
    C. it is concerned with the law

40. In Egypt, Eritrea, and Mali, roughly what percent of women have been circumcised (genitally mutilated)?
    A. 1-2 percent
    B. 7-8 percent
    C. 94-97 percent

41. The most severe form of female circumcision is _____.
    A. infibulation (also called pharonic circumcision)
    B. sunna circumcision
    C. clitoridectomy (removal of the clitoris along with the labia minora)

42. The short term health consequences of female genital mutilation (FGM) include shock, hemorrhage, infection, and even death.
    A. True   B. False

43. Female genital mutilation is most common in _____.
    A. parts of the Arab peninsula and in sub-Saharan Africa
    B. Latin America
    C. the Far East
    D. Western Europe

CHAPTER 8

Social Structure of the Family

Today sociologists all agree that the family is the one social institution that occurs without exception in all societies. Indeed the family is one of the few cultural universals that occur in the whole of the human experience. While the family does exist in some form in all societies, the structure of the family varies from one culture to the next. For example, the family in traditional Mexican society today is the end result of several hundred years of evolution and in more recent times has been affected by the Spanish culture, the Spanish government, the teachings of the Catholic church, and the impact of Mexican culture and traditions. In view of the Mexican family's need to adapt to this complex of social, historical, and economic forces a number of social structures have evolved over time.

Family Structures

From the sociological perspective the family can be viewed as the basic unit of kinship consisting of a man and a woman who are bound by a socially recognized contract and includes any children that they may have. It is clear that many variations of the family exist in American society today and can include such non-traditional family units as occur in same sex marriages, mutual cohabitation, and group marriages. In American society a man and a woman can formalize a marital relationship by means of a civil contract, a religious ceremony, or a combination of these socially acceptable means of bonding. The family structure that results is referred to as the **nuclear family,** or sometimes as the conjugal family.

The **conjugal family** consists of two generations, as the husband and wife are considered the first generation and their children constitute the second generation. By definition the conjugal family is limited to two generations (i.e. the parents and their immediate children), although several attenuated nuclear family forms are possible. While children view their parents as their family of orientation, when they marry and have children they establish a family of procreation. The **family of orientation** is the family into which you were born and is the social unit that formed the basis for your early socialization into the community and society. On the other hand, the **family of procreation** is the family that you form when you get married. Obviously it is referred to as the family of procreation because the traditional expectation was that when a couple gets married they are expected to procreate. But in the sociological sense this would include any children you have or adopt. This development cycle starts all over when your children marry and start their own family of procreation (See Figure 8.1 below).

In terms of increased complexity in social organization we can move from the basic nuclear family structure and observe that a more complex form of social organization occurs in the **extended family.** By definition the traditional extended family consists of three or more generations and includes grandparents, unmarried children, married sons, their spouses, and their children (See Figure 8.2 below).

In a traditional society, like Mexico, the extended family may consist of four generations, although it usually only contains three

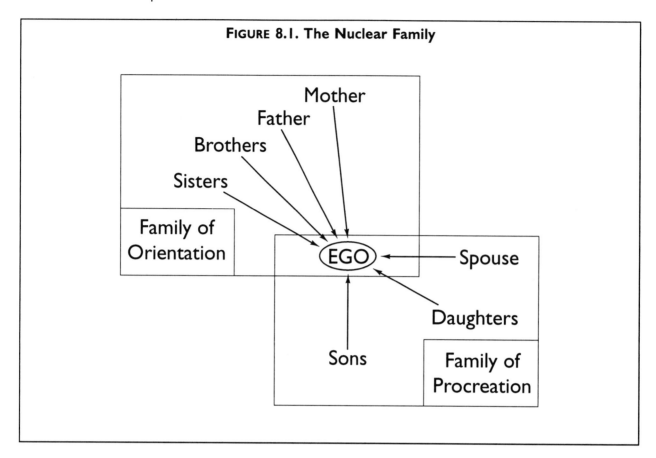

FIGURE 8.1. The Nuclear Family

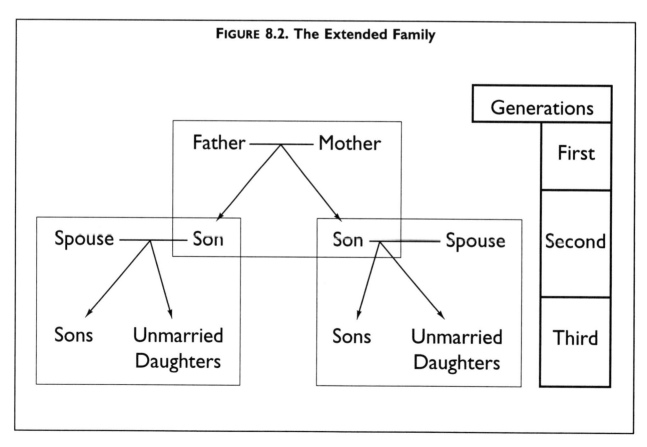

FIGURE 8.2. The Extended Family

generations, namely the grandparents, their children and their grandchildren. The extended family may be residentially consolidated (in which case they would live on the same plot of land or even share household structures, for example) or it can take a non-residential form (where the extended family members simply live in the same neighborhood or community). The extended family is sometimes referred to as a **consanguine family.** Consanguine simply means that a group of individuals are related by blood, as the term derives from the Latin word sanguine, meaning "of the same blood."

Cross Cultural Marriage Patterns

Cultural norms, social expectations, and established laws in American society today hold that one man should only be married to one woman at any given time. This cultural expectation is referred to as marital **monogamy.** However, widowed persons and, as occurs more frequently today, divorced persons are allowed to remarry. In more recent times the term **serial monogamy** is used to describe the tendency of people to remarry following divorce. At the other end of the marital spectrum we have the practice of **polygamy,** or plural marriage in which one person is allowed to have two or more spouses at the same time. Polygamy can take two basic forms, either polygyny or polyandry. By far the most common form of polygamy in all societies today is referred to as **polygyny** and is the cultural practice that allows a man to have two or more wives. **Polyandry** is a rare form of polygamy and allows a woman to have two or more husbands.

As a cultural option polygamy was far more common in ancient and more traditional societies and evolved as a survival mechanism and as a cultural adaptation. However, when various societies accepted plural marriages as a legitimate option, it usually took the form of polygyny, that is the practice of allowing a man to have two or more wives at the same time. For example, polygyny was the only form of plural marriage allowed among the Aztecs. And as a rule polygyny was only practiced by powerful

and wealthy men and served as an indication of their social standing and prestige in the community. Therefore the more wives that a man could have and support in Aztec society gave him more power and prestige in the community.

The most common form of polygyny in Aztec society, and in most societies where polygyny was allowed, was **sororal polygyny.** Sororal polygyny occurs when a man is married to two or more sisters. In their ethnographic studies of Mexican culture anthropologists have found the existence of sororal polygyny in Chan Kom (Redfield and Rojas, 1962:87-98), Ojitlan (Weitlaner, 1951:441-451), Chalchihuitan (Guiteras, 1961:199-206), and in Cancuc (Guiteras, 1947:12).

Sororal polygyny usually results from the cultural provision known as the **levirate.** The levirate was a rather common cultural formation in pre-industrial and traditional societies that required a widow to marry the brother of her deceased husband. In practice the levirate was not only an acceptable custom but a cultural expectation among well-to-do Aztecs. In fact the levirate accounts for most of the polygynous relationships that occurred in Mesoamerican societies (Soustelle, 1963:112). In more recent times anthropologists have discovered that the levirate is still practiced in certain areas of Mexico; as was true in Chalchihuitan (Guiteras, 1947:204) and in the village of Cancuc (Guiteras, 1947:12). The social function of the levirate allowed a family to maintain its name, titles, and property over a longer period of time, that is in spite of the demise of one of its male members. This practice also insured that the members of his extended family would provide for the children of a deceased brother. The basis for this cultural adaptation was the socially accepted view that children were their father's property and should remain within his family's kinship structure for all time. All of these considerations were of vital importance in traditional societies that lacked state or national laws and social welfare structures to insure the care and protection of children over the long term, and particularly in cases where one or both of their parents experienced an untimely death.

The rarest form of polygamy is polyandry.

Polyandry is the cultural option that allows a woman to have two or more husbands simultaneously. Although polyandry has occurred historically and is an acceptable cultural practice in certain societies today, it is none-the-less a rather rare form of social bonding. For example, in his now classic study of marriage and the family in various cultures throughout the world Murdock found that only two societies allowed for the practice of polyandry (Murdock, 1949:26-28). Interestingly enough, when polyandry occurs it is usually a societal reaction to an acute shortage of women. Ironically the shortage of women in those societies where polyandry occurs is often the result of the practice of female **infanticide** (Van den Berghe, 1979:62). It is also true that when polyandry occurs it most frequently takes the form of **fraternal polyandry,** in which case the woman's husbands are brothers.

Descent and Authority Patterns

Historically, **patrilineal descent** is the most common means of determining family origins, that is the determination of descent along the male line of the family. In the long term patrilineal descent is always assumed, while matrilineal descent is always a certainty. **Matrilineal descent** is traced along the female line of the family. **Bilateral descent** patterns occur in those societies where both families play an equally important role in the determination of descent patterns. This is the most common form of decent in American society today. In contrast, bilateral descent has symbolic value in the Mexican cultural tradition and this is the reason that married Mexican women keep their family surname and simply add their husband's surname to their surname (Foster, 1961:1178). In contrast, the use of hyphenated surnames is a relatively new idea in American society.

The residential location of nuclear and extended families has always played an important role in determining the nature of social relationships within the family and the relationships that exist between related families. For example, in a traditional society like Mexico, **patrilocal residence** is the most common residential pattern and usually occurs when

newlyweds move into the groom's father's household (Beals, 1946:178; Foster, 1948:264-265; Friedrich, 1965:193-195; Parsons, 1936:66-96). However, the most common residential pattern for newlyweds in American society today is **neolocal residence.** This residential pattern occurs when a committed couple establishes an independent household.

The least common residential pattern among newlyweds or committed couples today is **matrilocal residence,** which occurs when the young couple moves in with the bride's family (Carrasco, 1964:200-201; Murphy, 1976:193-194; Nutini, 1968:203-206). This residential pattern rarely occurs in traditional Mexican society or in American society and is often viewed askance. Even greater opprobrium is reserved for those who enter **beena marriages.** A beena marriage is a nuptial agreement by which the groom is actually adopted into his wife's family with the stipulation that any children and all property will ultimately remain with the wife's family.

As with residential location, the male lineage predominates in most cultures around the world and so it is the case in the Mexican cultural tradition. This is particularly true in terms of the **sex roles** within the family as they relate to issues of authority and dominance. Historically, **patriarchy** has played a significant role in the growth and development of the Mexican American family. It is from this heritage that the stereotype of male dominance within the family has evolved.

Matriarchy is the least common form of marital authority found in most societies around the world today. When matriarchy occurs it usually occurs when the wife/mother becomes a single parent (usually following divorce) or when the eldest male of the extended family (usually the grandfather) dies and the eldest female (i.e., the grandmother) is the sole survivor. Under these circumstances the grandmother assumes the position of authority in the extended family, that is at least symbolically (Murphy, 1976:192). It is at this final stage in her life that she is treated as the matriarch of the family. But in view of the ever increasing divorce rates in American society today, more families are assuming the single parent matriarchal form (Elsasser, 1980).

Social Structure of the Nuclear Family

It is an established fact that the nuclear family is a cultural universal and serves as the basis for all forms of social organization. Therefore it is not surprising that the nuclear family was the basic unit of social organization among the Aztecs of ancient Mexico and all other preindustrial societies. For example, among the Aztecs the independent nuclear household was used as the most fundamental source of tribute and social responsibility. The head of the household in Aztec society was the eldest male and he was responsible for any land and property owned by the family. And of utmost importance he was held responsible for the payment of the annual tribute to the state (Carrasco, 1964:188).

For similar reasons the nuclear family constituted the very basic unit of social organization during the Mexican colonial period. Invariably the nuclear family in traditional Mexican society was patriarchal, patrilineal, and patrilocal in form. As is true in all traditional societies, Mexican society was strictly a male-dominated society where women and children were kept under the absolute control of the male head of the family.

In contrast to commonly held views and social stereotypes the nuclear family in traditional Mexican society was actually small, as the family size ranged from four to five and a half members (Nutini, 1967:387). This means that on average there were two to three children per household. Undoubtedly the small size of the nuclear family was related to the high infant mortality rates that were prevalent during this period. The probability of an infant surviving beyond the critical fifth year of life was no better than fifty-fifty. Women typically gave birth to six to eight children, but only three or four survived to adulthood (De Leon, 1982:28-29; Nutini, 1967:387).

The most comprehensive distinction that can be made in terms of nuclear family types in a traditional society is to determine whether the nuclear family is independent or dependent. An **independent nuclear family** is one that has established its own independent living quarters and has demonstrated its economic and social independence. In most Mexican vil-

lages slightly less than half of all nuclear families could be classified as independent nuclear family households (Nutini, 1968:183). In contrast, **dependent nuclear families** reside within an extended family network and are dependent on the social and economic resources of the extended family for their day-to-day survival.

The determination whether a nuclear family is dependent or independent is often a function of the family's developmental process. This is true since most nuclear families begin their existence as dependent families and only after they accumulate sufficient resources to leave the protection and support of the extended family, do they establish their independent households (Nutini, 1968:203). This process stems from the Mexican custom and social expectation that newlyweds will move into the groom's father's household and will remain there until they can establish an independent residence. On average 75 to 90 percent of all nuclear families can trace their origins to an extended family unit (Nutini, 1967:388). It is estimated that between 20 to 30 percent of all families in Mexican society can be classified as extended families (Friedrich, 1965:193; Lewis, 1951:60; Nutini, 1965:125; Redfield and Rojas, 1962:91; Rojas, 1945:81).

It should be clear that the independent nuclear family is a mature family structure, as it has had time to establish its economic independence, to rear children, and to develop social relationships in the community. This process of growth and development means that most young couples will spend several years with the groom's parents. With hard work and the accumulation of resources, the young couple will gradually gain their independence from the extended family and move out on their own, for this is the cultural expectation that has evolved over the years (Foster, 1961:1179-1180).

Types of Nuclear Families

Beyond the consideration of whether a nuclear family is dependent or independent, it is also possible to delineate five types of nuclear families that are commonly found in traditional and modern families around the world. The five family types are:

1. the incipient nuclear family,
2. the simple nuclear family,
3. the aggregated nuclear family,
4. the complex nuclear family,
5. the polygynous nuclear family (See Figure 8.3 below).

In turn, each of these nuclear families will differ in terms of (1) whether they are dependent or independent, (2) whether they have children living in the home or not, and (3) whether they have other relatives or non-relatives living with them. Clearly these structural characteristics can reveal a great deal of information about how each of these families is different in terms of its adaptation to a variety of social, cultural, and economic circumstances.

The first type of nuclear family structure is very common and is known as the **incipient nuclear** family. This nuclear family type consists of only the husband and wife. Since newlyweds typically follow the traditional patrilocal residential pattern, most incipient nuclear families are also dependent nuclear families. This pattern prevails in more traditional societies today, since it is unusual for newlyweds to establish neolocal residences (Carrasco, 1963).

FIGURE 8.3. Nuclear Family Types				
Types of Families	Dependent/ Independent	Other Children	Relatives	Non-Relatives
1. Incipient Nuclear Family	Dependent	–	–	–
2. Simple Nuclear Family	Dependent/ Independent	+	–	–
3. Aggregated Nuclear Family	Independent	+	+	–
4. Complex Nuclear Family	Independent	+	+	+
5. Polygynous Nuclear Family	Independent	+	+	–

While patrilocal residence provides newlyweds with certain economic advantages, the most important of which is free housing, it also means that they must relinquish their personal freedom and social and economic independence. In the traditional setting newlyweds are usually given a small bedroom, as space in the extended family household is at a premium. In practice household accommodations are allocated according to the hierarchical principle within each family, that is the eldest sons are given priority in the selection of rooms and the use of household facilities (Nutini, 1968:178). In return for their accommodations newlyweds are expected to perform a variety of domestic chores. In actual practice this usually means that the daughter-in-law is under the direct supervision and control of her mother-in-law and the daughter-in-law quickly discovers that her living conditions are less than ideal in this traditional family setting (Salovesh, 1976).

One aspect of life in the extended family that can make things difficult for the young couple is that the son is usually required to work for his father as long as they remain in his household. And if the son is employed outside the family farm or business he is expected to relinquish his earnings to his father. Since his father is the ultimate authority in the household it is left to his best judgment to determine how the money will be spent and how much of an allowance he will give to his son (Nutini, 1968:206-207).

While the incipient nuclear family is dependent upon the protection and resources of the extended family, this is not always the case for the **simple nuclear family.** The simple nuclear family also began as a dependent family. But since they have children and greater economic resources at their disposal they can afford to move out on their own. This familial transition represents the overall pattern of social maturity within the extended family and can be seen as a move along the continuum of social improvement and economic independence.

However, not all simple nuclear families leave the security of the extended family. In some situations as the nuclear family matures and accumulates its own resources adjustments are made by the head of the household to insure greater freedom and independence for the nuclear family. For example, they may construct an additional room to the house for the growing family. By this time their relationship has matured and the son is allowed to keep his earnings and he is only expected to give his father enough money to help cover the day-to-day household expenses. At the same time his puerile spouse has had time to work out an amiable relationship with her in-laws and is learning to enjoy the closeness and security of the extended family.

However, the members of the simple nuclear family do not necessarily abandon the security of the extended family at the first opportunity, since the benefits of living in an extended family sometimes outweigh the disadvantages and inconveniences. This initial transition experience often sets the pattern for the other sons in the extended family. Usually the members of the extended family join forces and build the next eldest son a separate room for his wife and children. In this manner the process of assistance and accommodation continues and the extended family matures and grows over time (Lomnitz, 1977).

By way of contrast the **aggregated nuclear family** has had time to assert its independence and no longer relies on the assistance or support of the extended family. The aggregated nuclear family consists of the parents, their children, and one or more close relatives (See Figure 8.3). In many ways this family structure is similar to the simple nuclear family, with the exception that it is maturer and has more economic resources from which to draw. The key characteristic of this family type is that they have invited one or more relatives to live with them. For example, the wife's widowed mother may move into the household, as she may have limited resources and may need a place to stay. The advantage for the family is that the resident grandmother can help with the childcare responsibilities and the domestic chores. Or it may happen that the aggregated nuclear family may take care of a cousin or a nephew in time of need, for it is a common practice for traditional families, like the Mexican families, to succor or otherwise 'adopt' close relatives who have fallen upon hard times. In practice these **informal adoptions** are not at all unusual when families must survive at the subsistence level of existence. Close relatives, like nephews and nieces, that are informally adopted by more stable family units may live in these households for a few months or, in some case, for several years. These informal adoptions represent one way in which a more fortunate family can help another family in their time of need. It would be most unusual for a family to deny a call for assistance from a relative in time of need (Lewis, 1959).

The **complex nuclear family** is similar to the aggregated family but with the difference that it also includes one or more non-relatives (See Figure 8.4). For example, the complex nuclear family might consist of five children, a paternal grandmother who takes care of the children and does most of the cooking, an orphaned cousin, and a widowed *comadre* (co-parent) of the grandmother. The complex nuclear family is always an independent nuclear family and has established itself as one of the more solvent families in the community. This family structure has evolved and matured over the years and is simply reacting to the basic needs of relatives and close friends.

An unusual nuclear family structure that is known to exist in certain preindustrial and traditional societies is the **polygynous nuclear family.** As revealed in our previous discussion, polygyny was practiced among the Aztecs and was also considered an acceptable cultural alternative during the colonial period. By definition polygyny allows a man to take several wives and his wives are expected to share the economic and social responsibilities of marriage and provide for any offspring resulting from these relationships. In general when polygyny occurs a man usually only takes two wives and this relationship is agreed to by all the parties involved. For example, one study of family life in a rural Mexican village found that nine percent of the married men were involved in polygynous unions (Nutini, 1968:305).

In terms of household arrangement, there are two types of polygynous structures. In the first type the husband and his wives occupy a common household and they constitute one independent polygynous family. This structural arrangement usually occurs in sororal polygyny and is also typical of polygynous unions where only two wives are involved. In sororal polygyny the co-wives are sisters and they share all the domestic chores and childcare responsibilities. In the second type of arrange-

ment the husband continues to live with his first wife in their established household and then finds another house (a *casa chica*) for his second wife, which is usually located at a propitious distance from the main house. The first wife in these polygamous relationships is always considered the legal wife, while the second wife plays a less conspicuous role in the family and in the community. Naturally these polygynous arrangements require the husband to have greater time and resources at his disposal in order to support two independent households (Lewis, 1959:202-203). But unfortunately, these domestic arrangements are not always as cordial or convenient as the relationships that exist in the independent polygynous households.

In view of its various forms the nuclear family is obviously a very flexible and adaptable social structure that provides for the survival of individuals who are forced to live under some rather harsh conditions. From its inception the nuclear family is given aid and assistance by the larger and more resourceful extended family. Eventually the nuclear family achieves its independence from the extended family and as it gains in strength and resources, it, in turn, offers aid to the less fortunate members of the kinship lineage. In sum, the nuclear family insures the survival of dependent family members who otherwise might not manage on their own.

Social Structure of the Extended Family

Without any doubt the most adaptive social structure for long term survival is the extended family. While the nuclear family can manage the day-to-day problems, it is the extended family that provides for the long-term survival of the family. For this reason the extended family continues to play a very important role in more traditional social settings, like those found in the rural areas of Mexico and the Spanish speaking segments of the American Southwest.

In the case of the evolution of Mexican society the origins of the extended family can be traced to the Aztec family as it emerged several hundred years prior to the Spanish conquest (Carrasco, 1971; 1976). As early as the sixteenth century slightly more than half of the Mexican population was living in extended family units (Carrasco, 1964:191). While the nuclear family is essential for the procreation and survival of any society, the extended family is clearly a requisite for the survival of the family from one generation to the next. The historical record demonstrates that the nuclear family is too small and lacks the strength and resources to survive over the long term. This, in a great part, explains why the extended family has played such an important role in the development of the family in Mexico.

By way of formal definition the extended family consists of three or more generations of individuals who are related by **consanguineous ties.** In its basic form the extended family consists of the husband and wife, their unmarried children, married sons, their spouses, and their grandchildren. In the Mexican tradition the extended family is most often based on **agnatic kinship** ties and as a result is primarily patriarchal, patrilineal, and patrilocal in its structure and orientation (See Figure 8.4).

Almost without exception the eldest male in the family lineage is considered the head of the extended family household and is ultimately responsible for the conduct and welfare of all the members of his family. The head of the household is the undisputed authority in the family and his orders must be obeyed (Nutini, 1968:214).

Strictly speaking the extended family is inherently hierarchical and requires that all family members play (depending on their position in the family) either a superordinate or subordinate role. The role that an individual plays in the extended family depends, for the most part, on their age and gender. Adherence to these basic rules of age and gender stratification is of utmost importance for the survival of the family, as failure to observe these basic rules of conduct will eventually result in the demise of the extended family as a smooth and efficient social unit.

Within our structural and cultural consideration of the extended family it is possible to describe four basic types of families. These four family types are:

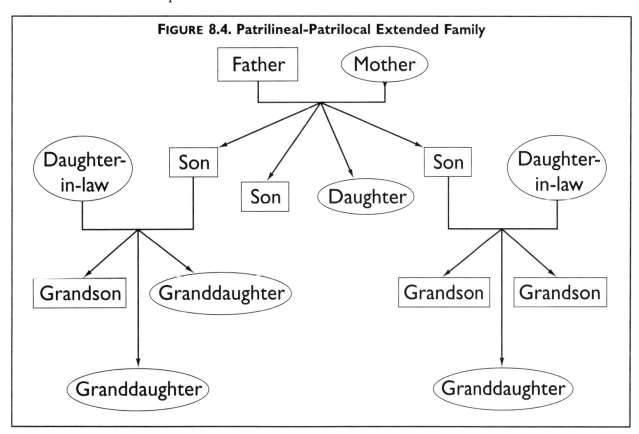

FIGURE 8.4. Patrilineal-Patrilocal Extended Family

1. the simple extended family,
2. the aggregated extended family,
3. the complex extended family,
4. the fraternal extended family (See Figure 8.5 below).

While each of these family structures is different in certain ways, primarily as a result of their adaptation to diverse social and economic circumstances, it is nonetheless true that each family type adheres to the established definition of the extended family. That is all of these families are based on the existence of consanguineous ties and they all include at least three generations of family members.

The most common form of the extended family, and the least complex structurally, occurs in the **simple extended family** and consists of the grandparents, their unmarried children, married sons and their spouses, and their children. The simple extended family is usually patrilocal, patriarchal, and patrilineal in its

orientation and social structure (See Figure 8.6). While the extended family can maintain its existence for more than three generations, it usually dissolves when the children from the third generation establish their own independent households. The demise of the extended family only means that the various nuclear families that once composed it have established independent households. These independent nuclear households will in turn serve as the basis for the creation of a new extended family structure. So the process of growth and development continues.

Within the context of a traditional cultural environment the extended family grows and develops out of sheer necessity. From the historical perspective the extended family structure in Mexico represents a concrete response to the basic need to survive in what can sometimes be a very harsh environment. For example, while boys and girls in this culture mature at a faster rate and are given adult responsibili-

FIGURE 8.5. Extended Family Types			
Type of Family	Children	Other Relatives	Non-Relatives
1. Simple Extended Family	+	−	−
2. Aggregated Extended Family	+	+	−
3. Complex Extended Family	+	+	+
4. Fraternal Extended Family	+	+	−

ties at a much earlier age than is normally the case in the United States, it is also true that their dependence on their parents and the support of their families is much greater. The closeness of these family relationships and their higher levels of dependency simply reflect the fact that life is much more difficult and tenuous at the subsistence level of existence. This is the reason that a young man must obtain his father's approval for marriage, as he understands that he cannot support his new bride from his own meager resources. From this basic relationship among social desires and needs and stark economic reality, it is clear why the extended family is so important in a traditional cultural environment and why the extended family structure has survived for hundreds of years.

Obviously, the extended family will survive and proliferate because it meets the social and economic needs of the second and third generations who constitute its form and structure. Therefore, in our example the head of household will determine if he can support an extra person, that is his son's new bride, and he also has to consider what additional provisions have to be secured in order to accommodate the new couple and the children who will inevitably follow. But the head of the extended family understands because he also had to approach his father and ask his permission to marry, thereby placing an additional strain on the meager resources of his father's family. So the cycle of marriage, family expansion, and growth continues from one generation to the next. Economic necessity and family obligations fuel this cycle of petition and dependence.

The process of growth continues from one son to the next and as each dependent nuclear family has children, the household accommodations of the extended family expand accordingly. With the passage of time and the accumulation of resources the dependent sons, each in their turn, will build separate dwellings for their families on the *ancestral paraje* (ancestral plot). By doing so, they achieve economic independence from their father's household, but they still have all of the advantages of physical propinquity to his household (Nutini, 1968:188). In view of this developmental pattern over three or four generations it is not uncommon to see a large house (that is the

main house) on the *ancestral paraje* surrounded by two or three smaller houses (Lomnitz, 1977:100-103).

If the sons are unable to build a house on their father's property, they will purchase a lot as close to the *ancestral paraje* as possible. In part this residential pattern derives from the Mexican family custom of subdividing a large lot into smaller plots, that are then given to each of the sons as they marry and start their own families (Foster, 1961:1180; Taylor, 1933:28-31). This traditional residential pattern of building on the *ancestral paraje* also explains why many families living on a particular block in the Mexican American community today are related to one another (Gonzales, 1985:21-27; Rubel, 1971:3-24).

In terms of the economic structure of the extended family two distinct patterns evolve; either the sons are totally dependent on their father for economic support or they lead an independent economic existence. While the issue of economic dependence or independence in the extended family is a matter of degree, most recently married sons do not have the economic resources to support a family. Consequently they must depend on their father's economic support.

As each son matures and as their economic position improves their dependence on their father decreases and their independence from the economic resources of the extended family increases. Over time each of the dependent nuclear families, within the extended family, gradually asserts its economic independence. For as long as they reside in the extended family household they are expected to contribute to the overall maintenance of the family by giving a portion of their earnings to their father and by making occasional contributions of food. In addition they are expected to volunteer their labor and participate in family construction projects.

In view of our discussion it is easy to understand how the extended family bonds people together and allows them to work for mutual support and survival. For this reason the extended family is the epitome of social exchange and altruistic consideration in human relationships. It is the giving and sharing of scarce resources to insure their mutual survival that promotes the imprinting of **familism,** that is the importance of human relationships and kinship ties. This also explains why the extended family plays such an important role in the lives of those who have experienced traditional extended family bonds, for it represents the essence of life in the family and in the community.

The Mate Selection Process

Sociologists have devoted a great deal of attention to the mate selection process, that is to the way that people select marital partners from the available pool of individuals that are available in any given social group. Some societies require that their members marry within their groups: a practice that is known as **endogamy.** Other societies require their members to marry outside their group, a practice known as **exogamy.** In the long term both of these mate selection rules work hand-in-hand to produce a balanced distribution of potential marriage partners in any given society.

The cultural rule that always sets a definite limit on endogamy is the **incest taboo.** In general the incest taboo is limited to the **primary relationships** that exist in the nuclear family, as it places a strict prohibition on sexual relationships between fathers and daughters, mothers and sons, and brothers and sisters. Some cultures extend the incest taboo to include all secondary relatives and sometimes it even includes the more distant tertiary relatives. **Secondary relationships** encompass those consanguineous ties that include first cousins, aunts, uncles, and grandparents. **Tertiary relationships** include those blood ties that extend to second and third cousins, great aunts, great uncles, and great grandparents (See Figure 8.6 below).

The incest taboo varies in its inclusion and exclusion of relatives from the connubial bond from one culture to another. For example, among the Aztecs marriage was prohibited within the *calpulli* (a territorial sector) and was always prohibited among members of the same clan (Vaillant, 1948:111). In most cases the *calpulli,* clan membership, and *appellido* (or surname) overlapped and were synonymous in ancient Mexico and they established the outer limits within which marriage was strictly prohibited (Carrasco, 1961).

For example, in pre-revolutionary Mexico the incest taboo eliminated anyone with the same surname or anyone from the same **barrio** as a potential marriage partner. During this period every barrio was associated with certain surnames and these surnames were associated with barrio membership (Nutini, 1961:71). In spite of these stringent rules of exogamy it is nonetheless true that on a larger scale most marriages took place within the village or *municipio,* as most Mesoamerican communities exhibited a strong propensity for endogamous relationships. It is reported that at least three out of four of all marriages took place within the village or municipio (Diebold, 1966:47-48; Nutini, 1967:399).

In addition to the territorial and clan considerations that served as the basis for the incest taboo, marriage was also prohibited between primary, secondary, or even tertiary relatives. Sometimes the incest taboo extended to fourth cousins, as was true in Tepoztlan (Lewis, 1951:76), Ojitlan (Weitlaner, 1951:443), Tzintzuntzan (Foster, 1948:249), and among the Maxatec Indians (Cowan, 1947:252). To this day the culture does not allow godchildren and godparents to marry or for god-siblings to marry without attracting social disapproval. This cultural prohibition on marriage between godchildren stems from the fact that the children of *compadres* (co-parents) cannot marry each other as they are considered spiritual brothers and sisters (Lewis, 1951:76).

Social Functions of the Family

As demonstrated in our previous discussion the extended family is not static but is in a continuous state of flux, as this allows for the introduction of new members and the release of long-term members as the extended family ages and matures. As a result most people live or have lived in an extended family at some point in their development and maturation (Diebold, 1966:41-45; Lomnitz, 1977:102; Nutini, 1965:123-127). For example, Carrasco found that agnatic kinship ties determined the domestic residence of four out of five dependent families in his study (Carrasco, 1964:198).

When examined structurally the primary difference between the simple extended family and the aggregated extended family is that in

FIGURE 8.6. Family Relationships

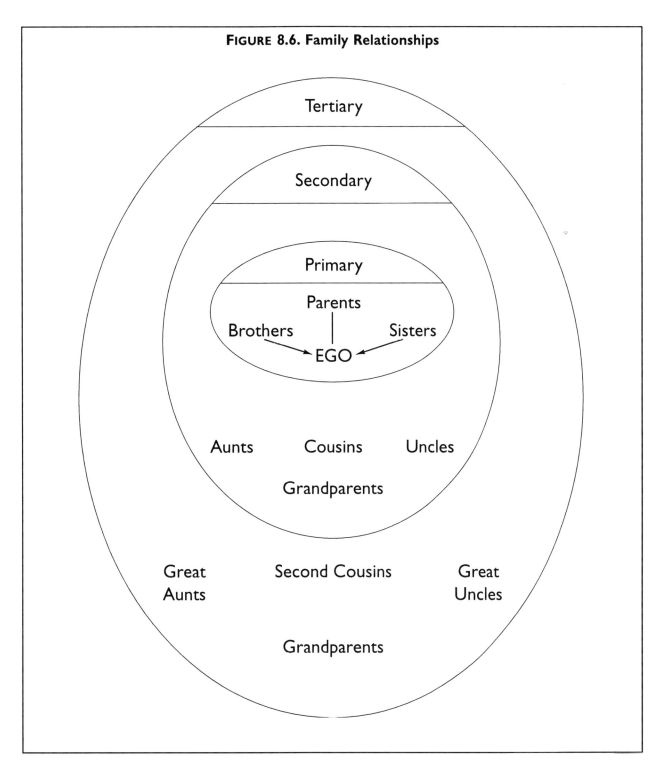

the latter type of family structure other relatives are present. Besides the grandparents and two or three dependent nuclear families, the aggregated extended family also includes other relatives who have taken up residence with the extended family, either on a temporary or a permanent basis. These relatives are usually lineage dependents who have agnatic ties with the head of the household and have called upon his altruistic feelings in their time of need. Usually these dependents are older relatives, who are beyond their productive years, or children and adolescents.

The term of residence of these older or younger extended family dependents is often permanent, as they tend to remain in the household until they expire, as in the former case, or until they assert their independence, as in the latter case. Relatives who are functioning adults are not as likely to attach themselves to a kinsman's extended family and when they do, their stay is usually temporary. The one exception to this pattern of temporary residence of functioning adult relatives occurs when a close relative has a child out of wedlock and lacks any means of support. Under these circumstances she will have few options but to call upon the largess of her kinsmen.

In a sense the extended family can be viewed as an informal social services agency that is functioning in an environment that has known very few sources of public assistance. Consequently the permanent residents in the extended family tend to be older relatives who can no longer take care of themselves or else they are the orphaned or abandoned children of close relatives. Other dependent relatives are the unfortunate widowed women with children or hapless unwed mothers.

Sometimes these attached relatives are children who have been given to their kinsmen by their parents. This phenomenon occurs when a family has more children than they can support. They simply call upon the largess of relatives who have more resources at their disposal. In effect an informal adoption takes place. These informal adoptions usually occur during infancy and the child is subsequently reared by an aunt and uncle, or by his/her grandparents. The child knows who his parents are but is simply told that due to some unfortunate circumstances his parents decided to allow another relative to rear him/her in their home. Once again the social acceptability of these informal adoptions is a practical solution to the economic hard times in a society that offers few social services for orphans and the needy.

Beena Marriages

Thus far in our discussion of the structural characteristics of the extended family we have demonstrated the universal prevalence of patriarchal dominance and patrilineal relationships. This structural pattern explains why a family will always turn to the male's side of the family for assistance and support. Therefore it would

be unheard of for a man in the Mexican culture to ask his wife's family for assistance, as this would inform his wife's kinsmen that he is incapable of supporting their daughter or sister. As a result a man will rarely call upon his affinal relatives for help in time of need but will always call upon his immediate family for assistance.

While it is true that agnatic bonds are almost universal and most extended families are patriarchal, patrilineal, and patrilocal, a small proportion are matrilocal. Here we have the unusual situation where the extended family is composed of a married couple, their unmarried children, and a married daughter with her husband and children. In the Mexican culture this familial anomaly is referred to as *irse de yerno* (i.e., to go as a son-in-law). This cultural adaptation is well known to anthropologists and is referred to as a beena marriage. A beena marriage occurs when a man has no sons but has several daughters and he invites the future husband of his eldest daughter to come and live with his family. In reality, the son-in-law is "adopted" into his family and as a result he acquires full membership in his father-in-law's lineage.

This anomalous situation is allowed to occur in a strong patrilineal-patriarchal society because it is an adaptive cultural mechanism that insures the survival of a man's lineage and family name, that is despite the fact that he does not have a son to carry on his family name or inherit his property. Within this cultural milieu a man without male issue is looked upon with pity; that is for having the "misfortune" of only having daughters. The cultural response is to allow a man to adopt his daughter's husband and this will help assuage his psychological urge to have someone whom he can treat as a son. In those cases where this cultural mechanism is applied the son-in-law is usually of a lower social status and is therefore willing to accept the fact that his father-in-law will always be the man in charge.

In addition to loosing a certain amount of social prestige and respect in the community, the adopted son-in-law also must accept the fact that he no longer belongs to his lineage of orientation and to the fact that he has been adopted into his wife's lineage. Therefore he is expected to give his allegiance and loyalty to a new set of kinsmen. This also means that he will forfeit his rights over his children, which is a very important consideration in the event of separation or divorce. In fact, his children take their maternal grandfather's surname and do not carry his surname (Nutini, 1968:205).

The Complex Extended Family

As with the other family types discussed thus far, the complex extended family evolved in response to a structural need in the family lineage (See Figure 8.6). The complex extended family consists of three or more generations; namely the grandparents, their unmarried children, their married sons and spouses, their grandchildren, one or more primary relatives, and one or more non-relatives. The fact that distinguishes the complex extended family from all other family types is that it includes non-relatives as members of the family.

In most complex extended families these non-relatives are often *compadres* or *amigos de confianza* (trusted friends) who have moved in with the extended family for a variety of reasons. This cultural phenomenon can be traced to the practice among wealthy Aztec families that typically included close friends, servants, and slaves as members of the extended family (Carrasco, 1964:205-206). To this day it is culturally acceptable, and not at all unusual, for large families to have one or more non-relatives living with them indefinitely.

For the most part these non-relatives are treated as members of the family and are given the same consideration as any member of the extended family. These non-relatives typically fall into one of three social categories: (1) **fictive kin** or family companion, (2) the *nana* (or nanny), and (3) the orphaned or attached poor.

In terms of their position and living condition in the extended family the fictive kin have the best living situation as they are often a contemporary of the matriarch of the family and are sometimes her *comadre*. Often the family companion is a woman who has lost her husband and lacks any means of support and will ask one of her close friends or *comadres* for support and is subsequently invited to move in with the extended family.

In those extended families with children and many chores to perform it is not unusual for them to have a *nana* to care for the children. The *nana* is usually permanently attached to the family, as she has no other means of support. For this reason she often plays a dual role as a *criada* (a servant or maid) and as a member of the extended family, as she is never treated like a maid. Sometimes *criadas* are drawn from the impoverished classes in the community, as they offer their domestic services in exchange for room and board. Once again the extended family has adapted itself to the needs of certain unfortunate members of the community who might otherwise be relegated to a life of penury.

Perhaps the most unfortunate of the attached non-relatives are the orphaned or attached poor. For the most part they have fallen upon hard times and in exchange for their labor they are treated as family members. If they are children or adolescents the family as a selfless act of altruism usually adopts them.

The Fraternal Extended Family

Of the four types of extended families found within the Mexican cultural milieu (See Figure 8.6), the fraternal extended family is somewhat rare. By way of description the fraternal extended family is formed when two or more brothers with their wives and children establish a common household (Murdock, 1949:33). In all the other extended families it is the husband-wife relationship or the parent-child relationship that unites the family. But in the fraternal extended family it is the brother-brother relationship that consolidates these families into an extended family unit. In this sense the fraternal extended family has a social structure that is similar to the nuclear family structure, inasmuch as it usually consists of two generations and lacks temporal continuity. However, like the other extended families consanguineous ties, rather than conjugal ties bind it.

For example, the typical social structure of the fraternal extended family may look like the graphic representation below. In this example, we have a three generational fraternal extended family, with family "A" representing the eldest brother in the family as the head of household. The eldest brother's family is the only one in the extended family unit that consists of three generations, as his son is married and lives in the household with his wife and daughter as a dependent nuclear family. In this example family "B" represents the second oldest brother with his wife and three sons and one daughter. Family "C" represents the youngest brother in the fraternal extended family and includes his wife, two daughters, and a son.

As with other family forms the fraternal extended family develops in response to changing circumstances that occur in the immediate social environment. The most common developmental pattern occurs when the head of an existing extended family dies, while two or more of his married sons are still living in the family household. In this case the brothers continue to share the household and live together as an extended family. In view of the strong patriarchal orientation of the Mexican culture it is the eldest son who will become the head of the fraternal extended family, for his-

torically the eldest son inherits all the real and chattel property (Carrasco, 1964:209). As the inheritor, the eldest son is expected to support his younger brothers and sisters. The primary reason for the existence of this cultural mechanism is the strong desire to keep the *ancestral paraje* intact.

Although the widowed mother may be recognized as the symbolic head of this newly formed fraternal extended family, as her opinion and advice is sought on all family matters, the major family decisions are made by her eldest son. However this established rule of patriarchal authority is sometimes modified as a result of the formation of a new fraternal extended family. Whereas custom dictates that the eldest son should take his father's place as the head of the household, sometimes it is the *xocoyote* (the last born son) who assumes the headship of the fraternal extended family (Nutini, 1968:211).

In these anomalous circumstances it is the youngest son who has remained in the family household until his father's death, at which

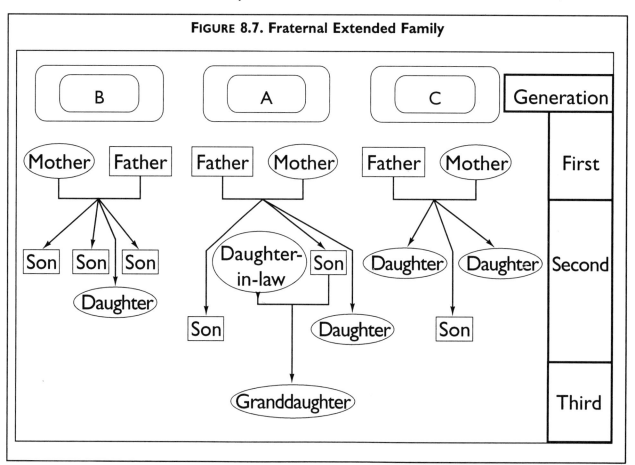

FIGURE 8.7. Fraternal Extended Family

time he is given the house, the property, and the social recognition as the new head of household. It then becomes the *xocoyote's* responsibility to take care of the house and family property and to provide for his widowed mother and any unmarried sisters who remain in the household. Usually his elder brothers have moved out of the house and have established their families. Therefore questions of authority and the ownership of family property are not as serious as they otherwise might be. The social and structural advantage of the *xocoyote* relationship is that the family property is not subdivided from one generation to the next, nor is the family property automatically inherited by the eldest son, as occurs under a system of **primogeniture.**

In some families the *xocoyote* pattern of inheritance is repeated over several generations and serves to maintain the family lineage for many years. The *xocoyote* pattern of the fraternal extended family is a version of the **stem family** pattern, found in various cultures, that allows the family estate to pass intact to a son chosen by the head of the family. The other sons either migrate, settle on family land in the same area, purchase their own land, sharecrop someone's land, or establish a household on land obtained from the spouse's family.

Conclusion

Following this review of the social structure of the family it should be clear that there is a direct relationship between individual survival and the ability of the family to meet these demands. Therefore as conditions change for the individual then the family also must change to accommodate and satisfy those needs as best it can, that is in view of the limited resources at its disposal.

For all practical purposes the family, as a structural unit in society is constantly changing and adapting to the changes that are always present in its immediate social, economic, and political environment. Therefore there is a close relationship between the demands placed upon the individual and the concomitant changes that occur in the social structure of the family. Consequently the social structure of the family reflects the social and economic conditions that make up its socio-cultural milieu. The family reflects these conditions since it is constantly changing to meet the demands placed upon it by its members and by the immediate environment.

Key Concepts

aggregated nuclear family
agnatic kinship
barrio
beena marriages
bilateral descent
complex nuclear family
conjugal family
consanguine family
consanguineous ties
dependent nuclear families
endogamy
exogamy
extended family
familism
family of orientation
family of procreation

female infanticide
fictive kin
fraternal polyandry
incest taboo
incipient nuclear family
independent nuclear family
informal adoptions
levirate
matriarchy
matrilineal descent
matrilocal residence
monogamy
neolocal residence
nuclear family
patrilineal descent

patrilocal residence
polygamy
polygynous nuclear family
polygyny
polyandry
primary relationships
primogeniture
secondary relationships
serial monogamy
sex roles patriarchy
simple extended family
simple nuclear family
sororal polygyny
stem family pattern
tertiary relationships

Internet Resources

http://www.familyweb.com/index.html

Document: Family Web

The Family Web is an information site, accessible to families all over the world. This web site discusses family matters such as pregnancy, infancy, parenting, and health.

http://www.acf.dhhs.gov/

Document: The Administration For Children and Families

This web page was developed by the U.S. Department of Health and Human Services. It frequently updates articles on children's issues and supplies information on Federal programs and legislation that affects children and parents.

http://www.childrensdefense.org/index.html

Document: Children's Defense Fund

This web site provides information on the organization, which acts as a voice for all children. The Children's Defense Fund web site also contains articles and other sources of information on minority children's issues.

http://www.plannedparenthood.org/

Document: Planned Parenthood

This web site gives location information for the local Planned Parenthood Centers throughout the United States. It also covers issues such as Roe vs. Wade, women's health, birth control, abortion, STD's, teen issues, and a section for parents.

http://www.buddybuddy.com/toc.html

Document: Partners Task Force for Gay and Lesbian Couples

This site offers a comprehensive list of articles and legislative issues covering same-sex marriage, including links to many other Right to Marry organizations. Furthermore, this web site discusses relationship issues between gay couples and other information, such as ceremonial marriage and domestic partnership.

http://www.divorce-online.com/

Document: Divorce Online

Divorce Online contains updated information on divorce. It explores the psychological, financial, and legal aspects of divorce. There is also a bulletin where people can discuss related topics, articles on certain divorce issues, and a professional referral service for people undergoing the process of divorce.

http://fostercare.org

Document: Foster Parents CARE (Child Advocates Resource Exchange)

Foster Parents Care is a non-profit organization dedicated to the internet community. Their web site provides resources for children and their guardians on issues of foster care and adoption. Go to the "Jump to:" box and select an area of interest (library, links, database, etc.).

Learning Exercise 8.1

Family Structures

The learning objectives of this chapter are for you to understand a sociological perspective on the family, especially the Mexican family. In so doing, this chapter allows the reader to compare the nuclear family with others types of family structure found in the world. Marriage is one of the most important relationships that make a world. Utilizing the concepts examined in this chapter answer the following questions.

1. Ask a married couple you know to keep track of the time they spend involved in household maintenance, children, outside work and leisure for a week. If you are married do this exercise on your own marriage. According to the different types of family structures discussed in this chapter, how would time be spent differently? Prepare a chart encompassing the activities of the husband and wife you examined. Discuss the differences in the time they used.

2. Describe and explain the differences between sororal poloygny and the levirate system. Why do these types of systems develop and what may replace these types of systems in the modern world? In what case are the woman's husbands brothers?

3. In your family of origin, what are the rules of descent, authority and locality? How are these rules different than beena marriages? Define a marriage and a family. How are nuclear family structure and extended family structures different? In what types of societies are they functional? What is the nature of the polygynous nuclear family?

4. Discuss how different types of family systems bond individuals together. How is a family a social system of exchange relationships? How is family the essence of life in reference to community and society?

5. What role does love have in mate selection? Describe to the reader the rules regarding mate selection. What is the function of the incest taboo?

Suggested Readings

Allen, Paula Gunn, *The Sacred Hoop: Recovering The Feminine In American Indian Traditions* (Boston: Beacon Press, 1986).

Billingsley, Andrew, *Black Families in White America* (Englewoods Cliffs, NJ: Prentice-Hall, 1968).

Ching, Frank, *Ancestors, 900 Years in the Life of A Chinese Family* (New York: Morrow, 1988).

Coontz, Stephanie, *The Way We Never Were: American Families and the Nostalgia Trap* (New York: Basic Books, 1992).

Glenn, Evelyn N., *Issei, Nisei, War Bride: Three Generations of Japanese American Women in Domestic Service* (Philadelphia: Temple University Press, 1986).

Gonzales, Juan L. Jr., *Racial and Ethnic Families in America* (Third Edition) (Dubuque, Iowa: Kendall/Hunt, 1998).

Hochschild, Arlie, *The Second Shift: Working Parents and the Revolution at Home* (New York: Viking, 1989).

Rubin, Lillian, *Families on the Faultline: America's Working Class Speaks about the Family, the Economy, Race and Ethnicity* (New York: Harper Collins, 1994).

Multiple-Choice Questions

1. Some examples of non-traditional marriages are:
   A. same sex marriages
   B. mutual cohabitation
   C. group marriages
   D. all of the above

2. In American society a man and a woman can formalize a marital relationship by means of:
   A. civil contract
   B. a religious ceremony
   C. a rite of passage
   D. both A and B

3. Of the sociological concepts listed below, which one(s) would describe the traditional family structure composed of a married man and a women living with their children?
   A. family of orientation
   B. conjugal family unit
   C. family of procreation
   D. consanguine family

4. Of the sociological concepts listed below, which one(s) would describe the traditional family structure composed of a married man and a women living with their grown children and their grandchildren?
   A. extended family unit
   B. conjugal family unit
   C. consanguine family
   D. both A and C above

5. Which of the following term(s) best describes marriage patterns in the United States today?
   A. monogamy
   B. polygamy
   C. serial monogamy
   D. polygyny

6. Select the one term that describes the most common form of plural marriages in societies around the world today.
   A. polyandry
   B. polygyny
   C. serial monogamy
   D. sororal polygyny

7. Select the one term that describes the least common form of plural marriages in societies around the world today.
   A. polyandry
   B. serial polygyny
   C. fraternal polyandry
   D. sororal polygyny

8. In ancient societies the primary purpose of the liverate custom was to:
   A. insure the birth of many sons
   B. keep a man's wives from being unfaithful
   C. insured that all the children remained in the extended family
   D. provide men with a variety of sexual partners

9. The most common form of family decent patterns in American society today is:
   A. patrilineal descent
   B. bilateral descent
   C. neolocal descent
   D. matrilineal descent

10. The least common form of family decent patterns in American society today is:
    A. patrilineal descent
    B. bilateral descent
    C. neolocal descent
    D. matrilineal descent

11. In a modern urban society the most common residential pattern following marriage is:
    A. matrilocal residence
    B. neolocal residence
    C. patrilocal residence
    D. primogeniture

12. In a rural traditional society the most common residential pattern following marriage is:
    A. matrilocal residence
    B. neolocal residence
    C. patrilocal residence
    D. primogeniture

13. This nuclear family type consist of only the husband and wife.
    A. the aggregated nuclear family
    B. the simple nuclear family
    C. the incipient nuclear family
    D. the complex nuclear family

14. This nuclear family type consist of only the husband and wife and their children.
    A. the aggregated nuclear family
    B. the simple nuclear family
    C. the incipient nuclear family
    D. the complex nuclear family

15. This nuclear family type consist of the parents, their children, and one or more close relatives.
    A. the aggregated nuclear family
    B. the simple nuclear family
    C. the incipient nuclear family
    D. the complex nuclear family

16. This nuclear family type consist of the parents, their children, one or more close relatives, and also includes one or more non-relatives.
    A. the aggregated nuclear family
    B. the simple nuclear family
    C. the incipient nuclear family
    D. the complex nuclear family

17. The extended family structure consist of how many generations?
    A. one
    B. two
    C. three
    D. three or more generations

18. Which one of the following is not a characteristic of the simple extended family?
    A. unmarried children
    B. married daughters and their spouses
    C. married sons and their spouses
    D. the grandchildren

19. Which of the following sociological terms describes intermarriage?
    A. endogamy
    B. exogamy
    C. monogamy
    D. beena marriages

20. Which of the following sociological terms describes the adoption of a son-in-law by his wife's family?
    A. endogamy
    B. exogamy
    C. monogamy
    D. beena marriages

21. When members of the same religious or ethnic group only marry members of their own group, what is this called by sociologists?
    A. endogamy
    B. exogamy
    C. monogamy
    D. beena marriages

22. Which of the following would be considered a primary relationship by sociologists?
    A. first cousins
    B. aunts and uncles
    C. brothers and sisters
    D. grandparents

23. Which of the following would be considered a secondary relationship by sociologists?
    A. great aunts and great uncles, and great grandparents
    B. aunts and uncles
    C. brothers and sisters
    D. grandparents

24. Which of the following would be considered a tertiary relationship by sociologists?
    A. great aunts and great uncles, and great grandparents
    B. first cousins
    C. mothers and sons
    D. grandparents

25. The incest taboo prohibits sexual relationships or marriage between?
    A. first cousins
    B. brothers and sisters
    C. second cousins
    D. depends on the cultural expectations

CHAPTER 9

Stratification and Society

Not being able to make that which is just strong, man has made
that which is strong just.

Pascal

■   ■   ■

There is a story in Boston that in the palmy days of the twenties, a
Chicago banking house asked the Boston investment firm of Lee,
Higginson & Co. for a letter of recommendation about a young
Bostonian they were considering employing. Lee, Higginson & Co.
could not say enough for the young man. His father, they wrote,
was a Cabot, his mother was a Lowell; farther back his background
was a happy blend of Saltonstalls, Appletons, Peabodys, and others
of Boston's First Families. The recommendation was given without
hesitation. Several days later came a curt acknowledgment from
Chicago. Lee, Higginson & Co. was thanked for their trouble.
Unfortunately, however, the material supplied on the young man
was not exactly of the type the Chicago firm was seeking. "We
were not," their letter declared, "contemplating using Mr.
_____ for breeding purposes."

Cleveland Amory, *The Proper Bostonians*

■   ■   ■

In ancient India, a young man, Stayakama Jabala, wanted to become a Brahmacharya. To pursue his ambition, he contacted a Brahman teacher. The teacher wanted to know his lineage because he only taught upper caste young men. He went to his mother to enquire about his lineage. His mother did not know it either because she had been a domestic servant con-stantly on the move and did not know the identity of his father (Gazetteer, Vol. IX. Part I.1901). Armed with this potentially damaging knowledge, Satyakama once again approached the teacher. Satyakama repeated the facts of his background as related to him by his mother. The teacher was so impressed by Satyakama's virtue that he initiated him as his student.

In this story, the love for truth established Satyakama as a true Brahman and successfully established his lineage (Ghurye 1969 and Census of India, Baroda. Vol.XXIII. Part II. 1891). It illustrates the fact that under special circumstances, individuals may move up in caste a stratification system (Census of India, Baroda. Vol.XVIII. Part I. 1901). Finally, the story demonstrates that systems of stratification are social constructions.

Shakespeare's (1987) last play, *The Tempest*, written in 1610-1611, is a complex tale of the relationship between the colonizer and the colonized. The play begins with a storm and in Act I, Scene II, we meet Prospero, accompanied by his daughter Miranda. Prospero had been the Duke of Milan and had been cheated out of his dukedom by his brother, whom he had trusted. The brother had taken away the dukedom of Prospero and exiled him by putting him in a rotten ship to sea during a tempest (storm). The ship marooned on an island owned by powerful witch, Sycorax, who had a son, "a freckled whelp, hag born" who is called Caliban. Prospero teaches Caliban to speak and he becomes Prospero's slave. But, Caliban is not happy as a slave and accuses Prospero of taking over his mother's island through sorcery. Caliban complains bitterly, arguing that Prospero had taken away everything that belonged to Caliban—including his identity. He also regrets that he had been naive in showing Prospero all the secrets of the island because ultimately, he, Caliban, was enslaved. Prospero retorts that Caliban is a lying ingrate and reminds him that it is he, Prospero, who taught Caliban everything he knows. Subsequently, Caliban hatches a plot to overthrow Prospero, but does not succeed.

This is the outline of Shakespeare's play and we only hear Prospero's voice telling us his version of the sequence of events. The rewritten version of the play is written from Caliban's perspective. In this version, Caliban is not a savage, but a rebel and a positive hero. The name Caliban (derived from the word cannibal) is not his real name, but one given by Prospero. Caliban in Prospero's version, is created as ugly, evil and treacherous. When he first sees Caliban, a character in the play asks, "What have we here? a man or fish?" (Hawkes 1986). In this question, Caliban's humanity is denied. In the revised version of the play, Caliban is not

a savage but a great historian (Cesaire 1986). Not only does Prospero take over everything that is rightfully Caliban's, but he also destroys Sycorax's matriarchal order. In these versions, Caliban overthrows the rule of Prospero and wins. Caliban accuses Prospero of establishing economic ascendancy by taking over what was rightfully his and justified the takeover on superior cultural and moral grounds.

The above example is an illustration of competing versions of reality. *The Caliban school of thought* identifies with Caliban and makes him the hero of resistant cultural movements. It is a commentary on the condition of the colonized. One third of the globe was under European control where indigenous peoples' culture and history had been written in defense of colonial practices. Colonial rule was justified on the grounds that the natives were savages and needed to be civilized. Cultural materialists have seized Caliban and made him a symbol of their own condition. In the new version, Caliban overthrows Prospero and **re-appropriates** his identity and culture (Saldivar 1995).

The above instance is an example of the cultural wars being waged in academia, often called the multicultural debate or part of the diversity program. The point to be made is that reality has many vantagepoints and the silenced voices of the formerly colonized are pressing to be heard.

What Is Social Stratification?

Social stratification is a system of ranking in society. Groups of people are arranged in a hierarchical order from high to low. Thus, the group that is on top receives greater benefits in the form of wealth, income, power, and prestige. Race, class and gender stratify American society. An individual's life chances are impacted by their membership in these categories. Social stratification creates and maintains inequality. Social stratification is universal in human societies.

Why Are Societies Stratified?

Stratification is necessary to allocate scarce resources such as wealth, income, power, and prestige. Through systems of stratification people are denied or provided access to these resources.

What Is the Purpose of Stratification Systems?

1. All forms of stratification are indicators of identification.
2. They all have social distance built into them and inform us with whom we ought to associate as well as whom we ought to avoid.
3. They all produce status.
4. They are all hierarchical.
5. They control access to scarce, yet widely valued, resources.

Minority Groups

A minority group is not a numerical category that is small. For if that were the case, then women in the United States would not be categorized as minorities because they outnumber men. A group of people denied equal access to the scarce resources of society is called a minority group (Gonzales 1996). The group is discriminated against based on ascriptive characteristics over which it has no control. Thus, African Americans, women, Mexican Americans, the disabled, Asian Americans, Native Americans, and elderly Americans are frequently denied opportunities because of prejudice based on social characteristics that are not seen in a positive light.

Prejudice and Discrimination

Prejudice is a negative attitude directed towards a minority group. Discrimination is the power to act in a manner to "exclude specific individuals or groups from certain rights, opportunities or privileges" (Gonzales 1996). Wellman (1993) argues that prejudice is not a psychological, but a social condition. Prejudice is an ideological defense to insure the maintenance of interests and privileges. Therefore, prejudice has an economic base. Prejudiced people do not focus on what people really fear; they mask it with words expressing concerns for "standards," etc. Different classes have different interests. For example, consider racial problems; whites who are professional do not care if some blacks should be raised from "unskilled to skilled category." It does not

matter to them, so they may be viewed as people who have no racial bias.

Discrimination is apparent when one looks at the income gap between black and white Americans. For men with bachelor degrees, black men make $764 for every $1000 that white men make. Black women at the same level as white women, make $966 for every $1000. The greater parity in women's income stems from the fact that women in general are discriminated against (Hacker 1995).

Systems of Social Stratification

Systems of social stratification closely correspond to the kind of society they develop in at a particular moment in time. Social stratification in a developing country will be different than in an industrialized country. In countries with an agrarian economy, the stratification will be traditional and simple. The social system will have more close-knit ties because of the reliance of the individual on the group. In sharp contrast, industrialized countries have a complex set of relationships where the individual does not need to rely on his or her group, but on organizations that provide services for money.

In an agricultural based society, **ascribed status** will be important. Ascribed status refers to qualities one is born with such as race, gender and age. The individual's inherited characteristics are significant. For instance, if one is a first-born son, then he will have a higher status than his younger male siblings. In a modern industrial society, **achieved status** will be valued. Achieved status refers to qualities an individual acquires through individual efforts during his/her life. An example of this would be becoming a doctor or a chief executive officer of a corporation. Achievement is measured in terms of acquiring certain skills, wealth, power and prestige. Achievement is said to be based on merit.

However, this is not completely true. If one is born in a rich family, then one has advantages that a child from a poor family does not have. Social status is never purely achieved or ascribed. It is a mixture of both. We will look at four major forms of stratification that continue to impact peoples' lives. They are caste, class, race/ethnicity and apartheid.

The Caste System

The caste system exists in India. The system is dated in antiquity. It is generally assumed that the caste system is the most rigid form of stratification the world has ever seen. This, as we will see is not true. The caste system has survived because it is extremely flexible and assimilative (Cox 1959). There are four major **varnas** or divisions in the caste system:

1. The Brahman caste (priests and scholars)
2. The Kshatriyas (warriors and nobles)
3. The Vaishayas (merchants and skilled artisans)
4. The Shudras (untouchables involved in degrading labor)

Several theories regarding the origin of caste have been advanced (Census of India. Vol.I. Part I. 1931:433). However, its origins are so old that they remain shrouded in mystery and do not help in explaining the caste system and its pervasive influence in the Indian sub-continent. Caste is best viewed as an evolving social system (Cox 1959). It could not have come into existence all at once. Its evolution took centuries and was formed while defending itself from the external influence of proselytizing religions and internal transformations (Census of India. Vol. XXIII. Part II. 1911:151-152). There is some scholarly consensus that the caste system was shaped by the conflict for power between the priest and warrior castes (Gazetteer of Bombay. Vol. IX. Part I. 1901:433-432).

What is Caste?

Scholars define caste in various ways. Bougle (1971) observes that caste has three tendencies: repulsion (keep a distance from those below one's caste), hierarchy, and hereditary specialization. Cox (1959) considers the multiplicity of custom-dictated hierarchies in particular localities as constituting a caste system. Caste divisions determine interaction, both actual and ideal (Beteille 1965). Caste is a flexible and dynamic form of social stratification. There is no central authority vested in a single spiritual Brahman (Dumont 1970). What exists within the caste society of India is a fluid

divine power vested in the Brahman caste, defined and defining social reality. The very continuation of the caste system in modern India is testimony to its flexible and recuperative powers (Chandra 1994).

It has been difficult to define caste. The census of India decided to use occupation to determine caste (Census of India. *Report*. Vol.I Part I.1911:366). The main objective was to ensure uniformity where none really existed. All that is really needed to form a caste is a bond of union, some form of mutual attraction (Census of India. *Report on the Operations*. Vol. XXIII. Part II. 1911:160). Occupational caste categorization does not really explain the caste system because it was an all encompassing organization. Goods and services were exchanged primarily on mutual-reciprocal acts which were constantly renewed and reaffirmed in ritual enactments of economic, political, sacral, and social obligations.

The true Brahman male is ritually defined. He is part medicine man and part magician in ritual enactments of his position and is specially learned in the *Vedas* (sacred texts) and astronomy. In the broadest sense, the Brahman is one who is virtuous (Gazetteer of the Bombay Presidency. Vol.IX. Part I. 1901: 437). The story of Satyakama Jabla, at the beginning of this chapter, bears testimony to caste principles in practice. There are Brahmans who are considered outcasts like the Shudras (Ibbetson 1916). Contrary to the stereotype, historically Brahmans and other castes ate meat. The Brahmans of *Bengal* and *Kashmir* (states in India) have always eaten meat (Beteille 1965 and Census of India. *Notes for Operations.* Vol. XVI. Part I. 1911:244).

Caste is best expressed in ritual. Ritual separation constitutes a major practice in the constant reaffirmation of caste membership. It is the obsession with ritual and its proper enactment that ultimately distinguishes caste from any other form of stratification and marks distinctions between castes (Beteille 1965). Once a Brahman stops being a Brahman, if he "drops his sacredotal character" and becomes a cultivator, then he too has to employ other Brahmans to perform priestly duties on his behalf (Ibbetson 1916 and Census of India. *Notes for Report.* 1911:89). Therefore, Ibbetson (1916) concludes, the four *Varnas* of the caste system are merely a "convenient symbol of social standing." It is then appropriate to view caste as a social institution rather than a purely religious, institution (Census of India. *Report on the Operations.* Baroda. Vol. XXIII. Part II. 1891:148).

Before the advent of the English, the caste system was often controlled by the king and he was considered the ultimate court of appeal. The king could, at will, shuffle the social rank of castes, alleviating or degrading groups of people from one caste to another and regulated intermarriage relationships between groups. Furthermore, the king could change the caste composi-

tion and rules, should the whim or necessity arise (Census of India. *Notes for Report.* 1911:91).

When the British colonized India, transactions were paid for in cash and that separated economic and, later, political functions of caste. These set the stage for rapid transformation of the Indian social system. The separation of economics from the fold of caste, hastened caste mobility for aspiring castes because, through money they could buy themselves out of lower caste status (Chandra 1994). Please read Box 9.1.

BOX 9.1

Caste Mobility in India: The Case of the Patidaar Community

In the past, caste mobility would take generations to achieve. The slow pace was due to narrow social horizons, a static economy, limited population movement as well as legal and ritual sanctions imposed by the Brahmanical caste system. **Sanskritization** was "the traditional principle idiom of social mobility" in traditional India. Economic mobility hastens caste mobility (Beteille 1981).

In 1891, Hindu castes were ordered in the following chronological order, Brahman (priest), Rajput (warrior), Bania (merchant), and Kunbi (polluted caste) (Census of India. *Report on the Operation.* Baroda. Vol.XXIII. Part II. 1891:159). In fact the Kunbis constituted the aboriginal tribes. They lived in the plains and considered themselves Hindus (Census of India. Report. Baroda. Vol. XXIV. Part I. 1891:122). The Kunbis spent extravagantly for their funeral ceremonies and relatively less on marriages (Gazetteer of the Bombay Presidency. Baroda. Vol.VII. 1883:59). They practised widow remarriage, polygamy, ate meat, and paid a bride price for their grown up wives (Census of India. *Report.* Baroda. Vol XVI. Part I. 1911:250-

251;303). The extravagant expense at funeral ceremonies, the practice of bride price, polygamy, and widow remarriage are in stark contrast to a Brahmanical marriage. They had accumulated wealth, but no high caste person would give their daughter in marriage to the Kunbis. They were not permitted to sit and eat with high caste people, even the touch of the Kunbi was said to "pollute the hand of his Brahman servant" (Census of India. Report. Baroda. Vol. XVIII. Part I. 1901:435).

The affluent section of the community had been Sanskritizing their life style. As more and more members of the community became affluent, they could afford the luxury of ritual purity collectively. Caste mobility is a collective phenomenon. For the bid to be successful, the entire caste must move up in the hierarchy, only then is it a collective, unifying, and durable change (Srinivas 1978, 1980; Cox 1959).

The Kunbis, who were not that well-off, began migrating to East Africa (Harding 1977). The upper castes would not migrate because the Hindu faith prohibited it as contact with

foreigners would pollute caste incumbents (Kondapi 1951). The British needed labor in East Africa to develop their colonies and encouraged lower caste members to migrate. The Kunbis thrived economically in East Africa and their large remittances back to India, improved the economic condition of the community. By 1931, the Patidaar community had done well economically, the world-wide depression prompted the Kunbis return to India to rejoin their affluent group. They had revolutionized their traditions and mode of worship and continued to claim a higher caste status with the census enumerators. They had become politically (the largest caste) and economically (the wealthiest group in the region) prominent (Chandra 1997). The Kunbis had consolidated their economic and political status and their claim to the Kshatriya (warrior) caste was accepted by the census with a nonchalant explanation, "The great agricultural communities, who seemed to dislike their old name of 'kanbi,' were thereupon shown under Patidaar" (Census of India. Report. Vol. XIX. Part I. 1931:394).

Class

A class system came into existence with the industrial revolution. There are two kinds of classes, *economic* and *political.* Economic class is based on accumulating wealth and material possessions. Political class is formed by a sizable number in a group of people claiming similar interests. Hence, ethnic minorities are a political class when they organize based on a common history, affiliation, and definition of ethnicity and demand concessions based upon common problems and issues. Political groups, based on their numbers, have economic clout for they can impact the outcome of elections. Therefore, political groups attempt to appease leaders of ethnic groups such as women's groups, African Americans, Latin Americans, Native Americans, Asian Americans and, recently, the gay and lesbian community and the disabled Americans.

The mobility in economic class may be rapid if an individual wins a lottery. Other avenues for moving up in the class hierarchy include pursuing a professional degree, conducting a lucrative business, etc.

How Are Classes Formed?

We will look at the ideas of Karl Marx and Max Weber to understand the formation of classes. Both Marx and Weber witnessed the industrial revolution and were trying to understand the transformation in people's lives. Marx's analysis focuses on conflict between two interest groups. He asserts that class struggle propels human society. In Marx's opinion, the root cause of all alienation is economic alienation. He says that capitalist society is inherently contradictory.

Karl Marx (1818-1883) analyzed the causes of the industrial revolution to formulate his theory of class formation. Marx was critical of the emerging new economic system as he saw people being dislocated from the moorings in tradition to life in anonymous urban centers. He saw poor people get poorer and suffer while the rich became richer.

Marx identified material conditions as being important in determining a person's consciousness and he focused on the private ownership of property as a cause of much human inequality. According to Marx, human society passes through four stages of development and each of them is determined by its **mode of production.**

Historical Materialism

Karl Marx

Marx's methodology is called *historical materialism.* People enter into relations of production against their will. The material condition of people's lives and the particular stage of historical development they find themselves in, determines their consciousness. In historical materialism, the four stages of evolution are the following:

1. *Asiatic Stage* In the asiatic mode of production everyone is a generalist. There is no specialization, although the land is held by the state and everyone is subordinate to the state.
2. *Ancient Stage* The ancient mode of production is characterized by slavery (Aron 1979).
3. *Feudal Stage* The feudal mode of production is characterized by serfdom.
4. *Bourgeois Stage* The bourgeois mode of production is the final stage, characterized by wage earning (Aron 1979).

The last stage interested Marx the most. It is in this stage that the different class positions of those who own the *means of production* and those who work for the owners, crystallize. Through the ancient and feudal stages, the laborers are not conscious of their common plight. However, in the fourth stage, the workers who work on the factory floor, realize their common condition. They develop a **class consciousness,** where they realize their class interests are different from those who own the means of production. Marx asserts that throughout the earlier stages, the two groups (the **haves** and the **have nots)** develop an antagonistic relationship which comes to a head in the capitalist mode of production. Antagonistic relationships develop because of the conflict inherent in the relationship (Aron 1979). The old system is destroyed as a new one comes into being. Thus each of these stages (including the capitalist mode of production) contains the seeds of its own destruction.

In all these stages, a person's labor, which is a natural part of the individual, is taken from the individual person by those people who own the means of production. The owners become rich by exploiting the workers' giving workers very little in exchange for their work. In the process, labor becomes a **commodity** and external to the worker.

Surplus Value

People essentially labored for what they needed. Everything that was produced by a person was consumed by that person. This is called *use value*. However, when one-person exploits other people for their labor, the exploiter takes (steals) another person's labor for less than its value. Peoples' labor then becomes an object outside of themselves (Marx 1967).

In the bourgeois mode of production, there is a value to labor that is "embodied in the form of some object," where human labor may be seen accumulated. The bourgeois's goal is profit. He has two objectives, both of which are related to profit. These goals are

1. to produce something of value to be sold as a commodity and
2. to be able to get a return that is greater than his initial investment.

The most important activity for the capitalist is how to accumulate more wealth. The solution for the bourgeoisie is to keep expanding the market share by brutal competition. However, to insure profitability, they decrease the wages and increase the workload of workers.

Meanwhile, the competition reduces the number of bourgeoisie as smaller enterprises are "swamped" by larger enterprises, thus swelling the numbers of the proletariate. The constant revolutionizing of the means of production leads to mechanization and the workers are paid even less. The workers receive fluctuating wages for their labor. The workers then become organized into unions and assume a revolutionary class identity and overthrow the bourgeoisie and their capitalist system. (Marx 1967). This scenario was Marx's vision of what he hoped the future held for the workers.

Alienation

Alienation is caused by the "private ownership of the means of production and the anarchy of the market" (Aron 1979). As argued above, work is no longer an expression of oneself, but becomes a means by which one earns a livelihood. Work becomes dehumanized and individuals lose control of their existence.

1. Thus, people become alienated from nature because they are not working for themselves, but for someone else.
2. Next, people become alienated from the process of production. Working on an assembly line production, the worker cannot claim that he or she completed the product. The worker worked on a tiny part of the product. There is no joy or pride in the work.
3. Workers are alienated from their fellow workers when there is little interaction at the work place. Competition for jobs divides one worker from another (tertius gaudens).
4. Finally, the worker is alienated from his or her "self." There is no meaning to the worker's life. The worker, in Marx's eyes, is like a robot working for wages.

Ultimately, Marx posited, the workers would break from pre-history and establish a new state in which there will be an end to antagonistic relations. The working class will rise spontaneously and will overthrow the capitalist class.

Max Weber

Max Weber's (1864-1920) concept of class development varied from Marx's theory of historical materialism. In many ways, it is said that Weber's work on the rise of capitalism is a continuous dialogue with the ghost of Marx (Coser 1977). For Marx, the material conditions determined consciousness; for Weber, it is the consciousness that determines existence.

The Protestant Ethic and The Spirit of Capitalism

Weber's most famous work is entitled *The Protestant Ethic and The Spirit of Capitalism.*

In this book, Weber puts forth an explanation for the rise of capitalism.

Weber studied religion and focused on the Calvinist sect in the Protestant faith. He focused on the doctrine of the Calvinists and looked at the role of asceticism, also known as self-denial. The Calvinists strongly believed in an afterlife and predestination. The afterlife was more important than this life because death is certain. What happens after death is significant. Unlike in other denominations the Christian faith, the Calvinists had a one-on-one relationship with God that was conducted in "deep spiritual isolation." However, people faced a dilemma: How was a person to know if he/she had been selected for salvation? This issue created a great amount of anxiety. This anxiety was resolved with the idea that God worked through the individual. This also meant the power was within the individual to construct his or her own destiny. The individual led a life of ascetic denial of worldly goods and accumulated wealth. The incentive to asceticism was the doctrine of predestination. To work and to accumulate wealth, but not use it for one's own pleasure, became the sign that one was selected for salvation. This accounts for the rise of capitalism (Weber 1996).

One difference between Marx and Weber is that Weber asserts that bureaucracies characterize modern society. To Weber, it does not matter who owns the means of production.

Social Action and Bureaucracy

For Weber, sociology is a science of social action. Weber stresses the importance of verstehen in understanding human social action. **Verstehen** refers to subjective understanding—to assuming the position of the other, to taking the role of the other so that one can decipher the subjective meanings that the participants attribute to their own actions and to their situation (Coser 1977).

Bureaucracies organize our lives. Bureaucracies, which we explore in some depth in another chapter, have several characteristics.

1. They co-ordinate activities
2. They are rational organizations
3. They are hierarchical
4. They have written rules that are impersonal; incumbents are governed by these rules

5. Appointments are based on specialized qualifications rather than on ascriptive criteria.

Bureaucracies are rational, but there is a problem where human relations are concerned. Human relations are depersonalized in a bureaucracy. This concept is very similar to Marx's concept of alienation.

Class, Status, and Power

For Weber, class is based on life style and consumption patterns rather than solely on the process of production and one's place within the production process. Weber's classes are *status groups* who form a community based on what constitutes a proper life style and the honor and esteem that is accorded to them by others. They are exclusive and maintain a social distance from inferiors. **Power** is not valued by individuals "for its own sake". It also entails honor. Thus, individuals commanding a large-scale bureaucratic organization have tremendous powers, even though their source of income is a salary (Coser 1977).

In a study regarding the perception of social class, Gonzales (1985) found that social status in the Mexican American community was viewed more favorably if traditional values of the Mexican culture were retained as opposed to those who had assimilated and adopted the American culture and life style. Those Mexican Americans who participated in community work were accorded prestige by other Mexican Americans. Frequently, one's friendships with such prominent individuals allowed them to bask in reflected glory. A person accorded high prestige did not necessarily belong to the upper class, but could be a member of the middle-class. This cross-cultural difference is important when viewing social class among immigrants and provides support for Weber's theory.

According to Mills (1956), power in the United States is centralized in the economic, political, and military, institutions. The leaders of these three wings of command actively socialize and collude when making decisions that influence national and international affairs. The people who control these bureaucracies see themselves as part of "the inner circle of the upper social classes". Others view them as powerful men.

Race and Ethnicity

There is a distinction between the concepts of race and ethnicity. We may note the following:

1. Race is a pre-World War II concept, while ethnicity is a post-World War II construct.
2. Race is said to be based on biological differences, while ethnicity is said to be based on cultural differences.
3. Race presupposes the inferiority of minorities when they are spoken of disparagingly as the other. Ethnicity is viewed positively and is also a mode of self-identification.
4. The inferior connotation of race was based on the manual labor that minorities were employed in as opposed to the superior races that were not involved in hard physical labor (the colonial experience).
5. Once the so-called racial groups acquired the *right to vote*, their political status transformed them into an ethnic group (Chandra 1994).

Origin of Racial Stratification

Although differences between groups of people, even differences within a group of people have been observed, racial stratification on a large scale really came about with the industrial revolution. The industrial revolution necessitated human contact from distant lands. The distances contracted as technology provided quicker and safer methods to navigate the seas and reach distant lands. As people came together, the physical differences became noticeable. These differences became significant when the groups were interested in the same thing, economic gain. For scholars, the "discovery" of America and the need for division of labor characterized the beginning of race relations where skin color becomes the hallmark of racial division (Chandra 1994; Williams 1990; Cox 1959). Although the differences are masked in cultural terms, they underlie an economic imperative (Steinberg 1989).

Imperialism and Colonization

Industrial development produced new technologies, but there was a continuous need for raw materials, cheap labor and new markets. This led to a race among the industrialized nations of the West to seek new locations to be profitable (Takaki 1989). These newly industrialized nations (England, France, and later Germany), moved towards the continents of Americas, Asia and Africa. People on these continents had an agrarian life style that was based on barter/exchange and they were subdivided into smaller groupings. The industrial nations of the West subdued these groups of people and colonized them by imposing western political, legal, religious, and economic institutions. They demarcated the differences between themselves and the indigenous populations by inventing the ideology of race and **manifest destiny.** The ideology of manifest destiny stated that the native populations were lazy and heathens and needed the civilizing influence of Christianity. The natives also needed to work to justify their need for existing on earth (Takaki 1989).

World System Theory

The world system theory is a second explanation for the hierarchy among nations and the resulting division of labor. The author of the theory is Wallerstein (1974), who states that a world system began developing in the sixteenth century. The **core** nations (Britain, France, Holland, and Gernamy) began to have capitalist development. Subsequently, *semi-peripheral* nations around the Mediterranean became dependent and involved in the trade with the core nations. The *peripheral* nations of Eastern Europe became part of the world system because they sold agricultural products to the core nations. The *external area* consisted of the continents of Asia and Africa. Asia and Africa had little capitalist development and were not connected to the core countries.

Williams (1990) extends the argument by demonstrating the movement of West Africans and Irish into the United States as part of the expansion of capitalist development and the manner in which these nations became a part of the world system. According to Williams, these countries, like the rest, traded their surplus, which was necessary to fuel capitalist growth. West Africa and Ireland had a surplus of manpower and the United States had a surplus of land, but little bullion or money in circulation. He further argues that the difference between the Irish and the Africans has been constructed on the voluntary and involuntary pattern of migration. West Africans were brought to the United States as slaves and were involuntary immigrants; whereas, the Irish were voluntary immigrants and, therefore, in a superior position.

Williams's analysis reveals that the dichotomy is erroneous because the Irish, too, were forced to leave their homeland like the West Africans. The Irish were not enslaved and brought in chains like the Africans, but they had little choice in the matter of leaving their home. The Africans were enslaved because they owned their parcels of land and had to be moved by force and violence so their land could be used for market production. The Irish peasants had already been dispossessed of their land. Their condition was not a simply the result of the failed potato crop, because there were other crops that had not been attacked by blight, and the potato could have been substituted, avoiding the widespread famine impacting this class. But, their condition had been deliberately created by the Protestant landlords to oust the peasants from the land.

There was little wage work available in Ireland or England because of the periodic slump in the capitalist economy. The peasants were desperately poor and their subsistence on the potato crop and its failure left them without a real choice. Either they remained in Ireland and faced slow, but certain, starvation and death or they agreed to move to the United States where there were economic opportunities in the developing industrial north-east (Williams 1994).

Internal Colonization

Blauner's (1972) emphasis is on the role of *internal colonization* in the United States. He argues that there is no difference where oppression occurs. Most minority groups in the United States immigrated because of the pressure in the countries where they were pushed out. The only group that really came to the United States voluntarily were the early European immigrants who had more autonomy than immigrant groups that came later.

Blauner demonstrates that the United States was developed on the principle of race determined by skin color. Even though it is true that the Irish, Italians and Jews experienced discrimination because of their religious faith, they had a distinct advantage of possessing

white skin and European ancestry. They had freedom of movement in the United States. The African Americans, Asians and Mexicans could not move freely. They were not classified as **free labor** because of their physical characteristics.

Since the indigenous Native American population resisted attempts at "dependent labor relationships," they were either killed or pushed out of the area. Europeans entered the labor force as "contract laborers" and were concentrated in the industrially developing northeast. It is also true that people of East European descent were in the heavy metals industry and the Jews concentrated in the garment industry; they were able to grow as institutions expanded (Steinberg 1989). Perhaps the most important factor was that they worked as wage labor.

African Americans worked in the rural south as slaves and were not paid for their labor. Asians and Mexicans were concentrated in the west where their labor was used for mining and building railroads. There was little opportunity for mobility. It was easier for people of European descent and they merged into American society when the next generation was born. For others, the labor systems weakened or destroyed their cultural ties because these could not be replicated under the plantation system for African Americans. Asians were not allowed to bring their wives and children. Nineteenth century United States policy of cultural genocide unleashed on Native Americans is a perfect example of internal colonization.

Other ethnic groups have won economic concessions because of their position in the economy. The status of the home country and its relations with the United States often determine the position of the minority group (Takaki 1989; Blauner 1972). This leaves the future of the Native American Indians in an awkward position because they do not have an independent nation to call their own (Blauner 1972).

Apartheid in South Africa

Apartheid became official in South Africa and lasted from 1948 to 1994 (Birmingham 1995). Apartheid was a system of legal segregation based on race. The inequality was a result of imperialism and colonialism where the growth of capitalism was inextricably linked to colonial conquest. This was necessary to transfer wealth from the colonized nations to the colonial powers. In order to do so, the colonial power developed political and ideological tools to facilitate an easier transfer of wealth. Biological and cultural theories of inferiority regarding the colonized took shape in a multitude of processes that are historical, psychological, religious and philosophical. The racial system in South Africa was legitimated through the passages of laws (Magubane 1979).

South Africa had an extremely repressive policy towards all non-Europeans. The Class Areas Act was passed in 1924 ("Bill to make provision for the reservation of residential and trading areas in urban areas for persons, other than natives having racial characteristics in common," (File #:88 (iii) 1921, 1924:11). The term "class" encompassed persons with common racial or physical characteristics. Here, as throughout the bill, the terms class and race are used interchangeably because the social system did not differentiate between the two. Both race and class had a symbiotic relationship where one defined the other, or, even the absence of one category clearly established it (Chandra 1994).

The absurdity of race classification was obvious in South Africa. White officials used "the pencil in the hair" technique to classify the population. If the pencil fell out when pushed into the hair, then the individual was colored. If it stayed there, then the "crinkly" hair was evidence of an African heritage. In a family, people were classified without any explanations. Couples who had married before the 1949 Mixed Marriage Act, before it became illegal to marry a person of another race, found their children assigned to one group or another. People appealed these classifications and by 1966, "one hundred and fifty thousand borderline cases" were waiting to be settled (Harrison 1981).

As in the American South, a small white majority ruled the vast black majority (DuBois 1985; Magubane 1979). The frequent use of violence keeps the natives *in their place.* In South Africa, the states' military became more oppressive as native Africans escalated class struggle. Similarly, in the United States, violence and the enactment of **Black Codes** became common place during the end of the **reconstruction** era (DuBois 1985). In both the case of South Africa and the southern United States, race was used for economic exploitation. Racism also served to keep poor black and white workers divided (DuBois 1985; Magubane 1979).

BOX 9.2

Comparison Between Caste and Race

Caste and race are often mentioned as possessing similar mechanisms of stratification by the caste school of race relations. The underlying similarity is posited on vaguely defined *caste-like* characteristics to define a social situation (Myrdal 1944; Dollard 1937) that does not constitute a comparable unit of comparison.

All forms of stratification have similarities at general levels and distinctions at micro levels.

1. Race operates according to real or imputed physical distinctions, caste on the basis of social reputation.

2. Caste is a pre-capitalist formation. Race is a result of division of labor in industrial society and supports capital development.

3. The Hindu caste system is a patriarchal system where the pedigree of the offspring is determined by the father's lineage (the story of Satyakama Jabala at the beginning of the chapter). In the racial system, one drop of black blood determines the race of the child.

4. The Brahman is designated a Brahman by ritual acts and the caste system is not based on visibility like the racial system.

5. Caste is inclusive, as is evidenced by the foreigners who have been integrated in the caste system, while race legislation excludes groups based on legislation.

6. There is mobility in the caste system. Theoretically, and in reality there is mobility in the theory of **Karma** and the transmigration of souls.

7. The substructures of caste are not available in racial slots, thereby leaving few avenues of negotiation open.

8. A network of reciprocal relationships constitutes the caste system. It is not a simple matter of 'black' and 'white'.
9. Caste incumbents maintain a strict separation within the system. A shudra would not be expected to

fight a Kshatriya war, unlike the racial system where members of the African group, though designated inferior, were involved in a diversity of domestic chores including fighting wars on behalf of the dominant group.

10. Caste members stand united as they stand to gain collectively from the labor of lower caste incumbents. All whites do not stand to gain uniformly from the dominance of a servile race.

The conflict of interest between the 40% English speaking and commerce controlling elite and the 60% Afrikaans speaking and politically controlling elite, pushed the ideology to extremes. Not all white South Africans stood to gain from a subservient Black race (Enloe 1973). The changing economic situation forces the dominant group to absorb ethnic minorities, if they are to maintain their competitive edge in the market. The economic position of minorities thus improves. This also occurs as a result of the scarcity of personnel from the dominant group (Hoetink 1975).

The Disability Movement

Historically, disabled individuals were a part of society. With the Civil War the casualty rate prompted the growth of institutions to house and look after the disabled. However, since they were considered charitable, "they became places of abuse, isolation, and segregation." By the end of the nineteenth century, there was considerable hostility directed towards the disabled.

Shapiro (1994) provides a history and analysis of the disability movement. The movement received a stimulus from an inadvertent clause, Section 504 of the Rehabilitation Act of 1973. Almost as an afterthought, some lawmaker had authorized $1.55 billion in federal aid to disabled individuals to be spent over a two year period. However, compliance with the law would cost billions more. Since the government was not about to enforce the law, activists staged a sit-in in San Francisco. This political act marked the beginning of the disability rights movement. But, the issue of cost continues to plague the implementation of programs.

They have "a hidden army" of supporters. The support they enjoy comes from a diversity of sources because even senators have relatives, friends and family members suffering from some form of disability. Lobbyists come from professional and parents' groups. Supporters, themselves, suffer from some disability. It is estimated that one in seven Americans suffers from a form of disability. President Bush had a disabled daughter who died a painful death from leukemia and his son suffers from a learning disability. President Bush became an ardent supporter.

On July 26, 1990, the Americans with Disabilities Act (ADA) became law and took effect in 1992. The group does not want pity, but rights. Laws alone do not guarantee inclusion; people's attitudes need to change. The traditional arguments that the costs are high in integrating the disabled are not true. It will cost society less, not more if the disabled are integrated in society.

Exchange Relationships That Make a World

Technological innovation and transportation costs are making it easier for people to move from one country to another. This movement of population is creating a multicultural world. Nowhere is this more apparent than in the United States.

The Role of Legislation

Migration and conquest have changed the demographic composition of a nation. Legislation has a dramatic impact on migration patterns. Thus, in 1882, a federal law was enacted that excluded further Chinese immigration into the United States for ten years. This law was renewed every decade until the passage of the 1924 law that banned all Asians from entering the United States (Gonzales 1990; Takaki 1989).

The sources of immigration to the United States have changed dramatically because of the passage of laws. The old immigrants, who came from 1820-1880, came from northwestern Europe. The new immigrants came between the years 1881-1920. This was, by far, the largest group and they came from eastern and southern Europe. The Depression and war years, 1921-1950, saw a dramatic decline in immigration. However, of those who came, two thirds continued to come from Western Europe. The immigration reform, between the years of 1951-1970, witnessed the arrival of refugees and war brides from Asia. In 1965, Congress passed liberal legislation. The Immigration Act of 1965 changed both the nature and source of immigrants. Most immigrants now come from Asia and Latin America (Gonzales, 1996; Ueda, 1994; Reimers, 1985).

The dramatic shift in population occurred as a direct result of the October 1965 Immigration and Nationality Act. The post war economy was booming and it became easy for those who argued for liberal legislation to make their case (Reimers 1985). The provisions of the act were aimed at

1. providing family unification
2. attracting skilled people with education
3. easing world problems arising out of political unrest and natural disasters
4. aiding international exchange programs
5. preventing undesirable people from entering the United States (Gonzales, 1996).

These liberal reforms were designed to attract European immigrants (Takaki, 1989). However, they had the unintended consequence of opening the doors to Asian and Latin American populations (Reimers, 1985).

Immigrants bring their culture to the United States. The American-born second generation seeks equality as American citizens. The second generation wants its version of events to be known, as our discussion about the revised version of *The Tempest* illustrates. Immigrants, whose culture is part of the resulting explosion of literature, culture, the arts, restaurants, and religious celebrations, enrich America.

BOX 9.3

The Unintended Consequences of Immigration Legislation

The *Braceros Program* came into effect in July 1942 and ended in December 1964. The Braceros program was initiated to deal with critical labor shortage that developed because of World War II. An estimated five million Mexicans participated in the Braceros Program. The unexpected outcome of the program was that it "stimulated the flow of undocumented aliens." Braceros were only hired to work in agricultural jobs. The farmers had to go through a formal process involving red tape and bureaucratic rules to sponsor a Bracero. Additionally, the farmers also had to post a $25 bond and pay a required $15 registration fee.

The campesinos (undocumented Mexican farm workers) had no such restrictions. They could also work in the non-agricultural sector of the labor market. The Immigration and Naturalization Service has observed the impact of this law on undocumented Mexican aliens (Gonzales 1996).

The refugee issue also underwent a drastic change as American presidents used provisions of Acts to admit refugees into the country. In 1968, the United States had agreed to conditions for admitting refugees under the UN Protocol on Refugees. But, Congress had not drafted rules and regulations for those seeking asylum. Nobody applied for asylum because there was no provision for this. Since the number of people seeking asylum was small, Congress drafted a provision for 5,000 to come under the asylum category in the 1980 Refugee Act. Carter had previously admitted 130,000 Cubans and Haitians without status; all of them became eligible to seek asylum. The 5,000 slots reserved for asylum seekers were not adequate for the Cubans and Haitians, not to mention the thousands of others like the Nicaraguans, Afghans, etc., who had been undocumented aliens who were only visiting or were students. They all began applying for asylum. The strategy was to get to the United States and apply for asylum. If the petition was denied, it could be appealed with the help of many church and civil rights groups, and perhaps one could remain in America for years. Refugees would seek asylum from outside the country; asylum seekers were in the country and were asking for a change in status (Reimers 1992).

Key Concepts

achieved status	mode of production	status group
alienation	power	surplus value
apartheid	prejudice	the "have nots"
ascribed status	race	the "haves"
Bania	Rajput	the ancient stage
Black Codes	reconstruction	the Asiatic stage
Brahman	semi-peripheral nations	the bourgeois stage
bureaucracy	caste	the Caliban school of
campesinos	class	thought
external area	class consciousness	the feudal stage
free labor	class formation	the Patidaar
historical materialism	commodity	*The Protestant Ethic and the*
internal colonization	core nations	*Spirit of Capitalism*
Karl Marx	discrimination	the Vedas
Kunbi	ethnicity	use value
manifest destiny	social stratification	verstehen
Max Weber	stages in the evolution of	world system theory
means of production	historical materialism	

Internet Resources

http://fswinfo.fsw.ruu.nl/soc/HG/ismf/index.htm

Document: International Stratification and Mobility File

This web site provides international sample survey data and mobility tables showing social stratification and social mobility.

http://www.ssc.wisc.edu/irp/

Document: Institute For Research On Poverty

This site, sponsored by the University of Wisconsin at Madison, analyzes poverty and social inequality in the United States. Readers have access to recent publications and can download their newsletter. Older publications and publications not copied electronically can be ordered through the web site.

http://www.umn.edu/irp/index.html

Document: Institute on Race and Poverty

The Institute on Race and Poverty, established by the University of Minnesota Law School in Minneapolis, posts articles and reports on their web site that analyze the impact of racial segregation and poverty in the U.S. This web site includes the following sections: Online Publications, Press Releases, Conferences and Events, Links, Recommended Readings, and Employment Opportunities.

http://aspe.os.dhhs.gov/poverty/poverty.htm

Document: U.S. Department of Health and Human Services: Poverty Guidelines, Research and Measurement.

This web site posts current explanations of Federal poverty measurements and features articles that discuss different poverty issues. It also links to the Census Bureau's list of poverty statistics in the U.S.

http://www.fedstats.gov/

Document: Fedstats

Fedstats allows the public to access statistics from many U.S. Federal Government agencies. To begin, link on to *Agencies*. Go to the left column and scroll down to "Internal Revenue Service: Statistics *of Income Division*." Link here to find interesting facts on wealth divisions in the U.S., such as the number of millionaires. This web page also provides links to other statistical agencies, including international web links.

http://psc.lsa.umich.edu/

Document: Population Studies

This web page, created by the University of Michigan, includes research on inequality and social mobility. Data and publications that are not accessible on-line can be ordered from this web page.

Suggested Readings

Cromwell, Adelaide M., *The Other Brahmins: Boston's Black Upper Class* (Fayetteville, AK: University of Arkansas Press, 1994).

Dill, Bonnie Thornton, *Across the Boundaries of Race and Class: An Exploration of Work and Family among Black Female Domestic Servants* (New York: Garland Publishng, 1994).

Dill, Bonnie Thornton, "'Making the Job Good Yourself:' Domestic Service and the Construction of Personal Dignity," in Ann Bookman and Sandra Morgen (Eds.) *Female Domestic Servants* (New York: Garland Publishing, 1994).

Domhoff, William G., *The Bohemian Grove and Other Retreats: A Study in Ruling-Class Cohesiveness* (New York: Harper and Row, 1974).

Domhoff, William G., *Who Rules America? Power and Politics in the Year 2000* (Mt. View, CA: Mayfield Publishing Company, 1998).

Feagin, Joe R., and Sikes, Melvin P., *Living with Racism: the Black Middle-Class Experience* (Boston: Beacon Press, 1994).

Gilbert, Dennis, and Kahl, Joseph A., *The American Class Structure: A New Synthesis* (Fourth edition) (Belmont, CA: Wadsworth, 1993).

Mendez, Jennifer Bickham, "Of Mops and Maids: Contradictions and Continuities in Bureaucratized Domestic Work," *Social Problems*, Vol. 45, No. 1 (February)1998: 114-135.

Ostower, F., *Why The Wealthy Give: The Culture of Elite Philanthropy* (Princeton, NJ: Princeton University Press, 1995).

Zweigenhaft, Richard L., and Domhoff, William G., *Diversity in the Power Elite: Have Women and Minorities Reached the Top?* (New Haven, CT: Yale University Press, 1998).

Learning Exercises

The learning objective of this chapter is for you to understand how and why human societies are stratified. The chapter also demonstrates the manner in which the world is, has been, and continues to be linked through economic trade. Not only are there hierarchical relations among people, but nations also are stratified based on resources and power. In the writing assignments below, you are to write a response to the questions or issues as indicated. Your answers to the written assignments are to be typed, double spaced, and stapled in the upper-left hand corner.

Learning Exercise 9.1
Writing Assignment

Answer the following questions in an essay in which you use some of the key concepts from the chapter. Please type your essay double spaced, and staple it in the upper left-hand corner. The essay should be at least two full pages in length.

1. Briefly define a minority group, colonizer, colonization, the caste system, achieved and ascribed status, the racial and ethnic forms of stratification, and apartheid. Please give an example of how four of these (your choice) are manifest in your life today.
2. Have you ever felt discriminated against in your life? How did you feel?
3. What were your views about the caste system in India before you read this chapter? Have you changed your view? Is caste stratification a flexible system? Please compare and contrast caste stratification with racial and class systems of stratification.
4. Please describe the relationship between the colonizer and the colonized. What do you think of the revised version of Shakespeare's *The Tempest*? Is it okay to rewrite the play? Why or why not?
5. Apartheid has now ended in South Africa. Do you think this will create chaos or anomie in the country? What was the ideological justification for apartheid? What was the reality?

■ ■ ■

Learning Exercise 9.2
Writing Assignment

Answer the following questions in an essay in which you use some of the key concepts from the chapter. Please type your essay, double-spaced, and staple it in the upper left-hand corner. The essay should be at least two full pages in length. Please answer these questions by thinking about current issues and how they are connected.

1. How are the concepts of class different for Marx and Weber? Who do you agree with more? Are there distinct characteristics of class visible in our society? What are they? How do patterns of consumption influence class relations?
2. How do prejudice and discrimination interact? Provide instances of structural discrimination still prevalent in our society.
3. How are race and ethnicity different? How does economic class influence each of these forms of stratification? How does your ethnicity help and obstruct your progress and life chances?

4. Should immigration into the United States be stopped? Describe the effect of legislation on the demographic composition of our country. Should immigrants become United States citizens quickly? Why or why not?
5. Were minority groups in the United States colonized? What were the forms of colonization as pertaining to different ethnic groups? How important was the role of legislation in the colonization process?
6. What is the difference between caste and race, class and caste, and race and class? What are the common elements in these forms of stratification? How do you view the current multicultural debate? What are its merits and demerits? What do you think about affirmative action?

■ ■ ■

Learning Exercise 9.3

Engaging in Sociological Research

Answer the following questions in an essay in which you use some of the key concepts from the chapter. Please type your essay, double-spaced, and staple in the upper left-hand corner. You are required to do extra research in the library in order to answer the questions below. The essay should be at least 8 full pages in length. Please answer these questions by thinking about current issues and how they are connected.

1. Marx's concept of alienation is fundamental to his critique of capitalism. Do you think it is a critical variable? State your reasons. Is there alienation in the United States? Have you experienced it? Please tell the reader about it. What, in your opinion, causes alienation? Is it actually the transformation from use value to exchange value that is responsible for alienation, or something else?
2. Surplus value is an important concept for Marx, Williams, and Weber. According to each of these theorists, what is the role of surplus value in the development of capitalism? What do you understand by using the concept of surplus value?
3. How were African Americans paid for their labor under slavery? Why were the Black codes enacted? Discuss the functions of the Black codes.

■ ■ ■

Learning Exercise 9.4

In-Class Group Discussion

Please think about these issues for a few minutes in silence. Then, the class will break up into the small groups. You are to engage in a discussion with your small group. How do they see these issues? It is important that you have a more or less even mixture of males and females, as well as people from different ethnic groups.

1. Is the United States a racist society? Why or why not? Is there a concept called "reverse discrimination?" Why or why is it not a valid concept?
2. Should illegal immigration be stopped? Why do undocumented aliens come to the United States.?

3. Does America have a racial caste system? What are the characteristics that constitute caste-like features?
4. Is the process of colonization still going on in the world in a different form?
5. How is the process of re-appropriating or recovering one's history helpful? What function does it have?
6. Why have the images of Asians changed in a positive direction? How is the model minority image harmful to Asians?

■ ■ ■

Multiple Choice and True-False Test

1. Social stratification is universal in human society.
   A. True.   B. False

2. Prejudice is _____.
   A. a negative attitude towards a minority group
   B. the power to act against a minority group
   C. an act to exclude a minority group
   D. seen as positive social attitude

3. Ascribed status is based on _____.
   A. education
   B. birth
   C. class
   D. immigration

4. Achieved status is based on _____.
   A. inheritance
   B. caste
   C. race
   D. merit

5. The Shudra belongs to the _____.
   A. warrior caste
   B. priest caste
   C. trader caste
   D. untouchable caste

6. The caste system evolved because of the _____.
   A. inclusion of foreigners
   B. rivalry between the Brahmans and the kshatriyas
   C. co-ordinating efforts of the Brahman and Kshatriya castes
   D. exclusion of the Shudra caste

7. It was difficult to define caste. The Indian census decided to base it upon _____.
   A. occupation
   B. skin color
   C. wavy hair
   D. height

8. Before the advent of the British, the caste system was controlled by the _____.
   A. Brahman priests
   B. Kshatriya kings
   C. Vaishaya traders
   D. farming castes

341

9. Once census enumeration of castes became official, the census became an avenue for _____.
    A. caste mobility
    B. spiritual mobility
    C. economic mobility
    D. political mobility

10. According to Marx, class consciousness emerges in the _____.
    A. socialist stage
    B. asiatic stage
    C. bourgeois stage
    D. feudal stage

11. According to Marx, surplus value is generated by _____.
    A. exploitation of workers
    B. use value and consumption
    C. the high consumption of workers
    D. workers greed

12. According to Marx, the bourgeois's only objective is _____.
    A. commodity exchange
    B. exploitation of workers
    C. profit
    D. all of the above

13. For Marx, alienation is caused by _____.
    A. economic alienation
    B. political alienation
    C. social alienation
    D. spiritual alienation

14. Bureaucracies are _____.
    A. rational organizations
    B. they co-ordinate activities
    C. they are hierarchical
    D. all of the above

15. Race and ethnicity are different based upon their _____.
    A. organization
    B. political participation
    C. skin color
    D. biological differences

16. Manifest Destiny is a doctrine for equal treatment.
    A. True   B. False

17. The world system theory was authored by _____.
    A. Marx
    B. Weber
    C. Wallerstein
    D. Williams

342

18. Williams argues that the Unites States., Africa, and Ireland became integrated in the world system by trading their _____.
    A. land
    B. surplus
    C. people
    D. money

19. The internal colonization model was first proposed by _____.
    A. Williams
    B. Wallerstein
    C. Cox
    D. Blauner

20. The indigenous population of the Americas is _____.
    A. African Americans
    B. Native Americans
    C. Asian Americans
    D. European Americans

21. Apartheid lasted in South Africa from the years _____.
    A. 1941-1968
    B. 1943-1978
    C. 1948-1994
    D. 1949-1992

22. To control blacks in the American South by the end of the Reconstruction period _____.
    A. black codes were enacted
    B. land was redistributed
    C. wealth was redistributed
    D. political power was granted

23. The Americans with Disabilities Act was passed in the year _____.
    A. 1989
    B. 1990
    D. 1993
    E. 1997

24. The source countries for immigration changed dramatically after the 1965 Immigration Act. The law brought unintended consequences which allowed this impact through the clause for _____.
    A. skilled professionals
    B. family unification
    C. refugee provision
    D. aid to international exchange programs

25. All Asian migration to the U.S. was banned in _____.
    A. 1920
    B. 1924
    C. 1932
    D. 1947

26. According to Takaki, the liberal immigration reforms of 1965 were designed to attract _____.
   A. Europeans
   B. Asians
   C. Mexicans
   D. Africans

27. The Braceros Program stimulated the migration of _____.
   A. farm workers
   B. professionals
   C. single women
   D. illegal migration

28. According to the split labor market theory, jobs are stable with benefits in the _____.
   A. primary labor market
   B. secondary labor market
   C. tertiary labor market
   D. all of the above

29. According to the split labor market theory, the working class is divided because of the actions of _____.
   A. capitalists
   B. higher wage workers
   C. lower wage workers
   D. racial minorities

30. Dominance is not only assured by ideology, but also by _____.
   A. prejudice and discrimination
   B. class action
   C. racial action
   D. legislative action

31. Prejudice is based on _____.
   A. the truth
   B. ideology
   C. limited information
   D. minority behavior

32. Push factors that stimulate migration are _____.
   A. better jobs out side
   B. religious freedom
   C. higher wages
   D. natural disasters in the home country

33. Groups are characterized as minority when they do not have _____.
   A. enough numbers
   B. too many children
   C. few women
   D. power

34. According to Marx, a class system is based upon the realtionship to _____.
    A. nature
    B. the means of production
    C. dominant groups
    D. minority groups

35. Marx's methodology is called _____.
    A. class conflict
    B. ideology
    C. historical materialism
    D. all of the above

36. The fourth stage in Marx's evolutionary model of society is _____.
    A. ancient stage
    B. bourgeois stage
    C. asiatic stage
    D. feudal stage

37. The model minority group is _____.
    A. Latinos
    B. Africans
    C. Native Americans
    D. Asians

CHAPTER 10

Race and Ethnicity: Relationships That Make a World

"You can write, you can write about what you know, your experience is valuable, who you are is valuable, and how you view the world and society and the cosmos is valuable. Put it down on paper, paint a picture, make a drawing, write music!"

Rudolpho Anaya, *Chicano Authors: Inquiry by Interview*

■ ■ ■

Rita Levi-Montalcini wanted to attend the university. Her father, however, believed that his daughters should be wives and mothers, not educated, career women. Rita persisted in her entreaties. Her father finally agreed to pay for her medical school education at the University of Turin in Italy. Rita enjoyed her studies, did very well in them, and she joined the teaching staff at the University of Turin after her graduation from medical school in 1936.

Soon, the Fascists came to power in Italy. Their anti-Jewish campaign forbade the Italian publishers to publish anything written by a Jewish writer. Rita, undeterred, published the results of her experiments in scientific journals in Belgium. The Fascists then barred Jews from Italian Universities. Rita went into hiding in a small Turin apartment, where she conducted experiments on the central nervous system of chick embryos in a make-shift laboratory set up in the bedroom. When the situation became even more intolerable, she fled Italy, taking her family with her.

While on the run from the Nazis, she continued to perform scientific experiments. Of necessity, she used the simplest of tools: a needle that she sharpened on a stone, alcohol (which she used to keep things sterile), eggs that she found in farmhouses and in barns, and a fifteenth-century portable microscope. She would not allow the children to scramble and to eat the eggs until she had finished performing her experiments on the chick embryos. This did not make her popular with her siblings who were not keen on the idea of eating eggs that had been used in scientific experiments.

Rita Levi-Montalcini's experiments elicited an invitation from Dr. Hamburger of Washington University in St. Louis. He was struck by Rita's repeat, in the simple Turin bedroom lab, of an experiment that he had originally conducted. Her results were similar to his results, but Rita drew very different conclusions from them. Hamburger invited her to visit him at Washington University, in St. Louis, to find out who was right. She accepted his gracious invitation, little guessing that she would stay there for almost twenty years. They did find out who was right. It was she.

The simple experiments on the central nervous system of chick embryos, begun while on the run from the Nazis, eventually led Rita Levi-Montalcini to discover *nerve growth factor* (NGF), a bodily substance that she proved affects cells in the immune and central nervous systems and that regulates the rate at which cells multiply. The discovery of NGF inaugurated a whole new line of fundamental scientific research. Subsequently, other nerve growth factors have been discovered. For her discovery of NGF, she was awarded both the top U.S. award, the Lasker, and the Nobel Prize in medicine (1986).

What Is a Minority Group?

As the concept is commonly used in contemporary American society, the term **minority group** can be applied to any recognizable racial, ethnic, religious, or gender group that has suffered a historical disadvantage as a result of an ingrained pattern of prejudice and discrimination. Following a consistent pattern of discrimination, the minority group experiences social isolation and segregation (Massey and Denton, 1993). Ultimately, minorities are avoided and rejected by the dominant group in society. Over the long term, these acts of discrimination and the acceptance of racial segregation are institutionalized and legalized as a direct result of social pressure, political action, and social legislation.

As a result of several decades of sociological research and scientific observations, it is now accepted by most sociologists who have studied race relations in the United States that there are five fundamental characteristics that determine minority group status (Wagley and Harris, 1958):

1. A minority group must have a history of unequal treatment.
2. A minority group must have distinctive physical or cultural characteristics.
3. Their membership in the group must be involuntary.
4. They experience in-group marriage.
5. They must be aware of their minority status.

Experience a History of Unequal Treatment

A minority group must have a history of being the object of prejudice, discrimination, **segregation** (the physical and social separation of different racial and ethnic groups) (Massey and Denton, 1993; Jackman, 1994), racism, sexism, **xenophobia** (fear of strangers or of foreigners) or **homophobia** (fear of homosexuals). **Racism** refers to a form of inequality wherein one racial group dominates another and legitimaizes this domination with ideologies that proclaim the **majority group**—that is, those who wield power in society—is superior physically, morally, intellectually, etc. (Lapchick, 1991; Feagin and Feagin, 1996). The majority group institutes a wide variety of practices, including laws, that protect their dominance (Daniels, 1997). **Sexism** refers to a form of inequality wherein one gender group dominates another and legitimates this domination with ideologies that proclaim that the majority group is superior physically, morally, intellectually, etc. In sexism, the majority group also institutes a wide variety of practices, including laws, that protect their dominance (Williams, 1995).

Unequal treatment of minority groups is based on the fact that the majority group has not only the means to discriminate against them, but also the social will and the economic and political ability to do so (Almaguer, 1994). Once minorities are selected for special treatment, the effects of prejudicial attitudes and the development of stereotypes virtually guarantee their unequal treatment (Churchill, 1994; Onishi, 1996). This pattern of long term discrimination is translated into laws and social policies that enforce their segregation and social isolation. Please read Box 10.1. In the final analysis, the legal institutions reflect their unequal treatment and ultimately justify subordination of minorities (Ropers, 1995).

Distinctive Characteristics

Probably the most important part of our definition of a minority group is that minorities must have some physical or cultural characteristics that differentiate them from the majority group. As you probably already guessed, this

BOX 10.1

Charlayne Hunter-Gault on the Importance of Role Models and Pursuing Your Vision

Charlayne Hunter-Gault is one of two students who desegregated the University of Georgia during the Civil Rights Movement in the United States. She became a successful national news correspondent. In the following excerpt from her autobiography, she recalls pursuing her vision of becoming a news reporter in the face of attempts at dissuasion:

I studied the comic-strip character Brenda Starr as I might have studied a journalism textbook, had there been one. I had been reading the funny papers, as we called them, all my life, and along with Dick Tracy and Dagwood, Brenda Starr was one of my favorite characters. I loved her sense of adventure, and the adventures she was always having as the star reporter on the *New York Daily Flash.* I especially loved the mystery and romance in her life, a lot of which was supplied by Basil St. John, a one-eyed connoisseur of black orchids. The fact that Brenda Starr was a redheaded, blue-eyed white woman who worked in an all-white newsroom did not even register with me until, one day during my senior year, I had a conversation about what I wanted to do after I graduated. "I want to be a reporter." By that time, I had been editor of the paper for two years—the first junior ever to be appointed to the position, thanks to Mrs. Evans.

"You better hang up those pipe dreams and go on over there to Spelman [a renowned college for African American females] and become a teacher," she told me in all seriousness. And while she didn't say it in so many words, it was clear to me what she meant: Journalism is a white man's profession; even your precious Brenda Starr is an exception! I later told Mrs. Evans about the conversation; she looked at me the way she usually did when she was about to cut with a verbal knife so sharp it left no visible marks, and said ever so sweetly, "Now, we know what to do with advice like that, don't we?"

Source: Charlayne Hunter-Gault, 1992.

would only seem logical in view of the fact that if you intend to discriminate against a particular person or group then you must select some unique physical or cultural characteristics of the individual or the group and focus attention on them. A quick review of the historical record makes it abundantly clear that racist societies always have found ways to make minorities appear different. And in their zeal to discriminate against minorities, some societies have even gone as far as to make them appear subhuman.

Involuntary Membership

Accident of birth is the basis for involuntary membership in a minority group. Therefore, membership is an **ascribed status,** since individuals are born into a minority group and minority membership identifies the individual in society. However, the most important thing to remember about minority group status is that a person is only a minority because society arbitrarily has defined membership in a particular group as having negative social conse-quences. The positive or negative characteristics associated with a particular set of physical attributes simply reflects society's definition of a minority group.

For example, the fact that a person is born with dark pigmentation will have certain social consequences for a person born in Lagos, Nigeria, a different outcome for someone born in New York City and yet another set of consequences for a person born in Montgomery, Alabama. Obviously, the accident of birth does have profound consequences for minorities, as minority group status has a direct impact on a person's life chances.

In-Group Marriage

The propensity for in-group marriage is another important characteristic of minority group status. **Endogamy** refers to the tendency of minorities to marry within their group. The opposite of endogamy is **exogamy,** or as we commonly say, intermarriage. In the United States, immigrants (who later on are identified as ethnic and racial groups) historically have practiced endogamy during their early period of settlement, when they often experience prejudice, discrimination, high levels of social isolation and enforced segregation. But, as minorities gain social acceptance their rate of exogamy increases. For this reason, the rate of exogamy (i.e., intermarriage) among minorities is often used by sociologists to indicate the level of social acceptance and the degree of assimilation of the minority. Please read Table 10.1 on the extent of intermarriage among Latinos.

TABLE 10.1. Latino Ethnicity of Wives and Husbands in the United States, 1996 (In Percents)

Ethnicity of wives	Same	Other Hispanic	Non-hispanic
All Hispanics	76	6	18
Mexican	82	3	15
Puerto Rican	67	10	23
Cuban	70	10	20
Ethnicity of husbands			
All Hispanics	79	6	15
Mexican	84	3	13
Puerto Rican	66	13	21
Cuban	70	19	11

Source: Adapted from del Pinal and Singer, 1997: Figure 10, p. 29.

With regard to African Americans, there has been a fairly sharp increase between 1980 and 1990 in the rate of intermarriage between blacks and whites, although it is still rare (Farley, 1997: 256). Young African American males are increasingly marrying white females. About 5.6 percent of young African American males who married in the 1980s had white wives, a considerable increase from the 1950s and 1960s when fewer than 1 percent of African males had white wives (Farley, 1997).

Awareness of Subordinate Status

While the observation that minorities must recognize that they are minorities may seem self evident, it happens that minority group status is not always recognized or even accepted by all of the members of the group. You have probably met someone in the past who refuses to accept the fact that they are an ethnic or racial minority. This can affect their self-concept and, for some, may result in an identity crisis. But, on the other hand, the acceptance of minority group status often results in greater social cohesiveness among minorities.

As a result of their small group research, social psychologists have discovered that strong identification with their minority status results in the development of a *consciousness of kind* among minorities. The social psychologist *Franklin Giddings* (1924) referred to **consciousness of kind** as a feeling of identification with others who are similar to oneself. As a result, minorities often develop an *esprit de corps*, a sense of brotherhood or a feeling that "we have a shared historical experience" (Northcott, 1948). In large part, this explains why you often notice that minority students on your campus seem to have a natural attraction for each other, as they share a consciousness of kind. Minority students just feel more comfortable around people who have had many of the same life experiences that they have had and therefore they "understand each other."

Types of Minority Groups

In view of the social and cultural diversity of American society today it is sometimes difficult to categorize all the minorities who are a part of the American cultural environment. But, despite the heterogeneity of American society most minorities can be assigned to at least one of five basic minority groups:

- A Racial Group
- An Ethnic Group
- A Nationality Group
- A Religious Group
- A Gender Group

Racial Groups

The concept of **racial groups** is based on the premise that people are different because of observed physical differences and because these physical differences result in specific social consequences for the members of these groups (Marger, 1994; Newman, 1995). The criteria used by anthropologists to define racial groups are often based on commonly observed physical differences, such as body size and shape, skin color, facial features, and the structure and color of hair (Banton, 1983: 32-59).

However, there are two important factors to

consider in any discussion of racial classifications. The first is that any single physical characteristic is not statistically exclusive to any racial group (Kalish, 1995). Therefore, any physical characteristic that is used to identify a racial group, such as skin color, tends to overlap from one racial group to another (Sandor, 1994; Scales-Trent, 1995). For example, you have probably noticed that Puerto Ricans come in all colors, from dark to brown to white. So, the question remains, what race are Puerto Ricans? The second point is that while these racial distinctions are strictly arbitrary classifications, they are nonetheless important because they produce social consequences (Marable, 1997: 112). In effect, observed physical differences, such as skin color, are only important because society has made them important and our culture has given them social significance (Zack, 1995).

Ethnic Groups

While the concept of racial group is strictly a biological concept, ethnic group is a cultural concept (Feagin, 1996). The concept of ethnic group is based on the distinctive cultural characteristics of a particular group. The most common tangible aspects of a culture are its language, religion, social customs, folklore, historical origins, community traditions, manner of dress, and traditional cuisine (Thompson, 1989: 21-46; Snipp, 1996).

As distinct from a racial group, an **ethnic group** is defined by its unique cultural characteristics and *not* by its physical characteristics (Alba, 1992). For example, the racial concept *Asian* refers to a large group of individuals who share a common gene pool, while the *ethnic* distinctions among the various Asian groups represent the specific *cultural* differences that exist among them. There *are* significant cultural differences among the Japanese, Chinese, and Koreans. Therefore, while each of these groups is culturally distinct, they are all genetically related. However, most Americans find it convenient to refer to all people from the Far East as Asians. This is a good example of how people often use a racial category, in this case Asians, as a convenient way of relating to diverse groups of people who, in fact, are culturally distinct. Sociologists note that in

doing this, people are using race as a **master status**—a status that overrides the importance and salience all other statuses the individual occupies (Benjamin, 1991). Asian is also used by individuals who are otherwise ignorant of the distinct ethnic differences among various Asian groups.

Nationality Groups

Historically, the term **nationality group** was applied to those immigrants who arrived in America during the latter part of the nineteenth century. Today, the term nationality group is still applied to those Americans who identify themselves as English, Irish, Germans, Italians, etc. As a concept, nationality group is a broad based term used to describe citizens of a particular country. The term nationality group derives from a person's political allegiance to, or origin from, a particular nation. Hence, the term nationality group is a political concept and an identity and is not necessarily synonymous with any particular ethnic or racial group, although this is most often the case. *Do you recall the furor a few years ago when the top Olympic skater from France was black? Do you recall the furor that hit Italy when Ms. Italy appeared to be black, thereby not fitting the commonly held stereotype of "Italian?" Can you think of other instances of stereotypes regarding nationality groups? Please tell us about them. What do these instances tell us about the societies in which they occur?*

Religious Groups

The recognition of religious groups as minority groups is particularly important when a religious group is in the numerical minority in any given society. For example, when we think of religious minorities in the United States today, we usually think of such groups as the Jews, the Mormons, the Hutterites, and the Amish. Only a few years ago, Catholics experienced blatant discrimination and were considered minorities in the United States. They still *are* considered as minorities in other countries, such as Northern Ireland. When there is an absence of *crosscutting social circles* and the presence of *reinforced cleavage,* the religious minority within a society tends to be recognized for its ethnic or racial composition. In these circumstances, the minority religious group also is synonymous with an ethnic or racial group. For example, religious groups (like the Jews, the Sikhs, and the Nation of Islam) have very strong racial and ethnic attachments.

Gender Groups

As a group, women are a minority in American society since they have experienced both prejudice and discrimination, they have a long history of unequal treatment, they clearly have distinctive physical characteristics, they are aware of their minority group status, and their membership in the group is involuntary (Frankenberg, 1993). The minority status of ethnic and racial women is particularly significant in American society, as these women are often the victims of **double jeopardy.** This means that minority women suffer from discrimination not only because they are women, but also because they are members of an ethnic or racial group (Jamieson, 1995). Please read Box 10.2.

BOX 10.2

Barbara Jordan on Making the Most of Double Jeopardy

Barbara Jordan has been cited as one of the ten most influential women in the state of Texas. She is an attorney, who served for many years as a member of the United States Congress. In this excerpt from her autobiography, she speaks about learning to make the most of her law school education:

So I was at Boston University in this new and strange and different world, and it occurred to me that if I was going to succeed at this strange new adventure, I would have to read longer and more thoroughly than my colleagues at law school had to read. I felt that in order to compensate for what I had missed in earlier years, I would have to work harder, and study longer, than anybody else. . . . I did my reading not in the law library, but in a library at my graduate dorm, upstairs where it was very quiet, because apparently nobody else studied there. So I would go there at night after dinner. I would load my books under my arm and go the library, and I would read until the wee hours of the morning and then go to bed. . . .

I was always delighted when I would get called upon . . . in class. But the professors did not call on the "ladies" very much. There were certain favored people who always got called on, and then on some rare occasions a professor would come in and would announce: "We're going to have Ladies Day today." . . . We were just tolerated. We weren't considered really top drawer when it came to the study of law.

At some time in the spring, Bill Gibson, who was dating my roommate . . . organized a black study group, as we blacks had to form our own. This was because we were not invited into any of the other study groups. There were six or seven in our group . . . and we would just gather and talk it out and hear ourselves do that. One thing I learned was that you had to talk out the issues, the facts, the cases, the decisions, the process. You couldn't just read the cases and study alone in our library as I had been doing; and you couldn't get it all in the classroom. But once you had talked it out in the study group, it flowed more easily and make a lot more sense. . . .

. . . I learned to think things out and reach conclusions and defend what I had said.

In the past I had got along by spouting off. Whether you talked about debates or oratory, you dealt with speechifying. But I could no longer orate and let that pass for reasoning because there was not any demand for an orator in Boston University Law School. You had to think and read and understand and reason. I had learned at twenty-one that you couldn't just say a thing is so because it might not be so, and somebody brighter, smarter, and more thoughtful would come out and tell you it wasn't so. Then, if you still thought it was, you had to prove it. Well, that was a new thing for me. . . . I really cannot describe what that did to my insides and to my head. I thought: I'm being educated finally.

Source: Barbara Jordan and Shelby Hearon, 1979.

The Creation of Minority Groups

Depending on the circumstances and the historical period, a minority group can move up or down the social scale and also can gain acceptance into the larger society or remain on its fringes (Omi and Winant, 1994). Historically, there are five fundamental methods by which minority groups are created:

1. Voluntary Migration
2. Involuntary Migration
3. Political Annexation
4. Colonial Expansion
5. Internal Colonialism

Voluntary Migration

In all the experiences of immigration, it is not unusual for new arrivals in a host society to be treated as outsiders, foreigners, and immigrants. This is the first step in the creation of a new minority by the method of voluntary migration. U.S. history is replete with dozens of examples of voluntary migration. *Can you think of one or two examples? Please tell us about them.* The process of acceptance and integration of immigrants into the host society is not always easy or quick. Some immigrants retain their minority status for decades.

Involuntary Migration

It should be clear to most that not all immigrants who arrive as voluntary migrants really emigrate of their own volition. For example, the Irish Catholics were voluntary migrants but they did not emigrate because they had a strong desire to leave their homeland; rather they were forced off their land and emigrated to avoid the death grip of starvation (Laxton, 1997). Similarly, in the story that opens this chapter, Rita Levi-Montalcini was a voluntary migrant, but she migrated not because she had a strong desire to leave her homeland, but because she wanted to avoid the Holocaust of the Nazis. Similarly, recently in Bosnia-Herzegovina, many people with ethnic group and religious affiliations that were despised by powerful others, fled particular geographical areas. Not because they wanted to leave their homeland, but because the alterna-

tive appeared to them to die (Schaefer, 1995). On the other hand, the African slaves who were brought to the New World in chains were clearly involuntary migrants (Frazier, 1957).

Political Annexation

Historically, it is common for those who are victorious in battle to claim the land of the vanquished. American history is replete with examples of territorial domination following a military victory. For example, the **Treaty of Guadalupe Hidalgo** (1848) ended the war between the United States and Mexico and forced Mexico to relinquish vast territories in the Southwest. The Mexicans living in these territories were considered racially inferior and were the victims of an untold number of acts of racism and violence. In a similar manner, the people of Puerto Rico and the Philippines were subjugated by the United States military and treated as racial minorities in their homeland.

Colonial Expansion

Many world history books refer to the period of **colonial expansion** as the period of "Exploration and Discovery." This refers to that historical period when the Europeans set out to claim and conquer all the territories in the New World. While their objective was to obtain more land, they also wanted to extract the raw materials from the conquered territories, ship them to the mother country, and thereby increase their wealth. But the key to their success was their ability to press the indigenous populations into forced labor.

The fact that these indigenous groups were all *People of Color* was particularly significant, as the European conquerors called upon a variety of racial theories to justify the subjugation of indigenous people throughout the world. If people could be made to believe that they were inferior and their only purpose in life was to serve as a source of cheap labor, obviously, this made it a lot easier for those who were intent on realizing their subjugation.

Internal Colonialism

The internal colonial model of race relations derives from the characteristics of classic colonialism. Under the system of **internal colonialism** there is no longer a need to create new minorities in foreign lands to use for cheap labor. Rather, these groups are now attracted to the mother country and are segregated within the society where their labor is exploited. In a real sense, internal colonies are created within the mother country (in this case the United States) and these labor reservations are popularly known as ghettos and barrios (Blauner, 1969).

The Definition of Prejudice

Prejudice refers to any unfavorable or negative *attitude* directed toward any person or group based on a set of assumed characteristics (Weitzer, 1997). Therefore, prejudice exists when any negative attitude is directed toward a particular individual or group. Prejudice is a universal phenomenon and occurs in all societies. In reality, no individual or society is free of prejudice.

Prejudice is usually based on a hostile or negative attitude toward a minority person, held by a member of the majority group. Although prejudice occurs in both minority and majority groups and can be directed from one group toward the other, the social consequences of prejudice are far more detrimental when held and acted upon by members of the majority group.

While prejudice is an individual characteristic reflecting certain psychological and social needs, it also reflects the values of the society in which we live. Therefore while prejudice is the result of the socialization process, it is also a significant part of our immediate social environment and an intrinsic characteristic of the society in which we live. Prejudicial attitudes are often held by the individual because they are the result of social expectations and tend to support the status quo.

Prejudice is based on any negative or hostile attitudes that a person may have against another person or group because of some perceived or assumed differences based on: (1) race, (2) ethnic origin, (3) religious identification, (4) gender, (5) social class, (6) age, or (7) sexual orientation. Prejudice is often based on inaccurate information or inflexible generalizations.

In sum, prejudice is most likely to occur among those individuals who are: (1) rigid in their thinking, (2) ignorant of racial and ethnic differences, and (3) are unwilling to accept those who are different from themselves. The likelihood of changing a prejudiced person is difficult because prejudice is often a rigid attitude that the prejudiced person will defend at all costs.

Theories of Prejudice

In reality, prejudice is unavoidable because it is learned in the family, in our peer groups, and in the general society. Therefore, prejudice is pervasive throughout society and every member of society is affected by prejudicial attitudes in one way or another — either as the perpetrators of prejudice or the victims of prejudice.

In an effort to understand the origins and tenacity of prejudice, sociologists have developed several theories regarding its existence and persistence. While a number of theories attempt to explain the pervasiveness of prejudice in society, the following five basic theoretical approaches serve as the basis for our understanding of prejudice:

1. The Exploitation Theory
2. The Scapegoating Theory
3. The Authoritarian Personality Theory
4. The Ecological Theory
5. The Linguistic Theory

The Exploitation Theory

The **exploitation theory** is most likely to take hold in those societies where there is a significant disparity in the power relationship between the majority group and various minority groups. This theory is applicable when one group dominates and takes advantage of another. It requires that the subordinate groups in society are kept in their proper place and they must bend their will to the needs and desires of the dominant group. This relationship creates tension and conflict between the majority and minority groups in society. Karl Marx viewed this as the systematic economic exploitation of the working classes.

Marx believed that the pervasiveness of prejudice in society is used by those in power to keep certain groups in subordinate positions. In capitalist societies, prejudice serves three key functions: (1) it justifies the exploitation of minorities, (2) it makes minorities feel inferior, and (3) it keeps minorities in their place.

The Scapegoating Theory

Scapegoating occurs when people place blame for their problems on some convenient, but powerless and innocent, person or group. The **scapegoating theory** holds that those who are unwilling to accept personal blame for their misfortunes will find another person or group to blame for their problems.

The term scapegoating derives from the practice among the ancient Hebrews, who observed an annual ritual where they symbolically placed all their sins on a goat that was then driven out into the wilderness. This purification rite served to rejuvenate the moral and religious health of the Jewish community. *Can you think of similar or analogous rituals in groups to which you, or someone you know, belongs? Please tell us about it.*

A closely related theory is the frustration-aggression hypothesis, proposed by John Dollard (1937). Dollard suggested that the frustration-aggression hypothesis served to explain the psycho-dynamics of scapegoating. Essentially, his theory held that when individuals are frustrated in their attempts to achieve a strongly desired goal, they tend to become aggressive. If they cannot retaliate against the source of their frustration—either because they cannot identify the source of their frustration, the source is considered too powerful, or they fear the consequences—then they will direct their growing frustration at some weaker or less threatening person or object. From the psychological perspective prejudice is considered a form of aggression and is viewed as a universal response to frustration. History reveals that, from time to time, various racial minorities were targets of frustration and victims of aggression and violence. The best known example of this was the mass extermination of the Jews in Nazi Germany. Hitler used the Jews as scapegoats for all the social ills of pre-war Germany.

Authoritarian Personality

A well-known approach to the study of prejudice in the United States is the authoritarian personality studies. Theodore Adorno and his colleagues did the pioneering work in the psychological study of prejudice in the late 1940's at the University of California, Berkeley.

The authors administered more than 2,000 interviews and psychological tests for this study. They found that *approximately ten percent of all Americans revealed strong authoritarian characteristics,* while *thirty percent demonstrated a strong propensity for authoritarianism.*

The **authoritarian personality** is represented by a personality type noted for (1) extreme conformity, (2) rigid thinking, (3) superstition, (4) toughness, (5) suppression of emotions, (6) strong adherence to convention, (7) submissiveness to authority, and (8) arrogance toward those whom they consider inferior. Research indicates that authoritarians are very insecure and seek security in social hierarchies and in strong identification with the group.

As adults, authoritarians are quick to treat everyone whom they perceive as inferior with distrust and disdain. They also rank high on Adorno's **F-scale** (Fascism scale), a psychological test used to measure levels of personal prejudice against others. A high score on the F-scale demonstrates a high correlation with anti-Semitic attitudes.

The Ecological Theory

In its basic form, the **ecological theory** holds that the immediate social environment has a direct impact on the attitudes and perceptions of all individuals. Therefore, if a person lives in surroundings where prejudice is part and parcel of everyday social interaction, then they are likely to share prejudicial attitudes, political perspectives, religious beliefs, and life goals.

An excellent example of this phenomenon was reported by *Thomas Pettigrew* (1959), who observed that whites in the south were more prejudiced against African Americans than whites in the north. However, he discovered that when southern students moved north to attend college they accepted the more liberal attitudes of their fellow Northern students as their own. On the other hand, when northern students transferred to southern universities, they very quickly accepted the more prejudicial attitudes of their southern classmates.

A more specific application of the ecological theory is the observation that racial attitudes are not only affected by regional differences, but also by organizational membership. This would include membership in segregated social, community, civic, recreational, and business organizations. It is clear that these organizations have a profound effect on people's social, political, and racial attitudes (Massaquoi, 1996).

Just as membership in private organizations can affect a person's racial attitudes, it is also true that the work environment has a significant impact on the maintenance of prejudicial attitudes. For this reason, the expression of prejudicial attitudes and the willingness to discriminate are usually situation specific. That is, people may express prejudicial attitudes and discriminate in one situation but *not* do so in another (Cose, 1996; Merton, 1949). This explains why most bigots will select a safe place to discriminate. African Americans, in particular, are very much aware of this form of closet bigotry (Sigelman and Welch, 1991: 47-66).

The Linguistic Theory

The **linguistic theory** is based on the premise that our language and cultural environment have a direct impact on our way of thinking and affect the development of our ideas and opinions. *Edward Sapir* (1921) and *Benjamin Whorf* are the researchers who developed the linguistic theory and promoted the renowned **Sapir-Whorf hypothesis.** This hypothesis holds that the language we use is more than just a medium for interpersonal communication; *it is also a framework or template for attributing meaning to social reality.* As such, language plays a very significant role in determining the social reality that we know and experience (Deutscher, 1973).

The integration of ethnic slurs and disparaging remarks in our linguistic repertoire is known as **ethnophaulism.** (Please see Driedger, 1996, on ethnophaulism in multi-ethnic Canada.) Even the use of essentially neutral words in our conversations sometimes has positive or negative connotations. For example, the word "black" historically has conveyed a negative connotation. Witches are dressed in black, some plagues are called black, death is associated with the color black, evil magic is black magic, and when people are ostracized we often say they are blacklisted or blackballed. On the other hand, the color white historically

has had positive connotations, such as in virginal bridal gowns, First Communion dresses, and even in soap (Moore, 1988: 269-279). Similarly, Asians have been portrayed in the West as yellow people. The color yellow has the negative connotation of referring to an individual who is cowardly, tricky, or otherwise untrustworthy (Moore, 1988: 270-271). Women have also have had to deal with negative appellations, such as girl, dame, broad, sister, chick, cupcake, fox, and even bitch (Baker, 1988: 280-295).

The Sapir-Whorf hypothesis holds that these connotations become a part of our cultural environment. Therefore, we need to be careful of the words we use. The sociological imagination and the Sapir-Whorf hypothesis enable us to appreciate that the old adage, "Sticks and stones will break my bones, but words will never hurt me," overlooks that fact that words are templates of meaning attribution, pieces of social structure that help us to construct the world in which we live. *The symbols that our words convey are very important in sorting out and eliminating prejudicial attitudes from our own lives.* Our attitudes and opinions *are* affected by our use of particular words to describe certain groups and by our association of specific words with certain negative characteristics or experiences. *Have you ever experienced ethnophaulism? Please tell us about one or two instances. How did the experience make you feel? What strategies have you found useful in dealing with ethnophaulisms? Please tell us about it.*

Stereotypes and Prejudice

The ability to sustain prejudicial attitudes over a long period of time is a reflection of an individual's dependence on stereotypes, which are a characteristic of prejudiced thinking. For without stereotypes, prejudice cannot exist. **Stereotypes** refer to any set of biased generalizations about an individual or group that are (1) unfavorable, (2) exaggerated, and (3) oversimplified.

Stereotypes are heuristic devices that allow the individual to sort people into certain slots, based upon a set of preconceived notions. While the use of stereotypes can make life less complicated, there are a number of serious problems with the use of stereotypes. Stereo-

Race and Ethnicity: Relationships That Make a World ■ 357

types can lead to many pitfalls, because they can (1) mislead us with false conceptions, (2) are often based on negative or biased information, (3) are emotionally anchored, (4) are difficult to change (even in the light of new information), and (5) they are easily adopted into our personality and psychological make-up (Stroebe and Insko, 1989: 4-30). Recent research indicates that whites who accept racial stereotypes express a desire for greater social distance from Peoples of Color than do whites who reject negative racial stereotypes (Krysan and Farley, 1993). Even though people may realize that their stereotypes are incorrect or baseless, they are nonetheless maintained because they represent the shared beliefs of the community (Pettigrew, 1982: 7-14).

Characteristics of Stereotypes

Following years of sociological and psychological research on the relationship between prejudice and stereotypes, it is now clear that stereotypes have five basic characteristics:

1. *Stereotypes are Self-Fulfilling*
   Because the social structure allows little room for change in the lives of some minorities, their lives become very predicable. For example, this is true of the urban poor, who have limited lifestyle options. Therefore their daily lives are monotonous and predictable and are often self-fulfilling.
2. *Stereotypes are Based on Selective Perception*
   Once people accept the credibility of a stereotype, they create a mind-set and search for characteristics that fit the original stereotype for that particular group. For these reasons, stereotypes often become self-fulfilling prophecies.
3. *Stereotypes are Most Often Negative*
   Historically when stereotypes are associated with racial and ethnic groups they are usually negative. This is the reason that the maintenance of stereotypes supports prejudicial attitudes.
4. *Stereotypes Result in Rejection and Social Isolation*
   Since stereotypes are often negative, they encourage a policy of avoidance and rejection, which leads to social isolation.

5. *Stereotypes are Based on a Kernel of Truth*
   Stereotypes are often accepted because they are based on a kernel of truth. Sometimes an anomalous characteristic of the group is selected and then projected to all members of that group.

Types of Discrimination

Discrimination occurs when an act, a status, or behavior elicits actions that exclude specific individuals or groups from certain rights, opportunities, or privileges. Therefore, *discrimination is an act* that results in the unequal treatment of an individual or a group based upon race, ethnicity, religion, gender, sexual orientation, age, or social class. **Individual discrimination**—such as individual racism, individual sexism—refers to unequal treatment of an *individual* based on race, ethnicity, religion, sexual orientation, age, or social class. On the other hand, **institutional discrimination** (sometimes referred to as **structural discrimination**) refers to the *business-as-usual practices* of organizations, groups, bureaucracies, and other institutions that result in the unequal treatment of an individual or a group based upon race, ethnicity, religion, gender, sexual orientation, age, or social class. Institutional discrimination is carried out by functionaries who implement the policies and procedures of the organizations to which they belong (Carmichael and Hamilton, 1967; Wilson, 1980, 1987, 1989; Margolis and Romero, 1998).

For example, a bank-loan officer may carry out the bank's policy of denying loans to people who live in certain neighborhoods. Those neighborhoods happen to be populated exclusively, or virtually so, by persons of Latino, African-American, or Native-American Indian descent. These loan policies, then, are characterized as institutional discrimination. Likewise, a business may fill its job vacancies by word-of-mouth practices. Since many people tend to associate in their recreational time disproportionately with persons whose social-class, ethnic, and racial memberships are similar to their own, advertising vacant positions by word-of-mouth tends to result in *social reproduction*. New hires are similar in demographic characteristics—including gender, race, ethnicity, age, and physical ability level—to those whom they replace. If the work place originally lacked females, Latinos, African-Americans, Native-American Indians, and so forth, word-of-mouth advertising of vacant practices almost guarantees that the imbalance persists indefinitely.

When discrimination occurs, frequently it is based on an existing prejudice, since discrimination is often the tangible expression of prejudice. However, it is possible for a person to discriminate without being prejudiced, as is exemplified in many forms of institutional discrimination. Conversely, it is also possible to be prejudiced without discriminating (Merton, 1949). But when, prejudice is acted upon it, is transformed into discrimination and this usually means that the victims of discrimination will experience negative consequences. (Please see Janie Victoria's study of how African American parents successfully teach their daughters to resist, rather than cope with, the sexism and racism they experience. This study is found in Leadbeater and Way, 1996.)

Discrimination is well known to all minorities. It is likely to affect them every day of their lives (Feagin and Sykes, 1994; Carger, 1996; Valdés, 1996; Stolzenberg and Tienda, 1997). The interest in the study of discrimination is related to the fact that unequal treatment and the deprivation of opportunities are so clear and their impact so immediate that they cannot be ignored. Therefore, it would be particularly instructive to focus on some of the most common types of discrimination, including (1) economic, (2) labor market, (3) educational, (4) housing, and (5) gender discrimination.

Economic Discrimination

Economic discrimination occurs when laws, public policies, or corporate policies have a differential impact on certain groups, putting them at an economic disadvantage. The most blatant form of economic discrimination occurs in the determination of the wage structure. All of the economic studies (to date) demonstrate that minorities and women have suffered, and continue to suffer, from a **wage gap differential.** This simply means that minorities and women are often paid less for doing the same

type of work. Because of wage discrimination, women typically receive about seventy-two percent of the wages that men receive for doing the same type of work (Bianchi and Spain, 1997). Likewise, African Americans and Latinos also suffer the effects of the wage gap differential (Simms, 1995; Wilson, 1997).

Economic discrimination can also occur in the nation's banking and mortgage institutions when minorities are in need of housing and in the insurance industry, where the need for automobile, home, and life insurance also places minorities at a severe economic disadvantage (Gonzales, 1991).

Labor Market Discrimination

Although the hiring practices of employers are carefully scrutinized to insure that they comply with government regulations regarding anti-discrimination provisions, it is still true that not all employers follow these rules and regulations. In fact, the best examples of the long term effects of institutional racism are most apparent in the hiring practices of employers (Bonacich, 1972, 1976; Amott and Matthei, 1991). One of the first areas of hiring discrimination can be seen in the role of employers as **gate keepers**, in that they always have the option of applying certain rules and regulations as they see fit. This results in blatant acts of discrimination in the labor market.

In view of the unemployment rate and growing economic instability, the labor market can best be described as an *employer's marketplace.* The primary reason that employers have the advantage is the simple fact that there are more people looking for work than there are jobs. Consequently, employers can be very selective in their hiring practices. These labor market conditions open an array of opportunities for employers selectively to eliminate certain groups from their labor force. Under these circumstances, the employer's position can be simply stated as, "Why discriminate, when you can eliminate?"

Educational Discrimination

In 1954, the Supreme Court ruled in *Brown vs. the Board of Education* that it is illegal to distinguish among racial groups for purposes of institutional discrimination in public

TABLE 10.2. Tenured Faculty at University of California (UC Campuses and in the California Public Community Colleges, by Race and Ethnicity, for Selected Years (Percent and Raw Total in Thousands) _____

Institution and years	African American	White American	Latino	Asian American	Native American	Total Percent	Total Number
UC System							
1977	1.8%	90.76%	2.55%	4.55%	0.34%	100%	6,505
1995	2.5%	82.68%	4.43%	10.10%	0.29%	100%	6,811
CA Public Community College System							
1984	4.90%	85.70%	5.30%	3.50%	0.60%	100%	15,604
1991	5.70%	81.02%	7.40%	5.00%	0.90%	100%	16,835

Source: Chancellor's Office, California Community Colleges; University of California Biennial Higher Education Staff Information (EEO-6) reports, as cited in Tierney, 1996: 127.

schools. Despite the fact that more than forty years have passed since the high Court's ruling on racial segregation in public schools, it is clear that most of the nation's schools remain highly segregated (Meier, et al., 1989: 49-57; Rothstein, 1995).

Another serious problem facing the nation's education system is the inordinately high drop-out rate among minority students. If the number of students who graduate from high school today is any indication of the success of public education, then we can only conclude that the system has failed to provide a quality educational experience for minority students (See Table 10.3 below).

Chicano novelist, playwright, short-story writer, and scriptwriter, *Rudolfo Anaya*, understands that discrimination in education may be blatant or subtle. As a child, he was reared by parents who spoke Spanish, and he was raised in an almost completely Latino background, speaking only Spanish at home. He did not learn English until he entered first grade. When authority figures such as educators and school administrators tell Chicano children that:

TABLE 10.3. Persons 14 to 24 Years Old by High School Graduate Status and Dropout Status, by Sex, Race and Hispanic Origin, 1995 (Numbers in Thousands) _____

	Persons 18 to 24 Years Old				
	Number	Number	Percent	High School Dropouts	
Race, Hispanic Origin, and Sex	All Persons Aged 18 to 24	Total High School Graduates₁	Of persons Aged 18 to 24 who are High School Graduates	Number	As a Percent of All Persons Aged 18 to 24
ALL RACES					
All Persons	24,900	20,125	80.8	3,471	13.9
Males	12,351	9,789	79.3	1,791	14.5
Females	12,548	10,338	82.4	1,679	13.4
WHITES All Persons	19,866	16,269	81.9	2,711	13.6
White Males	9,980	8,001	80.2	1,430	14.3
White Females	9,886	8,271	83.7	1,281	13.0
BLACKS All Persons	3,625	2,788	76.9	522	14.4
Black Males	1,660	1,247	75.1	235	14.2
Black Females	1,965	1,541	78.4	287	14.6
HISPANICS All Persons	3,603	2,112	58.6	1,250	34.7
Hispanic Males	1,907	1,106	58.0	653	34.2
Hispanic Females	1,696	1,011	59.6	598	35.4

Source: Adapted from U.S. Bureau of the Census, Current Population Survey.
Online: www.census.gov, Table A-5/May 3, 1998.
1. High school graduates are persons who have completed 4 years of high school or more.

they are at a disadvantage because they don't have command of the English language, . . . the more they begin to believe it; you build in a self-fulfilling prophecy. That is not right! . . .

We have . . . a rich culture, rich tradition. . . . a rich literary tradition. So we have to change that around *y en vez de decir que no tenemos el talento* [and instead of saying that we don't have the talent], say "You can write, you can write about what you know, your experience is valuable, who you are is valuable, and how you view the world and society and the cosmos is valuable. Put it down on paper, paint a picture, make a drawing, write music!" (Rudolfo Anaya, as cited in Bruce-Novoa, 1980).

Housing Discrimination

The history of urbanization in America is also the history of housing segregation, for as our nation became more urbanized, it also became more segregated. According to all the housing studies, the United States is highly segregated residentially today (Draden, 1986; Momeni, 1987, 1990). The high level of residential segregation demonstrates that anti-discrimination laws in housing are ineffective (Jiobu, 1988: 107-148). Residential segregation is the norm in American society today. It is not uncommon to find African American families, with above average incomes, living in areas were the property values and quality of housing are far below what would be expected statistically (Gonzales, 1988; 1989). In contrast, it is difficult to locate white families living in neighborhoods where the housing values are as incongruous with their income and level of education (Fong, 1996; Jackman and Jackman, 1986).

Gender Discrimination

Although women constitute 52 percent of the nation's population, they are a minority group and historically have experienced a wide range of discriminatory practices. Since the dawn of civilization, women have been considered the subordinate gender and have been treated as second class citizens (Bell and Blumenfeld, 1995; Chafetz, 1974: 108-152).

Perhaps the best known area of gender discrimination occurs in the area of wages and compensation for work (Mezey, 1992: 91-108). In view of a long history of discrimination against working women and the fact that wom-

en's work never has been given the same value as men's work, it is not surprising that women are still paid less than men for doing the same work (Chafetz, 1990: 45-63). Even the most recent income data reveal that women earn about seventy-two percent of what men earn, for doing the same kind of work and with the same level of experience and education (Bianchi and Spain, 1997). Simply stated, it is clear that women continue to serve as a source of cheap labor for American entrepreneurs.

Besides being paid less than men for comparable work, women also are segregated in certain occupations, such as secretaries, school teachers, health care workers, domestics, assembly line workers, and operatives. (Please read Table 10.4.) These jobs, historically, have offered the lowest wages and the fewest benefits for the skill levels and education required. More recent comparative studies have also found that when men are employed in these 'pink' collar jobs, they usually are paid more and they tend to experience more rapid and consistent promotions (Reskin and Hartmann, 1986).

Race and Ethnicity in the United States

The African American Experience

The first black immigrants arrived in Jamestown in 1619 as indentured servants. After serving their masters for a period of time, usually seven years, they were free to live and work on their own (Franklin, 1967: 46-49; Meier and Rudwick, 1966: 36-37). That is, they were free to live and work in the American colonies until Virginia legalized slavery in 1661. Their enslavement was justified on the basis that they were a separate species and therefore were "beasts of burden" (Gossett, 1965: 28-53; Jordan, 1968: 179-265).

By 1800, the lives of slaves were limited to back-breaking work on the plantations (Stamp, 1956: 34-85). In the eyes of white society, the slave family did not exist, as the father of a slave was "unknown" and the slave family had no legal standing. The master had the right to sell any slave, even children (Elkins, 1968: 55; Tannenbaum, 1946: 75-77). From the master's perspective, the slave family was a self-generating

TABLE 10.4. Sex Segregation in the Workplace in the United States: Top Five Occupations for Men and Women, 1995

Sex And Occupation	Number Employed	Percent Occupation Female
WOMEN		
Salesperson, Retail and Personal Serivces	4,338,128	65.6
Secretary	3,310,585	98.5
Cashier	2,159,784	79.2
Pre-School, Kindergarten, and Elementary School Teachers	2,039,32	91.2
Registered Nurse	1,840,587	93.1

	Number Employed	Percent Occupation Male
MEN		
Construction Worker	4,980,746	97.7
Mechanic	4,014,426	96.2
Truck Driver	2,732,255	95.5
Salesperson, Retail and Personal Services	2,274,872	34.4
Engineer	1,771,544	91.6

Source: Adapted from U.S. Bureau of Commerce, Bureau of the Census, 1996: 405-407.

institution that produced a never-ending supply of free labor (Stamp, 1956: 245-251).

During the ante bellum period (1815-1860), slave resistance and rebellions were a daily part of life. Besides burning barns, sabotaging equipment, and maiming livestock, the slaves took advantage of every opportunity to escape from a life of bondage. They were assisted in their flight for freedom by the *Abolitionist Movement* and the work of the *underground railroad* (Sorin, 1972: 21-37, 77-98). But, it was *Nat Turner's rebellion* in Virginia (1831) that struck terror into the hearts of all Southerners (Litwack, 1961: 230-246). Also, *John Brown's* raid at *Harpers Ferry* (1859) galvanized the South and brought the slavery question to the forefront of the political arena.

By the time Lincoln took office in February of 1861 seven states already had seceded from the Union. As part of his military strategy, President Lincoln issued the **Emancipation Proclamation** on January 1, 1863, as he wanted to deprive the South of their slave power.

The South not only was defeated in battle, its whole infrastructure and economy were destroyed. As a result, times were very difficult for the **Freedmen** (a sexist term for recently emancipated slaves). Jobs were scarce and most had to resort to *sharecropping*, a life that was only slightly better than slavery (Franklin,

1967: 311). In an attempt to deprive them of their political and civil rights, the **Ku Klux Klan** was organized in Tennessee in 1866 (Stamp, 1965: 199). Within a few years, the Klan had established a terrorist organization in each of the former slave states. In the public sector, the system of institutional segregation known as *Jim Crow* was adopted (1868) and was used to insure that blacks and whites would not have to share the same public facilities, such as trains, bathrooms, restaurants, lodging facilities, public swimming pools, and schools (Woodward, 1966: 12-29).

In an effort to escape the terror and violence experienced in the South many blacks moved north in a desperate attempt to find new opportunities and to experience peace and tranquillity (Meier and Rudwick, 1966: 189-192). At about the same time the termination of immigration during the First World War and the labor needs of the war time economy offered thousands of African Americans an opportunity to learn new skills and to take jobs in the industrial sector of the economy (Drake and Cayton, 1970: 46-64; Spear, 1967).

But, unfortunately, many blacks found that life in the Northern cities was harsh and fraught with danger. Please read Box 10.3. They were not always welcomed and some became the victims of racial violence. As early

BOX 10.3

Malcolm X on Constructing an Education in a Racist Society

Malcolm X is a martyr of the Civil Rights Movement. In the following excerpt from his autobiography, he speaks about constructing a viable education for himself under difficult circumstances:

I've never been one for inaction. Everything I've ever felt strongly about, I've done something about. I guess that's why . . . I . . . began writing to people . . . I never got a single reply . . .

It was because of my letters that I happened to stumble upon starting to acquire some kind of a homemade education.

I became increasingly frustrated at not being able to express what I wanted to convey in letters that I wrote. . . . In the street, I had commanded attention when I said something, but now, trying to write simple English, I not only wasn't articulate, I wasn't even functional. . . .

Many who today hear me somewhere in person, or on television, or those who read something I've said, will think I went to school far beyond the eighth grade. This impression is due entirely to my prison studies.

. . . [E]very book I picked up had few sentences which didn't contain anywhere from one to nearly all of the words that might as well have been in Chinese. When I just skipped those words, of course, I really ended up with little idea of what the book said. So I had come to the

Norfolk Prison Colony still going through only book-reading motions. . . .

I saw that the best thing I could do was get hold of a dictionary—to study, to learn some words. I was lucky enough to reason also that I should try to improve my penmanship. It was sad. I couldn't even write in a straight line. It was both ideas together that moved me to request a dictionary along with some tablets and pencils from the Norfolk Prison Colony school.

I spent two days just riffling uncertainly through the dictionary's pages. I'd never realized so many words existed! I didn't know *which* words I needed to learn. Finally, just to start some kind of action, I began copying.

In my slow, painstaking, ragged handwriting, I copied into my tablet everything printed on that first page, down to the punctuation marks.

I believe it took me a day. Then, aloud, I read back, to myself, everything I'd written on the tablet. Over and over, aloud, to myself, I read my own handwriting.

I woke up the next morning, thinking about those words—immensely proud to realize that not only had I written so much at one time, but I'd written words that I never knew were in the world. Moreover, with a little effort, I also could remember what many of these words meant. I reviewed the words

whose meaning I didn't remember. . . .

I was so fascinated that I went on—I copied the dictionary's next page. And the same experience came when I studied that. With every succeeding page, I also learned of people and places and events from history. Actually the dictionary is like a miniature encyclopedia. Finally the dictionary's A section had filled a whole tablet—and I went on into the B's. That was the way I started copying what eventually became the entire dictionary. . . .

I suppose it was inevitable that as my word-base broadened, I could for the first time pick up a book and read and now begin to understand what the book was saying. Anyone who has read a great deal can imagine the new world that opened. Let me tell you something: from then until I left that prison, in every free moment I had, if I was not reading in the library, I was reading on my bunk. You couldn't have gotten me out of books with a wedge. . . . Months passed without my even thinking about being imprisoned. In fact, up to then, I never had been so truly free in my life.

. . . Not long ago, an English writer telephoned me from London, asking questions. One was, "What's your alma mater?" I told him, "Books."

Source: Alex Haley and Malcolm X, 1965: 170, 171, 172-173, 179. Emphasis in original.

as 1908, a riot broke out in Springfield, Illinois, when a black man was wrongly accused of raping a white woman. In the end several black businesses and homes were torched and two

black men were lynched. A riot in East St. Louis in 1917 lasted several days and resulted in the death of 39 blacks and nine whites. During the *Red Summer* of 1919, more than 26 riots broke out across the country. One of the worst of these riots occurred in Chicago and resulted in the death of 23 blacks and 15 whites (Grimshaw, 1969).

With the collapse of the stock market in October of 1929, the living and working conditions of African Americans took a turn for the worse. To their detriment, the national economy did not improve until the outbreak of World War II. The war effort generated sufficient public pressure to change some discriminatory laws against African Americans. In 1942, the Congress of Racial Equality (CORE) was founded in Chicago. CORE members were the first to use "sit-ins" to desegregate restaurants in Chicago, Baltimore, and Los Angeles. In 1946, President Truman created the Presidential Committee on Civil Rights and two years later he issued an executive order desegregating the armed forces.

Until the end of the Second World War, it was common practice for homeowners to sign legally binding contracts called **restrictive covenants** that prohibited homeowners from selling their homes to certain undesirable individuals. The practice of restrictive covenants insured that housing for People of Color would be restricted to certain areas of the city (Gonzales, 1996: 46). In 1948, the Supreme Court ruled in *Shelly vs. Kraemer* that the courts could not legally enforce these restrictive covenants. And in 1954 the high court ruled in *Brown vs. the Topeka Board of Education* that racially separate schools were inherently unequal (Blaustein and Zangrando, 1968: 414-467).

Most would agree that the Civil Rights Movement started on December 1, 1955, in Montgomery, Alabama, when Rosa Parks, a Black seamstress, refused to give up her seat to a white man on a crowded bus (Gonzales, 1991: 213-219). A week later, the *Montgomery Bus Boycott* was in full swing. The boycott lasted a full year and in the end, the Supreme Court ruled that racial segregation on public transportation was unconstitutional. But perhaps more important, the boycott resulted in the founding of the Montgomery Improvement Association, headed by *Martin Luther King Jr.* (King, 1958). And as a result of his involvement

in the boycott, Dr. King gained national recognition and went on to become the leader of the Civil Rights Movement.

Sociologist *Reynold Farley* examines trends in residential segregation in the United States since the end of the World War II (Farley and Frey, 1994; Farley in Clayton, 1996: Chapter 3; Frey and Farley, 1996, Farley, 1997). Please read Table 10.5 on The Most Segregated and Least Segregated Metropolitan Areas in the United States, 1980 and 1990. Farley, a sociologist and *demographer* (one who studies population structure), finds that the *segregation of African Americans remains higher than that of Latinos and Asians*. However, he also finds that there have been some *improvements* in the extent of black-white segregation in the 1970s, 1980s, and 1990s. Farley cites the following as factors leading to a reduction in the extent of residential segregation (1997):

A softening of racist attitudes among whites. A half-century ago, national samples of urban whites were asked if there should be separate parts of the city for African Americans to live in. Eighty percent of whites endorsed racial segregation, whereas by the 1990s, fewer than one in five did so (Farley, 1991:1).

1. **New federal policies.** In the 1970s, Congress enacted and strengthened the enforcement provisions regarding the Fair Housing Law and other measures that govern mortgage lending and community investment.

3. **New housing construction.** New housing constriction that lacked a reputation for racial discrimination was built at a rapid rate.

4. **Growth of African American middle-class.** In 1968, when the Fair Housing Law was first enacted, only 8 percent of African American households had incomes of $50,000 or more (in constant 1994 dollars), whereas now about 17 percent of these households qualify. The percent of households that has social and economic characteristics that minimize the probability of white flight from neighborhoods fully doubled between 1970 and 1990.

TABLE 10.5. The 10 Most Segregated and Least Segregated Metropolitan Areas: Blacks and Whites, 1980 and 1990

1980		1990	
Metropolitan Area	Index of Dissimilarity₁	Metropolitan Area	Index of Dissimilarity₁
MOST SEGREGATED			
Bradenton, FL	91	Gary, IN	91
Chicago, IL	91	Detroit, MI	89
Gary, IN	90	Chicago, IL	87
Sarasota, FL	90	Cleveland, OH	86
Cleveland, OH	89	Buffalo, NY	84
Detroit, MI	89	Flint, MI	84
Ft. Myers, FL	89	Milwaukee, WI	84
Flint, MI	87	Saginaw, MI	84
Ft. Pierce, FL	87	Newark, NJ	83
West Palm Beach, FL	87	Philadelphia, PA	82
LEAST SEGREGATED			
Jacksonville, NC	36	Jacksonville, NC	31
Lawrence, KS	38	Lawton, OK	37
Danville, VA	41	Anchorage, AL	38
Anchorage, AL	42	Fayetteville, NC	41
Lawton, OK	43	Lawrence, KS	41
Fayetteville, NC	43	Clarksville, TN	42
Honolulu, HI	46	Ft. Walton Beach, FL	43
Anaheim, CA	47	Cheyenne, SY	43
San José, CA	48	Anaheim, CA	43
Colorado Springs, CO	48	Honolulu, HI	44

Source. Farley and Frey, 1994.
1. If all whites lived on entirely white blocks and all blacks lived on entirely black blocks, the index of dissimilarity equals 100. If race made absolutely no difference regarding place of residence, the index of dissimilarity equals zero.

The Latino Experience

As of 1996, Latinos or Hispanics comprise about 11 percent of the United States population. Numbering 29 million, the Latino population is expected to grow to about 100 million in 2050, and by 2005 it is projected to outnumber the African American population. Latinos already comprise about 4 out of ten school-age children in California (Pinal and Singer, 1997: 10). As of 1996, 64 percent of all Latinos in the U.S. are Mexican Americans, 11 percent are Puerto Rican Americans, and 4 percent are Cuban Americans. Fourteen percent of Latinos come from Central and South America, and 7 percent originate from "other" countries (U.S. Census Bureau, Current Population Survey, March, 1996).

Where Latinos Live

Latinos live in every state, although, historically, their population in concentrated in nine states: California, Texas, Florida, Illinois, New York, New Jersey, Arizona, New Mexico, and Colorado. As of the mid-1990s, these nine states account for about 85 percent of the Latino population. In 1996, the largest population of Latinos lives in California. Nine million Latinos, or about one out of three, live in California. About 5 million Latinos live in Texas, about half that number live in New York, about 2 million live in Florida, and 1 million live in Illinois. Latinos constitute 39 percent of New Mexico's population, 28 percent of California's 31 million residents, 27 percent of Texas's 18 million population, about one-fifth of Arizona's 4 million population.

Persons of Mexican origin are concentrated in the Southwest, although Illinois has a large Mexican American community in the Chicago area. Since the nineteenth century, Mexican Americans have migrated to the heartland of the nation, first to work in agriculture and on the railroads, and later to fill other jobs. Mexican Americans are more than 75 percent of Latinos in California, Texas, Illinois, and Arizona, and over half of Latinos in Colorado and New Mexico.

Puerto Ricans are the largest Latino group in New York. Cubans are the largest Latino group in Florida, where they are 38 percent of Latinos, followed by Central and South Americans (25 percent), Puerto Ricans (16 percent), and Mexican Americans (15 percent) (U.S. Bureau of the Census, 1996).

The Mexican Americans

With a population of over 16 million, Mexican Americans are the largest group of Latinos, accounting for six out of ten Latinos in the United States. Mexican American history began with the signing of the *Treaty of Guadalupe Hidalgo* in 1848, which ended the war between the United States and Mexico. This treaty gave the United States control of vast territories in the Southwest (Acuña, 1988: 5-15). One of the most important provisions of the treaty granted American citizenship to all Mexican nationals who remained in the area for one year following the ratification of the treaty. It is estimated that approximately 75,000 Mexicans thereby became American citizens (Moquin and Van Doren, 1971: 241-249).

During the early 1880s, the federal government encouraged the development of railroads, irrigation systems, and agricultural development in the Southwest. These projects required a large source of cheap, tractable labor (Fernandez, 1977: 97). To this end labor contractors were sent into Mexico. They encouraged thousands of Mexicans to leave their homeland and to work instead in the southwestern deserts (Cardoso, 1980: 58; Gamio, 1930; Gonzales, 1985: 1-18). By the late 1880s, 70 percent of the section crews and 90 percent of the extra gangs on the railroads were made up of Mexican laborers (McWilliams, 1968: 168). By 1910, they accounted for 95 percent of the farm workers harvesting crops in the Rio Grande Valley (Texas), the Salt River Valley (Arizona), and the Imperial Valley (California) (Reisler, 1976: 49-90).

The violence of the *Mexican Revolution* (1910-1924) prompted thousands of Mexicans

to cross the border (Cline, 1963: 24-30). Between 1900 and 1929, more than 710,000 Mexicans crossed the border. By 1920, the permanent Mexican population in the United States reached half a million. However, their economic well-being was upset by the *Great Depression.* With the failure of businesses and the loss of thousands of jobs, Mexican Americans were among the hardest hit. In many cities, they were blamed for the economic crisis, the lack of jobs, and the abuse of relief services (Hoffman, 1974; Meier and Rivera, 1972: 164).

The labor needs of the World War II spurred a renewed interest in Mexican labor. The U.S. government signed an agreement with Mexico to sponsor a *Bracero Program,* which guaranteed the availability of Mexican contract laborers during the war (Cockcroft, 1986: 67-75; Galarza, 1964). However, this program was in effect until 1968. During the entire period, more than five million Braceros worked as temporary contract laborers in the United States (Samora, 1975: 72).

After the war, some Mexican American veterans were given an opportunity to enter the nation's colleges and universities. Many of these college graduates went on to take white-collar jobs and professional positions. As a result of their educations and experiences, many became the leaders of their communities in the 1960s and 1970s.

The Puerto Ricans

The Puerto Ricans are the second largest group of Latinos, with a population of 2.7 million. Like the Mexican Americans, the Puerto Ricans can trace their origins to the Spanish conquest. In fact, Columbus "discovered" Puerto Rico during his second voyage to the New World in November of 1493. The Spanish began to colonize the island in 1510 (Hauberg, 1974: 13). By 1530, most of the 50,000 Indians on the island of Puerto Rico had died from overwork and the effects of various European diseases (Moscoso, 1980: 22-23). In an attempt to offset this labor shortage, the Spanish turned to the slave trade. By 1846, there were 51,000 slaves in Puerto Rico, out of a total population of 440,000 (Cordasco, 1973: 4).

--- BOX 10.4 ---

Gendered Transitions: Mexican American Immigration and Settlement Experiences

Through a rich ethnographic analysis of 26 immigrant households in a barrio in Northern California, sociologist Pierrette Hondagneu-Sotelo recently has published an insightful analysis of Mexican migration and settlement experiences. Pierrette Hondagneu-Sotelo focuses on how gender relations and the activities of women interact with the migration experiences of Mexican men and women. She then relates these migration experiences to modifications in gender relations both within families and the broader social world.

Hondagneu-Sotelo identifies the following three types of migrant behavior in her sample:

1. *Family stage migration.* In this pattern, husbands migrate as sojourners and the wives and families join them at a later date. This pattern comprised the majority of migrant behavior in her sample. Left in Mexico, wives learned to act autonomously and make decisions on behalf of themselves and their children. They became more assertive as a result. Over time, these women helped to consolidate female networks, which facilitated the migration of other females with information, job contacts, and economic assistance. Once in the United States, these wives played a greater role than before migration in household negotiations and in community activities outside of the home.

2. *Family unit migration.* In this pattern, entire families migrate at once.

3. *Individual migration.* In this pattern, individual men and women migrate alone, although they often are assisted by kinship networks both in Mexico and the United States.

Source: Pierrette Hondagneu-Sotelo, 1994.

Following the sinking of the *battleship Maine* in Havana Harbor, Congress declared war on Spain on April 21, 1898 (Golding, 1973. 94). *The Treaty of Paris,* which ended the war, was signed a year later and, Puerto Rico has since existed as a colony of the United States.

As a result of their colonial status, Puerto Ricans were given the right to travel to mainland United States. During the early period, very few Puerto Ricans migrated to the mainland, as their population did not exceed 12,000 in 1920 (Chenault, 1938: 53). By 1940, there were no more than 70,000 mainland residents (Senior, 1953: 130). But, with the introduction of commercial airline service between San Juan and New York City following World War II, the number of Puerto Ricans migrating to the mainland increased dramatically (Senior, 1965: 39). It is estimated that during the *Great Migration* (1946 to 1964), a total of 615,000 migrants arrived (U.S. Civil Rights, 1976: Table 8). Most of these migrants left Puerto Rico to escape the dire poverty of their homeland and to find jobs in the urban centers of America (Maldonado, 1980: 47; Uriciuoli, 1996).

The Cuban Americans

Cuban Americans are the third largest Latino group, with a population of just over a million. However, they did not arrive in the United States in any significant numbers until after Fidel Castro came to power in January of 1959. The rule of the communist government convinced many businessmen and professionals to leave Cuba. In view of the elite status of many of these refugees, they are now referred to as the *Golden Exiles* (Portes, et al, 1977).

During this first period of migration, between January 1959 and October 1962, a total of 215,000 refugees arrived. But, their flow was all but terminated following the *Cuban Missile Crisis.* As a result, only 74,000 refugees escaped communist Cuba between November 1962 and November 1965. In December of 1965, the United States and Cuba signed an agreement that allowed some refugees to be airlifted to Miami. During the period of these *Vuelos de la Libertad* or *freedom flights* (December 1965-April 1973) a total of 340,000 Cuban refugees arrived in America (Pedraza, 1996; Pinal and Singer, 1997: 23). Overall,

---
BOX 10.5

American Hero Raul Julia on the Importance of Extensivity and of Identities Transcending Primordial Attachments

Puerto-Rican American Raul Julia received numerous Tony nominations for his performances on Broadway. He appeared in many films, including Moon Over Parador, Presumed Innocent, *and* Romero. *He also was active in the Hunger Project, an international organization dedicated to ending hunger on this planet. In the interview exerpts below, Raul Julia voices the importance of ties of association and their role in solidifying identities that transcend primordial attachments:*

I acted in my first play when I was five years old. The play was in Spanish and I was the devil competing with a student, a farmer, and a hunter to capture the heart of a fair maiden. During the opening performance, I remember choosing to let go and risk being foolish. I fell to the floor and started rolling all over the stage like I was having a fit. No control. Everyone was stunned because this was not in the script. Suddenly, I got up and started saying my lines. I've been acting and taking risks ever since.

. . . Many years ago I had to choose between doing what I loved—acting—or going into my father's restaurant business in Puerto Rico. Choosing an acting career was a financial risk and besides, being a successful actor in the United States was as unlikely as being

a prince in a fairly tale. I chose to do what I loved, no matter what. What's the point of doing anything you don't love? It's not worth it. . . .

I was attracted to The Hunger Project in 1977, when for the first time in my life, I realized that we could actually end hunger on the planet.

I feel I have a responsibility beyond myself and my family to others who are starving. I have the good fortune to be able to feed my family. I imagine myself looking for work, not finding any, and not being able to provide food. That is happening right now for many people. All that is needed to end this tragedy is the commitment of people like you and me.

My commitment to end hunger inspires my acting. When I'm tired, disgusted, bored, or just don't feel like it, I remember that the more successful I become, the more of a difference I can make. Since I am now committed to something more than self-gratification, my work becomes finer. I am still learning and growing, of course, and contribution brings a different quality to my work.

Many of my high school Jesuit teachers had been tortured while they were imprisoned in China. The General of the Jesuit Order had been at Hiroshima when they dropped the bomb.

The primary thing that I learned from the Spanish Jesuits is that a hero is someone who goes beyond himself to make a difference for other people.

Going beyond yourself includes going beyond your cultural background. It is best to educate yourself about your background, be proud of who you are, and be accurate and knowledgeable when you communicate about it. Once you are knowledgeable and proud of your culture, you can go beyond yourself and become whatever you want to be. Transcending your background allows you to be free and proud.

I don't go around waving a flag saying that I am "Mr. Puerto Rico." I have that background and I am proud of it. I love Puerto Rico, I love my culture, and I love my background. I am first a human being who happened to be born into that background. If we see it that way, we can appreciate the diversity and, at the same time, enjoy our heritage more. The planet is small enough. It is now time for everyone on the planet to be human beings together.

Source: Raul Julia, as quoted in Ellis, 1997:340

from January 1959 to April 1973, a total of 629,000 Cuban refugees were admitted (Gonzales, 1992: Table 7.1).

Cuba has been the major source of political refugees to the United States from our hemisphere. For the period from the end of World War II to 1995, Cubans account for more than

90 percent of the 597,000 refugees and asylees from the Americas who have been granted permanent residence (U.S. Immigration and Naturalization Service, 1995: 183).

A new wave of Cuban immigrants entered the United States in 1980. More than 125,000 Cubans arrived in Florida from Cuba's Mariel

Harbor. They accounted for more than 85 percent of Cuban immigrants to the United States during the decade of the 1980s (Pinal and Singer, 1997: 24).

Economic conditions in Cuba worsened in the 1990s when the collapse of the Soviet Union ended vital foreign aid and trade. These hard times encouraged individuals to attempt to make it into the United States through any means possible, including attempting to make the 90-mile voyage from Cuba to Florida in makeshift boats called *balsas.* These refugees commonly were known as boat people or *balseros.* In 1994, thousands of *balseros* headed for the United States. While many of these refugees were allowed to remain in the United States, current U.S. policy is to return them to Cuba (del Pinal and Singer, 1997: 24).

The Asian Experience

The five major Asian American groups in the United States today are the Chinese, Japanese, Filipinos, Asian Indians, and Koreans (Min, 1994). While there are other Asian American groups, they tend to be more recent arrivals and their numbers are still relatively small.

The Chinese Americans

Among Asian immigrants, the Chinese were the first to arrive in America. They first settled in the United States in 1850, when their population here was only 789. By 1860 their population soared to over 34,000 (Lee, 1960: 21). Like thousands of other fortune seekers the Chinese were attracted to California by the *gold rush.* But they quickly diversified and were employed as factory workers, construction workers, fishermen, farmers, wood cutters, cigar makers, restaurant workers, wagon and cart builders, brickmakers, masons, and garment workers (Sandmeyer, 1939: 20-21). In addition they started a number of new businesses (Coolidge, 1909: 359; Takaki, 1989: 87-88) and, of course, helped build the transcontinental railroad (Saxon, 1971: 62).

Unfortunately their welcome was short-lived. Before long they were viewed as unwelcome competitors in the labor market and often served as scapegoats for the social and economic problems of the day. As early as 1859, unemployed laborers in San Francisco organized themselves into *Anti-Coolie Clubs,* and in a few years the Anti-Chinese Movement had unanimous public support (Daniels, 1962: 16).

The public's agitation, along with the support of the politicians, eventually resulted in the passage of various anti-Chinese laws at the local, state, and federal levels. All of these laws were intended to make life difficult for the hapless Chinese (Chinn, 1969; Wu, 1972; Chen, 1980; Chan, 1991). In view of the termination of Chinese immigration, those who remained were doomed to a lonely existence in a *bachelor society,* as only a few were allowed to bring their wives with them (Coolidge, 1909: 17-21). The critical shortage of women denied them the opportunity to produce a second generation of American citizens who could have formed the basis for a stable and thriving Chinese American community (Tsai, 1986: 41).

The Japanese Americans

The first group of 148 Japanese arrived in Hawaii in 1868 as contract agricultural laborers (Yoneda, 1971). By the turn of the century, there were more than 60,000 living in the Pacific islands (Petersen, 1971: 11). By 1909 there were more than 30,000 Japanese farm workers in California (Iwata, 1962). In 1910, the Japanese population on the mainland reached 72,157 (Ichioka, 1988: 48; Naka, 1913: 1).

The *Gentleman's Agreement* of 1908 prevented further immigration from Japan. However, they were allowed to send for their wives. This provision resulted in the proliferation of *proxy marriages,* whereby an immigrant's family would find a suitable wife and send her to America (Daniels, 1988: 125-129). Their wives were popularly known as *picture brides* (Kimura, 1988: 142-144). Between 1909 and 1923 a total of 45,706 Japanese females arrived in America (Glenn, 1986: 31; Matsui, 1922: 15-17). The historical significance of the picture bride program was that it not only insured the development of a stable community of Japanese immigrants, but it also resulted in the birth of a second generation of native born American citizens. This is clear when we consider that by 1940 two-thirds of the Japanese in America were native-born (Hale, 1945: 173). As citizens, the **Nisei,** the second generation, were in a better position to integrate themselves into the dominant American culture, which helped the Japanese community set roots in American society (Modell, 1968: 79; Smith, 1948: 253).

But, before long the Anti-Asian Movement was revived, and it made life difficult for the Japanese. The passage of the *Alien Land Law* of 1913 prohibited aliens from purchasing or owning land (Buell, 1924: 285). In 1922, the Supreme Court ruled in the *Ozawa case* that the Japanese were not "free white persons" and therefore were ineligible for citizenship (Takaki, 1989: 208). But, the final act of legal discrimination came with the passage of the *Omnibus Act* of 1924, effectively putting an end to all Asian immigration (Ichihashi, 1932; Hirschman and Wong, 1991).

However, the zenith of racial antipathy was reached during the World War II when more than 110,000 Japanese, two out of three of whom were American citizens, were rounded up and placed in *internment* camps (Bosworth, 1964; Daniels, 1971). They were stripped of all land and property and incarcerated because they were considered a threat to national security (Murphy, 1955; Petersen, 1971: 87). Forty years later, the federal government issued an apology for its internment practices, agreeing to award $20,000 to each person who had been placed in an internment camp (Daniels, 1993).

The Filipino Americans

The relationship between the United States and the Philippines is unique inasmuch as the United States gained control of the Philippines as a result of the *Treaty of Paris* (1899), which officially ended the Spanish American War. As a result of this treaty, Filipinos were considered *U.S. nationals,* and were allowed to immigrate without any restrictions, that is until public pressure forced Congress to pass the *Tydings-McDuffie Act* in 1934, limiting Filipino immigration to fifty per year (Melendy, 1977: 17-24).

As was true of other Asian groups, the Filipinos were viewed as a source of cheap labor for the burgeoning agricultural industry in the United States. Initially, they were hired as contract laborers by the Hawaiian Sugar Planters Association, where they worked in the cane fields and on the pineapple plantations (Clifford, 1967). Between 1909 and 1920, a

total of 33,273 Filipinos arrived in Hawaii and between 1921 and 1932 a total of 85,163 arrived (Sharma, 1984: 339).

By 1930, there were 27,000 Filipinos living in California and six out of ten were farm workers, while the others were employed as domestic servants and in manufacturing (Almirol, 1985: 52-59; Cal DIR, 1930; Rabaya, 1971: 190). As with the Chinese before them, the Filipinos were predominately young, single, or unaccompanied men without their families (Melendy, 1976: 104). Very few Filipino women immigrated, and, as a result, the number of Filipino families in California was rather small (Gonzales, 1992: 102-107).

Like other Asians, the Filipinos were also subjected to brutal racism and mob violence. The level of racial violence increased during the Great Depression, when the Filipinos were viewed as scapegoats for a whole host of social problems (Gonzales, 1991: 160). During this period, several Filipino farm workers lost their lives when their *colonias* were attacked by angry white mobs (De Witt, 1979; Chan, 1991: 48; Melendy, 1967).

Filipinos were not allowed to send for their wives and families until after the World War II. Those who served in the U.S. military during the war were permitted to send for their families and some veterans were allowed to apply for U.S. citizenship (Buaken, 1943; Vallangca, 1987: 34-76). This marked a very significant change in the life of the Filipino community, for now they were allowed to start their families and establish their own ethnic communities in America (Boyd, 1976: Table 1).

The Asian Indians

The fourth largest group of Asian Americans are the Asian Indians. The Asian Indians began their immigration to America at the turn of the century. Between 1904 and 1911, a total of 6,100 arrived. Nine out of ten of these pioneers were *Sikhs* from the Punjab. The Sikhs were attracted to California by the prospect of becoming independent farmers (Jacoby 1956: 7, 160; Millis, 1911). Since very few women immigrated during this early period, the Sikhs established a community of single men and pooled their economic resources and labor power to lease and buy farmland and equipment. Within a few years, many became prosperous independent farmers in the northern Sacramento Valley (Gonzales, 1986).

As with other Asian immigrants, the Asian Indians quickly became the targets of racist attacks and discriminatory laws that were intended to make life difficult for them and to terminate their immigration (Hess, 1974: 580-582). The Immigration Act of 1917, known as the *Pacific Barred Zone* was specifically intended to terminate all immigration from India, Burma, and Siam (Chandrasekhar, 1982; Hess, 1969: 62-64). But even more devastating was the Supreme Court's decision in the *Thind case*, ruling that Asian Indians were not "free white persons" and therefore were ineligible for American citizenship (Garner, 1927; Scott, 1923).

The ban on Asian Indian immigration was not lifted until after the World War II (1946) with the passage of the *Luce-Celler Bill.* This bill also restored their naturalization rights. But, more important was the fact that women and children were now allowed to immigrate and they were able to establish their families in America. Between 1945 and 1965, a total of 6,371 Asian Indians arrived and most of these were women and children (Gonzales, 1992: Table 5.2; Ireland, 1966: 469).

The Korean Americans

In December of 1902, the first group of Koreans arrived in Hawaii, where they were hired as contract workers (Pomerantz, 1984: 294-295). By the time the Korean government banned immigration to Hawaii in 1905, a total of 7,226 Koreans had settled into plantation life (Chai, 1981; Kim, 1934; Patterson, 1977).

In comparison, the number of Korean immigrants who arrived in the mainland was small. Most settled in California, where they worked on the railroads, in agriculture, as domestics, or as entrepreneurs (Choy, 1979: 129-132; Givens, 1939: 48). In 1920, there were only 1,677 Koreans living in the mainland, and by 1930, their population had only increased to 1,800 (Kim, 1971: 26; Ryu, 1977).

Today, the new wave Korean immigrants are predominantly urban, educated, and very likely to come from professional or technical backgrounds. In effect, they have the skills, education, and experience that are most needed by American employers (Takaki, 1989: 436-445). The social and economic characteristics of new wave Korean immigrants reflect the changes that were introduced by the *Immigration Reform Act of 1965* (Hurh, 1974; Ryu, 1977; Min, 1996).

Perhaps the most dramatic impact of the Immigration Reform Act on the flow of Korean immigrants to America was that it allowed for family reunification. This provision meant those immediate relatives of permanent legal resident aliens and naturalized citizens would be given a higher preference for immigration. However, it is important to note that a significant number (as high as 50 percent) of the immigrant visas issued to immediate relatives in Korea are given to Korean children who are adopted by American families (Mangiafico, 1988: Table 8.3).

The multiplier effect of the family reunification provision in the new immigration law is clear when we consider the flow of Korean immigrants between 1950 and 1990. For example, between 1950 and 1964, a total of 15,049 Koreans arrived in the United States, but between 1970 and 1979 a total of 240,398 were admitted (Koo and Yu, 1981). In effect this ten year period accounts for almost four out of ten (36.7 percent) of all Korean immigrants admitted between 1965 and 1991.

The Native American Experience

Native Americans are the one group that did not have the traditional immigration experience, although the first inhabitants of North America crossed the land bridge from Asia some 35,000 years ago (Dennis, 1977: 1). When the first white settlers arrived in America, it is estimated that there were some 300 distinct linguistic and cultural systems among Native Americans (Olson and Wilson, 1984: 9-10; Oswalt, 1973: 22). As a result of exposure to various European diseases, forced labor, removal, and outright massacres, their population dropped from approximately one million at the time of discovery to fewer than a quarter of a million (237,000) by 1900 (Cook, 1976: 44-53; Stuart, 1987: Table 3.2; Table 3.4; Mohak, 1992).

Initially, the U.S. government treated Native American tribes as independent nations and they were encouraged to sign treaties with the government. At the time, the tribes were large and well organized, such as the Iroquois, Seneca, Onondaga, Oneida, and the Mohawks (Wax, 1971: 13-16). In 1824 Congress created the Bureau of Indian Affairs (BIA) and counted on it to deal with the "Indian problem." In 1830, Congress approved the *Indian Removal Act,* which authorized the government's removal of all Indian tribes to the west of the Mississippi River. As anticipated, this plan met with considerable resistance from the Indians. For example, it cost the lives of 1500 soldiers (and countless Indians), ten years (1832-1842), and $50 million to remove the Seminoles from Florida. Likewise, the Cherokees were forced marched from Georgia to the Indian Territory in Oklahoma (1838-1839) and almost one out of four Indians died from starvation, disease, or injuries (Hagan, 1961: 66-91; Olson and Wilson, 1984: 39-41).

The Bureau of Indian Affairs managed the reservation system and was held responsible for the health and welfare of all Native Americans, who were considered wards of the state. They were relegated to a condition of almost total dependency (Takaki, 1993). This relationship resulted in a number of abuses and in the end they were not given the opportunity to learn the skills they needed for survival (McNickle, 1973; Noley, 1990).

In 1953, Congress passed the *Termination Act,* giving notice that the government was getting out of the "Indian business" (Wax and Buchanan, 1975). The Act sponsored a Voluntary Relocation Program, with the objective of getting Indians off the reservations and into the cities. In retrospect, this was an attempt by the government to deposit their Indian problem on the cities (Red Horse, et al, 1978). By 1968, more than 100,000 Indians had received services under this program and more than 200,000 were actually relocated to such urban centers as Los Angeles, Oakland, Oklahoma City, Tulsa, Dallas, Denver, and Seattle. However, many Native Americans were not given the government assistance they were promised. The services that were available were often inadequate (Bachman, 1992). As a result thousands were unable to find work, housing, or receive needed medical attention (Cornell and Kalt, 1990). Some became homeless in the cities, while others returned to the reservations disappointed and broken (Officer, 1971).

As enumerated by the U.S. Bureau of the Census, the Native American population in the United States increased from 792,000 in 1970 to 1,364,033 in 1980 to 1,878,285 in 1990. These increases are large, representing a 70 percent growth rate for the 1970s and over 35 percent for the 1980s. These increases are much larger than can be accounted for by natural increase (excess of births over deaths) or by immigration of indigenous peoples from Canada, South America, and Central America. Demographers who have studied this situation all arrive at the same conclusion. *The increase is due to changes in self-identification.* That is, people who previously did not identify themselves as Native Americans began to do so.

What caused this massive shift in self-identity? Sociologist *Joan Nagel* pulls together various types of evidence—interviews with Native American political activists, census data, and primary and secondary sources on the history of Native American Indian political activism—to argue that the most important factor that accounts for the resurgence of ethnicity is Native American political activism (1996), particularly the *Red Power Movement* of the 1970s. According to Nagel, the Red Power Movement captured the hearts and attention of Native Americans and non-Indians alike, leading to a surge in changes in self-identification and to a Native American cultural renaissance.

Race Relations in American Society

An excellent question to ponder is whether the quality of life for racial and ethnic groups in the United States has improved over the past twenty or thirty years, given the sacrifices made by those involved in the Civil Rights Movement.

One of the most important measures of social progress in American society is the economic position of minorities (Coakley, 1990; Eitzen and Sage, 1993). Specifically, we have to ask the question whether minorities have experienced an improvement in their standard of living over the past twenty or thirty years (Jiobu, 1990: 27-92). The ability of an individual to earn an income sufficient to support a family is essential for all Americans, yet the income data reveal that, as a group, women earn 72 percent of what men earn (Bianchi and Spain, 1997: 1-2). Data reveal that in the past twenty years this wage gap differential has lessened. An important question to answer is, *"Why has the male/female wage gap lessened?"*

Data consistently reveal that the wage gap has declined primarily because blue-collar *males are earning less and not because females are earning more.* Thus, Suzanne Bianchi, a professor of Sociology at the University of Maryland, notes that the de-industrialization of America has resulted in the elimination of many well paying blue-collar jobs that had been held primarily by males (Bianchi and Spain, 1997). The blue-collar jobs that have replaced them in the labor force do not pay nearly as well. This has resulted in blue-collar males, overall, earning less (in constant dollars) than they did twenty or thirty years ago, even though the incomes of chief executives of large corporations have increased considerably during the same time period. In 1980, African American males earned 87 percent of what white males earned and in 1990 African American males earned 85 percent of what white males earned. Thus, for African American males, the wage gap widened between 1980 and 1990, a situation also experienced by American Indian, Latino, and foreign-born Asian males. To quote sociologist and demographer Reynolds Farley of the Population Studies Center at the University of Michigan, "the net cost of being a minority [male] in terms of earnings was greater in 1990 than in 1980" (1997: 247).

Even more depressing is the consideration that black women earn only about one-third (37 percent) of what white men earn (Farley and Allen, 1987: Table 10.4). Additionally, while 77 percent of white families earn $25,000 or more per year, this holds true for 62 percent of Cuban American families, 51 percent of African American families, and 49 percent of Mexican American families (Pinal and Singer, 1997: 40). Please read Table 10.6, Family Income and Poverty Rates in the United States, 1995, by Race and Ethnicity. Despite their apparent progress in some social domains, college educated women today still only earns as much as white men with high school diplomas (Paul, 1989: 15). And, post-1990 census analyses reveal that the rate of poverty among Latino families—roughly 60 percent of whom are Chicano—"has surpassed that of African American families in 1994 and 1995, an unprecedented trend since statistics on Latino poverty have been compiled" (Saenz, 1997: 205-206).

The economic condition of minorities certainly brings the issue of social progress into question (Cohn and Fossett, 1995; D'Amico and Maxwell, 1995). For example, in 1970, 33.5 percent of black families were living below the poverty level and by 1995 their poverty level was 26 percent. Similarly, as of 1995, over one out of four (28 percent) Mexican American families live below the poverty level, and half (49 percent) of these families are supported by women, while two out of five (38 percent) Puerto Rican families live below the poverty level. At the same time, this compares to only

TABLE 10.6. Family Income and Poverty Rates in the United States, 1995, by Race and Ethnicity, in Percents

Race or Ethnic Group	Family Income		Percent Below Poverty Line		
	Under $10,000	$25,000 or more	All Families	Female-Headed	Elderly[1]
Total	7	72	11	32	6
Non-Hispanic					
White	5	77	6	22	4
Black	19	51	26	45	17
Latinos	16	49	27	49	18
Mexican	15	47	28	50	18
Puerto Rican	26	45	36	64	19
Cuban	10	62	16	29	12

Source: Adapted from Pinal and Singer, 1997: Table 9, p. 40.
1. Householder is aged 65 or older.

one out of ten white families (U.S. Census, 1988: Table 2; Pinal and Singer, 1997).

In 1995, Latino median family income was $24,600, well below that of non-Hispanic whites ($45,000). This was the first time since 1972 that Latino family income was below that of African Americans ($26,000) (Pinal and Singer, 1997: 38). Despite the common perception that Asian Americans are doing well in American society, it is still the case that Filipino men earn only 62 percent of what white men earn, Chinese men earn 68 percent, and Korean men earn 82 percent. These figures are particularly startling given that, on an annual basis, Asian men spend more time on the job than do white men (Cabezas and Kawaguchi, 1988; Jiobu, 1988: 179-206; Takaki, 1989: 475-476).

One of the primary reasons for the lack of social and economic progress for many minorities is the simple fact that they historically have been relegated to the lowest paying jobs. Therefore, no matter how hard they work or how many hours they put into their jobs, their incomes are hardly adequate to support their families. In effect the majority of ethnic Americans are still concentrated in the lowest wage sectors, that is in the secondary and tertiary

labor markets (Gonzales, 1984). For instance, Latinos are much more likely than whites or blacks to hold blue collar jobs. In 1996, almost three-fourths (73 percent) of Latino males worked in lower-skilled jobs—in construction or service jobs, in agriculture, or in factories—compared with 66 percent of African American males and less than half of white males (del Pinal and Singer, 1997:36). Fully 82 percent of foreign-born Latino males worked in these jobs in 1996, a percentage well above that for U.S. born Latino males. Seven out of ten (68 percent) Puerto Rican men are blue collar workers and most are employed as common laborers, operatives, and service workers (U.S. Census, 1988: Table 2). Likewise, seven out of ten (67 percent) Native Americans are concentrated in low paying blue collar jobs.

Many minorities have jobs that offer few benefits. While Latinos constitute about 11 percent of the U.S. population, they are 23 percent of the 41 million Americans who have no health insurance. Fully one-third of Latinos—about 9.5 million people—are not covered by medical insurance, in comparison with about one-fifth of African Americans and one-tenth of whites (del Pinal and Singer, 1997).

TABLE 10.7. California Residents Enrolled in Public Institutions of Postsecondary Education, by Institutional System and Race/Ethnicity, 1979 and 1995 (Percent and Raw Total)

Institution and Years	African American	White American	Latino	Asian American	Native American	Total Percent	Number
UC System₁							
1979	3.97%	78.29%	5.66%	11.57%	0.50%	100%	113,701
1995	4.43%	48.34%	13.51%	32.71%	1.01%	100%	147,757
CSU System₂							
1979	7.36%	73.39%	8.92%	8.98%	1.36%	100%	215,457
1995	21.19%	41.62%	16.54%	16.92%	3.72%	100%	344,660
CA Public Community College System₃							
1979	9.37%	71.99%	11.13%	6.06%	1.46%	100%	980,516
1995	7.73%	52.20%	22.13%	16.59%	1.36%	100%	945,369
Total							
1979	8.57%	72.77%	10.29%	7.01%	1.36%	100%	1,309,674
1995	10.62%	49.27%	19.90%	18.32%	1.89%	100%	1,437,786

Source: California Postsecondary Education Commission, 1996; adapted from Tierney, 1996: 128.

1. The University of California (UC) system is the most selective of the three public systems. It is the most research oriented and it grants PhDs in many fields of study.

2. The California State University system (CSU) is less selective than the University of California system but more selective than the system of public community colleges in the state.

3. The California Public Community College System is the least selective of the public systems of higher education in the state.

To be sure, slightly more than one-fourth of Hispanic males work in white-collar professional jobs, such as managers, sales, technical and administrative support staff. This percent is well below the 34 percent of African American males and 51 percent of white males who hold such jobs (del Pinal and Singer, 1997: 37). As we have seen, there has been progress in terms of equal opportunities in the housing market. Nonetheless, numerous audit studies sponsored by the U.S. Department of Housing and Urban Development, as well as numerous studies conducted by private-sector research agencies, document that black home seekers often are treated differently than whites (Yinger, 1995; Farley, 1997: 251). They are shown fewer homes, are provided with less information about financing options, and are more often steered to black or mixed neighborhoods. African American home seekers who have applied for mortgages from federally chartered institutions are more likely to be turned down than are ostensibly similar white applicants (Goering and Wienk, 1996; Farley, 1997).

To make matters worse People of Color and women have historically been the last hired and the first fired. For comparative purposes, it is interesting to note that the average unemployment rate during the Great Depression (1930-1940) was 19 percent. The overall unemployment rate for African Americans (18.1 percent) and Puerto Ricans (16.5 percent) is about two and a half times as high as that of Anglo Americans (7.1 percent) (1992). But *the true unemployment rate among minorities is actually higher, as many minorities get discouraged and drop out of the labor market.* It is also a well-known fact that the unemployment rate among black, Puerto Rican, and Native American youth is between 30-40 percent.

As a group, minorities are also more likely to suffer from chronic unemployment, as they are unable to find jobs that will provide them with a stable source of income. Minorities are also more likely to hold temporary or part-time jobs. They are the under-employed members of the American labor force. And yet, others have made the point that minorities are the working poor, since their wages do not provide them with sufficient income to pull them above the poverty level (Hill, 1989: 65). Some have referred to them as the new American **underclass,** a term which signifies that

despite their best efforts to improve their economic situation, they probably never will escape from the clutches of poverty (LaVally, 1992: 6, 24; McLoyd, 1990: 316).

As a result of their inability to find jobs that will allow them to support their families, many minority families are plagued by a whole host of social and economic problems. For example, in 1996, while single females headed 21 percent of white families with children, the corresponding figures are *33 percent for Latino families* and *58 percent for African American families* (U.S. Bureau of the Census, Current Population Reports, 1997, Table 11). In 1992, sixty-eight percent of all births in the black community occurred among young unmarried women (U.S. Bureau of the Census, 1996; U.S.Bureau of the Census, 1995, p. 7). To make matters worse, seven out of ten of these female-headed families live below the poverty level, which means that a very significant proportion of black youth are relegated to a life of poverty and pain (McLoyd, 1990: 317; Swinton, 1990: 33-37).

The inability of Puerto Ricans to find meaningful work that would, at least, provide them with a subsistence wage also has resulted in the disruption of their families. Almost half (44 percent) of all Puerto Rican families are headed by women (Schick and Schick, 1991: Table 1), and only half (52 percent) of Puerto Rican children under eighteen live in a two parent household (Bean and Tienda, 1987: Table 6.8). Overall, two out of five (38 percent) families and two out of three (65 percent) female-headed households in the Puerto Rican community live below the poverty level (Schick and Schick, 1991: 221). It is clear that the high rate of female-headed households and the prevalence of poverty in the Puerto Rican community are directly related to their inability to find jobs that will allow them to support their families at a socially acceptable standard of living.

Race and Ethnicity in Other Societies

Ethnicity and National Identification

As the attentive reader recalls, the term nationality group is a political concept and an identity and is not necessarily synonymous with any particular ethnic or racial group.

While identification with collectivities as large as the nation is always problematic, the history of voluntary migration to the United States suggests that many immigrants, by the second generation, assimilate sufficiently that they view themselves as Americans. When asked, *"Who are you?"* in reference to national identity, the answer of the second-generation tends to be, "I am an American," followed by ethnic identity. The nation is an important *and preva-lent* personal identity across demographic groups in America, and it is disseminated and reinforced by all major institutions, from families to schools to the state. In America, loyalty to the nation also is an important cultural value across major demographic groups.

Ethnicity and National Identification in Africa, in the Russian Federation and in the Newly Forming States of Central and Eastern Europe

In certain geographical regions in Africa, the Russian Federation, and Central and Eastern Europe, national identity is socially constructed differently than it is in America. This should not surprise us, when we consider that their social, economic, political, and intellectual history differs significantly from that characteristic of the West in general and of America, in particular.

The societies of the Russian Federation and of Central and Eastern Europe originated from tribes that developed into chiefdoms and then kingdoms, linked together by vassalages. Historically, as the Roman Empire disintegrated, poor transportation and communication made it difficult to govern over large areas. Powerful military leaders (lords) distributed conquered territory to their followers (*vassals*), who in turn owed their lords certain rights and duties, such as dispute resolution on the lands held in vassalage, support in terms of human power and equipment in warfare, a certain percentage of the taxes, and so forth. The vassals often became lords in their own right by further dividing the territory among *their* followers. Social life came to be centered on large agricultural estates called *manors. Peasants*, also known as *serfs*, were agricultural laborers tied to, and dominated by, their lords, who, in turn, have rights, duties and obligations to *their* lords, and so on. This highly decentralized

system of rule and of social, political, and economic rule is known as *feudalism.* Relations among lords are hierarchical in feudalism (Lachmann, 1991: 114).

The relationship among the nation, identification with the nation, and cultural identities is complex. History, values, norms and language influence this relationship. For example, when tribalism evolved into the city-state among the ancient Greeks, the ancient Greeks called the city-state *polis*, or city community; and in the Greek language, *ethnos* means nation or people. Thus, a **nation** can be defined as a group of people who share a common identity, tradition, history, aspirations, interests, language, religion, and culture (Kourvetaris, 1997: 64).

Under Russian feudalism, identifications were primordial and they did not extend very far. Individuals identified with kinship and village. Villages were essentially ethnically homogeneous settlements. Individuals identified with their family group, with their ethnic group, with their religion, with their occupation, and with the norms and values of their village and kinship. People in a village needed each other if they were to survive against a very frigid climate and against the various hardships brought to them by invaders. Identity, then, was a composite of specific ethnic values and norms essentially local and primordial in scope. Even ties between the village and the political center of the state were problematic. For example if we were to ask a peasant in Russia during the eighteenth century, *"Who are you?"* he or she might answer, "I am a Jew, the son (daughter) of Smyth, in the village Rostov, with loyalty to the Czar." Identity under feudalism tended to be narrow and specific to region and hierarchy.

These factors gave Russians a sense of isolation, a fear of disorder, and an *elective affinity* for strong leaders. Weber uses the term elective affinity to refer to cultural elements that occur together with some regularity; for instance, he argued that in the West there was an elective affinity between the values of ascetic Protestantism and the rise of capitalism.

In attempting to understand ethnic nationalism in Russia and in the newly emerging states of Eastern and Central Europe today, it is important to comprehend that their sense of isolation and separation from important traditions prevalent in the West is profound. Unlike Western Europe, *they missed the Renaissance, the Protestant Reformation, and the Enlightenment.* In short, they missed the cultural factors seminal in creating those cultural elements called "progressiveness" in Western societies (Humphries, 1998).

Russia's history is a history of invasion. The Turks, the Mongol Horde, the Swedes, the Finns, the French, and the Germans have invaded Russia. These invasions, which came mainly from the West, have increased Russians' fear of foreigners. Their fear of foreigners, **xenophobia,** manifests itself in many ways, including a wariness of current Western ideas (e.g., participatory democracy, and free or open economic markets).

Once a huge empire with deep historical roots, Russia's history is also a history of ethnic groups. There are many ethnic groups in the Russian Federation, where over eighty different languages are spoken on a daily basis. The Russian Federation and each of its autonomous republics has its majority group and many minority groups.

After the 1917 revolution, the Union of Soviet Socialist Republics legally recognized the equality of each separate ethnic group. Lenin wrote extensively on what is now called, "The National Question." In 1945, after *the Great Patriotic War* (more commonly known in the West as World War II), Estonia, Latvia, Ukraine, and Belarus were compelled to become a part of the Union of Soviet Socialist Republics. Each Republic in the Soviet Union owed loyalty to the central state in Moscow.

With the collapse of the Soviet Union in December of 1991, these societies, with their own separate ethnic and cultural identities, disconnected economically and politically from Russia. In Estonia, for example, ethnic Russians now must register as *alien residents,* even though many were in fact born in Estonia. In order to understand the social and political significance of mandatory registration, you need to know that historically ethnic Russians occupied a position of relative privilege in the hierarchy of ethnic stratification in Russia that extends back at least as far as the fifteenth century A.D. They were the majority group. They now find themselves treated as members of a *pariah group.* Weber uses the term pariah group to refer to groups or collectivities that are despised or

otherwise highly denigrated. This abrupt change in status has elicited a movement for (ethnic) nationalism among ethnic Russians in the Russian Federation. Similarly, in Yugoslavia and Czechoslovakia, diverse ethnic groups and language groups had been forged by war and conquest into nations possessing geographical and political boundaries. Before the imposition of nationhood, relations among ethnic groups in each of these societies were distant, cold, and sometimes overtly hostile.

As we have discussed previously in this textbook, authoritarian states tend to increase egalitarian cultural values. Authoritarian political regimes in the former Soviet Union, Czechoslovakia, and Yugoslavia enacted and rigidly enforced egalitarian norms and values. This approach led to relatively peaceful relations among ethnic groups. With the collapse of these authoritarian states (a change in imperative order), primordial attachments once again gained salience. Primordial identities—of tribes, village, region—long denied as legitimate bases of self-identification by an authoritarian state, experienced resurgence. *Primordial identities became the personal identities of many members of many ethnic groups.* These groups then lobbied for and, in numerous instances, fought for independent nation status.

Under socialism, authoritarian regimes had preserved ethnic identities in certain geographical territories. The collapse of authoritarian regimes was particularly likely to lead to demands for independent nation status in such areas or to a questioning, if not a renegotiation, concerning the centralized nature of power in Moscow.

Many of the conflicts in the world today—in Eritrea, within Kazakhstan, in the Middle East, in Bosnina and Herzegovina, in Croatia, in the Chechyna Republic in Russia, and in Albania, for example—are the products of conflicts between and among local cultural political elites blended with ethnic group identity issues. Please read Box 10.6, Ethnicity and Overlapping Social Circles in Eritrea. Major questions in these conflicts center around what group controls the natural resources, the political resources, the educational resources, the military resources, the economic resources, the health-care resources, and so forth; what language and religions shall be practiced; and "who are we."

─── **BOX 10.6** ───

Ethnicity and Overlapping Social Circles in Eritrea

Eritrea is a small, multiethnic, newly independent nation located in the Horn of Africa. Eritreans have been colonized by three states—Italy, the United Kingdom, and Ethiopia. In 1991, the armed wing of the Eritrean People's Liberation Front (EPLF) was successful in gaining independence from Ethiopia, a country twenty times its size that had occupied Eritrea for some seventeen years and which had attempted to stop the movement for independence by pitting Eritrea's many ethnic groups against each other. This ploy is known as *tertius gaudens.* Since 1991, the EPLF has been engaging in the task of turning Eritreans into citizens of a multi-ethnic state whose geographical boundaries are identical to those that characterized Eritrea when it was an Italian possession.

Eritrean society is characterized by overlapping social circles. There is widespread ethnic mixing and intermarriage. Ethnic, regional, and religious boundaries overlap and intersect.

There are many ethnic groups in Eritrea. The two largest are the Tigrinya and the Tigré. *The Tigrinya* are mainly highland dwellers who are Christian. *The Tigré* are mainly lowland dwellers who are Muslim. The Tigré and Tigrinya together constitute about 80 percent of a total population of roughly 3 million persons. The EPLF's initial support came mainly from these two ethnic groups whose languages share the same script. The EPLF approached other ethnic groups in Eritrea via cultural troups performing songs and dances in the various ethnic languages of the country, languages that in essence had been outlawed under

the Ethiopian occupation, which began in 1952. The smallest ethnic group are *the Rashaida.* They are nomads and are only a few thousand in number. The literacy rate among the Rashaida is low in comparison with that of other ethnic groups.

In the barren south of the country are found the Afar. *The Afar* ethnic group spreads across the borders of Eritrea into neighboring Ethiopia and Djibouti. The Afar was divided in its support for the EPLF during the struggle for independence. Some Afar supported Ethiopia while others wanted an independent Afar state. The current government of Ethiopia has dealt with this situation by granting de facto autonomy to the Afar.

The Ethiopian regime conducted all school instruction and public business in *Amharic,* the official language of Ethiopia. They also collected and burned textbooks in both Arabic and Tigrinya.

During its long struggle for independence, the Arab world was Eritrea's main source of outside support. Also, many peasants in Eritrea were (and still are Muslim). Unlike the Ethiopian rulers, the EPLF recognized the equal importance of Arabic and Tigrinya as languages in Eritrea. All senior officials of the EPLF were required to become bilingual. Textbooks were printed and distributed in six of the nine main ethnic languages found in Eritrea and also in English.

The present policy of the Eritrean government is for all elementary school instruction to be carried out in the main language of the area, and all elementary school students are expected to become literate

both in Tigrinya and Arabic. Tigrinya is the prevalent language for the majority of the political, military, business, and intellectual elites in Eritrea. Secondary and higher education are both conducted in English. And, the government is committed to the survival of the Arabic language as well. Why?

When the Eritrean war for independence from Ethiopia began in 1961, few Eritreans spoke Arabic. However, starting in 1964, hundreds of thousands of Eritreans fled into Arabic speaking Muslim states where they took refuge during the thirty-year war for independence. Most of the children born in these refugee camps now speak Arabic as their first language. A number of people who are members of Eritrean minority ethnic groups now have self-identities not as Eritreans, and not as Saho or Nara— which are minority ethnic groups in Eritrea—but as Muslims, which is an Arabic nationality.

The EPLF has been successful in recruiting sizable numbers of Eritrean ethnic minority group members into its ranks. The EPLF has been successful in retaining sizable numbers of Eritrean ethnic minority group members as well as in retaining as members many Tigrinya and Tigré. The EPLF also took care to ensure that "at least one representative" of each ethnic group "was on the governing Central Committee of the EPLF" (Pateman, 1997: 39).

Constructing a liberal multi-ethnic society is never unproblematic. Eritrea is making remarkable progress in this direction.

Source: Adapted from Pateman, 1996.

For example, in the Republic of Tatarstan, which is one of the fifteen autonomous republics comprising the Russian Federation, the issue of cultural and national identity still is not settled, especially with reference to the relationship of the Republic of Tatarstan to the central power in Moscow. A poll conducted in August of 1994 by the MacArthur Foundation for Peace Studies (which is an American institute) sheds some light on ethnic relations in Tatarstan. Please read Table 10.8, Personal Identity in Tatarstan.

In this survey, over one-third of Russians (36.1 percent) but less than 3 percent of Tatars identify with the ethnic (cultural) identity of Russian. Six out of ten Tatars (59 percent) but only two out of ten Russians identify with the ethnic (cultural) identity of Tatar. This situation reflects the fact that both Tatars and Russians have separate cultural identities, values, customs, and habits. For instance, Tatars are Muslims where Russians tend either to be non-believers or Orthodox Christians. Quite importantly, Table 10.8 reveals that fully three out of ten Tatars (31.9 percent) and a similar proportion of Russians (35.3 percent) identify themselves both as Russian *and* Tatar. In other words, roughly one out of three Russians and a similar proportion of Tatars identify equally with the cultures of Russia and Tatarstan. One out of three is equally at home in both cultural worlds. *This bespeaks an enormous amount of integration between these two cultures in the cities.* This integration is seen in residential housing, such as in Kazan, the political capitol of Tatarstan, where housing is ethnically integrated to a great extent. There is no obvious domination of one group by another linguistically, in the sense of having an "official language" for the city or for the Republic of Tatarstan. In fact, in accordance with legislation passed in 1992 both Tatar and Russian languages are taught in public secondary schools (high schools), colleges, and universities. A very important index of ethnic integration is the rate of intermarriage. In Kazan, there is a high rate of Tatar-Russian intermarriage. This bespeaks healthy ethnic group relations in the urban areas.

In the nonurban areas, the situation is different. Villages are culturally homogeneous. A village is Tatar *or* it is Russian. Each village has strong traditional norms and values. In the

TABLE 10.8 Personal Identity in Tatarstan "Do you identify yourself as a Russian Citizen or a Tatarstan Citizen?"

	Tatars	Russians[1]
Both as Russian and Tatarstan	31.9	35.3
More as Tatarstan Citizen	59.0	19.0
More as Russian Citizen	2.7	36.1
Difficult to Answer	6.4	9.6
TOTAL	100%	100%
N = 1000		

1. The Russian language has two meanings for the term Russian. *Rossisky* is used for "Russian Citizen" while *Russky* is used for Russian ethnicity.

village, inter group marriages are forbidden by cultural customs. In the village, people speak only their native languages. That is, in Tatar villages, people speak Tatar; in Russian villages, people speak Russian. Many Tatars and Russians live and die in these villages. Village life is collective and communal, with kinship and patriarchy being the dominant norms guiding behavior of village members. Farming is still collectivized, with no movement toward privatization. In other words, in the villages, personal identities remain primordial, local, traditional, and narrow in scope; they do not extend very far beyond the village.

An important minority ethnic group, both in Russia and Tatarstan, are the Jews. Jews are not considered *Russky* (Russian ethnicity) but they are considered as *Rossisky* (Russian citizen). After 1991, Mosques and Orthodox Christian churches, some thousands of years old and well-preserved under the authoritarian regime, were returned to parishioners and worshipers. However, in Kazan, state officials have refused to return the Synagogues to the Jewish community. There have been numerous requests, all of them denied by "the authorities." The lack of support for, and the presence of discrimination against, the Jewish community may be related to the history of anti-Semitism in Russia. Also, this reluctance could be a remnant of resentment. Under socialism, there was a hidden envy toward Jews who were migrating to Israel or the United States. Russkies and Tatars had the impression that other citizens were not as successful under socialism in their attempts at out-migration. Whatever the reasons, Jews do not have a place to worship, and thereby, to support each other culturally as well as spiritually. This discrimination, of course, has led to more Jews migrating out of Russia and Tatarstan.

In terms of daily interaction in Kazan, individuals *are* aware of ethnicity. They know who is Tatar, Russian, and Jewish. These cultural identities are also personal and interactional identities. In their "free time," Tatars tend to interact more with other Tatars than with either Russians or Jews. Russians tend to interact more with other Russians than with either Tatars or Jews, and so forth. Additionally, terms of ethnic reference and identification are abundantly and pervasively embedded in daily conversations among persons of all ethnicities in Kazan. That is, in conversations, one commonly hears such phrases as "Mark the Jew," "Alexander the Russian," "Alsue the Tatar." *What do we make of this particular piece of social structure?*

That, as you may have anticipated, depends upon one's perspective. Some observers maintain that the unfettered use of ethnic identifiers in daily life in Kazan carries no negative connotations whatsoever. Of course, other observers, using a different way of knowing, come to other conclusions. For instance, the Sapir-Whorf hypothesis alerts us to the importance of language as a piece of social structure. From the *point of view of the Sapir-Whorf hypothesis, the unfettered use of ethnic identifiers in daily discourse is significant and important.* The pervasive use of ethnic identifiers in the daily discourse of people in a large, densely populated, culturally and ethnically diverse setting *continually reminds social actors of who is who in terms of ethnicity.* Their use and prevalence are important pieces of social structure that maintain both group boundaries and long standing patterns of identity and role allocation. The high degree of pluralistic integration that is found in Kazan may have been facilitated by the relative isola-

tion of Kazan from Moscow (a center of ethnic Russian domination), the East (with strong strains of Islamic nationalism) and the West.

Conclusion

As we prepare for life in the twenty-first century we realize that many of the same historical patterns of racial violence and conflict that have plagued our nation are starting to repeat themselves (Feagin, 1991; Kim, 1993; Barringer et al., 1993; Feagin and Sikes, 1994; Noble, 1995). A day does not pass that we do not read about or hear of some act of racial violence in our schools, an act of discrimination on the job, or a racial incident on the street. Once again, it appears that the tolerance of blatant acts of racism and racial violence is increasing. And, as in the past, some politicians are taking advantage of the deteriorating racial climate in America and are attempting to use it to further their own selfish political objectives. Even more appalling, is the fact that hate groups and old racist organizations are attracting more attention, becoming bolder in their actions, and are attracting new members.

Obviously, these are difficult times for racial and ethnic minorities in America, but this is also a time of unity and of cooperation. This is a time for strong leadership, organization, and vigilance in all ethnic communities. Even more important is the consideration that this is the time for all Americans to support the beliefs described by the famous sociologist Robert Merton in his article "Discrimination and the American Creed," that is, the belief in equality, justice, and democracy for all Americans regardless of their religious beliefs, their race, or their ethnicity (Merton, 1949). When Americans deny these rights to one individual or group, they place the rights of all Americans in jeopardy.

Key Concepts

Abolitionist Movement
Alien Lien Law (1913)
alien resident
Anti-Coolie Clubs

authoritarian personality
bachelor society
Barbara Jordan
Battleship *Maine*

Benjamin Whorf
Bracero Program
Brown vs the Board of Education

characteristics of a minority group
characteristics of stereotypes
Charlayne Hunter-Gault
colonial expansion
colonias
consciousness of kind
creation of minority groups
crosscutting social circles
Cuban missile crisis
discrimination
double jeopardy
ecological theory
economic discrimination
Edward Sapir
elective affinity
Emancipation Proclamation
employer's market place
endogamy
ethnic group
ethnophaulism
exogamy
exploitation theory
feudalism
Franklin Giddings
F-scale
gatekeepers
gender discrimination
gender group
Gentleman's Agreement (1908)
gold rush
Golden Exiles
Great Depression
Great Migration
Harper's Ferry
homophobia
housing discrimination
in-group marriage
Indian Removal Act (1930)
individual discrimination
internal colonialism

internment
Immigration Reform Act of 1965
involuntary membership
involuntary migration
John Brown
Kazan
Ku Klux Klan (1866)
labor market discrimination
Luce-Celler Bill
majority group
Malcolm X
manors
Martin Luther King, Jr.
master status
Mexican Revolution (1910-1924)
nation
Nat Turner's rebellion
nationality group
Omnibus Act (1924)
out-group marriage
Pacific Barred Zone
peasants
pariah group
People of Color
picture brides
polis
proxy marriages
race relations in American society
racial group
racism
Raul Julia
Red Summer
reinforced cleavage
religious group
restrictive covenant
Rita Levi-Montalcini
Rudolfo Anaya
Sapir-Whorf hypothesis

scapegoating theory
segregation
serfs
sexism
sharecropping
Shelly vs. Kraemer
Sikhs
stereotypes
structural discrimination
Tatar
Termination Act (1953)
the African American experience
the Asian Indians
the Chinese Americans
the Cuban Americans
the economic position of minorities
the Filipino Americans
the Native American experience
the Great Patriotic War
the Ozawa case
the Puerto Ricans
the Thind case
theories of prejudice
Theodore Adorno
Thomas Pettigrew
Treaty of Guadalupe Hidalgo
Treaty of Paris (1899)
types of discrimination
Tydings-McDuffie Act (1934)
types of minority groups
U.S. nationals
underclass
underground railroad
vassals
voluntary migration
wage gap differential
xenophobia

Internet Resources

http://resi.tamu.edu/index.html

Document: Race and Ethnic Studies Institute

This web site from Texas A&M University reports current research on race and ethnicity in the United States. The Race and Ethnic Studies Institute also lists conferences on minority issues and features the latest scholarly publications.

http://www.brad.ac.uk:80/bradinfo/research/eram/eram.html

Document: The ERaM Programme (Ethnicity, Racism, and the Media)

The ERaM Programme analyzes the media treatment of ethnicity and provides an international forum. Readers may subscribe to the e-mail listing and receive or contribute to the ongoing discussion of ethnicity in the media.

Civil Rights

http://www.aclu.org/

Document: ACLU (American Civil Liberties Union)

This site features legislation and other information of current issues such as immigrants rights, racial equality, lesbian and gay rights, and women's rights. This page also instructs individuals needing legal assistance how to contact their local ACLU office.

http://www.nyise.org/blackhistory/index.html

Document: NYISE (The New York Institute For Special Education)

After entering this web site, click on the picture of Malcolm X and Martin Luther King Jr. You will be sent to the Historic Audio Archives where you can listen to a series of speeches by Martin Luther King, Malcolm X, and John F. Kennedy. The NYISE home page also includes a link to the National Civil Rights Museum and many links to other African American web sites.

http://www.adl.org

Document: Anti-Defamation League Online

The Anti-Defamation League web site posts their newsletter regularly and keeps an accessible file of past issues including the monitoring of hate-groups. This site also provides information on the organization's regional offices and a section where patrons can report incidents.

http://www.hatewatch.org/

Document: Hate Watch

Hate Watch monitors hate group activities on the web. This site posts the latest news articles (both nationally and internationally) on hate crime, and includes detailed information on specific hate groups that publish on the web. Furthermore the Hate Watch web site lists steps that readers can take to fight against the groups, and also a chat room where readers discuss issues relating to hate crimes and hate groups.

African-American

http://www.naacp.org/index.html

Document: NAACP

This site includes a description of the NAACP's projects, an "issue alert" section, and membership information. The web site also lists the NAACP representatives in each local community and how to contact them.

http://www.he.net/~awe/intro2.htm

Document: Aframian WebNet

The Aframian WebNet provides an extensive list of links of African American issues in the arts, business, education, politics, sports, etc. This site also includes a monthly top ten African American web links section and continually adds current links to its web site.

http://lcweb.loc.gov/exhibits/african/afam001.html

Document: The African American Mosaic

This web site is part of the Library of Congress Resource Guide, and features an in-depth study of black history in the United States.

Chicano/Latino

http://www.latino.com/

Document: LatinoLink

Besides articles on latino issues, bulletin boards, and chat forums, this web site also provides many links to other Latino-related sites.

http://latino.sscnet.ucla.edu/

Document: Chicano/Latino Electronic Network (CLNet)

This site was created by the UCLA Chicano Studies Research Center and UC Santa Barbara's Linguistic Minority Research Institute. CLNet offers links to libraries in the United States with Latino collections. CLNet contains a "Latino Virtual Museum," information on Latino communities, and a list of national Latino organizations. This site also catalogs employment information in the areas of Latino and ethnic issues, a calendar which lists conferences, meetings, and other events connected to Latino issues. To learn more about various Latino populations in the United States and Chicano Studies syllabi, click on Research Center, the Statistical Center, and the Student Center.

http://www.iprnet.org/IPR/index.html#menu

Document: Institute for Puerto Rican Policy

This web site publishes policy reports and data for Puerto Rican and other Latino communities. Statistics of Puerto Ricans in urban communities, over 500 Puerto Rican organizations, and related links are also listed on the Institute's web page.

http://www.laker.net/nike/megalinks.html

Document: The Cuba Megalinks Center

The Cuba Megalinks Center frequently updates their web site which offers a wide variety of Cuban American information including links to bibliographies, news articles, organizations, history, religion, and political sites. Much of the information is available in both Spanish and English.

Native American

http://www.doi.gov/bureau-indian-affairs.html

Document: Bureau of Indian Affairs: U.S. Department of the Interior on the Web

Bureau of Indian Affairs is the Federal Government agency that administers programs for federally recognized Native American tribes. This site keeps track of legislative issues, lists of tribes, geneological research, and other Native American Services. In addition this site offers great links to other Native American web sites.

http://www.tucson.ihs.gov/

Document: Indian Health Services

The Indian Health Services is an agency within the Department of Health and Human Services. Their web page provides the latest health care information to health care providers. This site also offers links to other Native American web pages.

http://www.wes.army.mil/el/ccspt/natamap/usa_pg.html

Document: Indian Land Areas Judicially Established 1978

This site presents a map of the United States divided by major regions. Click on a region in the U.S. and the region will appear with a list of all the local tribes.

http://www.mcn.net/~wleman/Cheyenne.htm

Document: Cheyenne Language Web Site

This site offers many different resources for learning Cheyenne, including an alphabet pronunciation guide, and a language reference materials page. There is also a disucssion of the Cheyenne history and language. Also click on Other Native American Resources, which contains links to many other home pages of Native American tibes, newspapers, and other Native American sites.

Asian Americans

http://www.mit.edu/activities/aar/aar.html

Document: Asian American Resources

This web site offers a forum for conversing with others on Asian American issues. It also contains a links section that lists clubs and organizations, media links, personal home pages, upcoming events, and other information.

http://www.asiacentral.com/ademo/ademo.htm

Document: We the American . . . Asians

By utilizing 1990 Census statistics, this site explores the major Asian-American groups and provides information on group education, work, and family statistics. Go to the 'Asian Ethnic Groups Demographics' section for statistical information on particular groups.

http://www.itp.berkeley.edu/~asam121/

Document: Interactive Chinese American History.

This site is a UC Berkeley Asian American studies project. Link to Timeline for a historical timeline of Chinese history in the United States. This web site also outlines immigration policies that affected Chinese immigrants, a bibliography section, and a link to UC Berkeley's undergraduate statitistics on admissions where readers can observe the number of Chinese American students (and other student populations) admitted to UC Berkeley in a given year.

http://www.janet.org/

Document: Japanese American Network

This web site is dedicated to sharing resources among Japanese American communitites. It offers links to Japanese art, government, civil rights, history, and more. There is also a bulletin board for people to read and post messages. This web site also encourages people to add Japanese-American links to the site, including personal homepages.

http://www.komerica.com/khome.htm

Document: Komerica

Komerica provides hundreds of links to Korean American issues on the internet in art, business, education, entertainment, news, sports, etc. This web page is posted in Korean and English.

http://www.filipinocommunity.com/index.html

Document: FilipinoCommunity.Com

This web site offers a vast resource of information on Filipino American communities. Included is historical and cultural information of Filipinos in the United States. Additionally, Filipino Community.Com contains a links section that lists government, entertainment, business, and many links to other categories.

Suggested Readings

Bacon, Jean, *Life Lines: Community, Family and Assimilation among Asian Indian Immigrants* (New York: Oxord University Press, 1996).

De Anda, R.M., (Ed.), *Chicanas and Chicanos in Contemporary Society* (Boston: Allyn and Bacon, 1996).

Daniels, Jessie, *White Lies: Race, Class, Gender, and Sexuality in White Supremacist Discourse* (New York: Routledge, 1997).

Foley, Douglas, E., *The Heartland Chronicles* (Philadelphia: University of Pennsylvania Press, 1995). An ethnographic account of Mesquaki Indiuan-White relations in Tama, Iowa.

Haslip-Viera, and Baver, Sherrie L., (Ed.), *Latinos in New York: Communities in Transition* (Notre Dame, IN: University of Notre Dame Press, 1996).

Hunt, Darnell M., *Screening the Los Angeles "Riots": Race, Seeing, and Resistance* (New York: Cambridge University Press, 1997).

Min, G.G., *Asian Americans: Contemporary Trends and Issues* (Thousand Oaks, CA: Sage, 1994).

Nagel, Joan, *American Indian Ethnic Renewal: Red Power and the Resurgenece of Identity and Culture* (New York: Oxford University Press, 1996).

Chapter Overview and Learning Exercises

The learning objectives of this chapter are for you to understand the importance of race and ethnicity, both in American society and globally. In so doing, you learned about the nature of racial, ethnic and minority groups and about unequal treatment, discrimination and prejudice.

Learning Exercise 10.1

Applying Sociology to Your Own Life

Please answer the following questions in an essay of not less than four typed, double-spaced, pages. Staple your paper in the upper left hand corner. In your answer, you should reflect upon the concepts and theories discussed in this chapter.

1. Please examine your own personal background and experiences. In so doing, please make note of at least one occasion when you personally experienced prejudice (attitude). For instance, this prejudice may have been directed your way by someone of the other gender, someone of another racial or ethnic group, or someone of your own racial or ethnic group.

2. Also, please make note in your relations with others when you engaged in discriminatory behavior toward (a) someone of the other gender, (b) someone of another ethnic group, (c) someone of your own ethnic group.

3. Write a three paragraph essay wherein you describe how you have been completely accepted by someone else. What did it feel like? How did it affect your behavior toward the person who accepted you?

4. Have you ever been completely unaccepted by someone else? If so, describe to the reader how it felt. What specific characteristics and/or behaviors, etc. indicated that the person was unaccepting of you? What characteristics indicate an unaccepting person?

5. How do you think people develop a capacity to accept people who are different than themselves? From your own experiences, how do people acquire tolerant and accepting attitudes about other ethnic groups, People of Color, whites, the physically disabled, the mentally challenged, and homosexuals. Discuss the sociological and psychological functions served by (a) prejudice, intolerance, and discrimination and those served by (b) acceptance of persons different than oneself. For instance, what are the personal and professional benefits of tolerant and accepting behavior, attitudes, and orientation?

6. In what way is your current level of tolerance, prejudice, and acceptance of others likely to represent a positive influence in your performance in the occupational career path of your choice? In what way would your current level be a cost to you professionally and personally?

■ ■ ■

Learning Exercise 10.2

Writing Assignment

Answer the following questions in an essay in which you use some of the key concepts from this chapter. Your essay is to be typed, double-spaced, and stapled in the upper left hand corner. Your essay should be no less than three full pages in length.

1. What are the relevant characteristics of a minority group? How are minority groups created? Can a minority group be numerically in the majority and still be a minority group? Why?
2. What are the theoretical relationships among segregation, prejudice, discrimination, and racism? Why are voluntary and involuntary migration important in the creation and maintenance of racism?
3. Outline three different theories of prejudice. What is the role of stereotyping in discrimination? What are the differences between institutional and personal racism and stereotyping?

■ ■ ■

Learning Exercise 10.3

Writing Assignment

Answer the following questions in an essay in which you use some of the key concepts from this chapter. Your essay is to be typed, double-spaced, and stapled in the upper left hand corner. Your essay should be no less than three full pages in length.

1. Describe to the reader the different types of discrimination. Have you experienced any of these? Please tell the reader about it. What factors seem to be responsible for the persistence of racism and discrimination against African Americans?
2. Compare and contrast ethnic group relations among groups in American society with ethnic group relations in Russia, Eastern Europe, and Central Europe. In what ways do ethnic group relations seem similar across these societies? In what ways do they seem different? How do you explain the similarities and the differences? Discuss the influence of feudalism in creating ethnic group relations. In what ways does feudalism differ from the social relations that came to predominate in the American society?

■ ■ ■

Name _____ Date _____

Multiple Choice and True-False Test

1. _____ is the physical and social separation of different racial and ethnic groups.
   A. Segregation
   B. Integration
   C. Xenophobia
   D. Endogamy

2. _____ is the fear of strangers or of foreigners
   A. Segregation
   B. Integration
   C. Xenophobia
   D. Endogamy

3. Homophobia is the fear of heterosexuals.
   A. True   B. False

4. Racism _____.
   A. is a form of inequality wherein one racial group dominates another
   B. is legitimized with ideologies that proclaim that the majority group is superior physically, morally, intellectually, and so on.
   C. Both of the above

5. Sexism _____.
   A. is a form of inequality wherein one gender group dominates another
   B. is legitimized with ideologies that proclaim that the majority group is superior physically, morally, intellectually, and so on
   C. both of the above

6. A review of the historical record _____.
   A. makes it abundantly clear that racist societies have found ways to make minorities appear different.
   B. sometimes have gone as far as to make minorities appear subhuman.
   C. both (A) and (B)

7. Endogamy refers to the tendency of minorities to marry within their group.
   A. True   B. False

8. The opposite of endogamy is exogamy
   A. True   B. False

9. The rate of exogamy among minorities _____ used by sociologists as an indication of their level of social acceptance and their degree of assimilation.
   A. is
   B. is not

10. With regard to African Americans in the United States there has been a fairly sharp increase between 1980 and 1990 in the black-white rate of intermarriage.
    A. True   B. False

387

11. The social psychologist, _____, referred to consciousness of kind as a feeling of identification with others who are similar to oneself.
    A. Sigmund Freud
    B. Franklin Giddings
    C. Malcolm X
    D. Lawrence Kohlberg

12. In large part, a consciousness of kind explains _____.
    A. why you often notice that minority students on your campus seem to have a natural attraction for each other
    B. why minority students just feel more comfortable around people who have had many of the same life experiences that they have had and therefore they "understand each other"
    C. None of the above
    D. Both (A) and (B)

13. The criteria used by anthropologists to define _____ is often based on commonly observed physical differences.
    A. ethnic groups
    B. racial groups

14. The concept of ethnic group is based on the distinctive _____ of a particular group.
    A. physical characteristics
    B. cultural characteristics

15. There are _____ cultural differences among the Japanese, Chinese, and Koreans.
    A. no
    B. significant

16. Historically, the term _____ was applied to those immigrants who arrived in America during the latter part of the nineteenth century.
    A. nationality group
    B. race

17. Catholics are considered as minorities in other countries, such as in Northern Ireland.
    A. True   B. False

18. African American women suffer _____.
    A. from racism
    B. from sexism
    C. double jeopardy

19. In recent years, in Bosnia-Herzegovina, _____.
    A. many persons with ethnic-group and religious affiliations despised by powerful others fled particular geographical areas.
    B. many people fled particular geographical regions because they feared for their lives.
    C. both of the above

20. African slaves who were brought to the new world in chains were clearly voluntary migrants.
    A. True   B. False

21. American history is replete with examples of territorial domination following a military victory.
    A. An example is the Treaty of Guadalupe Hidalgo.
    B. The Mexicans living in Guadalupe Hidalgo were considered racially inferior and were the victims of an untold number of acts of racism and violence.
    C. The people of Puerto Rico and the Philippines were subjugated by the United States military and treated as racial minorities in their homeland.
    D. All of the above
    E. None of the above

22. Many American high school world history books refer to the period of colonial expansion as the period of "Exploration and Discovery."
    A. This period refers to that historical era when the Europeans set out to claim and conquer all the territories in the New World.
    B. Europeans wanted to extract the raw materials from the conquered territories.
    C. A key to European success was their ability to press the indigenous populations into forced labor.
    D. All of the above
    E. None of the above

23. Under the system of internal colonialism, the dominant group creates new minorities in foreign lands so as to take advantage of their cheap labor.
    A. True   B. False

24. Internal colonies have been created within the United States and these labor reservations are popularly known as ghettos and barrios.
    A. True   B. False

25. _____ refers to any negative or hostile attitudes that a person may have against another person or group because of some perceived or assumed differences based on race, ethnic origin, age, religious identification, social class, gender, and sexual orientation.
    A. Discrimination
    B. Prejudice

26. Recent research indicates _____.
    A. that whites who accept racial stereotypes express a desire for greater social distance from Peoples of Color.
    B. whites who reject negative racial stereotypes desire less social distance from People of Color
    C. both (A) and (B)

27. *Individual* discrimination refers _____.
    A. to unequal treatment of an *individual* based on race, ethnicity, religion, sexual orientation, age, or social class
    B. to the denial of human rights by the state
    C. to the intentional use of force and violence
    D. all of the above

28. Which of the following is/are true regarding *institutional* discrimination or structural discrimination?
    A. It refers to the business-as-usual practices of organizations, groups, bureaucracies, and other institutions that result in the unequal treatment of an individual or a group.
    B. Institutional discrimination is carried out by functionaries who implement the policies and procedures of the organizations to which they belong.
    C. It accounts for a large part of discrimination and injustice in American society.
    D. All of the above.

29. All economic studies to date demonstrate that minorities and women do not suffer, and they will continue not to suffer, from a wage gap differential
    A. True   B. False

30. Economic discrimination can occur in the nation's banking and mortgage institutions when minorities are in need of housing; and in the insurance industry, where the need for automobile, home, and life insurance also places many minorities at a severe economic disadvantage.
    A. True   B. False

31. A serious problem facing the nation's education system is the high drop-out rate among minority students.
    A. True   B. False

32. During the ante-bellum period (1815-1860), _____.
    A. slave resistance and rebellions were a part of life.
    B. slaves were assisted in their flight for freedom by the Abolitionist Movement and the work of the underground railroad.
    C. both of the above

33. It was _____ in Virginia (1831) that struck terror into the hearts of Southerners.
    A. the creation of the Democratic Party
    B. the underground railroad
    C. Nat Turner's rebellion

34. In an attempt to deprive African Americans of their political and civil rights, the _____ was organized in Tennessee in 1866.
    A. John Birch Society
    B. Republican Party
    C. Ku Klux Klan
    D. Heritage Foundation

35. Farley, a demographer, finds that in the United States _____.
    A. the segregation of African Americans remains high
    B. there have been some improvements in the extent of black-white segregation
    C. the segregation of African Americans has not improved in the last 30 years
    D. both (A) and (B)

36. As of 1996, 64 percent of all Latinos in the United States are _____.
    A. Mexican Americans
    B. Puerto Rican Americans
    C. Cuban Americans

37. The _____ are the second largest group of Latinos in the United States.
    A. Mexican Americans
    B. Puerto Rican Americans
    C. Cuban Americans

38. The Treaty of Paris made _____ a colony of the United States.
    A. Guam
    B. the Philippines
    C. Puerto Rico
    D. Hawaii
    E. Alaska

39. _____ are the third largest Latino group in the United States.
    A. Mexican Americans
    B. Puerto Rican Americans
    C. Cuban Americans

40. The Gentleman's Agreement of 1908 prevented further immigration from _____.
    A. the Philippines
    B. Mexico
    C. Puerto Rico
    D. Japan

41. The first human inhabitants of North America _____.
    A. arrived with Christopher Columbus in 1492
    B. crossed a land bridge from Asia some 35,000 years ago

42. From a sociological point of view, an important measure of social progress in American society is the economic position of minorities
    A. True   B. False

43. Data consistently reveal that in the United States the wage gap between males and females
    A. has declined primarily because blue-collar males are earning less and not because females are earning more.
    B. has declined primarily because women are earning more

44. In the United States de-industrialization has resulted in blue-collar males, overall, earning _____ they did twenty or thirty years ago while the incomes of chief executives of large corporations _____ during the same time period.
    A. more than; have decreased considerably
    B. less than; increased considerably
    C. just as much (in constant dollars) as; also remained the same (in constant dollars)

45. The societies of the Russian Federation and of Central and Eastern Europe originated from tribes that developed into chiefdoms and then kingdoms, linked together by vassalages.
    A. True   B. False

46. As the Roman Empire disintegrated, _____.
    A. poor transportation and communication made it difficult to govern over large areas
    B. powerful military leaders (lords) distributed conquered territory to their followers (*vassals*), who in turn owed their lords certain rights and duties such as dispute resolution on the lands held in vassalage
    C. the vassals often became lords in their own right by further dividing the territory among *their* followers
    D. all of the above
    E. none of the above

47. In certain geographical regions of the Russian Federation and in Central and Eastern Europe national identity is socially constructed differently than it is in America.
    A. True   B. False

Crime and Deviance

Nonconforming Relationships That Make a World

"Curiouser and curiouser!" cried Alice.

Lewis Carroll, *Alice's Adventures in Wonderland and Through the Looking Glass*

■ ■ ■

Despite falling crime rates . . . crime remains an urgent issue for
most Americans. Crime routinely appears at or near the top of
surveys asking Americans to name the most important issues facing
the country.

Jean Johnson, *"Americans' Views on Crime and Law Enforcement"*

■ ■ ■

Police records inform us that shortly before
1:00 PM on March 24 1998, Andrew Golden,
age 11, pulled a fire alarm inside Westside
Elementary School in Jonesboro, Arkansas.
Andrew then ran outside and joined Mitchell
Johnson, age 13, in the woods near the school.
When teachers and pupils filed out of the
school building, the doors locked shut behind
them. Andrew and Mitchell then opened fire
from a distance of over 80 yards. Using 3 rifles
and 7 handguns, the boys fired 22 shots in
about 4 minutes. One female teacher and four
female pupils were killed. Another teacher and
nine female pupils were wounded. Police captured both Andrew and Mitchell within 15
minutes of the shootings. (Adapted from *Time*
Magazine, April 6, 1998).

This horrifying news catapulted people all
across America into a frenzy of introspection.
The incident once again showed the propensity
towards violence and crime that exists in the
nation. The news media saturated the country
with detailed information about life in rural
Arkansas, the families of the two kids, and
sparked a renewed interest in gun control. A
spirited debate began on what would be just
and reasonable punishment for these young
killers. Despite recent research which shows
that the incidence of nearly all categories of
violent crime has been declining, such incidents show that there is ample reason to continue to be concerned about crime, and to find
ways in which our society can deal with it.

What Is Deviance?

Sociologists always have been passionately interested in the study of deviance. Most agree that **deviance** can be defined as the violation of significant social norms. Deviance is associated with forms of behavior—or with qualities of the individual or of a collectivity—that are disvalued or discredited by salient audiences. The term deviance covers a broad spectrum of behavior. It suggests violent murder, child abuse, and drug addiction, but also includes tattoos, pierced tongues, or a proclivity towards nude beaches. Deviant behavior can include any behavior that salient audiences view as being eccentric, dangerous, outlandish, or abhorrent.

If there were very few deviants in an otherwise well ordered society, we could explain deviance as an individual aberration. But, given the multitude of deviants of various types, the phenomenon of deviance can be explained satisfactorily only as a characteristic of societies and groups, where it is created and sustained by the structure, systems, processes, and qualities of these societies and groups.

Deviance is a universal phenomenon. All societies and cultures, at all periods of time, have experienced deviant behavior. Of course, what is defined as deviant behavior reflects the valued norms and code of conduct of a given society or culture. This makes it necessary for sociologists to examine the viewpoint of both the deviants and the "straights" who are responding to them.

John Curra (1993) sets up three models of deviance. The **moral model** explains deviance as something caused by external temptations or inner compulsions that sway the weak. In this model, deviance is defined as a character flaw. The individual is stripped of willpower, and has a weak conscience. Thus, moral training and increased supervision are recommended to harness the weakness of flesh, thereby strengthening the spirit. In contrast, the **medical model** explains deviance by reference to a medical metaphor. Defects in social structure (or other causes of deviance) are viewed as pathogens which can be eliminated from the body social. Eliminating the agents that cause the "diseases" of crime and deviance will reduce or eliminate the phenomena of deviance and crime from our midst. With the current medical research in areas like homosexuality, alcoholism, obesity, violence, etc., this model has led to a phenomenon referred to as *the medicalization of deviance.* The third model, the **sociological model,** begins with the assumptions that no act is inherently deviant in itself and that social definitional processes, which frequently are conflictual in nature, label certain acts as deviant. The definition of deviant vs. normal behavior changes based on the type of society, culture, and the period of time in which it exists. Deviance is a form of social conflict, with those in positions of power and control able to define the less powerful as deviant. This model explains deviance as a purposeful choice of activities and lifestyle made by some. Those making such choices are stigmatized by others, and this, in turn, may lead to a collective response from the deviants.

Definition of Crime, Criminal Law, and Juvenile Delinquency

Although crime is difficult to define due to a lack of agreement on its meaning, a legal definition will suffice. A **crime** refers to as an intentional act or omission that violates the provisions of criminal statutory or case law, occurs without defense or justification, and is deemed to be a felony or misdemeanor by the state (Reid, 1996). Some characteristics of criminal law are that the state assumes the role of the plaintiff, and perpetrators pay for the consequences to society, not to the individual. Most of the time, criminal law is specific with regard to the offense and the prescribed punishment. Uniformity across social class is intended in its application. Finally, it requires that penal sanctions to reinforce punishment are used by the state.

In the United States, **juvenile delinquency** is an umbrella term that refers to youth below the age of majority (usually a child until the age of 18, though different states have different criteria by which minors are defined) who have been determined (adjudicated) by a family or juvenile court to be juvenile delinquents. Juvenile delinquents are minors

- who have committed offenses that would be crimes if they were adults (larceny, theft, burglary, robbery, motor-vehicle theft, and so forth)

- who have been neglected, dependent, abused, or abandoned by their parents or other legal adult guardians
- who are *status offenders*—that is, they have engaged in **status offenses,** actions that would be legal were they adults, but which are prohibited on the basis of age. Examples of status offenses include running away from home, engaging in sexual relations, being truant, drinking alcohol, smoking cigarettes, violating curfew, and being "beyond control" of parents or other legal adult guardians (sometimes called being *incorrigible*).

Juveniles account for much of the crime in the United States. Please read Table 11.1, "The Percent of Arrests Involving Juveniles for Various Crimes in the United States, 1996." Juveniles account for one-third of the arrests for property crimes and juveniles account for 53 percent of the arrests for arson. The corresponding figures for burglary (37 percent), motor-vehicle-theft (53 percent), and robbery (32 percent) are also substantial.

Formal vs. Informal Means of Social Control

The social control of individuals is a major concern for all societies. Laws are seen as a formal method of social control. Durkheim believed that the division of labor in society was influenced by the amount of complexity in society. Formal laws were not necessary in traditional societies which had few competing and conflicting interests. As societies went from being simple to more complex, they shifted from *mechanical* (the less complex society, with high levels of cultural integration) to *organic solidarity* (the more complex society with functional interdependence). This led to a transformation from repressive to restitutive sanctions, ultimately leading to a formal system of social control, governed by laws. However, a limitation of social control is that formal laws cannot take care of all contingencies. Formal laws cannot control the behavior of all individuals in every situation. Its sanctions can only be applied by organized political agencies.

TABLE 11.1. The Percent of Arrests Involving Juveniles, for Various Crimes in the United States, 1996.

Offense or Offense Category	Percent of Arrests Involving Juveniles[1]
All Arrests	19
Crime Index Total	31
Violent Crime Index	19
Property Crime Index	35
Arson	53
Vandalism	44
Motor Vehicle Theft	42
Burglary	37
Larceny-Theft	34
Robbery	32
Disorderly Conduct	26
Weapons	24
Liquor Laws	23
Sex Offense	18
Other Assaults	18
Forcible Rape	17
Murder	15
Aggravated Assault	15
Drug Abuse	14
Vagrancy	13
Drunkenness	3
Prostitution	1
Driving Under the Influence	1

Source: Adapted from U.S. Department of Justice, Officer of Justice Programs, Office of Juvenile Justice and Delinquency Prevention, Juvenile Justice Bulletin, "Juvenile Arrests 1996," (November 1997): 3.
1. Persons under the age of 18.

Most social control is informal. This includes education about a socially acceptable way of life, imparted to individuals through the agencies of socialization such as the family, peer group, mass media, religion, and so forth. Other informal means are the folkways, mores, traditions, and values of society. Also included under informal social control are a disapproving look, a frown, gossip, shaming, **social ostracism**—exclusion from mainstream societal activities—and even banishment from the group. Socialization and informal social control often result in the internalization of norms that discourage the individual from indulging in deviant behavior. Picture yourself on a dark, lonely street with a frail 80-year-old frail lady, knowing that she is carrying a large bundle of cash. Even in this reasonably "safe" situation conducive to a "successful" crime, not many of us would club this old lady on the head and rob her of her money.

A recent incidence of social ostracism at the national level was seen in the case of O.J. Simpson that we analyzed in an earlier chapter. Though acquitted of the charge of murdering his wife, Nicole Brown, and her friend, Ron Goldman, Simpson faced considerable social ostracism because large segments of the public thought he was guilty. These audiences refused to buy books written by him, to watch the TV shows he produced, or even to play golf with him in some instances.

Theories of Deviance and Crime

Sociologists divide theories of deviance and crime into broad categories. These are biological, structural-functional, symbolic interactionist and social conflict theories. Each approaches the study of deviance and crime from a different perspective.

Biological Theories

Biological theories of deviance and crime emphasize that deviant behavior is biologically determined. During the 19th century, the acceptance of biological theories was strong, and there has recently been a resurgence in this mode of explanation of crime. This category also includes the psychological explanations of crime.

Among the popular early biological explanations was the theory of an Italian surgeon, *Cesare Lombroso* (1835-1909), who was influenced by Darwin's theory of evolution. To Lombroso, criminals were literally born that way. He used the word atavism to describe them. The term **atavism** conveys that criminals were not as far along in the process of evolution, and were thus more animal like. He studied the prison population, and identified the common physical characteristics of these criminals, such as beady, shifty eyes, protruding foreheads, prominent jaws, hairiness, and unusually long arms (all of which made them more apelike). These physically inferior human specimens could not be reformed easily. In order to protect society, long prison sentences were handed out to these savages.

Of course, the major flaw in Lombroso's theory was that he only examined the physical characteristics of the prison population without having a control group of those outside the prison. When later studies, such as those by *Charles Goring* (1913), included both the prison and the outside populations, no differences were found in physical characteristics.

Body Structure and Delinquency

Prominent among researchers of the idea that there is a relationship between body build and delinquency, *William H. Sheldon*'s (1949) research among juvenile males lead him to a three part categorization of body types, which he termed endomorph, ectomorph, and mesomorph. Sheldon believed his research indicated that there was a relationship between body build and personality characteristics (temperaments). **Endomorphs** have soft, round, plump physiques and tend to be relaxed, easy going, and extroverted. **Ectomorphs** are thin, and agile of form, introverted, sensitive, and subject to worrying. **Mesomorphs,** on the other hand, are hard and built muscularly and are more likely to be aggressive, assertive, extroverted, and action seekers. Sheldon concluded that *mesomorphs* are the most likely to engage in delinquent activities. Similarly, *Sheldon Glueck* and *Eleanor Glueck* (1956) corroborated William Sheldon's research by finding that mesomorphic body types are more highly correlated with delinquency.

A major problem in explanations relating body types to delinquency according to many sociologists is an inability on the part of researchers to take environmental factors into account. For instance, perhaps the *mesomorph* is expected by the juvenile group to assume a position of importance due to his physique, which ultimately becomes a *self-fulfilling prophecy* resulting in higher levels of delinquent involvement.

Genetic Research

Since biological studies emphasized the inherited nature of behavior, it stands to reason that individuals with identical genes (identical twins) should behave alike. One of the most recognized studies of twins was conducted by *Karl O. Christiansen* (1977), who examined the incidence of criminal behavior among 3,586 twins between 1881 and 1910 in one region of Denmark. He concluded that the probability that if one twin was criminal, the identical twin would also be criminal too was 35 percent. But since both the identical twins live in the same environment, the influence of the environment on criminal behavior comes into question. This issue was taken up by *Sarnoff Mednick* et. al. (1986), who examined a sample of 72,000 from Denmark's adoption register. Research results indicated that one cannot ignore the impact of genetic factors in explaining criminal behavior. The major criticism of this study has been the fact that Danish adoption agencies tend to place children in homogeneous environments. Thus a child from a lower-middle-class family would be placed in a similar socio-economic situation. This may muddy the results but does not deter the researchers from emphasizing the link between genetics and crime.

Chromosomal Abnormality

In recent years, chromosomal abnormality explanations, such as the XYY syndrome, have been the subject of much research. The Y chromosome is male and the X, female. Males are born with XY chromosomes, while females are XX. Thus, the XYY male has an extra Y chromosome. Research published in Scotland by *P.A. Jacobs* et. al. (1965) reports a significantly greater number of inmates with the extra Y chromosome. A major criticism of this theory is the small sample size of these studies. Also, since the extra chromosome leads to lowered intelligence levels in males, the argument for the consequences of the latter is that XYY chromosome males are not intelligent enough to avoid being caught.

A Critique of Biological Theories

Some common problems of biological explanations include the following:

■ If society defines and changes what it considers to be deviance and crime, how can individuals have a genetic propensity towards the violation of laws? An example of changes in definition comes from the American Psychiatric Association, which during the 1970s redefined homosexuality from being a mental sickness to simply a life

choice. Similarly, what is defined as deviant in one society may be considered entirely normal or even desirable from the cultural perspective of another. While some deemed the bombing of Unites States military facilities by certain Middle Eastern groups to be "terrorist" activities, the other side considered them "heroic" acts of patriotism.

■ Most of these theorists reflect sociologist *Sue Titus Reid's* (1996) **dualistic fallacy** notion, which assumes that criminal (defined as prisoners) and non-criminal (defined as non-prisoners) categories for individuals are mutually exclusive. Yet it is possible that many individuals are not exclusively deviant. Instead, many people may "drift" between law abiding and law violating behaviors (Matza, 1964). Research tells us that only very small proportions of people who break the law become incarcerated in a penal institution.

■ The assumption that all biological differences are inherited is flawed. Some biological differences may be due to prenatal environment, injury, or inadequate diets.

■ These explanations also exhibit a social class bias. The official definition of deviance and crime is unquestioned. These explanations assume that crime is found primarily amongst the poor.

Psychological Theories

Before the development of more scientific theories of criminal behavior, demonology was a popular explanation. Individuals were thought to be possessed by evil spirits leading them to commit crimes. The only way to eliminate the behavior was to eliminate the spirits. In modern literature, various psychological, psychiatric, and psychoanalytical theories have one common trait: search for criminal pathology in the human personality, where measurable traits distinguish the criminal from the non-criminal. History is replete with examples from the reporting of the mass media, which is quick to assign a mental disorder to those engaging in criminal activities, especially when it is a heinous crime. A case in point is that of Susan Smith, a white single-mother living in Union, South Carolina, who, in the summer of 1994, put seat belts on her two small children and intentionally let the car roll into a lake, thereby drowning both children. She blamed an un-identified black man for the incident. After being arrested, she was considered to be "mentally ill" by the public and the media. The prospect of a mother intentionally killing her young, healthy, defenseless children is so horrific that the media and the public assumed that the perpetrator of such repulsive action must be seriously mentally ill.

Freudian Theories of the Personality

Sigmund Freud (1930) emphasized the importance of the unconscious. To him and his followers, most criminality was motivated by the unconscious, and may be a consequence of the repression of personality conflicts and unresolved conflicts from early childhood. Freud originated the concept of the **Oedipus complex,** which, is the desire of male children for sexual relations with the mother. Since this is blocked by the father, the result is hostility to male authority symbols. Unconscious motivation, which may be due to harsh toilet training or premature weaning as a child, may also lead to adult criminality. Crime is considered a substitute response when original goals are blocked. Individuals may also be engaging in crime due to an unconscious desire to be caught and punished (an expression of thanatos, the death wish). A critique is that most of Freudian theory is highly abstract and has not lent itself to empirical verification. Despite its popularity and significant impact on theoretical analysis, most of these hypotheses have not been verified. Added to this is the generic critique of psychoanalytic theory, which is the belief that most people do change and grow beyond childhood experiences.

Intelligence and Crime

Closely associated with other psychological approaches is the linking of crime to **IQ** (intelligence quotient). *Travis Hirschi* and *Michael Hindelang* (1977) found roughly a nine-point difference in the IQ of delinquents vs. non-delinquents. *IQ* was more important in predicting official delinquency than social class, and all other things being equal, the lower the verbal IQ of these juveniles, the higher the tendency to relapse into the criminal activity. Similarly, *James Q. Wilson* and *Richard Herrnstein* (1985) argued for a clear and consistent link between criminality and low verbal intelligence. This research was later extended by *Richard Herrnstein* and *Charles Murray* (1994), who explore the impact of intelligence on success in life and also elaborate on the relationship among criminal behavior, dependence on welfare, and economic achievements. Some of the researchers in this field discuss inherent IQ differences between races and ethnic minorities, which they see as leading to high levels of delinquency and crime in these subcultures

Of course this approach to explaining crime has several major criticisms, chiefly the allegation of racism. One basic criticism of IQ tests is that they are culturally biased. Very few researchers examine IQ as an exclusively genetically determined phenomenon without any influence from environmental factors.

Major criticisms of the psychological explanations, in general, include a lack of attention to the social conditions and life situations, and too much emphasis on the individual personality. Crime is treated as if it were a physical condition, instead of a socially and legally defined act.

Structural-Functional Analysis

This group of sociological explanations looks towards the organization and structure of society for explanations of deviant and criminal behavior. Some crime is seen as functional—even inevitable. The idea is that the structure and processes of life in society generate criminality.

The Functions of Deviance

Emile Durkheim focused on the role of deviance in strengthening and integrating society. He viewed deviance as normal, functional, and necessary. For Durkheim, deviance is an omnipresent feature of social life, a requisite for the existence of a stable social order. Here are four functions of deviance:

1. *Group solidarity function.* Deviance increases social solidarity and leads to coalescing the group against the deviant. In the face of this common enemy, the social bonds of the "insiders" are strengthened against the "outsiders." **Outsider** is a term coined by Becker to refer to the deviant

who is not part of the in-group of society. A tightening of moral boundaries and eventual rejection of the deviant are the end result. An example of this is the case of Richard Allen Davis, arrested for raping and killing 12 year old Polly Klas in Petaluma, California. An army of volunteers joined the father in looking for the killer. Public sentiment in the case was so strong that, even after the case was resolved with the conviction of Davis, a foundation was set up which was named after the little girl. A major objective of this foundation is to help find missing children.

2. *Boundary maintenance function.* Responding to deviance helps define the moral boundaries of society. Sanctions against the deviant teach us what to avoid. While specific forms of deviance may vary, some forms of deviance must exist in every society to sustain the "us" vs. "them" sentiment, thereby affirming the cultural values and norms that sustain morality.

3. *Reduction of tension function.* Deviance works as a safety valve for strains within society. By scapegoating the weirdoes, hippies, skaters, welfare moms, or homosexuals, society is able to drain off some of its own contradictions and problems.

4. *Innovative functions.* Societies which are extremely efficient at regulating and controlling deviance are vulnerable to inflexibility. Thus, the deviant may be helping society by challenging the foundation of old and outdated rules. The deviant rule-breaker of today may be hailed as an innovator of new rules tomorrow. This helps society accept and incorporate social change in a positive manner. Some concepts of deviance which have changed dramatically in the last 50 years or so are women in the work place, egalitarianism between the sexes, sexuality of the elderly, etc. Today perhaps, it is the soccer mom in the traditional cookie-baking role who may be considered a deviant!

Strain Theory: Robert Merton

According to *Robert Merton* (1957), social structure and conditions that generate discrepancies between societal goals and the means available for their achievement produce deviance in society. He relates the emphasis in American society on high material aspirations and the unavailability of legitimate means for member of all sectors of society to achieve them as creating a strain. Deviance is a normal product of such a society. This theory generates five different modes of adaptation by different personality types. The **conformist** accepts the culturally prescribed goals of society (economic success, etc.), and also the societally acceptable means of achieving them (education, hard work, deferred gratification, etc.). This mode of adaptation produces no crime.

The **innovator** accepts the culturally prescribed goal of success, but either rejects legitimate means or seeks illegitimate means to achieve them. Innovators look for a short cut to success. Examples of criminals here would be the bank robber, street hustler, drug dealer, and individuals involved in organized crime. This mode of adaptation generates the greatest amount of deviance and crime, and is particularly useful in explaining lower class criminality.

The **ritualist,** on the other hand, accepts the conventional means of society but no longer reaches for the goal of financial success. The ritualist may perform his or her job with minimally acceptable amounts of diligence and competence, so as to avoid being fired (if working for another) and so as to stay in business (if self-employed). The term "burn out" sometimes is used to describe the ritualist, as is the term the "mindless bureaucrat," who is so obsessed about the rules and regulations of the organization that he or she forgets the significance behind those rules and simply ends up going through the motions.

The **retreatist** rejects both the socially approved goals and means of conventional society. The term "drop out" sometimes is used to describe the retreatist. Examples of retreatists may include alcoholics and drug addicts, and perhaps some of the homeless.

And finally, the **rebel** rejects both the goals and means prescribed by conventional society and substitutes alternate ones. The new goals may be achieved through setting up a cult, engaging in revolutionary activities, or simply conjuring up a new social order based on personal assumptions about society. Members of *Heaven's Gate,* a cult in San Diego, California, believed that a spaceship would accompany the 1997 arrival of the Hale-Bopp comet, and that the inhabitants of this spaceship would take them from Earth. As the arrival of the comet drew near, the cult members drank poison, laid down in their beds and waited for transport to the spaceship. Other groups, called the **survivalists,** believe in the imminence of mass annihilation by atomic war. They live in caves in the deserts of Arizona and New Mexico and in other parts of the country; store canned food, bottled water, ammunition, and batteries, and they wait for the inevitability of world destruction, after which they will be the only survivors. The rebels, thus are strongly a part of the counter-culture.

Criticisms of Merton's Strain Theory

Merton's theoretical analysis has been received very well in both sociology and criminology and has spawned a number of subcultural theories to be discussed in the next section. Nonetheless, some social scientists criticize this perspective on the following grounds:

1. Strain theory places too much emphasis on the criminality of the lower classes, without much discussion about rule breaking by the elite. His theory fails to explain white-collar criminality by a Michael Milken or a Carl Icahn who broke laws, even though they were worth millions of dollars.
2. Strain theory assumes that there is uniform commitment to culturally prescribed goals. Strain theory ignores the pluralistic and heterogeneous nature of American society and cultural values.
3. Strain theory is geared to address materialistically-oriented crime and does not examine or explain crimes of violence or "victimless crime."

Deviant Subcultures

Richard A. Cloward and *Lloyd E. Ohlin* (1960) accepted Merton's basic assumptions about deviance and extended Mertonian concepts to a *theory of differential opportunity,* whereby deviance results from a lack of avail-

able legitimate *and the presence of illegitimate opportunity.* This theory focuses on three types of subcultures—criminal, conflict, and retreatist. In *criminal subcultures,* which exist primarily in lower-class neighborhoods, successful criminal models are available as a source of inspiration to others. They are willing to assist the young in committing crimes and impart knowledge deemed necessary for this profession. The dominant theme in *conflict subcultures* is violence, which is used to gain status in the group. These neighborhoods are populated by conventional society failures, and social controls are weak. These disorganized neighborhoods generate youth who turn to violence due to extreme frustration. The *retreatist subculture,* populated mainly by alcoholics and drug addicts, simply accepts the drop-outs from the first two subcultures.

Albert Cohen (1971), critiqued Merton's theory as being too individualistic. Cohen perceives lower-class delinquency as resulting from a reaction to middle class values. Compared to his middle class counterparts, the lower class boy lives for the moment, feels deprived of status, has low self-esteem and numerous adjustment problems. So he constructs a subculture that rejects middle class values. This subculture is **nonutilitarian** (stealing for a kick, not because of the economic value of goods), *negativistic* (breaking or opposition to the norms of society) and **malicious** (deriving joy from other people's discomfort). Other central points of this culture are autonomy and short-term hedonism (if it feels good, do it). Finally, since middle-class values threaten the self-esteem of this boy, an attack on middle class symbols provides much relief and joy.

Lower-Class Focal Concerns: Walter B. Miller

While *Walter B. Miller* (1970) accepts the existence of lower class delinquent subcultures, he proposes that lower-classes do not approach the world the same way as the more affluent classes. The question for Miller is not one of reversing or rejecting middle class values like economic success, education, or happiness. The question for Miller is, "On what do youth focus their attentional resources?"

Miller appreciates that *we* humans *have*

limited attentional resources. For instance, research on memory and information processing indicates that people's short-term memory can hold five to seven "chunks" of information, plus or minus two, at any given time. This aspect of human memory is so well established that it is known as *Miller's law.* When our short-term attentional resources are filled up, they are not available for investment elsewhere.

Miller develops a class-based explanation of delinquency that suggests that working-class youth fill their attentional resources—which he terms **focal concerns**—with very different material than do those in more affluent classes. Miller views the lower classes as characterized by unstable marriages, female-headed households, and a lack of economic and child-rearing support from fathers. The following are the lower class focal concerns identified by Miller:

1. *Trouble* Instead of achievements, getting into trouble and staying out of trouble are major issues that consume a lot of time and energy for this group. Trouble may involve sexual entanglements, criminal behavior, problems at school and so forth.
2. *Toughness* refers to a maniacal emphasis on physical strength and masculinity, on using physical violence as a preferred mode of dispute resolution.
3. *Smartness* refers to "street smartness"—the ability to manipulate and to outwit others.
4. *Fate* refers to an external locus of control. Lower classes tend to feel a lower sense of control over destiny. Good and bad happenings in the life do not have much correlation with personal ability, effort, or direction of their lives.
5. *Autonomy* refers to a low tolerance for being in a subordinate position in a status hierarchy. As a result, it manifests itself in a rejection of and hostility towards authority figures like parents, judges, teachers, police officers, supervisors, etc. Statements like "I am my own person, I do not have to listen to anybody" typify this approach to social life.
6. *Excitement* Compared to the somewhat evenly regulated rhythm of middle class life, which revolves around work, family, and conventional leisure activities, the lower-classes are thrill seekers whose lives are characterized by long bouts of boredom alternating with periods of high excitement—fighting, drinking to excess, engaging in illegal activities, and so forth. Excitement can lead to trouble.

The main theme of Miller's lower-class focal concerns approach is that people who expend their attentional resources on trouble, toughness, smartness, excitement, fate, and autonomy have few attentional resources remaining to develop approaches to life that maximize the probability that one will be successful in the conventional social order. People who expend their attentional resources on Miller's focal concerns disqualify themselves from successful participation in the conventional social order and increase the probability that they will engage in deviant and law-violating behaviors.

Criticisms of Miller's Lower-Class Focal Concerns Approach

Miller's lower class focal concerns approach to understanding deviance has been criticized on a number of grounds, including the following (Vold and Barnard, 1986):

■ Values of middle-class boys are no different than the values he ascribes to lower class boys. In fact, in contemporary society, trouble, toughness, smartness, fate, autonomy, and excitement seem to be the values of all juveniles.
■ Most research since Miller indicates that poor parents tend to raise their children with similar values as the middle-classes.
■ Miller ignores the effects of economic deprivation on these juveniles, and consequently he engages in what *William Ryan* terms blaming the victim (Ryan, 1971). *Blaming the victim* is an umbrella term used by sociologists to refer to social psychology refers to by the two concepts, *group–serving bias* (ultimate attribution error) and fundamental attribution error.

Attributions are explanations we give for things—for our own behavior, the behavior of others, events in the world. When explaining the actions of others, we commit **the fundamental attribution error** when we overestimate the importance of personal dispositions (temperament, personality) and underestimate the importance of situational or social-structural factors. Group-serving bias (ultimate attribution error) refers to the tendency to perceive both the groups and social categories to which one belongs and which one uses as positive reference groups in favorable terms. One of its manifestations is a tendency to give members of the groups and social categories to which one belongs, and which one uses as positive reference groups, the benefit of the doubt in situations where the evidence may be perceived as ambiguous. In short, the sociological concept blaming the victim refers to locating the source or cause of an individual's (or group's) suffering within the person (or group) itself.

- In addition, this approach has been critiqued for ignoring the delinquency of upper-classes and females.

Techniques of Neutralization

Gresham Sykes and *David Matza* (1957) provide a technique of neutralization approach that disagrees with Albert Cohen's (1964) assumption that delinquents are opposed to societal norms. Sykes and Matza argue that if this had been the case, delinquents would not exhibit shame or guilt when caught. Some delinquents admire law-abiding citizens, recognize that the dominant value system is moral, and distinguish between "suitable" targets and others. Instead of being totally committed to delinquency, most delinquents act out **subterranean values,** which exist side by side with mainstream values. Matza's theory uses the **soft determinism** approach to explaining human behavior, which suggests that though human behavior is influenced by external forces, the element of free will and responsibility for the individual cannot be denied. Since humans are neither entirely constrained nor entirely free, they exist in a state of limbo, which translates into the delinquent's drifting between conventionality and crime. Thus, even though delinquents are committed to the conventional moral order, they may "drift" into delinquency. In these situations, youths may use techniques of neutralization to avert their responsibility in subjecting others to harm.

What Sykes and Matza discuss as tech-niques of neutralization, students of psychology might study under the rubric of ego defense mechanisms. **Techniques of neutralization** are procedures that people use to place one's super ego (conscience) on "hold," so that one may break norms; afterwards, one bring one's conscience back "online" and resumes living in the conventional moral order.

The techniques of neutralization discussed by Sykes and Matza are the following (1957):

- *Denial of responsibility* One assigns blame to something outside of one's self. One assigns blame to one's social class, home life, lack of affection, etc.
- *Denial of victim* Since the person who got hurt was also a criminal, or immoral, or a member of an out-group, the behavior is justified. The victim "had it coming."
- *Denial of harm* One admits to engaging in the behavior but denies that any harm was done. For instance, one redefines stealing as "borrowing," rape as "sewing wild oats," and property destruction as youthful enthusiasm (e.g., "Boys will be boys").
- *Condemnation of the condemners* In logic, this technique is called making an *ad hominem argument*—an argument aimed against the person. "Ad" is Latin for "at" and "hominem" is Latin for "person" or "man." So, an ad hominem argument is one that appeals to personal prejudices, interests, or emotions rather than to reason. In other words, "If you don't like the message, attack the messenger." For example,
  - ✔ "The reason I got an F on the math exam is because I am not a teacher's pet; only geeks are teacher's pets."
  - ✔ "Police officers are corrupt, and judges are crooked. I don't have an alcohol problem. The reason I got three tickets within the past four weeks for driving under the influence is because the cops have it in for me. Besides, the police have a monthly quota of tickets they must write and they have to give them to somebody. I am just unlucky."
- *Appeal to higher loyalties* One justifies one's action through appeals to one's gang or neighborhood. That to which one is loyal is viewed as more important than law-abiding behavior.

Among the contributions of this theory is the idea of soft determinism—the notion that we cannot meaningfully divide juveniles into delinquents and nondelinquents.

Social Control Theories

Social control theories focus on the question, "How is conformity to the norms of the conventional social order possible?" These theories focus on the mechanisms by which society elicits conformity and maintains social control over individuals. Among the more popular is *social bond theory*, developed by *Travis Hirschi* (1969). Hirschi starts from the observation that it is conformity, not deviance, that needs explaining. Situated well within the positivistic Durkheimian tradition, Hirschi's theory views conformity as resulting from an individual's bonds to the conventional social order. Hirschi's perspective, which he originally tested with high school youth in a multi-ethnic west-coast city, views the bond to the conventional social order as having four parts, which he terms attachment, commitment, involvement, and belief. As used by Hirschi, these terms are neologisms. In this perspective, to the extent that the social bond is strong, we are deflected from deviant actions of various sorts; to the extent that the social bond is weak, we are unconstrained, free to commit a variety of deviant acts.

- *Attachment* refers to positive reciprocal affect to persons in the conventional social order. For instance, you care about your mother and she cares about you. You care what your father thinks about you, and he cares what you think about him. Hirschi identifies three types of attachment that are important for youth in industrial societies—attachment to parents, peers, and school. Strong attachments to parents, peers, and school lowers the probability of delinquent activities.
- *Commitment* refers to investing resources (e.g., of time and attention) in the conventional social order. For instance, one has spent years building a reputation as an honest, dependable person. One has studied diligently so as to be accepted to the college or university of one's choice. One has too much to lose by deviant behavior.

- *Involvement* is the sociological equivalent of the folk saying that "Idle hands are the devil's workshop." Involvement refers to the extent to which adults situated in the conventional social order adequately supervise youthful social and leisure activities. The more youth participate only in activities that are supervised by conventional adults, the lower the probability of deviant behavior.
- *Belief* refers to the extent to which one views conventional authority (teachers, parents, police, laws, and so forth) as legitimate. Hirschi's research indicates that belief is correlated not with social class but with attachment—especially attachment to parenting figures at a young age.

Hirschi's research documents that attachment to parents, peers, and school reduces delinquency. His research also finds that social class is a weak predictor of delinquency. In addition, his theory suggests that youths with a positive attitude towards their conventional accomplishments are more likely to believe in the conventional laws and moral rules of society. For instance, Hirschi's research documents that there is an inverse relationship between high school performance and delinquency rates.

Hirschi's bond theory has been well received. In general, criminologists and sociologists always have emphasized the importance of societal rules, familial relationships, community involvement, and peer group attachments.

Criticisms of Hirschi's Social Control Theory

- Hirschi's social control theory assumes that attachment to all peers reduces delinquency. Subsequent research examined attachment to conventional peers vs. attachment to criminal peers and concluded that only those attached to conventional peers were less likely to be delinquent (Mathur and Dodder, 1989).
- It is difficult to differentiate between involvement, commitment, and belief. They all seem to express a connection to conventional society.
- Hirschi's social control theory has been crit-

icized for not looking at societal origins of crime and for focusing instead on individual variations from societal norms.

Learning Theories

This group of theories has its origin in the Chicago School of Sociology. Of these, *Edwin H. Sutherland*'s (1883-1950) theory of *differential association* is one of the most influential. Sutherland (1947) proposes the following:

- Criminal behavior is learned in a process of interaction with others.
- Most of the learning takes place within intimate social groups.
- This learning includes techniques of committing the crime, along with specific direction of motives, drives, rationalizations and attitudes.
- The specific direction of motives and drives is learned from a definition of the legal code as favorable or unfavorable.
- A person becomes delinquent because of an excess of definitions favorable to the violation of laws over definitions unfavorable to violation of law.
- Differential association may vary in frequency, duration, priority, and intensity.

The emphasis here is not on examining the reasons for crime in society, but rather on how criminal attitudes and behavior are learned and transmitted. Thus in his book, *The Professional Thief* Sutherland writes that learning crime is similar to learning any other activity in life (1937). Even though this theory was formulated to explain criminal behavior, in reality, it explains all behavior.

Differential association has been criticized for being too vague, not testable, overly deterministic about social learning, and ignoring human choices in social action. After all, it is entirely probable that two children raised in the same milieu by their parents grow up making entirely different choices about their lives. Similarly not everyone living in inner city neighborhoods becomes a criminal.

Routine Activities Theory

This theory by *Lawrence E. Cohen* and *Marcus Felson* (1979) is tied to the notion of social disorganization. This approach believes that crime can be explained as a concurrence of three elements: likely offenders, suitable targets, and the absence of capable guardians. Thus the volume of criminal activities is influenced by the nature of everyday interactions. For example, transition from a traditional to an industrial society has resulted in many changes, leading to an increase in certain types of crime. Now that an increasing number of women are in the work force, more homes are empty during the day, leading to greater incidence of day time burglaries. Burglars may also find homes empty due to smaller family sizes, an increase in recreational activities outside the home, and longer vacations taken by families. Similarly, parents—Cohen and Felson actually specify "mothers"—being away from the home during the day leads to **latch key kids**—children who go home after school where there is no care giver until the parents return from work. This corresponds to an increase in delinquent activities by these children, such as drug abuse and other forms of deviance. To exacerbate the situation, affluent societies generate lots of small goods, which are easy to steal. This approach concentrates on where crime takes place, not why. The biggest failure of this theory has been its failure to explain the motivation of the offender.

All structural-functional theories tend to assume that there is general agreement in society about norms, values and cultural standards. However, the next section elaborates on the extremely nebulous nature of deviance and conformity.

Symbolic-Interaction Analysis and Labeling

One of the most important sociological principles is the extent to which our conception of self is shaped by our interaction with others. *George Herbert Mead* (1934) argues that the self-image of a child is developed through interaction with parents, peers, teachers, and others. Mead and other symbolic interactionists emphasize the micro-analysis of human behavior. The labeling theories discussed in this chapter have as their intellectual foundation the work of Mead, *Charles Horton Cooley*, and other symbolic interactionists. Symbolic interactionism is a way of understanding social life which became quite popular in American sociology during the rebellious sixties, when a number of social sociologists started to question the very foundation assumptions about criminal behavior. This era in American history is characterized by massive political and social struggle.

Many sociologists, during the 1960s, recognized that deviance was not just a matter of rule breaking. If we want to understand the phenomenon of deviance, they stressed, we must explore *who* makes the rules and how they are enforced. The focus of attention became the **moral entrepreneurs,** a term coined by Becker (1966). *Moral entrepreneurs* are individuals who generate and enforce morality in society. In contrast to biological and other theories, where the question addressed is, "Who is likely to engage in crime?," the question asked by labeling theories is, "Why are the social actions of some persons, but not of others, labeled as deviant?" **Labeling theory** refers to a group of theories that concentrate on who gets labeled as deviant or criminal in society and on who is in charge of the labeling process.

The following are some of the basic tenets of labeling theory (Schrag , 1971):

- No act is intrinsically criminal.
- Criminal definitions are enforced in the interest of the powerful in society.
- A person does not become a criminal by violating laws, he only becomes one when so designated by authorities.
- One cannot separate deviants and non-deviants into different groups, because everyone violates the law sometime or another.
- Important factors in the process of getting labeled are: age, socio-economic status, race, gender, etc.
- The process of labeling eventually produces a deviant identity, where the individuals self label themselves as deviants.

Edwin Lemert distinguishes between primary and secondary deviance (1967). According to this viewpoint, most of us have engaged in some deviant activity for which we never get caught. Engaging in deviant behavior that is not responded to by persons in positions of formal or informal authority is **primary deviance.** *Can you think of a couple of instances where you have engaged in primary deviance? Please tell us about it.* Labeling theory is not interested in primary deviance, in *why* we initially commit deviant behaviors. Labeling theory, however, is very interested in the social responses to deviant behavior and in the consequences of those responses.

Secondary deviance is associated with the psychological impact on the individual of being caught, and labeled (nut, weirdo, crazy, burglar, hooker, and so forth). The stigma from being processed by the criminal justice system or mental health institutions certainly has an impact in developing a deviant identity. Lemert suggests that instead of deviance leading to social control, it is really the reverse.

In order to understand the concept of secondary deviance, let us approach the concept developmentally and by means of an example. A child takes a piece of candy from a store without paying for it and does not get apprehended by an authority figure (primary deviance). The child takes a pen from a school mate with no intention of returning it. The child later takes something else of more value from another person. Eventually, the child is apprehended by an authority figure. This process is repeated many times. Eventually the child comes to think of himself or herself in terms of the norm-breaking behaviors. In Meadean language: the child becomes that which she or he is addressed. In other words, the child experiences an *identity transformation.* He or she comes to think of himself/herself—"Who am I?"—as someone who steals. This identity becomes a master identity, a core part of the self. Then, the child commits an act consistent with the deviant identity. Committing an act consistent with a deviant identity is *secondary deviance.*

Thus, if one were a fly on the wall and observed Samantha shoplifting a candy bar from the local market, one would not thereby know whether this is an act of primary deviance or an act of secondary deviance. One would need to know more about her social and identity history to determine whether a given act is primary or secondary deviance. *Can you think of instances of secondary deviance from your own life or from the life of someone you know? Please use the space below to tell us about it.*

Secondary Deviance

_____

_____

_____

_____

_____

_____

_____

_____

_____

_____

_____

_____

_____

_____

_____

_____

_____

_____

Stigma

The onset of secondary deviance may lead to the emergence of a *deviant career* (Goffman, 1963). *Erving Goffman* argues that individuals labeled as deviant have **spoiled identities.** He parallels the stigmatization process of labeled deviants to someone with a physical or mental handicap. People tend to respond negatively to both these categories of people. The label "deviant" leads to **stigma**—an attribution, a social definition that is discrediting for a person or group. Stigma can have major consequences for the self-concept and self-identity of individuals and collectivities. For example, laws whereby those convicted of child molestation are required to register with the police have been enacted in some jurisdictions in California. In some of these communities, the police inform the community about these deviants whereabouts. Although the intention behind such laws is to protect the community, in reality, this powerful negative label has lead to many problems for the individuals who are labeled, even though some of them committed the crime over 30 year earlier and have never repeated it.

Harold Garfinkel (1956) analyzes the consequences of a **public degradation ceremony**, a process whereby an individual is formally stigmatized in a public setting. Degradation ceremonies include a spectrum of activities ranging from the 19th century witch-hunts in Salem, Massachusetts, to the arrest and booking of people at police stations, to criminal trials, to trials for mental-health competency. For instance, when Tommy asks a question of the instructor in his Chemistry 101 class, and the instructor belittles Tommy in front of the class, the instructor has subjected Tommy to a degradation ceremony. Other students, wary of being subjected to such ridicule, may be less likely to ask questions of the instructor in class. *Please reflect on your life course. Can you think of an instance or two wherein you—or someone you know—has experienced a public degradation ceremony? Please use the space below to tell us about it.*

Public Degradation Ceremony

Labeling and Mental Illness

Application of labeling theory is particularly useful while analyzing the area of mental illness. *Thomas Scheff* (1966) believes that mental illness has become a catchall category for a variety of behaviors that violate the norms of everyday social interaction. These behaviors may include how one talks, gestures, postures, etc. The setting in which these behaviors take place is crucial. Thus, it is perfectly acceptable to have a protracted conversation with Jesus in a church, while doing the same in a public bus is problematic. Without labeling, this **residual deviance**—violating the norms of everyday social interaction—would be ignored. Labeling begins the process of transforming the rule breaker into a person who is defined by significant or powerful audiences as mentally ill. The following seven factors are important contributors to labeling:

1. the degree of rule breaking
2. the amount of rule breaking
3. the visibility of rule breaking
4. the power of the rule breaker
5. social distance between rule breaker and control agents
6. the tolerance level of a particular community to rule breaking, and
7. the availability of alternate nondeviant roles.

While the first two factors relate to the behavior of the individual, the last five are social factors, factors that exist independently of the rule breaker. Thus social factors may outweigh the influence of individual factors, leading to a career in residual deviance. A powerful rule breaker was Albert Einstein, who was so absent-minded that he would call his secretary to find out his home telephone number! Of course, this residual deviance was accepted and forgiven in a brilliant scientist. In professors, such behavior frequently is accepted or forgiven, as is manifested in the sobriquet, "the absent-minded professor." Similar persistent behavior from an average person might have an entirely different response.

In a seminal work entitled "Being Sane in Insane Places," *David L. Rosenhan* presents field-generated data that he gathered to test the propositions of labeling theory (1973). He wanted to study the impact of labels on individuals. He placed eight pseudo-patients in several different mental hospitals. When asked about symptoms, all reported a symptom of schizophrenia that of hearing voices. Schizophrenia is a severe mental disorder whereby a person suffers a major break with reality. For instance, one sees people and things that others do not see and hears voices that others do not here. Schizophrenia frequently is accompanied by major delusions. For instance, one thinks that one is Stalin's daughter, or that one personally owns the university one is attending or the mental hospital in which one is living.

After admission to the mental hospital, all pseudo-patients acted normally. Their length of stay in the mental hospital averaged nineteen days. The pseudo patients soon found that their normal behavior was interpreted by staff members as in concordance with the diagnosis of schizophrenia. Routine everyday interpersonal frictions were seen as signs of personal instability. Even note taking by the pseudo patients while observing the situation was defined as a pathological sign of a deeper disturbance. What was even more interesting is that the real patients in the institutions were not so easy to fool. They suspected that the pseudo patients did not belong there and were either researchers or journalists. Staff members on the other hand, remained oblivious to the true situation. This research emphasizes the importance of labeling in our lives.

In fact, psychiatrist *Thomas Szasz* (1961) went as far as to say that the label of insanity, which seems to be applied to those whose interpretation of reality is different from that of larger society, should be abandoned. Illness could only be of the body, not the mind use: so mental illness is a "myth" according to Szasz. He maintains that being different in thought and action may be irritating to members of society, but is no ground for designating someone as being sick. To do so simply shows that the powerful enforce conformity to their standards and values. The recent case of Theodore Kazynski, also known as the Unabomber, illustrates this point. Kazynski lived for over ten years, unwashed and unkempt, in a Montana cabin without running water, or electricity, or any other modern conveniences. The points only strengthened the public opinion that he must be mentally ill. What is perhaps even more fascinating is that, globally speaking, more than 40 percent of the world's population lives this way routinely and considers it perfectly normal.

Szasz's radical viewpoint has generated a lot of controversy. He is praised by some for exploring issues relating to the social construction of mental illness, while others disagree with the notion that all mental illness is fictional.

There are many important negative consequences of labeling, including the following:

- Professional psychiatrists are predisposed to using medical labels, learned as a part of their profession, even though the individual may not deserve it.
- The deviant label by the juvenile and the adult justice systems results in the labeled person being cut off from former conventional roles and may result in the development of a deviant self-identity, which in turn may lead to a career in deviance and crime. A deviant label frequently results in a lack of access to conventional opportunities such as jobs, rejection by conventional society, and rejection by family and friends.
- Goffman (1963) refers to **courtesy stigma,** whereby friends and associates of the deviant also suffer negative consequences.

Criticisms of Labeling Theory

Even though may theorists passionately dwell on the consequences of labeling, research in this area has produced mixed results. These theories have also spawned some generic criticisms.

- An overly passive view of the individual who is seen as a victim of societal sanctions. That people have free will is not recognized here. Everybody, including the extremely powerless, have the volition to reject negative labels, and not follow a deviant lifestyle, should they wish to do so. They could fight back, reject, deny, or renegotiate these identities.
- Too much sympathy for the underdog. After all, these individuals engaged in primary deviance on their own, without being labeled, and end up hurting people with their

crime. Conversely, many people become serious criminals without ever having been caught, or labeled.

- Labeling theorists recommend **radical non-intervention** (Schur, 1971), since official labeling only stigmatizes and does no good. Radical non-intervention, a termed introduced by Edwin M. Schur, refers to intervening as little as possible with deviants so that negative labeling does not occur. But proponents of the deterrence theory take exception to this view. They believe that this lenient approach would take away the fear of retribution by society, leading to an increase in crime and delinquency rates.
- Some deviants like to be labeled negatively and enjoy the status they derive from this process within their subculture. An example could be some inner city youth, for whom visits to juvenile hall may be a symbol of **machismo** and a **rite of passage** to an anticipated future life of crime. A rite of passage is a symbolic event or ritual that signals a move from one phase of life to another. The deviant label may also be useful to protesters against a government, who wish to attract attention to the unjust situation.
- Radical criminologists critique labeling theory for ignoring the crimes of the powerful (white collar crime) and focusing instead on crimes of the lower strata.

The next theoretical perspective concentrates on why some activities are defined as deviant and on who is in charge of this definitional process.

Social Conflict Analysis: Whose Law? and Whose Order?

Conflict theory has a long, illustrious tradition in sociology, a tradition that can be traced to Karl Marx, Ralf Dahrendorf (1959), and George Vold (1958) among others. The traditional theories of crime generally emphasize the positive functions of law and support the belief that deviants and non-deviants can be separated into different groups. Thus, consensus theorists perceive widespread agreement with regard to the benefits of the rule of law and with regard to why there are laws. Laws help to maintain social order and the rule of law is designed to benefit all members of the community. In contrast, conflict theorists believe that laws are enacted by the powerful to exert control over the powerless. Conflict theorists assume an ongoing struggle between a variety of social, religious, political, ethnic, and economic factions. The questions asked by conflict theorists are, "Who has the power to create and enforce laws? Whose interests do these laws serve? Do both the wealthy and the poor get their interests served by the justice system?" In short, **social conflict analysis** refers to a group of theories that emphasize the inequity of power among different groups and social categories. According to these theories, the structure of society is geared to protect the interests of the rich and powerful.

Marx (1930) believed that the state is biased toward the wealthy and the powerful. Marx viewed society as divided into two groups: the owners of the means of production (the bourgeoisie) and the workers (the proletariat) who sell their labor to the owners of the means of production. Private property is the result of the owners collecting surplus after paying wages. All the institutions in society, such as the political, legal, educational, and economic establishments, are viewed by conflict theorists as existing to protect the interests of the wealthy, capitalistic class. In this framework, crime may be viewed as an act of political rebellion by the poor against exploitation and as an expression of hostility towards the bourgeoisie. Crime is retaliation against the upper classes for the theft and treachery which have been perpetrated against the proletariat. In this viewpoint, the distress of the proletariat restricts their options and gives them very few choices. Stealing is among the choices they have. Marx argued that **capitalism,** an economic system characterized by a free market economy and the private ownership of property and of the economic means of production, is to be blamed for all crime. In this viewpoint, the only way to get rid of crime is to overthrow the capitalist system through social revolution.

As early as 1938, *Thorsten Sellin* wrote about the relationship between cultural conflict and crime. Since the cultural beliefs of immigrants were different than those of the larger American society in many instances, what was acceptable behavior in those cultures was deemed to be illegal in America. This culture conflict generated a lot of crime. An example of culture conflict is the practice of genital mutilation of young girls in some middle-eastern and African countries. A behavior perfectly within social and legal bounds in those countries is looked at with horror and would lead to prosecution in this country. This is also true for the religious and cultural practice of polygyny (having two or more wives at the same time), a practice that is perfectly legal in certain societies but illegal United States.

Sellin also distinguishes between primary and secondary conflict. **Primary conflict** occurs when the norms of two cultures clash, while **secondary conflict** arises out of the evolution of a single culture. A good example of primary conflict comes from the Gulf War. Several American soldiers, although prohibited from drinking alcohol while they were stationed on Saudi Arabian soil, in fact got into trouble with the authorities for violating this rule. Similarly, American female soldiers got in trouble when they wore trousers and did not cover their bodies from head to toe while on trips outside the military base. There are many examples of secondary conflict. Abortion, death penalty, ban on guns, welfare reform, views on homosexuality are only a few examples of secondary conflict in the United States. A recent newspaper article reported that the city of Berkeley, California, had decided not to provide free berths at the city owned marina to the Boy Scouts' organization. The Boy Scouts' bylaws require that members be "morally straight" and do their "duty to God." Since the city of Berkeley has a policy barring discrimination based on sexual or religious orientation, the policies of the Boy Scouts led to a loss of privileges for them (San Francisco Chronicle, April 18, 1998).

Please reflect on your own life. Can you think of a couple of examples of primary conflict that you have experienced? Please tell us about it. Can you think of a couple of examples of secondary conflict that you have experienced? Please use the space below to tell us about it.

Primary Conflict and Secondary Conflict

_____

_____

_____

_____

_____

_____

_____

_____

_____

_____

_____

_____

_____

_____

_____

_____

Vold (1958) suggests that the power to decide what is legal or illegal rests with groups that have legislative power. Crime is a consequence of conflict between various groups. This includes crimes due to political protests, labor problems, and racial and ethnic hostility. Statistics showing recent increases in hate crime corroborate his viewpoint. Vold explains the increase in juvenile gang activity as arising out of the conflict between the youth and adults. However, his theory does not explain spontaneous violence or property crime for personal gain.

The Social Reality of Crime: Law, Order, and Power

According to *Richard Quinney* (1980), enactment and enforcement of law are mechanisms used by powerful audiences to control social reality. Those in positions of power and control construct realities which are accepted by all of us. He calls this the **politics of reality.** Quinney presents six propositions that outline the relationship between crime and social order:

1. Crime is a definition of human conduct created by authorized agents in a politically organized society.
2. Criminal definitions are used to depict behaviors that are inconsistent with the interests of society's segment with the power to form public policy.
3. Those groups in society that have the power to shape the enforcement and administration of criminal law also apply the criminal definitions.
4. Behavior patterns in structured societies are organized in relation to criminal definitions, and, within this context, individuals engage in behavior that has a relative probability of being defined as criminal.
5. Conceptions of crime are devised and diffused in the segments of society using several means of communication.
6. Formulation and application of criminal definitions construct the social reality of crime, the development of behavior patterns related to criminal definitions, and the construction of criminal conceptions.

In other writings, Quinney (1974) describes criminal law as an instrument which is used to perpetuate and to maintain the existing social order. In advanced capitalistic societies, this is accomplished through a variety of institutions and agencies, which are set up by a government elite to look after the interests of the ruling classes. From this viewpoint, the solution to the crime can be achieved only by overthrowing capitalism and creating a socialist social order.

William J. Chambliss agrees that the conflict model provides the most relevant framework for understanding the functioning of legal institutions in a society that is complex, stratified, and bureaucratic (Chambliss and Zatz, 1994). He anticipates that as capitalistic societies get more industrialized, the gap between the rich and the poor will increase, and penal law will expand its efforts to coerce the poor into submission. Crime diverts the attention of the lower-classes away from the exploitation they experience, and directs it towards the members of their own social class. Chambliss predicts much lower rates of crime in socialist societies where the class struggle would be less intense.

Another proponent of the power and control concept is *Austin Turk* (1976), who suggests that divergence between and among individuals leads to conflict because each party is trying to promote its own views. This leads to a conscious struggle over the distribution of resources. People with similar beliefs band together and develop similar understandings and commitments, leading to the development of stratification systems. This results in economic exploitation, which is sustained by political domination. Turk urges the study of the differences between the statuses and roles of legal authorities and subjects. The universal phenomenon of inequity between these groups is assumed to be essential for social order. Crime is simply a label imposed on the powerless in society as the struggle for political power.

To Turk, application of criminal labels involves several processes. Criminalization is more likely to take place when the subordinate groups are less sophisticated. Criminalization is also more likely if there is consonance in the professed beliefs and behavior of the dominant groups. In other words, if the dominant groups say stealing is wrong, they do not steal themselves.

Critique of Conflict Theory

While social conflict theories have made a significant contribution towards explaining the origins of some criminal laws and types of crime, it has been attacked from many sides. Some of the criticisms are presented here:

- Conflict theories talk a lot about the ruling class in America. Is there really a ruling class, or is the United States a **pluralistic society,** with power widely distributed and shared among a number of different groups?

- Conflict theories emphasize conflicts between and among various groups (e.g., conflicts about the nature and types of laws) and ignore consensus about many social issues.

- Conflict theory is less effective in explaining conventional street crime, such as murder, assault, robbery, and burglary.

- The implications of conflict theories are that inequity of power and control among social classes generates crime. But, we know that deviance and crime are universal phenomena, regardless of the social or political system that exists.

- Empirical verification of conflict theory has proved difficult. When tested, research has provided mixed results on various aspects of these theories.

--- BOX 11.1 ---

Violence and Crime in Russia Today: Anomie and Capitalism

In the Russian Federation the relationship between the new rich and the state is a tug of war. The new rich influence state policies through bribes, murder, and extortion (Moscow News, No 9, 1995). For its part, the official state apparatus uses force and imprisonment to keep the new rich outside the political chain. Crime, as it is defined by a corrupt, ill-equipped national federal army, is purely subjective and is used to negatively label those in powerless positions who attempt to become part of the new rich.

In order to understand crime and violence in Russia today, it is necessary to know that under the old regime—the Union of Soviet Socialist Republics— youth gang cooperatives had emerged to provide scarce and widely-valued goods and services to those who could pay hard Western currency. The scarce and widely valued goods and services they provided included access to information and consumer items of

many sorts—personal computers, computer software, jeans, automobiles, video tape cassette recorders, and video tapes (VHS) to name just a few. Some of the members of these youth gangs became wealthy, members of a class known as the new rich. After the fall of the Soviet Union, the youth gang members vied for social position with other elements of the new rich and with other elements of the population. The fight among the old youth gang-cooperatives (the new rich) and those who are in power (the bureaucrats and other government officials who, even under the old regime, had been engaged in what in the United States we term as thievery)—now fuels crime. This fight among contending players for position is referred to in the United States as "Russian Mafia" violence and as Russian Mafia-induced social unrest.

It should be noted that prior to the spread of perestroika from Moscow, old-line Com-

munists and others with bureaucratic power never believed that any type of capitalism could be successful in the Soviet Union. As perestroika spread from Moscow to the periphery, and as the Soviet Union disintegrated, anomie spread throughout a land that spans 11 time zones, that is home to over 100 ethnic groups, and that in its 1,000 year history never has known and never has had markets (as markets are known in capitalist societies). The rules guiding human behavior came under attack. The new rules were not clear, were not fully accepted by all audiences, and were not widely institutionalized across segments of the population. In other words, what emerged is a classical example of anomie in Emile Durkheim's sense of that term. Moreover, in contrast to the West, many of the issues that emerged as part of this anomie—who is in control of what; what type of economy, tax code, legal structures, and banking will prevail; what type of governing structures will prevail, what type of federalism will prevail; what is the relationship of the center to the periphery; what is the place and content of law in relation to other institutions such as the economy, and so forth—will not be legitimately addressed until the federal government establishes a lawful disinterested third party with the authority to resolve contractual disputes. Privatization schemes and the overall thrust of perestroika have failed to ensure that profits will not be confiscated and that private property will be protected by the state and its representatives and servants. The representatives and servants of the state include public officials. Privatization efforts and the overall thrust of perestroika have failed to ensure that public officials will, if need be, use the coercive power of the state to protect private property, to protect individual rights, and to settle contractual conflicts.

Anomie manifests itself in many ways today in the newly emerging states of Eastern and Central Europe. Many of the very same bureaucrats and public officials who, under the old regime, used to enforce laws against such *economic crimes* as capitalism and private property, now are in the business of stealing and of selling state property for personal gain. While the KGB might have thrown a few of its files into the streets of Moscow and sold out some of its double agents to the West, the current Interior Ministry has the power and authority to define and to redefine what is, and what is not, criminal. Without a history of rationalization (Weber), a standardized body of laws, a system of accountability, and a new constitution that defines the limits of the state's authority and of the newly-permitted business activities, individuals conducting routine business today have no guarantee that the rules governing business today will be in effect, or enforced, by the state tomorrow.

Source: Harry L. Humphries, "Old Youth Gangs and the New Rich in Russia," Western Social Science Association Annual Meeting, Albuquerque, New Mexico, April 24, 1997.

Criticisms of Marxian conflict criminology include the following (Klockars, 1979):

- This perspective relates all problems of justice to the economic interest of classes. After social class, the legal order and capitalism are blamed for everything.
- This perspective tends to find fault with everything associated with the American state and its legal and economic systems, while completely ignoring its good laws.
- This perspective recommends the overthrow of the capitalistic society to usher in socialism as the only way to reduce crime. It completely ignores crime in the socialist states such as the concentration camps filled with criminals in the former Soviet Union, or domestic repression in Cuba which has led to overflowing prisons.

Despite these strong criticisms, social conflict analysis remains extremely popular and has resulted in much research on various aspects of laws and the machinations of the criminal justice system.

Crime

On Definitions of Crime

The earlier section defined crime from a legal perspective. Many sociologists go beyond a legal definition and use other definitions or conceptions of crime. For instance, some alternative perspectives define crime in terms of the type of victim (child abuse), type of offender (white collar crime), object of crime (property crime), or the method of criminal activity (organized crime). But, as we saw earlier, what is defined as crime changes with society, culture, and time period. Societal values are also reflected in what gets emphasized versus what gets devalued. The term **criminalization** refers to the process whereby something that was not illegal before (e.g., the manufacturing and sale of alcohol, possessing marijuana, engaging in insider trading) is made illegal through the enactment of laws. The recent criminalization of drunk driving is a case in point.

We now examine the agencies involved in the collection of criminal statistics and the documents they generate, and we examine how the nature of those data might influence the perception of who is a "criminal."

Sources of Data on Crime in the United States

The FBI is the primary agency for data collection on crime. It gathers statistics on crime known to the police from over 16,000 city, county, and state law enforcement agencies, covering about 95 percent of the population. This information is published in the *Uniform Crime Reports* (UCR). The UCR has two main parts, known as Part I and Part II indices. Please read Box 11.2. Part I offenses include the more serious "street" crimes against property and persons, while crimes considered less serious by the FBI are listed in Part II of the UCR.

There are many criticisms of the UCR. A lot of crime occurs that does not get reported to the police. This is known as **the dark figure of crime.** Thus, fully 72 percent of the rapes and attempted rapes that occur do not get reported to the police, 67 percent of the personal thefts, and almost half (49 percent) of household robberies (U.S. Department of Justice, 1996:3). Please read Table 11.2, "The Dark Figure of Crime in the United States, 1994." Fully 64 percent of crimes that happen in the United

States do not get reported to the police and hence do not appear in the Uniform Crime Reports. Common reasons for not reporting crime to the police include people viewing their victimization as a personal matter and the belief that the police can do nothing about solving the crime and bringing its perpetrator(s) to justice.

TABLE 11.2.   The Dark Figure of Crime in the United States, 1994: Percent of Crimes Not Reported to Police, by Offense Type ___

Type of Offense	Percent Not Reported to the Police
Rape/Attempted Rape	72
Robbery	45
Aggravated Assault	48
Simple Assault	64
Personal Theft	67
Household Robbery	49
Motor-Vehicle Theft	22
All Crimes	64

Source: Adapted from Craig Perkins and Patsy Klaus, Criminal Victimization, 1994 (Washington, D.C.: U. S. Department of Justice, (April) 1996: 3.

The UCR, the most widely cited source of data on crime in America, is criticized for the categories of crimes that it includes and excludes. Crimes that are prominent in these

---

_____ **BOX 11.2** _____

Offenses Reported in the Uniform Crime Reports

Index Or Part I Offenses

Violent Offenses	Property Crimes
Murder and non negligent manslaughter	Burglary
Forcible rape	Larceny-theft
Robbery	Motor vehicle theft
Aggravated assault	Arson

Partial List Of Part II Offenses

Embezzlement	Sex Offenses
Simple Assault	Motor Vehicle Theft
Bribery	Weapons Violation
Fraud	Stolen Property
Gambling	Prostitution
Robbery	Stolen Property
Drug Offenses	Sex Offenses
Vandalism	Drug abuse Violations

Source: Adapted from the Uniform Crime Reports, 1997.

indices are violent and property crimes, in essence crimes committed by those of the lower socio-economic strata. Little attention is paid to collecting data on "victimless" crime or white collar crime. Among the Part I and Part II indices, the only white-collar crimes included are embezzlement, fraud, and arson. Thus, no attempt is made to stay abreast of "crime" rates for government corruption, price fixing, computer fraud, false advertising, etc., which are primarily middle- and upper-class crimes. Similarly, data on organized crime, perceived by many as widely prevalent in this society, are not collected by the UCR. Critics of the UCR charge that it is no wonder when we examine the socio-demographic characteristics of criminals, we find that they are predominantly male, young, minority, and from the lower socio-economic groups. Concentrating exclusively on the UCR categories of crime leads to distortion of the results. The Index Crimes of the UCR include only serious violent and property crimes.

Diverse methods of crime data collection have been developed to offset these and many other criticisms of the UCR. Among them, the *National Incident Based Reporting System* (NIBRS) includes the relationship between the victim and the perpetrator, use of alcohol and drugs by the perpetrator, information on the type of weapon used and the demographic characteristics of the victims. The *National Crime Victimization Survey* (NCVS), conducted by the Bureau of Justice Statistics, interviews 60,000 households and collects data directly from the victims. This facilitates gathering of information about underreported crimes such as rape. Studies based on *self-report data* collect information about delinquency and crime by directly approaching the respondents and asking for information about their criminal activities. And finally, the *National Youth Survey* conducts longitudinal studies with juveniles, collecting data on their criminal activities.

The Costs of Crime

There are many costs of crime. These include the following six (Conklin, 1997):

1. *Direct loss of property:* Property is destroyed by arson, vandalism, etc.

2. *Transfer of property:* A transfer of property takes place from the victim to the perpetrator, as in cases of burglary, robbery, and theft.

3. *Costs related to criminal violence:* These includes lost wages of victims, unemployment compensation for victims, fees paid to doctors for physical and psychological therapy, funeral expenses for victims of homicide, etc.

4. *Illegal expenditures:* These redirect money from the legitimate economy to the selling of illegal goods and services, like gambling, drugs, prostitution, and pornography.

5. *Enforcement costs:* These include the cost of operating the criminal justice agencies. If crime rates were lower, this money could be used where it makes a more positive contribution.

6. *Prevention and protection costs:* These include money spent on locks; bars; security systems for homes, businesses, and cars; private security personnel at shopping malls, etc.

On Typologies of Crime

Crime typologies have been set up in several different ways. A popular one divides crime in to following categories: conventional crime (which includes violent and property crime), white collar crime, hate crime, victimless crime, and organized crime.

Conventional Crime

Violent Crime

Violent crimes are crimes against persons involving violence or threat of violence. The four major types of violent crimes are murder, forcible rape, robbery and assault. Rates of violent crime in the United States exceed those in most other industrialized nations. The Federal Bureau of Investigation publishes the UCR that are based on crimes known to the police.

According to the UCR (1997), about 1.7 million violent crimes were reported to law enforcement in 1996. This represented a decrease of 6 percent from 1995, and was the lowest total recorded in the 1990s. The United States saw a 7 percent decrease of violent crime in the cities during the period of 1995-1996. A look at the regions shows us that 39 percent of all violent crime in 1996 was accounted for by the south, 24 percent by the west, 20 percent by the midwest, while the northeast region at 17 percent showed the lowest rates. The highest incidence of violent crime was seen in the summer months of July and August, and the lowest violent crime was recorded for February. The year, 1996, also registered the lowest rate of violent crime since 1987.

Table 11.3, "Violent Crimes in the United States, 1996," presents a distribution of violent crime as reported in the 1997 Uniform Crime Reports. To the extent that a weapon is used in violent crime in America, the preferred weapon of choice is firearms, used in 29 percent of all murders, robberies and aggravated assaults, collectively. Please read Box 11.3, "United States Outpaces Other Nations in Gun Deaths."

Statistics also indicate the intraracial nature of murder. In cases involving one victim and one offender, 93 percent of African American victims were slain by a member of their own race. Similarly 85 percent of all white murders were intraracial in character. Both males (89 percent) and females (90 percent) were most often slain by males.

TABLE 11.3. Violent Crimes in the United States, 1996.

Type of Offense	Percent of Violent Crimes
Aggravated Assault	61
Robberies	32
Forcible Rape	6
Murder	1
TOTAL	**100**

Source: Uniform Crime Reports, 1997.

The 1996 clearance rate for violent crime showed an *increase* of 2 percent from that for 1995. Here are **the 1996 clearance rates for UCR violent crimes:**

Murder 67 %
Robbery 27%
Forcible rape 52%
Aggravated assults 58%

Violent crime accounted for 5 percent of all arrests in the United States in 1996. Those arrested were predominantly male (85 percent), white (55 percent), and adult (81 percent). The period 1995-1996 showed a 4 percent decline in arrests for violent crime, with the primary decline-taking place in rural counties. This time period also showed a decline of

─── **BOX 11.3** ───

United States Outpaces Other Nations in Gun Deaths

A government study found that the United States has the highest rate of gun deaths (murders, suicides, and accidents) among the world's 36 richest nations. While the United States rate for gun deaths was 14.24 per 100,000 people in 1994, Japan had the lowest rate, at .05 per 100,000 people. This study was conducted by the Centers for Disease Control and Prevention and is the first comprehensive international look at gun-related deaths. Among the reasons given by the center to explain the high rates in the US were an easy access to guns and the societal acceptance of violence. The center wants to treat gun deaths as a health hazard.

Gun Related Deaths Per 100,000 People in Selected Countries in 1994.

United States	14.24
Brazil	12.95
Mexico	12.69
Northern Ireland	6.63
Canada	4.31
England and Wales	0.41
South Korea	0.12
Japan	0.05

Source: *San Francisco Chronicle*, April 18, 1998.

6 percent for juvenile arrests, and a 3 percent decline for adult arrests. Criminologists have provided several reasons for this phenomenon of lower crime rates. Demographic changes, due to the "graying of America" are reducing the number of youth in this society, a group which accounted for a large percentage of criminal activity. Additional reasons given involve stricter laws (e.g. the three strikes law) and more stringent policing.

Property Crime

BOX 11.4

Thieves Beat Couple To Steal Beanie Babies

A collector of popular Beanie Babies dolls and her husband were clubbed on the head with a metal pipe and robbed of a box of the bean-filled dolls and $1000 in cash at their store.

Source: San Francisco Chronicle, April 12, 1998.

Property crime includes the offense of burglary, larceny-theft, motor vehicle theft, and arson. The UCR (1997) show that property crime dropped to its lowest level since 1986, and dropped by 2 percent from the previous year's level. During 1996, 40 percent of all property crime took place in the southern states, followed by the Western states (24 percent), midwestern states (22 percent), and northeastern states (15 percent). This pattern is similar to the pattern for the regional distribution of violent crime, where Southern states had topped the list, while the northeast had the lowest incidence of crime. Also similar is the pattern for the months when the most and least property crime took place. July and August produced the highest figures, while February recorded the lowest. There were an estimated 4,445 property crimes for every 100,000 US residents. The 1996 property crime rate was 10 percent lower than the 1987 rate. Nonetheless, over 15 billion dollars worth of property was stolen in 1996 (UCR, 1997).

The clearance rate for property crimes is far lower than that for crimes of violence. Compared to clearance rate of 47 percent for violent crime, the clearance rate for property crime is 18 percent. In 1996, 13 percent of all arrests resulted from property crime. For this year, 72 percent of all arrested for property crimes were male, and 65 percent of the total were males over the age of 18.

Hate Crime

Hate crime, also known as a bias crime, is defined by the UCR as a criminal offense committed against a person, property, or society which is motivated, in whole, or in part by the offender's bias against a race, religion, ethnic/national origin group, or sexual orientation group. Table 11.4 indicates the distribution of hate crimes by type of offense.

In 1996, fully 63 percent of all hate crimes were motivated by racial bias, 12 percent by sexual orientation, 11 percent due to ethnic reasons, and 14 percent were based on religious bias. Racially motivated hate crimes have been increasing in recent years.

TABLE 11.4. Hate Crimes in the United States, 1996

Crimes Against The Person:	
Intimidation	56%
Simple assault	24%
Aggravated assault	20%
Total	**100%**
Crimes Against Property:	
Destruction, damage, vandalism	86%
Other	14%
Total	**100%**

Source: Uniform Crime Reports, 1997.

Victimless Crime

Victimless crime refers to a consensual crime that lacks a complaining participant (Schur 1965). These offenses involve a willing participant. The crimes included here are drug use, gambling, prostitution, pornography, and assisted suicide. However, some social scientists argue that the term "victimless" crime is a misnomer: some of the participants to the crime, or others, may be viewed as victims.

Organized Crime

John E. Conklin (1997) defines **organized crime** as criminal activity by an enduring structure or organization that pursues profits through illegal means. Bureau of Justice Statistics (1988) lists some characteristics of organized crime:

- *Organizational continuity:* These groups ensure that they can survive the death or incarceration of their leaders and that they can take advantage of changing opportunity structures.
- *Hierarchical structure:* Usually headed by a single leader, organized crime tends to include members of many "families" working together.
- *Restricted membership:* Usually a demonstration of loyalty is demanded, the commitment is lifelong, and membership is along racial or ethnic lines.
- *Criminality/violence/power:* Key goals of power and control are achieved through criminal activities, intimidation, and violence.
- *Legitimate business involvement:* is used to "launder" money from illegal activities.
- *Use of specialists:* Specialists of many types are part of organized crime—tax accountants, attorneys, bomb makers, assassins, and arsonists, to name but a few.

White Collar Crime

The term white-collar crime was originally coined by Edwin Sutherland in an address to the American Sociological Association in 1939. As originally used by Sutherland, the term **white-collar crime** refers to activities of moral or administrative disrepute committed by respectable individuals of high social status during the course of their professions. Sutherland's original definition has been widely rejected today.

Two points are worth noting. First, most of the offenses that Sutherland and other sociologists term white-collar crimes actually were not, and still are not, violations of statutory criminal law. To the extent white collar "crimes" tend to result in court action, these court actions take place either in civil or administrative law proceedings. Second, due to changes in technology and mass communication, not only the upper classes, but the lower-classes as well have access to opportunities to commit white-collar crime.

A widely accepted contemporary definition comes from *Herbert Edelhertz,* who defines white collar crime as an illegal act or a series of illegal acts committed by non-physical means for the purpose of obtaining money and property (1970). White collar crime is distinguishable conceptually from corporate crime. **Corporate crime** is committed by individuals in formal organizations for the benefit of the formal organization. Thus, financial embezzlement by employees for their *own* benefit is white collar crime, while false advertising of a company's products is corporate crime. Some examples of corporate crimes are income tax evasion, bribery, extortion, insider trading, and anti-trust violations. Examples of white collar crime are employee theft and embezzlement.

Sociologists, particularly those of a conflict orientation, tend to lament the fact that white-collar crime traditionally generates very little attention. It is an axiom of conflict theory that the financial and social costs to society occasioned by white-collar crime exceed those occasioned by "street" property crimes which receive a lot of attention in the Uniform Crime Reports. Several reasons are proffered for the lack of attention to white-collar crime:

- *Labeling theorists* explain this is an example of the group-serving bias. The dominant classes in the country downplay deviance and crime committed by their own group, and concentrate instead on the crimes committed disproportionately by the lower classes. In a classic article, sociologist *Alexander Liazos* criticizes American sociologists for concentrating on norm breaking among the powerless and oppressed segments of the population—nuts, sluts, and perverts—to the neglect of more serious and harmful deviance among the powerful and affluent groups. Examples of deviance among the affluent include inequitable taxation, racism, sexism, and environmental pollution. Sociologists, Liazos laments, have tended to ignore unethical, illegal, and socially destructive activities of powerful groups and individuals.
- *Conflict theorists* perceive the interests of the dominant classes as differing from those of the working classes. According to this point of view, all the institutions of society

preserve the interests of those in positions of power and control. Crime by the upper classes is either ignored or is not taken seriously. Hence, quite generally crime by the powerful results in very little stigma for the perpetrator.

- *Street crime elicits personal fear of injury.* Even though injury from a faulty product may be even more serious, there is a widespread lack of dread from white collar activities.
- *The diffused costs of white collar crime.* While the economic cost of white collar crime is enormous, this cost is diffused and usually is not perceived directly or significantly by individuals.

Female Criminality

Among numerous socio-demographic variables, gender is, and has been, the best predictor of criminality. A lower incidence of criminal activities on the part of women is, and has been, a universal phenomenon in all cultures. Earlier, innate differences between men and women (i.e. men are stronger and naturally more aggressive and violent) were given as reasons for these gender differences. However, recent increases in female crime, especially

property offenses and white collar crime, have criminologists paying greater attention to female criminality.

Mary Daly and Meda Chesney-Lind (1988) point out three major gender-related issues for criminologists. These are:

1. *The generalizability problem* Are theories of deviance and crime, developed mostly by explaining offenses committed by males and tested using male subjects only, applicable to females? Examples include Travis Hirschi's theory of the social bond and Walter B. Miller's focal concerns approach—both of which originally were developed using exclusively male research subjects.
2. *Gender socialization* Traditional criminology explains the inequity between male and female crime rates as a consequence of biology and gender role socialization in society. Thus aggression by males is considered normal and acceptable, while similar behavior in women is labeled as a failure to control impulses. Some feminists argue that these explanations ignore the inequity of power between the sexes.
3. *The gender-ratio problem* Some feminist

--- **BOX 11.5** ---

Gender, Crime, and Corrections in the United States, 1995.

- During the past 31 years, the number of women in state or federal prisons in the United States has risen *599 percent*—dramatically—from 11,170 in 1976 to 78,067 in 1997 (Bureau of Justice Statistics, Bulletin, January 1998). During the same time period, the number of men in state or federal prisons in the United States increased 327 percent—from 266,830 in 1976 to 1,140,189 in 1997 (Bureau of Justice Statistics, Bulletin, January 1998). Of course, the number of sentenced prisoners per 100,00 U.S. residents is still far higher for males than fe-

males. While 835 males are under the jurisdiction of state or federal correctional authorities in the United States, the corresponding figure for females is 52. (Bureau of Justice Statistics, Bulletin, January 1998). From the research-methods chapter: Beware the small N. When the total number of cases is small to begin with, a modest increase in absolute numbers registers as a large—and sometimes, staggering—percentage increase.
- Men are more likely to be arrested for violent crimes, while women are more like-

ly to be arrested for property crimes.
- Women are more likely to be labeled as deviant across cultures because there are stricter controls on the behavior of women.
- According to the UCR report for 1995, females account for 26 percent of all arrests (Uniform Crime Reports, 1995: 213).

Source: Bureau of Justice Statistics, Bulletin, "Prison and Jail Inmates at Midyear 1997," January 1998; United States Department of Justice, Federal Bureau of Investigation, Crime in America, *Uniform Crime Reports*, 1995: 213.

scholars chide criminologists for perceiving women as the weaker, passive, and unambitious sex and they predict that with the liberation of women from the domestic role and with greater participation by women in the work force, there will be an eventual convergence of crime rates between males and females. Other scholars, including feminist scholars, do not expect the female crime rates to approach the levels of males, even if females were to achieve parity with males in the labor force and in the domestic division of labor.

Power-Control Theory

In power-control theory, *John Hagan* (1989) presents an interesting viewpoint on female delinquency. In distinguishing between patriarchal and egalitarian households, he states that the socialization of girls is different in each setting. In the former, girls internalize the passivity from mothers who in turn control them with greater levels of supervision than they do the boys. This results in lower delinquency for them than their brothers. In general, egalitarian households have a greater likelihood of mothers working outside the home, resulting in greater autonomy for them, but

also less supervision for the daughters. This increases the chances of delinquent behavior by the daughters. Thus, the theory predicts lower delinquency rates for lower-class families that are more likely to be patriarchal, and greater delinquency rates for middle class families that are more likely to be egalitarian. Research in this area has produced mixed results.

Many exciting new perspectives on female criminality have led to great advances in this area. This topic is gaining increasing importance due to the rise in female criminality rates and due to the reorientation of the topic due to the feminist theory discourse.

The Criminal Justice System

Formal social control in America is maintained by the agencies of the criminal justice system. This section discusses three components of the system: the police, courts, and the punishment philosophies for those convicted that are reflected in the correctional system (e.g., jails and prisons).

Table 11.5 provides nationally representative data on Americans' level of respect for and

---

BOX 11.6

A Variety of Feminist Perspectives on Crime

- *Liberal feminism* Gender rate differences in crime are attributable to traditional gender role socialization. Thus, higher crime rates for women during the 60's and beyond are a consequence of changing socialization patterns for women, and are caused by an increasing number of opportunities for crime.
- *Marxist feminism* The rise of industrialization, for males predominantly, leads to a move outside the home for economic production. This further perpetuates patriarchy. Women become valued for their 'reproduction of labor power,' and

typically start working at low paying jobs. Poverty leads to crime. They also suffer from an increase in rape and other violence under the system of capitalism.
- *Radical feminism* Biology is a major reason for patriarchy, as women are physically weaker than men. Men control women's sexuality by rape, domestic violence, battering, and pornography.
- *Socialist feminism* Interaction of social class and gender influences the development of crime and the operation of the criminal justice system. Types of crimes committed by upper

class men are different (e.g. white collar crime) than the types of crimes engaged in by poor women (e.g. prostitution, bogus check writing).
- *Women of color feminism* Here, the emphasis is on the interaction of gender, race, and class. It is noted that crime rates of African American females are higher than those for white women, as are the victimization rates. Differentials in treatment by the criminal justice system of women of color is emphasized.

Source: Adapted from Barkan, 1997.

confidence in various institutions. Fully 64 percent of Americans have a great deal or quite a lot of respect and confidence in the military, and 58 percent feel that way about the police. However, only one American in 5 has a great deal or quite a lot of respect and confidence in the criminal justice system.

TABLE 11.5. Americans' Level of Respect and Confidence in Selected Institutions, 1995

"I am going to read you a list of institutions in American society. Would you tell me how much respect and confidence you, yourself, have in each one—a great deal, quite a lot, some, or very little?"

Institution	Percentage of Americans having a great deal or quite a lot of confidence and respect in the institution
Military	64
Police	58
Presidency	45
Supreme Court	44
Banks	43
Medical System	41
Public Schools	40
Television News	33
Newspapers	30
Organized Labor	26
Congress	21
Big Business	21
Criminal Justice System	20

Source: Jean Johnson, "Americans' Views on Crime and Law Enforcement: Survey Findings," National Institute of Justice Journal, (September) 1997: 9-14. Adapted from Exhibit 1, p. 11.

The Police

Policing is the first stage of the criminal justice process. The first modern police force in the United States was organized in Boston during the year 1837. It was based on the British system. The current police force in the United States is organized at four levels. These are:

- Municipal police departments
- County sheriff's departments
- State police departments
- Federal police departments.

Marxist criminologists view the police as a tool of the upper-classes, used to maintain order and control over working classes. Police are, after all, the ultimate representative of the state and the government. Several studies on this issue have shown that the criminal justice system does respond to perceived threats to the social order. A study by *Pamela Irving Jackson* and *Leo Caroll* (1981) found that the racial composition of a city's population has an impact on the amount of expenditure on its police force. Cities with greater concentrations of African American populations were found to spend more on police salaries, operations, and capital expenditures than cities with lower concentrations. Similarly, cities with greater levels of political activity by African Americans show higher levels of police expenditure.

The Working Personality of the Officer

Even though a majority of time spent by the police is on activities like directing traffic and other mundane activities, police, in general, fear for their safety and are aware of the potential threat of injury. Because of this, sociologist *Jerome H. Skolnick* (1975) argues that police officers develop a distinct working personality, attributable mainly to the structure of the environment they encounter on the job. The dangers in their working environment cause the police to become suspicious of, and hostile to, the public. They also recognize the discretionary power they possess while encountering the public. All these variables reinforce mutual loyalty and generate cynicism and authoritarianism towards the public, ultimately resulting in greater levels of violence towards them.

One of the areas in which police have discretion is in making arrests. Studies indicate that the following factors influence the decision made:

- Seriousness of the offense
- The "intimacy" factor. Perpetrators are more likely to be arrested if they are strangers.
- Hostility of the perpetrator.

- Minority status.
- Expectations of the bystanders. Arrest is more likely to take place if the bystanders seem to expect it.

Please read Table 11.6. Most Americans (74 percent) are of the opinion that the police in their communities treat blacks and whites equally. However, while this perception is held by 76 percent of whites, it is held by less than half of African Americans. Forty-two percent of African Americans (but only 11 percent of white Americans) believe that the police in their communities mostly treat blacks worse than whites. For example, about half of African Americans (53 percent) have the perception that police racism and falsification of evidence in criminal cases is common among members of their local police forces. Only 15 percent of white Americans feel this way. (Please read Table 11.7.)

TABLE 11.6. Americans' Opinions About Police Treating Community Members Equally, by Race, In Percents, 1995

"As far as you know, do the police in your community mostly treat blacks worse than whites, or both races about equally?"

Response Option	General Public	Blacks	Whites
Mostly blacks worse than whites	14	42	11
Mostly equally	74	47	76
Mixed (Volunteered)	02	11	01
Don't know (Volunteered)	10	0	12

Source: Source: Jean Johnson, "Americans' Views on Crime and Law Enforcement: Survey Findings," *National Institute of Justice Journal*, (September) 1997: 9-14. Adapted from Exhibit 2, p. 12.

Deterrence and the Police

A major justification for the existence of the police force is the notion of deterrence—the notion that police presence allegedly reduces crime. Several studies have examined the effect of police presence on crime. Research studies by criminologists support the following observations:

- Patrol cars do *not* deter much crime.
- Police officers on foot patrol reduce the fear of crime.

TABLE 11.7. Americans' Opinions About Police Behavior, by Race, In Percents, 1995

"From what you know, is the kind of improper behavior by police described on the Fuhrman tapes (racism and falsification of evidence) common among members of your local police force, or not?"

Response Option	General Public	Blacks	Whites
Yes, common	20	53	15
No, not common	64	32	70
Don't know (Volunteered)	16	16	15

Source: Source: Jean Johnson, "Americans' Views on Crime and Law Enforcement: Survey Findings," *National Institute of Justice Journal*, (September) 1997: 9-14. Adapted from Exhibit 2, p. 12.

- Greatly increasing the number of police and arrests during "crime crackdowns" does reduce crime.
- Police patrol makes little impact on criminal activities which usually take place out of the view of the street.
- The cost of police is very high in relation to the financial savings achieved due to deterrence.

Varieties of Policing

James Q. Wilson (1978) describes three distinct styles of policing.

1. **The service style** emphasizes community relations. This style exists largely in homogeneous communities in middle-class suburbs.
2. **The watchman style** emphasizes patrolling and maintaining order and it exists in a highly political environment.
3. **The legalistic style** emphasizes extensive and accurate record keeping and it does not provide for much police discretion.

The Courts

After arrest, the onus of responsibility, with regard to the guilt or innocence of the suspect, falls on the court system. In the United States, the criminal courts are highly *decentralized*. Each state has its own criminal court system, as does the federal government. The decentralized nature of the court systems in this country is captured by the concept of *a dual court system*—which means that there are both state and federal courts.

While criminal courts in the United States may be different depending on the state, all states have both trial courts and appellate courts. Some states allow the trial courts to hear felony as well as misdemeanor cases. In other states, one level of the court hears felony cases, while another level of the court hears misdemeanor cases. All states have appeal courts, usually called the State Supreme Court.

The criminal court systems of the United States are *adversarial.* This means that the defendant is legally presumed innocent until proven guilty beyond a reasonable doubt. The prosecuting attorney attempts to prove that the defendant is guilty. In many other countries, the criminal courts are *inquisitorial,* which means that the defendant is presumed to be legally guilty, and the burden of proof is on the defense to prove the innocence of the defendant.

The federal court system has three levels: the district, the circuit and United States Supreme Court—which is the highest. The prosecuting attorney presents the case for the government and is responsible for securing the evidence against the defendant. The Sixth Amendment of the United States Constitution provides the right to counsel, so the accused has the right to a defense attorney in felony cases. In cases where the accused does not have the finances to hire an attorney, the counsel may be provided at government expense.

A bail system may be used to guarantee a defendant's presence at trial. In this way, the accused is allowed to be released in the community until the time of trial. Sometimes, preventive detention is used to ensure that the accused does not flee or injure himself or others. However, preventive detention may also be achieved by the court by setting an unusually high bail.

Plea Bargaining

Plea bargaining is an informal process of negotiation, whereby the prosecutor and the defense attorney reach an agreement on a guilty plea (usually a reduced charge) and a sentence. *Douglas A. Smith* (1986) concludes that more than 85 percent of all felony cases in American courts result in guilty pleas. A major reason for the use of this process is the heavy caseloads that burden all involved parties in

the criminal justice process. However, plea bargaining has many critics. *John E. Conklin* (1997) lists some of the criticisms. These are:

- Innocent defendants are often coerced into pleading guilty in order to get a more lenient sentence.
- Since plea bargaining goes on behind closed doors, it keeps the judicial process out of public view, thereby increasing the chance of abuse.
- The defendant is not sure that the judge will hand out the agreed upon sentence.
- Since the sentence handed out is less harsh, offenders do not get their "just desserts," leading to a subversion of the deterrent and incapacitating effect of punishment.

Sentencing Disparity

The types of sentences imposed range from the death penalty, incarceration, probation, split sentence, restitution and victim compensation, to community service, fines, and probation. **Probation** is a sentence whereby an alleged or adjudicated adult or juvenile offender is free to remain in the community, provided that the person meets certain conditions of behavior (e.g., remains drug free, does not associate with known felons, obeys the law). A major problem with the American court system is **sentencing disparity**—wherein persons accused of similar offenses, with similar criminal records, receive different sanctions from the court. Significant variations occur across judges, jurisdictions, and states. Many observers are concerned that in a justice system where all accused persons are to be treated equally before the law, that factors such as race, gender, and social class may influence sentencing.

Research on the relationship between race and sentencing has produced mixed results. That African Americans constitute about 13 percent of the Unites States population but are 50 percent of the incarcerated population, suggesting gross racial discrimination to some observers and critics of the court system. Research also has indicated that the complex role of race during the sentencing process is influenced by a number of other variables. Among them: the type of crime, race composition of the offender and victim, and the relationship between the offender and victim. *Cassia Spohn* (1994) concludes that the harshest penalties are meted out to African American males accused of sexually assaulting either white females or African American females who were strangers to them. The most lenient treatment according to Spohn occurs when white males are accused of sexual assault of a white female or an African American male who was facing charges from an African American acquaintance (1994).

Observers concerned about sentencing disparity make a distinction between direct discrimination and organizational discrimination. In *organizational discrimination* (which is a synonym for institutional discrimination) members of the lower socio-economic classes (which include a number of minority populations) have problems getting bail, are more likely to be convicted, are less likely to hire a private attorney, and are more likely to get longer prison sentences.

Another concern for many observers relates to the possible influence of race on capital punishment. (Please read Table 11.8, "Persons Under Sentence of Death in the United States, by Race/Ethnicity, 1996," and Table 11.9, "Executions in the United States, by Race/Ethnicity and Method of Execution, 1977-1996.") Research results consistently suggest that race plays a significant role in getting the death penalty (Keil and Vito, 1989). Thus, African Americans (who are 13 percent of the U.S. population) constitute 42 percent of those currently living under the sentence of death. Of the 358 persons executed between 1977 and

1996, fully 37 percent (N = 134) were African Americans.

Even though mixed results have been found regarding the relationship between social class and sentencing, evidence does exist regarding the impact of social class on both the length of sentence and on decisions by juries. And finally, recent studies examining the role that gender plays during the sentencing process point to a decline of gender as an influential factor. *Kathleen Daly* (1994) provides an alternate explanation for traditional studies that found a gender difference in sentencing. What initially appeared to be greater leniency towards females perhaps results from the fact that compared to males, females were less likely to commit serious crimes.

Punishment Philosophies

The final section of this chapter reflects on the justifications for punishment. Four different perspectives are the following:

Retribution

This philosophy is based less on personal feelings and more on general principles of ethics. Commonly associated with *lex talionis,* the principle of an eye for an eye and a tooth for a tooth which was expressed in the code of Hammurabi in the eighteenth century B.C., **retribution** is an act of moral revenge, in which the society subjects an offender to suffering comparable to that caused by the offense. A principle of justice underlying retribution is that people deserve to be punished if they break the law. This principle is expressed in the saying, "Don't do the crime if you can't do the time." This principle is commonly referred to as *just desserts.*

Retribution is analytically distinguishable from *vengeance,* which is private and does not possess the backing of the state. Retribution provides just desserts to the offender—if people break the law, they deserve to be punished—and thereby justice prevails.

Deterrence

This principle is based on the Enlightenment notion that human beings are rational and calculating, and that individuals will be prevented from crimogenic activities if they

TABLE 11.8. Persons Under Sentence of Death in the United States, by Race/Ethnicity, 1996.

Race/Ethnicity	Persons Under Sentence of Death in 1996	
	Number	Percent of Total
White	1,561	48.5
Black	1,349	42
Hispanic	259	8
Native American	24	0.7
Asian	18	0.6
Other	8	0.2
TOTAL	**3,219**	**100**

Source: Adapted from U.S. Department of Justice, Bureau of Justice Statistics Bulletin, "Capital Punishment 1996," (December) 1997: 1.

TABLE 11.9. Executions in the United States, by Race/Ethnicity and Method of Execution, 1977-1996

Method of Execution	Race/Ethnicity of Persons Executed, 1977-1996				
	White	Black	Hispanic	Native American	Asian
Total	200	134	21	2	1
Lethal Injection	123	70	20	2	1
Electrocution	66	61	1	0	0
Lethal Gas	6	3	0	0	0
Hanging	3	0	0	0	0
Firing Squad	2	0	0	0	0

Source: Adapted from U.S. Department of Justice, Bureau of Justice Statistics Bulletin, Capital Punishment 1996," (December) 1997: 12.

recognize that the pains of punishment outweigh the joys of crime. Two types of deterrence used are general and specific (sometimes called "special) deterrence. *General deterrence* is based on the notion that the dissemination of information about the severity of punishment and the imposition of that punishment on those who violate the law serves as an example to currently law-abiding members of the community. For example, Pat steals a car. In accordance with the principle of general deterrence, Pat is punished so that currently law-abiding members of the community will not steal automobiles. In *specific* (or special) *deterrence*, on the other hand, punishment demonstrates to the perpetrators of crime that the pains of punishment outweigh the pleasures of crime. The idea here is that people will not again engage in actions if the punishment for those actions outweigh the benefits. Via punishment, the quon dam perpetrator learns that "Crime does not pay." In accordance with the principle of specific deterrence, then, Pat is punished so that Pat will not steal automobiles any more.

Most research on the topic of deterrence indicates that the *celerity* and certainty of punishment are more important than its severity in deterring crime. The celerity (speed) of punishment refers to the quickness with which punishment follows law violating behavior. In terms of deterrence, punishment should follow swiftly on the heels of crime. The *certainty* of punishment refers to the probability of being punished if one breaks the law. In terms of achieving deterrence, there should be a high probability that people are punished if they break the law. Of course, Americans also hold

values that get in the way of swift and certain punishment. Some of these values are the right of due process of law and freedom from unlawful search and seizure. *Can you think of other values that get in the way of applying state punishment swiftly and with certainty? Please tell us about it.*

Rehabilitation

This modern approach developed out of research in the social sciences which views crime as a product of social conditions and personal pathologies. The emphasis here was on introducing education programs, psychotherapy sessions, drug and alcohol counseling, job training, and vocational rehabilitation programs, all within the confines of the institution. These intervention strategies would result in a reformed individual who has the necessary skills to reintegrate back into the world outside of the institution. Thus, reduction in crime would be achieved by changes in personality, abilities, attitudes, values, or behavior. However, most research on recidivism rates for these offenders shows no significant differences from those in control groups, who did not receive help from rehabilitation programs. In the long term, these programs seem to achieve very little in reshaping attitudes and behavior.

Societal Protection

Societal protection entails rendering the offender incapable of committing further offenses by incarceration or, in extreme cases, through execution. A recent increase in the length of sentences and in the number of executions corroborates the popularity of this approach.

Summary and Conclusion

Americans are both fascinated and horrified by deviance and crime and want to understand why people engage in it. In this chapter, we introduced various social-science approaches to the study of deviance, crime, criminal law, juvenile delinquency, and criminal justice. Crime and deviance are explored from many vantage points, including those of biology, political science, psychology, philosophy, and sociology. You are introduced to a variety of approaches for understanding deviance, crime, delinquency and criminal and juvenile justice

within the discipline of sociology. Social conflict theory, symbolic interactionism and structural-functional analyses are presented and assessed. You have been introduced to various approaches of defining deviance, crime, criminal law, and juvenile delinquency and have learned about formal and informal means of social control. We examined the nature and extent of crime in the United States and examined the types of crime. Next, the working of the agencies of the criminal justice system were explored. The chapter finally concludes with a critical look at different philosophies of punishment.

Key Concepts

Albert Cohen
Albert Quinney
Alexander Liazos
anomie
appeal to higher loyalties
atavism
attachment
attribution
autonomy
belief
biological theories of deviance
blaming the victim (William Ryan)
capitalism
Cassia Spohn
Cesare Lombroso
characteristics of organized crime (John E. Conklin)
Charles Horton Cooley
commitment
condemnation of the condemners
conflict subculture
conformist
corporate crime
correctional institutions
courtesy stigma
crime
criminal justice system
criminal subculture
criminalization
critique of conflict theories of deviance
dark figure of crime
David L. Rosenhahn

denial of harm
denial of responsibility
denial of victim
deterrence
deviance
deviant career
dual court system
dualistic fallacy (Sue Titus Reid)
Durkheim on the functions of deviance
ectomorphs
Edwin H. Sutherland
Edwin Lemert
endomorphs
Erving Goffman
excitement
fate
female criminality
feminist perspectives on crime
focal concerns
fundamental attribution error
liberal feminism on crime
malicious
Marxist feminism on crime
mechanical solidarity
mental illness as a myth
mesomorphs
moral entrepreneur
National Crime Victimization Survey
National Incident Based/Reporting System (NIBRS)
negativistic
nonutilitarian

Oedipal complex
organic solidarity
organizational discrimination in sentencing
organized crime
Part I offenses
Part II offenses
philosophies of punishment
pluralistic society
primary conflict (Thorsten Sellin)
primary deviance
probation
property crimes
public degradation ceremony
radical feminism on crime
radical nonintervention (Edwin M. Schur)
rebel
rehabilitation
residual deviance
retreatist
retreatist subculture
retribution
Richard A. Cloward and Lloyd E. Ohlin
rite of passage
ritualist
Robert Merton: strain theory
status offender
status offense
stigma
subterranean values
survivalists

symbolic interactionist theories
of deviance
techniques of neutralization
the costs of crime
the courts
the legalistic style of policing
the medical model of deviance
the moral model of deviance
the police
The Professional Thief
(Sutherland)
the service style of policing
the significance or
consequences of labels

the sociological model of
deviance
the watchman style of policing
theory of differential
opportunity
Thomas Scheff
Thomas Szasz
Thorsten Sellin
toughness
trouble
Uniform Crime Reports (UCR)
varieties of policing (James Q.
Wilson)

vengeance
victimless crime
violence and crime in Russia
today
Violent Offenses
Walter B. Miller
white-collar crime (Edwin
Sutherland)
William H. Sheldon
William J. Chambliss
women of color feminism on
crime
XYY chromosome

Internet Resources

http://www.usdoj.gov/

Document: United States Department of Justice

This site offers information on the Department of Justice. Readers can access government legal matters, research areas such as drug inforcement laws, immigration laws, etc.

http://www.fbi.gov/homepage.htm

Document: Federal Bureau of Investigation

The FBI's homepage contains information on the top 10 most wanted by the FBI, major investigations, information on fugitives, FBI cases, and the history of the organization.

http://www.ncjrs.org/homepage.htm

Document: Justice Information Center: A Service of the National Criminal Justice Reference Service.

This site is an expansive reference center that features documents, world wide web sites, agencies, and other information resources on crime. The page is divided up into sections such as "Corrections," "Courts," and "Juvenile." The database can also be searched through their catalog and keyword searches.

http://www.icpsr.umich.edu/NACJD

Document: National Archive of Criminal Justice Data

This site provides over 500 criminal justice data collections, other data on crime and justice, and quantitative data. This web page also offers specialized collections and data sets.

http://www.nvc.org

Document: National Victim Center

The National Victim Center's web site gives information on violent crimes that occur in the United States. Viewers have access to their library of violent crime statistics and other educational resources. This web site also gives information on whom and where people who become victims of violent crime should call.

http://www.nida.nih.gov/

Document: NIDA (National Institute on Drug Abuse)

NIDA frequently updates their web page and publishes on-line drug research. The site also provides information on commonly abused drugs, agency tri-annual reports, publications, conference dates, and web links.

http://www.ncadp.org/

Document: NCAADP (National Coalition to Abolish the Death Penalty)

The NCAADP is a national organization that fights to abolish the death penalty at the federal and state levels. They offer many facts about the death penalty and arguments against executions. This site also provides links to other death-penalty web links.

http://www2.jfa.net/jfa/

Document: Justice For All

Justice For All updates their page weekly. They advocate for victims' rights and work to educate and inform the public and criminal justice system on these issues. For their pro death-penalty views, link to **alt.activism.death-penalty.** Also link to Death Penalty and Sentencing Information for further discussion on the death penalty, which includes articles, bibliographies, and web links.

Suggested Readings

Benedict, Jeff, *Public Heroes, Private Felons: Athletes and Crimes Against Women* (Boston: Northeastern University Press, 1997)

Benson, Michael L., and Cullen, Francis T., *Combating Corporate Crime: Local Prosecutors at Work* (Boston: Northeastern University Press, 1998).

Brownmiller, Susan, *Against Our Will: Men, Women, and Rape* (NY: Simon and Schuster, 1975).

Cabana, Donald A., *Death at Midnight: The Confession of an Executioner* (Boston: Northeastern Univerity Press, 1998).

Chesney-Lind, Meda, and Sheldon, Randall G., *Girls, Delinquency, and Juvenile Justice* (Second efition) (Belmont, CA: West/Wadsworth, 1997).

Douglas, John D., and Olshaker, Mark, *Obsession* (NY: Scribner, 1998).

Felson, Marcus, *Crime and Everyday Life* (Second edition) (Thousand Oaks, CA: Pine Forge Press, 1998).

Felson, R.B., "Big People Hit Little People: Sex Differences in Physical Power and Interpersonal Violence," *Criminology,* Vol. 34, 1996: 433-452.

Jenness, Valerie, and Broad, Kendal, *Hate Crimes: New Social Movements and the Politics of Violence* (NY: Aldine de Gruyter, 1997).

Marshall, Joseph, *Street Soldier: One Man's Struggle to Save a Generation—One Life at a Time* (New York: Delta (Dell), 1996).

Ressler, Robert K.; Burgess, Ann W.; and Douglas, John E., *Sexual Homicide: Patterns and Motives* (New York: Lexington Books, 1988).

Upchurch, Carl, *Convicted in the Womb: One Man's Journey from Prisoner to Peacemaker* (New York: Bantam Trade Paperback, 1996).

Learning Exercise 11.1

Application of Sociological Analysis to Social Life

Answer the following questions in an essay of not less than three typed, double-spaced, pages. Staple your paper in the upper left corner. In your answer, you should reflect upon the concepts and theories of deviance and criminology discussed in this chapter.

1. Define deviance from a sociological perspective and contrast it with the general public's definition and understanding. Is deviance completely relative or are there some behaviors that are universally and absolutely deviant?
2. We have discussed that deviance and criminal behavior may vary by society, culture and time. What are some of the ordinary and everyday behaviors that may be considered deviant and/or criminal if they took place in a different setting or time?
3. People often become deviant for failing to understand and/or accept that the group's official norms may not be the real norms. The difference is between ideal vs. real culture. Can you think of any example of this contradiction?

■ ■ ■

Learning Exercise 11.2

In-Class Learning Exercise

In your group play the following game. Each member of the group is to take a half sheet of $8\frac{1}{2} \times$ 11-inch paper. Without consulting with each other, each person is to write one deviant label on her or his paper (e.g. crazy, criminal, weirdo, etc.). Please write or print clearly and in letters sufficiently large that others can readily decipher what you have written. Then, fold your piece of paper in fourths, so that the handwriting on the paper is not visible. Then, put the pieces of paper into a hat, paper sack, or empty book bag. Each member of the group, one at a time, is to withdraw one of those pieces of paper (with eyes closed) and to read the paper (silently). At this point it is important that each member does not reveal to other members what label he/she has selected. After each member has had an opportunity to read (silently) the label he/she has selected, you are to engage in pantomime—one at a time—in front of your group's members.

Group members attempt to guess which deviant label the person is modeling. After the deviant label has been guessed, the next person to the right role plays the deviant label he/she selected. The group members attempt to guess which deviant label the person is modeling—until each member of your group has had an opportunity to play a deviant label which the other members of the group attempt to identify.

After each student has had an opportunity to role play a deviant label, each student is to write an essay describing the role and how playing that deviant role—tell the reader what the deviant role was— made you feel. Why do you think you felt this way?

■ ■ ■

Writing Opportunity

Please develop well thought-out answers to the following questions using terms and concepts from this course and from this chapter. In your answers, you should reflect upon the concepts and theories of deviance and criminology discussed in this chapter. This exercise is to be no less than three pages in length. All papers are to be typed, double-spaced, and stapled in the upper left corner.

1. Contrast the functionalist theory of social control with the conflict theory of deviance and control. How do norms make social life possible?
2. Distinguish a sociological perspective (functionalism, conflict, or labeling) on deviance from a biological and psychological perspective. Please explain Szasz's controversial idea of the myth of mental illness. Have you ever known anyone who suffered a great deal from mental illness? Please explain the situation to the reader. Do Szasz's notions of mental illness as a myth seem to fit the example you have just described? Why or why not? Do you agree with Szasz that mental illness is a myth? Please explain your position and your reasons for it to the reader.
3. Recent years have seen a strong societal backlash against cigarette smoking in America. How would Durkheim describe the functions of this deviance for society?
4. Compare and contrast three sociological theories of crime or deviance. Which theory do you find particularly useful or meaningful in terms of explaining why people engage in crime or deviance? Explain your position. Also, which theory do you find particularly unappealing or weak, and why?
5. In examining the four philosophies of punishment, which one makes the most (and least) sense to you and why?

■　■　■

In-Class

1. First, ask the class to select a form of deviance. Write their selection on the board. Then, the class breaks up into their groups. Each group should select someone to act as note-taker for the group. Each group should select someone to act as spokesperson for the group. The spokesperson may be the note-taker or another member. Each group is to develop explanations for the chosen form of deviance using labeling, functionalist, social control, and social conflict theories. After all groups have constructed their explanations, a spokesperson from each group presents their group's case to the class.

2. Have the instructor of the class obtain a movie or the instructor may have you rent a video that demonstrates deviant behavior (e.g., "The Bird Cage," "Shawshank Redemption," "The Silence of the Lambs," "Barbarians at the Gate," and so on). Watch the videotape. Then, each group is to analyze the video/movie using at least four different perspectives (e.g., labeling theory, functional analysis, social control theory, conflict theory). Each group should present their findings in a paper before the class. This exercise may be executed as an individual learning exercise, in which case, the student should write an essay of no less than four typed, double-spaced pages. Analyze the movie/video from four different theoretical perspectives. Which theoretical perspective or combination of perspectives do you find the most and least satisfactory in understanding the social dynamics portrayed in the video, and why?

■ ■ ■

Learning Exercise 11.5

Writing Assignment

Answer the following questions in an essay not less than three typed, double-spaced pages. In your answer you should reflect upon the concepts and theories of deviance and criminology discussed in this chapter.

1. Think of a situation in which you felt like being a deviant, but did not do so. Use Hirschi's control theory to explain why you did not deviate. Now, think of a situation in which you felt like being a deviant, and did so. Use Hirschi's control theory to explain why you did deviate.
2. Sutherland asserts that we learn deviant and criminal definitions—like anything else—through interaction with others. In your associations and interactions, what impact do your friends' behavior have on you?
3. Can you think of a positive labeling experience you have had and its impact on you? How different would it be if this experience was a negative one and you had political or economic power?

■ ■ ■

Multiple Choice and True-False Test

1. Select the sociological term for the violation of significant social norms.
   A. Crime
   B. Deviance
   C. Law violation
   D. Juvenile delinquency

2. Select the term for the violation of norms, formally enacted in to criminal law.
   A. Juvenile delinquency
   B. Deviance
   C. Crime

3. What is the term for the formal system that responds to the alleged violations of the law using police and the courts?
   A. The criminal justice system
   B. Socialization
   C. The normative system.

4. Using Lombrosso's theoretical position, which of these statements would you agree with?
   A. Social structure generates deviance.
   B. The XYY chromosome causes males to be aggressive.
   C. Criminals are throwbacks in the process of evolution.
   D. Criminals can not be physically distinguished from non-criminals.

5. According to Sheldon, which of the following body types is most likely to be delinquent?
   A. Metamorphosis
   B. Ectomorphs
   C. Endomorphs
   D. Mesomorphs

6. Which one of these is a criticism of the biological theories of deviance and crime?
   A. Categories of criminals and non-criminals in society are not mutually exclusive.
   B. These theories show a social class bias by explaining the crimes of the lower classes.
   C. Too much sympathy for the underdog.
   D. All of the above
   E. Both (A) and (B)

7. Which of the following statements is/are true regarding psychological explanations of crime?
   A. Psychologists have demonstrated some connections between personality patterns and crime.
   B. Some research indicates a correlation between IQ and delinquency.
   C. They search for criminal pathology in the human personality.
   D. All of the above are true.
   E. Both (A) and (C)

8. Durkheim proposed several functions of deviance. Which of the following is **not** one of them?
   A. Deviance provides employment for a large section of the workforce.
   B. Deviance clarifies boundaries between the deviants and the non-deviants.
   C. Deviance leads to social solidarity.
   D. Deviance acts as a safety valve for strains within society.

9. What is the term used by Merton to refer to the rejection of cultural goals and means, and the advocation of alternatives?
   A. Conformity
   B. Rebellion
   C. Ritualism
   D. Reductionism

10. What is the term used by Merton to refer to an acceptance of culturally prescribed goals, while seeking illegitimate means to achieve them?
    A. Innovation
    B. Ritualism
    C. Rebellion
    D. Retreatism

11. Which of the following punishment philosophies, strives to change the attitudes, personality, and skill set of the offender?
    A. Rehabilitation
    B. Concurrent sentencing
    C. Legalistic policing
    D. Societal protection

12. According to Cloward and Ohlin's theory, _____.
    A. criminal subcultures are more likely to exist in upper class neighborhoods.
    B. retreatist subcultures involve individuals who retire to a life of conventionality after many years in crime
    C. the dominant theme in conflict sub-cultures is violence, which is used to gain status in the group.
    D. white collar crime is widely prevalent in lower income neighborhoods.

13. Which of Miller's focal concerns reflects the desire for freedom, expressed as a resentment towards authority figures?
    A. Fate
    B. Autonomy
    C. Smartness

14. Which of Miller's focal concerns reflects youths' emphasis on physical strength and masculinity?
    A. Toughness
    B. Fate
    C. Cyberphilia
    D. Hyperplasia
    E. In loco parentis

15. Which term refers to revenge by society on the perpetrator?
    A. Reintegration
    B. Retribution
    C. Rehabilitation
    D. Redistribution

16. According to Cohen, which of the following values are characteristics of lower class subculture?
    A. Attachment, commitment, involvement, belief
    B. Nonutilitarian, negativistic, malicious
    C. Criminal, conflict, retreatist
    D. Fate, trouble, smartness

17. According to Matza, which one of the following is **not** a technique of neutralization?
    A. Appeal to higher loyalties
    B. Denial of responsibility
    C. Condemnation of condemners
    D. Attachment to conventional society

18. What is/are some of the main concepts of Hirshi's social bond theory?
    A. Attachment to parents, peers, and school decreases delinquency
    B. Immigrant neighborhoods suffer from social disorganization
    C. There is no difference in the IQ scores of delinquents and non-delinquents
    D. All of the above

19. Which one of the following is a criticism of Hirschi's theory of the social bond?
    A. Too much sympathy for the underclasses.
    B. This theory does not look at societal origins of crime, but rather at individual variations from societal norms.
    C. If society determines what is criminal, how can criminality be biological?

20. What is the basic theme in Cohen and Felson's routine activity theory?
    A. Involvement and belief in conventional society reduce delinquency.
    B. Inner city slums are more likely to generate crime.
    C. Volume of crime is influenced by the nature of everyday interactions.
    D. Conformity, not deviance, needs an explanation.

21. Which one of these statements is **not** a part of labeling theory?
    A. No act is intrinsically criminal.
    B. Socio-economic factors are not important in the labeling process.
    C. Criminal definitions are imposed in the interest of the powerful in society.
    D. The process of labeling may produce a deviant identity.

22. What is Goffman's term for a powerful and negative social label that radically changes a person's social identity and self-concept?
    A. Negative label
    B. Label
    C. Stigma

23. What would you believe if you agreed with Szasz's approach to deviance?
    A. Mentally ill people are physically sick also.
    B. Mental illness is a myth.
    C. The real level of insanity in the United States is much higher than the psychiatrist profession would suggest.
    D. Mental illness is tied to unemployment rates.

24. According to Spohn, in the United States, which of the following situations led to the harshest sentences from the criminal justice system?
    A. White male accused of sexual assault on a white woman.
    B. African American male accused of sexual assault of a white woman.
    C. African American male accused of sexual assault of an African American woman who was a stranger.
    D. White males accused of sexually assaulting an African American female.

25. Into which two categories does Marx categorize social classes in capitalist society?
    A. Bourgeoisie/proletariat
    B. Saints/roughnecks
    C. Nominalists/populists
    D. Idealists/materialists

26. According to Thorsten Sellin's theory of culture conflict, _____ refers to conflict that results from the clash between the immigrant's original culture and US culture.
    A. primary
    B. secondary
    C. tertiary

27. What is the precise term for the legal negotiation in which the prosecution reduces defendant's charge in exchange for a guilty plea?
    A. Charge bargaining.
    B. Pretrial observation
    C. Plea bargaining.
    D. Determinate sentencing.

28. Which of the following is/are criticisms conflict theories of deviance?.
    A. Power in the United States is shared by diverse groups.
    B. Conflict theory focuses primarily on conventional street crime.
    C. These theories ignore existing consensus on many laws.
    D. All of the above.
    E. Both (A) and (C)

29. If you believe in Sutherland's differential association theory, what would you do to reduce crime?
    A. Increase the relative frequency of association with those who discourage norm violations.
    B. Remove the ability of the criminal justice system to label people.
    C. Remove stigma from deviant labeling.
    D. Change the focal concerns of the lower classes.

30. Regarding white collar crime, which of the following is/are **false?**
    A. Costs to society from white collar crime are minimal.
    B. When white collar criminals are charged and convicted, they usually go to prison for a long time.
    C. Most white collar cases are heard in civil or administrative courts rather than in courts of criminal law.
    D. The American public, in general, does not fear white collar crime nearly to the extent that they fear "street" crime.
    E. Only (A) and (B).

31. A person accused of _____ is suspected of carrying out a crime motivated by racial bias.
    A. robbery
    B. burglary
    C. a hate crime

32. Which one of the following is *not* a method of data collection about the extent of crime in America?
    A. Uniform Crime Reports
    B. National Incident Based Reporting System
    C. National Police Academy

33. Burglary is an example of what type of crime?
    A. Crime against the person
    B. Crime against property
    C. Hate crime
    D. Organizational crime

34. According to Wilson, the three different styles of policing are _____.
    A. Watchman, democratic, libertarian
    B. Legalistic, democratic, socialist
    C. Watchman, legalistic, service
    D. Democratic, efficient, political

35. Gender and crime data suggest _____.
    A. Women are more likely to be perpetrators rather than victims of crime.
    B. Arrest rates for men and women are the same.
    C. More than 55 percent of property crimes are engaged in by females.
    D. The incidence of crime for females is low compared to that for men.

36. In the United States, which of the following statements about violent crime is **false** for 1996?
    A. Violent crime rates have fallen by 6 percent from the rates for 1995.
    B. The northeastern region has the highest rates of violent crime.
    C. The highest incidence of violent crime takes place during the summer.
    D. The lowest rate for violent crime is during February.

37. Which one of the following is **not** a feminist perspective on crime?
    A. Radical feminism
    B. Courtesy feminism
    C. Liberal feminism
    D. Socialist feminism

38. Clearance rates for property crime are higher than clearance rates for violent crime.
    A. True
    B. False

CHAPTER 12

Groups, Organizations, Bureaucracy, and Work

Relationships of Power and Exchange That Make a World

"Colonel," he declared, "I don't give a rat's ass what you say: I am
not going."

Richard A. Gabriel and P. L. Savage, *Crisis in Command: Mismanagement in the Army*

■ ■ ■

The general spirit of bureaucracy is the secret, the mystery,
preserved within itself by the hierarchy and against the outside
world by being a closed corporation.

Karl Marx, "Contribution to the Critique of Hegel's *Philosophy of Right*"

■ ■ ■

After standing in line at the Kazan train station for thirty minutes, it is now Harry's turn to talk with the ticket agent at the Intourist Office. This American Fulbright Scholar is on a simple errand. He needs to exchange a ticket bought two days before for another, because the plans for his trip to Rostav-na-Donu have changed.

The ticket agent speaks into a microphone: "Nyet! (No) It is not done here. You must go to the downtown Intourist Office." The American replies, "But they told me to exchange my tickets here on the day of my departure." The ticket agent raises her voice, saying, "I told you, it is not done here; and, besides, there are no more first-class tickets available. Next person, please."

He tries to reason with her: "Why would they, in the downtown office, tell me to come to the train station on the day of my departure to exchange my tickets then?" Raising herself out of her chair, the ticket agent points her finger directly at Harry's nose, saying, "I told you, it is not done here. Move on."

Highly frustrated and tired, Harry walks the five miles to the downtown ticket office. He finds the door of the Intourist Office locked. A signs reads "CLOSED FOR LUNCH." The door finally is unlocked. Three people are in line ahead of him. After forty-five minutes, it is

447

finally his turn. The agent who originally gave him instructions to go to the train station is unavailable. Another agent listens patiently to his story. She spends some minutes phoning several people, acting as if this were the first time anything like this had happened. She moves papers around on the counter, opens and closes her registration book, and then she begins the paper work to exchange his tickets. With a sigh of relief, Harry realizes that he has a chance to fulfill his obligation to lecture at Rostov University. He can take a train there this very night.

After twenty minutes the clerk informs him: "The ticket will cost you an additional 12,000 Rubles. You have passed the six-hour deadline before your trains departs. I have been able to get you another first-class ticket." In complete astonishment he replies: "I was here two days ago to exchange my ticket. A clerk in this office told me to go to the train station on the day of my departure to make the exchange. It is unfair that I have to pay for the clerk's misinformation." The clerk says nothing. She shrugs her shoulders. Her eyes are unfocused. Harry pays. He takes the precious three pieces of paper that the clerk hands him. He needs these as receipts if he is to be reimbursed for his expenses by the U.S. Embassy in Moscow.

Bureaucracy, social organizations, and *groups* penetrate our everyday lives in numerous ways. We tend to spend our lives in the presence of, and in interaction with, others. In this chapter we take a close sociological look at various types of groups (voluntary associations), group structures (bureaucracy), group characteristics (size), and processes (exchange, leadership) that we experience in our daily lives.

Georg Simmel (1858-1918): Insights into the Dynamics of Social Life

German sociologist Georg Simmel (1858-1918) (sounds like GAY-oich or GAY-oig ZIMel) is one of the more perceptive observers of social life. He formed his views in opposition to the structural sociology of writers like Auguste Comte. Simmel, a forerunner of the Chi-

cago school of sociology, viewed society as a web of interactions among people. His sociology stresses interaction. For instance, his analysis of power emphasizes that the powerful could not exercise power without the complicity of their subordinates. Simmel emphasizes the sociological point that power is an interaction, a point that we explore further later in this chapter. In Simmel's sociology, even social structures are to be viewed as interactions between and among individuals (Abercrombie, Hill, and Turner, 1994: 378).

Formal Sociology

His proposed method of studying interaction is sometimes termed *formal sociology* because it emphasizes the form of social interaction rather than its content. Simmel maintains that it is possible to isolate the *form* of social interactions from its *content*. Apparently very different interactions with very different contents can be shown to have the same *form*. For instance, Catholics celebrating Mass, feminists celebrating the twenty-fifth anniversary of the U.S. Supreme Court's *Roe vs. Wade* decision, and recovering alcoholics attending a meeting of Alcoholics Anonymous are apparently different interactions with differing contents. However, they do have the same form, in that they all are examples of rituals that increase the solidarity of the participants. Likewise, the relationship between Michelangelo (1475-1564) and the Pope and the relationship between peasant and landlord in present-day Argentina are apparently different relationships, yet they have the same form in that both are examples of patronage relationships. At the level of concrete description, there would seem little in common between the early psychoanalytic movement in Vienna, Austria, and the early Communist movements in either Russia or China (Coser, 1997: 179). If one attends to the typical forms of interaction among members of these groups, one observes that they all reveal the structural features of the **sect**. A sect is a small, voluntary, exclusive group that demands total commitment from its followers, that emphasizes its separateness from the world of the vulgar, and that views itself as possessing esoteric knowledge not available to nonmembers.

Social Type

Simmel applies formal sociology to the analysis of social types. A **social type** is a consensual or group-generated conception of a role (e.g., stranger, social climber, sexual predator, redneck, the renegade, the "poor," etc.) that is not fully apprehended by reference to formal definitions. You cannot look up the definition of a particular social type in a dictionary and thereby receive the social information conveyed by the concept. Social types are road maps to structures of role expectations that otherwise are largely invisible. Social actors need to learn these role expectations in order to be able to participate effectively and insightfully in groups (Klapp, 1958; Coser, 1977: 182).

The role of *the stranger* or of *the newcomer*—from immigrants, to the new kid on the block, to the college freshman—is a good example of a social type. The newcomer or the stranger is a person who arrives (on your campus, on your block, at your school, etc.) and who is there now. She or he is *in* the group but not fully a member *of* it. The individual who occupies this role is identifiable by other individuals within the group.

The role of newcomer/stranger allows group members to know (1) how to behave toward him/her, and (2) allows the group to interpret and to understand the stranger/newcomer's behavior. Group members assign the stranger or newcomer a role that no other members of the group may play.

What is this role? The stranger/newcomer is perceived by members as distant, in that she or he does not know the particularistic roles, norms, and traditions of the group. The stranger is not yet fully part of its solidary order, is not yet fully part of the "we." By virtue of her or his partial involvement in the group, she or he approaches the unique practices of the group with an attitude of "objectivity." Confidences that must be withheld from more closely related persons may be shared with the newcomer/stranger because these confidences are not likely to have consequences. Thus, Jim may share with a stranger that he is severely depressed and suicidal, although he cannot bring himself to share this information with his wife whom he dearly

loves. Being near yet distant, the stranger frequently is called upon as a confidant. For similar reasons, strangers or newcomers may be more acceptable, as well as more "objective" as judges, arbiters or negotiators between conflicting parties (spouses, siblings, juveniles, labor vs. management, aggrieved prisoners vs. prison administrators, etc.) because they are not tied to, dependent upon, or beholden to either of the contending parties. The stranger (e.g., counselor, therapist, negotiator) is the ideal intermediary in the traffic of emotions, politics, and economics.

Group Size and Social Relations: Monad, Dyad, Triad

Monad

One participant is a **monad**. A monad is not a group.

Dyad

In Simmel's terminology, a **dyad** is an elementary form of a group. A dyad is a primary group composed of two participants. For illustrative purposes only, let us call one of the participants "A" and the other, "B." A dyadic relationship differs from all other types of groups in that each of the two participants is confronted by only one other participant, not by a collectivity. Participant "A" confronts participant "B," or visa versa. There is but this one possibility for interaction and for communication, whether verbal or non-verbal, within a dyad.

There are several sociological characteristics about dyads that are worth noting.

First, the dyad inherently is unstable as a structure, because withdrawal of one participant destroys or "kills" the group.

Second, as we have seen, as used by Simmel, a dyad is not just any group of two participants. A dyad is a *primary group* that consists of two people. In a primary group, relationships among participants are *diffuse*, which means that the participants know each other in the range of roles they occupy. They know each other as students; as daughters or as sons; as neighbors; as spouses; as participants or as non-participants in certain religious rituals; as members of a community, and so forth. They know each others' fears, desires, tri-

umphs, and shortcomings. They have no secrets from each other. Members of a primary
relationship also are likely to regard each other
as ends rather than as means to an end. For
instance, Sally and Martha are best friends.
They have a primary-group relationship. Sally
interacts with Martha because she likes Martha, because the interaction is a worthwhile
end in itself, *not* because she wants to borrow
Martha's lecture notes.

Third, members of a primary group no
longer are strangers. They no longer have the
inherent freedom of the stranger or of the
newcomer to pursue interests not governed by
the other participant's affiliation.

Fourth, primary group members are what
we might term friends. In our daily lives we
make distinctions between friends and acquaintances. Intimate friends share a primary-
group relationship; they form a dyad. Acquaintances do not. Acquaintances have
secondary-group relations with each other.

Relations among members in a secondary
group are *segmental,* which means that the
participants know each other in a limited range
of roles, or parts of the roles, that they occupy.
In the story that opens this chapter, the Intourist clerks in Kazan, Russian Federation, knew
our American Fulbright scholar, Harry, only as
a client who wanted to trade-in his railway
tickets. They didn't even know that he is a
Fulbright scholar. Nor did they know him as,
or interact with him in his role as, a sibling,
colleague, friend, or in his roles as a husband,
lecturer, professor, community member, and so
forth. As secondary-group participants, their
relations are segmental.

Secondary-group social relations also are a
means to an end rather than an end in themselves. Harry interacts with the Intourist clerks
not as an end in itself, but as a means to
exchange his railway tickets. The clerks interact
with him, not because such interaction is intrinsically pleasing or meaningful, but because
he showed up at their office as a client. Interacting with him is simply part of their jobs, one
small part of earning a paycheck. The participants in a secondary relationship do not invest
emotionally in secondary relationships as they
do with primary relationships. Secondary relationships are distant, not intimate.

The Triad: Qualitative Changes in Social Life

The addition of one other person transforms the dyad into a **triad.** A triad is a group
with three participants. For illustrative purposes, let us call the participants of a triad "A,"
"B," and "C." Simmel asserts that the apparently simple fact of adding one participant
creates important qualitative changes.

1. *Increased possibilities of communication.*
   In a triad, for the first time, processes are
   possible that previously could not take
   place. For instance, the task of communication, both verbal and nonverbal, now has
   three possibilities (A↔B, B↔C, A↔C)
   rather than one.
2. *Possibility of asserting group domination
   over its members.* Second, in the triad, as in
   all associations involving more than two
   participants, the individual faces the possibility of being outvoted by a majority. In
   other words, the triad is the smallest structure in which the group as a whole can
   assert its will (can achieve domination)
   over its members.
3. *Manifesting the dialectics of social life.*
   The apparently simple fact of adding a
   third member to a group generates for the
   first time, and in its simplest form, the
   dialectics that inform all social life—the
   dialectic of freedom and constraint, of individualism and collectivism, of segmenta-
   tion and self-fulfillment. We shortly explore this phenomenon in more detail.
4. *Other qualitative changes in group life.*
   Fourth, Simmel claims that the larger the
   group (a) the less intense the interaction,
   (b) the more stable the group, and (c) the
   greater the level of individual freedom.

Role of the Third Party in Conflict Situations

Simmel defines *conflict* as all types of op-
positions, including competition, rivalry, jealousy, physical attacks, and so forth. What is the
role of the third party in a triadic conflict
situation? Simmel suggests that there are at
least four possibilities when conflict arises.
First, the third party may be a *mediator.* The

mediator is an objective individual, to whom two participants in conflict present their case. Taking no participant's side, the mediator encourages expression. In modern societies, in a dyadic marriage conflict, the mediator may be a marriage counselor. In another instance, it might be a court judge. In some societies, as in the Russian Federation, a mediator may be a trusted friend. Members in conflict may become more objective in their perceptions with the assistance of an impartial mediator who seeks to moderate passions that threaten to tear the group apart.

A second possibility is an *arbitrator*. For Simmel, the arbitrator is a participant from whom partisans in conflict seek favor and support. In family situations, a child may seek arbitration from one parent to settle a conflict with a sibling. Members frequently become more oppositional and stubborn in the presence of an arbitrator.

A third possibility is *tertius gaudens* (joy of the third). This occurs when the third party tries to turn to her/his/its advantage a disagreement between the two other participants. Finally, a fourth possibility is *divide et impera* (divide and rule), whereby the third party intentionally creates a conflict between the other two participants in order to maintain dominance over them. We see this strategy in management-worker relations, where the owners of factories (or of agricultural fields) keep workers divided over issues of race, ethnicity, culture, and wages, thereby allowing the owner to dominate the workers. Similar tactics can be observed among white-collar workers (e.g., faculty vs. university administrators or governing boards).

Of course, the role of the third party is unstable. A dyad can form intense bonds that exclude the third party. Sometimes the dyad withdraws from the triad, a phenomenon known as *dyadic withdrawal.* While larger groups have a tendency to be more stable than smaller groups, they also have a propensity to break down in to monads, dyads, and triads. Simmel suggests that in every social relation there is an aspect of superordination (supraordination) and subordination that contains a dimension of power. Group relations often are characterized by evolving, shifting, coalescing, and destabilizing coalitions of dyads, triads, or

monads. Triads and dyads are, for Simmel, potential bases for interpersonal, intra-societal, and inter-societal conflict.

The Dialectics of Social Life

Simmel's sociology is informed by a dialectical approach that focuses on dynamic interconnectedness *and* on the conflicts among the social units he analyzes. Simmel's sociology stresses both interconnections (solidarities) *and* tensions (conflicts) between the individual and the collectivity. For Simmel and for Freud, the socialized individual always remains in a dual relation with society: she or he is "incorporated within it and yet stands against it. The individual is, at the same time, within society and outside it" (Coser, 1977: 184). The individual is *simultaneously* both a social link in a larger social structure *and* for the self (an autonomous center). For Simmel and for Freud, there is no escaping this inherent tension between the individual and the collectivity. It is part of the price of social life.

Simmel maintains that society *both* liberates *and* constrains the individual. It's not a matter of one *or* the other; it's a matter of both, simultaneously. For Simmel, only in and through institutional forms do human beings attain freedom from the encompassing demands of dyadic relations; yet this freedom "is forever endangered by these very institutional forms" (Coser, 1977: 184). This notion is not as strange as it might at first appear. As we have seen, dyadic social relations are, according to Simmel, intense in that they absorb the participants and their psychological and attentional resources. The participants in a dyad are dependent upon each other for the fulfillment of their needs. This is a heavy burden. Dyadic structures, according to Simmel, hold the individual in bonds of solidary, normative, imperative, and exchange relations unparalleled in intensity by large groups. Large groups characterized by secondary relations free the individual, if you will, from the "tyranny" of dyadic bonds. By and large, we invest ourselves only segmentally in secondary groups, which liberates us to devote our energies—of time, and those that are psychological, social, political, economic, intellectual, and so forth—elsewhere. We develop this idea when we discuss voluntary associations.

It is worth noting that in Simmelian sociology, nothing is pure—not social forms, not social types, not primary groups, and so forth. To Simmel, sociation always involves love *and* hatred, attraction *and* repulsion, harmony *and* conflict, liberation *and* constraint. Human social relations, in other words, are characterized by dialectics, by strain, by *ambivalence*. A mother both loves *and* is constrained by her children. A wife may simultaneously love *and be repulsed by* her husband. A student is *both* attracted to *and* repulsed by the process of learning. Well before feminists of the latter twentieth-century argued that all heterosexual sexual relations in patriarchal societies involve an element of coercion, of force, and hence may be regarded as forcible rape, Simmel observed that erotic relations, are

> woven together of love and respect, or disrespect . . . of love and an urge to dominate or the need for dependence. . . . What the observer or the participant . . . divides into two intermingling trends may in reality be only one (Simmel, 1908: 40, as cited in Coser, 1977: 184).

in other words, *all* social relations are dialectical, the intimate *and* the distant ones, those of a primary-group or dyadic nature and those of a secondary-group variety. Even intimate relationships have areas of distance—a wife may have some secrets even from her husband; lovers do not necessarily share all aspects of their lives with their beloved, and so forth. If you are looking for "either/or" answers—something is *either* this *or* that—you will not find them in Simmelian sociology. According to Simmel, the web of social life is too complex to be apprehended in the absence of dialectics.

The Functions of Conflict in Social Life

Simmel often is termed a "conflict" sociologist. In the Simmelian view (as in the Freudian view), conflict not only is inescapable in social life, it has positive functions. Conflict is "good" for individuals, social relationships, and for society. Even though the participants may suffer various forms of stress and distress, emotional and otherwise, Simmel believes the old adage that "whatever does not kill you makes you stronger." Even though outside observers or even the participants themselves may perceive a conflictive relationship in wholly negative terms, Simmel argues that conflict has latent positive functions. These include the following:

1. *Ties that bind.* Conflict (like power) is a form of sociation. It is essential to appreciate social conflict frequently is based on reciprocal roles, not on unilateral imposition. (If you do not know the meaning of the word "reciprocity," or its adjectival form, "reciprocal," please look it up in a dictionary. Remember, words are power. Become powerful.) Reciprocity is an elementary form of social life.

   For example, as we write this chapter, the U.S. Secretary of State is traveling in Europe to meet with heads of state, to try to marshal their support for military action against Iraq, in the event that the Iraqi head of state, Saddam Hussein, continues to refuse to allow representatives of a United Nations team to inspect certain parts of his country for prohibited "weapons of mass destruction." The United States claims the authority (the legitimate power) to engage in unilateral military action in this matter. Nonetheless, because this claim is viewed as spurious by some member nations, the U.S. seeks the approval of western European, Russian, and Middle-Eastern member nations, so that military action, if engaged in, will be perceived as a legitimate form of social conflict instead of being perceived by member countries as unwarranted military aggression by a mighty nation against a small state. Social conflict ties the parties to the social fabric even in the face of their disagreement.
2. *Safety valve.* Conflict allows negative feelings to be expressed. This permits potentially explosive situations to become defused. Ethnic-, class-, interpersonally-, culturally-, and regionally-based resentments can become violent, unless they are expressed in interaction and defused.
3. *Grievance clarification.* Conflict may clarify perceived grievances. Once the points of contention are clearly out in the open, participants may be more able to work towards their mutual resolution.

4. *Increased self-esteem.* Conflict may lead to a strengthening of the position for one or more parties to the conflict, thereby increasing the participant's self-esteem and dignity (Coser, 1977: 185).

5. *Mutual respect and understanding.* The participants may learn from their diversity to form relationships based on mutual respect and understanding.

Simmel and Marx on Exchange in Social Life

Many twentieth-century social theorists view exchange—tit for tat—as a basic ingredient of social life, as one of the things that makes a world. A propensity toward exchange flows from the fact that in many groups the distribution of scarce yet widely-valued resources is unequal. In these circumstances social actors have different levels or amounts of resources with which to bargain. Social actors with resources valued by others are in a position to strike a better bargain, particularly if the others who value their resources lack equally valued resources to offer in return (Turner, 1991: 298). This is the situation faced, for instance, by the proletariat in relation to the owners of capital according to Marxian theory. As American sociologist Jonathan Turner of University of California, Riverside, phrases this:

> Capitalists have the power to control the distribution of material rewards, whereas all that workers have is their labor to offer in exchange. Although labor is valued by the capitalist, it is in plentiful supply, and thus no one worker is in a position to bargain effectively with an employer. As a consequence, capitalists can get labor at a low cost and can force workers to do what they want. As capitalists press their advantage, they create the very conditions that allow workers to develop resources—political, organizational, ideological—that they can then use to strike a better bargain with capitalists . . . (Turner, 1991: 298)

Exchange Principles in Marxian Theory

Jonathan Turner identifies four principles or dynamics of exchange in Marx's view of social life in capitalist society (Turner, 1991: 299). Let us examine each of these.

1. *Those who need scarce and valued resources that clearly identifiable others possess but who lack equally scarce and valued resources to offer in return are in a weak exchange position.* They are dependent upon, and vulnerable to, those who control these resources. For example, Mary is married to Tom. They live in Houston. Tom, who speaks English, has a well-paying, secure job. Mary does not speak English. She is illiterate. She has no family near her other than her husband. She and her husband have three children under four years of age. Mary has no friends. She belongs to no church and to no other support groups. Mary is in a weak exchange position relative to her husband. She is dependent upon Tom for the fulfillment of her needs and for the fulfillment of many of their children's needs.

2. *Those who control valued resources have power over those who do not.* The point here is that the power of one social actor relative to another actor is directly related to the capacity of one actor to monopolize the valued resources needed, or desired by, other actors. Tom currently has a monopoly on resources valued by Mary and his children. He is in a powerful position.

3. *Those with power will exercise it.* They try to extract more resources from those who are dependent upon them. In the story that opens this chapter, the clerk in the downtown Kazan Intourist Office charges Harry, the American Fulbright scholar, an extra 12,000 Rubles to exchange his ticket, even though the official rules specify that no fine or fee is due.

The clerk can discern that the young man is a "foreigner," someone outside her sense of we-ness; that he is an American, and hence someone, by her personal operational definition, in possession of surplus wealth; and, by deciphering his body language and broken Russian speech, that he is desperate to obtain the train tickets to which she is the conduit. The clerk is in a strong position relative to this client.

She exercises power, the ability to get her way in the face of his opposition. The young man defers to her definition of the situation to

454 ■ Chapter 12

her power. She accepts both his display of "respect" and the extra 12,00 Rubles that will show up nowhere on the official books. The young man gets the train tickets and the receipts. This social interaction is a clear example of an exchange relationship.

4. *Those who press their advantage* **in this manner create the seeds of their own destruction, or at least the seeds of revolt.** Those who are dependent upon the monopolizers of valued and scarce resources (a) organize in ways designed to increase the value of their resources, or failing that, (b) organize in ways that enable them to coerce those on whom they are dependent.

The great American novelist Samuel Langhorne Clemens (1835-1910) appreciates the operation of exchange relations in social life. He writes perceptively about them in *Life on the Mississippi* (1904: 75-84), a book about his two-and-a-half years as a riverboat-pilot's apprentice. He formed his own pen name from *mark twain*, "an expression used by Mississippi riverboat pilots in sounding the shallows for minimum navigable depths" (Morris, 1969: 1385).

In *Life on the Mississippi* Twain tells us that riverboat pilots both had, and needed, a tremendous amount of knowledge about the river in order to navigate it safely. This knowledge earned them a good living. There came a time, however, when there were more pilots than boats going up and down the great river. In this situation, the pilots became dependent upon the captains of boats for employment. Riverboat captains were *the* source of employment for riverboat pilots.

Now in a strong position, captains pressed their advantage. Although pilots would quote a price for a trip, say, from New Orleans to St. Louis, as $250, a shrewd captain could make a more frugal deal. He would go to a flop house in New Orleans, locate an unemployed pilot, and offer him $50 and a jug of whisky for the round-trip. The captain could find pilots willing to accept the offer. The exploitation of riverboat pilots by captains eventually became so severe that the riverboat pilots finally organized. They successfully formed an union that—by keeping the number of available river

pilots in a favorable ratio to the number of boats and the amount of cargo going up and down the mighty river—helped them to regain a sense of pride, elevated self-self-esteem, a comfortable standard of living, and good benefits for retirement.

A really interesting thing that Twain relates is that the power position switches once the down-but-not-out pilot and the calculating captain are on the river (1904: 75). The able pilot of our story is driving the boat at a snail's pace straight up the middle of the river. That's as fast as a riverboat could go, as long as it was in the middle of the stream, fighting the whole vast force of the mighty river. The enterprising young captain reckons that at this rate he'd die of old age before he got the boat with its precious cargo to St. Louis, a trip that normally takes only a week. What a pilot *can* do is to take the boat over to the side of the river. The current isn't flowing as swiftly there, and the pilot can drive the boat along the side of the river. That way the boat travels swiftly. The captain *knows* this and demands to know why they are in the middle of the stream.

The pilot responds that it's much *safer* there. The captain notes that they could go *faster* if they were traveling up the side of the mighty river, like all the other boats that were leaving them behind. The able pilot replies that those other boats have very expensive pilots on them, $250 pilots, and *they* know and are able to spot and to avoid colliding with all the shifting sand bars, snags, shoals, rocks, and so forth on the river. All the $50-and-a jug-of-whisky pilots know is that *the river is deepest in the middle*. The captain offers him an additional $150 and the pilot agrees to travel up the side of the river. In this situation, you see, the power is reversed, because the pilot has a scarce and highly-valued resource that the captain needs.

Social Exchange in Simmelian Theory

Georg Simmel emphasizes that exchange is a fundamental form of social interaction engaged in by individuals and by collectivities (Simmel, 1907). This type of interaction is a manifestation of rational calculation in human affairs, and it may characterize any domain of human interaction, including the most intimate. As Jonathan Turner observes, for Simmel social exchange involves four elements (1991: 299-300):

1. A social actor desires a valued resource that she/he does not have.
2. An identifiable other possesses the valued resource.
3. The offer of a valued resource to secure from the identifiable other the desired object.
4. Acceptance of this offer by the possessor of the desired object.

Several additional points follow from this portrayal of exchange in social life (Turner, 1991: 300-301). These are summarized in nearby Table 12.1. Their thrust is that Simmel views social interaction as occurring because actors value each other's resources. The value of a resource is a function of many factors, including an actor's idiosyncratic needs and the scarcity of the object. Power is part of the exchange process. An actor who has resources that are valued by another is in a position to extract compliance from those seeking these resources. Much social interaction involves attempts to manipulate the level of availability of a desired resource and to conceal an actor's level of need for a desired resource. Tension is inherent in social exchange, and it can manifest itself in various forms, including social conflict.

Because these points are somewhat abstract, we will make them more concrete for you by means of an example. Let us use exchange theory to examine the processes of flirtation and of dating in the United States. Simmel maintains that flirtation and dating are, or may be viewed as, forms of exchange.

Let us say that two members of the opposite sex are strangers to each other yet are mutually attracted to each other. Perhaps they attend the same college or university. Simmel maintains that flirtation is allusive (suggestive) and has implicit, even if unstated, cultural rules of acceptance and of refusal. Let us say that these two actors flirt with each other and that, after a passage of time, arrange to have a first date. The first date is an interaction of two strangers, of people who do not as yet form a group. Both individuals, in an choreography of gesture-language and body language, engage in a suspenseful game, often uneasy, with a great deal of social distance, of allusive promises and withdrawal. The social actors alternate between the possibilities of acceptance and of withdrawal and rejection. There are intimations, suggestions, hopes and fears, but neither of the participants is deprived of all hope. If the two strangers develop mutual intimacy, they no longer are strangers and they begin to form a primary group.

Further Observations on the Importance of Group Size

The tale of the American Fulbright scholar that opens this chapter illustrates that large-scale organizations touch our everyday lives. It also illustrates the impersonal, segmental, and *instrumental* nature of secondary-group relationships. Harry interacts with the Intourist clerk not as an end in itself but because he wants to exchange one train ticket for another. The interaction is a means to an end; it is instrumental. This tale also illustrates the oper-

TABLE 12.1. Exchange Principles in Simmelian Theory _____

1. *Attraction.* The more social actors perceive as valuable one another's respective resources, the more likely an exchange relationship is to develop among these actors.
2. *Value.* The greater a social actor's need for a resource of a given type, and the greater the scarcity of that resource, the greater the value placed on that resource by the social actor.
3. *Power.* (3a) The more valuable a social actor perceives the resources of another social actor, the greater is the power of the latter over the former. (3b) The more a social actor's resources can be used in many types of exchanges (e.g., beauty, writing ability, money), the greater are that actor's options and power in social exchanges.
4. *Tension.* Many social exchanges involve attempts to conceal both (4a) the intensity of a social actor's need for a resource of a given type and (4b) the availability of a resource of a given type. A lot flows from this, including a fundamental *tension* that can erupt into other social forms, including conflict.

1. *Source:* Adapted from Table 14-1, Turner, 1991: 301.

ation both of *exchange* and of *power* (imperative order) relationships in formal organizations like state bureaucracies. The Intourist Office is part of a vast state bureaucracy in Kazan.

A **formal organization** is a secondary group whose goal is the achievement of explicit objectives or tasks. Formal organizations may be large or small in size. Bureaucracy is a particular system of administration and of formal organization. The term **bureaucracy** comes from the French word *bureau*, which translates into English as desk, table, or office, and the Greek word *kratos*, which means power. Thus, bureaucracies are offices arranged in a hierarchy based on legal or legitimate power.

Bureaucracies tend to arise whenever the activities of a large number of people need to be coordinated in order to attain an explicit goal. Bureaucracies have existed since the emergence of the first cities (and states) in Mesopotamia, Sumer, and ancient Egypt roughly five thousand years ago. They reached a high level of sophistication in the pre-industrial Empires of Rome, Byzantium, and China.

Characteristics of Bureaucracy

According to Max Weber, these are the characteristics of bureaucracy as an *ideal type* (1949):

1. Explicit procedural rules with a hierarchical authority structure (e.g., chain of command in the U.S. Army, Navy, Marines, Air Force, or Coast Guard), with clearly delineated areas of command and of responsibility.
2. A high degree of specialization and a clearly defined division of labor, with tasks officially distributed as duties attached to an office.
3. Formal, written rules govern the decisions and actions of the organization.
4. Impersonal relationships exist among organizational members and between organizational members and clients.
5. A specialized administrative staff maintains the organization and its official communication system.
6. Recruitment and promotion occur on the basis of merit (e.g., ability, technical knowledge), seniority, or both—so that

officials typically anticipate a long-term career in the organization.
7. The salary of office holders is fixed. There is a separation between private and official income.
8. The discreet characteristics noted above are tied into a coherent whole by *rationalization*. For Weber, notion of rationalization in bureaucracy embraces two somewhat different ideas (Abercrombie, Hill, and Turner, 1994: 38). First, bureaucracy maximizes technical efficiency. Second, bureaucracy is based on **rational-legal authority.** A system of social control or of authority is rational legal if it is accepted by its members because they view its rules as "rational, fair, and impartial—a 'legal-rational' value system" (Abercrombie, Hill, and Turner, 1994: 38).

Weber's definition of bureaucracy is an ideal type. A specific organization may meet many but not all of its criteria and still be a bureaucracy. For instance, social-science research documents that *informal relations* are important in bureaucracies. They serve to insulate their workers from some of the impersonal relations typical of bureaucracy, and they can either assist or impede the attainment of organizational goals. Particularistic considerations of age, gender, race, ethnicity, religious affiliation, social class, and so forth may undermine both recruitment and promotion on the basis of universalistic meritocratic principles. At the informal level, patrimonial rule—arbitrary, capricious rule based on the preferences of persons who occupy positions of power—may operate in bureaucracies. The separation between private and official income also may become blurred. For instance, a Vice President of a large company may buy a house well under normal market value because it was built with the sweated unpaid labor of workers in his chain-of-command. Members of a bureaucracy may fail to blow the whistle due to fears of reprisals or to fear of breaking bureaucratic norms of secrecy. The culture of a bureaucracy may impede efficiency. (Please read nearby Box 12-1, "Bureaucracy in an Insurance Company.") In other words, a formal organization may differ from Weber's ideal type and yet be an instance of bureaucracy.

—— BOX 12.1 ——

Bureaucracy in an Insurance Company

Sociologist Linda Smircich has conducted a study of the culture of the executive staff in an insurance company (1983). This case study illustrates that formal organizations may differ from, and even may have cultures contrary to, Weber's pure type and still be bureaucracies. It also illustrates that inefficiency may permeate bureaucracies at the highest administrative levels.

In this particular organization, a dominant cultural belief was that differences, problems, challenges, and conflicts between or among members of the organization should not be admitted, brought out into the open, and should not be brought to the attention of the boss for resolution. From the top down, people were socialized to appreciate that surface conformity and equanimity

were prized by the President of the company. The President of the company wants things that way. The company President wants to be the change agent. Change in operating procedures should be a top-down affair, period. These beliefs contributed to coordinated yet restrained interaction among the members of the organization and to "an aura of passivity among the staff members" (Smircich, 1983: 57-58). The weekly staff meetings were viewed by the staff as a hollow affair, important to the President, who relishes the opportunity to fluff his feathers, to "hold court" to the captive audience who showers him with deference by their mere presence and silent acceptance of his directives. From the staff's point of view these meetings

were an "empty" formality, where nothing of substance was ever accomplished. The members internalized, or at least complied with, the cultural definition of the situation.

These relationships are can work against (a) efficiency of procedures (b) recruitment and promotion on the basis of universalistic principles, and (c) a clearly defined division of labor. These relationships may lead to a high turn-over of employees. Those who remain may experience *alienation*, the subjective sense of powerless, of being separated from the fruits of their labor. Eventually, employees in this situation may suffer from chronic job "burnout" and low self-esteem or they may engage in collective action to redress perceived grievances.

Please reflect upon your own life in terms of personal experiences with bureaucracies. Which bureaucracies have touched your life? Select two of the bureaucracies you mention. For each one please explain to us the ways in which it conforms to, and differs from, the ideal type bureaucratic structure. Can you think of some instance wherein you experienced bureaucracies as burdensome and as inconvenient? For example, have you had to wait in long lines to enroll for classes, to pay your university fees, to purchase tickets for a concert or theater performance, to apply for or to receive assistance from a social-service agency, or to report a crime to the police? Please tell us about it.

Group Polarization, and Groupthink in Formal Organizations

Many conflicts emerge, become apparent, and grow as people on various sides of an issue talk with like-minded others about the issue. What is the

effect of group discussion on the preexisting attitudes and opinions of group members? Under which circumstances do groups impede effective decision making? Under which circumstances do groups facilitate effective decision making?

Group Polarization

Social science research helps us better to understand and to predict the effects of groups on our behaviors, actions, attitudes, and opinions. Over 300 field studies and small-group experimental studies indicate that there is a tendency, known as **group polarization,** for group discussion to accentuate the members' pre-existing tendencies and attitudes (Moscovici and Zavalloni, 1969; McCauley and Segal, 1987; Colman, 1991; Pascarella and Terenzini, 1991; Whyte, 1993; Myers, 1996: 332; Hunt, 1997). Group polarization occurs in communities, juries, neighborhood street gangs, voluntary associations, and in committee meetings in formal organizations. For example, if Susie is pro-choice on the issue of abortion and

Sam is pro-life and they both attend a public debate on abortion rights, both Susie and Sam's attitudes are likely to be *strengthened* by the debate experience. Susie will leave the debate even more pro-choice than previously, and Sam, more pro-life. Their initial inclinations have been enhanced, strengthened.

Analyses of terrorist organizations around the world also reveal the workings of group polarization. **Terrorism** refers to the use of violent acts, or the use of the threat of violence, to create fear, dread, alarm, or coercion, usually against government, among those who identify with the victims, in order to achieve objectives (which frequently are political in nature). Research indicates that terrorism emerges as people whose shared grievances bring them together engage in social interaction regarding those grievances. Over time, as they repeatedly interact in isolation from outside, moderating influences, their views become more extreme. Out of such group dynamics emerge violent and criminal acts on a magnitude of which the individuals, left to their own devices, might never have contemplated or executed. These acts include counterfeiting, armed robbery, bombing, murder, assassinations, and the deployment of weapons of mass destruction (Colman, 1991a, 1991b; Flynn and Gerhardt, 1995).

Informational Influence and Normative Influence

Two explanations of why groups intensify the members' pre-existing attitudes have survived scientific scrutiny (Deutsch and Gerard, 1955; Myers, 1996: 336). One of these is **informational influence**—conformity based on people accepting as correct, evidence about reality that is presented by other people (Deutsch and Gerard, 1955). A desire to be *correct* produces informational influence. I agree with you because I think you are correct. You exerted informational influence on me.

Informational influence involves more than merely *hearing* the evidence provided by others. *Active participation* in discussion is important, creating far more attitude change than does mere passive listening (Brauer, Judd, and Gliner, 1995; Tesser, Martin, and Mendolia, 1995). As David Myers reminds us,

[W]hat people *think* in response to a message is crucial . . . Even just *expecting* to discuss an issue with an equally expert person holding an opposing view can motivate people to marshal their arguments and thus to adopt a more extreme position (1996: 337; emphasis in the original).

Another explanation for group polarization is **normative influence,** which is conformity based on a social actor's desire to fulfill others' expectations and thereby to gain social acceptance (Deutsch and Gerard, 1955). Normative influence has its basis in the solidary order. When students tell me that they are attending the university because their parents expect them to attend college, they are telling me that their parents are exerting normative influence in their lives in important ways. Former President of the United States John F. Kennedy recalls that when he entered Congress he was told that "The way to get along, is to go along" (1956: 4). A desire to belong to a group, then, can lead social actors to go along with the group's opinions, attitudes, and lines of social action. This conformity, in informational influence, frequently assumes the form of **compliance**—outwardly agreeing but inwardly disagreeing.

Groupthink

There is a tendency, termed **groupthink** (Janis, 1971, 1982; Janis and Mann, 1977), for highly solidaristic groups that are structured in particular ways to suppress dissent in the interests of group harmony. This can result in flawed decision making processes that, in turn, produce flawed decisions. The flawed decision-making processes characteristic of groupthink account for the following major fiascoes:

- The explosion of *The Space Shuttle Challenger* on January 28, 1996 (Esser and Lindoerfer, 1989; Magnuson, 1986)
- The bombing of Pearl Harbor in December, 1941
- The Bay of Pigs Invasion of Cuba in 1961 by 1400 CIA-trained Cuban exiles
- The Vietnam War
- The Watergate cover-up that resulted in President Nixon's resignation from office

Recipe for Groupthink

Social psychologist Irving Janis, who coined the term groupthink, believes that these fiascoes were bred by decision making groups that had certain characteristics that maximized the probability that groupthink would occur. These include the following three:

1. *highly cohesive group* Not all decision-making groups are equally susceptible to groupthink. Highly cohesive groups, whose members value their membership, are particularly vulnerable. When newly elected President Kennedy and his advisers were planning the Bay of Pigs Invasion, he and his advisors enjoyed a strong camaraderie.
2. *isolate the group from dissenting viewpoints* During the planning of the Bay of Pigs invasion, arguments critical of the invasion were systematically suppressed, avoided, or excluded.
3. *directive leadership* The leader lets members know which decision she or he prefers. President Kennedy let his advisors know early in the discussions that he favored the Bay of Pigs invasion.

Symptoms of Groupthink

Irving Janis identifies eight symptoms of groupthink (Janis and Mann, 1977; Turner, Pratkanis, Probasco, and Leve, 1992; Turner and Pratkanis, 1994). These symptoms arise as group members attempt to sustain a sense of positive group feeling in the face of a threat. For example, a threatened President Nixon and his trusted advisors planned a cover-up of the Watergate burglary of the offices of the Democratic Party. The following are the symptoms of groupthink:

1. *Illusion of invulnerability* Group members think that there is no way that they could fail. They discredit or dismiss all threats that may be perceived.
2. *Occupy the moral high ground* Group members have an unquestioned confidence in the moral correctness of their decision. They ignore or discount evidence that might suggest that their position is morally or ethically questionable.

3. *Underestimate the opposition* Group members underestimate the opposition. President Kennedy and his advisors perceived Castro's military as so incompetent or weak and his popular support so thin that a small force of amateur invaders could easily topple his regime.
4. *Rationalization* Group members utilize the ego defense mechanism of rationalization, whereby they concoct intellectual rationales or excuses for their freely chosen actions.
5. *Pressures towards conformity* Group members who dare to dissent are ridiculed and rebuffed by the leader, perhaps by logical argument, but at times by sarcasm aimed at the individual personally.
6. *Self-censorship* Group members withhold or discount their own misgivings. For example, Arthur Schlesinger, advisor to President Kennedy, reproached himself after the Bay of Pigs debacle

   for having kept so silent during those crucial discussions in the Cabinet Room, though my feelings of guilt were tempered by the knowledge that a course of objection would have accomplished little save to gain me a name as a nuisance. I can only explain my failure to do more than raise a few timid questions by reporting that one's impulse to blow the whistle on this nonsense was simply undone by the circumstances of the discussion (1965: 255; as cited by Janis, 1972: 40)

7. *Illusion of unanimity* Group pressures to conform and the tendency for group members to engage in self-censorship produce an illusion of total agreement. This illusion of total agreement, in turn, is perceived by group members as affirming the correctness of the group's decision.
8. *Mindguards* Irving Janis uses the term **mindguard** to refer to the function of those group members who prevent information that would call into question the correctness, wisdom, efficiency, efficacy, ethical quality, or morality of the group's decision or proposed plan of action from being presented to or considered by the group. For example, prior to the Bay of Pigs invasion, the Secretary of State, Dean Rusk, withheld from the advisory group and

from the President intelligence experts' warnings against the invasion.

Preventing Groupthink: Social Organization

The sociological way of knowing stresses that a group is more than the sum of its parts, more than the sum of its members' personality characteristics. A group, as we see in the Merei play-group experiments, is a power greater than the self. A group is capable of affecting the way we conceive of and evaluate self, others, and the social and physical world around us; it is capable of deflecting lines of action that a person might otherwise engage in and of encouraging other forms of social action. Janis draws our attention to the specific ways decision-making groups in voluntary and in involuntary associations can organize so as to prevent groupthink. Janis isolates several concrete social practices or pieces of social organization useful in this regard (Janis, 1982: 477-501). We now look at each of these in turn.

1. *Knowledge transmission* Inform group members about groupthink, its causes and consequences.
2. *Impartial leadership* The leader remains impartial during the deliberations of the decision-making group, in both verbal and non-verbal communication remaining neutral with regard to which decision she or he may prefer. During deliberations the leader refrains from endorsing any position.
3. *Encourage group members to formulate and to share with group members objections, criticisms, doubts, concerns* Make it clear that it is the duty of each member to share with the group concerns, doubts, criticisms, and objections about proposed lines of action that could be raised by salient audiences with the group.
4. *Rotation of devil's advocate status* A **devil's advocate** is a position the incumbent of which opposes an argument or line of action with which she or he does not necessarily disagree so as to determine its validity. On a rotating basis one or more members of the group is assigned this role.
5. *On a staggered basis, invite outside experts to attend the group's meetings* The

duty of the outside experts is to use their expertise to challenge the group's views.

6. *Divide the decision-making group into subgroups* The subgroups meet separately, independently. Each subgroup works independently and simultaneously on the same issue. Each subgroup has its devil's advocate. Outside experts are invited to attend each subgroup's meetings on a staggered basis. Each subgroup formulates a plan and a decision. Each subgroup, after reaching a preliminary decision, calls a meeting wherein members are asked to express any doubts, concerns, etc. that remain. Then, the various subgroups meet together and air their differences.
7. *Rival groups* When the issue concerns relations with a rival group, take time to (a) identify and to assess possible actions and positions by the rival and by the rival's allies; (b) recognize and asses warning signs—signs that indicate that the proposed line of action is unwise, and (c) identify various possible responses and actions by the rival.
8. *Utilize feedback from trusted associates* Encourage group members confidentially to seek a trusted associate's assessment of the group's deliberations. Report the feedback to the group.
9. *Final draft* After reaching a preliminary decision, the groups meets again. The purpose of the meeting is to air concerns, doubts, reservations, and assessments that remain, that may have gone unexpressed.

Bureaucracy: Alienation, Self-Estrangement, and Rationalization

The perceptive and attentive reader recognizes Irving Janis' suggestions regarding how to structure a decision-making group so as to avoid groupthink as an example of **rationalization**—the development of greater standardization, coordination, and consistency in organizational structure; the substitution of explicit formal, procedures for earlier spontaneous, arbitrary, capricious, erratic approaches. It is worth noting that while Weber saw rationalization as a master trend in Western capitalist society, he nonetheless was highly ambivalent concerning the rationality of modern society. On the one hand, Weber appreciates that without the economic rationality created by the efficient social organization of large capitalist bureaucracies, not much would be accomplished in the modern world. We *do* receive our mail in three days. We mass produce food to feed millions of people. Bureaucracies accomplish their specific tasks. On the other hand, Weber acknowledges and laments certain effects of bureaucratic rationality on human behavior and on the individual. These effects include rigid conformity to impersonal rules and self-estrangement. With the development of a Protestant work ethic, people are rewarded for hard sustained work, but within a large impersonal bureaucracy, people become replaceable cogs in a huge depersonalized machine.

Karl Marx: The Clandestine Culture of Bureaucracy

In one of his early writings, "Contribution to the Critique of Hegel's *Philosophy of Right*," Marx presents a unique analysis and criticism of modern bureaucracy (1844). Like Weber, Marx perceives that the internal structure of bureaucracy is based on authority, power, and hierarchy. Bureaucracy, in striving for goals and its reason for existence, develops its own clandestine culture. In doing so, all social relations and all information and knowledge within each level of bureaucracy become deceptive in character. To use a metaphor, bureaucracy may be likened to an onion, and each of its layers is a layer of deception.

Deception, according to Marx, is a universal feature of bureaucracy—a feature, in other words, found in pre-capitalist, capitalist, and non-capitalist bureaucracies. Secrecy, and its cousin, mystification, are found both within the hierarchical organization and in its relationship to the public. Being open and honest in bureaucratic social relations is seen as betrayal to bureaucratic authority. This is especially true in relationship to the public. Bureaucracy becomes a "secret" society within a larger society.

For example, in American society, *whistle blowers*—i.e., those who expose corruption within public or private bureaucracies—often become unemployable. Exposing mistakes, cor-

ruption, waste and so on are viewed as disloyal and traitorous behavior contravening bureaucratic norms of conformity and secrecy.

Marx on Bureaucratic Alienation

Marx saw the lives of bureaucrats as empty and uninteresting and their whole careers as oriented toward conforming to rules of hierarchical authority. In *Robert K. Merton's* terminology, bureaucrats become *ritualists*, zealous conformists opposed to social change. Marx characterizes modern bureaucrats' career lives as sterile, apathetic, barren, indifferent, impotent, and alienated. Their lives are oriented toward the collection and retention of secret information which they may use for their own career advancement or to hurt potential rivals who seek to displace them. Marx's concept of bureaucratic alienation is quite similar to what Weber means by economic rationality and self-estrangement. Alienation, economic rationalization, and self-estrangement may be inherent feature of all modern societies.

Bureaucratic Inertia

Bureaucratic inertia refers the condition wherein and the processes whereby formal organizations that no longer perform the functions they were originally designed to accomplish remain in existence and establish new goals for themselves. For example, the army of the Russian Federation right now is characterized by bureaucratic inertia. In the former Soviet Union a large standing army was necessary to defend huge national borders and to put down popular uprisings. It also provided employment and a means of upward mobility for hundreds of thousands of people. After the breakup of the Soviet Union and the end of "the cold war," this large standing army has lost its original purpose, is a tremendous financial drain on the Federation, has not as yet found new goals to justify its existence, and has yet to be dismantled. Another example of bureaucratic inertia is the KGB (the USSR Committee of State Security). This agency once controlled the geographical movement of the population and the production of internal passports. Those functions no longer exist, but the agency, with cosmetic changes of name, still exists. In the wake of the Soviet Union's collapse, the KGB was divided into the foreign and domestic organizations that exist today—the foreign Intelligence Service (SVR) and Federal Security Service (FSK). In other words, the KGB formed new goals and directions relating to national security (Leighton, 1996).

Robert Michels (1876-1936)

Another German sociologist, Robert Michels, maintains that all modern bureaucracies have the tendency to develop into highly specialized structures wherein a small number of people, the top-level bureaucrats, rule over the many lower-level bureaucrats (1915). He refers to this tendency as the **iron law of oligarchy.** **Oligarchy** is the rule of the many by the few. In all bureaucratic formal organizations, maintains Michels, it is inevitable that a well organized bureaucratic minority rule over an apathetic, disorganized, majority, even in a democracy.

Michels' analysis, combined with those of Weber and Marx, present us with a critical assessment of bureaucracy in particular and of the hierarchical and oligarchic nature of modern societies in general. All three social theorists stress that private and public bureaucracies are not democratic in nature and are antithetical to democracy and to the expression of individualism.

In American society the problems inherent in bureaucracy are moderately subdued, according to Weber, through substantive rationalization, and, according to de Tocqueville, through voluntary associations, a topic to which we now turn. In American society individuals learn to remedy or alleviate the problems caused by bureaucracies through individual solutions (self-reliance, individualism) and through participation in voluntary associations.

Voluntary Associations

Many Americans belong to voluntary associations. Please read nearby Table 12.2. A **voluntary association** is a specialized formally organized group, membership in which is a matter of choice and from which members are free to resign. Etzioni (1975) stresses that a voluntary association is a normative organization that individuals voluntarily join in order to pursue morally, and in some cases professionally, approved goals. Boy Scouts of

TABLE 12.2. National Non-Profit Associations in the United States, by Number and Type, 1994

Total	22,512
Trade, Business, Commercial	3,768
Agricultural	1,119
Legal, Governmental, Public Administration, Military	781
Scientific, Engineering, Technical	1,347
Educational	1,289
Cultural	1,904
Social Welfare	1,852
Health and Medical	2,331
Public Affairs	2,169
Fraternal, Foreign Interest, Nationality, Ethnic	548
Religious	1,227
Veteran, Hereditary, Patriotic	577
Hobby, Avocational	1,555
Athletic, Sports	838
Labor Unions	245
Chambers of Commerce	169
Greek and Non-Greek Letter Societies	353
Fan Clubs	458

Source: Maurer and Sheets, Vol. 1, Part I, 1998: vii.

America, Girl Scouts of America, the American Sociological Association, the Lion's Club, the Chamber of commerce, the Red Cross, the American Mental Health Association, Kiwanis, Veterans of Foreign Wars, the American Legion, the PTA, volunteer fire departments, and emergency rescue groups are examples of voluntary associations. A voluntary association differs from an **involuntary association,** which is a specialized formally organized group, membership in which is based on compulsion and from which members are not free to retire. Examples of involuntary associations are prison populations, patients in secure mental hospitals, and a conscripted army or navy.

Please reflect on your own life. When you were a child did you belong to any voluntary associations? Which ones? Do you currently belong to any voluntary associations? Which ones? Please tell us about it.

Alexis de Tocqueville on the Role of Voluntary Associations in America

One of the earliest and most interesting studies of voluntary and involuntary associations and of bureaucracy comes from French political and social analyst Alexis de Tocqueville

(1805-1859). A French aristocrat, de Tocqueville was commissioned by the French government to investigate the nature of social organization and culture in American life, which continental Europeans referred to as an "experiment in self-government." He visited the United States in 1831 to 1832 and published his observations a few years later. His views on the negative psychological effects of solitary confinement in our prisons were reported with Gustave de Beaumont in *On the Penitentiary System in the United States* (1833). His observations about the role of voluntary associations in the process of democratic self-government appear in *Democracy in America*, which was published in two parts in 1835 and 1840.

In *Democracy in America*, de Tocqueville points out that bureaucrats are recruited from many social strata, which allows the possibility both of social mobility and a decreased likelihood of bureaucrats becoming rich nobles who would pass their inherited class positions onto their offspring. Self-government, he claimed, was a mechanism that could reduce the negative consequences of an impersonal state bureaucracy. In addition, de Tocqueville claimed that the character of Americans evolved from an opposition to the hierarchy of European feudal bureaucracy. By separating church from state, America limited the power of the state bureaucracy.

Americans, de Tocqueville claimed, were leery of, and opposed to, a strong centralized state that could control the lives of the individual (Hamilton, Madison, and Jay, 1787-1788). These orientations to the world created a very anti-bureaucratic and anti-state culture. In the U.S. Constitution itself, Americans explicitly ban titles of nobility. What Americans created was a very decentralized state in comparison to the ones in Eastern Europe and Asia.

Individuals in American society claim individualism, freedom, and self-reliance as important values. For most Americans taking care of their own problems and achieving economic and emotional self reliance are important goals of socialization. Americans associate becoming dependent on state agencies (bureaucracies) with the loss of both freedom and self respect. As de Tocqueville points out Americans

acquire the habit of always considering themselves as standing alone, and they are apt to imagine that their whole destiny is in their own hands. (1954: 11)

In contrast, in the Russian Federation, people view themselves as fundamentally interconnected with others. The family, the kinship, and the village are integral parts of who one is. One expresses oneself though these attachments. These attachments extend into, and find expression within, state bureaucracies. From this perspective interdependence with one's parents and with state bureaucracy is viewed not as intrusive and burdensome but as the very vehicle that makes social- and self-fulfillment possible. In the Russian Federation, which lacks both a tradition of economic rationalization and a tradition of voluntary associations, people look automatically to state bureaucracies for the solution to everyday problems like employment, health care, housing, and so forth. Bureaucracy permeates all levels of everyday reality in Russian society. Impersonal authoritarian state bureaucrats are culturally perceived as those whose legitimate responsibility it is to solve everyday problems.

De Tocqueville stresses that one of the unique characteristics of American society in comparison with other societies is the proliferation of voluntary associations. He was profoundly impressed by the extent to which voluntary associations are an integral part of a culture that is distinctly American.

By the mid 1950s there were slightly fewer than 9,000 voluntary associations in this country. In 1997 there were over 22,000 of them (Maurer and Sheets, 1998). Currently, seventy percent of Americans belong to at least one voluntary association, and one out of four belongs to *four or more* of them. Through their voluntary associations, Americans contribute more than 100 million hours each year to community service (Maurer and Sheets, 1998: vii). There is nothing like this in Eastern Europe or in the Far East.

De Tocqueville believes that voluntary associations are sources that both school and involve individuals in self-government. For instance, in the United States, voluntary associations are organized on the basis of simple democratic principles. Each club has a president, vice president, secretary, and so on. Members vote for candidates for these offices on the basis of one member, one vote, and candidates are elected to office on the basis of a simple majority of votes. Those who "run" for office seek support from other members, to whom they present their views on critical social and political issues. This type of democratic process gives birth to potential local, state, and national leaders. Participation in voluntary associations teaches Americans how to reach and to govern through consensus. Voluntary associations cultivate capable oppositional leaders with political abilities.

Membership in voluntary associations, says de Tocqueville, gives rise to and perpetuates local democracy while fulfilling both individual and societal needs. Voluntary associations, he stresses, also become autonomous powers that compete with, and that limit the power of, the state. For example, voluntary organizations like the Lion's Club were founded in the early part of the twentieth century to assist those who were seeing impaired. Members come from different social strata and from different occupational backgrounds and now include a significant number of females. They focus resources on one activity. They form community groups that have both intended and unintended consequences. The intended consequence is the development of a large sum of money to help those in the community who need special care as a result of being visually impaired. Thus, they both compete with and assist state bureaucracies, like state welfare agencies, in helping those in need of care.

For de Tocqueville the unintended consequences are the development of local decentralized groups that integrate individuals from many different cultural and religious backgrounds. Voluntary associations, in other words, perform the latent function of providing both integration and overlapping circles of social support for persons not related by primordial ties. They serve as networks of friendships that provide a basis for community. They are important community resources independent of state bureaucracy, and they are incubators of democracy.

Imperative Order in Human Groups

Leadership, whether bureaucratic or otherwise, primarily is concerned with the coordination of group activities toward group goals (Theodorson and Theodorson, 1969: 227). In sociology **leadership** is defined as the exercise of influence or power in human collectivities (Abercrombie, Hill, and Turner, 1994: 233). **Influence** may be defined as the ability to effect a voluntary change in a social actor's behavior, attitudes, or opinions through *persuasive* action (Theodorson and Theodorson, 1969: 202). The term influence thus suggests the exercise of persuasion not coercion. American *Robert Bierstedt* (1950) regards influence as different than power, in that *power* is *coercive* whereas influence is persuasive.

There are many types of leadership. Max Weber emphasizes traditional, rational-legal, and charismatic leadership. We first examine these forms of leadership. Then we examine expressive (socio-emotional, social) and task (instrumental) leadership, formal and informal leadership, and several styles of leadership: democratic, authoritarian, and laissez-faire.

Types of Leadership

Traditional, Rational-Legal, Charismatic, Formal, and Informal

Max Weber identifies three types of leadership that correspond to different forms of authority. **Traditional leaders** lead by virtue of custom or practice. The monarchy in England in an example of traditional rule, as is the rule of the Pharos in Egypt. **Rational-legal leadership** is based on expertise and implemented on the basis of formal written rules. This type of leadership typically is found in modern large business enterprises. **Charismatic leaders** lead by virtue of the extraordinary characteristics (charisma) attributed to them by their followers. Examples of charismatic leaders include Joan of Arc, Christ, Buddha, Alexander the Great (356-323 BC), Mohondas Gandhi (1869-1948), John Fitzgerald Kennedy, Malcolm X, Jim Jones, David Koresh, and Elvis Presley.

A charismatic leader may or may not hold an office to which authority is attached in a

Groups, Organizations, Bureaucracy, and Work ■ 465

formal organization. When a person is the incumbent of a status—an office, a position—to which authority is attached in a formal organization, we speak of *formal authority* and of **formal leadership**. The incumbent of such a position is a formal leader. For example, Bill Clinton currently is the incumbent of the position (status, office) of President of the United States. As such, he is viewed by many as the *Leader* of the Free World. He definitely is the *formal* political *leader* of the United States.

Leadership, is concerned with the coordination of group activities toward group goals. As formal leader, the President of the United States addresses the Union and presents a political agenda for the Congress of the United States to implement. Whether Congress in fact implements the President's agenda, the President has made the attempt to coordinate group activities and resources toward group goals. He has exercised formal leadership.

In contrast, **informal leadership** emerges when individuals are valued by a group because they conform to its norms and contribute to achieving the task of the group. In other words, informal leadership emerges when followers develop social cohesion and subgroup norms of loyalty around a particular individual. In informal leadership, the right to lead stems from one's position in the solidary structure of the group. Informal leadership has its basis of legitimation in the solidary order, in cultural elements that lack embodiment as formal organizational structures.

Jesus and Buddha are charismatic religious leaders who did not hold formal positions in a hierarchy. They are informal charismatic leaders. In contrast, Alexander the Great (356-323 BC), who had conquered an immense empire by the age of 32, is a charismatic leader who also held a position of formal traditional authority, that of King of Macedonia (336-323 BC). So, too, John F. Kennedy is a charismatic leader who held a position of legal authority, that of President of the United States (1961-1963). Similarly, Cesar Chavez, Mexican-American civil-rights leader and founder in the mid 1960s of the United Farm Workers (UFW), is a charismatic leader who also held a position of legal authority, that of President of the United Farm Workers, in which capacity in the 1970s he "pushed through landmark [Califor-

nia] state laws that, for the first time anywhere in the U.S. gave legal protection to farm workers seeking to unionize and made them eligible for unemployment insurance" (Zachary, 1995).

Charismatic leadership is inherently unstable, in the sense that it is difficult to transfer it to others. Political authorities in many parts of the modern world realize this. They arrest, kill, or exile charismatic leaders of social movements that challenge the legitimacy of their rule, that oppose their political or economic policies, or that otherwise seek political, economic, or cultural redress. Thus, the white government of South Africa under apartheid arrested and imprisoned Steven Biko and Nelson Mandela for many years. In the United States, the Federal Bureau of Investigation, under the leadership of J. Edgar Hoover, performed illegal wire-taps, engaged in covert investigations of and in campaigns of moral discreditation against the charismatic civil-rights leader Martin Luther King, Jr. In the Peoples Republic of China, the Beijing government has waged a comprehensive campaign to quash the remnants of China's pro-democracy movement that culminated in 1989 in the Tianamen Square demonstrations. Virtually all leaders whom the government could locate, following the completion of their prison sentences for participation in the protests, either have been jailed again, detained without charge, or exiled abroad (Chen, 1995).

Although inherently fragile and unstable, charismatic authority can be a vehicle that instigates fundamental and widespread social change. The Beijing government in the Peoples Republic of China appreciate this. Political scientist Andrew Nathan of Columbia University notes that Beijing "fears that if it were to allow even one . . . [charismatic leader and] dissident . . . to criticize the government, 'It's like the emperor has no clothes—it could take off like wildfire' " (Chen, 1995). Similarly, Christianity—which ushered in profound cultural, political, and economic changes—was started by the charismatic son of a carpenter. The modern civil-rights movement in this country was spearheaded by a charismatic civil-rights leader, Dr. Martin Luther King, Jr. It, in turn, inspired the Catholics of northern Ireland to form a civil-rights movement of their own, wherein they petitioned their government for the vote, for fair employment and housing practices, and for other basic civil liberties previously denied them on the basis of religious affiliation.

Expressive and Instrumental Leadership

Research indicates that in newly-formed (neonatal) problem-solving groups, two sorts of problems emerge over time, the *external* or *task problem* and the *internal* or *socio-emotional* problem (Bales, 1950; Gibb, 1950; Slater, 1955). As members focus on solving a problem, social relations within the group begin to fray. People get mad at each other, say unkind things, or say things in an unkind way, for instance. The group then focuses on mending social relations for a while. After the social fences are mended, the group resumes working on a solution to the task problem. This back-and-forth movement is commonly found in problem-solving groups: members work on the task, then mend social fences, resume work on the task, again mend social fences, and so forth. There is a tendency in small groups for these different functions—*socio-emotional leadership* and *task leadership*—to be performed by different persons. In other words, task and socio-emotional influence are largely independent of each other. Socio-emotional leadership is also called *expressive leadership*. Task leadership is also called *instrumental leadership*.

Social-science research indicates that different people are chosen as leaders and as friends (e.g., Gibb, 1950; Argyle, 1994). This in part is a reflection that task and socio-emotional influence are largely independent. Friendships in groups are formed among status equals (McPherson and Smith-Lovin, 1987).

Styles of Leadership: Democratic, Authoritarian, Laissez-Faire

Socio-emotional leaders often have a style that is termed **democratic.** They both welcome and solicit input from group members and use that information in formulating decisions, which are reached through consensus. Morale of members tends to be higher if their leader has a democratic leadership style.

In contrast, **authoritarian** leaders impose policies, techniques, and activities on the group. The case study of the insurance company in Box 12.1 illustrates an authoritarian leadership style. The members of the company know that, regardless of the input they give in a meeting, the boss will do as he sees fit. This sometimes is called a "top-down" leadership style. In this ideal type, group goals and directions stem from the leader and flow in a one-way stream to the other members. The authoritarian leaders tend to remain aloof from the other members of the group.

Authoritarianism tends to be produced by certain socialization experiences (Argyle, 1994: 53), including little physical punishment coupled with permissiveness for aggression and sex. Authoritarian leaders tend to be strong in power motivation, highly competitive, and more aggressive than the average person. This aggression may be active or passive. Authoritarian leaders try to dominate in groups, and they surround themselves with people they can dominate, a preference that is manifest in their hiring preferences. Not too surprisingly, authoritarian leaders tend not to be liked much by other members of the group. British sociologist Michael Argyle indicates that highly authoritarian leaders also tend to have high blood pressure, poor health, low self-esteem, and a large appetite for the consumption of alcohol (1994).

Laissez-Faire is French for "non-intervention" or "leave it alone." **Laissez-Faire** leaders encourage group members to reach their own decisions. They are only minimally involved in the group's decision-making process, intervening only when asked to do so. Other group members may like the laissez-fair leader because she or he does not flaunt power, is not highly critical, and does not make excessive demands. However, groups with laissez-fair leaders tend not to accomplish much, tend to stop working when the leader is away, and they become disorganized, directionless, and adrift (Siiter, 1991: 126).

The Measurement and Meaning of Leadership in Groups

What factors influence who is perceived as the leader of a task-oriented group?

1. *Verbal communication: priority of talk.* People who speak first have a greater likeli-

hood of being perceived as the leader (Hollander, 1985:506).

2. ***Verbal communication: amount of talk.*** In task-oriented collectivities like juries, committees, and work groups, a J-shaped distribution of the amount of talk emerges fairly quickly (Stein and Heller, 1983). One person talks most. Particularly in large groups, the majority of members speak very little, if at all. Moreover, when the top person speaks, she or he speaks to the whole group. When a low-ranked member speaks, she or he speaks to the top person (Argyle, 1994: 51; Bales, et. al, 1951). Studies of jury deliberations indicate that the top three people account for most of the discussion. The other members process the information by listening (Argyle, 1994).

The way leaders manage to talk more is, at least in part, by getting in first whenever there is a pause. They have a short reaction time for speech (Skvoretz, 1988).

The quantity of talking, not its quality, seems more important in perceptions of who is a leader (Hollander, 1985: 505). Perhaps this in itself is part of the explanation as to why some research indicates less emergence of women as leaders in mixed-sex groups (Lindzey and Aronson, 1985). For, contrary to the folk wisdom that when a woman is talking a man "can't get a word in edgewise," ample bodies of clinical and field research indicate that in mixed-sex groups, it is males who do most of the talking, who control the topic of the conversation, and who interrupt females far more than they are interrupted by them (Zimmerman and West, 1975). In mixed-sex groups, it is females who can't get a word in edgewise, which, in turn, influences perceptions of leadership.

People who talk the most are also the most influential. Stein and Heller's meta-analysis of seventy-seven studies indicates that rate of participation correlates overall .69 with leadership status based on the ratings of group members (1983). The other group members like what these people have to say, reinforce their utterances with signs of approval (body language), and give them high approval ratings as leaders (Ridgeway and Berger, 1986).

3. ***Task behavior.*** People who become leaders establish their dominance in the domain of task behavior, not in the domain of socio-emotional leadership (Ridgeway and Berger, 1986; Ridgeway and Johnson, 1990; Argyle, 1994 54). Influential members contribute more to the group task than lowly-ranked members.

4. ***Non-verbal communication.*** While those who have established their position tend to be more relaxed, those individuals who are seeking leadership in a group tend to use a special pattern of non-verbal communication (Ridgeway, 1987; Argyle, 1988; 1994: 54-55). This pattern includes the following behaviors:

- standing at a height, facing the group
- at full height, hands on hips, expand chest
- gazing a lot, staring down, looking while talking
- non-smiling face
- touching others
- voice loud, low-pitched
- gestures pointing at others or their property (Argyle, 1994: 55).

5. ***Seating position.*** In same-sexed groups, people who sit at the head of the table tend to be perceived as leaders. American sociologist Fred L. Strodtbeck and associates conducted a classic series of jury-simulation studies in which they note a market positional effect (Strodtbeck, James, and Hawkins, 1958; Strodtbeck and Hook, 1961). In arriving at a choice of foreperson, those jurors who initially sat at the head of a rectangular table were significantly more likely to be selected as foreperson. Further analysis revealed that persons selected as foreperson also tended to be higher up the socio-economic ladder in terms of education, occupation, and income than other members of the jury. Strodtbeck and associates infer that sitting at the head of the table was a self-selected behavior associated with high social position.

6. ***Gender.*** There appear to be strong differences in leadership perception on the basis of sex or gender. Natalie Porter, Florence

Geis, and Joyce Jennings Walstedt conducted a study of leadership perception using undergraduate college students as research subjects (1983). They showed the undergraduates a series of pictures. Each picture was represented as depicting a group of graduate students working together on a research project. In each picture, the individuals portrayed are sitting around a rectangular table. The researchers ask the undergraduates to take a pen-and-paper test of their first impressions of these pictures.

What are the results? *When the groups pictured are single sexed*, male and female respondents overwhelmingly select the individual sitting at the head of the table as the individual who contributes the most (i.e., as leader). *When the groups pictured are mixed sexed*, a male sitting at the head of the table is perceived as the leader by the overwhelming majority of students of *both* sexes, while a female sitting at head of table is ignored as leader by the majority of students of *both* sexes. A female sitting at head of table is, as the authors phrase it, *invisible*. A majority of students of both sexes select a male as contributing the most. As we are about to enter the next millennium there seems to be a strong expectation among both sexes that in mixed-sex groups that the leader should be a male. Seating position appears to facilitate perception of being a leader for males but not for females.

The Behavior of Followers

In the verbal domain, followers tend to do the opposite of the leaders. Followers exhibit bending posture, deferential head-nods, low volume of voice, smiling, and looking while the leader is speaking (Argyle, 1994: 55). Verbally, followers speak less, interrupt less, and address high-status individuals such as the leader rather than the whole group; on the whole, they do so politely.

Both field and experimental research indicate that low-status members communicate a lot with high status members and do so in a rewarding, deferential, approval-seeking way, particularly if they had shown a desire to move upwards (Kelly, 1951; Hurwitz et. al., 1960; Shaw, 1971; Argyle, 1994). This has been interpreted as a substitute for real upward mobility.

Ridgeway and Johnson argue that hierarchy inhibits the expression of disagreement by low-status members; high-status members are more likely than low-status ones to voice their disagreement with the task leader (1990).

Leadership Style and Group Effectiveness

Is one leadership style more effective than another? Both field and experimental research do *not* indicate that one form of leadership is inherently "better" than another or that one form of leadership is "right" and others "wrong." Rather, the weight of research suggests six things.

1. *The social situation.* The social situation is a powerful determinant of what style of leadership is more effective (e.g., Berkowitz, 1953; Gibb, 1969; Hare, 1976: 278-303; Argyle, 1994). The style of leadership required in responding effectively to an emergency situation, such as the Oklahoma City bombing of 1994, may be different than that which is effective in other, more ordinary circumstances. The style of leadership that is effective in a start-up company is different than the style that is most effective in an established, multi-million-dollar company. As tasks in a group change, so may the leadership (Carter and Nixon, 1949). An example from real life has been found in delinquent gangs. As they shift their activities from law-violating behavior to sports (e.g., football, soccer), the leadership also changes (Argyle, 1994: 54).

2. *Expectations of the members of the group.* If members of a group expect, anticipate, and positively value a particular style of leadership (e.g., democratic, authoritarian), the group tends to be more effective if the members' expectations are met.

3. *Level of societal complexity.* There seems to be a relationship between the level of technology or level of societal complexity and type of leadership. Hunting and gathering types of groups, societies, and social organizations tend to be characterized by a more *decentralized* leadership, while pastoral, agricultural, and industrial societies

tend to be characterized by more *centralized* leadership. Leadership in hunting and gathering societies also tends to be more *democratic* than in pastoral, agricultural, and early industrial societies. Feudal societies (urban-agrarian) societies tend to be characterized by highly authoritarian types of leadership. Leadership in industrialized democracies tends to be in the middle. In industrial democracies like the United States and England, leadership tends to be more authoritarian than in hunting and gathering societies but more democratic than that typical of feudal societies.

4. *Expressive component.* Expressive leadership is an important component in effective leadership in many situations. A great body of research in military, industrial, sports, and other settings indicates that effective leaders *combine* expressive and instrumental styles of behavior (Stouffer, 1949; Wilson, 1986; Argyle, 1989). The effective leader indicates the path to be pursued *and* is concerned for the group members. For instance, Stouffer and associates discovered that the most effective leadership style is provided by military officers, often non-commissioned officers, who form primary-group relations with the soldiers in their command (1949). They provide clear direction regarding the mission of the group and they provide emotional support, minimize stress, and emphasize harmony. This combination of elements enables them to act as an effective group even under conditions of extreme hardship and stress.

5. *Group cohesion.* Group cohesion around the leader is an important ingredient of effective leadership. Military research, for instance, indicates that the leaders of tank crews are effective *only when the tank crews are cohesive.* An effective tank crew must have task leadership *and* cohesion (Stouffer, 1949; Fiedler and Meuwese, 1963; Argyle, 1989).

6. *Alignment of goals.* If a larger organization is to achieve its formal goals, there has to be some kind of alignment between the demands placed upon members of the group by persons in positions of formal authority and the demands that the group places upon itself in the informal leadership structure. For instance, in armies around the world, the creation of solidarity in the immediate fighting unit is no guarantee of military performance in battle. Why? There is every chance that the norms of the primary group will conflict with the aims of the larger organization. This lack of alignment of goals can result in snatching defeat out of the jaws of victory. Recognition of this is one of the reasons for the system of political vigilance in many communist armies, where the *zampolit* (political officer) seeks to ensure that the aims of the group conform to and do not deviate from those of the larger organization.

Military historian Richard Holmes documents that alignment between the demands placed on members of fighting units by the higher command and those that the group places upon itself in its informal leadership structure ubiquitously has been problematic. They have been known to diverge throughout the known history of military engagements. For example, the norm of the immediate fighting group may rate the survival of the group and its members as all-important. In this situation, individuals who encourage the group to fight may be met with suspicion, hostility, and violence (1984: 317). Researchers Gabriel and Savage give a fairly recent example of practices that have gone on for centuries, when they note that sometimes during the American military involvement in Viet Nam,

> officers' legitimate concern for the safety of their own men persuaded them that they were morally right in declining to go into action. In June 1966 a company commander in 2nd Battalion, 327th Infantry, firmly refused to risk his men without adequate supporting fire. "Colonel," he declared, "I don't give a rat's ass what you say: I am not going.' (As quoted in Holmes, 1984: 318)

Commanding officers are aware of this problem. Sometimes they attempt to deal with it through raw power alone. For example, Brigadier-General Frank Crozier was commanding a battalion of the Western Front during World War I. He became aware that soldiers he had sent out on patrol sometimes avoided combat by going a short distance from camp, waiting until they were due back in, and, upon returning, simply reported that they had no contact with the enemy. He therefore insisted that each of his patrols brought back a section of German barbed wire, to prove that they had in fact reached it. The Brigadier General was chagrined to learn that one of this own company commanders kept a roll of the wire in his dugout and would, from time to time, give pieces of it to his men which enabled them to avoid their next patrol (Ashworth, 1980).

Power, Influence, and Leadership as Socially Structured

When sociologists speak of imperative order as one of the relationships that makes a world, we use terms like power, influence, leadership, and authority. A sociological view stresses the *socially structured nature* of power in social life. Power and leadership are not just about, or even primarily about, being bigger or having more guns than another social actor. Size and fire power can have a lot to do with power, but a basic sociological point about imperative order is its socially structured character. Power is socially organized.

A Case Study: Hungarian Sociologist Ferenc Merei's Classic Research

Let us introduce you to the subject of the socially organized nature of power by means of classic small-group research involving children between ages 4 and 11 in same-sex play groups. Hungarian sociologist **Ferenc Merei** studied power among children in these situations (1949), much as Swiss social scientist Jean Piaget studied child development.

Measures of Power

Merei and his associates used two main indices of power, influence, and leadership in the play groups. One is the ratio of orders given to the number of orders taken. For instance, each time Ralphie says, "Emily, you be the Mommy and I'll be the daddy," and Emily says "OK," that's recorded as an order given by Ralphie and as an order taken by Emily. The ratio of the number of orders you give relative to the number of orders you take is a measure of your power in the group. It is a measure of

your capacity to be "effectively bossy," as these researchers would say.

Another measure of power in the Merei play groups is the number of times other children imitate you relative to the number of times you imitate other children. A large amount of influence that goes on among very young children in play situations is measured by means other than direct verbal statements (Garber, Alibali, and Goldin-Meadow, 1998). This is because in many cases very young children do not talk to each other very much. So, if you see one little child piling up blocks and another child comes along and starts piling up blocks, the initiator of the action has more power in the piling up blocks game.

Remove the Leaders and Let Play Groups Emerge Anew

In these ways Merei and his associates identified two categories of children, leaders and followers. Next, the researchers separate the leader from the non-leader children and let the non-leader children form play groups. These new play groups are composed of children none of whom had been leaders in the previous play groups.

An assemblage of non-leader children is considered as a group when it develops a realatedness (solidary order) with norms, habits, and traditions of its own (normative order) that it enforces. In other words, Merei let the children play together until they formed a social structure. Much as in the migrant camps observed by Steinbeck a leadership structure (imperative order), rituals, and routines emerge in these groups. They develop a jargon of their own. For instance, in one group, a child may call the play dough "doughy doughy," and the other kids in the group pick up that term. From then on, the kids in that group, instead of calling it play dough as their mothers and the teacher do, instead refer to it as "doughy doughy." "Let's play doughy doughy." That's an example of kids developing their own traditions.

Another tradition that develops in the groups concerns seating order, who sits where , so that every day when the teacher says, "Children, it's time to play blocks!," the children would sit around the table in the same order. If someone sat in someone else's chair, the mis-seated child is evicted by the members of the group. Other traditions that developed in these groups concern a division of play toys (who plays with what), group ownership of certain objects and of ceremonies concerning their use, verbal and non-verbal expressions of belonging together, and sequence of games (the temporal order in which games are played). In other words, solidary, normative, and imperative order emerged in these groups—solidarity in the form of kids knowing and liking each other, normative order in the form of rules of behavior that are part of their roles in the group, and imperative order in that the kids themselves enforce their rules and traditions.

What's coming next?

Insert Previously-Proven Leaders into the Groups

Merei and associates place one the 26 previously-proven effectively-bossy children into each of the play groups that had developed its own social organization. Merei makes sure that the previously-proven leader he inserts into each group is one to two years older than the other children in each play group. If there's a group of four- and five-year-old children, Merei inserts a previously-proved leader who is six years old. For each group, there is a year-and-a-half's difference in age between the other kids and that the newly inserted previously-proven leader.

Merei then observes the previously-proven leaders attempt to take over these groups. What happens?

Results of Take-Over Attempts

In Merei's own words: *"[C]onfronted by a group having its own traditions, the [previously proven] leader proves weak; this, in spite of the fact that . . . he is [physically larger and] stronger than any one member of the group"* (Merei, 1949: 25; italics in original). The previously proven leader also takes on the habits and traditions of the children in the group. For example, the group may have been playing a ritualized game of climbing up the slide. The newly inserted previously proven leader might suggest: "Don't play climb-up-the-slide. Play climb-up-the-slide-part of the slide instead of climb-up-the-stairs part of the slide." The other children

simply play "climb up the slide" and hit him on the way down. Almost without exception, Merei finds these 26 older and stronger previously-proven leaders unable to direct the activities of the groups. The children ignore him or her, except in one case.

There was one child—a year and a half older than the average age of the other children in the group—who was able simply to take over the group. Let us call this child Alex. Alex gave orders. They followed. Alex modeled. They imitated. Alex decided what to play, in what order, and how to play it. The rules Alex introduced took the place of those the group previously had.

In only one instance did this occur. That instance itself makes interesting analysis, because this group was very special in several ways. For one thing, it was a group that already had been subject top three previous take-over attempts by older children within three days. In three days, three different previously-proven leaders had tried, unsuccessfully, to foist their initiative upon this group and had tried to change its rituals. Against these three leaders, the group was able to preserve its customs, rejecting their suggestions against all the enticing and aggression these would-be leaders could perpetrate upon the group. However, the struggle *exhausted* the group.. The struggle exhausted the group, weakened it, in the sense that it weakened its cohesion (solidarity), its normative order, its imperative order.

Social scientists indicate that groups as well as individuals may be described as exhausted. Thus, the Deputy Head of England's Royal Military Academy, Sandhurst, makes precisely this point in a sociological analysis of soldiers in battle. In an analysis of those conditions and factors that exhaust both individuals and the immediate fighting units and the formations in which they are situated, Richard Holmes describes military fighting units as following the same curve of

apprehensive enthusiasm, efficiency, over-confidence and exhaustion as the soldiers who compose them, . . . with the same tragic consequences . . . [Sustained siege and bombardment] may so lacerate the fabric of a unit that is cohesion [solidary order] and self-discipline [normative order] disappear. This process is likely to be accompanied by . . . large-scale failure in battle (1985: 222, 333).

Similarly, in the Merei play groups, members had been expending so much energy during the previous three days in attempting to maintain the old traditions, in attempting to ignore the onslaughts of the dangerous and threatening older child who was in the group, that finally, on the fourth day, they gave up and accepted the leadership of this child who totally dominated the group from then on.

The exhaustion of the group manifested itself in a number of ways. The children more often played by themselves than collectively as a group. Let's say the children had been "playing house." Instead of playing house collectively as a group, each child played house, separately and singly, side by side. In other words, the old traditions are still formally there, but the members of the group observed them singly, by themselves. Collective play, collective observance of ritual, had broken down. *Collective play broke down first; only then could a previously-proved effectively-bossy child take over the group.*

Patterns in Outcomes of the Take-Over Attempts

So, in one group that was in a weakened, socially disorganized condition, a previously-proven leader was able to take over. In all other groups, the previously-proven leader was in some sense defeated. Merei observes four major patterns in these other take over attempts. We now examine each of these.

1. *The totally assimilated.* In the totally assimilated pattern, the older and stronger previously-proven leader child is unable to make a dent in the group. The child is able to exert no successful leadership at all. The child simply becomes a new member of the group and totally accepts its traditions.
2. *The order giver.* The order-giver pattern is more frequent. According to this pattern, the older and stronger previously proven leader child enters the group and attempts to take over. This child gives orders, makes suggestions, bosses everybody. The children carefully avoid this person, ignore her/his orders, and carry on in their traditions. Soon, the older and stronger previously-proven leader child finds him/herself alone. Once that happens, the child

changes tactics. The child joins the group in its activities, quickly learning its rituals, expressions, habits, and games. Soon this child is ordering the others to do what they would have done anyway. For example, let's say that in this group, the first thing that happens when they first get together is that they play "slide." This child realizes that this is the tradition of the group and learns to come in and the first thing that she/he says is "Hey, let's play slide!" and the other kids say "Good idea" and play slide. So, the previously-proven leader child is telling them to do precisely the same things in precisely the same order in precisely the same way that they've been doing them all along.

3. *The proprietor.* A third style of incorporation observed by Merei in these groups is that of the proprietor. The proprietor accepts all the traditions of the group and even accepts the leadership of the other children. However, this child successfully asserts ownership of the play resources. For instance, if someone says, "Let's play dough," the would-be leader says: "Good idea. I'll let you all use my play dough," and then proceeds to get the group's play dough and puts it out there for all to play with. This child is asserting a leadership role by asserting the ownership of the resources.

More than one of the contributors to this textbook once belonged to a Department of Social Science where the Department Secretary claimed just this type of leadership in the group. She asserted ownership of the Departmental resources — public space in the Departmental office, paper, ink cartridges for the laser printer, pass-word codes for the departmental personal computers, pencils and so forth. She claimed ownership these resources, and faculty would have to gain access to them through her. The official head of the Department, the Department Chair, would not cross the secretary in this regard.

A variation on the proprietor pattern of leadership is the assertion of personal ownership of the group's traditions. In this variation the children in the group may say

"Let's build a fort out of Leggos" and the previously-proven leader says "Good idea. How do *you* build a fort out of Leggos?" They show him and he builds one exactly like that. Then, when all the other member of the group admire the fort and ask "Where'd you learn to build a fort like that?," the previously-proven leader child says, "Oh, I'm just good at building forts, I guess." There's an acceptance in the group, in other words, of the fiction that they didn't just teach him how to build a fort just like that.

4. *The diplomat.* A final category of assimilation is that of the diplomat. The diplomat is a child with a tremendous amount of social skills. The diplomat becomes proficient in the traditions of the group and then changes them. This child is what we elsewhere have called a charismatic leader. After having learned the group's traditions, he diplomat, essentially says, "Tradition says . . . but *I* say unto you . . ."

    Let us look at the sequence of events. The child goes into the group. The group is playing blocks. The child says, "Playing blocks is a dumb thing. I don't want to play blocks. Let's play slide." The kids just ignore this child and continue playing blocks. Then the previously proven leader child says, "I'll tell you what: Let's play blocks," and the other children might not say anything because playing blocks is precisely what they are doing. The previously-proven leader child then watches carefully, learns the traditions of the group, becomes proficient at participating in them with the group. After several sessions, this child has become proficient at giving orders within the confines of the group's old traditions and only then proceeds to introduce minute changes. For example, she joins in the traditional block game of the group but demands that the blue side of the block always is on top. This child then becomes the leader of the traditional activities thus changed. It is important to note here that it is only after having accepted the former traditions and having demonstrated competence in conforming to them that the previously-proven leader is able to break through those traditions and to modify or change them.

Group Characteristics and Outcomes of Take-Over Attempts

Which of the four patterns emerges—that of total assimilation, of order giving, of proprietorship, or of diplomacy—depends not only on the size, strength, and personality characteristics of the previously-proven leader but on the characteristics of the group itself. Merei identifies three group characteristics that influence the outcome of take-over attempts.

1. *The degree of crystallization of traditions.* Some groups developed their own forms of social structure over an extended period of time, and therefore these groups had what Merei called more crystallized social structure. The more crystallized the social structure, the more difficult it was for a previously proven leader to become anything other than totally assimilated.

2. *The extent of collaborative play.* The extent of collaborative play refers to the extent to which the group's traditions are collective and involve everybody playing the same games together as a group, as opposed to being organized into dyads, triads, monads, and so forth. The greater the extent of collaborative play, the more difficult it was for a previously-proven leader to come in and successfully take over leadership of the group.

3. *The extent of a group's cohesion.* Whether previously-proven, older leaders could come into these groups and take over one or another degree of leadership in the groups depended on how cohesive the group was. The less cohesive the group, the greater the likelihood that a previously-proven older leader could come in and successfully take over leadership of the group.

What are the bases of power in the Merei play groups? On what does the power of the members of the groups rest? What is the basis of the absence of power in the previously proven leaders? In the last analysis, power in these groups rests on familiarity with the group's culture. The disadvantage of the newly-inserted would-be leaders is that they are unfamiliar with the group's traditions and culture. The more the would-be leaders learn the group's traditions and culture, the more they are able to reassert themselves as powerful figures. Similarly, the group as a group is able to resist the influence of a much older and stronger person because the group shares something that the new would-be leader does not have—knowledge of the cultural traditions of the group, or to phrase this somewhat more sociologically, control over the resource of cultural knowledge. So, we learn from the Merei play group experiments that shared cultural knowledge in a group of people can be a resource on which power is based. We have more to say about this shortly.

The study of power in the Merei play groups gives us a better appreciation that power is something that is socially organized and is founded on more than mere brute strength or physical prowess. Because power is socially organized, it also is fragile. Let us explore the fragile nature of power before we analyze the bases of power in groups.

Power as Fragile

Power is fragile. This notion might at first glance appear somewhat strange to us. We are accustomed to thinking of fine porcelain, tea cups, and crystal as fragile. But power?

The fragile nature of power follows from the fact that it is socially organized. *If the social organization on which power is based breaks down, then the power itself breaks down.* One implication is that *power is never unproblematically based on sheer physical force.* The famous social historian Richard Henry Tawney recognized this over sixty-five years ago when he wrote that power

is both awful and fragile, and can dominate a continent, only in the end to be blown down by a whisper. To destroy it, nothing more is required than to be indifferent to its threats, and to prefer other goods to those which it promises. Nothing less, however, is required also. (1931: 176)

Fragging: Ancient and Recent

Fragging specifically refers to the purposive killing of a comrade in arms by another through the use of a fragmentation grenade. The term also refers quite generally to the purposive killing of one comrade in arms by another through the use of small arms of whatever variety. Military historians indicate

that fragging is an ancient practice. For instance, the armies of the Roman Empire, of Napoleonic France, of First World War Russia, and of Australians during World War II were marred by fragging. So, too, were American forces in Southeast Asia during the 1960s and 1970s. Military historians indicate that with regard to Army personnel in Viet Nam, "the incidence of fragging peaked in 1971, with no less than 333 confirmed incidents and another 158 possible ones" (Holmes, 1985: 329). Richard Gabriel and P.L. Savage suggest that over one thousand U.S. officers and Non Commissioned Officers (NCOs) were killed by fragging in Viet Nam and speculate that as many as twenty percent of the American officers killed in that war may have died at the hands of fellow American soldiers (1979). A similar practice in the U.S. Air Force or Navy was *fodding*—the deliberate use of foreign object damage to kill a fellow military comrade. This form of lethal sabotage could be accomplished, for example, by placing a washer in an air intake. The more general point is that fragging and fodding tend to be preceded by the collapse of solidary and normative organization in the small fighting units. This brings us to the topic of the sources of power.

The Sources of Power

How, as indicated in a quote that opens this chapter—"Colonel, . . . I don't give a rat's ass what you say: I am not going"—was a company commander able to refuse a direct order from his commanding officer to take his men into military action? On what was his power based? How could the group members in the Merei play groups resist the power of the previously proven leader? What are the bases of power in the Merei play groups? Let us use exchange theory to formulate some possible answers (e.g., Blau, 1964; Emerson, 1972; Heath, 1976; Blau, 1977; Cook and Emerson, 1978; Cook, Emerson, Gillmore, and Yamagishi, 1983; Cook and Emerson, 1984; Blau, 1984; Blau and Schwartz, 1984; Emerson, 1987; Blau, 1988; Friedman and Hechter, 1988; Hechter, 1987; Hechter, 1988). Since Tawney already has said that all it takes to resist power is a whisper, one may rephrase this question as: "What do you have to whisper in order to resist power?" Exchange theory suggests that you can whisper one of four things (Blau, 1964: 115-142; Turner, 1991).

1. *Have something the power holder needs.* One way to resist power is to have something the power holder needs. One can offer inducements not to exercise power. For instance, one might say to a federal prosecutor: "Give me immunity from prosecution, put me and my entire family on the Federal Witness Protection Program for the rest of our lives, and I'll tell you everything you want to know." Or a lieutenant might say to a commanding officer: "Colonel, You don't want to arrest me, to put me through a court martial and send me to prison. Why not? Well, I have these pictures of you, of your eminence yourself, committing adultery, having oral sex with an intern or with animal or with underage boys" or whatever. The lieutenant offers the Colonel inducements not to exercise his power.
2. *Have alternatives to the power-holder's resources.* Another way to resist power is to have alternatives to the power-holder's resources. One thereby can obtain what the power-holder has somewhere or somehow else. Thus, one spouse may say to another: "It's OK if you divorce me, dearest, because I can earn a six-digit salary, after taxes, on my own and there is this really supportive attractive somebody who has been and is interested in sharing my company." In this example, the spouse has alternatives to the power holder's resources.
3. *Use of counter force.* A third way of resisting power is counter force. The Colonel orders you to take your troops into battle and kick him in the teeth or shoot him between the eyes with your pistol.
4. *Be indifferent to the rewards and punishments that the power holder can offer.* A final way to resist power is to be indifferent to the rewards and punishments that the power holder offers. The lieutenant feels that anything—even death, or court martial and prison—would be preferable to taking his troops into battle without adequate supporting fire. The lieutenant is indifferent to the fate that awaits him is he fails to take his troops into battle.

Those are four ways of resisting power. The converse of those things are sources of power. In other words, you have power over somebody who can't resist you. What are those things, then, that give you power?

1. *The principle of least interest.* One thing that gives a person power is indifference to the things that the power holder offers you. This sometimes is called the *principle of least interest:* the social actor with the least interest in a relationship is viewed as wielding the most power in that relationship. For instance, a young man might say to a young woman: "Marry me and I'll take care of you," and she says, "No thank you, I can take care of myself just fine." She is indifferent to those things—companionship, caring, financial support—that the young man is offering her. She has more power in their relationship.
2. *Monopoly over satisfying another social actor's needs.* Another thing that gives a social actor power is having a monopoly over satisfying another social actor's needs. For instance, if a wife has no job, has no close friends and no family nearby, and she has no money in the bank and none stashed away at home, and she is illiterate, and her husband is the only one she knows who can satisfy her needs, then she is in a weak position relative to her husband. Many wives in analogous situations in the United States stay with physically and psychologically abusive husbands. Houses for battered women, by breaking the husband's monopoly over needs satisfaction, restore some power to the wife.

   The principle of maintaining a monopoly over needs satisfaction is followed to a great extent by the official government in the People's Republic of China and it was followed by the government in the former Soviet Union. In these countries, the government strives to maintain a monopoly of access to scarce yet widely-valued goods and services (e.g., a University education, access to fine consumer goods, to travel both within and outside of the country, etc.). Its citizens receive access to these goods and services through this one source, which gives the government considerable power over many of its citizens. In the former Soviet Union, as the government monopoly of access fell apart, so, too did the government itself.

3. *Coercion.* This point has two parts, both of which concern the use of force. First, if you are bigger than the other social actor—have more guns, fire power, physical prowess, etc.—and are able to lick that social actor in all sorts of physical encounters, then one may successfully impose one's will and successfully oppose opposition through force, which is a form or manifestation of power.

Second, there may be external constraints (normative constraints) that do not permit the use of force, which gives the physically weaker social actor greater power. In other words, *constraints on the use of force* are a source of power to social actors who control other resources. For instance let us suppose that you are a small person physically and that you are not adept at the martial arts. Let us also suppose that you own a jewelry store that has lots of precious gems in it. Let us also assume that there are some physically big people in the community who desire to take these gems without paying for them. Let us further assume that there are external constraints that do not permit the use of force. Ideally, those constraints deprive the bigger social actors of the possibility of taking your valued resources through force. Thus, *law and order* are a source of power to people who control other resources. Ideally, for instance, law and order prevent physically larger people from resisting eviction by an aged, physically infirm landlord, and it prevents a muscled gangster with a gun from forcing a jeweler to hand over a diamond ring at gun point.

4. *Supporting values.* A fourth source of power is located in supporting values—values that induce or entice others to value the resources that power holders have to offer. If I am a diamond merchant, values that induce you highly to prize diamonds are a source of power for me. Many values can be sources of power. Materialistic values that entice people positively to value money and what it can buy

fortify the power of employers, who are the primary source of money for many employees. Revolutionary ideologies that define the successes of a revolutionary movement as beneficial for the individual members of the movement fortify the position of the leaders of revolutionary movements. The value of "enlightenment" that entices people to desire that rarefied state is a source of power to various purveyors of it (e.g., scientology, universities, gurus, counselors).

Summary: Power Rests on the Control of Resources

We may summarize the foregoing analysis on the sources of power by noting that power rests on the control of valued resources. We may classify the types of power, then, according to the types of resources on which it rests. Military power rests on the control of military resources, educational power rests on the control of educational resources, political power rests on the control of political resources, and so forth. Other kinds of power rest on the control of other resources. These include violence (e.g., Green Beret, ninjas, Marines, Navy Seals), love, prestige, and knowledge of cultural resources. All of these things can be sources of power. Knowledge of the river was a source of power for Mississippi river-boat pilots. In the Merei play groups, knowledge of cultural traditions was an important basis of power. This was also true among the Chinese literati in traditional China.

Work

Work for paid employment is an important part of many Americans' lives. Whether we are working in bureaucratic or non-bureaucratic settings, the majority of us perceive it as very important to derive a feeling of accomplishment from paid employment that is useful to society. (Please read nearby Tables 12.3 and 12.4.)

A Global Economy, Technology, and Personalizing Bureaucracy

The forces of social change may humanize the depersonalized nature of modern bureaucracies. The information revolution has estab-

TABLE 12.3. Perceptions in United States of Importance of Feeling of Accomplishment in Job, for Selected Years, in Percents.

"Would you please look at this card and tell me which one thing on this list you would most prefer in a job? Which comes next? Which is third important? Which is fourth most important? Work important and gives a feeling of accomplishment."

Year

RESPONSE	1972-1982	1983-1987	1988-991	1993	1994
Most	54%	53%	54%	54%	53%
Next	19	20	21	17	19
Third	15	16	13	17	14
Fourth	12	11	12	12	14
Total₁	100%	100%	100%	100%	100%

1. May not total to 100 due to rounding.
Source: General Social Survey, 1994.

lished new norms for production and for communication. The micro-chip personal computer can rapidly process information that mainframe computers located in corporate centers used to process. The personal computer is highly flexible and mobile. The development, production, and deployment of fiber optics have expedited and expanded the system of communication. Combined with satellite technology, these tools allow people to communicate globally instantly.

These technological changes mean that what used to be accomplished through formal systems of bureaucracy—and which used to take weeks, months, and years—can be accom-

TABLE 12.4. Perceptions in United States of Importance of a Job That Is Useful to Society, for Selected Years, in Percents.

"Would you please look at this card and tell me which one thing on this list you would most prefer in a job? Which comes next? Which is third important? Which is fourth most important? A job that is useful to society."

RESPONSE	YEAR 1988-1991
Very Important	28%
Important	48
Neither Important Nor Unimportant	17
Not Important	4
Not Important at All	0
Can't Choose or No Answer	3
Total₁	100%

1. May not add to 100 due to rounding
Source: General Social Survey, 1994.

plished in seconds, minutes, and days. For example, it used to take weeks to receive the result for tests like the Graduate Record Examination, the Scholastic Aptitude Test, the Academic College Test and for psychological evaluations such as the Minnesota Multiphasic Personality Inventory. These results now can be calculated within minutes after the examinations have been taken. More importantly, it is no longer necessary for business people, managers, college professors, medical doctors, lawyers, scientists, truck drivers, and secretaries and so on to travel to a central location to conduct their professional work activities. They may simply work out of their homes, automobiles, trucks, and recreational vehicles.

Many college professors, for example, conduct lectures over interactive television utilizing modern technology so that they may serve larger groups of people who may not otherwise be able to take college courses or to earn a college degree. Please read Table 12.6. Even advanced professional degrees—such as a Ph.D. in Social Work— are being offered via the Internet. So, whether as undergraduates or as graduate students, instead of students coming to the university, the university now is increasingly available to them in their homes or in a nearby location. Instead of agonizing about inadequate parking, day-care arrangements for children or for aging relatives, students now have convenient access to higher education through modern technology. This process is now occurring on a global scale, even in Russia between Russian and American universities.

TABLE 12.5. Fastest Growing Occupations Projected to Have the Largest Numerical Increase In Employment Between 1996 and 2006, by Level of Education and Training. _____

Fastest Growing Occupations	Education/Training Required	Occupations Having The Largest Numerical Category Increase In Employment
	First Professional Degree	
Chiropractors		Lawyers
Veterinarians and veterinary inspectors		Physicians
Physicians		Clergy
Lawyers		Veterinarians
Clergy		Dentists
	Doctoral Degree	
Biological scientists		College and university faculty
Medical scientists		Biological scientists
College and university faculty		Medical scientists
Mathematicians and all other Mathematical scientists		Mathematicians and all other mathematical scientists
	Master's Degree	
Speech-language pathologists and audiologists		Speech-language pathologists and audiologists
Counselors		Counselors
Curators, archivists, museum Technicians		Psychologists
Psychologists		Librarians, professional
Operations research analysts		Operations research analysts
	Work Experience Plus Bachelor's or Higher Degree	
Engineering, science, and Computer systems managers		General managers and top executives
Marketing, advertising, and public relations managers		Engineering, science, and computer systems managers
Artists and commercial artists		Financial managers
Management analysts		Marketing, advertising, and public relations managers
Financial managers		Artists and commercial artists
Fastest Growing Occupations	**Education/training Required**	**Occupations Having the Largest Numerical Category Increase In Employment**
	Bachelor's Degree	
Data base administrators and computer support specialists		Systems analysts
Computer engineers		Teachers, secondary school
Systems analysts		Data base administrators and computer support specialists
Physical therapists		Teachers, special education
Occupational therapists		Computer engineers
	Associate Degree	
Paralegals		Registered nurses
Health information technicians		Paralegals
Dental hygienists		Dental hygienists
Respiratory therapists		Radiologic technologists and technicians
Cardiology technologists		Health information technicians

Work Experience Plus
Bachelor's Degree or Higher

Food service and lodging managers	Clerical supervisors and managers
Teachers and instructors, Vocational education and training	Marketing and sales worker supervisors
Lawn service managers	Food service and lodging managers
Instructors, adult education	Teachers and instructors, vocational education and training
Nursery and greenhouse managers	Instructors, adult (nonvocational) educational

Source: ***The 1998-1999 Occupational Outlook Handbook,*** Bureau of Labor Statistics, 1998.

These new technologies allow clients and professionals to have face-to-face interactions without clients having to wait for a long time in impersonal office lobbies. Medical doctors and other health-care delivery personnel can now communicate through modern technology with people who live in rural areas that are under-staffed by medical experts. They can provide diagnostic and other services to people in rural areas via these new technologies. It could be that in the future the medical doctor will once again make house calls but do so via fiber optics and a personal computer.

The success of the Japanese-style of man-agement and evaluation-research of successful U.S. corporations both indicate that employees are better motivated workers if they are includ-ed in the decision-making process within small primary-group settings in the work place (Vo-gel, 1979; Argyris, 1960, 1964, 1967, 1985, 1990, 1993; Peters and Waterman, 1982; Fisher and Ury, 1986; Morita, 1986; Drucker, 1988, 1992, 1993a, 1993b,1995, 1996). In other words, decentralized decision-making struc-tures enhance employee satisfaction. Many American companies are examining and incor-porating the Japanese model of bottoms-up

management: the use of work teams, quality circles, sharing responsibilities by allowing the planning and design of work to be initiated from the bottom rather than the top, giving workers ownership and profit-sharing in the corporation, job rotation, and group advance-ment rather than individual promotion. The quality of Japanese products, including auto-mobiles, has created a healthy reminder of the efficacy of these management principles. The "secret" of their huge success lies in the nature of their social organization, the way their com-panies are put together.

The Hawthorne studies conducted by soci-ologist Elton Mayo and associates at the West-ern Electric Company's Hawthorne Works in Chicago from 1924 to 1932 demonstrated that employer-employee relations are an important factor in human motivation. Employee satisfac-tion and productivity increase when workers perceive that their employers are concerned about their well being and perceive them as important elements in the process of produc-tion.

Economist Jeremy Rifkin suggests that the recent down-sizing of modern corporations and the leveling of hierarchical bureaucracies

TABLE 12.6. Public and Private Higher Education's Institutional Plans for Distance Education, 1995.

Institutional type	Institutional plans for distance education, in Percents		
	Currently Offering	*Planning to offer within 3 years*	*Not offering or planning to offer*
Public 2-year	58%	28%	14%
Private 2-year	2	14	84
Public 4-year	63	23	14
Private 4-year	12	27	61

Source: U.S. Department of Education, National Center for Education Statistics, Postsecondary Quick Information System, Survey on Distance Education Courses Offered by Higher Education Institutions, 1995 (Washington: .S. Government Printing Office, 1995).

may signal a fundamental change in the organization of production. Rifkin notes that the future of the global economy is dependent on the new information-age computer technologies that are shaping and re-shaping work. These technologies, and the social organization of production around them, hold a variety of challenges. Many managers, secretaries, accountants, and others have been "leveled" out of their former jobs.

These technologies form the basis of those occupations in the United States that are expected to be the fastest growing during the period 1996-2006. *The Occupational Outlook Handbook, 1998-1999*, published by the U.S. Bureau of Labor Statistics of the U.S. Department of Labor (1998), indicates that over the 1996-2006 period, total employment is expected to increase by 18.6 million jobs, a 14 percent increase. This rate of growth is much slower than during the previous ten-year period, 1986-1996, when growth was 19 percent and the economy gained over 21 million jobs. Health services, business services, and social services will account for fully one-half of the new jobs created between 1996-2006. Manu-

facturing's share of total jobs is expected to continue to decline.

Professional specialty occupations are projected to increase the fastest and to add the most jobs—4.8 million. These are the jobs for which college education is required. *Service workers* are expected to add 3.9 million jobs. These two groups of occupations are at opposite ends of the educational attainment and earnings ladders. These two groups are expected to provide one-half of projected job growth over the 1996-2006 period. Please see Table 12.7.

Summary

In this chapter we review several sociological perspectives on the nature of groups, formal organizations, bureaucracy, and the processes of power and exchange in social life. Contrary to the forecasts of Karl Marx, Max Weber, and Robert Michels regarding the increase in alienation, self-estrangement, and depersonalization in modern bureaucracies, the social harnessing of technological change is restructuring the work place, making it more flexible and

TABLE 12.7. **The Fifteen Fastest Growing Occupations in the United States, 1996-2006. (Numbers in Thousands of Jobs)**

Occupation	Employment change, 1996-2006		Most significant source of training
	Number	*Percent*	
Database administrators, computer support specialists, and all other computer scientists	249	118	Bachelor's degree
Computer engineers	235	109	Bachelor's degree
Systems analysts	520	103	Bachelor's degree
Personal and home-care aides	171	85	Short-term on-the job training
Physical and corrective therapy assistants and aides	66	79	Moderate-term on-the job training
Home health aides	378	76	Short-term on-the job training
Medical assistants	166	74	Moderate-term on-the job training
Desktop publishing specialists	22	74	Long-term on-the job training
Physical therapists	81	71	Bachelor's degree
Occupational therapy assistants and aides	11	69	Moderate-term on-the job training
Paralegals	76	68	Associate's degree
Occupational therapists	38	66	Bachelor's degree
Teachers, special education	241	59	Bachelor's degree
Human-services workers	98	55	Moderate-term on-the job training
Data processing equipment repairers	42	52	Postsecondary vocational training

Source: The Occupational Outlook Handbook, 1998-1999 (Washington, D.C.: U.S Government Printing Office, 1998).

allowing individual workers to be more autonomous. The newly emerging states of Eastern Europe remind us both of the fragile nature of power and that the dynamics captured by Michel's concept of the iron law of oligarchy are not immune to popular uprisings and to the social harnessing of the forces of technological change. A democratic society, de Tocqueville reminds us, requires a value system that constrains the coercive activities of the state. Voluntary associations in the United States are an important part of the relationships that make democracy possible for us. Your excursion into sociological ways of knowing enables you to appreciate more fully that participating in voluntary associations satisfies more than personal needs. You are now more able than you were a few short weeks ago to look for and to perceive all the relationships that make a world.

Key Concepts

acceptance
alexis de Tocqueville
alienation
arbitrator
authoritarian leadership
bureaucracy
characteristics of bureaucracy
charismatic leadership
compliance
de Tocqueville on functions of
    voluntary associations
democratic leadership
devil's advocate
dialectics of social life
diffuse relationships
divide et impera
dyad
dyadic withdrawal
exchange principles in Marxian
    theory
expressive leadership
Ferenc Merei's classic studies
    on power in same-sexed
    children's play groups
fodding
formal leadership
formal organization
formal sociology
functions of conflict in social
    life
Georg Simmel
group
group characteristics
    influencing the outcomes of
    take-over attempts

group polarization
group polarization
groupthink
humanizing the work place
imperative order in human
    groups
influence
informal leadership
informal relations
informational influence
instrumental leadership
involuntary associations
leadership
leadership and non-verbal
    behavior
leadership and seating position
leadership and task behavior
leadership and the amount of
    talk
leadership and the priority of
    talk
Marx and Simmel on exchange
    in social life
mediator
mindguard
monad
normative influence
oligarchy
perception of leadership and
    gender
power
preventing group think
primary group
qualitative changes in social life
    that occur with a triad

rational-legal authority
rational-legal leadership
recipe for groupthink
Robert K. Merton on
    bureaucracy and ritualism
Robert Michels: iron law of
    oligarchy
role of the third party in
    conflict situations
Simmel on elements of
    exchange in social life
Simmel on the role of the
    stranger
social organization
socio-emotional leader
    task leader
terrorism
tertius gaudens
the diplomat
the Hawthorne studies
the Japanese style of
    management
the measurement and meaning
    of leadership in groups
the methodology of Ferenc
    Merei's studies of power in
    children's play groups
the order giver
the proprietor
the sources of power
the totally assimilated
traditional leadership
triad
voluntary associations
whistle blowers

Internet Resources

Museums of Art (Voluntary Associations)

http://www.metmuseum.org

Metropolitan Museum of Art

http://boston.com/mfa

Boston Museum of Art

http://www.Christusrex.org

Sistine Chapel

http://www.paris.org.Musees/Louvre

The Louvre

http://www/nmaa.si.edu:80

The National Museum of American Art

Other Formal Organizations

http://www.un.org

Document: The United Nations

http://www.cdc/gov

Document: The Centers for Disease Control (CDC)

http://www.world-health.net/

Document: World Health Net

http://www.usdoj.gov/

Document: U.S. Department of Justice

Suggested Readings

Bernhardt, Annette, and Handcock, Mark S., "Women's Gains or Men's Losses? A Closer Look at the Shrinking Gender Gap in Earnings," *American Journal of Sociology,* Vol. 101, No. 2, (September) 1995: 302-328.

De Freitas, Gregory, "Unionization Among Racial and Ethnic Minorities," *Industrial and Labor Relations Review,* Vol. 46, 1993: 284-301.

De Mente, Boye (Ed.), *Japanese Etiquette and Ethics in Business* (Fifth edition) (Lincolnwood, IL: NTC Business Books, 1987).

Hodson, Randy and Sullivan, Tersa A., *The Social Organization of Work* (Belmont, CA: Wadsworth Publishing Company, 1990).

Holzer, Harry J., *What Employers Want: Job Prospects for Less-Educated Workers* (New York: Russell Sage Foundation, 1996).

Jasso, Guillermina, "Assessing Individual and Group Differences in the Sense of Justice," *Social Science Research,* Vol. 23, 1994: 368-406.

Johnson, Cathryn, "Gender, Legitimate Authority, and Leader-Subordinate Conversations," *American Sociological Review,* Vol. 59, 1994: 122-135.

Kanter, Rosabeth Moss, *Men and Women of the Corporation* (New York: Basic Books, 1993).

Rifkin, Jeremy, *The End of Work: The Decline of the Global Labor Force and the Dawn of the Post-Market Era* (New York: Putnam and Sons, 1995).

Learning Exercises

The learning objective of this chapter is for you to understand the nature of groups, formal and informal organization, power, leadership, exchange, and the impact of technology in the modern world. Americans sometimes have difficulty understanding the impact of social organization in our live. Americans tend to use the concept of individualism in understanding human social action. In other words, there is a tendency for us to individualize and to personalize our everyday lives and experiences. In this chapter we see that as we progress through our lives we belong to and interact with various organizations. Many of these organizations presently are in the vortex of an information revolution, an event in which you are both participant and benefactor.

For many workers the Information Society has arrived. Many workers are not yet equipped to understand or to use the hardware or software of personal computers, nor are they yet prepared to use the information available via personal computers. These workers are at a disadvantage in the labor market. Many workers did not expect that the primary social organizations they worked for would unemploy them. A sociological imagination that enables you to understand the potentialities and pitfalls of social organization, including work organizations, is a valuable resource that will benefit you as you participate in the new high-technology frontier of the twenty-first century.

Learning Exercise 12.1

Writing Assignment

Answer the following questions in an essay of not less than two-and-a-half typed pages. In this essay you are to reflect upon ideas, concepts, and ways of knowing presented throughout this textbook.

1. Consider what an education is, how it can affect a person's self-concept and view of the world; how education can refocus a person's sense of well-being; how an education can affect a person's ideas about work, leisure, values, and the life of the mind.
2. Consider what "human nature" is as it is defined and expressed throughout this textbook and course.
3. Consider what "work" and "leisure" are as they express or satisfy human nature.
4. Consider what your education means in reference to the views you have of human beings and in terms of what you have learned from your families, communities, and society.

■   ■   ■

Learning Exercise 12.2

Sociology and Your Everyday Life

Answer the following questions in an essay of not less than four typed pages. Your answers are to be typed, double-spaced, and stapled in the upper left-hand corner.

1. Describe for the reader some examples of primary and secondary group relations in your own life. What does it mean "to be ourselves" in a primary group? Describe some of the groups you belong to on campus or in your community. Has your reference group changed since coming to _____. (Please insert in the blank spaces in the questions of Learning Exercise 12.2 the name of the college or university you now are attending.)

What was it like to go home for Christmas after your first academic term at college? Do your friends at home understand your experiences at _____. What do you talk about? Does high school seem far away now?

2. Give the reader some examples of group formation in your experiences at _____. How did your group form? How does Simmel's analysis of groups help you to understand social relations in your group experiences?

3. With whom do you spend your leisure time? (With whom do you hang out?) Describe what it is like when a new person wants to join your group. Can you see how conflict within a group may be positive? What types of leaders do you have in your group? If you are in a team sport (or in a church group or in a voluntary association of any sort), describe to the reader how leadership emerged. Can you see new leaders developing? What are the behavioral markers of "wanna-be" leaders (emergent leadership)?

4. Many conflicts emerge, become apparent, and grow as people on various sides of an issue talk with like-minded others about the issue. What is the effect of group discussion on the preexisting attitudes and opinions of group members? Under which circumstances do groups impede effective decision making? Under which circumstances do groups facilitate effective decision making?

5. Group polarization occurs in communities, juries, neighborhood street gangs, voluntary associations, and in committee meetings in formal organizations. Describe to the reader two examples of group polarization from your own life. In the instances that you describe, why did group polarization occur? Describe to the reader two examples of informational influence and of normative influence from your own life.

■ ■ ■

Learning Exercise 12.3

Writing Assignment

Answer the following questions in an essay of not less than four typed pages. Your answers are to be typed, double-spaced, and stapled in the upper left-hand corner.

1. Summarize for the reader Weber, Marx, de Tocqueville, and Michel's perspectives on formal organizations and bureaucracy. We take for granted the benefits of bureaucracy. What are they? Some Americans argue that bureaucracy and government are barriers to their freedom. What if bureaucracy and government suddenly collapsed? What would happen? How does bureaucracy create a social and political climate conducive to political and social stability?

2. Please reflect upon your own life in terms of personal experiences with bureaucracies. Which bureaucracies have touched your life? Select two of the bureaucracies you mention. For each one please explain to us the ways in which it conforms to, and differs from, the ideal type bureaucratic structure. Can you think of some instance wherein you experienced bureaucracies as burdensome and as inconvenient? For example, have you had to wait in long lines to enroll for classes, to pay your university fees, to purchase tickets for a concert or theater performance, to apply for or to receive assistance from a social-service agency, or to report a crime to the police? Please tell us about it.

3. Voluntary associations are the products of a civil society where individuals join an organization in order to serve their communities and in order to fill perceived individual needs. They are organizations that provide overlapping circles of solidarity. Without them, a lot would go

unaccomplished in our society. Do you belong to a voluntary association? How many? Which ones? Select two of them. What social worth does your organization provide for the community? (An answer of "no social worth, none" is unacceptable here. Think of something, even a latent function. Engage your sociological imagination.) How do you personally benefit from your membership in these organizations?

4. Has one of your family members or friends been laid-off because of technology? Tell the reader about it. How do they see their future? (As bright, as dismal, or what?) Are they prepared for the Information Society? Are *you* prepared for the Information Society? What do you need to know and to understand to be prepared for the future?

■ ■ ■

Multiple-Choice and True-False Test

1. The sociology of Georg Simmel _____.
   A. sometimes is called formal sociology because it stresses the form of social interaction rather than its content
   B. applies formal sociology to the analysis of social types
   C. is informed by a dialectical approach that focuses on the dynamic interconnectedness and on the conflicts among the social units he analyzes
   D. all of the above
   E. none of the above

2. A _____ is a small, voluntary exclusive group that demands a high level of commitment from its followers, that emphasizes its separateness from the world of the vulgar, and that views itself as possessing esoteric knowledge not available to nonmembers.
   A. sect
   B. bureaucracy
   C. secondary group
   D. monad
   E. social type

3. A _____ is a consensual or group-related conception of a role (e.g., stranger, social climber, sexual predator, redneck, the "poor," etc.) that is not fully apprehended by reference to formal definitions.
   A. sect
   B. bureaucracy
   C. secondary group
   D. monad
   E. social type

4. Which of the following is true of the role of the stranger or of the newcomer? The newcomer or stranger _____.
   A. is *in* the group but not fully a member *of* it
   B. The person who occupies this role is identifiable by other individuals within the group
   C. Group members assign the stranger or newcomer a role that no other members of the group may play.
   D. all of the above
   E. none of the above

5. A monad is a group.
   A. True   B. False

6. A primary group consisting of two participants is a _____.
   A. monad
   B. dyad
   C. triad
   D. secondary group
   E. reference group

7. Members of a primary relationship are more likely to regard each other as
   A. means to an end outside of the relationship
   B. ends rather than as means to an end outside of the relationship

8. Relationships among members of a _____ group tend to be segmental and characterized by specificity rather than by diffuseness.
   A. primary
   B. secondary

9. According to Simmel, the apparently simple fact of adding one more participant to a dyad creates important qualitative changes. Which of the following is/are among the qualitative changes that emerge(s) with the formation of a triad?
   A. increased possibilities of communication
   B. possibility of asserting group domination over its members
   C. manifestation of the dialectics of social life
   D. all of the above
   E. Both (A) and (B)

10. According to Simmel, the possible role of a third party in triadic conflict includes _____.
   A. mediator
   B. arbitrator
   C. tertius gaudens
   D. all of the above
   E. none of the above

11. According to Simmel, all social relations are dialectical. the intimate ones and the distant ones, those of a primary-group nature and those of a secondary-group variety.
   A. True   B. False

12. According to Simmel, social conflict may _____.
   A. bind the parties to the conflict to the social fabric even in the face of their disagreement
   B. have a safety-valve function
   C. clarify grievances
   D. lead to mutual respect and understanding
   E. all of the above

13. Many twentieth-century social theorists view exchange as a basic part of social life.
   A. True   B. False

14. Attraction, value, power, and tension are exchange principles in Simmel's theory.
   A. True   B. False

15. The tale of Harry, the American Fulbright scholar who tries to exchange train tickets in Kazan, the Russian Federation, illustrates _____.
   A. that dealing with bureaucracy may be frustrating
   B. the instrumental, impersonal, segmental nature of secondary relationships
   C. that secondary relationships have been eliminated under communism
   D. all of the above
   E. both (A) and (B)

16. The term *Gesellschaft* comes from the French word *bureau*, which translates into English as desk, table, or office.
   A. True   B. False

17. Bureaucracy is based on charismatic authority.
   A. True   B. False

18. Research indicates that *informal relations* _____ important in bureaucracies.
   A. are
   B. are not

19. A *formal organization* is a secondary group whose goal is the achievement of explicit objectives or tasks.
   A. True   B. False

20. According to Max Weber, bureaucracy is based on this type of authority.
   A. traditional
   B. laissez-faire
   C. rational-legal
   D. charismatic

21. According to Weber, as an ideal type, bureaucracy is characterized by _____.
   A. explicit procedural rules and a hierarchical authority structure
   B. clearly delimited areas of command and of responsibility
   C. patrimonial rule
   D. all of the above
   E. both (A) and (B)

22. According to Weber, as an ideal type, bureaucracy is characterized by _____.
   A. the salary of office holders is fixed
   B. recruitment and promotion on the basis of merit
   C. impersonal relations among organizational members and between organizational members and clients
   D. tasks officially distributed as duties attached to an office
   E. all of the above

23. The term *bureaucracy* is derived from _____.
   A. the French word, *bureau*, which translates into English as desk, office, or table,
   B. the Greek word *kratos*, which translates into English as power
   C. both of the above
   D. none of the above

24. As a form of social organization, bureaucracy _____.
   A. is a uniquely American form of social organization
   B. has existed since the emergence of the first cities and states in Mesopotamia, Sumer, and ancient Egypt
   C. did not exist before the twentieth century
   D. both (A) and (C)

25. For Weber, the notion of *rationalization* in bureaucracy embraces two somewhat different ideas. These are _____.
   A. technical efficiency, rational-legal authority
   B. patrimonial rule, charismatic leadership
   C. laissez-faire authority, anarchy as an ideal
   D. democratic leadership, full freedom of individual expression

26. According to Karl Marx, *deception* is a universal feature of bureaucracy, a feature found in pre-capitalist, capitalist, and non-capitalist bureaucracies.
    A. True   B. False

27. *Bureaucratic inertia* refers to those who expose corruption within public or private bureaucracies.
    A. True   B. False

28. The KGB (the USSR Committee of State Security) is an example of _____.
    A. bureaucracy
    B. bureaucratic inertia
    C. both of the above

29. The term iron law of oligarchy was coined by _____.
    A. Karl Marx
    B. George Herbert Mead
    C. Robert Michels
    D. Max Weber
    E. Georg Simmel

30. A *voluntary association* is a specialized formally organized group, membership in which is a matter of choice and from which members are free to resign.
    A. True   B. False

31. According to Alexis de Tocqueville, _____.
    A. by separating church from state America increased the power of the state bureaucracy
    B. Americans preferred a strong, centralized central government that could direct the lives of the individual, while European countries favored decentralization of governmental functions
    C. both of the above
    D. none of the above

32. According to Alexis de Tocqueville, Americans associate becoming dependent on state agencies (bureaucracies) with the loss of freedom and of self respect.
    A. True   B. False

33. In the Russian Federation, people associate becoming dependent on state agencies (bureaucracies) with the loss of freedom and of self respect.
    A. True   B. False

34. Alexis de Tocqueville stresses that the proliferation of voluntary associations is

    _____.
    A. characteristic of most societies
    B. a unique characteristic of American society

35. According to de Tocqueville, voluntary associations in America _____.
    A. fulfill individual and community needs
    B. cultivate capable oppositional leaders with political capabilities
    C. involve individuals in self government
    D. compete with, and limit the power of, the state
    E. all of the above

36. Voluntary associations, according to de Tocqueville, voluntary associations in America provide both integration and overlapping circles of support for persons not related by primordial ties.
   A. True   B. False

37. American sociologist Robert Bierstedt regards power as different than influence in that power is _____ whereas influence is _____.
   A. persuasive; coercive
   B. laissez-faire; based on coercion
   C. coercive; persuasive

38. Charismatic leaders rule by virtue of _____.
   A. custom
   B. formal written rules
   C. the extraordinary characteristics attributed to them by their followers

39. Task leadership also is termed _____ leadership.
   A. socio-emotional
   B. expressive
   C. instrumental

40. _____ leaders are only minimally involved in the group's decision-making process, encourage group members to reach their own decisions, and intervene only when asked to do so.
   A. Laissez-Faire
   B. Authoritarian
   C. Democratic

41. _____ leaders both welcome and solicit input from group members and use that information in formulating decisions which are reached through consensus.
   A. Laissez-Faire
   B. Authoritarian
   C. Democratic

42. _____ leaders impose policies, techniques, and activities on the group.
   A. Laissez-Faire
   B. Authoritarian
   C. Democratic

43. British sociologist Michael Argyle indicates that authoritarian leaders _____.
   A. tend to be produced by certain socialization experiences
   B. tend to be strong in power motivation and highly competitive
   C. tend to have high blood pressure, poor health, and drink a lot of alcohol
   D. tend not to be liked much by other members of the group
   E. all of the above

44. In a task-oriented group, Pat speaks first; talks a lot in a loud, low-pitched voice; contributes a lot to task behavior; touches other members a lot; and sits at the head of the table. You have taken an introduction to sociology course, so you recognize these as behavioral markers of _____.
   A. leadership behavior
   B. anomie
   C. a person occupying a position of low power in the group
   D. a sociopath

45. Research indicates that the *quantity* of talking, not its quality, seems more important in perceptions of who is a leader.
    A. True   B. False

46. Bodies of clinical and field research indicate that in mixed-sex groups, it is _____ who do most of the talking, who control the topic of the conversation, and who interrupt _____ far more often than they are interrupted by them.
    A. females; males
    B. males; females

47. In task-oriented groups, people who become leaders establish their dominance in the domain of socio-emotional leadership, not in the domain of task behavior.
    A. True   B. False

48. In task-oriented groups, when the leader speaks she or he tends to speak to the whole group, and when a low-ranked member speaks, she or he tends to speak to _____.
    A. to the whole group
    B. to the leader

49. In task-oriented groups, hierarchy tends to _____.
    A. inhibit the expression of disagreement by low-status members; high status members are more likely than low-status ones to voice their disagreement with the task leader
    B. have no effect on behavior
    C. inhibit the expression of disagreement by high-status members; low status members are more likely than high-status ones to voice their disagreement with the task leader

50. The social situation is a powerful determinant of what style of leadership is more effective.
    A. True   B. False

51. There seems to be a relationship between the level of technology or level of societal complexity and type of leadership. Hunting and gathering societies tend to be characterized by a more _____ leadership than pastoral, agricultural, and industrial societies.
    A. centralized
    B. decentralized

52. Leadership in industrialized democracies tends to be more _____ than in hunting and gathering societies but more _____ than that typical of feudal societies.
    A. democratic; authoritarian
    B. decentralized; authoritarian
    C. centralized; democratic
    D. both (A) and (B)

53. Group cohesion around the leader is an important ingredient of effective leadership.
    A. True   B. False

54. In classic research on power in children's same-sex play groups, Hungarian sociologist Ferenc Merei and associates insert a larger, older, previously-proven-leader child into already established same-sex play groups of children between 4-11 years of age. Describe the results of these take over attempts.
    A. "Might makes right." (*Macht hat Recht.*) The effectively bossy older child almost always is successful in taking over the leadership role of the established play groups.
    B. "Survival of the fittest." The bigger, older child beats the younger children into submission almost always.
    C. "Cultural knowledge is power." Almost without exception, the older and stronger previously-proven leaders are *unable* to direct the activities of the established groups and was in some sense defeated.

55. Groups as well as individuals may be described as *exhausted.*
    A. True   B. False

56. Which of the following describe(s) the patterning of results in the take-over attempts in the Merei play groups?
    A. the totally assimilated
    B. the order giver
    C. the proprietor
    D. the diplomat
    E. all of the above

57. The take-over attempts in the Merei play groups were influenced by the degree of crystallization of traditions.
    A. True   B. False

58. The extent of collaborative play did not influence the results of the take-over attempts in the Merei play groups.
    A. True   B. False

59. A big insight of the Merei play-group research is that power in human groups is primarily based on brute strength and physical prowess.
    A. True   B. False

60. *Fragging* refers to the purposive killing of a comrade in arms by another through the use of small arms of whatever variety (e.g., a fragmentation grenade, hand gun, etc.).
    A. True   B. False

61. Use of counter force, having alternatives to the power-holder's resources, having something the power holder needs, and being indifferent to the rewards and punishments that the power holder can offer are ways of resisting power according to exchange theory
    A. True   B. False

62. The social actor with the least interest in a relationship is viewed as wielding the most power in a relationship. This is termed _____.
    A. habeas corpus
    B. anomie
    C. the principle of least interest
    D. group think

63. The results of the General Social Survey indicate that among Americans it is important that their jobs _____.
   A. give them a feeling of accomplishment
   B. are useful to society
   C. both of the above
   D. none of the above

64. Over the 1996-2006 period in the United States, which occupations are projected by the U.S. Department of Labor to increase the fastest and to add the most jobs?
   A. service occupations
   B. professional specialty occupations
   C. occupations at opposite ends of the educational attainment and earnings ladders
   D. all of the above

65. The social harnessing of computer technologies (technological change) is restructuring the work place in the United States.
   A. True   B. False

66. Fragging and fodding tend to be preceded by the collapse of the solidary and normative organization in the small fighting units.
   A. True   B. False

67. Group polarization refers to the tendency for group discussion to accentuate members' pre-existing tendencies and attitudes.
   A. True   B. False

68. Freddie is pro save the rain forest, and Sam is pro economic development (Sam, in other words, favors cutting down the rain forest). Sam and Freddie attend a public debate on the rain forest issue. The *group polarization* perspective predicts which of the following results? After the public debate, _____ than before attending the debate.
   A. Freddie is more pro economic development, and Sam is more pro save the rain forest
   B. Freddie is more pro save the rain forest, and Sam is more pro economic development
   C. no change in intensity of attitude
   D. both Freddie and Sam are alienated from the issues and no longer care about the issues, one way or the other

69. The use of violent acts, or the use of the threat of violence, to create fear, dread, alarm, or coercion, usually against government among those who identify with the victims in order to achieve objectives which usually are political in nature is called _____.
   A. quality circles
   B. management by objectives
   C. terrorism
   D. rationalization

70. _____ is influence based on a social actor's desire to belong to a group.
   A. Normative influence
   B. Informational influence

71. _____ is influence based on a social actor's accepting as correct, evidence about reality that is presented by other people.
   A. Normative influence
   B. Informational influence

72. Groupthink refers to highly solidaristic decision-making groups tending to _____.
    A. make better decisions than lowly solidaristic groups
    B. increase dissent in the interests of achieving a sound decision
    C. decrease dissent in the interests of group harmony, resulting in flawed decision making practices that, in turn, produce flawed decisions

73. An illusion of invulnerability, a perception among group members that they occupy the moral high ground, an underestimation of the opposition, self-censorship,and pressures toward conformity are behavioral markers or symptoms of _____.
    A. quality circles
    B. management by objectives
    C. alienation

Glossary

absolute score Please see **raw score,** below.

acceptance Conformity that is both public and private; one has internalized the norm and agrees with it and one conforms to it in public.

accidental sample A type of non-probability sample. Please see **convenience sample,** below.

achieved status A position (status) we earn through our own efforts, merit, or skill. For instance, in order to become a medical physician in this country, one must successfully complete many years of study, must take state licensing examinations, and so forth.

administrative system A territorial unit, such as a town, city, county, parish, or state, that is defined by its political boundaries.

agent of socialization A person, institution, or other social entity engaging in socialization. An agent of socialization may be a person, such as a parent, sibling, or day-care attendant. An agent of socialization may be a group, such as a youth group or youth gang, or even an institution, such as a school, a family court, a work place, or the mass media.

aggregate As a form of collectivity, an aggregate refers to a gathering of persons in physical proximity who have come together temporarily and who lack any social organization or lasting patterns of interactions. An example would be strangers waiting at a street corner to cross the street. Also refers to a number of persons who share one or more characteristics (e.g., income level, eye color) but who are not socially organized; in this sense, it is used as a synonym for social category.

aggregated nuclear family This family type has had time to assert its independence and no longer relies on the assistance or support of the extended family. It consists of the parents, their children, and one or more close relatives.

agnatic kinship Family or kin relationships that are traced through the male line of descent.

alienation Subjective sense of being separated from the fruits of one's labor, of being powerless. The powerlessness of the proletariat, according to Karl Marx.

altruistic suicide refers to an adult who is in sound mind taking her or his own life. It is termed as altruistic by Emile Durkheim if the act is motivated by an individual's desire to serve the perceived interests of the collectivity; it is found in societies that de-emphasize the importance of the individual.

anarchy Collapse or absence of imperative order or of political authority; from the Greek, "anarkhia," which translates into English as "without a ruler."

androgyny Gender roles characterized by equal amounts of traditionally masculine and traditionally feminine personality traits. (Sandra L. Bem)

annexation Occurs when a dominant group incorporates the territory of another country politically, usually by military force.

anomic suicide Suicide motivated by the anxiety induced by *anomie.* A term coined by Emile Durkheim. Please see **anomie,** below.

anomie A term used by Emile Durkheim referring to the normative order in a social setting: one or more norms or complexes of norms no longer are clear and hence guidelines for acceptable and proper behavior no longer are clear. Tends to be perceived by individuals as an uncomfortable state and to induce anxiety as an emotional or psychological response. Not to be confused with **anarchy.**

anonymity A research subject has this when the researcher is unable to identify a particular response with a particular research subject.

antagonistic relations Relations: two groups of people who have the same interests in an object but not the same access to it.

anticipatory socialization Learning the rights, duties, obligations, values, and outlook typical of a particular role before one occupies the role. (Robert K. Merton and Alice Kitt, 1950)

antithesis A clash of contradictions; the second stage or phase of the dialectical process, according to Marx.

apartheid A system of legal segregation based on race in South Africa. It lasted from 1948-1994.

applied sociology A pragmatic approach to a sociological way of knowing, this type of sociology utilizes a variety of sociological approaches, principles, and methods to solve social problems. Includes clinical sociology, the application of sociological skills and methods in therapeutic practice with individuals and groups.

area sample A type of probability sample. A type of sample selected on the basis of geographical location. The total area to be sampled is divided up into geographical areas, from which a random sample is selected. These, in turn, are divided into areas, from which a random sample is selected. From these areas, a randomly chosen set of cases is studied. Sometimes called **multi-stage cluster sampling.**

artificial will Human relations are founded on rational calculation rather than on spontaneous attraction; characteristic of Gesellschaft. (Ferdinand Toennies)

ascetic denial Self denial of worldly, material goods.

ascribed status A position (status) we earn through no efforts of our own; a status based on birth. Race, sex, age, noble status are examples of ascribed status.

assimilative To be integrative. The caste system includes all.

association Used as a neologism to refer to two or more groups whose memberships cross-cut or overlap; an elementary basis of solidarity. These groups, by virtue of their overlapping memberships, are characterized by what are termed *cross-cutting circles* or *overlapping social circles, cross-cutting solidarity,* or *overlapping solidarity.*

atavism This term, as used by Lombroso, suggests that criminals are situated lower down the evolutionary ladder than law-abiding humans and hence are more animal like.

attraction Positive affective attraction to another person.

authoritarian A leadership style; in this ideal type, the leader imposes policies, techniques, and activities on the group; group goals and directions stream from the top and flow in a one-way stream to the other members.

authority legitimate power (Weber)

autokinetic effect or **autokinetic phenomenon:** A perceptual illusion. In the dark one tends to perceive a stationary point of light as moving.

axiom Statement whose truth is either self-evident to a scientific community or so well established that it is accepted unquestioningly by a scientific community; these form the foundation of a theory.

backstage behavior Behavior in which the actors rest from their performances, debrief, discuss and analyze their performances, and plan future ones.

band A territorially based community that is smaller than a tribe; the most elementary form of human community, often found among nomadic and semi-nomadic peoples.

barrio A Spanish speaking neighborhood or community.

base-rate information Information (or data) that applies (apply) to or that describes (describe) most people.

beena marriage This is a nuptial agreement by which the groom is actually adopted into his wife's family with the stipulation that any children and all property will ultimately remain with the wife's family.

Bengal State in east India.

bilateral descent This occurs in those societies where both families play an equally important role in the determination of descent patterns.

biological theories As applied to the topic of deviance, this group of theories suggests that deviance is biologically determined—e.g., by brain structure, body build, hormones, genes, and so forth.

birth cohort All persons born in a given year.

Black codes During the period of reconstruction in the American South from 1860-1880, the few gains made by African Americans were nullified by the enactment of these codes which were a thin mask for violence and intimidation against them. Incidents of lynching increased as the dominant group saw the freeing of the slaves as a threat to the status quo.

blaming the victim A concept that suggests that people sometimes explain the suffering of a person (or a group) as due to personal defects (laziness, insobriety) and thus they underestimate the importance of situational or social structural causes.

boundary maintenance function The social response to deviance helps to affirm cultural norms an values that sustain society.

bourgeoisie Those who own the economic means of production, according to Karl Marx; the capitalist class.

Brahmacharya An unmarried student under the tutelage of a Brahman teacher.

Brahman A caste consisting of priests

bride wealth A sum of money or property brought to the marriage by the family of the groom; to whom it is given varies.

bureaucracy A large-scale formal organization with a hierarchical system of offices having a rational-legal chain of command, recruitment into which and promotion within which occur on the basis of meritocratic universalistic procedures. Emphasis is placed on discipline, impersonal procedures, efficiency, centralized authority, rationality, and technical knowledge. (Weber)

capitalism An economic system characterized by a free market economy and the private ownership of property.

capitalist patriarchy A society where men are in-charge of all the important societal processes, specially the economy. Politically women are in a subordinated socio-economic position because the economic structure is controlled by men.

case study A research method for studying social phenomena through a thorough analysis of an individual case or unit. The case may be a person, a group, an event, an episode, a community, a society, etc.

caste A group defined by means of entrée and egress. One gets into a caste by being born into it and one gets out of a caste through death. Traditional India had a non-racial caste system. South Africa under apartheid had a racial caste system. Caste also refers to a major type of stratification system, caste stratification. A system of stratification in India.

caste panchayat Local governing bodies of the village or sect in India.

causal reasoning Reasoning about cause and effect.

cell In a statistical table, the place for each entry of data.

charismatic authority Legitimate power (authority) based on extraordinary characteristics attributed to a leader by her or his followers.

charismatic leadership The exercise of influence or power in human collectivities on the basis of the extraordinary characteristics attributed to a leader by followers.

the Chicago school Between the world wars, sociological analyses produced by University of Chicago sociologists had several distinctive characteristics that lent this name to a new type of sociology. This body of work is heavily influenced of the ideas of George Herbert Mead, as well as by the ideas of German sociologists Toennies and Simmel; it relies heavily on a research method based on detailed observations of the daily life of the people being studied.

class This term, as a referent to the concept of social class, is variously defined by sociologists. Its definition can vary both within and between paradigms. According to Weber, it refers to those who have similar life chances; a rough index of which in modern capitalist classes is *income*. According to

Weber, it is one of three main dimensions of stratification; the other two are **status** and **power.** Karl Marx, however, defined objective social class in terms of one's relations to the economic means of production.

class consciousness Awareness of a common class situation shared with other individuals.

classical experimental design An experiment characterized by random assignment of research subjects to the experimental and control groups.

clinical sociology Please see **applied sociology.**

collectivism A concept that gives priority to defining self in terms of group affiliations and gives priority to the goals of the group over one's own personal wants, desires and goals.

column In a statistical table, the vertical listing of data in a series of categories, of which have a common classification.

column caption In a statistical table, a title that describes the common classification of the data listed in the columns.

column heading Please see **column caption.**

column marginals In a contingency table, the raw and percent frequency distributions found along the column edges or margins of the table.

commodity An object that is bought and sold in the open market. External to a human being.

common conscience Characteristic of mechanical solidarity, according to Durkheim. What you believe, I believe, we all believe.

common sense Cultural traditions or folk knowledge as a way of knowing. These form a body of shared and somewhat standardized explanations of a variety of phenomena and contain "solutions" for everyday problems (Just say "No" to drugs).

comparison group In a quasi-experiment, the group to which the experimental group is compared. Members are not assigned to experimental and comparison group on the basis of random assignment.

complex nuclear family Is similar to the aggregated family but with the difference that it also includes one or more non-relatives.

compliance One publicly acts in accordance with a norm but privately disagrees with the norm.

concept Mental construct, a word or set of words that express the general nature of something or the relationship among things; the building-blocks of theory and of variables.

confidentiality A research subject has this when a researcher can identify a particular response with a particular research subject but promises not to do so publicly.

conformist An individual who accepts the goals and means of conventional society. (Robert K. Merton)

conformity Change in behavior or attitudes or beliefs as a result of perceived or actual group influence or pressure. Two types of conformity are **acceptance** and **compliance.**

conjugal family (1) Consists of two generations, as the husband and wife are considered the first generation and their children constitute the second generation; (2) Form of family that consists of husband, wife, and their dependent children and that has loose relations with other family members. This term was developed by American sociologist William Goode in response to a debate within American sociology concerning whether the "nuclear" family (consisting of husband, wife, and dependent children) is actually isolated and ubiquitous.

colonial expansion Many history books refer to this period as the period of "Exploration and Discovery;" an historical period when the Europeans set out to claim and to conquer the territories of the New World.

consanguine family This simply means that a group of individuals are related by blood, as the term derives from the Latin word *sanguine,* meaning "of the same blood."

consanguineous ties Refers to individuals who are related by blood or by common ancestors.

consciousness awareness

consciousness of kind A feeling of identification with others who are similar to oneself (Franklin Giddings).

conspecifics Others of one's own species.

constrictedness An orientation to the world that focuses inward; persons with this orientation are more focused on themselves and their own needs and they pay scant attention to others; at best they reserve a sense of obligation to help others in need to a small circle, from which most others are excluded. (Samuel P. Oliner and Pearl M. Oliner)

construct validity The extent to which a measure relates to other variables as predicted by a theory.

content validity The extent to which a measure covers the range of meanings included in a concept.

contingency table A bivariate statistical table. Please see **cross-tabulation table.**

control group In an experiment, the group that is not exposed to the manipulation of the independent variable.

convenience sample A type of non-probability sample. Also known as an *accidental sample* or as an *incidental sample.* Sampling on a catch-as-catch-can basis. Interviewing the first 20 people to walk through the main entrance of the Student Center a Monday morning in order to find out what students at your college or university feel about a particular issue is an example of convenience sampling, accidental sampling, incidental sampling.

cooperation A social construct; a consistency between what the individual is doing and what others are doing.

core countries The countries that are at the leaders and centre of capitalist development.

corporate crime Crime committed by individuals in formal organizations for the benefit of the formal organization.

correlation A relationship between two or more quantitative variables, such that an increase or decrease in the magnitude of one variable is associated with the magnitude of the other(s); when two variables are highly correlated, it is possible to predict the magnitude of one variable from a knowledge of the magnitude of the other

counter culture A subculture that rejects key norms and values of the conventional society in which they are located. Sometimes also called a *contra culture.*

courtesy stigma Negative labeling of the friends and relatives of a deviant.

crime Intentional act or omission of an act that violates the provisions of criminal statutory law. (legal definition)

criminalization Refers to the process whereby something that was not illegal before (e.g., the manufacturing and sale of alcohol, possessing marijuana, engaging in insider trading) is made illegal through the enactment of laws. The recent criminalization of drunk driving is a case in point.

criterion-related validity The extent to which a measure is correlated with an external criterion; the greater the extent to which a measure relates to an external criterion, the greater its validity.

critically self conscious To be critically self conscious means to be able to perceive things (including yourself and the social world) as broken down into their fundamental constituent "parts". The parts of the social world are many and include major institutions (e.g., the family, political order, education, religion, the economy, human sexuality) and processes (e.g., ritual; stratification; normative, solidary, exchange, and imperative orders).

cross-tab Shortened expression for a **cross-tabulation table.**

cross-tabulation table A method of ordering and of displaying data, so that a cross-tabulation of two or more variables is presented; the table presents the raw number of cases and the percent of cases falling into each combination of categories of the two or more variables.

cult of true womanhood A Victorian idea defining women as fragile and helpless. It also emphasized that women's place was at home and that their primary responsibility was to raise children and to look after the house.

cultural capital The extent to which an individual or a group has absorbed the dominant culture. The greater the extent to which an individual or group has absorbed the dominant culture, the greater its cultural capital (Bourdieu, 1973).

cultural element Please see cultural trait, below.

cultural lag One "part" of society changes at a different rate than at least one other "part" of society.

cultural pluralism Please see **pluralism,** below.

cultural trait In a particular analysis or study, the simplest identifiable and significant unit of a culture. Also called a *cultural element.*

cultural universal A cultural trait found in virtually every society.

culture All material and non-material human-made products that are transmitted from one generation to another.

culture shock Disorientation experienced by people who come into contact with a culture perceived as significantly different than their own.

customary law The manner in which traditional practices are conducted in the present day.

deduction Logical model in which specific hypotheses are developed on the basis of general principles. Traditional model used in the scientific method.

defense mechanism In Freudian theory, a technique used by the **ego** to defend itself against anxiety.

definition of the situation The process whereby one examines and evaluates a situation before arriving at a decision regarding the meaning or nature of a situation and before deciding which actions and behaviors are appropriate. The term was first used by W.I. Thomas and Florian Znaniecki in *The Polish Peasant in Europe and America* (Vol. 1) (Chicago: University of Chicago Press, Chicago, 1918).

de-individuation Loss of self-consciousness and of evaluation apprehension.

demand characteristic In research, cues that signal to the research subjects what behavior is expected of them.

democratic A leadership style; the leader solicits and welcomes input from group members and reaches decisions through consensus.

demographic Pertaining to the study of populations.

demography The study of population structure, including birth rates, death rates, and migration.

dependent nuclear family Refers to a nuclear family that resides within an extended family network and that is dependent on the social and economic resources of the extended family for their day-to-day survival.

dependent variable The effect or result; often represented symbolically by the letter Y, as in X causes Y (the result). In the statement, "Floods cause damage," damage is the dependent variable.

deviance Violation of significant social norms. (Durkheim)

deviant career Occurs when an individual internalizes a deviant label given by salient audiences and takes on a life of deviance and crime.

devil's advocate In a group, it is a position, whose incumbent opposes an argument or line of action with which she or he does not necessarily disagree so as to determine its validity.

dialectic This concept expresses the view that change (history) depends on the clash of contradictions. Karl Marx used this term. His ideas concerning it were influenced greatly by Hegel. The dialectical process according to Marx was viewed as consisting of three stages or phases: the **thesis, antithesis,** and **synthesis.**

direct relationship In reference to a correlation or association, please see **positive relationship.**

discrimination An *act* that results in the unequal treatment of an individual or a group based on race, ethnicity, religion, gender, sexual orientation, age, or social class.

disvirgined A term used by Aman, a Somali female, to describe the first time she was to engage in sexual intercourse with her husband.

domination The right to command and the duty to obey (Weber, from the German word, *Herrschaft*).

dowry Gifts in cash and kind furnished by the bride's family to the bridegroom's family on the occasion of marriage. This is a custom in India and in other countries.

dualistic fallacy A concept that assumes that criminal and noncriminal categories are mutually exclusive for individuals.

double jeopardy In race and ethnic relations, this concept means that minority women suffer from discrimination not only because of their gender but also because they are members of an ethnic or racial group.

dyad A primary group consisting of two participants.

dysfunction Functionalism uses this term to refer to those instances in which one or more parts of society (or of another system) operate in such a way that they disturb, hinder, threaten, undermine, or destroy the survival and stability of the system. Of course, what is viewed as functional for one part of the system may be dysfunctional for another part of the system. Synonymous with negative function. For example, incest is dysfunctional for the family.

economic means of production The property necessary for economic production. (Karl Marx). According to Marx, one's objective relation to the economic means of production determines one's objective social class.

economic order The complex of roles and norms organized about the production, distribution, and consumption of goods and services. That "part" of society that provides for the material needs and demands of the members of society.

economy The dominant form of economic activity in a society. Examples of different types of economies are hunting and gathering economy, nomadic pastoral economy, horticultural economy, settled agricultural economy, and modern industrial economy.

ectomorph An individual with a thin, agile physique who tends to be introverted, sensitive, and subject to worrying. (William Sheldon)

ego According to Freud, the part of the personality that is largely conscious and that mediates between the demands of the **id** and **superego;** Latin word for "I."

ego defense mechanism Please see **defense mechanism,** above.

egoistic suicide According to Emile Durkheim, this type of suicide is due to a strong value system, weak group integration, and an overwhelming sense of personal responsibility.

endogamy A norm that requires people to marry within their own social or cultural group. There are many forms of endogamy—ethnic endogamy, racial endogamy, social class endogamy, religious endogamy, and so forth.

endomorph Individual with soft, round, plump physique who tends to be relaxed, easy going, and extroverted.

the Enlightenment The eighteenth century in Western Europe, named after a philosophical movement concerned with the critical examination of previously accepted doctrines, paradigms, and institutions from a point of view known as **rationalism.**

epistemology The science of knowing and of knowledge: its origins, nature, and limits.

ethic A principle of good or of right conduct.

ethics The study of the general nature of morals and of concrete moral choices.

ethnic group . . . An anthropological concept based on the distinctive *cultural* characteristics of a particular group (Gonzales, 1990: 7) or aggregate.

ethnocentrism Tendency to view the norms, values, and institutions of one's culture as right and as preferable to those of other cultures.

ethnography An empirically based analytical description of social life.

ethnomethodology Founded by Harold Garfinkel, a school of sociology concerned with how people understand the bases of their behaviors in everyday life.

504   ■   Glossary

exchange order The order of *quid pro quo,* three Latin words meaning, depending on the translation "this for that" or, more colloquially, "tit for tat."

exchange value When one exchanges one commodity for another, especially through the medium of money.

exogamy This norm requires that people marry outside of their own social or cultural groups. There are many forms of exogamy—ethnic exogamy, racial exogamy, social class exogamy, religious exogamy, and so forth. Exogamy commonly is termed *intermarriage.*

experiment An investigation in which there is controlled manipulation of the independent variable by the investigator and precise observation and measurement both of the variables and of the results.

experimental group In an experiment, the group that is exposed to the manipulation of the independent variable.

experimental mortality Refers to research subjects dropping out of a study; it is a source of internal invalidity.

exploitation Taking undue advantage of the helplessness of an individual

extended family The traditional extended family consists of three or more generations and includes grandparents, unmarried children, married sons, their spouses, and their children.

extensivity An orientation to the world that focuses outward towards others and that emphasizes both the common humanity of all persons as well as an ethical obligation to help all persons in need. (Samuel P. Oliner and Pearl M. Oliner)

external locus of control Perceiving oneself as lacking in free will, agency, or choice and as buffeted a out by forces over which one has no control.

exuvial magic *Exuviae* is the plural form of a Latin noun that literally translates into English as the cast-off skins or coverings of various animals, including snakes. (*Exuvium* is the singular form of the noun.) More generally, the term refers to any part of an animal—a cast-off scab, eyelash, strand of hair, piece of a hoof, or an entire organ (such as the heart, liver, etc.). Please see **magic,** below. Belief in this type of magic is prevalent in hunting and gathering societies. In exuvial magic, if a shaman has even a part of a person (her or his *exuviae)* the shaman is believed to be able to control the entire person by performing certain rituals.

face validity If a measure makes sense as an indicator of a concept, it has face validity. Sometimes also called logical validity.

false consciousness According to Karl Marx, persons with **false consciousness** fail to perceive two things: (1) that they have interests in common with all others whose relation to the economic means of production is the same as theirs and (2) that their common interests are both differnt than and opposite to those who own the economic means of production.

familism The belief and practice that make the family and its values and relationships the top priority in the lives of its members.

family of orientation The family into which you were born; the social unit that formed the basis for your early socialization into the community and society.

family of procreation The family that you form when you get married.

female circumcision Mutilation of the vagina. Clitoridectomy is excising the clitoris and inner labia of a girl, usually prior to reaching puberty.

feminism A political concept pertaining to women's political activity and writing on behalf of women.

feminist dialect This term focuses on the construction of knowledge which is always biased in societies in which women are oppressed. This term suggests that knowledge to be authentic must take into account not only the vantage point of the dominant classes but should recognize that there is a complex reality of unequally empowered groups who form shifting coalitions and/or stand opposed vis-à-vis other groups.

feral An adjective referring to a person who, according to legend, has been reared apart from humans, usually by animals. Romulus and Remus, the legendary founders of Rome are examples of feral children.

fictive kin Refers to those relationships where individuals who are not related by blood ties or ancestry treat each other as if they were related.

field research A way of knowing that examines people as they go about their everyday lives.

fixation In Freudian theory, this is said to occur if a disproportionate amount of libidinal energy is invested in a particular bodily orifice, and personality is dominated by the traits associated with that level of development; as a result, psycho-sexual maturity is not attained.

focal concerns A concept used by Walter B. Miller to delineate the central attentional foci in the lives of the lower classes.

focus group research A research method wherein a small number of people are brought together to engage in guided discussion of a topic.

formal leadership In a **formal organization** the incumbent of a position to which authority is attached. The incumbent of the office of President of the United States, for example, is the *formal* political *leader* of this country.

formal organization A secondary group whose goal is the achievement of explicit objectives or tasks.

fraternal polyandry A form of polygamy in which the woman's husbands are all brothers.

free labor Wage labor.

frequency A number of occurrences of a particular value or category of a variable in a data set.

frequency distribution A classification of data showing the raw or absolute number of occurrences of each subdivision, category, or value of a variable.

frontstage behavior Behavior in which the actor seeks to put on a definite "performance" for a specific audience. (Erving Goffman)

function Functionalism uses this term to refer to those instances in which one or more parts of society (or of another system) operate in such a way that they contribute to the survival and stability of the system. For example, the (or a) function of gift giving is to re-enforce solidary order. Synonymous with positive function or eufunction.

fundamental attribution error In explaining the behavior of others, the tendency to over estimate the importance of personal dispositions (temperament, personality) and under estimate the importance of situational or social structural factors.

gate keepers A concept used in the study of structured inequality to refer to the role of majority group members who, in their role as employers, have the option of applying certain rules and regulations as they see fit, thus discriminating against minorities in the labor market.

Gemeinschaft According to Ferdinand Toennies, the type of society founded on natural will: relationships are warm, personal, direct, diffuse, and are a positive end in themselves. As distinguished from Gesellschaft.

gender identity The inner sense of self that "I am male" or "I am female."

gender roles Expectations of behavior (roles) attached to one's perceived sexual status of male or female.

generalized other The attitudes and expectations of behavior held by the larger social group.

Gesellschaft According to Ferdinand Toennies, the type of society founded on artificial will: relationships are founded on rational calculation; relationships are a means to an end; relationships are cold, impersonal, indirect, and segmental.

gesture According to George Herbert Mead, any vocalization or physical movement that conveys eaning and that evokes a response in one or more persons.

glass-ceiling A barrier through which top opsitions may be viewed but cannot be attained.

great famine of 1866 A famine in India in 1866 while India was under the British raj.

group A collection of two or more individuals with the following characteristics: (1) sustained interaction, (2) shared goal(s); and (3) solidarity (a sense of we-ness"). The sociological position is that a group is more than the sum of its parts.

group polarization Group-produced enhancement of members' pre-existing attitudes, opinions, and tendencies.

group-serving bias Also known as the **ultimate attribution error.** The tendency to perceive in favorable terms both the groups and social categories to which one belongs and which one uses as a positive reference groups. One of its manifestations is a tendency to give members of the groups and social categories to which one belongs and which one uses as positive reference groups the benefit of the doubt in situations where the evidence may be perceived as ambiguous.

groupthink Flawed decision making processes, usually found in highly solidaristic decision-making groups that are structured in particular ways, that flow from the leader's desire for harmony and the suppression of dissent. (Irving Janis)

Gujarat A state in west India.

hate crime Also known as a bias crime, hate crime is defined by the Uniform Crime Reports of the Federal Bureau of Investigation as a criminal offense committed against a person, property, or society and which is motivated, in whole, or in part by the offender's bias against a race, religion, ethnic/national origin group, or sexual orientation group.

the "haves" The group of people who own the means of production and who are wealthy capitalists.

the "have nots" The group of people who have nothing but their labor to sell; workers.

the Hawthorne effect The confounding effects on research outcomes due to research subjects' responses to being studied.

the Hawthorne studies Studies conducted at the Western Electric Company's Hawthorne Works in Chicago from 1924 to 1932 by Elton Mayo and a Harvard University research team. These studies demonstrated the importance of informal social organization in the work place.

historical materialism (1) Karl Marx's materialistic conception of social change and history. History and social change happen due to the status quo (thesis) clashing with its internal contradictions (antithesis), and out of this clash emerges something new (synthesis), which, with the passage of time, becomes the thesis. The thesis then clashes with antithesis, etc. (2) Karl Marx's methodology which focuses on the evolution of human societies based on the method of production.

homophobia A fear of homosexuals.

hypothesis A tentative, testable statement asserting a relationship between two or more **variable**s; the statement is intended to be tested empirically and either verified or rejected. A scientific hypothesis is derived from a theoretical system and from the results of prior research.

the "I" The part of the self that is unsocialized; the spontaneous, self-interested part of the self, according to George Herbert Mead; as distinguished from "the me."

id According to Freud, the part of the personality that is innate and that contains our sexual and aggressive drives; the part of our personality where the pleasure principle resides.

ideal type A conceptual model or schema used to analyze social phenomena. (Max Weber)

identification (1) One's sense of self as rooted in group membership(s). (2) In Freudian theory, neutralizing the threat of an aggressor or of a more powerful person or group by adopting the characteristics of the aggressor.

identity One's sense of self; the various labels and characteristics one attributes to one's self.

identity group Established, institutionally defined groups that have a sense of identity. Examples would include persons who have AIDS (acquired immune deficiency syndrome), American females, persons of old money, and heads of state.

ideology An idea or set of ideas held by a social group (or groups or society) that reflects, defends, justifies, rationalizes the institutional commitments and interests of that collectivity.

imperative function Functionalism uses this term to refer to those functions which, in the final analysis, contribute to the well-being and overall functioning of the entire social system.

imperative order The various forms of domination and behaviors related thereto. Major paradigms in sociology view imperative order, its nature, importance, effects, manifestations, and the level of consensus with regard to its legitimacy, quite differently.

incest taboo This norm prohibits a sexual or marital relationship between individuals who are in too close in proximity to one another in terms of their kin relationship

incipient nuclear family This nuclear family type consists of only the husband and wife. They are often newlyweds.

independent nuclear family A nuclear family that has established its own independent living quarters and has demonstrated its economic and social independence.

independent variable The cause; often represented symbolically by the letter X, as in X causes Y (the result). In the statement, "Floods cause damage," floods is the independent variable.

indigenous Native or local to the area.

individual discrimination Unequal treatment of an *individual* by another individual based on race, ethnicity, religion, sexual orientation, age, or social class.

individualism A concept that gives priority to defining self in terms of personal attributes and to one's own wants, desires and goals over those of the group (Myers, 1993:213).

induction Logical model of reasoning from specific instances to general principles.

infanticide An acceptable practice in some cultures that allows for the killing of offspring under certain circumstances. This is usually limited to female infants.

infibulation Paring and surgical closure of the outer labia during female circumcision.

influence The ability to effect "a voluntary change" in a social actor's behavior, attitudes, or opinions through persuasive action (Theodorson and Theodorson, 1969: 202).

informal adoptions Close relatives, like nephews and nieces, are sometimes informally adopted by more stable family units and they may live in these households for a few months or, in some case, for several years.

informal authority The right to command and the duty to obey that are not rooted in formal organization (rational-legal authority), in tradition (traditional authority), or in the followers' belief in the extraordinary character of their leader (charismatic authority). The basis of legitimation of informal authority rests in cultural elements that lack embodiment as formal organizational structures.

informal leadership Leadership refers to the coordination of group activities toward group goals. Informal leadership emerges when individuals are valued by a group because they conform to its norms and contribute to achieving the task of the group. Informal leadership, like informal authority, has its basis of legitimation in cultural elements that lack embodiment as formal organizational structures.

informational influence Conformity based on accepting evidence about reality provided by other people. A person goes along with the group because she or he believe the group to be correct. (Deutsch and Gerard, 1955)

in-group Any group whose members have a strong sense of identification with and loyalty to the group and a sense of exclusiveness toward nonmembers.

in-group bias A tendency to favor persons who are members of one's in-group; a tendency to favor one's own group.

innovator In Robert K. Merton's typology of adaptations, an individual who accepts the goals of conventional society but who uses illegitimate mean s to attain them.

institution A concept referring to an interrelated system of roles and norms organized around meeting important social needs or tasks. Examples of institutions are the economy, the family, education, the political order, the military, and religion.

institutional discrimination This concept, sometimes referred to as **structural discrimination,** refers to the everyday practices and policies of organizations, groups, bureaucracies, and other institutions that result in the unequal treatment of an individual or a group based on race, ethnicity, religion, gender, sexual orientation, age, or social class. This form of discrimination is carried out by functionaries who implement the policies and procedures of the organizations to which they belong.

instrumentation effects The confounding effects that repeated measures of the dependent variable can have on research outcomes.

internalization The process whereby social rules, norms, values, and statuses become internal to the individual, part of the individual's sense of self.

internal colonialism A model of race relations wherein colonies—popularly known as ghettos and barrios—are created *within* the mother country; the labor of those residing in these internal colonies is exploited by the majority group. (Blauner)

internal locus of control Perceiving oneself as possessing free will, agency, or choice and as master of one's own life and fate; one believes that one's actions make a difference in one's life.

internal validity The extent to which the results of a research study accurately depict whether the independent variable actually caused the dependent variable.

interval measures Refers to level of measurement that has all the characteristics of ordinal measures (mutual exclusiveness, exhaustiveness, rank-order), plus equal distance between measures.

inverse In reference to a correlation or association, please see **negative relationship.**

involuntary association A specialized formally organized group, membership in which is based on ascription or compulsion and from which members are not free to retire. A conscripted army and prison populations are examples of involuntary associations.

iron law of oligarchy The tendency in modern bureaucracies and in societies, including in democracies, for the few to rule the many. (Robert Michels)

isolation A term indicating that women lead isolated lives, spending most of their time with people who are in significant ways unlike them (children).

judgmental sample A type of non-probability sample. Please see **purposive sample.**

juvenile delinquency In the United States, this is an umbrella term that refers to youth below the age of majority who have been determined (adjudicated) by a family or juvenile court to be minors who (a) have committed an offense that would be crimes were they adults; (b) have been neglected, dependent abused, or abandoned by their parents of other adult guardians; or (c) are have engaged in actions (called **status offenses)** that would be legal were they adults but which are prohibited on the basis of age (e.g., smoking cigarettes, consuming alcohol).

the Kallars A lower caste in India. It arose as a result of persons of various castes eating within sight of each other in a common soup kitchen set up by the British during the great famine of 1866 in India. These persons had engaged in behavior stringently prohibited by the caste system.

Karma The Hindu ideology that one should do one's duty without expecting rewards.

Kashmir A state in Northern India.

Koran The sacred text of the followers of the Islamic faith.

labeling theories A group of theories that concentrates on who gets labeled as a deviant or criminal and on who is in charge of the labeling process.

Kshatriya warrior caste.

Kunbi Original tribal name of the peasants now known as the Patidars.

laissez-faire A leadership style; the leader is minimally involved in the group decision-making process, encourages group members to reach their own decisions, and intervenes only when asked to do so.

language A virtually universal form of human behavior involving symbolic communication through a culturally accepted system of (sound, gesture) patterns that have standardized meanings.

latch key kids Children who come home from school to homes with no caregiver until the parents return from work.

latent function The often-time hidden, unrecognized, and unintended consequences of a social institution, behavior, event, policy, etc.

Latino A person of Hispanic descent. The term emphasizes similarities among apparently diverse aggregates of people, including but not limited to persons who trace their descent to Cuba, Spain, Mexico, Puerto Rico, El Salvador, Brazil, Argentina, Guatemala, etc.

leadership The exercise of influence or power in social collectivities.

legal authority Please see **rational-legal authority,** below.

legal leadership Please see **rational-legal leadership,** below.

levirate A rather common cultural formation in pre-industrial and traditional societies that required a widow to marry the brother of her deceased husband.

libido In Freudian theory, the force of life. Libido's aim is the satisfaction of instinctual drives toward survival, pleasure, and avoidance of pain.

logical validity Please see **face validity,** above.

longitudinal data Data on the same persons or sample across time.

looking-glass self . . . The process whereby one acquires a sense of self (identity): we come to know or to define ourselves by internalizing our perceptions of the reaction of others to us. Coined by Charles Horton Cooley.

loyalty Attraction to groups *qua* groups.

lynching Legally defined as three or more people getting together to kill a man. A term applied to the murdering by hanging of African American men in the South.

machismo An exaggerated sense of masculinity stressing attributes like physical courage, virility, domination of women, and aggressiveness or violence.

macro With reference to levels of analysis, large scale. Macro sociological analysis focuses on large-scale structures, such as large-scale institutions (e.g., work, leisure, the media, family, government, the economy), entire societies, or groupings of societies.

magic A way of knowing. The use of rituals that are believed to be successful in manipulating supernatural forces for a desired result. In magic, if the proper ritual is performed appropriately by the designated functionary the supernatural forces are compelled to do what is asked of them.

malicious In deviance, deriving joy from other peoples' discomfort or suffering.

mammy In the slavery era, African American women who worked as domestics in the plantation house and who served as a nanny for the master's children. The mammy was depicted as fat and jolly. However, she was a strict matriarch when it came to her own family.

manifest destiny The idea that it was the duty of Europeans to civilize the "savage" native.

manifest function The purposive and intended outcomes of a social institution, behavior, event, policy, etc.

marginal distributions The **row marginals** and **column marginals** of a contingency table.

master status A position in a group (status) that overrides in importance and salience the other statuses that an individual (or a group) occupies. For instance, in contemporary America, a felony conviction often is a master status for an individual.

material conditions Pertaining to tangible goods produced by a culture.

material culture All human-made material objects that are passed across generational lines.

matriarchy Describes a family structure in which the mother, or eldest female, is the head of household.

matrilineal descent The determination of descent along the female line of the family.

matrilocal residence This residential pattern occurs when the young couple move s in with the bride's family.

the "me" The socialized part of the self that has internalized the community's notions of appropriate behavior, according to George Herbert Mead.

measure of central tendency Central tendency refers to the grouping of data around the center or middle of a distribution or array of data and, hence, to what is typical or "average" in a data array. There are several measures of the average.

measurement Assignment of symbols, usually numbers, to the properties of objects or events. Accurate and precise measurement is crucial to the way of knowing called the scientific method.

mechanical solidarity Societies held together by similarities, by things they have in common, characterized by a **common conscience.** (Emile Durkheim)

median This measure of central tendency is the "middle" value in an array or series of values; half of the values in the array are above the median, and half are below it.

medical model The **medical model** explains deviance by reference to a medical metaphor. Defects in social structure (or other causes of deviance) are viewed as pathogens which can be eliminated from the body social. Eliminating the agents that cause the "diseases" of crime and deviance will reduce or eliminate the phenomena of deviance and crime from our midst.

meso With reference to levels of analysis, in between micro and macro. Meso sociological analysis focuses on medium-scale structures, such as a voluntary organization (e.g., a particular gang), a bureaucracy (a state-university system of higher-education or a particular university within such a system; a particular Girl-Scout troop), or a system of ritual within a formal organization (e.g., ritual in Alcoholics Anonymous, Synanon, or Gamblers Anonymous).

mesomorphs Individuals whose body build in the middle. These individuals are not skinny like **ecto-morphs,** nor are they plump or fat like **endomorphs.** Mesomorphs are muscular in body build and more likely to be aggressive, assertive, and extroverted action seekers according to William Sheldon and other researchers.

methodology The logic of science as a way of knowing. Within sociology, methodology includes the procedures of empirical investigation, the relationship of theory and research, the process of theory construction, the analysis of the assumptions of sociology and of science.

micro With reference to level of analysis, small scale. Micro sociological analysis focuses on small-scale structures, such as on dynamics in dyads or triads, or the ways in which meanings emerge out of interactions among people.

mindguard A concept coined by Irving Janis to refer to the function of those group members who keep information that would call into question the correctness, wisdom, efficiency, efficacy, ethical quality, or morality of the group's decision or proposed plan of action from being presented to or considered by the group.

minority group A concept that can be applied to any recognizable racial, ethnic, religious, or gender group that has suffered a historical disadvantage as a result of an ingrained pattern of prejudice and discrimination.

mirror-image perceptions Often held by parties in conflict; reciprocally held views where each side attributes similar virtues to itself and similar flaws to the other side. Thus, one side may view itself as peace-loving, fair, moral, and reasonable and the other side as war-mongering, biased, evil, and unreasonable.

mode of production Method of producing goods and services.

monad One person. Not a group.

monogamy The cultural expectation that one man should only be married to one woman at any give time.

moral entrepreneurs Social actors—individuals, groups, or collectivities—who generate and enforce morality in society. (Becker)

moral model A perspective that locates the cause of deviance in external temptations or inner compulsions that sway the weak into deviance.

morbidity Illness, disease.

nationality group A broad based term used to describe citizens of a particular country; the term derives from a person's political allegiance to, or origin from, a particular nation.

natural will Relationships are founded on spontaneous attraction; characteristic of Gemeinschaft. (Ferdinand Toennies)

negative relationship A statistical relationship (also known as a statistical **association** or statistical **correlation)** between two or more variables is called **negative** or **inverse** if as one variable (let us call it "X") *increases* in magnitude or frequency, the other variable (let us call it "Y") *decreases* in magnitude or frequency. In the United States, educational attainment and unemployment are negatively related: the more education one has, the lower the probability that one is unemployed; and, the lower one's level of educational attainment, the greater the probability that one is unemployed.

negative sanction A punishment; a stimulus whose effect is to reduce (or to eliminate) the frequency or magnitude of the behavior with regard to which it is applied.

neolocal residence This residential pattern occurs when a committed couple establishes an independent household.

nominal measures Variables whose attributes have only the characteristics of mutual exclusiveness and exhaustiveness are measured at the nominal level.

non-material culture All human-made material objects that are transmitted across generational lines. Sometimes called *symbolic culture.*

nonprimordial group All groups that are not primordial.

non-probability sample A sample in which it is not possible to determine the probability that each case in the population has of being included in the sample.

nonutilitarian In reference to deviance, this term refers to deviance that does not result in economic gain for the perpetrator.

norm A rule of behavior that is backed by positive and negative sanctions.

normative order The various forms of norms (e.g., folkway, more) and the behaviors related thereto (whose effect or intent is to reinforce, build, undermine, or destroy it and to replace it with something different) constitute normative order. Major paradigms in sociology view normative order, its nature, importance, effects, and manifestations importance quite differently.

nuclear family Consists of two generations, as the husband and wife are considered the first generation and their children constitute the second generation.

Oedipus complex Sexual attraction of boys for their mothers. (Freud)

oligarchy Rule of the many by the few.

operationalize Please see **operationalization.**

operationalization Set of precise, detailed instructions for how a researcher measures concepts and variables.

ordinal measures Have all the characteristics of nominal variables (mutual exclusiveness, exhaustiveness), plus they may be logically rank order from smaller to larger, less to more, younger to older, lower to higher, and so forth.

organic solidarity Solidarity based on a division of labor and interdependence. (Durkheim)

organized crime Criminal activity pursued by an organization for the purpose of economic gain.

out-group All nonmembers of an in-group.

outsider A term coined by Becker to refer to the deviant who is not part of the in-group in society.

paradigm A fundamental framework for making sense out of (and for attributing meaning to) happenings, events, and objects in the social world. Some major or emerging paradigms in American sociology include functionalism, feminist theory, conflict theory, world-systems theory, symbolic interactionism, and postmodernism.

participant observation Field-research method wherein the researcher joins and participates in a group, culture, subculture, or counter-culture, and over time, investigates, in great detail the group's attitudes, values, norms, structure, and views of the world from that group's perspective.

particularism Refers to the orientation of one individual (or social actor) to another on the basis of the special nature of their relationship to each other (for instance,, membership in the same group or category: they both have blue eyes). If a judge sentences a person leniently because the person is her nephew, the judge is applying *particularistic* standards.

patriarchy (1) Describes a family structure in which the father, or eldest male, is the head of household; (2) Social order based on male supraordination: males are superior to females in class, status, and power.

patrilineal descent The determination of descent along the male line of the family.

patrilocal residence This residential pattern occurs when newlyweds move into the groom's father's household.

patrimonial rule Arbitrary, capricious, erratic rule. Characteristic of many feudal social orders, which also are known as urban-agrarian or as agrarian societies. Also known as **patrimonialism.**

patrimonialism Please see **patrimonial rule.**

peer group Primary group composed of persons who have roughly equal status.

People of Color An umbrella term referring to indigenous people; European conquerors called upon a variety of racial theories to justify the subjugation of indigenous people throughout the world.

The personal is political A slogan coined in the 1960s in the United States when women began to speak openly about subjects that had been taboo. Women spoke about issues like rape, incest, domestic and other forms of violence.

philosophy As a way of knowing, philosophy is concerned with the problems of value, ethics, and aesthetics and also with the nature of knowledge, meaning, truth, reality, and the ultimate nature of humans and of humans' relation to the universe.

pluralism (1) A paradigm that assumes that power is widely dispersed in society; or (2) a perspective on relations between culturally different groups that "holds that cultural heterogeneity is a goal that should be achieved by society. This position allows for cultural differences within society so long as these differences do not interfere, or otherwise conflict, with the principal norms and values of the dominant culture." (Gonzales, 1990: 56)

political order The complexes or bundles of norms and roles that serve to maintain social order, to provide the means for changing the legal or administrative systems, and to exercise the power to compel conformity to the existing structure of authority. Also known as imperative order.

politics of reality Albert Quinney used this term to describe the dominance of the upper classes by means of which they define and construct social reality.

polyandry A rare form of polygamy that allows a woman to have two or more husbands.

polygamy Plural marriage in which one person is allowed to have two or more spouses at the same time.

polygynous nuclear family This arrangement allows a man to take several wives and to provide for any offspring resulting from these relationships; the wives are expected to share the economic and social responsibilities of marriage.

polygyny The cultural practice that allows a man to have two or more wives at the same time; a form of plural marriage; a male having more than one wife at a time.

population The total number of cases with a given characteristic or characteristics, or all members of a given class or set.

positive relationship A statistical relationship (also known as a statistical **association** or statistical **correlation**) between two or more variables is called **positive** or **direct** if as one variable (let us call it "X") *increases* in magnitude or frequency, so too does the other variable (let us call it "Y"); as X *decreases* in magnitude or frequency so too does Y. In the United States, educational attainment and income are positively correlated.

positive sanction A reward; a stimulus whose effect is to increase the frequency or magnitude of the behavior with regard to which it is applied.

positivism A term introduced into sociology by Auguste Comte. A philosophic position that science only can deal with observable entities perceived directly by the senses (sight, hearing, touch, etc.). According to positivism, knowledge must be derived only through sensory experience. The methods of the physical sciences are considered the only valid means for obtaining genuine knowledge. Please see **scientific method.**

power The ability to get one's way even in face of opposition (Max Weber).

pragmatism Philosophical view that stresses that concepts and actions should be analyzed and evaluated in terms of their practical consequences. In this view, actions and concepts designed to accomplish a desired goal are appropriate by reason of the goal they are designed to accomplish and need no theoretical rationale.

predestination The idea that everything that happens on the earth is pre-ordained.

prejudice Any unfavorable or negative attitude directed toward any person or group based on a set of assumed characteristics.

primary conflict Occurs when the norms of two or more cultures clash. (Thorsten Sellin)

primary deviance Engaging in deviant behavior that is not responded to by persons in positions of formal or informal authority.

primary group A group with common standards of behavior or values and direct, frequent contact among its members. Its members engage in a wide variety of activities with each other and many aspects of each individual's personality are involved" in her or his relations with the members of the group. Relations among members are *ends* in themselves, not means to ends. Members of a primary group are interested in and know about a wide range of aspects of each others' lives and they have a broad range of mutual rights and duties. In other words, the relationship is *diffuse* The family, the rural community, and the small old-fashioned neighborhood in large cities or in small towns are examples of a primary These groups are considered as primary because they have the earliest and the most profound influence on a person's socialization and development.

primary relationships With regard to the family, these relationships exist in the nuclear family. Examples include the relationships that occur between fathers and daughters, mothers and sons, and brothers and sisters.

primary socialization Socialization that occurs during the first few years of life.

primogeniture Refers to a system of inheritance in which all of the property and titles of the father are given over to his first born son.

primordial group A group that comes first in our experience—family, race, ethnicity, community, territorial group, etc.

probabilistic reasoning Reasoning based on probability not certainty. "Probability" refers to the likelihood that out of a specific number of mutually exclusive and equally likely events a given result will occur. For example, in a deck of 52 playing cards, the probability that you will select the Ace of spades—given that there is one Ace of spades in a deck of 52 cards—is $1/52 = .0192$. You have slightly less than 2 chances out of 100 or about 1 chance in 50 of selecting the Ace of spades.

Probabilistic reasoning and probabilistic knowledge then are *not* based on certainty but on probability. This type of reasoning and knowledge enables us to say that *if X occurs, then Y is more (or less) likely to occur.* Thus, "If I study diligently and consistently for my Chemistry exam, I will be more likely to get a good grade on the test" is a probability statement. So, too is the statement "If I stop smoking tobacco, I will be less likely to get lung cancer." Probabilistic reasoning does *not* allow us to say that if X occurs Y will occur or even that Y will probably occur.

probability sample A sample drawn in accordance with probability theory.

probation In the United States, a criminal or juvenile-justice sentence whereby an alleged or adjudicated juvenile or adult offender is free to remain in the community, provided that the person meets certain conditions of behavior (e.g., remains drug free, does not associate with known felons).

projection In Freudian theory, a variety of **defense mechanism** whereby one attributes to another a property of oneself; thereby, one can blame the other person instead of feeling guilty oneself.

proletariat Those who sell their labor to the bourgoisie, according to Karl Marx.

prolocutorship A person assumes the position of spokesperson for an alleged common interest. A prolocutor is not necessarily an appointed or elected official of a formal organization, although such a person may also be a prolocutor.

proselytize Attempting to convert people to a belief.

public degradation ceremony A public process that results in stigma for an individual.

pull factors Factors that attract immigrants to a country.

purposive sample A type of non-probability sample. Also known as a *judgmental sample.* The researcher selects cases to be included in the sample on the basis of her/his own *judgment* about which ones will be most representative or useful. A *focus-group* could be used to generate a menu of cases to be selected as a sample.

push factors Factors that induce immigrants to leave their homeland.

quantitative analysis Logical and statistical techniques used to break something down into its constituent parts for individual study, and for drawing inferences based on precise measurement, and enumeration.

quantitative data Data in numerical form.

quota sample A type of non-probability sample. The researcher selects cases to be included in the sample on the basis characteristics specified in advance (e.g., age, sex, ethnicity, social class, political-party affiliation), so that the total sample will have the same distribution of characteristics as is presumed to exist in the target population.

race Please see **racial group,** below.

racial group A group or aggregate defined on the basis actual or imputed physical differences, such as facial features, the color and structure of the hair, skin color, and body shape and size (Gonzales, 1990: 6).

racism A form of inequality wherein one racial group dominates another and legitimates this domination with ideologies that proclaim that the **majority group** is superior physically, morally, intellectually, etc Racism may be individual or institutional.

radical nonintervention A term introduced by Edwin M. Schur which refers to intervening as little as possible with deviants so that negative labeling does not occur.

random assignment In an experiment, research subjects are assigned randomly to one of two experimental conditions: to the experimental group, wherein they are exposed to the independent variable, or to the control group, where they are not exposed to the independent variable. Each research subject has the same chance of being assigned to one condition as to the other. Also known as **randomization.**

randomization Please see **random assignment,** above.

random sample A type of probability sample. A sample in which every case in the population has an equal probability of being included in the sample. Sometimes called simple random sample.

ratio measures Refers to a level of measurement that has all the characteristics of interval measures (mutual exclusiveness, exhaustiveness, rank-order, equal distance between measures) plus an absolute or true zero.

rationalism Philosophical doctrine that reason and logical thinking are the only basis of valid knowledge. Rationalism thus rejected religious revelation as a valid way of knowing. It also rejected empirical investigation and experience as sources of genuine knowledge. Not to be confused with **rationalization.**

rationalization (1) In Weberian theory, the substitution of explicit formal, written rules and procedures for earlier spontaneous, arbitrary, capricious, erratic approaches; the development of greater standardization, coordination, and consistency in organizational structure. Weber saw this as the master trend of Western capitalist society. Not to be confused with **rationalism.** (2) In Freudian theory, a variety of **defense mechanism,** an intellectual rationale or excuse for what was a freely chosen action.

rational-legal authority Legitimate power the legitimationos which rests on a system of formal laws designed to regulate behavior rationally and to attain specified goals. Also called **legal authority.** (Weber)

rational-legal leadership The exercise of influence in human collectivities on the bais of a system of formal laws designed to regulate behavior rationally and to attain specified goals. Also called **legal leadership.**

raw score In a cell of a statistical table, a score that reveals how much of the characteristic of interest is possessed by an individual or by an event, object, etc.; any datum that provides an absolute, not relative, assessment of one's position on a quantitative variable.

reaction formation One's anxiety about something (e.g., Susie is attracted romantically to someone who has already spurned her) is kept at bay by overtly assuming the opposite (e.g., "I dislike/hate/am indifferent to that person."). This is a brittle, fragile defense unless buttressed with a lot of supports.

reappropriation Used in a political sense, this term means to take back that which had been taken from one. For instance, to take one's rightful place or to rewrite history from the point of view of previously oppressed groups.

rebel In Robert K. Merton's typology of adaptations, an individual who rejects the goals and means of conventional society and who replaces them with others.

reconstruction Pertaining to the period after the Civil War. In 1861 African Americans were promised political emancipation. During the years 1861-1880, some scholars argue that **black reconstruction** was the reconstruction of servitude.

reduction of tension function With regard to deviance, the notion here is that deviance works as a safety valve to drain off societal contradictions and problems.

reference group A group or social category whose members we use to evaluate our own behavior. Reference groups serve three functions: (1) normative, in that they let the individual know what behaviors, attitudes, beliefs, and values are appropriate; (2) evaluative, in that they provide a standard of comparison by means of which an individual may reach an appraisal of her/his abilities and behavior; and (3) identity, in that an individual has some sense of identity with the reference group, even if the individual does not belong to it and even if the individual's conception of the group and its values is inaccurate. Coined by Herbert Hyman.

regression to the mean The tendency for extreme scores to move toward the average (mean); a source of causal invalidity.

reinforced cleavage Multiple lines of group membership are superimposed; the opposite of overlapping social circles. Makes for more extreme conflict when social conflict does erupt.

reliability A measuring instrument and research method have reliability to the extent that the same or similar results are obtained when another researcher uses the same or similar measuring instrument on the same or similar sample or population.

religion A way of knowing; religion is found in virtually all societies and is viewed as differing from magic in its relationship between the supplicant and the deity (the supernatural). In magic, the petitioner is viewed as being in control: If the shaman performs the appropriate ritual correctly, the supernatural forces are viewed as compelled to grant what is requested. In contrast, in religion, the deity is viewed as being in control: The petitioner or the shaman (priest, mullah, rabbi, etc.) may perform the appropriate ritual correctly and yet the god(s) may refuse to grant the request. In religion, the god(s) answer, but their answer may be "No."

repression In Freudian theory, a **defense mechanism** whose aim is to prevent an idea, wish, anxiety, impulse, image, or other mental element from becoming conscious; and rejecting a mental element from consciousness to unconsciousness.

repulsion There is social distance between castes. The upper castes repel any contact with the lower castes.

research Systematic and objective study of a problem for the purpose of deriving general principles. In research, the investigation is guided by, or responds to, previously collected data.

residual deviance A term coined by Thomas Scheff to refer to the violation of the norms of everyday social interaction.

resocialization Socialization that represents a radical change in the person, that tears down one's old world view, beliefs, values, and conceptions of self, and replaces them with a new ones.

retreatist In Robert K. Merton's typology of adaptations, an individual who rejects the goals and means of conventional society.

retribution A philosophy of punishment based on general principles of ethics, whereby the state issues punishment if people violate the law. The notion is that such punishment is due and proper if one violates the law.

rite of passage A symbolic event or ritual that signals a move from one phase of life to another.

ritual A culturally standardized set of actions that have symbolic meaning and that are performed by persons and on occasions prescribed by tradition; the acts and words that comprise a ritual vary little if at all from one occasion to another.

role Expectations of behavior. A role attaches to a status.

role conflict Incompatibility *between* two or more roles.

role distance Detaching the performer from the role she or he is performing. (Erving Goffman)

role playing Acting in a manner that one perceives as appropriate for a role one is occupying.

role strain Incompatibility of the expectations *within* a role.

role taking Taking the point of view or attitudes of another person by imaginatively perceiving oneself as the other person, in order to be able to anticipate that person's actual or likely behavior.

row In a statistical table, the horizontal listing of data in a series of categories, of which have a common classification.

row caption A title that describes the common classification of the data listed in the rows of a statistical table.

row heading Please see **row caption.**

row marginals In a contingency table, the raw and percent frequency distributions found along the row edges or margins of the table.

salvation In reference to religious beliefs, the deity granting peace and harmony.

sample Part of a population.

Sanskritization Adoption of a Brahmanical life style, especially their ritual observations.

sati Customary practise in India where women immolated themselves on their deceased husband's funeral pyre.

schizophrenia A mental disorder wherein one suffers a major break with reality. One hears voices others do not hear and sees things others do not see. Frequently this disorder is accompanied by delusions of grandeur. For instance, one thinks one that one is Napoleon or Stalin's daughter or that one owns the university that one is attending.

science A way of knowing that attempts to develop general principles about a finite range of phenomena on the basis of empirical observations made through the senses and so stated that they can be tested—and either rejected or accepted—by any competent person.

scientific knowledge Knowledge gained by means of the scientific method

scientific method Building a body of scientific knowledge through observation, generalization, and verification. It consists of the following steps: (1) problem definition;(2) statement of the research problem in terms of a particular theoretical framework and relating the research problem to findings of previous research; (3) Statement of research problem as an hypothesis or as hypotheses; (4) Selecting an appropriate methodology or methodologies; (5) data collection; (6) data analysis: conclusion regarding the research hypothesis, and relating the conclusion(s) to the original body of theory with which the study began.

secondary analysis The use of an available data resource by a researcher to study a problem different than that for which the data originally were collected.

secondary conflict A term developed by Thorsten Sellin to refer to conflict that arises out of the evolution of a single culture. There are many examples of secondary conflict. The issues of abortion, the death penalty, a ban on guns, welfare reform, and views on homosexuality are a few examples of secondary conflict in the United States.

secondary group A non-primary group. Relations among secondary-group members are (1) segmental—members know each other only in a limited range of roles; and (2) instrumental, a means to an end (e.g., You say "Hi" to Sally not because you like her but because you want to borrow her lecture notes).

secondary relationships Encompass those consanguineous ties that include first cousins, aunts, uncles, and grandparents.

secondary socialization Socialization that occurs after the first few years of life.

sect A small, voluntary exclusive group that demands total commitment from its followers, emphasizes its separateness from the vulgar world, and views itself as possessing esoteric knowledge unavailable to nonmembers.

segregation The physical and social separtation of different racial and ethnic groups.

self Identity; a conception of who one is and of who one is not.

self-control A social construct; the individual considers others and actively directs her- or himself in relation to those others.

self-handicapping An ego-defense mechanism; creating a ready excuse for failure.

self-serving bias The tendency for people to perceive *themselves* in favorable terms.

serial monogamy Describes the tendency of people to remarry following divorce. Therefore they have two or more marriages in sequence.

sex roles Gender based behavioral modes and expectations.

sexism An to an individual's or a group's (1) prejudicial attitudes and discriminatory behaviors towards people because of their sex or gender; or (2) institutional practices that subordinate people on the basis of sex or gender. Although sexism is less overt in this country than it was, say, thirty years ago, it is by no means absent.

sexy Jezebel A stereotype about African American women portraying them as seductresses who can never be raped because they are always ready for sex.

shaman A priest or healer (doctor) in hunting and gathering societies.

Shudras Lowest caste in traditional India. Members of this caste engage in menial tasks that are considered extremely polluting. Hence, members of this caste are polluted and "untouchable."

sign A cue or stimulus that is associated with, or that evokes, a response to something else that is not physically present at the time.

silence A concept in women's scholarship signifying the subordinate status of women as a group. The concept refers to the coercing of women to keep quiet, a form of social control which perpetuates injustice and oppression.

simple extended family Consists of the grandparents, their unmarried children, married sons and their spouses, and their children.

simple nuclear family This family structure has children and greater economic resources at its disposal and they can afford to move out on their own.

snowball sample A type of non-probability sample. Each person interviewed is asked to suggest a few other people for interviewing. Often used in field-research.

social category A plurality of persons who do not form a group but who do have at least one similar social characteristic or status in common, e.g., sex, age, race. Examples of social categories would be females, males, working women, African Americans, whites, computer scientists, the unemployed, missionaries, teenagers, etc. Synonyms are **aggregate** and **social aggregate.**

social conflict Conscious struggle between groups (or social categories, social aggregates, institutions, etc.) over resources.

social conflict analysis Refers to a group of theories that emphasize the inequity of power among different groups and social categories (including social classes). According to these theories, the structure of society is geared to protect the interests of the rich and powerful.

social construction The manner in which societal institutions create gender differences based on traditional social practices and create images that keep women in subordinate positions based on gender affiliation.

social dynamics Social change (Auguste Comte)

social fact A social phenomenon; it is distinct from an individual phenomenon, from a biological phenomenon, and from a psychological phenomenon, according to Emile Durkheim. Social facts, according to Durkheim, should be explained only by other social facts.

social form German sociologist Georg Simmel distinguishes between the *form* and the *content* of social phenomena. The *forms* of social interaction—e.g., intimacy and distance; subordination, superordination; conflict and cooperation; centralization and decentralization—are the proper domain of sociological analysis, according to Simmel. As with Weber's concept of **ideal type,** the social forms found in the real world are never pure. Thus, conflict as well as cooperation frequently are found in a troubled marital relationship. "Pure" forms are **ideal types**—constructs that are never realized in the real world but which nonetheless are useful tools of analysis.

social organization Please see **social structure,** below.

social ostracism Exclusion from mainstream societal activities.

social statics Complexes of norms (institutions) or "parts" of society that are vital parts of society and that provide for stability and order in society. A term used by Auguste Comte.

social stratification Method by which societies allocate scarce yet widely-valued resources.

social structure Stable and recurring patterns of social relations. Also known as social organization.

social type A consensual or group-generated conception of a **role** (e.g., stranger, social climber, sexual predator, redneck, the renegede, the "poor," etc.) that is not fully apprehended by formal definitions. You cannot look up the definition of a particular social type in a dictionary and thereby receive the social information conveyed by the concept. Social types are road maps to structures of role expectations that otherwise are largely invisible. Social actors need to learn them in order to be able to participate effectively and insightfully in groups (Klapp, 1958; Coser, 1977: 182).

socialization Process whereby we learn roles and norms, develop the capacity to conform to them, and develop a conception of self.

society A group of people with a common culture who occupy a particular territorial area, have a sense of unity, and who regard themselves as different than non-members.

sociolinguistics The study of how language varies by social contexts.

sociological model With regard to deviance, a viewpoint that stresses that deviance is defined by society, culture, and the period of time in which it is situated.

sociology The scientific study of how and why we form groups, live together in small ones (like our families) and in larger ones (like the military) and it encompasses the functioning of whole societies and the social, economic, cultural, political and technological relationships within, between, and among societies.

soft determinism With regard to an understanding of human behavior, this viewpoint stresses that human behavior is influenced by forces external to the individual and by the free will of the individual.

solidarity The sense among members of a collectivity that those persons who are members are different, for better or for worse, that persons who are not members.

solidary order The various forms of solidarity (cohesion) and the behaviors related thereto (that reinforce, build, undermine, or destroy it) constitute solidary order. Major paradigms in sociology view solidary order and its importance quite differently.

sororal polygyny Occurs when a man is married to two or more sisters.

spoiled identity Stigma resulting from the labeling process leads to regative responses from people.

spurious A relationship between two variables is said to be spurious when it is actually accounted for (caused by) the relationship of the two variables to a third. For instance, the relationship between the number of fire trucks present at a fire and the amount of monetary damage is spurious: the cause of both variables is size of fire.

statistical association (or **statistical correlation, statistical relationship**) The strength (e.g., strong, medium, weak) and direction of a relationship between two or more variables. There are many measures of statistical association.

status The term *status* has more than one meaning in sociology. (1) Position in a group. In this sense, power and roles attach to a status. In the sociological view, one wields power because one is the incumbent of a position to which power attaches. (2) deference, esteem, honor (Max Weber).

status offense In juvenile justice in the United States, an action that would be legal if one were an adult but which is prohibited on the basis of age.

stem family A family pattern which, while based on a nuclear family structure, also includes one or more relatives who are considered part of the family.

stigma An attribution, a social definition, that is discrediting for a person or group.

Stockholm syndrome, the Hostages identify with, or experience feelings of empathy toward, the hostage takers and displace their frustration and aggression toward the authorities.

Stonewall riot Named after a nightclub, the Stonewall Inn, in Greenwich Village, New York. In 1969, gay patrons at the Stonewall Inn resisted arrest by police officers, thereby setting off a gay civil-rights movement in this country.

stratified sample A type of probability sample. Useful method of sampling a population with great diversity, providing that you have access to sampling frames for each of the sub-groups in the population. The purpose of stratified sampling is to divide the population into homogeneous sub-sets, and then within each sub-set randomly to select appropriate numbers of elements. In diverse populations, this sampling method obtains a greater degree of representativeness.

structural discrimination Please see **individual discrimination,** above.

structural functinalism Sometimes called consensus theory. Refers to a group of theories that suggests that society has as structure that fulfills a purpose. These theories assume that there is consensus in society about norms, values, and laws.

structural view Perceiving social structure as consisting of "parts," and perceiving the parts as interrelated.

subculture The more or less different folkways, mores, material and non-material traits developed by a group within a society.

subjectivity In women's scholarship this term refers to women's personal experiences and how they see and interpret their situations and lives.

sublimation Diverting the energy of the **id** to ends no longer sexual and no longer aggressive.

subterranean values Values that tend to be hidden from persons living in the conventional social order but which exist side by side with mainstream values.

substructure The economic foundation of society. (Karl Marx)

superego According to Freud, the part of our personality that contains notions of right and wrong that we have internalized from our significant others who live within a particular historical period and a specific culture; our conscience.

superstructure All parts of society *other than* the economy. Includes arts, religion, the state, government, social classes, gender relations, law, norms, the exchange order, politics, the family, education, and so forth. The *superstructure* is viewed as caused by the economic **substructure.** (Karl Marx)

supportive social systems Parts of social structure that provide individuals with social support and that positively integrate individuals into communities and into their society. A term from Emile Durkheim.

survey research A quantitative field-research method wherein a researcher systematically (1) gathers data about individuals or collectivities through the use of an interview or questionnaire administered to a population or a sample, (2) analyzes the resulting data through statistical analyses, and (3) interprets the results.

survivalists A group of individuals who believe in the imminent mass destruction of the country by atomic war.

symbol A sign that evokes a uniform social response form one or more audiences; anything that stands for (represents) something else.

symbolic interactionism This paradigm stresses the importance of language, gestural communication, and role taking in the formation of the mind, self, and society. It also tends to stress the importance of subjective understanding as a way of knowing.

synthesis The emergence of something new; the third stage of the dialectical process, according to Marx.

systematic sample A type of probability sample. Every Kth element in the sampling frame is chosen for inclusion in the sample. If the sampling frame is a list of all 6,000 students enrolled at a particular college or university, and you want to have a sample of 300, then : 6,000 divided by 300 = 20. You select every 20th element for inclusion in your sample.

It is a good idea to get a random start. So, pick a random number from 1 to ten. Use that number as the first case, and then select every 20th person following it. This method technically is termed a *systematic sample with a random start.*

techniques of neutralization Procedures that people use to place one's conscience on "hold," so that one may break norms; afterwards, one brings one's conscience back online and resumes living in the conventional moral order.

technology The segment of culture, including knowledge and tools, used by humans (and by some non-human primates) to manipulate the physical environment in order to attain a desired practical result.

terrorism The use of violent acts or the use of the threat of violence to create fear, dread, alarm, or coercion, usually against government, among those who identify with the victims, in order to achieve objectives (which frequently are political in nature).

tertiary relationships Include those blood ties that extend to second and third cousins, great aunts, great uncles, and great grandparents.

tertius gaudens "Divide and conquer," or "the joy of the third." Already existing cleavages both between and among the constituent groups in a population are reinforced and accentuated, thereby making it far more likely that the various groups would fight among themselves rather than against those who actually are dominating and exploiting them.

theodicy Religious explanation of the relationship between humans and the god(s)

theory A set of interrelated principles and definitions that conceptually organize selected aspects of the empirical world in a systematic fashion.

thesis The way things are, the status quo. According to Karl Marx, the first stage of the dialectical process.

total percents In a contingency table, the percentages in the marginals sometimes are called total percents because they are derived by dividing each frequency by the total sample size and multiplying the result by 100.

traditonal authority Legitimate power based on custom or tradition.

traditional leadership The exercise of influence based on custom or tradition.

Treaty of Guadalupe Hildago This treaty (1848) which ended the war between the United States and Mexico forced Mexico to relinquish vast territories in the Southwest.

triad A group consisting of three members.

tribe A preliterate community or collection of communities occupying a common geographical area and having a similar language and culture.

ultimate attribution error Please see **group-serving bias,** above.

universalism Refers to the orientation of one individual (or social actor) to another on the basis of generalized standards or principles of behavior rather than on any special relationship that may exist between them. If a special relationship exists between persons in a situation defined as appropriately universalistic, the persons are expected to ignore the particularistic relationship.

unobtrusive methods Research methods that do not intrude on the phenomena being studied.

urban-agrarian Type of society in which no more than about ten percent of the total population lives in cities and in which the rest of the population are agricultural laborers tied to and dominated by an urban elite; on all dimensions important in the study of stratified inequality, the most unequal of types of societies known to social and behavioral scientists. (Gideon Sjoberg, Robert Redfield)

validity The correspondence between what a measuring instrument is supposed to measure and what it actually measures. To the extent that a measuring instrument measures what it is supposed to measure, to that extent it has validity.

value An abstract, generalized conception of what is desirable, to which members of a group feel a strong, positively-toned commitment and which serves as a standard for selecting and evaluating concrete means, goals, rules, and actions.

value inconsistency Incompatibility or conflict between or among values.

variable A characteristic that has different degrees of magnitude or different categories. Thus, sex or gender is a variable, whose categories are male and female; education is a variable, and one may have different amounts of it.

verstehen Subjective understanding; empathetic understanding. A term used by Max Weber.

victimless crime Refers to consensual crime that lacks a complaining participant. (Edwin Schur)

violent crime According to the Uniform Crime Report of the Federal Bureau of Investigation, a crime against persons involving violence or threat of violence.

voluntary association (1) Reaching out beyond a primordial membership to establish common cause; a non-primordial form of solidarity. (2) A specialized formally organized group, membership in which is a matter of choice and from which members are free to resign.

wage gap differential In gender, ethnic, and race relations, this concept refers to the fact that minorities and women often are paid less than members of the majority group for doing the same type of work.

welfare queen A stereotype about African American and other minority women who have children and live on welfare. The condition allegedly is passed on from generation to generation from mother to daughter. Studies show this is not true.

we-ness As in a sense of "we-ness." Please see **solidarity,** above.

white collar crime "Crime" engaged in by affluent people of high moral respectability in the course of their legitimate occupations. (Sutherland)

work-restriction norms Informal rules (norms) that workers develop that seem to help them cope with difficulties on the job; sometimes called *gold-bricking* by out-group members.

xenophobia A fear of strangers or foreigners.

Yanomamo An ancient hunting and gathering people in South America.

References

Aafke, Komter, and Vollebergh, Wilma, "Giftgiving and the Emotional Significance of Family and Friends," *Journal of Marriage and the Family,* Vol. 59, (August) 1997: 747- 757.

Aaker, Jennifer L, and Maheswaran, Durairaj, "The Effect of Cultural Orientation on Persuasion," *Journal of Consumer Research,* Vol. 24, (December) 1997: 315-328.

ABC News, February 2, 1995.

Abbey, A., "Acquaintance Rape and Alcohol Consumption on College Campuses: How are They Linked?" *Journal of American College Health,* Vol. 39, 1991a: 165-169.

Abbey, A., "Misperceptions of Friendly Behavior as Sexual Interest: A Survey of Naturally Occurring Incidents," *Psychology of Women Quarterly,* Vol. 11, 1987: 173-194.

Abbey, A., "Misperception as an Antecedent of Acquaintance Rape: A Consequence of Ambiguity in Communication Between Women and Men," in A. Parrot (Ed.), *Acquaintance Rape* (New York: John Wiley, 1991b).

Abercrombie, Nicholas, Hill, Stephen, and Turner, Bryan S., *The Penguin Dictionary of Sociology* (Third edition) (London: Penguin Books, 1994).

Acker, Joan, Berry, Kate, and Esseveld, Joke, "Objectivity and Truth: Problems in Doing Feminist Research," *Women's Studies International Forum,* Vol. 6, 1983: 423-435.

Acuña, Rodolfo, *Occupied America: A History of Chicanos* (Third edition) (New York: Harper & Row, 1988)

Adam, B., "Structural Foundations of the Gay World," in S. Seidman (Ed.), *Queer Theory/Sociology* (Massachusetts: Blackwell Publishers Inc., 1996), pp. 111-126.

Adams, Susan; Kuebli, Janet; Boyle, Patricia A., and Fivush, Robyn, "Gender Differences in Parent-Child Conversations about Past Events: A Longitudinal Investigation," *Sex Roles,* Vol. 33, Nos. 5/6, 1995: 309-323.

Adler, J., "The Tutor Age," *Newsweek,* March 30, 1998: 47-50.

Adorno, Theodore W., E. Frenkel, E., Levinson, D.J., and Sanford, R.N, *The Authoritarian Personality* (New York: W.W. Norton & Company, 1950).

Ainsworth, Mary D., "Attachment: Retrospect and Prospect," in C.M. Parkes and J. Stevenson (Eds.), *The Place of Attachment in Human Behavior* (London: Tavistock, 1982).

Ainsworth, Mary D., "Attachments Beyond Infancy," *American Psychologist,* Vol. 44, 1989: 709-716.

Alba, Richard, "Ethnicity," in in Edgar F. Borgatta and Marie L. Borgatta, (Eds.), *Encyclopedia of Sociology* (New York: Macmillan and Company, 1992), pp. 547-584.

Almaguer, Tomas, *Racial Fault Lines: The Historical Origins of White Supremacy in California* (Berkeley: University of California Press, 1994).

Almirol, Edwin B., *Ethnic Identity and Social Negotiation: A Study of a Filipino Community in California* (New York: AMS Press, 1985).

Alwin, D.F., "Historical Changes in Parental Orientations to Children," in N. Mandell (Ed.), *Sociological Studies of Child Development,* Vol. 3 (Greenwich, CT: JAI Press, 1990).

American Sociological Association, *Code of Ethics* (Washington, D.C.: American Sociological Association, 1989).

Amory, Cleveland, *The Proper Bostonians* (New York: E.P. Dutton, 1947).

Amott, Teresa, and Matthaei, Julie, *Race Gender, and Work: A Multicultrueal Economic History of Women in the United States* (Boston: South End Press, 1991).

Anderson, Elija, *Streetwise: Race, Class, and Change in an Urban Community* (Chicago: The University of Chicago Press, 1990).

Anderson, Kristin L., "Gender, Status, and Domestic Violence: An Integration of Feminist and Family Violence Approaches," *Journal of Marriage and the Family,* Vol. 59, (August) 1997: 655-669.

Anderson, M.L.C., "High Juvenile Crime Rate: A Look at Mentoring as a Preventive Strategy," *Criminal Law Bulletin,* Volume 30, 1994: 1.

Andersen, Margret, *Thinking About Women: Sociological Perspectives on Sex and Gender* (New York: McMillan Publishing Co., 1993).

Anderson, M.L., *Thinking About Women* (Fourth edition) (Boston: Allyn and Bacon, 1997).

Anderson, Perry, *Lineages of the Absolutist State* (London: New Left Books, 1974).

Anderson, Perry, *Passages from Antiquity to Feudalism* (London: New Left Books, 1974).

Anson, Ofra and Anson, Jon, "Surviving the Holidays: Gender Differences in Mortality in the Context of Three Moslem Holidays," *Sex Roles,* Vol. 37, Nos. 5/6, 1997: 381-399.

Anthony, T., Cooper, C., and Mullen, B., "Cross-Racial Facial Identification: A Social-Cognitive Interaction," *Personality and Social Psychology Bulletin,* Vol. 18, 1992: 296-301.

Antonio, Robert J. and Glassma, Ronald, *A Weber-Marx Dialogue* (Lawrence: The University of Kansas Press, 1985).

Anzaldua, G., *Borderlands* (San Francisco, CA: Aunt Lute Books, 1987).

Archer, D., Iritani, B., Kimes, D. B., and Barrios, M., "Face-ism: Five Studies of Sex Differences in Facial Prominence," *Journal of Personality and Social Psychology,"* Vol. 45, 1983: 725-735.

Archer. S. L., "A Feminist's Approach to Identity Research," in G. R. Adams, T.P. Gullotta, and R. Montemayor (Eds.), *Adolescent Identity Formation* (Newbury Park, CA: Sage Publications, 1992).

Argyle, Michael, *Bodily Communicatrion* (Second edition) (London: Methuen, 1988).

Argyle, Michael, *Cooperation: The Basis of Sociability* (New York: Routledge, 1991).

Argyle, Michael, *The Psychology of Happiness* (London: Methuen, 1987).

Argyle, Michael, *The Psychology of Social Class* (London: Routledge, 1994).

Argyle, Michael, *The Social Psychology of Everyday Life* (London: Routledge, 1992).

Argyle, Michael, *The Social Psychology of Work* (Second edition) (Harmondsworth, England: Penguin, 1989).

Argyris, Chris, *Integrating the Individual and the Organization* (New York: Wiley, 1964).

Argyris, Chris, *Knowledge for Action: A Guide to Overcoming Barriers to Organizational Change* (San Francisco: Jossey-Bass, 1993).

Argyris, Chris, *Overcoming Organizational Defenses: Facilitating Organizational Learning* (Boston: Allyn and Bacon, 1990).

Argyris, Chris, *Personality and Organization: The Conflict Between System and the Individual* (New York: Garland, 1987).

Argyris, Chris, *Some Causes of Organizational Ineffectiveness Within the Department of State* (Washington, D.C.: U.S. Government Printing Office, 1967) (Center for International Systems Research, Occasional Papers, Number 2, U.S. Department of State, Department of State Publication 8180).

Argyris, Chris, *Strategy, Change, and Defensive Routines* (Boston: Pitman, 1985).

Argyris, Chris, *Understanding Organizational Behavior* (Homewood, IL: Dorsey Press, 1960).

Aries, Phillip, *Centuries of Childhood: A Social History of Family Life* (New York: Random House, 1960).

Aron, Arthur, Paris, Meg, Aron, Elaine N., "Falling In Love: Prospective Studies of Self-Concept Change," *Journal of Personality and Social Psychology,* Vol. 69 (1995): 1102-112.

Aron, R., *Main Currents in Sociological Thought* (Vol. I) (New York: Frederick Ungar Publishing Company, 1976).

Aronson, Ronald, *After Marxism* (New York: Guilford Press, 1995).

Aschaffengurg, Karen, and Maas, Ineke, "Cultural and Educational Careers: the Dynamics of Social Reproduction," *American Sociological Review,* Vol. 62, 1997 (August) 1997: 573- 587.

Aseltine, Robert H. Jr., "A Reconsideration of Parental and Peer Influences on Adolescent Deviance," *Journal of Health and Social Behavior,* Vol. 36, (June) 1995: 103-121.

Ashley, Joann, *Hospitals, Paternalism, and the Role of the Nurse* (New York: Teachers College Press, 1977).

Ashworth, Tony, *Trench Warfare, 1914-18: The Live and Let Live System* (London: Holmes and Meier, 1980).

Babad, E., Bernieri, F., and Rosenthal, R., "Students as Judges of Teachers' Verbal and Nonverbal Behavior," *American Educational Research Journal,* Vol. 28, 1991: 211-234.

Babbie, Earl, *The Practice of Social Research* (Seventh edition) (Belmont, CA: Wadsworth Publishing Company, 1995).

Bachman, Ronet, *Death and Violence on the Reservation: Homicide, Family Violence, and Suicide in American Indian Populations* (New York: Auburn House, 1992).

Back, Les, *New Ethnicities and Urban Culture: Racisms and Multiculture in Young Lives* (New York: St. Martin's Press, 1996).

Bacon, Jean, *Life Lines: Community, Family and Assimilation among Asian Indian Immigrants* (New York: Oxord University Press, 1996).

Bahr, Howard M., Chadwick, B.A, and Strauss, J.H., "Discrimination Against Urban Indians in Seattle," *The Indian Historian*, Vol. 5, No. 4, 1972: 4-11.

Bakalian, Anny, *Armenian-Americans: From Being to Feeling Armenian* (New Brunswick, NJ: Transaction, 1993).

Bakan, Abigail, and Stasiulis, Daiva, "Making the Match: Dopmestic Placement Agencies and the Racialization of Women's Household Work," *Signs*, Vol. 20, 1995: 303-335.

Baker, Robert, "'Pricks' and 'Chicks': A Plea for 'Persons,'" in Paula S. Rothenberg (Ed.), *Racism and Sexism: An Integrated Study* (New York: St. Martin's Press, 1988), pp. 280-295.

Bales, Robert, *Interaction Process Analysis* (Cambridge, MA: Addison-Wesley, 1950).

Baltzell, E. Digby, *Philadelphia Gentlemen: The Making of a National Upper Class* (Philadelphia: University of Pennsylvania Press, 1979).

Baltzell, E. Digby, *The Protestant Establishment: Aristocracy and Caste in America* (New York: Vintage Books, 1968).

Banks, Dwayne A., "The Economics of Death? A Descriptive Study of the Impact of Funeral and Cremation Costs on U.S. Households," *Death Studies*, Vol. 22, No. 3, (April/May) 1998: 269-285.

Bankston III, Carl L., Caldas, Stephen J., and Zhou, Min, "The Academic Achievement of Vietnamese American Students: Ethnicity as Social Capital," *Sociological Focus*, Vol. 30, No. 1, (February) 1997: 1-16.

Banton, Michael, *Racial and Ethnic Competition* (London, England: Cambridge University Press, 1983).

Barak, Gregg, *Integrating Criminologies* (Boston: Allyn and Bacon, 1998).

Bard, M., *Shadow Women* (Kansas City: Sheed and Ward, 1990).

Barkan, Steven E., Criminology: A Sociological Understanding (Upper Saddle River, NJ: Prentice Hall, 1997), pp. 242-244.

Barnes, Grace M., and Farrell, Michael P., "Parental Support and Control as Predictors of Adolescent Drinking, Delinquency, and Related Problem Behaviors," *Journal of Marriage and the Family*, Vol. 54, (November) 1992: 763-776.

Barnes, Virginia Lee, and Boddy, Janice Patricia., *Aman: The Story of a Somali Girl* (New York: Pantheon Books, 1994).

Barnett, M.A., "Empathy and Related Responses in Children," in N. Eisenberg and J. Strayer (Eds.), *Empathy and Its Development* (Cambridge, England: Cambridge University Press, 1987).

Barricklow, D., "Women in the Media: With Few Exceptions, Sexist Stereotypes Endure," *The Ford Foundation Report*, Vol. 22, 1992, pp. 17-19.

Barringer, H.R., Gardner, R.W., and Levin, M.J., *Asians and Pacific Islanders in the United States* (New York: Russell Sage Foundation, 1993).

Barry, Dave, "Bored Stiff," *Funny Times* (January, 1995), page 5, as cited in David Myers, *Social Psychology* (Fifth edition) (NY: McGraw-Hill, 1996), p. 201).

Bauken, Manuel, "Life in the Armed Forces," *New Republic*, Vol. 109, 1943: 279-280.

Baumeister, R.F., *Meanings of Life* (New York: Guilford, 1991).

Baumrind, Diana, "New Directions in Socialisation Research," *Psychological Bulletin*, Vol. 35, 1980: 639-652.

Baumrind, Diana, "Parental Disciplinary Patterns and Social Competence in Children," *Youth and Society*, Vol. 9, 1978: 239-276.

Beals, Ralph L., *Cheran: A Sierra Tarrascan Village* (Washington, D.C.: Institute of Social Anthropology, Smithsonian Institution, Publication No. 2, 1946.

Beals, Ralph L., "Problems in the Study of Mixe Marriage Customsm" in Robert E. Lowie (Ed.), *Essays in Anthropology Presented* to A.L. Kroeber (Berkeley: University of California Press, 1936), pp. 7-13.

Beauvoir, Simon de, *The Second Sex* (London: Jonathan Cape, 1953).

Beard, Charles A., *An Economic Interpretation of the Constitution of the United States* (New York: Free Press, 1962).

Becker, Howard S., *Boys in White: Student Culture in Medical School* (Chicago: University of Chicago Press, 1961).

Becker, Howard S., *The Outsider: Studies in the Sociology of Deviance* (New York: The Free Press, 1966).

Becker, J., *Mentoring High-Risk Kids* (Minneapolis, MN: Johnson Institute, 1994).

Beteille, A., *Caste, Class and Power* (Berkeley: University of California, 1965).

Beteille, A., "The Future of the Backward Classes." in *Perspectives* (Vol. 1) (New Delhi: Indian Council for the Future, 1981): 15.

Bell, Linda A. and Blumenfeld, David (Eds.), *Overcoming Racism And Sexism* (Lanham, MD: Rowman & Littlefield, 1995).

Bell, P. Inge, *This Book Is Not Required* (Fort Bragg, CA: The Small Press, 1991).

Bellah, Robert M. Madsen, Richard, Sullivan, William M., Swidler, Ann, and Tilton, Steven M., *Habits of the Heart: Individualism and Commitment in American Life* (New York: Harper and Row, 1985).

Bem, Sandra Lipsitz, "Androgyny vs. the Tight Little Lives of Fluffy Women and Chesty Men," *Psychology Today,* September, 1975: 58 62.

Bendix, Reinhard, *Max Weber: An Intellectual Portrait* (New York: Anchor Books, 1962).

Bendix, Reinhard, and Roth, Guenther, *Scholarship and Partisanship: Essays on Max Weber* (Berkeley: University of California Press, 1971).

Benedict, Jeff, *Public Heroes, Private Felons: Athletes and Crimes Against Women* (Boston: Northeastern University Press, 1997)

Benedict, Ruth, *Patterns of Culture* (Boston: Houghton Mifflin, 1934).

Benjamin, Lois, *The Black Elite: Facing the Color Line in the Twilight of the Twentieth Century* (Chicago: Nelson-Hall, 1991).

Benson, Michael L., and Cullen, Francis T., *Combating Corporate Crime: Local Prosecutors at Work* (Boston: Northeastern University Press, 1998).

Berger, Bennett M., Review of *Ordinary Knowledge: An Introduction to Interpretative Sociology* by Michael M. Maffesoli. Translated by David Macey (Cambridge: Polity Press, 1996), in *American Journal of Sociology,* Vol. 103, No. 1, (July) 1997: 273-275.

Berezin, Mabel, "Cultural Form and Political Meaning: State Subsidized Theater, Ideology, and the Language of Style in Fascist Italy," *American Journal of Sociology,* Vol. 99, 1994: 1237-1286.

Berger, Peter, *Invitation to Sociology: A Humanistic Perspective* (New York: Doubleday & Co., Inc., 1963).

Berger, Peter, and Lukmann, Thomas, *The Social Construction of Reality: A Treatise in the Sociology of Knowledge* (New York: Anchor Books Inc., 1966).

Berkman, L.F., and Syme, S.L., "Social Networks, Host Resistance, and Mortality: A Nine Year Follow-up Study of Alameda County Residents," *American Journal of Epidemiology,* Vol. 109, 1979: 186-204.

Bernhardt, Annette, and Handcock, Mark S., "Women's Gains or Men's Losses? A Closer Look at the Shrinking Gender Gap in Earnings," *American Journal of Sociology,* Vol. 101, No. 2, (September) 1995: 302-328.

Berscheid, Ellen, "Interpersonal Attraction," in Gardner Lindzey and Elliot Aronson, *The Handbook of Social Psychology* (Third edition) (New York: Random House, 1985).

Bettelheim, Bruno, *Uses of Enchantment* (New York: Vintage Books, 1977).

Beutel, Ann M., and Marini, Margaret Mooney, "Gender and Values," *American Sociological Review,* Vol. 60, (June) 1995: 436-448.

Bian, Yanjie, "Bringing Strong Ties Back In: Indirect Ties, Network Bridges, and Job Searches in China," *American Sociological Reveiw,* Vol. 62, (June) 1997: 366-385.

Bianchi, Suzanne M., and Robinson, John, "What Did You Do Today? Children's Use of Time, Family Composition, and the Acquisition of Social Capital," *Journal of Marriage and the Family,* Vol. 59, (May) 1997: 332-342.

Bianchi, Suzanne, and Spain, Daphne, "U.S. Women Make Workplace Progress," *Population Today,* Vol. 25, No. 1, (January) 1997: 1-2.

Bierstedt, Robert, "An Analysis of Social Power," *American Sociological Review,* Vol. 15, 1950: 730-738.

Billig, M., and Tajfel, H., "Social Categorization and Similarity in Intergroup Behaviour," *European Journal of Social Psychology,* Vol. 3, 1973: 27-52.

Birmingham, D., *The Decolonization of Africa* (Athens, OH: Ohio University Press, 1995).

Bishop, John H., "The Impact of Previous Training on Productivity and Wages," in L. Lynch (Ed.), *Training and the Private Sector: International Comparisons* (Chicago: University of Chicago Press, 1994).

Blalock, Hubert, M. Jr., *Social Statistics* (New York: McGraw Hill, 1972).

Blalock, Hubert M. Jr., *Social Statistics* (Revised second edition) (New York: McGraw Hill, 1979).

Blau, Peter M., *Cross-Cutting Social Circles* (Orlando, FL: Free Press, 1984).

Blau, Peter M., *Exchange and Power in Social Life* (New York: Wiley, 1964).

Blau, Peter M., *Inequality and Heterogeneity: A Primitive Theory of Social Structure* (New York: The Free Press, 1977).

Blau, Peter M., "Microprocesses and Macrostructure," in Karen S. Cook (Ed.), *Social Exchange Theory* (Beverly Hills, CA: Sage Publications, 1987), pp. 83-100.

Blau, Peter M., *Structural Contexts of Opportunities* (Chicago University of Chicago Press, 1994).

Blau, Peter M., "Structures of Social Positions and Structures of Social Relations," in Jonathan Turner (Ed.), *Theory Building in Sociology* (Newbury Park, CA: Sage, 1988).

Blauner, Robert, "Internal Colonialism and Ghetto Revolt," *Social Problems*, Vol. 16, 1969: :393-408.

Blauner, Robert, *Racial Oppression in America* (New York: Harper and Row, 1972).

Blaustein, Albert P. and Zangrando, Robert L., *Civil Rights and the American Negro: A Documentary History* (New York: Washington Square Press, 1968).

Blazer, Dan G., "Social Support and Mortality in an Elderly Community Population," *American Journal of Epidemiology*, Vol. 115, 1982: 684-694.

Bloch, H.A., and Neiderhoffer, A., *The Gang: A Study in Adolescent Behavior* (New York: Philosophical Library, 1958).

Bloch, Marc, *Feudal Society* (Chicago: The University of Chicago Press, 1961) (Originally published, 1940).

Bloch, M.N., "Young Girls and Boys Play at Home and in the Community: A Cultural-Ecological Framework," in M.N. Bloch and A.D. Pellegrini (Eds.), *The Ecological Context of Children's Play* (Norwood, NJ: Ablex, 1989), 120-154.

Blumberg, Rae Lesser, *Stratification: Socioeconomic and Sexual Inequality* (Dubuque: Wm. C. Brown Company Publishers, 1978).

Blumer, Herbert, *Symbolic Interactionism: Perspective and Method* (Englewood Cliffs: Prentice-Hall, 1969).

Bochner, S., "Cross-cultural Differences in the Self-Concept: A Test of Hofstede's Individualism/Collectivism Distinction," *Journal of Cross-Cultural Psychology*, Vol. 25, 1994: 273-283.

Bodvarsson, Örn, and Gibson, William A., "Economics and Restaurant Gratuities: Determining Tip Rates," *The American Journal of Economics and Sociology*, Vol. 56, (April) 1997: 187-204.

Boivin, Michel, and Hymel, Shelley, "Peer Experiences and Social Self-Perceptions: A Sequential Model," *Developmental Psychology*, Vol. 33, No. 1, 1997: 135-145.

Boli, John, and Thomas, George, "World Culture in the World Polity: A Century of International Non-Governmental Organization," *American Sociological Review*, Vol. 62, (April) 1997: 171-190.

Bonacich, Edna, "Advanced Capitalism and Black-White Relations in the United States: A Split Labor Market Interpretation," *American Sociological Review*, Vol. 41, 1976: 34-51.

Bonacich, Edna, "A Theory of Ethnic Antagonism: The Split Labor Market," *American Sociological Review*, Vol. 37, 1972: 547-549.

Bonacich, Philip, "Communication Dilemmas in Social Networks: An Experimental Study," *American Sociological Review*, Vol. 55, 1990, pp. 427-447.

Bonilla-Silva, Eduardo, "Rethinking Racism: Toward a Structural Interpretation," *American Sociological Review*, Vol. 62, (June) 1997: 465-480.

Bonilla-Silva, Eduardo and Lewis, Amanda, "The 'New Racism': Toward an Analysis of the U.S. Racial Structure, 1960s-1990s," 1997, Department of Sociology, University of Michigan, Ann Arbor, MI. Unpublished manuscript.

Bosworth, Allan R., *America's Concentration Camps* (New York: Bantam Books, 1964).

Bothwell, R.K., Brigham, J.C., and Malpass, R.S., "Cross-Racial Identification," *Personality and Social Psychology Bulletin*, Vol. 15, 1989: 19-25.

Bougle, C., *Essays on the Caste System* (Translated by D.Pocock) (Cambridge, England: Cambridge University Press, 1971).

Boulton, Michael J., "Partner Preferences of British and Asian and White Girls and Boys on the Middle School Playground," *Journal of Research in Childhood Education*, Vol. 11, No. 1, 1996: 25-34.

Boulton, M.J., and Smith, P.K., "Ethnic, Gender Partner, and Activity Preferences in Mixed Race Schools in the UK: Playground Observations," in C. Hart (Ed.), *Children on Playgrounds: Research Perspectives and Applications* (Albany, NY: State University of New York Press, 1993), pp. 210-237.

Boulton, M.J., and Smith, P.K., "Liking and Peer Perceptions Among Asian and White British Children," *Journal of Social and Personal Relations*, Vol. 13, 1996: 163-177.

Bourdieu, P., "Cultural Reproduction and Social Reproduction," in R. Brown (Ed.), *Knowledge, Education, and Cultural Change* (London: Tavistock, 1973), 71-112.

Bourne, Peter G., *Men, Stress and Vietnam* (Boston: Little Brown, 1970).

Bowlby, John, *Attachment and Loss* (Second edition) (New York: Basic Books, 1982).

Bowles, Samuel and Gintis, Herbert, *Schooling in Capitalist America: Educational Reform and the Contradictions of Economic Life* (New York: Basic Books, 1976).

Boyd, Monica, "Oriental Immigration: The Experience of the Chinese, Japanese, and Filipino Populations in the United States," *International Migration Review*, Vol. 10, 1976: 48- 60.

Boyer, Richard and Morais, Herbert, *Labor's Untold Story* (New York: United Electrical, Radio and Machine Workers of America, 1965).

Brabant, Sarah, and Mooney, Linda, "Sex Role Stereotyping in the Sunday Comics: A Twenty Year Update," *Sex Roles*, Vol. 37, Nos. 3/4, 1997: 269-281.

Branch, C.W., and Newcomb, "Racial Attitude Development Among Young Black Children as a Function of Parental Attitudes: A Longitudinal and Cross-Sectional Study," *Child Development*, Vol. 56, 712-721.

Brauer, J., Judd, C.M., and Gliner, "The Effects of Repeated Expressions on Attitude Polarization During Group Discussions," *Journal of Personality and Social Psychology*, Vol. 68, 1995: 1014-1029).

Braun, Denny, *The Rich Get Richer: The Rise of Income Inequality in the United States and the World* (Chicago: Nelson-Hall Publishers, 1991).

Braun, Kathryn L., and Nichols, Rhea, "Death and Dying in Four Asian American Cultures: A Descriptive Study," *Death Studies*, Vol. 21, No. 4 (July-August) 1997.

Braverman, Harry, *Labor and Monopoly Capital* (New York: Monthly Review Press, 1974).

Brett, D., and Cantor, J., "The Portrayal of Men and Women in U.S. Television Commercials: A Recent Content Analysis and Trends Over 15 Years," *Sex Roles*, Vol. 19, 1988: 595-609.

Bridges, J.S., "Pink or Blue: Gender-Stereotypic Perceptions of Infants as Conveyed by Birth Congratulations Cards," *Psychology of Women Quarterly*, Vol. 17, 1993: 193-205.

Brigham, J.C., and Malpass, R.S., "The Role of Experience and Contact in the Recognition of Faces of Own and Other-Race Persons," *Journal of Social Issues*, Vol. 41, 1985: 139- 155.

Brody, Leslie R., and Hall, Judith A., "Gender and Emotion," in Michael Lewis and Jeanette Haviland (Eds.), *Handbook of Emotions* (New York: Guilford Press, 1993).

Brown, David L., and Tandon, Rajesh, "The Ideology and Political Economy of Inquiry: Action Research and Participatory Research," *Journal of Applied Behavioral Science and Technology: An International Perspective*, Vol. 19, 1983: 277-294.

Brown, Lyn Michael, and Gilligan, Carol, *Meeting at the Crossroads: Women's Psychology and Girls' Development* (Cambridge, MA: Harvard University Press, 1992).

Brown, Roger, *Social Psychology* (New York: Free Press, 1965).

Brown, Roger, *Social Psychology* (London: Collier Macmillan, 1986).

Browning, J., and Dutton, D., "Assessment of Wife Assault with the Conflict Tactics Scale: Using Couple Data to Quantify the Differential Reporting Effect," *Journal of Marriage and the Family*, Vol. 48, 1986: 375-379.

Brownmiller, Susan, *Against Our Will: Men, Women, and Rape* (NY: Simon and Schuster, 1975).

Bureau of Justice Statistics, *Report to the Nation on Crime and Justice: The Data* (Second edition) (Washington D.C.: U.S. Department of Justice, 1988).

Bruce-Novoa, Juan D., *Chicano Authors: Inquiry by Interview* (Austin, Texas: University of Texas Press, 1980).

Buckley, Walter, "Social Stratification and the Functional Theory of Social Differentiation." *American Sociological Review*, Vol. 23, 1958: 369-375.

Buell, Raymond L., *Japanese Immigration* (New York: World Peace Foundation, 1924).

Bukowski, W.M., Gauze, C., Hoza, B., and Newcomb, F., "Differences and Consistency Between Same-Sex and Other-Sex Peer Relationships During Early Adolescence," *Developmental Psychology*, Vol. 29, 1993: 255-263.

Burris, Val, "Introduction," in "The Structural Influence in Marxist Theory and Research," *Insurgent Sociologist*, Vol. 9, 1979: 4-17.

Burris, Val, "The Political Partisanship of American Business: A Study of Corporate Action Committees," *American Sociological Review*, Vol. 52, 1987: 732-744.

Buss, Andrea, "The Economic Ethic of Russian-Orthodox Christianity: Part II-Russian Old Believers and Sects," *International Sociology*, Vol. 4, 1989: 447-472.

Butler, J., *Gender Troubles: Feminism and the Subversion of Identity* (London: Routledge, 1990).

Butterfield, Fox, "Historical Study of Homicide and Cities Surprises the Experts," *The New York Times*, October 23, 1994.

Butterfield, Fox, "Number of Homicides Drops 11 Percent in U.S.," *The New York Times*, June 2, 1997.

Cabana, Donald A., *Death at Midnight: The Confession of an Executioner* (Boston: Northeastern University Press, 1998).

California Postsecondary Education Commission, *Enrollment by Institution* (Sacramento, CA: California Postsecondary Education Commission, October 8, 1996) (Report ID: EnInstPr).

The CIA World Fact Book http://www.odci.gov/cia/publications/nsolo/factbook/global.htm

Cal, DIR, *Facts About Filipino Immigration into California* (Sacramento: California Department of Industrial Relations, 1930).

Cameron, Bradley, "The Modification of Authoritarian Traits in Police Officers," Department of Social Science, 1997, Pittsburg State University, Pittsburg, KS.

Campbell, Bernard G., *Humankind Emerging* (Fifth edition) (Boston: Scotts, Foresman, 1988).

Cancian, Francesca, and Armstead, Cathleen, "Participatory Research," in Edgar F. Borgatta and Marie L. Borgatta, (Eds.), *Encyclopedia of Sociology*, Vol. 3 (New York: Macmillan and Company, 1992), pp. 1427-1432.

Cann, Arnie, and Vann, Elizabeth D., "Implications of Sex and Gender Differences for Self: Perceived Advantages and Disadvantages of Being the Other Gender," *Sex Roles*, Vol. 33, Nos. 7/8 1995: 531-541.

Caplan, Nathan; Whitmore, John K.; and Choy, Marcella, "Indochinese Refugee Families and Academic Achievement," *Scientific American*, Vol. 266, (February) 1992: 36-42.

Cardoso, Lawrence A., *Mexican Emigration to the United States, 1897-1931: Socio-Economic Patterns* (Tucson: University of Arizona Press, 1980).

Carger, Chris Liska, *Of Borders and Dreams: a Mexican American Experience of Urban Education* (New York: Teachers College Press, 1996).

Carmichael, Stokley, and Hamilton, Charles V., *Black Power: The Politics of Liberation in America* (New York: Vvintage Books, 1967).

Carpenter, C.J. Houston, A.C., and Serpa, L., "Children's Use of Time in their Everyday Activities During Middle Childhood," in M.N. Bloch and A.D. Pellegrini (Eds.), *The Ecological Context of Children's Play* (Norwood, NJ: Ablex, 1989).

Carr, Dara, *Female Genital Cutting: Findings from the Demographic and Health Surveys Program* (Calverton, MD: Macro International, 1997).

Carrasco, Pedro, "El Barrio y la Regulacion del Matrimonio en un Pueblo del Valle de Mexico en el Siglo XVI," *Revista Mexicana de Estudios Antropologicos*, Vol. 16, 1961: 7-26.

Carrasco, Pedro, "Family Structure of Sixteenth Century Tepotzlan," in Robert A. Manners (Ed.), *Process and Pattern in Culture* (Chicago: Aldine Publishing Company, 1964)

Carrasco, Pedro, "The Joint Family in Ancient Mexico," in Hugo G. Nutini, et al (Eds.), *Essays on Mexican Kinship* (Pittsburgh: University of Pittsburgh Press, 1974).

Carrasco, Pedro, "A Note on Residence," *American Anthropologist*, Vol. 65, 1963: 487-488.

Carrasco, Pedro, "Social Organization in Ancient Mexico," in Robert Wauchope (Ed.), *Handbook of Middle American Indians*, Vol. 10 (Austin, TX: University of Texas Press, 1971).

Carter, L.F., and Nixon, M., "An Investigation of the Relationship Between Four Criteria of Leadership for Three Different Tasks," *Journal of Psychology*, Vol. 27, 1949: 245-261.

Cash, T.F., *What Do You See When You Look in the Mirror? Helping Yourself to a Positive Body Image* (New York: Bantam, 1995).

Cash, Thomas F., and Henry, Patricia E., "Women's Body Images: The Results of a National Survey in the U.S.A.," *Sex Roles*, Vol. 33, Nos. 1/2, 1995: 19-28.

Cash, T.F., and Pruzinsky, T. (Eds.), *Body Images: Development, Deviance, and Change* (New York: Guilford Press, 1990).

Census of India, Report on the Operations. Baroda. Vol. 23 (Part II), 1891: 148, 154-155, 159.

Census of India, Report, Baroda. Vol. 18 (Part I), 1901: 435-436.

Census of India, Notes for Report, 1911: 89

Census of India, Report, Vol.I (Part I), 1911:36, 366

Census of India, Notes for Report, Vol. 16 (Part I), 1911: 244.

Census of India, Report, Baroda, Vol 16 (Part I), 1911: 250-251, 303.

Census of India, Vol. 23 (Part II), 1911: 151-152.

Census of India, Report on the Operations, Vol. 23 (Part II), 160.

Census of India, Vol. 1 (Part I), 1931: 433.

Census of India, Report, Vol 19 (Part I), 1931: 394.

Cerulo, Karen A., "Symbols and the World System: National Anthems and Flags," *Sociological Forum,* Vol. 8, 1993: 243-271.

Cesaire, A., *A Tempest* (Translated by R. Miller) (New York: Ubu Repertory Publications, 1986).

Chagnon, Napoleon A., *Yanomamo* (Third edition) (New York: Holt, Reinhart and Winston, 1983).

Chai, Alice, "Koren Women in Hawaii, 1903-1945," in Hilah Frances Thomas and Rosemary Skinner Keller (Eds.), *Women in New Worlds* (Nashville, TN: Abingdon,. 1981).

Chalkley, Kate, "Female Genital Mutilation: New Laws, Programs Try to End Practice," *Population Today,* Vol. 25, No. 10, (October) 1997: 4-5.

Chambliss, William J., and Zatz, M., *Making Law: Law, State, and Structural Contradiction* (Bloomington: Indiasa University Press, 1994).

Chambliss, William J., "The Saints and the Roughnecks," *Society,* Vol. 11, (November- December) 1973: 24-31.

Chan, S., *Asian Americans* (Boston: Twayne, 1991).

Chan, Sucheng, *Asian Californians* (San Francisco: MTL/Boyd & Fraser, 1991).

Chance, June E., "Faces, Folklore, and Research Hypotheses," Presidential Address to the Midwestern Psychological Association Convention, 1985.

Chandler, Alfred D. Jr., "The United States: Seedbed of Managerial Capitalism," in Frank Hearn (Ed.), *The Transformation of Industrial Organization: Management, Labor, and Society in the United States* (Belmont, CA: Wadsworth Publishing Co., 1988).

Chandra, V.P., "The Present Moment of the Past: An Analysis of Caste, Class, and Ethnic Formation," State University of New York at Stonybrook, unpublished dissertation, 1994.

Chandra, V.P., "Remigration: The Return of the Prodigals, An Analysis of the Impact of Cycles of Migration and Remigration on Caste Mobility," *International Migration Review,* Vol. 31, No. 1, 1991: 162-170.

Chandra, V.P., "Till Death Us Do Part: Gift-Giving as a Determinant of Status," Unpublished manuscript, Department of Sociology and Social Services, California State University, Hayward, 1998.

Chandrasekhar, Sripati, *A History of United States Legislation with Respect to Immigration from India to America* (La Jolla, CA: Population Review Publications, 1982).

Chapman, Stanley H., "W.E.B. Du Bois," in Lachmann, Richard, *The Encyclopedic Dictionary of Sociology* (Fourth edition) (Guilford, Connecticut: The Dushkin Publishing Group, 1991).

Charon, Joel M., *Symbolic Interactionism: An Introduction, An Interpretation, An Integration* (Sixth edition) (Upper Saddle River, NJ: Prentice Hall, 1998).

Chassin, Laurie, and De Lucia, Christian, "Drinking During Adolescence," *Alcohol, Health and Research World,* Vol. 20, No. 3, 1996: 175-180.

Chen, Jack, *The Chinese of America* (San Francisco: Harper & Row, 1980).

Chen, Kathy, "China Defies Pressure on Human Rights: Dissident's Trial Reflects Belief Economics Will Rule," *Wall Street Journal,* December 11, 1995: p. A8.

Chenault, Lawrence, *The Puerto Rican Migrant in New York City* (New York: Columbia University Press, 1938).

Chesney-Lind, Meda, and Sheldon, Randall G., *Girls, Delinquency, and Juvenile Justice* (Second edition) (Belmont, CA: West/Wadsworth, 1997).

Children's Defense Fund, *Child Poverty in America* (Washington, D.C. Children's Defense Fund, 1994).

Chinn, Thomas (Ed.), *A History of the Chinese in California: A Syllabus* (San Francisco: Chinese Historical Society of America, 1969).

Chirot, Daniel, *Social Change in the Modern Era* (New York: Harcourt Brace Jovanovich College Publishers, 1986).

Chodorow, N., *The Reproduction of Mothering: Psychoanalysis and the Sociology of Gender* (Berkeley: University of California Press, 1978).

Choy, Bong-youn, *Koreans in America* (Chicago: Nelson-Hall, 1979).

Christiansen, Karl O., "A Review of Studies of Criminality among Twins," in Sarnoff A. Mednick and Karl O. Christiansen (Ed.), *Biosocial Bases of Criminal Behavior* (New York: Gardner Press, 1977).

Churchill, Ward, *Indians Are Us? Culture and Genocide in Native North America* (Monroe, ME: Common Courage Press, 1994).

Cialdini, Robert, *Influence: How and Why People Agree to Things* (Glenview, IL: Scott Foresman, 1984).

Clark, Russell D., III, and Hatfield, Elaine, "Gender Differences in Receptivity to Sexual Offers," Unpublished manuscript, Department of Psychology, Florida State University, Tallahassee, Florida, 1981.

Clark, Reginald M., *Family Life and School Achievement: Why Poor Black Children Succeed or Fail* (Chicago: University of Chicago Press, 1983).

Clausen, John A., "A Historical and Comparative View of Socialization Theory and Research," in J.A. Clausen (Ed.), *Socialization and Society* (Boston: Little, Brown, 1968).

Clayton, Jr., Obie, *An American Dilemma Revisited: Race Relations in a Changing World* (New York: Russell Sage foundation, 1996).

Clifford, Mary D., "The Hawaiian Sugar Planters Association and Filipino Exclusion," in J.M. Saniel (Ed.), *The Filipino Exclusion Movement, 1927-1935* (Quezon City: University of the Philippines, Institute of Asian Studies, 1967), pp. 11-29..

Clinard, Marshall B., and Meier, Robrt F., *Sociology of Deviant Brehavior* (New York: Harcourt Brace, 1992).

Clinchy, B. M., "The Development of Thoughtfulness in College Women: Integrating Reason and Care," *American Behavioral Scientist,* Vol. 32, 1989: 647-657.

Cline, H. F., *Mexico: Revolution to Evolution: 1940-1960* (New York: Oxford University Press, 1963).

Clinton, Catherine, *The Plantation Mistress: Woman's World in the Old South* (New York: Pantheon Books, 1982).

Cloward, Richard A., and Ohlin, Lloyd E., *Delinquency and Opportunity: A Theory of Delinquent Gangs* (New York: Free Press, 1966).

Coakley, Jay J., *Sport in Society: Issues and Controversies* (Fourth edition) (St. Louis: Times Mirror/Mosby, 1990).

Cockcroft, James D., *Outlaws in the Promised Land: Mexican Immigrant Workers and America's Future* (New York: Grove Press, 1986).

Cohen, Albert K., *Delinquent Boys: The Culture of Gangs* (New York: Free Press, 1955).

Cohen, Lawrence E., and Felson, Marcus, "Social Change and Crime Rate Trends: A Routine Activities Approach," *American Sociological Review,* Vol. 44, 1979: 588-608.

Cohen, Lawrence, E., and Machalek, Michard, "The Normalcy of Crime: From Durkheim to Evolutionary Ecology," *Rationality and Society,* Vol. 6, 1994: 286-308.

Cohen, Stanley, *Visions of Social Control* (Cambridge, England: Polity Press, 1985).

Cohen, Stephen F., *Bukharin and the Bolshevik Revolution* (New York: St. Martin's Press, 1973).

Cohn, S., and Fossett, M., "Why Racial Employment Inequality is Greater in Northern Labor Markets: Regional Differences in White-Black Employment Differentials," *Social Forces,* Vol. 74, 1995: 511-542.

Colley, Ann; Griffiths, Deborah; Hugh, Michelle; Landers, Kirsten; and Jaggli, Nicole, "Childhood Play and Adolescent Leisure Preferences: Associations with Gender Typing and the Presence of Siblings," *Sex Roles,* Vol. 35, Nos. 3/4, 1996: 233-243.

Collins, Randall, "An Asian Route to Capitalism: Religious Economy and the Origins of Self-Transforming Growth in Japan," *American Sociological Review*, Vol. 62 (December), 1998:843-865.

Collins, Randall, *Conflict Sociology* (New York: Academic Press, 1975).

Collins, Randall, "Conflict Theory," in Edgar F. Borgatta and Marie L. Borgatta (Eds.), *Encyclopedia of Sociology*, Vol. 1 (New York: Macmillan Publishing Company, 1992), pp. 288-290.

Collins, Randall, *Theoretical Sociology* (San Diego: Harcourt Brace, Janovich, 1988).

Colman, A.M., "Crowd Psychology in South African Murder Trials," *American Psychologist*, Vol. 46, 1991a: 1071-1079.

Colman, A.M., "Psychological Evidence in South African Murder Trials," *The Psychologist*, Vol. 14, 1991b: 482-486.

Comte, Auguste, *The Positive Philosophy of Auguste Comte* (London: Bell, 1896). (Originally published in French in 1838).

Conklin, John E., *Criminology* (Boston: Allyn and Bacon, 1997).

Connor, Walter, D., "The Soviet Working Class: Changes and Its Political Impact." in Michael Paul Sacks and Jerry G. Pankhurst (Eds.), *Understanding Soviet Society* (Boston: Unwin Hyman, 1988).

Cook, Karen S.; Emerson, Richard; Gillmore, Mary R.; and Yamagishi, Toshio, "The Distribution of Power in Exchange Networks," *American Journal of Sociology*, Vol. 89, 1983: 275-305.

Cook, Karen S., and Emerson, Richard, "Exchange Networks and the Analysis of Complex Organizations," *Research in the Sociology of Organizations*, Vol. 3, 1984: 1-30.

Cook, Sherburne F., *The Population of the California Indians 1769-1970* (Berkeley: University of California Press, 1976).

Coolidge, Mary R., *Chinese Immigration* (New York: Arno Press, 1969). (Originally published, 1909).

Cooley, Charles Horton, *Human Nature and the Social Order* (New York: Schocken, 1964). (Originally published, 1902).

Cooley, Charles Horton, *Social Organization* (New York: Schocken, 1962) (Originally published, 1909)

Copetas, Craig A., *Bear Hunting with Politburo: A Gritty First-Hand Account of Russia's Young Entrepreneurs—and Why Soviet-Style Capitalism Can't Work* (New York: Simon and Schuster, 1991).

Cordasco, Francesco, *The Puerto Ricans 1493-1973: A Chronology & Fact Book* (Dobbs Ferry, NY: Oceana, 1973).

Cornell, S., and Kalt, J.P., "Pathways from Poverty: Economic Development and Institution Building on American Indian Reservations," *American Indian Culture and Research Journal*, Vol. 14, 1990: 89-125.

Corey, Lewis, *The Crisis of the Middle Class* (New York: Covici Friede Publishers, 1935).

Coronel, S. and Rosca, N., "For the Boys: Filipinas Expose Years of Sexual Slavery by the US and Japan," *Ms.*, (November/December) 1993: 10-15.

Cose, Ellis, *Color Blind* (New York: Harper, 1996).

Cose, "We're So Terribly Sorry," *Newsweek*, April 6, 1998: 31.

Coser, Lewis A., "Conflict: Social Aspects," in David L. Sills (Ed.), *International Encyclopedia of the Social Sciences* (New York: Macmillan and Free Press, 1968), pp. 232-236.

Coser, Lewis A., *The Functions of Social Conflict* (New York: Free Press, 1956).

Coser, Lewis A., *Masters of Sociological Thought: Ideas in Historical Context* (Second edition) (New York: Harcourt Brace Jovanovich, 1977).

Coughlin, Chris, and Vuchinich, "Family Experience in Preadolescence and the Development of Male Delinquency," *Journal of Marriage and the Family*, Vol. 58, (May) 1996: 491-501.

Cousins, Steven, "Culture and Selfhood in Japan and the US," *Journal of Personality and Social Psychology*, Vol. 56 (January), 124-131.

Covington, Martin V., and Beery, Richard G., *Self-Worth and School Learning* (New York: Holt, Rinehart, and Winston, 1976).

Cowan, Florence Hansen, "Linguistic and Ethnological Aspects of Mazateco Kinship," *Southwestern Journal of Anthropology*, Vol. 3, No. 3, 1947: 247-256.

Cox, O.C., *Caste, Class and Race* (New York: First Monthly Review Press, 1959).

Cox, Steven, *Police, Practice Perspectives, Problems* (Boston: Allyn & Bacon, 1996).

Crabb, Peter .B., and Bielawski, Dawn., "The Social Representation of Material Culture and Gender in Children's Books," *Sex Roles,* Vol. 30, 1994: 69-79.

Crew, Keith, "How Much Is 'Very'?," in Rubin, Allen, and Babbie, Earl, *Research Methods for Social Work* (Second edition) (Pacific Grove, CA: Brooks/Cole Publishing Company, 1993), p. 344.

Cromwell, Adelaide M., *The Other Brahmins: Boston's Black Upper Class* (Fayetville, AK: University of Arkansas Press, 1994).

Curra, John, *Understanding Social Deviance: From the Near Side to the Outer Limits* (New York: Harper Collins, 1993).

Curtiss, Susan, *Genie: A Psycholinguistic Study of a Modern-Day "Wild Child"* (New York: Academic Press, 1977).

Dahrendorf, Ralf, *Class and Class Conflict in Industrial Society* (Stanford, CA: Stanford University Press, 1959).

D'Amico, R., and Maxwell, N.L., "The Continuing Significance of Race in Minority Male Joblessness," *Social Forces,* Vol. 73, 1995:" 969-991.

Daly, Kathleen, *Gender, Crime, and Punishment* (New Haven CT: Yale UniversityPress, 1994).

Daly, Kathleen, and Chesney-Lind, Meda, "Feminism and Criminology," *Justice Quarterly,* Vol. 5, 1988: 497-538.

Daly, M., *Gyn/Ecology: The Metaethics of Radical Feminism* (Boston: Beacon Press, 1979).

Daniels, Jessie, *White Lies: Race, Class, Gender, and Sexuality in White Supremacist Discourse* (New York: Routledge, 1997).

Daniels, Roger, *Asian America: Chinese and Japanese in the United States Since 1850* (Seattle: University of Washington Press, 1988).

Daniels, Roger, *Concentration Camps, U.S.A* (New York: Holt, Rinehart & Winston, 1971).

Daniels, Roger, *The Politics of Prejudice: The Anti-Japanese Movement in California and the Struggle for Japanese Exclusion* (Berkeley: University of California Press, 1962).

Daniels, Roger, *Prisoners Without Trial: Japanese-Americans in World War II* (New York: Hill and Wang, 1993).

Darwin, Charles, *The Expression of Emotions in Man and Animals* (Chicago: Chicago University Press, 1965). (Originally published, 1872).

Darwin, Charles, *The Origin of Species* (New York: A Mentor Book, 1958). (Originally published, 1859).

Davies, G.H., Ellis, H.D., and Shepherd, J. (Eds.), *Perceiving and Remembering Faces* (London: Academic Press, 1981).

Davies, Peter (Ed.), *The American Heritage Dictionary of the English Language* (New York: Dell Publishing Company, 1976).

Davis, Kingsley, *Human Society* (New York: The Macmillan Company, 1948).

Davis, Kingsley, "The Sociology of the Parent-Youth Conflict," *American Sociological Review,* Vol. 5 (1940): 523-535.

Davis, Kingsley, "The Sociology of Prostitution," *American Sociological Review,* Vol. 2, 1937: 744 755.

Davis, Kingsley and Moore, Wilbert, "Some Principles of Stratification," *American Sociological Review,* Vol. 10, No. 2, 1945: 242-249.

Davis, M.H., Franzoi, S.L., and Wellinger, P., "Personality, Social Behavior, and Loneliness," presented at the American Psychological Association annual meeting, Los Angeles, CA, (August) 1985.

De Freitas, Gregory, "Unionization Among Racial and Ethnic Minorities," *Industrial and Labor Relations Review,* Vol. 46, 1993: 284-301.

De Leon, Arnold, *The Tejano Community, 1836-1900* (Albuquerque, NM: University of New Mexico Press, 1982).

de Maris, Alfred, "The Dynamics of Generational Transfer in Courtship Violence: A Biracial Exploration," *Journal of Marriage and the Family,* Vol. 52, 1990: 219-231.

de Maris, Alfred; Pugh, Meredith D., and Harman, Erika, "Sex Differences in the Accuracy of Recall of Witnesses of Portrayed Dyadic Violence," *Journal of Marriage and the Family,* Vol. 54, (May) 1992: 335-345.

De Mente, Boye (Ed.), *Japanese Etiquette and Ethics in Business* (Fifth edition) (Lincolnwood, IL: NTC Business Books, 1987).

del Pinal, Jorge and Singer, Audrey, "Generations of Diversity: Latinos in the United States," *Population Bulletin,* Vol. 52, No. 3, (October) 1997: 2-48.

Dean, Alfred, Kolody, Bohdan, and Wood, Patricia, "Effects of Social Support from Various Sources on Depression in Elderly Persons," *Journal of Health and Social Behavior,* Vol. 31, 1990: 148-161.

Decker, Paul T., Rice, Jennifer King, and Moore, Mary T., *Education and the Economy: An Indicators Report* (Washington, D.C.: U.S. Department of Education, National Center for Education Statistics, 1997).

Dekovic, Maja, and Geeris, Jan R.M., "Parental Reasoning Complexity, Social Class, and Child-Rearing Behaviors," *Journal of Marriage and the Family,* Vol. 54, (August) 1992: 675- 685.

Dennis, Henry C., *The American Indian 1492-1976: A Chronology & Fact Book* (Second edition) (Dobbs Ferry, NY: Oceana Publications, 1977).

Denzin, Norman K., *The Research Act* (Third edition) (Englewood Cliffs, NJ: Prentice Hall, 1989).

Denzin, Norman K., *Symbolic Interactionism and Cultural Studies: The Politics of Interpretation* (Oxford, England: Blackwell, 1992).

Derksen, Linda, and Gartrell, John, "Scientific Explanation," in Edgar F. Borgatta and Marie L. Borgatta (Eds.), *Encyclopedia of Sociology,* Vol. 4 (New York: Macmillan Publishing Company, 1992), pp. 1711-1720.

Deutsch, Morton and Mary E. Collins, *Interracial Housing: A Psychological Evaluation of a Social Experiment* (Minneapolis: University of Minnesota Press, 1951).

Deutsch, M., and Gerard, H.B., "A Study of Normative and Informational Social Influence Upon Individual Judgment," *Journal of Abnormal and Social Psychology,* Vol. 51, 1955: 629-636.

Deutscher, Irwin, *What We Say/What We Do: Sentiments and Acts* (Glenview, IL: Scott, Foresman, 1973.

De Witt, Howard, "The Watsonville Anti-Filipino Riot of 1930: A Case Study of the Great Depression and Ethnic Conflict in California," *Southern California Quarterly,* Vol. 61, 1979: 291-302.

Diebold, A. Richard Jr., "The Reflection of Coresidence in Mareno Kinship Terminology," *Ethnology,* Vol. 5, No. 1, 1966: 37-79.

Dill, Bonnie Thornton, *Across the Bpimdaries of Race and Class: An Exploration of Work and Family among Black Female Domestic Servants* (New York: Garland Publishng, 1994).

Dill, Bonnie Thornton, " 'Making the Job Good Yourself:' Domestic Service and the Construction of Personal Dignity," in Ann Bookman and Sandra Morgen (Eds.) *Female Domestic Servants* (New York: Garland Publishing, 1994).

Dines, Gail, and Humez, Jean M. (Eds.), *Gender, Race, and Class in Media* (Newbury Park, CA: Sage Publications, 1995).

DiPrete, Thomas A., and Nonnemaker, K. Lynn, "Structural Change, Labor Market Turbulence, and Labor Market Outcomes," *American Sociological Review,* Vol. 62, (June) 1997: 386-404.

Dollard, John, *Caste and Class in a Southern Town* (New York: Doubleday Anchor Book, 1957). (Originally published, 1937).

Domhoff, William g., *The Bohemian Grove and Other Retreats: A Study in Ruling-Class Cohesiveness* (New York: Harper and Row, 1974).

Domhoff, William G., *The Higher Circles* (New York: Vintage Press, 1971).

Domhoff, William G., *The Powers That Be* (New York: Vintage Press, 1979).

Domhoff, William G., *Who Rules America?* (Englewood Cliffs: Prentice-Hall, 1967).

Domhoff, William G., *Who Rules America? Power and Politics in the Year 2000* (Mt. View, CA: Mayfield Publishing Company, 1998).

Donovan, Marjorie E., "About Face in Science," *The Practice of History and Social Science,* No. 27, (Spring) 1992: 1-10.

Donovan, Marjorie E., "Boadicea Leads Revolt Against Roman Rule," in John Powell (Ed.), *Chronology of European History, 15,000B.C. to 1996* (Pasadena, CA: Salem Press, 1998), pp. 143-146.

Donovan, Marjorie E., "Ascribe If You Can and Let Who Must Achieve: High Schools and White-Collar Work in Nineteenth-Century America," unpublished Ph.D. dissertation, Department of Sociology, University of California, Davis, 1977.

Donovan, Marjorie E., "Compulsory and Mass Education," in F. M. Magill (Ed.), *Survey of Social Science: Sociology* (Pasadena, CA: Salem Press, 1996).

Donovan, Marjorie, "Culture Gives Meaning to Behavior," in Marjorie Donovan, *Instructor's Manual with Test Bank to Accompany Sociology: An Everyday Life Approach* by Ernest K. Alix (Minneapolis/St. Paul, MN: West Publishing Company, 1995), pp. 24-26.

Donovan, Marjorie E., "Male and Female Perceptions of Women in Science," Midwest Sociological Society, 1990.

Donovan, Marjorie E., "A Sociological Analysis of Commitment Generation in Alcoholics Anonymous," *British Journal of Sociology*, Vol. 79, 1984: 411-418.

Donovan, Marjorie E., "Syndication Turns *Star Trek* into a Cult Classic," in Frank N. Magill (Ed.), *Great Events from History II: Arts and Culture* (Pasadena, CA: Salem Press, 1993), pp. 2260-2264.

Dornbusch, S.M., et. al., "The Relation of Parenting Style to Adolescent School Performance," *Child Development*, Vol. 58, 1987: 1244-1257.

Doty, C. Steward, "How Many Frenchmen Does It Take To . . . ," *Thought and Action*, Vol. 11, 1995: 85-104.

Douglas, John D., and Olshaker, Mark, *Obsession* (NY: Scribner, 1998).

Douvan, E., and Adelson, J., *The Adolescent Experience* (New York: Wiley, 1966).

Downey, Douglas B., "When Bigger is Not Better: Family Size, Parental Resources, and Children's Educational Performance," *American Sociological Review*, (October) 1995: 746-761.

Draden, Joe T., "Accessibility to Housing: Differential Residential Segregation for Blacks, Hispanics, American Indians, and Asians," in Jamshid A. Momeni (Ed.), *Race, Ethnicity, and Minority Housing in the United States* (New York: Greenwood Press, 1986), pp. 109-126.

Drake, St. Clair and Cayton, Horace R., *Black Metropolis: A Study of Negro Life in a Northern City* (New York: Harcourt, Brace & World, 1970).

Draper, H., *Karl Marx's Theory of Revolution* (New York: Monthly Review Press, 1978).

Dreidger, Leo, *Multi-Ethnic Canada: Identities and Inequalities* (New York: Oxford University Press, 1996).

Driscoll, R., Davis, K.E., and Lipitz, M.E., "Parental Interference and Romantic Love: The Romeo and Juliet Effect," *Journal of Personality and Social Psychology*, Vol. 24, 1972: 1-10.

Drucker, Peter F., *The Executive in Action* (New York: Harper Business, 1996).

Drucker, Peter F., *Managing for the Future: The 1990s and Beyond* (New York: Truman Talley Books, 1993a).

Drucker, Peter F., *Managing in a Time of Great Change* (New York: Truman Talley Books/Dutton, 1995).

Drucker, Peter F., *Post-Capitaist Society* (New York: Harper Business, 1993b).

Drucker, Peter F., "What We Can Learn From Japanese Management," in Frank Hearn (Ed.), *The Transformation of Industrial Organization: Management, Labor and Society in the United States* (Belmont, CA: Wadsworth, 1988).

Dubois, A., *Hindu Manners, Customs, and Ceremonies* (Oxford: The Clarendon Press, 1906).

DuBois, W.E.B., *Black Reconstruction in America: 1860-1880* (New York: Atheneum, 1985).

Du Bois, William E.B, *The Philadelphia Negro* (Philadelphia, PA: University of Pennsylvania Press, 1899).

Du Bois, William E.B., *Souls of Black Folk* (New York: Crest, 1972). (Originally published, 1903).

Dufur, Mikaela, "Race Logic and 'Being like Mike': Representations of Athletes in Advertising, 1985-1994," *Sociological Focus*, Vol. 30, No. 4, (October) 1997: 345-356.

Dumont, L., *Homo Hierarchicus* (Chicago: University of Chicago Press, 1970).

Dunn, Judy, "The Beginnings of Moral Understanding: Development in the Second Year," in Jerome Kagan and Sharon Lamb (Eds.),*The Emergence of Morality in Young Children* (Chicago: University of Chicago Press, 1987), pp. 91-112.

Dunn, Judy, *The Beginnings of Social Understanding* (Oxford: Blackwell, 1988).

Durkheim, Emile, *The Division of Labor in Society* (New York: Free Press, 1964). (Originally published, 1895).

Durkheim, Emile, *The Elementary Forms of Religious Life* (New York: Free Press, 1965). (Originally published, 1917).

Durkheim, Emile, *The Rules of the Sociological Method* (New York: Free Press, 1964).

Durkheim, Emile, *Selected Writings,* (Cambridge, England: Cambridge University Press, 1972) (Anthony Giddens, Editor)

Durkheim, Emile, *Socialism* (New York: Collier Press, 1958).

Durkheim, Emile, *Suicide* (New York: Free Press, 1966). (Originally published, 1897).

Eccles, Jacquelynne S., Jacobs, Janise E., and Harold, Rena D., "Gender Role Stereotypes, Expectancy Effects, and Parents' Socialization of Gender Differences," *Journal of Social Issues*, Vol. 46, 1990: 183-201.

Edelhertz, Herbert, *The Nature, Impact, and Prosecution of White-Collar Crime* (Washington, D.C.: U.S. Government Printing Office, 1970).

Edelman, Murray, *Constructing the Political Spectacle* (Chicago: University of Chicago Press, 1988).

Edleson, J.L., and Brygger, M.P., "Gender Differences in Reporting of Battering Incidences," *Family Relations,* Vol. 25, 1986: 377-382.

Edwards, C.P., "Behavioral Sex Differences in Children of Diverse Cultures: The Case of Nurturance to Infants," in M. Pereira and L. Fairbanks (Eds.), *Juveniles: Comparative Sociology* (Oxford University Press, 1991).

Edwards, Harry, *The Struggle That Must Be: An Autobiography* (New York, Macmillan Publishing Company, 1980).

Edwards, Richard, *The Contested Terrain: The Transformation of the Workplace in the Twentieth Century* (New York: Basic Book, Inc., 1979).

Efron, David, *Gesture, Race, and Culture* (The Hague: Mouton, 1972).

Ehrenreich, Barbara, *Fear of Falling: The Inner Life of the Middle Class* (New York: Harper, 1990).

Ehrenreich, Barbara, and Ehrenreich, John, "The Professional Managerial Class," in Pat Walker (Ed.), *Between Labor and Capital* (Boston: South End Press, 1979).

Eichler, Margrit, *Non-Sexist Research Methods* (Boston: Allen & & Unwin, 1988).

Eisenstadt, S.N., *Power, Trust, and Meaning: Essays in Sociological Theory and Analysis* (Chicago: University of Chicago Press, 1995).

Eitzen, D. Stanley, and Sage, George H., *The Sociology of North American Sport* (Fifth edition) (Dubuque, IA: Brown, 1993).

Elsasser, Nan; Mac Kenzie, K.; and Y. Tixier y Vigil, Y., *Las Mujeres: Conversations from a Hispanic Community* (Old Westbury, NY: The Feminist Press, 1980).

Elder, G.H., "Structured Variations in the Child Rearing Relationship," *Sociometry,* Vol. 25 1962, 241-262.

Elkins, Stanley M., *Slavery: A Problem in American Institutional and Intellectual Life* (Second edition) (Chicago: University of Chicago Press, 1968).

Eliot, Thomas Stearns, *Notes Towards the Definition of Culture* (New York: Harcourt, Brace, 1949).

Elis, H.D., "Theoretical Aspects of Face Recognition," in G.H. Davies, H.D. Ellis, and J. Shepherd (Eds.), *Perceiving and Remembering Faces* (London: Academic Press, 1981).

Ellis, Albert, *How to Live with and without Anger* (New York: Reader's Digest Press, 1977).

Ellis, Albert, *Humanistic Psychotherapy: The Rational-Emotive Approach* (New York: McGraw-Hill, 1973).

Ellis, Albert, "Techniques of Handling Anger in Marriage," *Journal of Marriage and Family Counseling,* Vol. 2 No. 4 (October) 1976: 305-315.

Ellison, Ralph, *Invisible Man* (New York: Random House, 1952).

Emerson, Richard, "Exchange Theory, Part I: A Psychological Basis for Social Exchange," and "Exchange Theory, Part II,: Exchange Relations and Network Structures," in J. Berger, M. Zelditch, and B. Anderson, (Eds.), *Sociological Theories in Progress* (New York: Houghton Mifflin, 1972), pp. 38-87.

Emerson, Richard, "Toward a Theory of Value in Social Exchange," in Karen S. Cook (Ed.), *Social Exchange Theory* (Newbury Park, CA: Sage, 1987: 11-46.

Emigh, Rebecca Jean, "The Spread of Sharecropping in Tuscany: The Political Economy of Transaction Costs," *American Sociological Review,* Vol. 62, (June) 1997: 423-442.

Engels, Frederick, *The Origins of the Family, Private Property and the State* (New York: International Press, 1975). (Originally published, 1884).

Enloe, C.H., *Ethnic Conflict and Political Development* (Boston: Little Brown and Company, 1973).

Epps, E., "Education of African Americans," in M.C. Alkin (Ed.), *Encyclopedia of Educational Research* (New York: Macmillan, 1992): 49-60.

Erikson, Bonnie H., "Culture, Class, and Connections," *American Journal of Sociology,* Vol. 102, No. 1 (July, 1996): 217-251.

Erikson, Erik , *Childhood and Society* (New York: W.W. Norton and Company, Inc., 1963). Originally published in 1950.

Erikson, Erik, *Identity: Youth and Crisis* (New York: Norton, 1968).

Erikson, Erik, *Identity and Life Cycle* (New York: W.W. Norton and Company, Inc., 1980).

Erikson, Kai, *All In Its Path: Destruction of Community in Buffalo Creek Flood* (New York. Simon Schuster, 1976).

Erikson, M.F., Sroufe, L.A., and Egeland, B., "The Relationship Between Quality of Attachment and Behavior Problems in Preschool in a High Risk Sample," in I. Bretherton and E. Waters (Eds.), *Monographs of the Society for Research in Child Development*, Vol. 50, 1985.

Ermakoff, Ivan, "Prelates and Princes: Aristocratic Marriages, Canon Law Prohibitions, and Shifts in Norms and Patterns of Domination in the Central Middle Ages," *American Sociological Review*, Vol. 62, (June) 1997: 405-422.

Esposito, John L., *Islam: The Straight Path* (Expanded edition) (New York: Oxford University Printing Press, 1991).

Esser, J.K., and Lindoerfer, J.S., "Groupthink and the Space Shuttle Challenger Accident: Toward a Quantitative Case Analysis," *Journal of Behavioral Decision Making*, Vol. 2, 1989: 167-177.

Etzioni, Amitai, *A Comparative Analysis of Complex Organizations: On Power, Involvement and Their Correlates* (Revised and enlarged edition) (New York: Free Press, 1975).

Evans-Pritchard, E. E., *Kinship and Marriage Among the Nuer* (Oxford, England: Clarendon, 1951).

Evans-Pritchard, E.E., *The Nuer* (Oxford, England: Clarendon Press, 1940).

Fals Borda, Orlando, *Knowledge and People's Power: Lessons with Peasants: Nicaragua, Mexico and Colombia* (New York: New Horizons Press, 1988).

Faludi, Susan, *Backlash* (New York: Anchor Books, 1992).

Farganis, James (Ed.), *Readings in Social Theory: The Classic Tradition to Post-Modernism* (New York: McGraw-Hill, 1996).

Farley, Reynolds, "Modest Declines in U.S. Residential Segregration Observed," *Population Today: News, Numbers, Analysis* (Vol. 25, No. 2, February 1997: 1-2.

Farley, Reynolds, "Racial Trends and Differences in the United Stqtes 30 Years after theCivil Rights Decade," *Social Science Research*, Vol. 26, No. 3, 1997: 235-262.

Farley, Reynolds, and Frey, William H., "Changes in Segregation of Whites from Blacks: Small Steps Toward a More Integrated Society," *American Sociological Review*, Vol. 59, No. 1 (1994): 23-45.

Feagin, Joe R., The Continuing Significance of Race: Anti-black Discrimination in Public Places," *American Sociological Review*, Vol. 56, 1991: 101-116.

Feagin, Joe R., *Racial and Ethnic Relations* (Fifth edition) (Upper Saddle River, NJ: Prentice- Hall, 1996).

Feagin, Joe R., and Beagin, Clairece Booher, *Social Problems: A Critical Power-Conflict Perspective* (Fourth edition) (Upper Saddle River, NJ: Prentice Hall, 1994).

Feagin, Joe R., and Sikes, Melvin P., *Living with Racism: the Black Middle-Class Experience* (Boston: Beacon Press, 1994).

Featherstone, Michael, *Global Culture: Nationalism, Globalization, and Modernity* (A *Theory, Culture, and Society* Special Issue) (Newbury Park, CA: Sage, 1990).

Feise, Barbara H.; Hooker, Karen A.; Kotary, Lisa; and Schwager, Janet, "Family Rituals in the Early Stages of Parenthood," *Journal of Marriage and the Family*, Vol. 55, (August) 1993: 633-642.

Felson, Marcus, *Crime and Everyday Life* (Second edition) (Thousand Oaks, CA: Pine Forge Press, 1998).

Felson, R.B., "Big People Hit Little People: Sex Differences in Physical Power and Interpersonal Violence," *Criminology*, Vol. 34, 1996: 433-452.

Fendrich, Michael; Mackesy-Amiti, Mary Ellen; Wislar, Joseph S.; and Goldstein, Paul J., "Childhood Abuse and the Use of Inhalants: Differences by Degree of Use," *American Journal of Public Health*, Vol. 87, No. 5 (May) 1997: 765-769.

Fernandez, M., "Domestic Violence by Extended Family Members in India," *Journal of Interpersonal Violence*, Vol. 12, No 3, (June) 1993: 433-455.

Fernandez, Raul, *The United States-Mexico Border: A Political Economic Profile* (Notre Dame, IN: University of Notre Dame, 1977).

Festinger, Leon, and Carlsmith, J. Merrill, "Cognitive Consequences of Forced Compliance," *Journal of Abnormal Social Psychology*, Vol. 58, 1959: 203-210.

Fiedler, F.E., and Meuwese, W., "Leader's Contribution to Task Performance in Cohesive and Uncohesive Groups," *Journal of Abnormal and Social Psychology*, Vol. 67, 1963: 83-87.

Figurski, Thomas J., "Moral Development," in Edgar F. Borgatta and Marie L. Borgatta (Eds.), *Encyclopedia of Sociology*, Vol. 3 (New York: Macmillan Publishing Company, 1992), pp. 1310-1318.

Filtzer, Donald, *Soviet Workers and the Collapse of Perestroika: The Soviet Labour Process and Gorbachev's Reform, 1985-1991* (New York: Cambridge University Press, 1994).

Fine, Gary Alan, *Kitchens: The Culture of Restaurant Work* (Berkeley and Los Angeles: University of California Press, 1996).

Fine, Gary Alan, "Naturework and the Taming of the Wild: The Problem of 'Overpick' in the Culture of Mushroomers," *Social Problems*, Vol. 44, No. 1, (February) 1997: 68-88

Finkelstein, N.W., and Haskins, R., "Kindergarten Children Prefer Same-Color Peers," *Child Development*, Vol. 21, 1983: 502-508.

Firestone, S., *The Dialectics of Sex: The Case for a Feminist Revolution* (New York: Morrow, 1970).

Fisch, Mark L., *Annual Editions: Criminology* (Dushkin/McGraw Hill, 1998).

Fisher, Claude S., "CENTENNIAL ESSAY: The Subcultural Theory of Urbanism: A Twentieth-Year Assessment," *American Journal of Sociology*, Vol. 101, No. 3 (November) 1995: 543-577.

Fisher, Roger and Ury, William, *Getting to Yes: Negotiating Agreement Without Giving In* (NY: Penguin Books, 1986).

Fleisher, Mark, *Beggars and Thieves* (Madison: University of Wisconsin Press, 1995).

Flynn, Kevin, and Gerhardt, Gary, *The Silent Brotherhood: The Chilling Inside Story of America's Violent Anti-Government Militia Movement* (New York: The Free Press, 1990)

Fogarty, G.J., and White, C., "Differences Between Values of Australian Aboriginal and non-Aboriginal Students," *Journal of Cross-Cultural Psychology*, Vol. 25, 1994: 394-408.

Foley, Douglas E., *The Heartland Chronicles* (Philadelphia: University of Pennsylvania Press, 1995).

Fong, Eric, "A Comparative Perspective on Racial Residential Segregation: American and Canadian Experiences," *Sociological Quarterly*, Vol. 37, No. 2, 1996: 199-226.

Forsyth, D., *Group Dynamics* (Second edition) (Pacific Grove, CA: Brooks Cole, 1990).

Foster, George M., "The Dyadic Contract: A Model for the Social Structure of a Mexican Peasant Village," *American Anthropologist*, Vol. 63, 1961: 1178.

Foster, George M., *Empire's Children: The People of Tzintzuntzan* (Washington, D.C.: Institute of Anthropology, Smithsonian Institution, Publication No. 6, 1948).

Foucault, Michel, *Discipline and Punish* (Translated by Alan Sheridan) (New York: Vintage, 1979).

Foucault, Michel, *Madness and Civilization: A History of Insanity in the Age of Reason* (Translated by Richard Howard) (New York: Mentor, 1967).

Frank III, Arthur W., "Ethnomethodology," in Richard Lachmann, *The Encyclopedic Dictionary of Sociology* (Fourth edition) (Guilford, Connecticut: The Dushkin Publishing Group, 1991), pp. 107-108.

Frankenberg, Ruth, *White Women, Race Matters: The Social Construction of Whiteness* (Minneapolis: University of Minnesota Press, 1993).

Franklin, John Hope, "A Brief History of the Negro in the United States," in John P. Davis (Ed.), *The American Negro Reference Book* (Englewood Cliffs, NJ: Prentice-Hall, 1966), pp. 1-95.

Franklin, John Hope, *From Slavery to Freedom* (New York: Vintage Books, 1967).

Frazier, E. Franklin, *The Black Bourgeoisie: The Rise of a New Middle Class in the United States* (New York: The Free Press, 1957).

Frazier, E. Franklin, *The Negro Family in Chicago* (Chicago: The University of Chicago Press, 1932).

Frazier, E. Franklin, *The Negro in the United States* (New York: McMillan Company Press, 1957).

Frazier, E. Franklin, *Race and Culture Contacts in the Modern World* (New York: Alfred A. Knopf, 1957).

Freedman, Jonathan, "The Long-term Behavioral Effects of Cognitive Dissonance," *Journal of Experimental Social Psychology*, Vol. 1, 1965: 145-155.

Freeman, J. (Ed.), *Women* (Fifth edition) (Mountain View, CA: Mayfield Pubblishing Company, 1995).

Freud, Sigmund, *Civilization and Its Discontents* (London: Hogarth Press, 1930).

Freud, Sigmund, *The Future of an Illusion* (New York: Doubleday Anchor Books, 1957). (Originally published, 1927).

Freud, Sigmund, *Gesammelte Werke* (Frankfurt am Maine: S. Fisher, 1985-1938). *Beyond the Pleasure Principle,* in Vol. 18 of Sigmund Freud, *Standard Edition of the Complete Psychological Works of Sigmund Freud* (New York: Norton, 1920).

Freund, Julien, *The Sociology of Max Weber* (New York: Vintage, 1969).

Frey, W.H., and Farley, R., "Latino, Asian and Black Segregation in U.S. Metropolitan Areas: Are Multi-Ethnic Areas Different?," *Demography,* Vol. 33, No. 1, 1996: 35-50.

Friedan, Betty, *The Feminine Mystique* (New York: Dell Publishing Company, 1963).

Friedman, Debra and Hechter, Michael, "The Contribution of Rational Choice Theory to Macrosociological Research," *Sociological Theory,* Vol. 6 (Fall) 1988: 201-218.

Friedrich, Paul, "A Mexican Cacicazgo," *Ethnology,* Vol. 4, 1965: 190-209.

Frihart, Dale M., Humphries, Harry L., and Cameron, Brad, "Using Law Enforcement Personnel in Drug Free Education," unpublished manuscript, Pittsburg State University, Department of Social Science, 1990).

Fritschner, Linda Marie, "Karate: The Making and the Maintenance of an Underdog Class," *Journal of Sport Behavior,* Vol. 1, 1978: 3-13.

Fromm, Erich, *Greatness and Limitations of Freud's Thought* (New York: Signet, 1980).

Fromm, Erich, *Marx's Concept of Man* (New York: Ungar Press, 1985).

Fuchs, Victor R., *Women's Quest for Economic Equality* (Cambridge, MA: Harvard University Press, 1988).

Funk, Jeanne, B., and Buchman, Debra, "Children's Perceptions of Gender Differences in Social Approval for Playing Electronic Games," *Sex Roles,* Vol. 35, Nos. 3/4, 1996: 219-231.

Furnham, Adrian and Bitar, Nadine, "The Stereotyped Portrayal of Men and Women in British Television Advertisements," *Sex Roles,* Vol. 29, Nos. 3/4, 1993: 297-310.

Gabriel, Richard A., and Savage, P.L., *Crisis in Command: Mismanagement in the Army* (New York: Hill and Wang, 1978).

Galarza, Ernesto, *Merchants of Labor: The Mexican Bracero Story* (San Jose, CA: The Rosicrucian Press, 1964).

Galbraith, John Kenneth, *The Nature of Mass Poverty* (Cambridge, MA: Harvard University Press, 1979).

Gamio, Manuel, *Mexican Immigration to the United States* (Chicago: University of Chicago Press, 1930).

Gamson, William, "Hiroshima, the Holocaust, and the Politics of Exclusion," *American Sociological Review,* Vol. 60, 1995: 1-20.

Gamson, William, *Talking Politics* (New York: Cambridge University Press, 1992).

Garber, Philip, Alibali, Martha Wagner, and Goldin-Meadow, Susan, "Knowledge Conveyed in Gesture is Not Tied to the Hands," *Child Developmnet,* Vol. 69, No. 1, 1998: 75-84.

Garcia, A.M., The Development of Chicana Feminist Discourse, 1970-1980," in V.L. Ruiz, and E.C. DuBois (Eds.), *Unequal Sisters* (Second edition) (New York: Routledge, 1994), pp. 531-544.

Garfinkel, Harold, "Conditions of Successful Degradation Ceremonies," *American Journal of Sociology,* Vol. 6, No. 2 (March) 1956; 420-424.

Garner, James W., "Denationalization of American Citizens," *American Journal of International Law,* Vol. 21, 1927: 106-107.

Gaskell, G., and Smith, P., "Group Membership and Social Attitudes of Youth: An Investigation and Some Implications of Social Identity Theory," *Social Behaviour,* Vol. 1, 1986: 66- 77.

Gates, H.L. (Jr)., *Loose Canons: Notes on the Cultural Wars* (New York: Oxford University Press, 1992).

Gazetteer of the Bombay Presidency, Baroda, Vol. 7: 1883: 59.

Gazetteer of Bombay, Vol. 9 (Part 1), 1901: 433-437.

Gazetteer of the Bombay Presidency, "Gujarat Population: Hindus," Vol. 9 (Part 1), 1901: 437-438.

Gecas, Victor, "Socialization," in Edgar F. Borgatta and Marie L. Borgatta, (Eds.), *Encyclopedia of Sociology* (New York: Macmillan Publishing Company, 1992), pp. 1863-1872.

Gerber, Theodore P., and Hout, Michael, "Educational Stratification in Russia During the Soviet Period," *American Journal of Sociology,* Vol. 101, No. 3 (November) 1995: 611-660.

Gerbner, George, "Television Violence: the Power and the Peril," in Gail Dines and Jean M. Humez (Eds.), *Gender, Race, and Class in Media* (Newbury Park, CA: Sage Publications, 1995), 547-557.

Gerbner, George; Gross, L.; Morgan, M.; and Signorielli, N., "Growing up with Television: The Cultivation Perspective," in J. Bryant and D. Zillman (Eds.), *Media Effects: Advances in Theory and Research* (Hillsdale, NJ: Lawrence Erlbaum, 1994).

Gerstel, N., and Gross, H.E., "Gender and Families in the U.S.: The Reality of Economic Dependence," in J. Freeman (Ed.), *Women* (Fifth edition) (Mt. View, CA: Mayfield Publishing Company, 1995), pp. 92-127.

Gerth, Hans H., and Mills, C. Wright, *From Max Weber: Essays in Sociology* (New York: Oxford University Press, 1974). (Originally published, 1946).

Ghurye, G.S., *Caste and Race in India* (Bombay: Popular Prakashan, 1969).

Gibb, C.A., "The Sociometry of Leadership in Temporary Groups," *Sociometry,* Vol. 13, 1950: 226-243.

Gibbs, Leonard E., *Scientific Reasoning for Social Work: Bridging the Gap Between Research and Practice* (New York: McMillan Publishing Company, 1991).

Gibbs, Nancy, "End of the Run," *Time,* June 27, 1994: 29-35.

Gibson, M. A., *Accommodation without Assimilation: Sikh Immigrants in an American High School* (Ithica, NY: Cornell University Press, 1989).

Giddens, Anthony, *The Class Structure of the Advanced Societies* (New York: Harper and Row, 1975).

Giddens, Anthony, *The Consequences of Modernity* (Stanford: Stanford University Press, 1990).

Giddens, Anthony, *The Constitution of Society: Outlines of the Theory of Structuration* (Berkeley: The University of California Press, 1984).

Giddens, Anthony, *Sociology: A Brief but Critical Introduction* (New York: Harcourt Brace, Jovanovich, Inc., 1982).

Giddings, Franklin, *The Scientific Study of Human Society* (Chapel Hill, NC: University of North Carolina Press, 1924).

Giddings, P., *When and Where I Enter* (New York: Bantam, 1984).

Gilbert, Dennis, and Kahl, Joseph A , *The American Class Structure: A New Synthesis* (Fourth edition) (Belmont, Ca: Wadsworth, 1993).

Gillespie, Marie, *Television, Ethnicity, and Cultural Change* (New York: Routledge, 1995).

Gilligan, Carol, "Adolescent Development Reconsidered," *New Directions for Child Development,* Vol. 37, 1987: 63-92.

Gilligan, Carol, *In a Different Voice* (Cambridge, MA: Harvard University Press, 1982).

Gilligan, Carol, "Two Moral Orientations: Gender Differences and Similarities," *Merrill-Palmer Quarterly,* Vol. 34, 1988: 223-237.

Gilmore, Samuel, "Culture," in Edgar F. Borgatta and Marie L. Borgatta (Eds.), *Encyclopedia of Sociology* (New York: Macmillan Publishing Company, 1992), Vol. 1, pp. 404-411.

Giordano, Peggy C.; Cernkovich, Stephen A.; and De Maris, Alfred, "The Family and Peer Relations of Black Adolescents," *Journal of Marriage and the Family,* Vol. 55, (May) 1993: 277-287.

Giordano, Peggy C., "The Wider Circle of Friends in Adolescence," *American Journal of Sociology,* Vol. 101, 1995: 661-697.

Givens, Helen Lewis, "The Korean Community in Los Angeles County," M.A. Thesis, University of Southern California, 1939.

Glaser, Barney G., and Strauss, Anselm, *The Discovery of Grounded Theory* (Chicago: Aldine, 1967).

Glassman, Ronald M., *Democracy and Despotism in Primitive Society* (Port Washington, NY: Kennicott Press, 1986).

Glenn, Evelyn N., Issei, Nisei, War Bride: *Three Generations of Japanese American Women in Domestic Service* (Philadelphia: Temple University Press, 1986).

Glueck, Sheldon, and Glueck, Eleanor, *Of Delinquency and Crime* (Springfield: Charles C. Thomas, 1974).

Goering, John, and Wienk, Ron (Eds.), *Mortgage Lending, Racial Discrimination, and Federal Policy* (Washington: Urban Institute Press, 1996).

Goffman, Erving, *Asylums: Essays on the Social Situation of Mental Patients and Other Inmates* (New York: Anchor Books, 1967).

Goffman, Erving, *Behavior in Public Places* (New York: Free Press, 1963).

Goffman, Erving, *The Presentation of Self in Everyday Life* (Garden City, New York: Doubleday Anchor, 1959).

Goffman, Erving, *Stigma: Notes on the Management of a Spoiled Identity* (New Jersey: Prentice Hall, 1963).

Goldberg, Susan, and Lewis, Michael, "Play Behavior in the Year-Old Infant: Early Sex Differences," *Child Development*, Vol. 40 1969: 21-31.

Golding, Morton J., *A Short History of Puerto Rico* (New York: New American Library, 1973.

Goldman, Paul, and Van Houten, Donald R., "Bureaucracy and Domination: Managerial Strategy in Turn-of-the Century American Industry," in Frank Hearn, *The Transformation of Industrial Organization: Management, Labor and Society in the United States* (Belmont, CA: Wadsworth Publishing Company, 1988).

Goleman, Daniel, *Emotional Intelligence* (New York: Bantam Books, 1995).

Gonzales, Juan L. Jr., *The Affordability of Auto Insurance Among Low Income Families in Los Angeles* (San Francisco, CA: Consumers Union, 1991b).

Gonzales, Juan L. Jr., "Asian Indian Immigration Patterns: The Origins of the Sikh Community in California," *International Migration Review*, Vol. 20, 1986.

Gonzales, Juan L. Jr., "Exogamous Marriage Patterns Among The Sikhs of California: 1904- 1945," *International Journal of Contemporary Sociology*, Vol. 25, Nos. 1 & 2, 1988.

Gonzales, Juan L. Jr., "The Growth of the Black Ghetto in Oakland: A Case of Residential Segregation, 1960-1988." Paper presented at the Annual Meetings of the Western Social Science Association, Albuquerque, NM, April, 1989.

Gonzales, Juan L. Jr., *The Lives of Ethnic Americans* (Dubuque, IA: Kendall Hunt, 1991a).

Gonzales, Juan L. Jr., *The Lives of Ethnic Americans* (Second edition) (Dubuque, IA: Kendall-Hunt Publishing Company, 1994).

Gonzales, Juan L. Jr., *Mexican and Mexican American Farm Workers: The California Agricultural Industry* (New York: Praeger, 1985).

Gonzales, Juan L. Jr., "The Pattern of Ethnic Residential Segregation in Oakland, California: 1940-1980." Paper presented at the Annual Meetings of the Western Social Science Association, Denver, CO, April, 1988.

Gonzales, Juan L. Jr., "Race Relations in the United States," *Humbolt Journal of Social Relations*, Vol. 19, (No. 2), 1993: 39-78.

Gonzales, Juan L. Jr., *Racial and Ethnic Families in America* (Dubuque, IA: Kendall/Hunt, 1992).

Gonzales, Juan L. Jr., *Racial and Ethnic Families in America* (Second edition) (Dubuque, IA: Kendall-Hunt Publishing Company, 1994).

Gonzales, Juan L. Jr., *Racial and Ethnic Groups in America* (Dubuque, IA: Kendall-Hunt Publishing Company, 1990).

Gonzales, Juan L. Jr., *Racial and Ethnic Groups in America* (Third edition) (Dubuque, IA: Kendall-Hunt Publishing Company, 1996).

Goodall, Jane van Lawick, *The Behavior of Free-Living Chimpanzees in the Gombe Stream Reserve* (London: Ballière, Tindall, and Cassell, 1968).

Goodall, Jane, *The Chimpanzees of Gombe: Patterns of Behavior* (Cambridge, MA: Belknap Press of Harvard University Press, 1986).

Goodall, Jane, *In the Shadow of Man* (Boston: Houghton Mifflin, 1971).

Goode, Erich, *Deviant Behavior* (Fourth edition) (Englewood Cliffs, NJ: Prentice Hall, 1994).

Goode, Erich, *Deviant Behavior* (Fifth edition) (Upper Saddle River, NJ: Prentice Hall, 1997).

Goode, William J., *The Family* (Second edition) (Englewood Cliffs, NJ: Prentice Hall, 1982).

Goode, William J., *World Revolution and Family Patterns* (New York: The Free Press, 1963).

Goodman, Mary Ellen, *Race Awareness in Young Children* (Revised edition) (New York: Collier, 1964).

Goodner, James, *Indian Americans in Dallas: Migrations, Missions and Style of Adaptation* (Minneapolis: University of Minnesota Press., 1969).

Goring, Charles, *The English Convict* (London: His Majesty's Stationary Office, 1913).

Gossett, Thomas F., *Race: The History of an Idea in America* (New York: Schocken Books, 1965).

Gottlieb, Martin, "Racial Split at the End, As At the Start," *New York Times* (Late New York Edition), October 4, 1995, p. A1.

Gottman, John, "Same and Cross-Sex Friendship in Young Children," in John Gottman and J. Parker (Eds.), *Conversation of Friends* (New York: Cambridge University Press, 1986).

Gourevitch, Philip, "Letter from Rwanda: After the Genocide," *The New Yorker,* December 18, 1995: 78-94.

Government of India, Document: Indians in South Africa, "Bill to Make Provision for the Reservation of Residential and Trading Areas in Urban Areas for Persons, Other Than Natives Having Racial Characteristics in Common," File #:88 (iii), 1921 and 1924: 11.

Greatbatch, David and Dingwall, Robert, "Argumentative Talk in Divorce Mediation Sessions," *American Sociological Review,* Vol. 62, (February) 1997: 151-170.

Greenberg, D.F. and Bystryn, M.H., "Capitalism, Bureaucracy, and Male Homosexuality," in S. Seidman (Ed.), *Queer Theory/Sociology* (Boston: Blackwell Publishers Inc., 1996), pp. 83-110.

Greer, G., *The Female Eunuch* (London: Verso, 1970).

Grimshaw, Allen D. (Ed.), *Racial Violence in the United States* (Chicago: Aldine, 1969).

Grodzins, Morton, *The Loyal and the Disloyal: Social Boundaries of Patriotism and Treason* (Chicago: University of Chicago Press, 1956).

Grossman, Jean Baldwin, and Garry, Eileen M., "Mentoring—A Proven Delinquency Prevention Strategy," *Juvenile Justice Bulletin,* (April) 1997 (Washington, D.C.: U.S. Department of Justice, Office of Justice Programs, Office of Juvenile Justice and Delinquency Prevention, 1997).

Grotpeter, Jennifer K., and Crick, Nicki, R., "Relational Aggression, Overt Aggression, and Friendship," *Child Development,* Vol. 67, 1996: 2328-2338.

Gudykunst, W.B., "Culture and Intergroup Processes," in M.H. Bond (Ed.), *The Cross-Cultural Challenge to Social Psychology* (Newbury Park, CA: Sage, 1989).

Guiteras-Holmes, Calixta, "Clanes y Sistema de Parentesco de Cancuc (Mexico," *Acta Americana,* Vol. 5, 1947: 1-17.

Guiteras-Holmes, Calixta, *Perils of the Soul: The World View of a Tzotzil Indian* (New York: The Free Press, 1961).

Gunter, B., and Svennevig, M., *Behind and in Front of the Screen* (London: John Libbey, 1987)

Gusfield, Joseph R., "Primordialism and Nationality, *Transaction,* Vol. 33, No. 2, (January/February) 1996: 53-57.

Hacker, A., *Two Nations: Black and White* (New York: Ballentine, 1995).

Hagan, Frank E., *Introduction to Criminology* (Chicago: Nelson-Hall, 1994).

Hagan, John, *Structural Criminology* (New Brunswick, NJ: Rutgers University Press, 1989).

Hagan, William T., *American Indians* (Chicago: University of Chicago Press, 1961).

Hagstrom, Warren O., "What is the Meaning of Santa Claus?," *The American Sociologist,* Vol. 1, 1966: 248-254.

Haigler, V.F., Day, H.D., and Marshall, D.D., "Parental Attachment and Gender-Role Identity," *Sex Roles,* Vol. 33, 1995: 203-220.

Hale, Robert M., "The United States and Japanese Immigration," unpublished Ph.D. Dissertation, The University of Chicago, 1945.

Haley, Aley and X, Malcolm, *The Autobiography of Malcolm X* (New York: Grove Press, 1965)

Hall, Edward T., *The Hidden Dimension* (New York: Doubleday, 1966).

Hall, Edward T., *The Silent Language* (Garden City, New York: Doubleday, 1959).

Hamilton, Alexander, Madison, James, and Jay, John, *The Federalist Papers* (New York: Bantam Books, 1982). (Originally published, 1787-1788).

Hampson, S.E., *The Construction of Personality* (Second edition) (London: Routledge, 1988).

Hannan, Michael, Tuma, Nancy Brandon, and Groenwald, Lyle, "Income and Marital Events," *American Journal of Sociology,* Vol. 82, 1977, pp. 186-211.

Hanson, Wynne, "The Urban Indian Woman and Her Family," *Social Casework,* Vol. 61, No. 8, 1980: 476-483.

Hanson, Wynne, "The Urban Indian Woman and Her Family," *Social Casework,* Vol. 61, No. 8, 1980: 476-483.

Hardiman, D., "The Crises of the Lesser Patidaars: Peasant Agitations in Gujarat 1917-1934," in D.A. Low (Ed.) *Congress and the Raj* (Columbia: South Asia Books, 1977).

Harlow, Harry F., "The Heterosexual Affectional System in Monkeys," *American Psychologist,* Vol. 17, 1962: 1-9.

Harlow, Harry F., and Harlow, Margaret Kuenne, "Social Deprivation in Monkeys," *Scientific American,* Vol. 207, 1962: 137-146.

Harlow, Harry F., Harlow, Margaret Kuenne, and Suomi, S.J., "From Thought to Therapy: Lessons from a Primate Laboratory," *American Scientist,* Vol. 59, 1971: 1-13.

Harlow, Harry F. and Zimmerman, R.R., "Affectional Responses in the Infant Monkey," *Science,* Vol. 130, 1959: 421-432.

Harré, Rom and Lamb, Roger (Eds.), *The Dictionary of Personality and Social Psychology* (Cambridge, MA: the MIT Press, 1986).

Harris, M. J., and Rosenthal, R., "Four Factors in the Mediation of Teacher Expectancy Effects," in R.S. Feldman (Ed.), *The Social Psychology of Education* (New York: Cambridge University Press, 1986).

Harris, Marvin, *Cannibals and Kings: The Origins of Cultures* (New York: Random House, 1977).

Harris, Marvin, *Cows, Pigs, Wars, and Witches: The Riddles of Culture* (New York: Vintage Books, 1975).

Harris, Marvin, *Cultural Materialism: The Struggle for the Science of Culture* (New York: Random House, 1978).

Harrison, Algea O., Wilson, Melvin N., Pine, Charles J., Chan, Samuel Q., and Buriel, Raymond, "Family Ecologies of Ethnic Minority Children," *Child Development,* Vol. 61, (No. 2) 1990: 347-362.

Harrison, D., *The White Tribe of South Africa* (Berkeley: University of California Press, 1981).

Haslip-Viera, and Baver, Sherrie L., (Ed.), *Latinos in New York: Communities in Transition* (Notre Dame, IN: University of Notre Dame Press, 1996).

Hatfield, Elaine, and Sprecher, Susan, *Mirror, Mirror . . . The Importance of Looks in Everyday Life* (Albany, NY: State University of New York Press, 1986).

Hauberg, Clifford A., *Puerto Rico and the Puerto Ricans* (New York: Twayne Publishers, 1974).

Hawkes, T., *That Shakespeherian Rag: Essays on a Critical Process* (London: Methuen, 1986).

Hawkins, J. David; Graham, John W.; Maguin, Eugene; Abbott, Robert; Hill, Karl G; and Catalano, Richard F., "Exploring the Effects of Age of Alcohol Use Initiation and Psychosocial Risk Factors on Subsequent Alcohol Misuse," *Journal of Studies on Alcohol,* Vol. 58, No. 3, (May) 1997: 280-290.

Hawthorn, Geoffrey, *Enlightenment & Despair: A History of Sociology* (London: Cambridge University Press, 1976).

Hazan, Cindy, "Attachment," in David Levinson (Ed.), *Encyclopedia of Marriage and the Family,* Vol. 1 (New York: Simon and Schuster Macmillan, 1995), pp. 40-50.

Hazan, C., and Hutt, M.J., "Continuity and Change in Internal Working Models of Attachment," (Ithica, NY: Cornell University Department of Human Development and Family Studies, 1993).

Heath, Anthony, *Rational Choice and Social Exchange* (Cambridge, England: Cambridge University Press, 1976).

Hechter, Michael, "Rational Choice Foundations of Social Order," in Jonathan Turner (Ed.), *Theory Building in Sociology* (Newbury Park, CA: 1988).

Hechter, Michael, *Principles of Group Solidarity* (Berkeley: University of California Press, 1987).

Heimsath, C.H., *Indian Nationalism and Hindu Social Reform* (Delhi: Oxford University Press, 1964).

Heller, Celia S. (Ed.), *Structured Social Inequality: A Reader in Comparative Social Stratification* (Second edition) (New York: Macmillan Publishing Co., 1987).

Henley, Nancy M., *Body Politics: Power, Sex, and Nonverbal Communication* (Englewood Cliffs, NJ: Prentice-Hall, 1977).

Herrnstein, Richard J., and Murray, Charles, *The Bell Curve: Intelligence and Class Structure in American Life* (New York: Free Press, 1994).

Heslin, Richard, and Patterson, Miles L., *Nonverbal Behavior and Social Psychology* (New York: Plenum Press, 1982).

Hess, Gary R., "The 'Hindu' in America: Immigration and Naturalization Policies and India," *Pacific Historical Review,* Vol. 38, 1969: 59-79.

Hess, Gary R., "The Forgotten Asian Americans: The East Indian Community in the United States," *Pacific Historical Review,* Vol. 43, 1974: 576-596.

Hewstone, M., "The Ultimate Attribution Error? A Review of the Literature on Intergroup Causal Attribution," *European Journal of Social Psychology,* Vol. 20, 1990: 311-335.

Hindelang, Michael J., Hirschi, Travis, and Weis, J.G., *Measuring Delinquency* (Beverly Hills: Sage, 1981).

Hippensteele, Susan K., and Chesney-Lind, Meda, "Race and Sex Discrimination in the Academy," *Thought and Action,* Vol. 11, (Fall) 1995: 43-66.

Hirschfeld, Lawrence A., *Race in the Making: Cognition, Culture, and the Child's Construction of Human Kinds* (Cambridge, MA: MIT Press, 1996).

Hirschi, Travis, *Causes of Delinquency* (Berkeley: University of California Press, 1969).

Hirschi, Travis, and Hindelang, Michael J., "Intelligence and Delinquency: A Revisionist Review," *American Sociological Review*, Vol. 42 (August) 1977: 571-587.

Hobbes, Thomas, *Leviathan* (Glasgow, Scotland: Fontana, 1962). (Originally published in 1651).

Hobfoll, S.E., *The Ecology of Stress* (New York: Hemisphere, 1988).

Hobson, J. A., *Imperialism* (Ann Arbor: The University of Michigan Press, 1972). (Originally 1902).

Hochschild, A., with Machung, A., *The Second Shift* (New York: Avon Books, 1989).

Hoetink, H., "Resource Competition, Monopoly, and Socioracial Diversity," in L.A. Despres (Ed.), *Ethnicity and Resource Competition in Plural Societies* (The Hague: Mouton Publishers, 1975).

Hoffman, Abraham, *Unwanted Mexican Americans in the Great Depression: Repatriation Pressures, 1929-1939* (Tucson, AZ: University of Arizona Press, 1974).

Hoffnung, M., Motherhood: Contemporary Conflict for Women," in J. Freeman (Ed.), *Women* (Fifth edition) (Mt. View, CA: Mayfield Publishing Co., 1995), pp. 162-181.

Hofstede, Geert, *Cultures and Organizations: Software of the Mind* (London: McGraw-Hill, 1990).

Hollander, Edwin P., "Leadership and Power," in Gardner Lindzey and Elliott Aronson, *The Handbook of Social Psychology* (Third edition) (New York: Random House, 1985): pp. 485-537.

Holmes, Richard, *Acts of War: The Behavior of Men in Battle* (New York: The Free Press, 1985).

Hooks, B., *Talking Back* (Boston, MA: South End Press, 1989).

Holstein, James A., and Gubrium, Jaber F., "Field Research Methods," in Edgar F. Borgatta and Marie L. Borgatta (Eds.), *Encyclopedia of Sociology* (New York: Macmillan Publishing Company, 1992), pp. 711-716.

Holy, Ladislav, *The Little Czech and the Great Czech Nation: National Identity and the Post-Communist Transformation of Society* (New York: Cambridge University Press, 1996).

Holzer, Harry J., *What Employers Want: Job Prospects for Less-Educated Workers* (New York: Russell Sage Foundation, 1996).

Hom, Harry, Jr., "Can You Predict the Overjustification Effect?," *Teaching of Psychology*, Vol. 21, 1994: 36-37.

Hondagneu-Sotelo, Pirrette, *Gendered Transitions: Mexican Experiences of Immigration* (Berkeley: University of California Press, 1994).

Hoover, Kenneth and Donovan, Todd, *The Elements of Social Scientific Thinking* (Sixth edition) (New York: St. Martin's Press, 1994).

Hossfield, K.J., "Hiring Immigrant Women: Silicon Valley's 'Simple Formula,'" in M. Zinn and B.T. Dill (Eds.), *Women of Color in US Society* (Philadelphia: Temple University Press, 1994), pp. 65-93.

Howes, C., "Same- and Cross-Sex Friendships: Implications for Interaction and Social Skills," *Early Childhood Research Quarterly*, Vol. 3, 1988: 21-37.

Hraba, Joseph, Dunham, Carolyn, Tumanov, Sergey, and Hagendoorn, Louk, "Prejudice in the Former Soviet Union," *Ethnic and Racial Studies*, Vol. 20, No. 3, (July) 1997: 613-627.

Hubbard, R., "Rethinking Women's Biology," in A. Kesselman, L.D. McNair, and N. Schniedewind (Eds.), *Women: Images and Reality* (Mt. View, CA: Mayfield Publishing Company, 1995b), pp. 25-30.

Hubbard, R., "Using Pregnancy to Control Women," in A. Kesselman, L.D. McNair, and N. Schniedewind (Eds.) *Women: Images and Reality* (Mt. View, CA: Mayfield Publishing Company, 1995a), pp. 25-30.

Huesmann, L. Rowell., Eron, Leonard, and Yarmel, Patty Warnick, "Intellectual Functioning and Aggression," *Journal of Personality and Social Psychology*, Vol. 52, No. 1, (January) 1987: 232-240..

Hughes, John A.; Martin, Peter J.: and Sharrock, W. W., *Understanding Classical Sociology* (London: Sage Publications, 1995).

Hughes, L.A., "'But that's Not *Really* Mean': Competing in a Cooperative Mode," *Sex Roles*, Vol. 19, 1988: 669 -6876.

Hum, Magi, *The Dictionary of Feminist Theory* (Columbus: Ohio State University Press, 1990).

Humphreys, Laud, *Tearoom Trade: Impersonal Sex in Public Places* (Chicago: Aldine, 1970).

Humphries, Harry L., "Durkheim, Weber and Marx on Socialism: A Reevaluation in Light of Recent Events in Eastern Europe," Paper presented at the Midwest Sociological Society Annual Meeting, 1992.

Humphries, Harry L., "Ethnicity and Nationalism in Russia and in the Newly Independent States of Central and Eastern Europe," College of Arts and Science Seminar, Pittsburg State University, April 7, 1998.

Humphries, Harry L., "Lessons From The Past: An Assessment of Russia's Progress Toward Market Economies," *Economic Institute Annual Publications* (Kazan, Russia: Kazan State University Press, 1995.

Humphries, Harry L., "Old Youth Gangs and the New Rich in Russia," Western Social Science Association Annual Meeting, Albuquerque, New Mexico, April 24, 1997.

Humphries, Harry L., "The Politics and Structure of Intermediary Class Positions: An Empirical Examination of Recent Theories of Class," unpublished Ph.D. dissertation, Department of Sociology, University of Oregon, 1984 (Ann Arbor, MI.: University Microfilms, 1984).

Humphries, Harry L., "The Rise of Sociology in Western Europe in Comparison to Eastern Europe," 1996, Social Science Department, Pittsburg State University, Pittsburg, Kansas. Unpublished manuscript.

Humphries, Harry L., Smith, Ronald W., and Preston, Frederick, "Alienation From Work: A Case Study of Casino Card Dealers in Las Vegas, Nevada." in R. Eadington (Ed.), *Gambling and Society* (New York: Charles C. Norton Publishers, Inc.: 1976), pp. 229-246.

Humphries, Harry R., unpublished sermon, 1984.

Hunt, Darnell M., *Screening the Los Angeles "Riots": Race, Seeing, and Resistance* (New York: Cambridge University Press, 1997).

Hunt, Geoffrey; Joe, Karen; and Waldorf, Dan, "Culture and Ethnic Identity Among Southeast Asian Gang Members, *Free Inquiry: Creative Sociology*, Vol. 25, No. 1, (May) 1997: 9-21.

Hunter Gault, Charlayne, *In My Place* (New York: Vintage Books, 1993). (Originally Published by Farrar, Straus, Giroux, 1992).

Hurh, Won Moo, "Comparative Study of Korean Immigrants in the United States: A Typology," *Korean Christian Scholars Journal*, (Spring) 1974: 60-69.

Hurtado, Aida, Gurin, Patricia, and Peng, Timothy, "Social Identities—A Framework for Studying the Adaptations of Immigrants and Ethnics: The Adaptations of Mexicans in the United States," *Social Problems*, Vol. 41, 1994: 129 - 151.

Hurwitz, J.I., Zander, A.F., and Hymovitch, B., "Some Effects of Power on the Relations Among Group Members," in D. Cartwright and A. Zander (Eds.), *Group Dynamics* (Second edition) (London: Tavistock, 1960).

Hyman, Herbert H., *Interviewing in Social Research* (Chicago: University of Chicago Press, 1954).

Hyman, Herbert H., "The Psychology of Status," *Archives of Psychology*, No. 269, 1942.

Ibbetson, Sir D., *Punjab Castes* (Lahore: Sh. Mubarak Ali, 1916).

Ichihashi, Yamato, *Japanese in the United States* (Stanford, CA: Stanford University Press, 1932).

Ichioka, Yuji, *The Issei: The World of the First Generation Japanese Immigrants, 1885-1924* (New York: The Free Press, 1988).

IMF, *International Monetary Fund: Quarterly Reports, 1995* (Paris: The World Bank, 1995).

Intons-Peterson, M. J., and Reddel, M., "What do People Ask About a Neonate?," *Developmental Psychology*, Vol. 20, 1984: 358-359.

Ireland, Ralph R., "Indian Immigration in the United States, 1901-1964," *Indian Journal of Economics*, Vol. 46, No. 183, 1966: 465-476.

Ishida, Hiroschi, Müller, Walter, and Ridge, John M., "Class Origin, Class Destination, and Education: A Cross-National Study of Ten Industrial Nations," *American Journal of Sociology*, Vol. 101 No. 1, (July) 1995: 145-193.

Itard, J.M.G., *The Wild Boy of Aveyron* (New York: Appleton-Century Crosfts, 1932).

Iwata, Masakazu, "The Japanese Immigrants in California Agriculture," *Agricultural History*, Vol. 36, 1962: 25-37.

Jackman, Mary R., *The Velvet Glove: Paternalism and Conflict in Gender, Class, and Race Relations* (Berkeley: Unibversity of California Press, 1994).

Jackman, Mary R. and Robert W. Jackman, in Jamshid A. Momeni (Ed.), *Race, Ethnicity, and Minority Housing in the United States* (New York: Greenwood Press, 1986), pp. 39-52.

Jackson, Linda A., and, Olivia, "Body Type Preferences and Body Characteristics Associated with Attractive and Unattractive Bodies by African Americans and Anglo Americans," *Sex Roles*, Vol. 35, Nos. 5/6, 1996: 295-307.

Jacobs, Jerry A. (Ed.), *Gender Inequality At Work* (Thousand Oaks, CA: Sage Publications, 1995).

Jacobs, P.A., Brunton, M., Melville, M.M., Brittain, R.P., and McClemont, W.F., "Aggressive Behaviour, Mental Sub-Normality, and the XYY Male," *Nature*, Vol. 208, 1965: 1351-1352.

Jacoby, Harold S., "A Half Century of Appraisal of East Indians in the United States," Sixth Annual College of the Pacific Faculty Research Lectur, University of the Pacific, Stockton, CA, 1956.

Jaeger, Gertrude, and Selznick, Philip, "A Normative Theory of Culture," *American Sociological Review*, Vol. 29, 1964: 653-669.

Jamieson, Kathleen Hall, *Beyond The Double* (New York: Oxford University Press, 1995).

Janis, Irving, L., "Counteracting the Adverse Effects of Concurrence-Seeking in Policy-Planning Groups: Theory and Research Perspectives," in H. Brandstater, Davis, J.H., and Stocker-Kreichgauer, G. (Eds.), *Group Decision Making* (New York: Academic Press, 1982), pp. 477-501.

Janis, Irving L., *Crucial Decisions: Leadership in Policymaking and Crisis Management* (New York: Free Press, 1989).

Janis, Irving L., "Groupthink," *Psychology Today*, November, 1971: 43-46.

Janis, Irving L., "Sources of Error in Strategic Decision Making," in J.M. Pennings (Ed.), *Organizational Strategy and Change* (San Francisco: Jossey-Bass, 1985).

Janis, Irving L., *Victims of Groupthink* (Boston: Houghton Mifflin, 1972).

Janis, Irving L., and Mann, L., *Decisonmaking: A Psychological Analysis of Conflict, Choice, and Commitment* (New York: Free Press, 1977).

Jaret, C., *Contemporary Racial and Ethnic Relations* (New York: Harper Collins, 1995).

Jasso, Guillermina, "Assessing Individual and Group Differences in the Sense of Justice," *Social Science Research*, Vol. 23, 1994: 368-406.

Jenness, Valerie, and Broad, Kendal, *Hate Crimes: New Social Movements and the Politics of Violence* (NY: Aldine de Gruyter, 1997).

Jet, "Opinion Poll Says Race Plays Role in O.J. Simpson Case," *Jet*, Vol. 86, (July 25, 1994): 16-18.

Jiobu, Robert M., *Ethnicity and Assimilation* (Albany: State University of New York Press, 1988).

Johnson, Cathryn, "Gender, Legitimate Authority, and Leader-Subordinate Conversations," *American Sociological Review*, Vol. 59, 1994: 122-135.

Johnson, C.B., Stockdale, M.S., and Saal, F.E., "Persistence of Men's Misperceptions of Friendly Cues Across a Variety of Interpersonal Encounters," *Psychology of Women Quarterly*," Vol. 15, 1991: 463-475.

Johnson, J. Randall, "Social Support," in Edgar F. Borgatta and Maire L. Borgatta, *Encyclopedia of Sociology*, Vol. 4 (New York: Macmillan and Company, 1992), pp. 1976-1979.

Johnson, Jean, "Americans' Views on Crime and Law Enforcement," U.S. Department of Justice, Office of Justice Programs, National Institute of Justice, *National Institute of Justice Journal*, (September) 1997: 9-14.

Jones, James, *Bad Blood* (New York: Free Press, 1981).

Jones, Philip W., *World Bank Financing of Education: Lending, Learning, and Development* (London: Routledge, 1992).

Jones, Richard Glyn, *The Mammoth Book of Killer Women* (New York: Carrol & Craf Publishers, Inc., 1993).

Jordan, Barbara, and Hearon, Shelby, *Barbara Jordan, A Self-Portrait* (Garden city, NY: Doubleday, 1979).

Jordan, Winthrop D., *White Over Black: American Attitudes Toward the Negro, 1550-1812* (Baltimore: Penguin Books Inc., 1968).

Joseph, P.S., *No Pity* (New York: Random House, 1994).

Jourad, Sidney M., "An Exploratory Study of Body Accessibility," *British Journal of Social and Clinical Psychology*, 1966, Vol. 5, 1966: 221-231.

Jouriles, E.N., and O'Leary, K.D., "Interspousal Reliability of Reports of Marital Violence," *Journal of Marriage and the Family*, Vol. 53, 1985: 419-421.

Julia, Raul, "Master Student Raul Julia," in Dave Ellis, *Becoming a Master Student* (Eighth edition) (Houghton Mifflin, 1997), p. 340.

Jussim, L., "Teacher Expectations: Self-Fulfilling Prophecies, Perceptual Biases, and Accuracy," *Journal of Personality and Social Psychology*, Vol. 57, 1989: 469-480.

Kabagarama, Daisy, *Breaking the Ice: A Guide to Understanding People from Other Cultures* (Boston: Allyn & Bacon, 1993).

Kadushin, Charles, "Friendship Among the French Political Elite," *American Sociological Review*, Vol. 60 (April), 1995: 202-221.

Kagan, Jerome, *Infancy: Its Place in Human Development* (Cambridge: Harvard University Press, 1978).

Kagan, Jerome, *Unstable Ideas: Temperament, Cognition, and Self* (Cambridge, MA: Harvard University Press, 1989).

Kalish, Susan, "Interracial Births Increase as U.S. Ponders Racial Definitions," *Population Today*, Vol. 23, No. 4, 1995: 1-2.

Kanter, Rosabeth Moss, *Commitment and Community: Communes and Utopias in Sociological Perspective* (Cambridge, MA: Harvard University Press, 1972).

Kanter, Rosabeth Moss, *Men and Women of the Corporation* (New York: Basic Books, 1977).

Karraker, Katherine Hildebrandt; Vogel, Dena Ann, and Lake, Margaret Ann, "Parents' Gender-Stereotyped Perceptions of Newborns: The Eye of the Beholder Revisited," *Sex Roles*, Vol. 33, Nos. 9/10, 1995: 687-701.

Kates, Gary, *Monsieur d'Eon Is a Woman: A Tale of Political Intrigue and Sexual Masquerade* (Boulder CO: Basic Books, 1996).

Katz, Jack, *Seductions of Crime: Moral and Sensual Attractions of Doing Evil* (New York: Basic Books, 1988).

Keil, Thomas J., and Vito, Gennaro F., "Race, Homicide Severity, and Application of the Death Penalty: A Consideration of the Barnett Scale," *Criminology*, Vol. 27 (August) 1989: 511-535.

Keirsey, David and Bates, Marilyn, *Please Understand Me: Character & Temperament Types* (Del Mar, CA: Prometheus Nemesis Book Company, 1984).

Kelling, George et. al., *The Kansas City Preventive Patrol Experiment* (Washington, D.C.: Plice Foundation, 1974).

Kelly, H.H., "Communication in Experimentally Created Hierarchies," *Human Relations*, Vol. 4, 1951: 39-56.

Kemper, K.A.; Sargent, R.G.; Drane, J.W.; Valois, R.F.; Hussey, J.R.; and Leatherman, T.L., "Black and White Adolescent Females' Perceptions of Ideal Body Size and Social Norms," *Obesity Research*, Vol. 2, 1994: 117-126.

Kennedy, John F., *Profiles in Courage* (New York: Harper, 1956).

Kephart, William M., and Zellner, William W., *Extraordinary Groups: An Examination of Unconventional Lifestyles* (New York: St. Martin's Press, 1998).

Kerbo, Harold R., *Social Stratification and Inequality: Class Conflict in Historical and Comparative Perspective* (Second edition) (New York: McGraw-Hill, 1991).

Kertzer, David I., *Ritual, Politics, and Power* (New Haven, CT: Yale University Press, 1988).

Kesselman, A.; McNair, L.D.; and Schniedewind, N. (Eds.), *Women: Images and Reality* (Mt. View, CA: Mayfield Publishing Company, 1995).

Khuzin, Fayas, *History of Tatar and Volga People*, unpublished Ph.D. dissertation, Department of History, Leningrad State University, St. Petersburg, Russia, 1995.

Kim, Bernice B., "The Koreans in Hawaii," *Social Science*, Vol. 9, No. 4, 1934: 409-413.

Kim, Elaine, H., "Home Is Where the *Han* Is: A Korean American Perspective on the Los Angeles Upheavals," in Robert Godding-Williams (Ed.), *Reading Rodney King: Reading Urban Uprising* (New York: Routledge, 1993), pp. 215-235.

Kim, E., "Sex Tourism in Asia: A Reflection of Political and Economic Inequality," *Critical Perspectives in third World America*, Vol. 2, No. 1, 1984: 214-231.

Kim, Uichol; Choi, Sang-Chin; Gelfand, Michele J., and Yuki, Masaki, et. al., "Culture, Gender, and Self: A Perspective from Individualism-Collectivism Research," *Journal of Personality and Social Psychology*, Vol. 69, No. 5, 1995: 925-937.

Kim, Warren Y., *Koreans in America* (Seoul, Korea: Po Chin Chai Printing Co., 1971).

Kimura, Yukiko, *Issei: Japanese Immigrants in Hawaii* (Honolulu, HI: University of Hawaii Press, 1988).

King, Martin Luther Jr., *Stride Toward Freedom: The Montgomery Story* (New York: Harper and Brothers, 1958).

Kingston, Maxine Hong, *Woman Warrior: Memoirs of a Girlhood Among Ghosts* (New York: Vintage Books, 1989).

Klapp, Orrin E., "Social Types: Process and Structrue," *American Sociological Review*, Vol. 23, No. 6, (December) 1958: 674-678.

Klein, Gillian, *Reading into Racism: Bias in Children's Literature and Learning Materials* (London, England: Routledge and Kegan Paul, 1985).

Klein, M.W., *Street Gangs and Street Workers* (Englewood Cliffs, NJ: Prentice Hall, 1971).

Klockars, Carl, "The Contemporary Crisis of Marxist Criminology," *Criminology*, Vol. 16 (Fall) 1979: 477-515.

Kluegel, James R., "Trends in Whites' Explanations of the Black-White Gap in Socio—economic Status, 1977-1989," *American Sociological Review*, Vol. 47, 1990: 512-525.

Knight, G.P., and Chao, C., "Gender Differences in the Cooperative, Competitive, and Individualistic Values of Children," *Motivation and Emotion*, Vol. 13, 19890: 125-141.

Knight, Kim H., Elfenbein, Morton H., and Messina, Julie A., "A Preliminary Scale to Measure Connected and Separate Knowing: The Knowing Styles Inventory," *Sex Roles*, Vol. 33, 1995: 499-512.

Kohlberg, Lawrence, "Stage and Sequence: The Cognitive-Developmental Approach to Socialization," in David A. Goslin (Ed.), *Handbook of Socialization Theory and Research* (Chicago: Rand McNally, 1969), pp. 347-480.

Kohlberg, Lawrence, Levine, Charles, and Hewer, Alexandra, *Moral Stages: A Current Formulation and a Response to Critics* (Basel, Switzerland: Karger, 1983).

Kohn, Melvin L., *Class and Conformity. A Study in Values* (Second edition) (Homewood, IL: Dorsey Press, 1977).

Kohn, Melvin L.; Naoi, Atsushi; Schoenbach, Carrie; Schooler, Carmi; and Slomczynski, Kazimierz M., "Position in the Class Structure and Psychological Functioning in the United States, Japan, and Poland," *American Journal of Sociology*, Vol. 95, 1990: 964- 1008.

Kohn, Melvin L., Slomczynski, Kazimierz M.; Janicka, Krystyna; Khmelko, Valeri; Mach, Bogdan W.; Paniotto, Vladimir; Zaborowski, Wojciech, et. al., "Social Structure and Personality Under Conditions of Radical Social Change: A Comparative Analysis of Poland and Ukraine," *American Sociological Review*, Vol. 62 (August) 1997: 614-638.

Kohn, Melvin L.; Slomczynski, Kazimierz; with Schoenbach, Carrie, *Social Structure and Self-Direction: A Comparative Analysis of the United States and Poland* (Oxford, England: Basil Blackwell, 1990).

Kondapi, C., *Indians Overseas 1938-1949* (New Delhi: Oxford University Press, 1951).

Koo, Hagen and Yu, Eui-Young, *Korean Immigration to the United States: Its Demographic Pattern and Social Implications for Both Societies* (Honolulu, HI: East-West Population Institute, 1981).

Kourvetaris, George A., *Political Sociology: Structure and Process* (Boston, MA: Allyn and Bacon, 1997).

Kowalski, Robin M., "Inferring Sexual Interest from Behavioral Cues: Effects of Gender and Sexually Relevant Attitudes," *Sex Roles*, Vol. 29, Nos. 1/2, 1993: 13-36.

Kraus, Linda A., Davis, Mark H., Bazzini, Doris, Church, Mary, and Kirchman, Clare M., "Personal and Social Influences on Loneliness: The Mediating Effect of Social Provisions," *Social Psychological Quarterly*, Vol. 56, 1993: 37-53.

Krueger, Richard, *Focus Groups* (Newbury Park, CA: Sage, 1988).

Krysan, Maria, and Farley, Reynolds, "Racial Stereotypes: Are They Alive and Well? Do They Continue to Influence Race Relations?" Paper presented at the Annual Meeting of the American Sociological Association, Miami Beach, Florida, August, 1993.

Kubey, R; Shifflet, M.; Weerakkody, N., and Ukeiley, S., "Demographic Diversity on Cable: Have the New Cable Channels Made a Difference in the Representation of Gender, Race, and Age?" *Journal of Broadcasting and Electronic Media*, Vol. 29, 1995: 459-471.

Kuhn, Thomas, *The Structure of Scientific Revolution* (Chicago: The University of Chicago Press, 1970).

Kupferberg, Feiwel, "Managing an Unmasterable Past," *Transaction*, Vol. 33, (January/February) 1996: 69-79.

Labov, William, *Sociolinguistic Patterns* (Philadelphia: University of Pennsylvania Press, 1973).

Lachmann, Richard (Ed.), *The Encyclopedic Dictionary of Sociology* (Fourth edition) (Guilford, CT: The Dushkin Publishing Group, 1991).

Lang, Eric, "Hawthorne Effect," in Edgar F. Borgatta and Marie L. Borgatta (Eds.), *Encyclopedia of Sociology* (New York: Macmillan Publishing Company, 1992), pp. 793- 794.

Lapchick, Richard E., *Five Minutes to Midnight: Race and Sport in the 1990s* (Lanham, MD: Madison Books, 1991).

Larrick, Nancy, "The All White World of Children's Books," *Saturday Review*, Vol. 48, (September 11) 1965: 84-85.

Larson, Mary Strom, "Sex Roles and Soap Operas: What Adolescents Learn About Single Motherhood," *Sex Roles*, Vol. 35, Nos. 1/2, 1996: 97-110.

Latané, Bibb, and Darley, John M., "Bystander Intervention in Emergency Situations: Diffusion of Responsibility," *Journal of Personality and Social Psychology*, Vol. 8, No. 4, 1968: 377-383.

Latané, Bibb, and Nida, Steve, "Ten Years of Research on Group Size and Helping," *Psychological Bulletin*, Vol. 89, 1981: 308-321.

Laumann, E.O., Gagnon, J.H., Michael, R.T., and Michaels, S., *The Social Organization of Sexuality: Sexual Practices in the United States* (Chicago: University of Chicago Press, 1994).

Lawler, Edward J., and Bacharach, Samuel B., "Comparison of Dependence and Punitive Forms of Power," *Social Forces*, Vol. 66, 1987: 446-462.

Lawrence, Richard, *School Crime and Juvenile Justice* (New York: Oxford University Press, 1998).

Lawrence, Richard, "School Performance, Peers, and Delinquency: Implications for Juvenile Justice," *Juvenile and Family Court Journal*, Vol. 42, 1991: 59-69.

Laxton, Edward, *The Famine Ships: The Irish Exodus to America* (New York: Henry Holt and Company, 1997).

Lazarsfeld, Paul, "Problems in Methodology," in Robert K. Merton (Ed.), *Sociology Today* (New York: Basic Books, 1959).

Leadbeater, Bonnie J. Ross, and Way, Niobe, *Urban Girls: Resisting Stereotypes, Creating Identities* (New York: New York University Press, 1996).

Leary, M.R., Nezlek, J.B., Downs, D., Radford-Davenport, J., Martin, J., and McMullen, A., "Self-Presentation in Everyday Interactions: Effects of Target Familiarity and Gender Composition," *Journal of Personality and Social Psychology*, Vol. 67, 1995: 664-673.

Le Bon, Gustave, *The Crowd* (London: Unwin, 1903).

Le Bon, Gustave, *La Psychologie Politique* (Paris: Flammarion, 1910).

Lee, C., and Slaughter-Defoe, D., "Socio-Cultural Influences in African American Education," in J. Banks and C. Banks (Eds.), *Handbook of Research on Multicultural Education* (New York: Macmillan, 1995).

Lee, Dorothy, "Lineal and Nonlineal Codifications of Reality," *Psychosomatic Medicine*, Vol. 12, (March-April) 1950: 89-97).

Lee, Rose Hum, *The Chinese in the United States of America* (Hong Kong: Hong Kong University Press, 1960).

Lemert, Edwin M., *Human Deviance, Social Problems and Social Control* (New York: Prentice Hall, 1967).

Leighton, Marian, "From KGB to MFA: Primakov Becomes Russian Foreign Minister," *Post-Soviet Prospects*, Vol. 4 (No. 2), (February) 1996. (http://www.csis.org/html/pspiv2.html)

Lengermann, P. and Niebrugge-Brantley, J., "Contemporary Feminist Theory," in G. Ritzer (Ed.), *Frontiers in Social Theory* (New York: Columbia University Press, 1990), pp. 400-443.

Lenin, V.I., *Selected Works* (New York: International Publishers, 1974).

Lenski, Gerhard, *Power and Privilege* (New York: McGraw-Hill, 1966).

Lenski, Gerhard, Nolan, Patrick, and Lenski, Jean, *Human Societies: An Introduction to Macrosociology* (Sixth edition) (New York: McGraw-Hill, 1991).

Lenski, Gerhard, Nolan, Patrick, and Lenski, Jean, *Human Societies: An Introduction to Macrosociology* (Seventh edition) (New York: McGraw-Hill, 1995).

Leppard, Wanda; Ogletree, Shirley Matile; and Wallen, Emily, "Gender Stereotyping in Medical Advertising: Much Ado About Something?" *Sex Roles*, Vol. 29, Nos. 11/12, 1993: 829-838.

Lerner, Jacqueline V.; Hertzog, Christopher; Hooker, Karen A.; Hassibi, Mahin; and Thomas, Alexander, "A Longitudinal Study of Negative Emotional States and Adjustment from Early Childhood through Adolescence," *Child Development*, Vol. 59, 1988: 356-366.

Lever, Janet, "Sex Differences in the Complexity of Children's Play and Games," *American Sociological Review*, vol. 43, 1978: 471-483.

Lever, Janet, "Sex Differences in the Games Children Play," *Social Problems*, Vol. 23, 1976: 478-487.

Levi-Montalcini, Rita, *In Praise of Imperfection: My Life and Work* (Translated by Luigi Attardi) (New York: Basic Gooks, 1998) (Translation of *Elogio dell'imperfezione*).

Levine, Rhonda F., and Lembcke, Jerry (Eds.), *Recapturing Marxism: An Appraisal of Recent Trends in Sociological Theory* (New York: Praeger, 1987).

Lewis, M., Feiring, C., McGuffog, C., and Jaskir, J., "Predicting Psychopathology in Six-Year-Olds from Early Social Relations," *Child Development*, Vol. 55, 1984: 123-136.

Lewis, Oscar, "The Culture of Poverty," *Scientific American*, Vol. 115, 1966: 19-25.

Lewis, Oscar, *Five Families* (New York: New American Library, 1959).

Lewis, Oscar, *Life in a Mexican Village: Tepoztlan Restudied* (Urbana: University of Illinois Press, 1951).

Liazos, Alexander, "The Poverty of the Sociology of Deviance: Nuts, Sluts, and 'Preverts,'" *Social Problems,* Vol. 20 (Summer) 1972: 103-120.

Lieberson, S., "A Societal Theory of Race and Relations," *American Sociological Review,* Vol. 26, 1961: 902-910.

Liebow, Elliot, *Tally's Corner: A Study of Negro Streetcorner Men* (Boston: Little Brown and Company, 1967).

Lin, Nan, and Ensel, Walter M., "Life Stresses and Health: Stressors and Resources," *American Sociological Review,* Vol. 54, 1989: 382-399.

Lin, Nan, Walter M., Vaughn, John C., "Social Resources and Strength of Ties: The Structural Factors in Occupational Status Attainment," *American Sociological Review,* Vol. 46, 1981: 393-405.

Linton, Ralph, *The Study of Man* (New York: Appleton-Century-Crofts, 1936).

Lips, H.M., "Gender-Role Socialization: Lessons in Femininity," in J. Freeman (Ed.), *Women* (Fifth edition) (Mt. View, CA: Mayfield Publishing Company, 1995), pp. 128-148.

Lipset, Seymour Martin, *Political Man: The Social Bases of Politics* (Second edition) (Baltimore: John Hopkins University Press, 1981).

Little, Daniel, *Varieties of Social Explanation: An Introduction to the Philosophy of Social Science* (Boulder: Westview Press, 1991).

Livingston, Jay, *Crime and Criminology* (Prentice Hall, 1996).

Litwack, Leon F., *North of Slavery: The Negro in the Free States, 1790-1860* (Chicago: University of Chicago Press., 1961).

Lofland, Lyn, *World of Strangers: Order and Action in Urban Public Space* (New York: Basic Books, 1973).

Loftus, Elizabeth, and Zanni, Guido, "Eye-witness Testimony: The Influence of the Wording in a Question," *Bulletin of the Psychonomic Society,* Vol. 5, 1975: 86-88.

Lombroso, Cesare, *Crime: Its Causes and Remedies* (Boston: Little, Brown, 1918). (Revised edition) (Originally published, 1899).

Lombroso, Cesare, "Introduction," in Gina Lombroso-Ferrero (Ed.), *Criminal Man According to the Classification of Cesare Lombroso* (New York: Putnam, 1911).

Lomnitz, Larissa A., *Networks and Marginality: Life in a Mexican Shantytown* (New York: Academic Press, 1977).

Luhman, Reid, *The Sociological Outlook: A Text with Readings* (Second edition) (San Diego, CA: Collegiate Press, 1989).

Lukes, Steven, *Emile Durkheim-His Life and Work: A Historical and Critical Study* (New York: Harper-Row, 1977).

Lundman, R.J., *Prevention and Control of Juvenile Delinquency* (Second edition) (New York: Oxford, 1993).

Lynch, Michael and Bogen, David, "Sociology's Asociological 'Core': An Examination of Textbook Sociology in Light of the Sociology of Scientific Knowledge," *American Sociological Review,* Vol. 62, (June) 1997: 481-493.

Lytle, L. Jean; Bakken, Linda; and Romig, Charles, "Adolescent Female Identity Development," *Sex Roles,* Vol. 37, Nos. 3/4, 1997: 175-185.

Maccoby, Eleanor, and Jacklin, Carol Nagy, "Gender Segregation in Childhood," in H. Reese (Ed.), *Advances in Child Development and Behavior* (New York: Academic Press, 1987), pp. 239-287.

McCarthy, John, and Zald, Mayer N., "Resource Mobilization and Social Theory: A Partial Theory," *American Journal of Sociology,* Vol. 82, 1977: 1212-1214.

McCauley, C.R., and Segal, M.E., "Social Psychology of Terrorist Groups," in C. Hendrick (Ed.), *Group Processes and Intergroup Relations,* Vol. 9 (Newbury Park, CA: Sage, 1987).

McCord, Joan, "The Cycle of Crime and Socialization Practices," *The Journal of Criminal Law and Criminology,* Vol. 82, No. 1 (Spring) 1991: 211-228.

McCord, Joan and McCord, William, "A Follow-Up Report on the Cambridge-Sommerville Youth Study, *Annals,* Volume 322, 1959b: 89-98.

McCord, Joan and McCord, William, *Origins of Crime: A New Evaluation of the Cambridge-Sommerville Youth Study* (New York: Columbia University Press, 1959a).

McKay, N.Y., "Remembering Anita Hill and Clarence Thomas: What Really Happened When One Black Woman Spoke Out," in T. Morrison (Ed.), *Race-ing Justice, En-gendering Power* (New York: Pantheon Books, 1992), pp. 269-289.

McNickle, D'Arcy, *Native American Tribalism: Indian Survivals and Renewals* (New York: Oxford University, 1973).

McPherson, J.M. and Smith-Lovin, L., "Homophily in Voluntary Organizations: Status Distance and the Composition of Face-to-Face Groups," *American Sociological Review,* Vol. 52, 1987: 370-379.

McWilliams, Carey, *North From Mexico: The Spanish-Speaking People of the United States* (New York: Greenwood, 1968).

Magnuson, E., "A Serious Deficiency?: The Rogers Commission Faults NASA's 'Flawed' Decisionmaking Process," *Time,* March 10, 1986: 40-42, international edition.

Macionis, John, *Sociology* (Englewood Cliffs, NJ: Prentice Hall, 1996).

Magubane, B.N., *The Political Economy of Race and Class in South Africa* (New York: Monthly Review Press, 1979).

Maldonado-Denis, Manuel, *The Emigration Dialectic: Puerto Rico and the USA* (New York: International Publishers, 1980).

Malinowski, Bronislaw, *Sex and Repression in Savage Society* (London: Routledge, 1927).

Mallet, Serge, *Essays on the New Working Class* (St. Louis: Telos Press, 1975).

Malthus, Thomas Robert, *Essay on the Principle of Population* (London: Reeves and Turner, 1872). (Seventh edition) (Originally published, 1798).

Mangiafico, Luciano, *Contemporary American Immigrants: Patterns of Filipino, Korean, and Chinese Settlement in the United States* (New York: Praeger, 1988).

Mann, J.W., "Rivals of Different Rank," *Journal of Social Psychology,* Vol. 61, 1963: 11-28.

Manza, Jeff, and Brooks, Clem, "The Religious Factor in U.S. Presidential Elections, 1960-1992," *American Journal of Sociology,* Vol. 103, No. 1 (July) 1997 38-81.

Maples, William R., and Browning, Michael, *Dead Men Do Tell Tales: The Strange and Fascinating Cases of a Forensic Anthropologist* (New York: Doubleday, 1994).

Marable, Manning, "What's in a Name? African American or Multiracial," *Black Issues in Higher Education,* March, 1997.

Marcinko, Richard, and Weisman, John, *Rogue Warrior* (New York: Simon & Schuster Inc., 1992).

Marcuse, Herbert, *One-Dimensional Man* (Boston: Beacon Press, 1964).

Marcuse, Herbert, *Reason and Revolution: Hegel and the Rise of Social Theory* (Boston: Beacon Press, 1969).

Marger, Martin R., *Race and Ethnic Relations: American and Global Perspectives* (Belmont, CA: Wadsworth, 1994).

Margolis, Eric, and Romero, Mary, "'The Department Is Very Male, Very White, Very Old, and Very Conservative'" The Functioning of the Hidden Curriculum in Graduate Sociology Departments," *Harvard Educational Review,* Vol. 68, No. 1, Spring 1998: 1-32

Markus, H., and Kitayama, S., "Culture and the Self: Implications for Cognition, Emotion, and Motivation," *Psychological Review,* Vol. 98, 1991: 224-253.

Marsden, Peter V., "Social Network Theory," in Edgar F. Borgatta and Marie L. Borgatta, *Encyclopedia of Sociology,* Vol. 4 (New York: Macmillan and Company, 1992), pp. 1887-1894).

Marshall, Joseph, *Street Soldier: One Man's Struggle to Save a Generation—One Life at a Time* (New York: Delta (Dell), 1996).

Martin, C.L., Wood, C.H., and Little, J.K., "The Development of Gender Stereotype Components," *Child Development,* Vol. 61, 1990: 1427-1439.

Martin, S.E., "Sexual Harassment: The Link Joining Gender Stratification, Sexuality, and Women's Economic Status," in J. Freeman (Ed.), *Women* (Fifth edition) (Mt. View, CA: Mayfield Publishing Company, 1995), pp. 22-46.

Martindale, Don, *The Nature and Types of Sociological Theory* (Second edition) (Boston: Houghton Mifflin Company, 1988).

Marwell, Gerald, "Experiments," in Edgar F. Borgatta and Marie L. Borgatta (Eds.), *Encyclopedia of Sociology,* Vol. 2 (New York: Macmillan Publishing Company, 1992), pp. 616-620.

Marx, Karl, *Capital* (Vol. 1) (Edited by F. Engels) (New York: International Publishers, 1967).

Marx, Karl, "Contribution to the Critique of Hegel's *Philosophy of Right,*" in Robert C. Tucker (Ed.), *The Marx-Engels Reader* (Second edition) (New York: W.W. Norton & Company, 1978), pp. 16-25. (Originally published, 1844).

Marx, Karl, Excerpts from "Preface to A Contribution to the Critique of Political Economy," "German Ideology," "Speech at the Graveside of Karl Mark by Frederich Engels," and "The Communist Manifesto," in Robert C. Tucker (Ed.), *The Marx-Engels Reader* (New York: Norton, 1972).

Marx, Karl, and Engels, Friedrich, *The Communist Manifesto* (New York: International Publishers, 1930).

Marx, Karl, and Engels, Friedrich, *The Communist Manifesto* (New York: International Publishers, 1948).

Masden, Jane M., "Historical Images of the Black Child in Children's Literature and Their Contemporary Reflections," *Minority Voice*, Vol. 4, 1980: 1-36.

Maslow, A., *Motivation and Personality* (New York: Harper, 1954).

Massaquoi, Hans J., "The New Racism: No Matter How High They Climb on the Ladder of Success, Black VIPs Say They are Far From Immune to Bigotry," *Ebony*, August, 1996: 56-60.

Massey, D. S., and Denton, N.A., *American Apartheid: Segregation and the Making of the Underclass* (Cambridge, MA: Harvard University Press, 1993).

Mathur, M., and Dodder, Richard A., "Delinquency and Attachment Bond in Hirschi's Control Theory," *Free Inquiry in Creative Sociology*, 1985.

Matsui, Shichiro, "Economic Aspects of the Japanese Situation in California," M.A. Thesis, Department of Economics, University of California, Berkeley, 1922.

Matteson, D.R., Differences Within and Between Genders: A Challenge to the Theory," in J.E. Marcia, A.S. Waterman, D.R. Matteson, S.L. Archer, and J.L. Orlofsky (Eds.), *Ego Identity* (New York: Springer-Verlag, 1993).

Matthews, J., "Class Struggle," *Newsweek*, March 30, 1998: 52-56.

Matute-Bianchi, Maria E., "Ethnic Identities and Patterns of School Success and Failure among Mexican-Descent and Japanese-American Students in a California High School: An Ethnographic Analysis, *American Journal of Education*, Vol. 95, 1986: 233-155.

Maughm, W. Sommerset, *On A Chinese Screen* (New York: Arno Press, 1977).

Maurer, Christine, and Sheets, Tara E. (Eds.), *Encyclopedia of Associations* (33rd Edition), Vol. 1, Part 2, *National Organizations of the United States*, Part 2, Sections 7-8, Entries 10229-22761 (Detroit, MI: Gale, 1998).

Maurer, Christine, and Sheets, Tara E. (Eds.), *Encyclopedia of Associations: An Association Unlimited Reference* (33rd edition), Vol. 1, *National Organizations of the U.S.*, Part I (Sections 1-6) Entries 1-10228 (New York: Gale, 1998).

Mayhew, Leon, *Society: Institutions and Activity* (Glenview, Illinois: Scott, Foresman and Company, 1971).

Mazella, C.; Durkin, K.; Cerini, E.; and Buralli, P., "Sex Role Stereotyping in Australian Television Advertisements," *Sex Roles*, Vol. 26, 1992: 243-259.

Mead, George Herbert, *Mind, Self and Society* (Chicago: University of Chicago Press, 1934).

Mead, Lawrence, *The New Politics of Poverty: The Nonworking Poor in America* (New York: Basic Books, 1992).

Mead, Margret, *The Coming of Age in Samoa* (New York: Dell, 1965). (Originally published, 1928).

Mead, Margaret, *Sex and Temperament in Three Primitive Societies* (New York: William and Morrow, 1935).

Mednick, Sarnoff A., et. al., "Genetic Factors in Criminal Behavior: A Review," in Dan Olweus et. al., (Eds.), *Research Theroies and Issues* (New Work: Academic Press, 1986).

Meier, August and Rudwick, Elliott M., *From Plantation to Ghetto* (New York: Hill and Wang. 1966).

Meier, Matt and Rivera, Feliciano, *The Chicanos* (New York: Hill and Wang, 1972).

Meier, Kenneth J., Stewart, J., Jr. and England, R. E., *Race, Class, and Education: The Politics of Second-Generation Discrimination* (Madison, WI: The University of Wisconsin Press, 1989).

Melendy, H. Brett, "California's Discrimination Against Filipinos, 1927-1935," in J.M. Saniel (Ed.), *The Filipino Exclusion Movement 1927-1935* (Quezon City: Institute of Asian Studies, University of the Philippines, 1967), pp. 3-10.

Melendy, H. Brett, "Filipinos in the United States," in Norris Hudley, Jr. (Ed.), *The Asian American: The Historical Experience* (Santa Barbara: Cleo Books, 1976).

Melendy, H. Brett, *Asians in America: Filipinos, Koreans, and East Indians* (Boston: Twayne Publishers, 1977).

Meltzer, Bernard N., Petras, John W., and Reynolds, Larry T., *Symbolic Interactionism: Genesis, Varieties and Criticism* (London: Routledge & Kegan Paul, 1980).

Memmi, Albert, *The Colonizer and the Colonized* (Boston: Beacon Press, 1965).

Memmi, Albert, *Pillar of Salt* (New York: Grossman Publishers, Inc., 1963).

Mendez, Jennifer Bickham, "Of Mops and Maids: Contradictions and Continuities in Bureaucratized Domestic Work," *Social Problems*, Vol. 45, No. 1 (February) 1998: 114-135.

Merei, Ferenc, "Group Leadership and Institutionalization," *Human Relations*, Vol. 2, 1949: 23-39.

Merton, Robert, "Discrimination and the American Creed," in R.M. MacIver (Ed.), *Discrimination and National Welfare* (Harper & Brothers, New York, 1949), pp. 99-126.

Merton, Robert K., "Social Structure and Anomie," *American Sociological Review*, Vol. 3, 1938: 672-682.

Merton, Robert K., *Social Theory and Social Structure* (Revised and enlarged edition) (Glencoe: The Free Press, 1957).

Merton, Robert K., *Social Theory and Social Structure* (New York: Free Press, 1968).

Merton, Robert K. and Kitt, Alice S., "Contributions to the Theory of Reference Group Behavior," in Robert K. Merton and Paul F. Lazarsfeld (Eds.), *Continuities in Social Research: The Studies in the Scope and Method of the American Soldier* (Glencoe, Illinois: Free Press, 1950).

Mezey, Susan G., *In Pursuit of Equality: Women, Public Policy, and the Federal Courts* (New York: St. Martin's Press, 1992).

Michels, Robert, *Political Parties: A Sociological Study of Oligarhical. Tendencies in Modern Democracy* (New York: Free Press, 1968) (Originally published, 1915).

Miller, Walter B., "Lower Class Culture as a Generating Milieu of Gang Delinquency," in Marvin Wolfgang, Leonard Savitz, and Norman Johnson (Eds.), *The Sociology of Crime and Delinquency* (New York: Wiley, 1970). (Originally published, 1958).

Millett, Kate, *Sexual Politics* (London, Virago, 1969).

Millis, H.A., "East Indian Immigration to British Columbia and the Pacific Coast States," *American Economic Review*, Vol. 1, 1911: 72-76.

Mills, C. Wright, *The Power Elite* (New York: Oxford University Press, 1956).

Mills, C. Wright, *The Sociological Imagination* (New York: Grove Press, 1959).

Mills, C. Wright, *White Collar.* (New York: Oxford University Press, 1951).

Min, P.G. (Ed.), *Asian Americans: Contemporary Trends and Issues* (Thousand Oaks, CA: Sage, 1994).

Min, Pyong Gap, *Caught in the Middle: Korean Merchants in America's Multi-Ethnic Cities* (Berkeley, CA: University of California Press, 1996).

Minsky, Marvin, *The Society of Mind* (New York: Simon and Schuster, 1986).

Miyake, K., Chen, S., and Campos, J.J., "Infant Temperament, Mother's Mode of Interaction, and Attachment in Japan: An Interim Report," in I. Bretherton and E. Waters (Eds.), *Monographs of the Society for Research in Child Development*, Vol. 50, 1985.

Model, John, "The Japanese American Family: A Perspective for Future Investigations," *Pacific Historical Review*, Vol. 37, 1968: 67-81.

Mohak, J., "Looking for Columbus: Thoughts on the Past, Present, and Future of Humanity," in M.A. Jaimes (Ed.), *The State of Native America* (Boston: South End Press, 1992)., pp. 439-444.

Molm, Linda, "Structure, Action, and Outcomes: The Dynamics of Power in Social Exchange," *American Sociological Review*, Vol. 55, 1990: 427-447.

Momeni, Jamshid A., (Ed.), *Homelessness in the United States—Data and Issues* (New York: Praeger, 1990).

Momeni, Jamshid A., *Housing and Racial/Ethnic Minority Status in the United States: An Annotated Bibliography with a Review Essay* (Foreword by Joe T. Darden) (New York: Greenwood Press, 1987).

Money, John, and Wiedeking, C., "Gender Identity/Role: Normal Differentiation and Its Transpositions," in B. B. Wolman and John Money (Eds.), *Handbook of Human Sexuality* (Englewood Cliffs, NJ: Prentice Hall, 1980), 269-284.

Moore, Barrington, *Social Origins of Dictatorship and Democracy* (Boston: Beacon Press, 1993).

Moore, Gwen, "Gender and Informal Networks in State Government," *Social Science Quarterly*, Vol. 73, (March) 1992: 46-61.

Moore, Gwen, "Structural Determinants of Men's and Women's Personal Networks," *American Sociological Review*, Vol. 55, 1991: 726-735.

Moore, John P., "Highlights of the 1995 National Youth Gang Survey," Office of Juvenile Justice and Delinquency Prevention, Fact Sheet #63, April, 1997 (Washington, D.C.: U.S. Department of Justice, Office of Justice Programs, Office of Juvenile Justice and Delinquency Prevention, 1997).

Moore, Robert B., "Racist Stereotyping in the English Language," in Paula S. Rothenberg (Ed.), *Racism and Sexism: An Integrated Study* (New York: St. Martin's Press, 1988), pp. 269-279.

Moquin, Wayne and Van Doren, Charles (Eds.), *A Documentary History of the Mexican Americans* (New York: Bantam Books, 1971).

Morgan, David L. (Ed.), *Successful Focus Groups: Advancing the State of the Art* (Newbury park, CA: Sage, 1993).

Morita, Akio, *Made in Japan: Akio Morita and SONY* (New York: E.P. Dutton, 1986).

Morris, Charles W. (Ed.), *Mind, Self and Society* (Chicago: The University of Chicago Press, 1934).

Morris, James, *Heaven's Command: An Imperial Progress* (New York: Brace Jovanovich, 1973).

Morris, William (Ed.), *The American Heritage Dictionary of the English Language* (New York: Houghton Mifflin Company, 1969).

Moscos, Charles C., and Butler, John Sibley, *All That We Can Be: Black Leadership and Racial Integration—The Army Way* (Boulder, CO: Basic Books, 1997).

Moscoso, Francisco, "Chiefdom and Encomienda in Puerto Rico: The Development of Tribal Society and the Spanish Colonization to 1530," in Adalberto Lopez (Ed.), *The Puerto Ricans: Their History, Culture and Society* (Cambridge: Schenkman Publishing Company, 1980).

Moscovici, Serge, and Zavalloni, M., "The Group as a Polarizer of Attitudes," *Journal of Personality and Social Psychology,* Vol. 12, 1969: 124-135.

Moscow News, English Translations. Weekly Editions, 1985-1995.

Moscow News, No. 9, 1995.

Mucha, Janusz, "American Indian Success in the Urban Setting," *Urban Anthropology,* Vol. 13, No. 4, 1984: 329-354.

Mullen, B., "Group Composition, Salience, and Cognitive Representations: The Phenomenology of Being in a Group," *Journal of Experimental Social Psychology,* Vol. 27, 1991: 297-323.

Mullen, B., Brown, R., and Smith, C., "In-group Bias as a Function of Salience, Relevance, and Status: An Integration," *European Journal of Social Psychology,* Vol. 22, 1992: 103-122.

Mummendey, A., and Simon, B., "Better or Different? III. The Impact of Importance of Comparison Dimension and Relative-In-Group Size Upon Intergroup Discrimination," *British Journal of Social Psychology,* Vol. 28, 1989: 1-16.

Munroe, R.L., and Munroe, R. H. "Effect of Environmental Experience on Spatial Ability in an East African Society," *Journal of Social Psychology,* Vol. 83, 1971:15-22.

Murdock, George Peter, "The Common Denominator of Cultures," in Ralph Linton (Ed.), *The Science of Man and the World Crisis* (New York: Columbia University Press, 1945).

Murdock, George Peter, *Social Structure* (Toronto, Canada: The Macmillan Company, 1949).

Murnane, Richard J., Willett, J.B., and Levy, Frank, "The Growing Importance of Cognitive Skills in Wage Determination," *Review of Econommics and Statistics,* (May) 1995: 251-266.

Murphy, Thomas D., *Ambassadors in Arms: The Story of Hawaii's 100th Battalion* (Honolulu, HI: University of Hawaii Press, 1955).

Murphy, Timothy D., "Marriage and Family in a Nahuatl-Speaking," in Hugo G. Nutini, et al (Eds.), *Essays on Mexican Kinship* (Pittsburgh: University of Pittsburgh Press, 1976).

Murray, Charles, and Cox, L.A., *Beyond Probation: Juvenile Corrections and the Chronic Offender* (Beverly Hills, CA: Sage, 1979).

Murray, Stephen O., *American Gay* (Chicago: University of Chicago Press, 1996).

Musgrove, Frank, *Youth and the Social Order* (Bloomington, IN: Indiana University Press, 1965).

Mwangi, Mary W., "Gender Roles Portrayed in Kenyan Television Commercials," *Sex Roles,* Vol. 34, Nos. 3/4, 1996: 205-214.

Myers, David G., *Social Psychology* (Fourth edition) (New York: McGraw-Hill, Inc., 1993).

Myers, David G., *Social Psychology* (Fifth edition) (New York: McGraw-Hill, Inc., 1996).

Myers, Isabel Briggs, and Myers, Peter, *Gifts Differing* (Palo Alto, CA: Consulting Psychologists Press, 1980).

Myrdal, Gunnar, *An American Dilemma: The Negro Problem and Modern Democracy* (New York: Harper & Brother, 1944).

Nagel, Joane, *American Indian Ethnic Renewal: Red Power and the Resurgence of Identity and Culture* (New York: Oxford University Press, 1996).

Nagel, Joane, "Constructing Ethnicity: Creating and Recreating Ethnic Identity and Culture," *Social Problems*, Vol. 41, 1994: 1562-176.

Naka, Kaizo, "Social and Economic Conditions Among Japanese Farmers in California," M.A. Thesis, University of California, Berkeley, 1913.

Nandi, Proshanta K., "Surveying Asian Minorities in the Middle-Sized City," in William T. Liv, (Ed.), *Methodological Problems in Minority Research* (Chicago: Pacific/Asian American Mental Health Research Center, 1982), pp. 81 - 92.

Nelson, Daniel, "The Forman's Empire," in Frank Hearn (Ed.), *The Transformation of Industrial Organization: Management, Labor and Society in the United States* (Belmont, CA: Wadsworth Publishing Company, 1988).

Nerlove, S. B., Munroe, R. J., and Munore, R. L., "Effects of Environmental Experiences on Spatial Ability: A Replication," *Journal of Social Psychology*, Vol. 84, 1971: 3-10.

Newman, David, *Sociology: Exploring the Architrectrue of Evcertyday Life* (Thousand Oaks, Ca: Pine Forge Press, 1995).

Nisbet, Robert A., *The Sociological Tradition* (New York: Basic Books, Inc., 1966).

Nisbet, Robert A., *Sociology as an Art Form* (New York: Oxford University Press, 1976).

Noble, K.B., "Attacks on Asian Americans on the Rise, Especially in California," *New York Times*, December 13, 1995: p.B13.

Noley, G., "The Foster Child of American Education," in N.R. Yetman (Ed.), *Race Relations in the 1980s and 1990s* (New York: Hemisphere, 1990), pp. 239-248.

Northcott, Clarence H., "The Sociological Theories of Franklin Henry Giddings," in Harry E. Barnes (Ed.), *An Introduction to the History of Sociology* (Abridged edition) (Chicago: The University of Chicago Press, 1948).

Nutini, Hugo G., "Clan Organization in a Nahuatl-Speaking Village in the State of Tlaxcala, Mexico," *American Anthropologist*, Vol. 63, No. 1, 1961: 71.

Nutini, Hugo G., "Polygyny in a Tlaxcalan Community," *Ethnology*, Vol. 4, 1965: 123-147.

Nutini, Hugo G., *San Bernardino Contla: Marriage and Family Structure in a Tlaxcalan Municipio* (Pittsburgh: University of Pittsburgh Press., 1968).

Nutini, Hugo G., "A Synoptic Comparison of Mesoamerican Marriage and Family Structure," *Southwestern Journal of Anthropology*, Vol. 23, 1967: 23:383-404.

O'Callaghan, Frances V.; Chant, David C; Callan, Victor J.; and Baglioni, A., "Models of Alcohol Use by Young Adults: An Examination of Various Attitude-Behavior Theories,:" *Journal of Studies on Alcohol*, Vol. 58, No. 5 (September) 1997: 502-507.

O'Connor, James, *The Fiscal Crisis of the State* (New York: St. Martin's Press, 1973).

Officer, James E., "The American Indian and Federal Policy," in In Jack O. Waddell and O.M. Watson (Eds.), *The American Indian in Urban Society* (Boston: Little, Brown, 1971), pp. 45-60.

Ofshe, Richard J., "Coercive Persuasion and Attitude Change," in Edgar F. Borgatta and Marie L. Borgatta, *Encyclopedia of Sociology* (New York: Macmillan Publishing Company, 1992), 212-224.

Ogbu, John, *Cultural Models and Educational Strategies of Non-Dominant Peoples* (New York: City College Workshop Center, 1989).

Ogbu, John, "Minority Education in Comparative Perspective," *Journal of Negro Education*, Vol. 59, 1990: 45-57.

Oliner, Samuel P., and Oliner, Pearl M., *The Altruistic Personality: Rescuers of Jews in Nazi Europe* (New York: The Free Press, 1988).

Olson, James S. and Wilson, Raymond, *Native Americans in the Twentieth Century* (Provo, Utah: Brigham Young University Press, 1984).

Olweus, D., "Aggression and Hormones: Behavioral Relationship with Testosterone and Adrenaline," in D. Olweus et. al. (Eds.), *Development of Antisocial and Prosocial Behavior* (Orlando: Academic Press, 1986).

Omi, Michael, and Winant, Howard, *Racial Formation in the United States: From the 1960s to the 1980s* (New York: Routledge and Kegan Paul, 1986).

Omi, Michael, and Winant, Howard, *Racial Formation in the United States: From the 1960s to the 1980s* (Second edition) (New York: Routledge, 1994).

Onishi, HN., "New Sense of Race Rises Among Asian Americans," *New York Times,* May 30, 1996, pp. A1, B6.

Ornstein, Allen C., and Levine, Daniel U., "Social Class, Race and School Achievement: Problems and Prospects," *Journal of Teacher Education,* Vol. 40, 1989: 3.

Osberg, Timothy, "Psychology is Not Just Common Sense: An Introductory Psychology Demonstration," *Teaching of Psychology,* Vol. 20, 1993: 110-111.

Ostower, F., *Why The Wealthy Give: The Culture of Elite Philanthropy* (Princeton, NJ: Princeton University Press, 1995).

Oswalt, Wendell H., *This Land Was Theirs: A Study of the North American Indian* (Second edition) (New York: John Wiley & Sons, 1973).

Otnes, Cele, Kyungseung, Kim, and Kim, Young Chan, "Yes, Virginia, There Is a Gender Difference: Analyzing Children's Requests to Santa Claus," *Journal of Popular Culture,* Vol. 28 1994: 17-29.

Pagel, Mark K., Erdly, William W., and Becker, Joseph, "Social Networks: We Get by with (and in Spite of) a Little Help from Our Friends," *Journal of Personality and Social Psychology,* Vol. 46, 1987: 1097-1108.

Painter, N.I., "Hill Thomas and the Use of Racial Stereotype," in T. Morrison (Ed), *Race-ing Justice, En-gendering Power* (New York: Pantheon Books, 1992), pp. 200-214.

Parcel, Toby L., "Secondary Data Analysis and Data Archives," in Edgar F. Borgatta and Marie L. Borgatta, *Encyclopedia of Sociology* (New York: Macmillan Publishing Company, 1992), pp. 1720-1728.

Parkin, Frank, *Class Inequality & Political Order: Social Stratification in Capitalist Communist Societies* (New York: Praeger, 1971).

Parnell, K.; Sargent, S.; Thompson, S.H.; Duhe, S.F.; Valois, R.F.; and Kemper, R.C., "Black and White Adolescent Females' Perceptions of Ideal Body Size," *Journal of School Health,* Vol. 66, 1996: 112-118.

Parsons, Elsie Clews, *Milta; Town of Souls* (Chicago: University of Chicago Press, 1936).

Parsons, Talcott, *Social Systems and the Evolution of Action Theory* (New York: Free Press, 1977).

Parsons, Talcott, *Societies: Evolutionary and Comparative Perspectives* (Englewood Cliffs, NJ: Prentice-Hall., 1966).

Parsons, Talcott, *Sociological Theory and Modern Society* (New York: The Free Press, 1967).

Parsons, Talcott, *The Structure of Social Action* (New York: McGraw-Hill, 1937).

Parsons, Talcott, *The System of Modern Societies* (Englewood Cliffs, NJ: Prentice-Hall, 1971).

Pascarella, Ernest T., and Terenzini, Patrick T., *How Colleges Affects Students: Findings and Insights from Twenty Years of Research* (San Francisco: Jossey Bass, 1991).

Pateman, Roy, "The Legacy of Eritrea's National Question," *Society,* Vol. 33, No. 6, (September/October) 1996: 37-42.

Patterson, G.R., "The Contribution of Siblings to Training for Fighting: A Microsocial Analysis," in D. Olweus et. al., (Eds.), *Development of Antisocial and Prosocial Behavior* (Orlando: Academic Press, 1986).

Patterson, Wayne, "The First Attempt to Obtain Korean Laborers for Hawaii: 1896-1897," in Hyung-Chan Kim (Ed.), *The Korean Diaspora* (Santa Barbara: Clio Press, 1977).

Pearce, Frank, *The Radical Durkheim* (London: Unwin Hyman, 1989).

Pedraza, Silvia, "Cuba's Regugees: Manifold Migrations," in Silvia Pedraza and Rubén Rumbaut, *Origins and Destinies: Imigration, Reace, and Ethnicity in America* (Belmont, CA: Wadsworth Publishing, 1996), pp. 263-279.

Perdue, C.W., Dovidio, J.F., Gurtman, M.B., and Tyler, R.B., "Us and Them: Social Categorization and the Process of Intergroup Bias," *Journal of Personality and Social Psychology,* Vol. 59, 1990: 475-486.

Perkins, Craig and Klaus, Patsy, *Criminal Victimization 1994* (Washington, D.C.: U.S. Department of Justice, (April) 1996.

Perrucci, Robert and Potter, Harry R. (Eds.), *Networks of Power: Organizational Actors at the National, Corporate, and Community Levels* (New York: Aldine de Gruyter, 1989).

Pescosolido, Bernice, Grauerhold, Elizabeth, and Milkie, Melissa, "Culture and Conflict: The Portrayal of Blacks in U.S. Children's Picture Books Through the Mid- and Late- Twentieth Century," *American Sociological Review,* Vol. 62, 1997: 443-464.

Petersen, William, *Japanese Americans* (New York: Random House, 1971).

Peters, Thomas J., and Robert. H. Waterman, *In Search of Excellence: Lessons From America' Best Run Companies* (New York: Warner Books, 1982).

Peterson, Richard, "Symbols and Social Life: The Growth of Cultural Studies," *Contemporary Sociology*, vol. 19, 1990: 498-500.

Petterson, Stephen M., "Are Young Black Men Really Less Willing to Work?," *American Sociological Review*, Vol. 62, (August) 1997: 605-613.

Pettigrew, Thomas F., "Prejudice," in S. Thernstrom et. al., (Eds.), *Harvard Encyclopedia of American Ethnic Groups* (Cambridge, MA: Harvard University Press, 1980).

Pettigrew, Thomas F., "Prejudice," in Thomas F. Pettigrew, et al. (Eds.), *Prejudice* (Cambridge, MA: Harvard University Press, 1982), pp. 1-29.

Pettigrew, Thomas F., "Regional Differences in Anti-Negro Prejudice," *Journal of Abnormal and Social Psychology*, Vol. 59, 1959: 28-36.

Pettigrew, Thomas F., "The Ultimate Attribution Error: Extending Allport's Cognitive Analysis of Prejudice," *Personality and Social Psychology Bulletin*, Vol. 55, 1979: 461-476.

Pfohl, Stephen, *Images of Deviance and Social Control: A Sociological Hisoty* (McGraw Hill, 1994).

Piaget, Jean, *The Language and Thought of the Child* (London: Kegan Paul, 1926).

Piaget, Jean, *The Moral Judgment of the Child* (Glencoe, Ill.: Free Press, 1965). (Originally published, 1932). (Translated by Marjorie Gabain).

Pieper, Josef, *Leisure: The Basis of Culture* (New York: Mentor Books, 1963).

Pierce, Kate, "Socialization of Teenage Girls Through Teen Magazine Fiction," *Sex Roles*, Vol. 29, Nos. 1/2, 1993: 59-68.

Piercy, M., "A Work of Artifice," in A. Kesselman, L.D. McNair and N. Schniedewind (Eds.), *Women: Images and Reality* (Mt. View, CA: Mayfield Publishing Co., 1995).

Pines, Maya, "The Civilization of Genie," *Psychology Today*, Vol. 15, (September) 1981: 28-34.

Platz, S.J., and Hosch, H.M., "Cross-racial/Ethnic Eyewitness Identification: A field Study," *Journal of Applied Social Psychology*, Vol. 18, 1988: 972-984.

Pleck, J.H., Sonenstein, F.L., and Ku, L.C., "Masculinity Ideology: Its Impact on Adolescent Males' Heterosexual Relationships," *Journal of Social Issues*, Vol. 49, 1993: 11-29.

Polivy, J.D., Garner, D. M., and Garfinkel, P.E., "Causes and Consequences of the Current Preference for Thin Physical Physiques," in C.P. Herman, M.P. Zanna, and E.T. Higgins (Eds.), *Physical Appearance, Stigma, and Social Behavior: The Ontario Symposium* (Vol. 3) (Hillsdale, NJ: Erlbaum, 1986).

Pomerantz, Linda, "The Background of Korean Emigration," in Lucie Cheng and Edna Bonacich (Eds.), *Labor Immigration Under Capitalism: Asian Workers in the United States Before World War II* (Berkeley: University of California Press, 1984), pp. 277-315.

Pomerleau, A., Bolduc, D., Malcuit, G., and Cossette, L., "Pink or Blue: Environmental Gender Stereotypes in the First Two Years of Life," *Sex Roles*, Vol. 22, 1990: 359-367.

Popielarz, Pamela A., and McPherson, J. Miller, "On the Edge or In Between: Niche Position, Niche Overlap, and the Duration of Voluntary Association Memberships," *American Journal of Sociology*, Vol. 101, 1995: 698-720.

Popper, Karl R. *The Logic of Scientific Discovery* (London: Hutchinson, 1959).

Population Reference Bureau, *Population Today*, Vol. 26, No. 6, (April) 1998: 5.

Porter, Natalie, Geis, Florence, and Walstedt, Joyce Jennings, "Are Women Invisible as Leaders," *Sex Roles*, Vol. 9, 1983: 1035-1049.

Portes, Alejandro, J.M. Clark, J.M., and Bach, R. L., "The New Wave: A Statistical Profile of Recent Cuban Exiles to the United States," *Cuban Studies/Estudios Cubanos*, Vol. 7, 1977:1-32.

Poulantzas, Nicos, *Classes in Contemporary Capitalism* (London: New Left Books, 1978).

Poulantzas, Nicos, *Political Power & Social Classes* (London: New Left Books, 1978).

Powell, William, "Austro-Hungarian and Balkan Settlement on the Cherokee-Crawford Coal Fields of Southeastern Kansas," Abstract and narration, Archives and Special Collection of Axe Library, Pittsburg State University, Pittsburg, KS, 1994.

Press, Andrea L., Book Review of Sut Jhally and Justin Lewis, *Enlightened Racism: The Cosby Show, Audiences, and the Myth of the American Dream* (Boulder, CO: Westview Press, 1992), *American Journal of Sociology*, Vol. 99, No. 1 (July) 1993: 219-221.

Price, John A., "The Migration and Adaptation of American Indians to Los Angeles," in Deward E. Walker Jr. (Ed.), *The Emergent Native Americans* (Boston: Little, Brown and Company, 1972), pp. 728-738.

Quigley, Lori A., and Marlatt G. Alan, "Drinking Among Young Adults: Prevalence, Patterns, and Consequences," *Alcohol, Health and Research World,* Vol. 20, No. 3, 1996: 185-191.

Quillan, Lincoln, "Prejudice as a Response to Perceived Group Threat: Population Composition and Anti-Immigrant and Racial Prejudice in Europe," *American Sociological Review,* Vol. 60, 1995: 586-611.

Quinney, Richard C., *Class, State, and Crime: On the Theory and Practice of Criminal Justice* (New York: Longman, 1980).

Quinney, Richard C. (Ed.), *Criminal Justice in America: A Critical Understanding* (Boston: Little Brown, 1974).

Rabaya, Violet, "Filipino Immigration: The Creation of a New Social Problem," in Amy Tachiki, et al (Eds.), *Roots: An Asian American Reader* (Los Angeles: UCLA Asian American Studies Center, 1971), pp. 188-200.

Red Horse, John G., Lewis, R., Feit, M., and Decker, J., "Family Behavior of Urban American Indians," *Social Casework,* Vol. 59, No. 2, 1978 :67-72.

Radke-Yarrow, Marian and Zahn-Waxler, Carolyn, "Roots, Motives and Patterns in Children's Prosocial Behavior," in Ervin Staub et. al., (Eds.), *Development and Maintenance of Prosocial Behavior* (New York: Plenum, 1984).

Range, Lillian M., and Stringer, Traci A., "Reasons for Living and Coping Abilities Among Older Adults," *International Journal of Aging and Human Development,"* Vol. 43, No. 1, 1996: 1-5.

Redfield, Robert and Rojas, Alfonso Villa, *Chan Kom: A Mayan Village* (Washington, D.C.: Carnegie Institute of Washington, Publication No. 488, 1962).

Redfield, Robert, "The Folk Society," *American Journal of Sociology,* Vol. 52, 1947: 293-308.

Reid, Sue Titus, *Crime and Criminology* (Eighth edition) (Dubuque, IA: Brown and Benchmark, 1996).

Reimers, D., "History of Recent Immigration Regulation," *Proceedings of the American Philosophical Society,* Vol. 136, No.2, 1992.

Reimers, D., *Still the Golden Door: The Third World Comes to America* (New York: Columbia University Press, 1985).

Reinharz, Shulamit, *Feminist Methods in Social Research* (New York: Oxford University Press, 1992)

Reisler, Mark, *By the Sweat of Their Brow: Mexican Immigrant Labor in the United States, 1900-1940* (Westport, CN: Greenwood, 1976).

Reskin, Barbara and Roos, Patricia, *Job Queues, Gender Queues: Explaining Women's Inroads into Male Occupations* (Philadelphia, PA: Temple University Press, 1990).

Reskin, Barbara and Hartmann, Heidi (Eds.), *Women's Work, Men's Work: Sex Segregation on the Job* (Washington, D.C.: National Academy Press, 1986)

Ressler, Robert K.; Burgess, Ann W.; and Douglas, John E., *Sexual Homicide: Patterns and Motives* (New York: Lexington Books, 1988).

Restak, Richard M., *The Mind* (New York, Bantam Books, 1988).

Reyes, Olga, and Jackson, Leonard A., "Pilot Study Examining Factors Associated with Academic Success for Hispanic High School Students," *Journal of Youth and Adolescence,* Vol. 22, 1993: 57-71.

Richey, M.H., and Richey, H.W., "The Significance of Best-Friend Relationships in Adolescence," *Psychology in the Schools,* Vol. 17, 1980: 536-540.

Ridgeway, Cecilia L., "Compliance and Conformity," in Edgar F. Borgatta and Marie L. Borgatta, *Encyclopedia of Sociology* (New York: Macmillan Publishing Company, 1992), pp. 277-282.

Ridgeway, Cecilia L., "Gender, Status, and the Social Psychology of Expectations," in P. England (Ed.), *Theory on Gender/Feminism on Theory* (New York: Aldine, 1993), pp. 175-198.

Ridgeway, Cecilia L., "Interaction and the Conservation of Gender Inequality: Considering Employment," *American Sociological Review,* Vol. 62, (April) 1997: 218-235.

Ridgeway, C.L., "Nonverbal Behavior, Dominance, and the Basis of Status in Task Groups," *American Sociological Review,* Vol. 52, 1987: 683-194.

Ridgeway, C.L., and Berger, J., "Expectations, Legitimation, and Dominance Behavior in Task Groups," *American Sociological Review,* Vol. 51, 1986: 603-617.

Ridgeway, C.L., and Johnson, C., "What is the Relationship Between Socio-Emotional Behavior and Status in Task Groups?," *American Journal of Sociology,* Vol. 95, 1990: 1189-1212.

Rifkin, Jeremy, *The End of Work: The Decline of the Global Labor Force and the Dawn of the Post-Market Era* (New York: Putnam and Sons, 1995).

Riley, Nancy E., "Gebder, Power, and Population Change," *Population Bulletin,* Vol. 52, No. 1, (May) 1997.

Ritzer, George, The *McDonaldization of Society* (Revised edition) (Thousand Oaks, CA: Pine Forge Press, 1996).

Ritzer, George, *Modern Sociological Theory* (Fourth edition) (New York: McGraw-Hill, 1966).

Robertson, Roland, *Globalization: Social Theory and Global Culture* (London, England: Sage, 1990).

Robins, Lee N., *The Vietnam Drug User Returns: Final Report* (Washington, D.C.: Government Printing Office, 1974).

Robinson, J.P., Shaver, P.R., and Wrightsman, L.S., (Eds.), *Measures of Personality and Social Psychological Attitudes* (San Diego, CA: Academic Press, 1991).

Robinson, R.J., Keltner, D., and Ross, L., *Misconstruing the Views of the "Other Side": Real and Perceived Differences in Three Ideological Conflict,* Vol. 18, Stanford Center on Conflict and Negotiation, Stanford University, 1991.

Rodin, Judith, "The Application of Social Psychology," in Gardner Lindzey and Elliot Aronson (Eds.), *The Handbook of Social Psychology* (New York: Random House, 1985), pp. 805-881.

Rodin, Judith, *Body Traps* (New York: Morrow, 1992).

Roethlisberger, F.J., and Dickson, William J., *Management and the Worker* (Cambridge, MA: Harvard University Press, 1939).

Rohlen, Thomas P., *For Harmony and Strength: Japanese White-Collar Organization in Anthropological Perspective* (Berkeley: University of California Press, 1979).

Rohrer, J.H., Baron, S.H., Hoffman, E.L., and Swander, D.V., "The Stability of Autokinetic Judgments," *Journal of Abnormal and Social Psychology,* Vol. 49, 1954: 595-597.

Rojas, Alfonso Villa, *The Maya of East Central Quintana Roo* (Washington, D.C.: Carnegie Institution of Washington, Publication No. 559, 1945).

Rollins, Boyd D., and Thomas, Darwin L., "Parental Support, Power, and Control Techniques in the Socialization of Children," in Burr., W.R.,; Hill, R.; Nye, F.I., and Reiss, I.L., (Eds.), *Contemporary Theories About the Family,* Vol. 1 (New York: Free Press, 1979).

Romero, M., *Maid in the U.S.A.* (New York: Routledge, 1992).

Rook, Karen, "The Negative Side of Social Interaction: Impact on Psychological Well-Being," *Journal of Personality and Social Psychology,* Vol. 46, 1984: 1097-1108.

Ropers, Richard B. and Pence, Dan J., *American Prejudice: With Liberty And Justice For Some* (New York: Insight Books, 1995).

Ropers, Richard B. and Pence, Dan J., *Class, Culture, And Race In American Schools: A Handbook* (Westport, CT: Greenwood Press., 1995).

Rose, Stephen J., *Social Stratification in the United States: The American Profile Poster* (Revised and expanded) (New York: The New Press, 1992).

Rosenhahn, David, "On Being Sane in Insane Places," *Science,* Vol. 179, 1973: 250 258.

Rosenthal, Robert, "Teacher Expectancy Effects: A Brief Update 25 Years after the Pygmalion Experiment," *Journal of Research in Education,* Vol. 1, 1991: 3-12.

Rosenthal, Robert, and Jacobson, Lenore, *Pygmalion in the Classroom: Teacher Expectations and Pupils' Intellectual Development* (New York: Holt, Rinehart, and Winston, 1968).

Rossi, Alice A., and Rossi, Peter H., *Of Human Bonding: Parent-Child Relations Over the Life Course* (New York: Aldine de Gruyter, 1991).

Rossi, Peter H., Berk, Richard A., and Lenihan, Kenneth J., *Money, Work, and Crime: Experimental Evidence* (New York: Academic, 1980).

Rossi, Peter H., and Nock, Steven L., *Measuring Social Judgments: The Factorial Survey Approach* (Beverly Hills, CA: Sage, 1982).

Rotter, J. B., "Generalized Expectancies for Internal versus External Control Reinforcements," *Psychological Monographs,* Vol. 80, 1966: 609.

Rotundo, E. Athony, *American Manhood: Transformations in Masculinity from the Revolution to the Modern Era* (Boulder, CO: Basic Books, 1994).

Rowe, Mary Budd, "Pausing Phenomena: Influence on the Quality of Instruction," *Journal of Psycholinguistic Research,* Vol. 3, 1974a: 203-224.

Rowe, Mary Budd, "Wait-Time and Rewards as Instructional Variables, Their Influence on Language, Logic, and Fate Control. Part one—Wait time," *Journal of Research in Science Teaching,* Vol. 11, 1974 b: 81-94.

Roy, Beth, *Some Trouble with Cows: Making Sense of Social Conflict* (Berkeley: University of California Press, 1994).

Rubel, Arthur, *Across the Tracks: Mexican Americans in a Texas City* (Austin, TX: University of Texas, 1971).

Rubin, Allen, and Babbie, Earl, *Research Methods for Social Work* (Second Edition) (Pacific Grove, CA: Brooks/Cole Publishing Company, 1993).

Rucker, C. E., and Cash, T.F., "Body Images, Body-Size Perceptions, and Eating Behaviors among African-Americans and White College Women," *International Journal of Eating Disorders*, Vol. 12, 1992: 291-300.

Rudakova, Natasha, unpublished interview, Kazan State University, Kazan, Russia, 1994.

Ruggiero, Karen M., and Taylor, Donald M., "Why Minority Group Members Perceive or Do Not Perceive the Discrimination That Confronts Them: The Role of Self-Esteem and Perceived Control," *Journal of Personal and Social Psychology*, Vol. 72, 1997: 373-389.

Russell, James W., *After the Fifth Sun: Class and Race in North America* (Englewood-Cliffs, NJ: Prentice-Hall, 1994).

Rymer, Russ, *Genie* (New York: Harper Perennial, 1994).

Ryan, William, *Blaming the Victim* (New York: Vintage Books, 1976).

Ryu, Jai P., "Koreans in America: A Demographic Analysis," in Hyung-chan Kim (Ed.), *The Korean Diaspora* (Santa Barbara: ABC Clio Press, 1977), pp. 205-228.

Saal, F.E., Johnson, C.B., and Weber, N., "Friendly or Sexy? It May Depend on Whom You Ask," *Psychology of Women Quarterly*, Vol. 13, 1989: 263-276.

Saenz, Rogelio, "The Demography of Chicanos," in R.M. De anda (Ed.), *Chicanas and Chicanos in Contemporary Society* (Boston: Allyn and Bacon, 1996).

Saenz, Rogelio, "Ethnic Concentration and Chicano Poverty: A Comparative Approach," *Social Science Research*, Vol. 26, 1997: 205-228.

Sahlins, Marshall, *Stone Age Economics* (Chicago: Aldine, 1972).

Sahlins, Marshall, and Service, Elman, *Evolution and Culture* (Ann Arbor: University of Michigan Press, 1960).

Sakamoto, Arthur, and Powers, Daniel, "Education and the Dual Labor Market for Japanese Men," *American Sociological Review*, Vol. 60, (April) 1995: 222-246.

Salagaev, Alexander, "Lecture Series on Crime in Russia," Sociological Research Laboratory, Kazan State University, 1995.

Salagaev, Alexander, "Lecture Series on Mind-Activities," Sociological Research Laboratory, Kazan State University, 1995.

Saldivar, J.D., *The Dialectics of Our America: Genealogy, Cultural Critique and Literary History* (Durham: Duke University Press, 1991).

Salovesh, Michael, "Postmarital Residence in San Bartolome de los Llanos, Chiapas," in Hugo Nutini, P. Carrasco and J. M. Taggart (Eds.), *Essays on Mexican Kinship* (Pittsburgh: University of Pittsburgh Press, 1976), pp. 207-217.

Saltzberg, E.A. and Chrisler, J.C., "Beauty is the Beast: Psychological Effects of the Pursuit of the Perfect Female Body," in J. Freeman (Ed.), *Women* (Fifth edition) (Mt. View, CA: Mayfield Publishing Company, 1995), pp. 306-315.

Samora, Julian, "Mexican Immigration," in Gus Tyler (Ed.), *Mexican Americans Tomorrow* (Albuquerque: University of New Mexico Press, 1975).

Samuels, Suzanne Uttaro, *Fetal Rights, Women's Rights: Gender Equality In The Workplace* (Madison, WI: University of Wisconsin Press, 1995).

Sandmeyer, Elmer C., *The Anti-Chinese Movement in California* (Chicago: The University of Illinois Press, 1939).

Sandor, Gabrielle, "The Other Americans," *American Demographics*, Vol. 16, No. 6, 1994: 36-41.

San Francisco Chronicle, April 12, 1998.

San Francisco Chronicle, April 18, 1998.

Santiago, A.M., and Wilder, M.G., "Residential Segregation and its Links to Monoirty Poverty: Tthe Case of Latinos in the United States," *Social Problems*, Vol. 38, 1991: 492-515.

Sapir, Edward, *Language* (New York: Harcourt, Brace & World, 1921).

Saxton, Alexander P., *The Indispensable Enemy: Labor and the Anti-Chinese Movement in California* (Berkeley: University of California Press, 1971).

Scales-Trent, Judy, *Notes of a White Black Woman: Race, Color, Community* (University Park, PA: Pennsylvania State University, 1995).

Schachter, Stanley, "The Psychology of Affiliation: Experimental Studies of the Sources of Gregariousness," *Stanford Studies in Psychology,* No. 1. (Stanford, CA: Stanford University Press, 1959).

Schachter, Stanley, "Social Cohesion," in David L. Sills (Ed.), *International Encyclopedia of the Social Sciences,* Vol. 2 (New York: The Macmillan Company and The Free Press, 1968), pp. 542-546.

Scharr, John H., "Loyalty," in David L. Sills (Ed.), *International Encyclopedia of the Social Sciences,* Vol. 9 (New York: The Macmillan Company and The Free Press, 1968), pp. 484-487.

Scheff, Thomas, *Being Mentally Ill: A Sociological Theory* (Second Edition) (New York: Aldine, 1984).

Schemer, Richard T., *Racial and Ethnic Groups* (New York: Harper Collins, 1993).

Scheafer, Richard T., *Race and Ethnicity in the United States* (New York: Harper Collins, 1995).

Schedroviksy, George, *Systematic Research* (Moscow: Moscow Press, 1990).

Schlenker, Jennifer; Caron, Sandra; and Halteman, Wiliam A., "A Feminist Analysis of *Seventeen* Magazine: Content Analysis from 1945 to 1995," *Sex Roles,* Vol. 38, Nos. 1/2, (January) 1998: 135-149.

Schlesinger, Arthur J., Jr., *A Thousand Days* (Boston: Houghton Mifflin, 1965).

Schneider, Dorothy, and Schneider, Carl J., *Sound Off! American Military Women Speak Out* (New York: Paragon House, 1992).

Schneider-Rosen, K., Braunwald, K.G., Carlson, V., and Cicchetti, D., "Current Perspectives in Attachment Theory: Illustration from the Study of Maltreated Infants," in I. Bretherton and E. Waters (Eds.), *Monographs of the Society for Research in Child Development,* Vol. 50, 1985.

Schrag, Clarence, *Crime and Justice: American Style* (Washington D.C.: Government Printing Office, 1971).

Schütz, A., "Entertainers, Experts, or Public Servants? Politicians' Self-Presentation on Television Talk Shows," *Political Communication,* Vol. 12, 1995: 211-221.

Schuman, Howard, "Survey Research," in Edgar F. Borgatta and Marie L. Borgatta (Eds.), *Encyclopedia of Sociology,* Vol. 4 (New York: Macmillan Publishing Company, 1992), pp. 2119-2127.

Schuman, Howard, and Presser, Stanley, *Questions and Answers in Attitude Surveys: Experiments on Question Form, Working, and Context* (New York: Academic Press, 1981).

Schur, Edwin M., *Crimes Without Victims: Deviant Behavior and Public Policy* (Englewood Cliffs, NJ: Prentice Hall, 1965).

Schur, Edwin M., *Labeling Deviant Behavior: Its Sociological Implications* (NY: Harper and Row, 1971).

Schwarzer, R., and Leppin, A., "Social Support and Health: A Meta-Analysis," *Psychology and Health,* Vol. 3, 1989: 1-15.

Scott, James Brown, "Japanese and Hindus Naturalized in the United States," *American Journal of International Law,* Vol. 17, 1923: 328-330.

Scott, James Brown, "Migration and Puerto Rico's Population Problem," *The Annals of the American Academy of Political and Social Science,* Vol. 285, 1953:130-136.

Schwendinger, Julia, and Schwendinger, Herman, *Sociologists of the Chair* (New York: Basic Books, 1974. Scott, James, *Weapons of the Weak* (New Haven, CT: Yale University Press, 1985).

Scull, Andrew, "Deviance and Social Control," in Neil J. Smelser (Ed.), *Handbook of Sociology* (Newbury Park, CA: Sage, 1988): 667-693.

Sellin, Thorsten, *Culture and Conflict and Crime* (New York: Social Science Research Council, 1938).

Senart, E., *Caste in India* (London: Methuen and Company, Ltd., 1930).

Senior, Clarence, *The Puerto Ricans: Strangers-Then Neighbors* (Chicago: Quandrangle Books, 1965).

Shakespeare, W., *The Tempest* (Edited by N. Fry) (New York: Penguin Books, 1987).

Shakin, M., Shakin, D., and Sternglanz, S.H., "Infant Clothing: Sex Labeling for Strangers," *Sex Roles,* Vol. 12, 1985: 955-964.

Shapiro, Jeremy J., and Hughes, Shelley K., "Information Literacy as a LiberalArt," *Educom Review,* Vol. 31, No. 2, (March/April) 1996.

Sharma, Miriam, "The Philippines: A Case of Migration to Hawaii, 1906 to 1946," in Lucie Cheng and Edna Bonacich (Eds.), *Labor Immigration Under Capitalism: Asian Workers in the United States Before World War II* (Berkeley: University of California Press, 1984), pp. 337-358.

Sharp, Vicki, F., *Statistics for the Social Sciences* (Boston: Little, Brown and Company, 1979).

Shaw, George Bernard, *Saint Joan* (New York: Penguin Books, 1946). (Originally published, 1924.)

Shaw, M.E., *Group Dynamics* (New York: McGraw-Hill, 1971).

Sheldon, William H., *The Varieties of Human Physique: An Introduction to Constitutional Psychology* (New York: Harper and Row, 1940).

Sheldon, William H., *The Varieties of Temperament* (New York: Harper and Row, 1942).

Sherif, Muzafer, "An Experimental Approach to the Study of Attitudes," *Sociometry*, Vol. 1, 1937: 90-98.

Shibutani, Tamotsu, *The Derelicts of Company K: A Sociological Study of Demoralization* (San Francisco: Jossey-Bass, 1978).

Shils, Edward, "Primordial, Personal, Sacred, and Civil Ties," *British Journal of Sociology*, Vol. 8, 1957: 130-145.

Shotola, Robert W., "Small Groups," in Edgar F. Borgatta and Marie L., Borgatta, *Encyclopedia of Sociology* (Vol. 4) (New York: Macmillan Publishing Company, 1992), pp. 1796-1806.

Shub, David, *Lenin: A Biography* (New York: Doubleday and Company, 1948).

Sigelman, Lee and Welch, Susan, *Black Americans' Views of Racial Inequality* (New York: Cambridge University Press, 1991).

Signorielli, N., and Lears, M., "Children, Television, and Conceptions about Chores: Attitudes and Behaviors," *Sex Roles*, Vol. 27 1991: 157-170.

Siiter, Roland, "Group Process," in Richard Lachmann, *The Encyclopedic Dictionary of Sociology* (Fourth edition) (Guilford, CT: The Dushkin Publishing Group, 1991), p.126.

Siiter, Roland, "Sociolinguistics," in Richard Lachmann, *The Encyclopedic Dictionary of Sociology* (Fourth edition) (Guilford, CT: The Dushkin Publishing Group, 1991), p.284.

Silverstein, Merril and Bengtson, Vern L., "Intergenerational Solidarity and the Structure of Adult Child-Parent Relationships in American Families," *American Journal of Sociology*, Vol. 103, No. 2 (September) 1997: 429-460.

Simmel, Georg, *Conflict: The Web of Group Affiliations* (Glencoe, Ill.: Free Press, 1955). These essays originally appeared as "Der Streit" and "Die Kreuzung sozialer Kreise" in Simmel's *Soziologie*, published by Duncker and Humblot, Berlin, 1908.

Simmel, Georg, *The Sociology of Georg Simmel* (Kurt Wolff, Editor and Translator) (New York: Press, 1950).

Simmel, Georg, *The Philosophy of Money* (Boston: Routledge & Kegan Paul, 1978). (Translated by T. Bottomore and D. Frisby) (Originally published, 1907).

Simms, Margaret C. (Ed.), *Economic Perspectives On Affirmative Action* (Washington,DC: Joint Center for Political and Economic Studies, 1995).

Simons, R.L.; Johnson, C.; and Conger, R.D., "Harsh Corporal Punishment Versus Quality of Parental Involvement as an Explanation of Adolescent Maladjustment," *Journal of Marriage and the Family*, Vol. 56, 1994: 591-607.

Singelis, Ted, Triandis, Harry C., Bhawuk, D.S., and Gelfand, Michele, "Horizontal and Vertical Dimensions of Individualism and Collectivism: A Theoretical and Measurement Refinement," *Journal of Comparative Social Science*, Vol,. 29 (August) 1995: 240-275.

Singerman, Diane, *Avenues of Participation: Family, Politics, and Networks in Urban Quarters of Cairo* (Princeton, NJ: Princeton University Press, 1995).

Sjoberg, Gideon, "Folk and 'Feudal' Societies," *American Journal of Sociology*, Vol. 58, 1952: 231-239.

Sjoberg, Gideon, "The Preindustrial City," *American Journal of Sociology*, Vol. 60, 1955: 438-441.

Sjoberg, Gideon, *The Preindustrial City: Past and Present* (New York: the Free Press, 1960).

Skinner, B.F. *About Behaviorism* (New York: Knopf, 1974).

Skinner, B.F., *The Behavior of Organisms: An Experimental Analysis* (New York: Appleton-Century, 1938).

Skinner, B.F., *Science and Human Behavior* (New York: Macmillan, 1953).

Skocpol, Theda, *States and Social Revolutions* (Cambridge, England: Cambridge University Press, 1979).

Skocpol, Theda, and Campbell, John L. (Eds.), *American Society and Politics: Institutional, Historical and Theoretical Perspectives* (New York: McGraw-Hill, 1995).

Skolnick, Jerome H., *Justice Without Trial: Law Enforcement in Democratic Society* (Second edition) (New York: Wiley, 1975).

Skvoretz, J., "Models of Participation in Status-Differentiated Groups," *Social Psychology Quarterly*, Vol. 51, 1988: 43-57.

Slater, P.E., "Role Differentiation in Small Groups," *American Sociological Review*, Vol. 20, 1955: 300-310.

Slaughter-Defoe, Diana T., and Carlson, Karen Glinert, "Young African American and Latino Children in High-Poverty Urban Schools: How They Perceive School Climate," *The Journal of Negro Education*, Vol. 65, No. 1, (Winter) 1996: 60-70.

Slavin, Robert E., and Karweit, Nancy C., "Effects of Whole Class, Ability Grouped and Individual Instruction on Mathematics Achievement," *American Educational Review Journal*, Vol. 22, 1985: 351-367.

Smircich, Linda, "Organizations as Shared Meanings," in Louis R. Podney et. al., (Eds.), *Organizational Symbolism* (Greenwich, CN: JAI Press, 1983), pp. 55-65.

Smith, Adam, *An Inquiry into the Nature and Causes of the Wealth of Nations* (London: Methuen, 1950). (Originally published, 1776).

Smith, Alan (Ed.), *Challenges for Russian Economic Reform*. (Washington, D.C.: Brookings Institute, 1995.

Smith, Bradford, *Americans From Japan* (Philadelphia: Lippincott, 1948).

Smith, Carolyn A., and Stern, Susan B., "Delinquency and Antisocial Behavior: A Review of Family Processes and Intervention Research," *Social Service Review*, Vol. 71, No. 3, (September) 1997: 82-420.

Smith, Douglas A., "The Plea Bargaining Controversy," *Journal of Criminal Law and Criminology*, Vol. 77 (Fall) 1986: 949-967.

Smith, Hedrick, *The New Russians* (New York: Vintage Press, 1993).

Sniderman, Paul, Fletcher, Joseph F., Russell, Peter H., and Tetlock, Philip E., *The Clash of Rights: Liberty, Equality, and Legitimacy in Pluralist Democracy* (New Haven, CT: Yale University Press, 1996).

Snipp, C.M., "Understanding Race and Ethnicity in Rural America," *Rural Sociology*, Vol. 61, 1996: 125-142.

Sobal, Jeffery, unpublished personal correspondence to Harry L. Humphries, Gettysburg College, 1981.

Sokol-Katz, Jan; Dunham, Roger; and Zimmerman, Rick, "Family Structure Versus Parental Attachment in Controlling Adolescent Deviant Behavior: A Social-Control Model," *Adolescence*, Vol. 32, No. 125 (Spring) 1997: 199- 216.

Somners-Flanagan, R., Somners-Flanagan, J., and Davis, B., "What's Happening on Music Television? A Gender-Role Content Analysis," *Sex Roles*, Vol. 28, 1993: 745-753.

Sorin, Gerald, *Abolitionism: A New Perspective* (New York: Praeger, 1972).

Sorokin, Pitrim, *Fads and Foibles in Modern Sociology and Related Sciences* (Chicago: Regnery, 1956).

Sorensen, Annemette, and Trapp, Heike, "The Persistence of Gender Inequality in Earnings In the German Democratic Republic," *American Sociological Review*, Vol. 60, (June) 1995: 398-406.

Soustelle, Jacques, *The Daily Life of the Aztecs: On the Eve of the Spanish Conquest* (Translated by Patrick O'Brian) Weidenfeld and Nicolson (1955).

Spates, James L., and Macionis, John J., *The Sociology of Cities* (Second edition) (Belmont, CA: Wadsworth, 1987).

Spear, Allan H, *Black Chicago: The Making of a Negro Ghetto* (Chicago: University of Chicago Press, 1967).

Spergel, Irving A., *The Youth Gang Problem: A Community Approach* (New York: Oxford University Press, 1995).

Spitz. René, "Hospitalism," *The Psychoanalytic Study of the Child*, Vol. I, 1945: 53-74 and Vol. II, 1947: 113-117.

Spohn, Cassia, "Crime and the Social Control of Blacks: Offender/Victim Race and the Sentencing of Violent Offenders," in George S. Bridges and Martha A. Myers (Eds.), *Inequality, Crime, and Social Control* (Boulder, CO: Westview, 1994), pp. 249-268.

Spradley, James P., and Mann, Brenda, J., *The Cocktail Waitress: Woman's Work in a Man's World* New York: John Wiley & Sons, Inc., 1974).

Springen, K. and Peyser, M., "The Rat Race Begins at 14," *Newsweek*, March 30, 1998: 54-55.

Srinivas, M.N., *Caste in Modern India and Other Essays* (Bombay: Asia Publishing House, 1978).

Srinivas, M.N., *India: Social Structure* (New Delhi: Hindustan Publishing Corporation., 1980).

Squire, Larry, *Memory and Brain* (New York: Oxford University Press, 1987).

Sroufe, L., "Infant-Caregiver Attachment and Patterns of Adaptation in Preschool: The Roots of Maladaptation and Competence," in M. Permutter (Ed.), *Minnesota Symposium in Child Psychology*, 1984.

Sroufe, L. A.; Bennett, C.; Englund, M.; Urban, J.; and Shulman, S., "The Significance of Gender Boundaries in Preadolescence: Contemporary Correlates and Antecedents of Boundary Violation and Maintenance," *Child Development*, Vol. 64, 1993: 455-466.

Stack, Carol, *All Our Kin: Strategies for Survival in a Black Community* (New York: Harper & Row, 1975).

Stack, Carol B., *All Our Kin: Strategies for Survival in a Black Community* (Boulder, CO: Basic Books, 1997).

Stamp, Kenneth M., *The Era of Reconstruction, 1865-1877* (New York: Vintage Books, 1965).

Stamp, Kenneth M., *The Peculiar Institution* (New York: Vintage Books, 1956).

Starr, Frederick S. (Ed.), *The Legacy of History in Russia and the New States of Eurasia* (New York: M.E. Sharpe, 1994).

Starr, Paul, *The Social Transformation of American Medicine* (New York: Basic Books Inc., 1982).

Steil, J.M., "Supermoms and Second Shifts: Marital Inequality in the 1990s," in J. Freeman (Ed.), *Women* (Fifth edition) (Mt. View, CA: Mayfield Publishing Company, 1995), pp. 149-161.

Stein, R.T. and Heller, T., "The Relationship of Participation Rates to Leadership Status: A Meta-Analysis," in H.H. Blumberg, et. al. (Eds.), *Small Groups and Social Interaction* (Chichester: Wiley, 1983).

Steinbeck, John, *The Grapes of Wrath* (New York: McGraw-Hill, 1939).

Steinberg, S., *The Ethnic Myth* (Boston: Beacon Press, 1989).

Stimson, Ardyth, "Interpersonal Attraction," in Edgar F. Borgatta and Marie L. Borgatta (Eds.), *Encyclopedia of Sociology* (New York: Macmillan Publishing Company, 1992), pp. 990- 994.

Stinchcomb, Arthur L., *Constructing Social Theories* (Chicago: University of Chicago Press, 1987).

Stokes, Joseph, and Levin, Ira, "Gender Differences in Predicting Loneliness from Social Network Characteristics," *Journal of Personality and Social Psychology,* Vol. 51, 1986: 1069-1074.

Stolzenberg, Ross M., and Tienda, Marta, "English Proficiency, Education, and the Conditional Economic Assimilation of Hispanic and Asian Origin Men," *Social Science Research,* Vol. 26, No. 1, (March) 1997: 25-51.

Storr, Anthony, *Solitude: A Return to the Self* (New York: Ballantine Books, 1988).

Stouffer, Samuel et al., *The American Soldier: Adjusting During Army Life* (Princeton: Princeton University Press, 1949).

Strasburger, V.C., *Adolescents and the Media: Medical and Psychological Impact* (Thousand Oaks, CA: Sage Publications, 1995).

Strodtbeck, Fred L., and Hook, L.H., "The Social Dimensions of a Twelve-Man Jury Table," *Sociometry,* Vol. 24, 1961: 397-415.

Strodtbeck, Fred L., James, R.M., and Hawkins, C., "Social Status in Jury Deliberations," in E.E. Maccoby, T.M. Newcomb, and E.L. Hartley (Eds.), *Readings in Social Psychology* (Third edition) (New York: Holt, 1958), pp. 379-388.

Stroebe, Wolfgang and Chester A. Insko, "Stereotype, Prejudice, and Discrimination: Changing Conceptions in Theory and Research," in Daniel Bar-Tal, C.F. Graumann, A.W. Kruglanski, and W. Stroebe (Eds.), *Stereotyping and Prejudice: Changing Conceptions* (New York: Springer- Verlag, 1989), pp. 3-34.

Stuart, Paul, *Nations Within a Nation: Historical Statistics of American Indians* (Westport, CN: Greenwood Press, 1987).

Stryker, Sheldon, "Identity Theory," in Edgar F. Borgatta and Marie L. Borgatta (Eds.), *Encyclopedia of Sociology* (New York: Macmillan Publishing Company, 1992), pp. 871-876.

Sutherland, Edwin H., *The Professional Thief* (Chicago: University of Chicago Press, 1937).

Sutherland, Edwin H., "White Collar Criminality," *American Sociological Review,* Vol. 5, No. 1 (February) 1940: 1-12.

Sutherland, Edwin H., and Cressey, Donald R., *Criminology* (Philadelphia: Lippincott, 1978).

Swadener, E.B., and Johnson, J.E., "Play in Diverse Social Contexts: Parent and Teacher Roles," in M.N. Bloch and A.D. Pellegrini (Eds.), *The Ecological Context of Children's Play* (Norwood, NJ: Ablex, 1989), pp. 214-244.

Sykes, Gresham, and Matza, David, "Techniques of Neutralization and Delinquency: A Theory of Delinquency," *American Sociological Review,* Vol. 22 (December) 1957: 664-670.

Szasz, Thomas S., *The Myth of Mental Illness* (New York: Harper and Row, 1961).

Szinovacz, M.E., and Egly, L.C., "Comparing One-Partner and Couple Data on Sensitive Marital Behaviors: The Case of Marital Violence," *Journal of Marriage and the Family,* Vol. 57, 1995: 995-1010.

Szymanski, Albert J., *The Capitalist State and the Politics of Class* (Boston: Winthrop, 1978).

Szymanski, Albert J., *Class Structure: A Critical Perspective* (New York: Praeger, 1983).

Szymanski, Albert J., "Crisis and Vitalization: An Interpretive Essay on Marxist Theory," in Rhonda F. Levine and Jerry Lembcke (Eds.), *Recapturing Marxism: An Appraisal of Recent Trends in Sociological Theory* (New York: Praeger, 1987).

Szymanski, Albert J., *The Logic of Imperialism* (New York: Praeger, 1981).

Szymanski, Albert J., "Racial Discrimination and White Gain," *American Sociological Review,* Vol. 41, 1976: 403-414.

Tajfel, Henri and Turner, Jonathan, "The Social Identity Theory of Intergroup Behavior," in S. Worchel and W.G. Austin (Eds.), *Psychology of Intergroup Relations* (Second edition) (Chicago: Nelson-Hall, 1986), pp. 7-24.

Takaki, Ronald, *A Different Mirror: A History of Multicultural America* (Boston: Little, Brown, 1993).

Takaki, Ronald, *Strangers From a Different Shore: A History of Asian Americans* (New York: Penguin Books, 1989).

Tannenbaum, Frank, *Slave and Citizen: The Negro in the Americas* (New York: Vintage Books, 1946).

Tarde, Gabriel, *The Laws of Imitation* (New York: Holt, Rinehart and Winston, 1903).

Tawney, Richard Henry, *Equality* (New York: Barnes and Noble, 1964). (Originally published, 1931).

Taylor, Jill McLean, Gilligan, Carol, and Sullivan, Amy M., *Between Voice and Silence: Women and Girls, Race and Relationship* (Cambridge, MA: Harvard University Press, 1995).

Tesser, A., Martin, L., and Mendolia, M., "The Impact of Thought on Attitude Extremity and Attitude-Behavior Consistncy," in R.E. Petty and J.A. Krosnick (Eds.), *Attitude Strength: Antecedents and Consequences* (Hillsdale, NJ: Erlbaum, 1995).

Theodorson, George A., and Theodorson, Achilles G., *A Modern Dictionary of Sociology* (New York: Barnes & Noble Books, 1969)

Thomas, George M., *Revivalism and Cultural Change: Christianity, Nation-Building, and the Market in the Nineteenth-Century United States* (Chicago, IL: University of Chicago Press, 1989).

Thomas, W.I., and Znaniecki, Florian, *The Polish Peasant in Europe and America* (Vol. 1) (Chicago: University of Chicago Press, 1918).

Thompson, E.P., *The Making of the English Working Class* (New York: Vintage Books, 1963).

Thompson, Leonard, *A History of South Africa* (Revised edition) (New Haven, CT: Yale University Press, 1995).

Thompson, Richard H., *Theories of Ethnicity: A Critical Appraisal* (New York: Greenwood Press, 1989).

Thompson, S.H., Sargent, R.G., and Kemper, K.A., "Black and While Adolescent Males' Perceptions of Ideal Body Size," *Sex Roles,* Vol. 34, 1996: 391-406.

Thorndike, R.L., "Review of *Pygmalian in the Classroom,*" *American Educational Research Journal,* Vol. 5, 1968: 707-711.

Thorne, B., *Gender Play: Girls and Boys in School* (Buckingham, England: Open University Press, 1993).

Thrasher, F.M., *The Gang: A Study of 1,313 Gangs in Chicago* (Chicago: University of Chicago Press, 1936).

Tice, Dianne M., Butler, Jennifer L., Muraven, Mark B., and Stillwell, Arlene, "When Modesty Prevails: Differential Favorability of Self-Presentation to Friends and to Strangers, *Journal of Personality and Social Psychology,* Vol. 69, 1995: 1120-1138.

Tierney, William, "Affirmative Action in California: Looking Back, Looking Forward in Public Academe," *Journal of Negro Education,* Vol. 65, No. 2, 1996: 122-132.

Time Magazine, April 6, 1998.

Tocqueville, Alexis de, *Democracy in America,* Vol. 1 (New York: Vintage Books, 1954). (Originally published in 1835, 1840).

Toqueville, Alexis de, and Beaumont, G. de, *On the Penitentiary System in the United States and Its Application to France* (Carbondale and Edwardsville, IL: Southern Illinois University Press, 1964). (Originally published, 1833).

Toennies, Ferdinand, *Gemeinschaft und Gesellschaft (Community and Association)* (Michigan: Michigan State University Press, 1957).

Torbet, Patricia McFall, et. al, *State Responses to Serious and Violent Juvenile Crime: An : Research Report* (Washington, D.C.: U.S. Department of Justice, Office of Justice Programs, Office of Juvenile Justice and Delinquency Prevention, 1997).

Triandis, H.C.; McCusker, C.: Betancourt, H.; Iwao, S.; Leung, K.; Salazar, JM., et. al., "An Etic-emic Analysis of Individualism and Collectivism," *Journal of Cross-Cultural Psychology,* Vol. 24, 1993: 366-383.

Trotsky, Leon, *The Russian Revolution* (New York: Doubleday Anchor Books, 1959).

Trow, Martin, "The Democratization of Higher Education in America," *European Journal of Sociology,* Vol. 3, 1962: 231-263.

Trow, Martin, "The Second Transformation of American Secondary Education," *International Journal of Comparative Sociology*, Vol. 2, 1961: 144-166.

Tsai, Henry S., *The Chinese Experience in America* (Bloomington: Indiana University Press, 1986).

Tucker, Robert C., *The Marx-Engels Reader* (Second edition) (New York: W.W. Norton & Company, 1978).

Tumin, Melvin, "Some Principles of Stratification: A Critical Analysis," *American Sociological Review*, Vol. 18, 1953: 387-94.

Turk, Austin, "Law as a Weapon in Social Conflict," *Social Problems*, Vol. 23 (February) 1976: 276-291.

Turk, Austin, *Political Criminality: The Defiance and Defense of Authority* (Beverly Hills: Sage Publications, 1986).

Turkle, Sherry, *Life on the Screen: Identity in the Age of the Internet* (New York: Simon and Schuster, 1995).

Turkle, Sherry, *The Second Self: Computers and the Human Spirit* (New York: A Touchstone Book Published by Simon & Schuster, Inc., 1984).

Turner, Jonathan H., *The Structure of Sociological Theory* (Fifth edition) (Belmont, CA: Wadsworth Publishing Company, 1991).

Turner, John C., "Social Identification and Psychological Group Formation," in H. Tajfel (Ed.), *The Social Dimensions: European Developments in Social Psychology*, Vol. 2 (London: Cambridge University Press, 1984).

Turner-Bowker, Diane, "Gender Stereotyped Descriptors in Children's Picture Books," *Sex Roles*, Vol. 35, Nos. 7/8, 1996: 461-488.

Turner, M.E., and Pratkanis, A.R., "Social Identity Maintenance Prescriptions for Preventing Groupghink: Reducing Identity Protection and Enhancing Intellectual Conflict," *International Journal of Conflict Management*, Vol. 5, 1994: 254-270.

Turner, M.E., Pratkanis, A.R., Probasco, A.R., and Leve, C., "Threat Cohesion, and Group Effectiveness: Testing a Social Identity Maintenance Perspective on Groupthink," *Journal of Personality and Social Psychology*, Vol. 63, 1992: 781-796.

Turpin, Jennifer E., *Reinventing the Soviet Self: Media and Social Change in the Former Soviet Union* (Westport, CT: Praeger, 1995).

Twain, Mark, *Life on the Mississippi* (New York: Harper, 1904).

Tylor, Edward B., *Primitive Culture: Researches Into the Development of Mythology, Philosophy, Religion, Art, and Custom.* 2 Vols. (London: John Murray, 1871). Volume 1: *Origins of Culture*

Ueda, R., *Post War Immigrant America: A Social History* (New York: St. Martin's Press, 1994).

United Nations, *Demographic Yearbook, 1994* (New York: United Nations, 1996).

United Nations, *The World's Women, 1970-1990: Trends and Statistics* (New York: United Nations, 1991).

United States Bureau of the Census, *Statistical Abstract of the United States 1996* (116th edition) (Washington, D.C.: U.S. Government Printing Office, 1996).

United States Bureau of the Census, Current Population Reports, *Household and Family Characteristics: March, 1996 (Update)*, PPL-66, 1997, Table 11. Online: http://www.census.gov.

U.S. Civil Rights, *Puerto Ricans in the Continental United States: An Uncertain Future* (Washington, D.C.: USGPO, 1976).

United States Department of Education, National Center for Education Statistics, Postsecondary Quick Information System, *Survey on Distance Education Courses Offered by Higher Education Institutions, 1995.* (Washington, D.C.: U.S. Government Printing Office, 1995).

United States Department of Justice, FBI, Crime in America, *Uniform Crime Reports, 1995:* 213.

United States Department of Labor, Bureau of Labor Statistics, *Future Occupation Growth.* February, 1996. Press Release 91-113 (Washington, D.C.: U.S. Printing Office, 1996).

United States Department of Labor, Bureau of Labor Statistics, *Occupational Outlook Handbook, 1998-1999* (Washington, D.C.: U.S. Government Printing Office, 1998).

United States Department of Labor, Bureau of Labor Statistics, *New 1996-2006 Employment Projections.* Data released December 3, 1997. Internet: http://stats.bls.gov.emphome.htm

United States Immigration and Naturalization Service, *Statistical Yearbook, 1995:* 91.

United States National Center for Health Statistics, *Current Estimates from the National Health Interview Survey, 1992* (Hyattsville, MD: The Center, 1992).

Upchurch, Carl, *Convicted in the Womb: One Man's Journey from Prisoner to Peacemaker* (New York: Bantam Trade Paperback, 1996).

Urberg, K.A., and Kaplan, M.G., "An Observational Study of Race-, Age-, and Sex-Heterogeneous Interaction in Preschoolers," *Journal of Applied Developmental Psychology*, Vol. 10, 1989: 299-311.

Uriciuoli, B., *Exposing Prejudice: Puerto Rican Experiences of Language, Race, and Class* (Boulder, CO: Westview, 1996).

van den Berghe, Pierre L., *Human Family Systems: An Evolutionary View* (New York: Elsevier, 1979).

van den Berghe, Pierre L., *Race and Racism* (New York: John Wiley and Sons, 1978).

van den Berghe, Pierre L., *South Africa: A Study in Conflict* (Middletown, CT: Wesleyan University Press, 1965).

van Ginneken, Japp, *Crowds, Psychology, and Politics, 1871-1899* (Cambridge, England: Cambridge University Press, 1992).

Vaillant, George C., *Aztecs of Mexico: Origin, Rise and Fall of the Aztec Nation* (Garden City, NY: Doubleday and Company, 1948).

Valdés, Guadalupe, *Con Respeto: Bridging the Distance Between Culturally Diverse Families and Schools* (New York: Tachers College Press, 1996).

Vallangca, Caridad C., *The Second Wave: Pinay & Pinoy (1945-1960)* (San Francisco, CA: Strawberry Hill Press, 1987).

Veblen, Thorstein, *Theory of the Leisure Class* (New York: Macmillan, 1899).

Veroff, J., Douvan, E., and Kulka, R.A., *The Inner American* (New York: Basic Books, 1981).

Villenas, Sophia, "The Colonizer/Colonized Chicana Ethnographer: Identity, Marginalization, and Co-optation in the Field," *Harvard Educational Review*, vol. 66, No. 4, (Winter) 1996: 711-731.

Vold, George, and Barnard, *Thomas, Theoretical Criminology* (Third edition) (New York: Oxford University Press, 1986).

Yinger, J., *Closed Doors, Opportunities Lost: The Continuing Costs of Housing Discrimination* (New York: Russell Sage Foundation, 1995).

Vogel, Ezra, *Japan as Number One: Lessons for America* (New York: Harper-Torchbooks, 1979).

Wagley, Charles Harris, Marvin, *Minorities in the New World: Six Case Studies* (New York: Columbia University Press, 1958).

Walder, Andrew, "Career Mobility and the Communist Political Order," *American Sociological Review* Vol. 60, 1995: 309-328.

Walens, Susann, *War Stories: An Oral History of Life Behind Bars* (Westport, CT: Praeger Publishers, Praeger Series in Criminology and Crime Control Policy, 1997).

Walker, A. and Parmar, P., *Warrior Marks: Female Genital Mutilation and the Sexual Blinding of Women* (London: Jonathan Cape, 1993).

Wallace, Walter, *The Logic of Science in Sociology* (New York: Aldine de Gruyer, 1971).

Wallerstein, Immanuel, *The Capitalist World Economy* (New York: Cambridge University Press, 1979).

Wallerstein, Immanuel, *The Modern World-System: Capitalist Agriculture and the Origins of the European World-Economy in the Sixteenth Century* (New York: Academic Press, 1974).

Wallerstein, Immanuel, *The Politics of the World Economy: The States, the Movements and the Civilizations* (Cambridge: Cambridge University Press, 1984).

Walsh, J., "Asian Women, Caucasian Men," *Image*, (December) 1990: 11-16.

Warner, Lloyd, *American Life: Chicago* (Chicago: University of Chicago Press, 1936).

Warr, Mark, "Parents, Peers, and Delinquency," *Social Forces*, Vol. 72 (September) 1993: 247-264.

Watson, James B., *Behaviorism* (New York: Norton, 1924).

Wattleton, F., "Teenage Pregnancy: The Case for National Action," *The Nation*, (July 24/31) 1989: 138-141.

Wax, Murray L. and Buchanan, Robert W., *Solving the Indian Problem: The White Man's* Burdensome Business (New York: New York Times Book Co., 1975).

Weber, Max, *Ancient Judaism* (Glencoe, IL: The Free Press, 1952).

Weber, Max, *Economy and Society: An Outline of Interpretive Sociology* (New York: Bedminister Press, 1968).

Weber, Max, *Max Weber on the Methodology of the Social Sciences* (Glencoe, IL: The Free Press, 1949). (Translated and edited by Edward E. Shils and H. Finch).

Weber, Max, *The Protestant Ethic and the Spirit of Capitalism* (New York: Charles Scribner's and Sons, 1930. (Originally published in German in 1904-1905 and in English in 1930).

Weber, Max, *The Religion of China* (New York: Macmillan, 1951).

Weber, Max, *The Religion of India* (Glencoe: The Free Press, 1958).

Weber, Max, *Social and Economic Organization* (New York: Free Press, 1922).

Weber, Max, *The Sociology of Religion* (Boston: Beacon Press, 1963). (Originally published in Germany in 1922 by J.C. B. Mohr under the title "Religions-soziologie," from *Wirtschaft und Gesellschaft)*

Weeks, J., "The Construction of Homosexuality," in S. Seidman (Ed.), *Queer Theory/Sociology* (Boston, MA: Blackwell Publishers Inc., 1996), pp. 41-63.

Weisstein, N, "Kinder, Küche, Kirche: Psychology Constructs the Female," in A. Kesselman, L.D. McNair, and N. Schniedewind (Eds.), *Women: Images and Reality* (Mt. View, CA: Mayfield Publishing Company, 1995), pp. 51-54.

Weitlaner, Robert J., "Notes on the Social Organization of Ojitlan, Oaxaca," in Homenaje al Dr. Alfonso Caso, S.A. (Mexico: Imprenta Nuevo Mundo, 1951).

Weitzer, Ronald, "Racial Prejudice Among Korean Merchants in African American Neighborhoods," *The Sociological Quarterly*, Vol. 38, No. 4, 1997: 587-606.

Werner, Emmy, "Vulnerability and Resiliency: A Longitudinal Study of Asian Americans from Birth to Age 30," Invited Address at the IXth Biennial Meeting of the International Society for the Study of Behavioral Development, Tokyo, July 15, 1987.

Werner, Emmy E., and Smith, Ruth S., *Vulnerable But Invincible: A Longitudinal Study of Resilient Children and Youth* (New York: Adams, Bannister, Cox, 1989).

Wesoloski, Wlodzimierz, "Some Notes on the Functional Theory of Stratification," *The Polish Sociological Bulletin*, Nos. 3-4, 1962: 5-6.

West, Donald J., and Farrington, David P., *Who Becomes Delinquent?* (London: Heinemann Educational Books, 1973).

Weyer, Edward Moffat, *The Eskimos: Their Environment and Folkways* (Gamden, CT: Archon Books, 1962).

Wharton, Amy S., "Structure and Agency in Socialist-Feminist Theory." *Gender & Politics*, Vol. 5, 1991: 373-389.

Wheeler, L., Reis, H., and Nezlek, J., "Loneliness, Social Interaction, and Social Roles," *Journal of Personality and Social Psychology*, Vol. 45, 1983: 943-953.

Wheeler, Peter, "The Naked and the Bipedal," in Tim Folger (Ed.), *Discover*, Vol. 14, No. 11, 1993.

Whitaker, Mark, "Whites v. Blacks," *Newsweek*, Vol. 126 (October 16, 1995): 28-31.

White, Merry, *The Material Child: Coming of Age in Japan and America* (Berkeley: University of California Press, 1994).

Whitehead, B., "Dan Quayle Was Right," *The Atlantic Monthly*, (April) 1993: 47-50ff.

Whitehead, John T., and Lab, Steven P., *Juvenile Justice: An Introduction* (Second edition) (Cincinnati, OH: Anderson Publishing Company, 1996).

Whyte, G., "Escalating Commitment in Individual and Group Decision Making: A Prospect Theory Approach," *Organizational Behavior and Human Decision Processes*, Vol. 54, 1993: 430-455.

Whyte, William Foote, "Advancing Scientific Knowledge Through Participatory Action Research,:" *Sociological Forum,* Vol. 4, 1989: 367-386.

Whyte, William Foote, *Street Corner Society: The Social Structure of an Italian Slum* (Second edition) (Chicago: University of Chicago Press, 1955).

Williams, Christine L., *Still a Man's World: Men Who Do "Women's Work"* (Berkeley: University of California Press, 1995).

Williams, C., *It's Time for My Story: Soap Opera Sources, Structure and Response* (Westport, CT: Praeger, 1992).

Williams, Robin, *American Society: A Sociological Interpretation* (Third edition) (New York: Alfred A, Knopf, 1970).

Williams, R., *Hierarchical Structures and Social Values: The Creation of Black and Irish Identities in the U.S.* (Cambridge, England: Cambridge University Press, 1990).

Williams, R., "Labor Migration in the World System: An Investigation into the Involuntary/Voluntary Distinction," *Research in Race and Ethnic Relations*, Vol. 7, 1994: 271-298.

Wilson, Edward O., *Sociobiology: The New Synthesis* (Cambridge, MA: Harvard University Press, 1975).

Wilson, George, "Payoffs to Power Among Males in the Middle Class: Has Race Declined in Significance?," *The Sociological Quarterly,* Vol. 38, No. 4, 1997: 607-622.

Wilson, James Q., *The Moral Sense* (New York: The Free Press, 1993).

Wilson, James Q., *Varieties of Police Behavior: Th Management of Law and Order in Eight Communities* (New York: Atheneum, 1968).

Wilson, James Q., and Herrnstein, Richard J., *Crime and Human Nature* (New York: Simon & Schuster, Inc., 1985).

Wilson, L.K., *Assertion and its Social Context,* unpublished Ph.D. Dissertation, University of Queensland, 1989.

Wilson, T., "Osage Women 1870-1980," in S. Chan, D.H. Daniels, M.T. Garcia, and T.P. Wilson (Eds.) *Peoples of Color in the American West* (Lexington: D.C. Heath and Company, 1994), pp. 182-196.

Wilson, William Julius, *The Declining Significance of Race: Blacks and Changing American Institutions* (Second edition) (Chicago: The University of Chicago Press, 1980).

Wilson, William Julius, "The Ghetto Underclass: Social Science Perspectives," **The Annals of the** *American Academy of Political and Social Science,* Vol. 501, 1989.

Wilson, William Julius, *The Truly Disadvantaged: The Inner City, The Underclass and Public Policy* (Chicago: The University of Chicago Press, 1987).

Wilson, William Julius, *When Work Disappears* (New York: Alfred A. Knopf, 1996).

Winant, Howard, *Racial Conditions: Politics, Theory, Comparisons* (Minneapolis, MN: University of Minnesota Press, 1994).

Wittfogel, Karl, *Oriental Despotism* (New Haven, CT: Yale University Press, 1957).

Wolf, Eric R., *Europe and the People Without History* (Berkeley: The University of California Press, 1982).

Wolf, Eric R., *Peasants* (Englewood Cliffs, NJ: Prentice-Hall, 1966).

Wolf, Eric R., *Peasant Wars in the Twentieth Century* (New York: Harper-Row, 1969).

Wolf, N., *The Beauty Myth: How Images of Beauty are Used Against Women* (New York: Morrow, 1991).

Wolfe, N., "The Beauty Myth," in M.L. Andersen and P.H. Collins (Eds.) *Race, Class, and Gender* (Second edition) (Belmont, CA: Wadsworth Publishing Company, 1995), pp. 417-422.

Wu, Cheng-Tsu (Ed.), *Chink! A Documentary History of Anti-Chinese Prejudice in America* (New York: World Publishing, 1972).

Woodward, C. Vann, *The Strange Career of Jim Crow* (New York: Oxford University Press, 1966).

Wright, Erik Olin, *Classes* (London: Verso, 1985).

Wright, Erik Olin, Baxter, Janeen, and Birkelund, Gunn Elisabeth, "The Gender Gap in Workplace Authority: A Cross-National Study," *American Sociological Review,* Vol. 60, (June) 1995: 407-435.

Wright, Erik Olin, and Martin, Bill, "The Transformation of American Class Structure, 1960-1980," *American Journal of Sociology,* Vol. 93, 1987:1-29.

Wright, Kevin N., and Wright, Karen E., *Family Life, Delinquency, and Crime: A Policymaker's Guide* (Washington, D.C.: Office of Juvenile Justice and Delinquency Prevention, 1994).

Wrong, Dennis H., "The Functional Theory of Stratification: Some Neglected Considerations," *American Sociological Review,* Vol. 24, 1959: 772-782.

Yang, Mayfair Mei-hui, *Gifts, Favors, and Banquets: The Art of Social Relationships in China* (Ithica, NY: Cornell University Press, 1994).

Yoneda, Karl, "100 Years of Japanese Labor History in the USA," in Amy Tachiki, et al, (Eds.), *Roots: An Asian American Reader* (Los Angeles: Asian American Studies Center, University of California, 1971), pp. 150-158.

Zachary, Pascal, "State of the Union: United Farm Workers Are Finding New Life After Chavez's Death," *Wall Street Journal,* December 19, 1995: pp. 1 and A6.

Zack, Naomi (Ed.), *American Mixed Race: The Culture of Microdiversity* (Lanham, MD: Rowman & Littlefield Publishers, 1995).

Zborowski, Mark, "Cultural Components in Responses to Pain," *Journal of Social Issues,* Vol. 8, 1952: 16-30.

Zeisel, Hans, "Disagreement over the Evaluation of a Controlled Experiment," *American Journal of Sociology,* Vol. 88, 1982: 378-389.

Zhou, Xueguang, Tuma, Nancy Brandon, and Moen, Phyllis, "Institutional Change and Job-Shift Patterns in Urban China, 1949-1994," *American Sociological Review*, Vol. 62, (June) 1997: 339-365.

Zietlin, Irving M., *Ideology and the Development of Sociological Theory.* (Fifth edition) (Englewood Cliffs: Prentice-Hall, 1994).

Zigler, E., and Child, I.L., "Socialization," in G. Lindzey and E. Aronson (Eds.), *The Handbook of Social Psychology,* (Second edition) Vol. 3 (Reading, MA: Addison-Wesley, 1969).

Zimmerman, Don, and West, Candace, "Sex Roles, Interruptions, and Silences in Conversation," in b. Thorne and N. Henley (Eds.), *Language and Sex: Difference and Dominance* (Rowley, MA: Newbury House, 1975).

Zukin, Sharon, *The Culture of Cities* (Cambridge, MA: Blackwell Publishers, 1995).

Zweigenhaft, Richard L., and Domnoff, William G., *Diversity in the Power Elite: Have Women and Minorities Reached the Top?* (New Haven, CT: Yale University Press, 1998).

SUBJECT INDEX

NAME INDEX